Lola Montez

YALE UNIVERSITY PRESS/NEW HAVEN AND LONDON

BRUCE SEYMOUR

Lola Montez

A LIFE

Copyright © 1996 by Bruce Seymour. All rights reserved. This book may not be reproduced, in whole or in part, including illustrations, in any form (beyond that copying permitted by Sections 107 and 108 of the U.S. Copyright Law and except by reviewers for the public press), without written permission from the publishers.

Designed by Nancy Ovedovitz and set in Century Expanded type by The Marathon Group, Inc., Durham, North Carolina. Printed in the United States of America by Vail-Ballou Press, Binghamton, New York.

Library of Congress Cataloging-in-Publication Data
Seymour, Bruce, 1946–
Lola Montez : a life / Bruce Seymour.
p. cm.
Includes bibliographical references and index.
ISBN 0-300-06347-4
1. Montez, Lola, 1818–1861. 2. Bavaria (Germany)—Kings and rulers—Mistresses—Biography. 3. Ludwig I, King of Bavaria, 1786–1868. 4. Mistresses—Germany—Bavaria—Biography. I. Title.
DD801.B383M687 1995
943'.307'092— dc20
[B]   95-36465
CIP

A catalogue record for this book is available from the British Library.

The paper in this book meets the guidelines for permanence and durability of the Committee on Production Guidelines for Book Longevity of the Council on Library Resources.

10   9   8   7   6   5   4   3   2   1

CONTENTS

Contents

PREFACE AND
ACKNOWLEDGMENTS

Lola Montez once claimed to be the subject of more biographies than any living woman, and she added that none of them came any nearer to being a biography of her than it did to being an authentic history of the man in the moon. The inaccuracy of biographies of this fascinating woman has continued, in large part because the subject was an incorrigible liar. The records of her life are scattered around the globe in the many places she lived and visited, and biographers have been largely content to rework Lola's lies about herself and make up some of their own. The few who made a serious effort to get at the truth were frustrated by her efforts to confuse the facts and by the fictions that some biographers had themselves invented.

When I began this biography, I quickly concluded that the record of her life was so deeply tangled in fiction that only by going back to original sources did I have any hope of finding the truth. The search for those sources has taken me to scores of archives and libraries on four continents and has resulted in some spectacular discoveries, particularly the wealth of material in the King Ludwig I Archive at the Bavarian State Library.

I have made a scrupulous effort to base Lola's story on sources contemporary with the events described. Whenever I have doubted the sources or whenever a lack of any documentation has forced me to speculate, I have tried to make that clear in the text. The first paragraphs of the biography, describing the thoughts of the Reverend Hawks, are a fiction based closely on Hawks's memoir of his brief association with Lola Montez; otherwise, I have invented nothing. All translations are my own. I think that the real story of the life of Lola Montez, told here for the first time, is at least as fascinating and incredible as Lola's own fictions or those of her previous biographers.

To assist anyone interested in pursuing the story of Lola Montez, I have deposited all of my notes and research materials with the Bancroft Library of the University of California, Berkeley. These thousands of pages include my transcribed notes, photocopies of newspapers and documents, and an earlier version of this biography, with additional material and more extensive citations. I have also added a critical bibliography and memoranda addressing some of the unanswered questions about Lola's life.

Writing this book would have been impossible without the help of many librarians and archivists. As custodians of the collective memory of mankind, they perform a priceless service that is rarely recognized and appreciated. It is impossible for me to thank each of them here individually, but my gratitude goes out to them for all they have done for me and for our civilization.

I would also like to express my thanks to a number of individuals and organizations who rendered special assistance in the work on this biography. Without my winnings on the television game show "Jeopardy!" it would have been impossible for me to devote four years of my life to the research and writing of this book, and I thank the producers and staff of Merv Griffin Productions for providing me with the opportunity to pursue Lola's story around the world.

The staffs of the Bavarian State Library, the Bavarian Central State Archives, and the Harvard Theatre Collection were particularly helpful in leading me through the extensive Lola Montez materials in their collections. I am grateful to them and to the other organizations and individuals who have allowed me to reproduce pictures or to quote from manuscripts in their collections.

My editor at Yale University Press, Heidi Downey, was faced with the daunting task of cutting a path through the dense undergrowth of my prose. I thank her for making the book more concise and readable.

Finally, I want to thank all the friends who have demonstrated extraordinary patience in listening to me babble about Lola Montez over the past four years. I know that they have concluded that I am Lola's final victim, seduced by charms that transcend time, and that they will be happier than I am that this project has come to an end. For even if it is almost with a sense of relief that I write my last lines about Lola Montez, I must admit that, despite her lies and her vanity, I will miss her.

1

FROM IRELAND TO INDIA

The Reverend Francis Lister Hawks appeared troubled as he walked down Manhattan's busy, muddy Seventeenth Street on a cold day in late December 1860. His uneasy thoughts focused not on the gathering storm of civil war but on a strange request from one of his parishioners at Calvary Episcopal Church. This woman had a childhood friend who was dying, a person Hawks had never met but whose reputation was known all too well to virtually everyone in the civilized world capable of reading a newspaper: Lola Montez.

The rector could recall more than a few amazing stories about Lola Montez, the woman who now requested his spiritual comfort in the face of death. She was variously reported to be a Spanish noblewoman, an Irish slut, or perhaps even a native New Yorker, but all accounts agreed that in her youth, not so many years ago, she had been a devastating beauty, enslaving the hearts of powerful and famous men as she danced seductively on stages all over the world. According to the stories, she had taken over the Bavarian government from old King Ludwig, her doting lover, and was transforming the kingdom into a model liberal state when murderous street mobs hired by reactionaries had forced her to flee. Her beauty was reputed to conceal a physical courage as great as any man's, and the cigarettes she constantly smoked characterized her disdain for conventional femininity. She could ride like an Amazon, was deadly with a pistol, and had horsewhipped more than

1

one man who had dared to impugn her character. Lola had seen, so the stories said, most of the known world and was as much at home in a hut in India as in a palace. Depending on which story you believed, Lola Montez was a living fury or feminine charm incarnate, a woman of imposing intellect or a common drab, the most amazing figure of her age or a greater humbug than Barnum. Troubled furrows creased the great bald pate above the Reverend Hawks's bushy eyebrows as he considered whether his mission to the dying woman would find him sharing the heartfelt confession of a truly penitent Christian or simply witnessing the pathetic desperation of a sinful whore whose only regret was that death would allow her to sin no longer.

The minister met his parishioner at her home on West Seventeenth Street, just off Fifth Avenue, and together they traveled the few blocks to 194 West Seventeenth, on the south side of the street, just short of Eighth Avenue. It was a middle-class district with respectable rooming houses, and the parishioner led the way up the stairs to a small rear apartment. Hawks stepped into a simple room, and in the flickering lamplight he looked down on the face of Lola Montez, once beautiful but now emaciated and wracked by suffering yet still vibrant, the dark blue eyes looming unnaturally large and expressive in the pale face framed by jet-black hair.

The rector must have wondered how the frail form before him could have excited the admiration and lust of kings and emperors, faced down angry mobs, and danced with abandon. But Lola had confessed to herself, "I have known *all* the world has to give—ALL!" Now, as she lay dying, she could look back on forty years filled with adventures sufficient for forty lifetimes.

Lola had once written that "our first feelings always remain our last memories," and for her those last memories would have been of an exotic childhood in India. The subcontinent's searing sun apparently had bleached from her memory her first three years, spent in the gray chill of Ireland. She arrived in India in the summer of 1823 with her father, an ensign in the British Army, and her mother, the illegitimate daughter of a pillar of Ireland's Protestant ruling class.

Some of his daughter's thirst for adventure must have come from Ensign Edward Gilbert, who had exchanged his safe but boring police duties in the discontented Irish hinterland for service with another regiment in India. Not only was India far more exotic than Ireland, but the pay there was better and went further; and an officer's chances for advancement, if he could withstand disease, the climate, and the rebellious natives better than did his superiors, were far greater than at home.

Gilbert was just twenty-six when he arrived in Calcutta, but he already had six years' service as an army officer behind him. Lola described him as having a handsome, boyish face, ornamented with light blond sidewhiskers and a thin mustache. His exact origins are a mystery, but he clearly sprang, legitimately or otherwise, from the nobility or well-to-do gentry.

He had arrived in County Cork with the Twenty-fifth Foot Regiment at the end of December 1818, and the regiment set about keeping down rebellion in King George's Irish domain. Cork had its attractions, and one of them was the Irish girls. Lola said that her father had a cheerful and engaging personality, and it may have been that personality as much as his youthful figure in the red uniform jacket and narrow trousers that attracted Eliza Oliver, a fourteen-year-old milliner's assistant. Oliver was a mighty name in both County Cork and adjoining County Limerick; the family had great land holdings and controlled most public offices and the parliamentary representation of the area. Eliza was proud of her origins in this powerful Protestant family even though she was illegitimate. Her father, Charles Silver Oliver, a former high sheriff of Cork and member of Parliament, had waited until he was past forty to marry, but while procrastinating he had sired four children by his mistress, Mary Green.

Eliza, or Elizabeth, as her father called her, was the youngest of Oliver's children by Mary Green. She was born in 1805, the same year her father finally took a well-born local heiress as his lawful wife and began begetting seven legitimate heirs to the Oliver name. But Eliza and her sister, Mary, and brothers John and Thomas all bore their father's name as well, and he saw to it that they were well taken care of, even after their mother died. The boys were apprenticed to grocers, and the girls were bound to Mrs. Hall, a milliner in Cork, so that they might support themselves honestly. And when Oliver died in 1817, he left each of his four "reputed" children £500, a considerable sum in those days, to be paid to them on their twenty-first birthday.

Ensign Gilbert was likely more impressed with Eliza Oliver's pretty face, dark eyes, and raven hair than with anything he might have learned about her father and her inheritance. The girl already had a woman's body, and in the spring of 1819 she demonstrated that fact—as well as her injudicious affection for the young officer—by becoming pregnant. Eliza had pride; she had to live with the shame of being illegitimate, and she seems to have been reluctant for all of Cork to note smugly that one of the bastards of the late

Charles Silver Oliver, M.P., was herself giving birth to a bastard, so it appears that she left the city to conceal her pregnancy. As Lola claimed Limerick as her birthplace, it is likely that her mother left the millinery to have her child in Limerick, where her brother Thomas probably was working.

If any record was made of the birth of the girl who would become a legend as Lola Montez, it has since disappeared. Lola would tell the King of Bavaria that she had been born on 14 February, and although she may have been lying to associate herself with the patron saint of lovers, she probably was born on about that date in 1820. Her mother gave the child her own first name and the father's last name.

At just about this time, Gilbert's regiment was moving out of Cork. Soldiers on police duty must be moved regularly to keep them from fraternizing with the people they are supposed to be suppressing, and the Twenty-fifth Foot was moving into the countryside farther north to discourage rebellion. But Eliza Oliver and Edward Gilbert returned to Cork so that they could be married on 29 April in Christ Church, where the Lord Mayor of Cork and all the Protestant elite of the city had their pews. And if anyone missed the posting of the notice, announcements were inserted in the newspapers so that all would know of the marriage of "Edward Gilbert, Esq., 25th Regiment to Eliza, daughter of late Charles Silver Oliver, Esq., of Castle Oliver, MP."

For the first two years of married life Gilbert was stationed in Ireland, mostly in County Boyle and County Sligo, but in 1822 Gilbert arranged to exchange his post with that of a new graduate of the Military Academy at Sandhurst, who had been assigned to the Forty-fourth Foot Regiment, already en route to India. In those days British trade with India was a monopoly of the British East India Company, a corporation that functioned as a quasi government in British-dominated parts of the subcontinent. The Honorable Company, as it was known, had its own army of native troops commanded by British officers, but these were supplemented by regiments of the regular British army. The regulars were regarded as far superior to the native soldiers, and in the general military reductions following the Napoleonic Wars, the War Office was happy to have employment for some of its regiments.

So the Gilberts traveled to England to arrange passage to India, and on 14 March 1823 they sailed from Gravesend, not knowing when they might return. In those days, before the Suez Canal was built, the voyage to India required about four months, with one or two stops for water and provisions. Gilbert arrived at Calcutta, the capital of the Presidency of Bengal, in the summer of 1823 to find that his new regiment had already been ordered to the garrison of Dinapore, near Patna, nearly four hundred miles up the Ganges.

After four months at sea, Gilbert and his wife could not have had much enthusiasm for setting out immediately with their small daughter on the arduous trip upriver, but it had been nearly a year since he had officially been transferred to the regiment, and any further delay in reporting for duty would be hard to justify. The family probably joined the last companies of the regiment departing from Calcutta and began the voyage in small boats up the Ganges. The expedition traveled only in daylight, averaging a little more than ten miles a day through the treacherous currents and shallows of the huge river. With the heat, the monsoon rains, the insects, and the tedious progress of the boats, the journey was anything but a pleasure trip. The natives who tended fields on the broad plain on both sides of the river were not fond of the foreigners, and they sold food to them only reluctantly.

Ensign Gilbert had come prepared for the tedium, bringing along ten volumes of *New British Theatre*, three volumes of Pope's works, *Rhyme and Reason, Essays on Physiognomy*, and a French grammar. With his colors and pencils and drawing kit, he was ready to capture the scenes of India, and in the evenings he could entertain his fellow travelers with his flute with silver fittings.

In spite of the discomfort and the slow progress of the boats, the travelers must have been fascinated by India's exoticism. The river stretched three miles wide in its main channel, and the landscape ranged from wide broad grassland to rich farms to forests filled with screeching gray apes. The Indians themselves, going about their daily lives along the waterway, must have seemed wonderfully strange to the Britons.

But for Ensign Gilbert the voyage was not the beginning of a great adventure. As the boats approached the great riverside market at Patna, he probably had begun to suffer the vomiting and diarrhea typical of the onset of cholera; and on 22 September, after the group had traveled the last few miles to the cantonment at Dinapore, Gilbert's name was entered in the muster rolls both as reporting for duty and as a casualty.

As a young, pretty officer's widow, Mrs. Gilbert would have had no problem finding suitors both in the regular British army and in the Honorable Company's regiments. She had a small widow's pension, but unless she remarried there would be little place for her, socially or economically, in the expatriate community in India.

According to Lola, her mother was a vain, self-centered woman who, though capable of devotion to her husband, was principally concerned with having people and movement around her; parties, balls, and society were the focus of her world. She was one of those unhappy women, Lola wrote, who suffer nervous prostration when left alone with their thoughts.

If that were the case, the widow Gilbert probably never seriously considered remaining in the remote and rugged outpost where she had buried her husband. Even if she were to remain in India, returning to Calcutta—the seat of the governor-general and of British society in the subcontinent—would certainly have been her goal. But as there was no regular passenger service on the river, she had to wait until a convoy of boats would be making the journey back.

The other officers' wives probably helped in caring for Eliza. She was old enough to sense the loss of her father, if not understand it, but the new faces, sights, and smells must have helped distract her from any grief she might have felt. Lola always accused her mother of neglecting her, leaving her in the care of indulgent Indian nursemaids, called *ayas*, who allowed her to become spoiled and undisciplined, and the pattern of her behavior probably was set while they were still at Dinapore.

A month after Gilbert's death the regiment auctioned his personal effects, and the proceeds, together with other money due the late officer, a total of £60, were paid over to his widow. That amount would have provided for the widow and her daughter for several months, but it came nowhere near paying for the voyage back to Great Britain. Whether or not the widow was inclined to mourn her husband for a full year, the only course of action likely to provide for her and her child was to find a new husband without delay.

The mother and daughter probably began the trip to Calcutta in November. It's possible that they even met the young Scot Lt. Patrick Craigie on the trip down the river. Craigie, of the Nineteenth Native Infantry Regiment of the British East India Company, had just been ordered back to Calcutta from his post as guard to the Company's political agent at the court in Jaipur, and he would have been traveling downriver past Dinapore at about this time.

Craigie was twenty-four and had been in India five years. He came from a large middle-class family of Montrose, on the east coast of Scotland. He was well liked by his fellow officers, and his superiors deemed him punctual, cheerful, and prompt in his duties. The young Scot was an impressive figure, and his oval face was framed by light-brown whiskers, perhaps grown to offset the prominent brow given him by a prematurely receding hairline.

Craigie had already begun to make a name for himself as an administrative officer capable of handling the myriad details involved in moving and supplying large bodies of troops.

A serious courtship seems to have developed between Craigie and the widow Gilbert by the following summer, when Craigie, at the request of Lt. Col. William Innes, was assigned to duty on the Sylhet frontier on what is now the northeastern border between Bangladesh and India. In Dacca on 16 August 1824, less than a year after burying her first husband, the nineteen-year-old Mrs. Eliza Gilbert became Mrs. Patrick Craigie.

Craigie had become attached not only to the Irish widow but also to her blue-eyed daughter, Lola wrote. It is certain that Lola's memories of her stepfather were far happier than those she had of her mother, and she always wrote of him with affection, saying that he kept her from ever missing her real father. Although her stepfather always referred to Eliza as "Mrs. Craigie's daughter," he was jolly and gentle and her principal source of happiness in their new household. His duties kept Craigie in the field far from home much of the time, and, if we are to believe Lola, her mother left her daughter largely to the care of the ayas. Lola later described herself as riding about on the hip of her nurse, half naked, constantly spoiled and praised.

Lola recounts that while her mother occupied herself with clothes and entertainments, the daughter had, under the smothering care of her aya, barely learned to walk, talk, or feed herself. The lushness of India, with its incredible variety of plant, animal, and human life, made a wonderful playground for the pampered but neglected girl, and Lola had fond memories not only of the birds and monkeys and flowers but also of daily life in India, of being bathed twice a day in the Houghly River, of the constant spectacle of the tradesmen, the dancers, the naked fakirs. "I always went barefoot," she wrote, "and my mind had never concerned itself with anything other than the strange and surprising spectacle that met the eye at every step in East India." She remembered chewing betel until her mouth was dyed bright red, and lying indoors on sweltering afternoons, listening in the shadow to the rhythmic swishing of the great ventilating fans, the *punkhas*, endlessly pulled by native boys who were paid pennies a day.

It was her stepfather, Lola said, who finally became concerned that six-year-old Eliza showed no signs of becoming anything other than a petted and half-wild animal. In late 1826 her carefree days in India came to an end. Lieutenant Craigie was appointed deputy assistant adjutant general at Meerut, near Delhi and more than a thousand miles from Calcutta, and at about the same time his former commander, Lieutenant Colonel Innes, decided to retire to England with his family. If Eliza were to be sent to Britain for schooling, as children of officers in India commonly were, this was the opportune time. In Meerut they would be too far from Calcutta to make arrangements easily for her passage. They were fortunate that Innes and his wife would be able to take charge of Eliza during the voyage back to Europe.

Craigie arranged for his stepdaughter to sail to London with the Innes family on the *Malcolm*. From London the child would be taken to live with Craigie's father in Montrose. Eliza was anything but happy about the prospect of leaving India. It was then, she later wrote, that she learned that no one is truly free and that the world is only a great prison.

Her mother set about enthusiastically packing lovely clothes and toiletries, which Lola would see as one more example of her mother's ability to find happiness in the vain and trivial. "Thus I parted from my first homeland," she would write, "full of poetic memories of the magical spectacle, the intoxicating dances, and left the company of those with whom I had spent my childhood."

The family had Christmas together, and on 26 December 1826, at Diamond Harbor, ninety miles downriver from Calcutta, where the *Malcolm* was anchored, the mother and stepfather embraced the girl for the last time. The mate noted in the log's passenger list, "Eliza Gilbert, daughter of Mrs. Craigie," the gangplank went up, the canvas snapped overhead, and the six-year-old waved a sad, painful goodbye to the only family and home she had ever known.

2

FROM CHILD TO WOMAN

Eliza was traveling in good company. Although he was an officer of the East India Company's army, not of the British Army, Lieutenant Colonel Innes was a Companion of the Order of the Bath, which meant that he was well bred, well connected, and well off. He, his wife, and their grown daughter had to deal with a moody, willful, and undisciplined six-year-old during the four-month journey. The *Malcolm* made one stop in Madras and then headed across the Indian Ocean, through storms and squalls, with the temperature dropping as the ship sailed southward. On 10 March it sighted Cape Agulhas, the southernmost tip of Africa, and began to sail north toward England.

The Inneses were patient and kind with their charge, but to Eliza they were strangers. In this alien world the girl demonstrated the volatility of temper and moods that would become one of her hallmarks. Eliza, accustomed to her two daily baths, must have found the water rationing on board just one more rude surprise. Fresh water was limited to five pints per day per passenger because it had to last until they reached the watering station at Saint Helena.

On 19 May 1827, after nearly five months at sea, the *Malcolm* landed at Blackwall, just down river from the Tower of London. Lola received heartfelt kisses from the colonel and his wife, which she took as a sign that all her moods and tantrums were forgiven, and was entrusted to the care of the relative who had come to escort her to Scotland.

To a child used to Calcutta, Montrose must have seemed alien and as still as death. Even the sun, low in the sky and rarely seen in the short, chill days of winter, was alien here. The town , with fewer than ten thousand inhabitants, lay on an estuary and tidal basin sheltered from the worst rages of the North Sea, between Dundee and Aberdeen. Eliza's stepgrandfather, also named Patrick Craigie, had been provost of the town four times during the Napoleonic Wars, retiring from the Town Council in 1816 to his druggist's practice. He and his wife, Mary, had had nine children in their thirty years of marriage, and the youngest was just six years older than the newcomer from India.

Lola recalled that the "arrival of the queer, wayward, little East Indian girl was immediately known to all Montrose. The peculiarity of her dress, and I dare say not a little eccentricity in her manners, served to make her an object of curiosity and remark; and very likely the child perceived that she was somewhat of a public character, and may have begun, even at this early age, to assume airs and customs of her own." Eliza was later remembered in Montrose for her uncontrollable love of fun and mischief; on one occasion, the locals recalled, she had amused herself during Sunday service in the red sandstone church in the High Street by silently sticking flowers into the wig of the old gentleman seated in the pew in front of her.

When she was eleven, her stepfather's older sister, Mrs. Catherine Rae, and her husband, William, moved south to Durham to establish a boarding school at Monkwearmouth. There is no way of knowing why Eliza went along, but she traveled to England with the couple late in 1831. Among the teachers engaged was a Mr. Grant, who taught drawing and who years later described the girl he had known:

> Eliza Gilbert . . . was at that time a very elegant and beautiful child of about ten or (perhaps) eleven; of stature rather promising to be tall than actually such for her age, but symmetrically formed, with a flowing graceful carriage, the charm of which was only lessened by an air of confident self-complacency—I might almost say of haughty ease—in full accordance with the habitual expression of her else beautiful countenance, namely, that of indomitable self-will—a quality which I believe had manifested itself from early infancy. Her features were regular, but capable of great and rapid changes of expression. Her complexion was orientally dark, but transparently clear; her eyes were of deep blue, and, as I distinctly remember, of excessive beauty, although bright with less indication of the gentle and

tender affections of her sex than of more stormy and passionate excitements. The mouth, too, had a singularly set character, far more allied to the determined than the voluptuous, and, altogether it was impossible to look at her for many minutes without feeling convinced that she was made up of very wayward and troublesome elements. The violence and obstinacy, indeed, of her temper gave too frequent cause of painful anxiety to her good kind aunt; and I remember, upon one occasion it was necessary, before Eliza could receive her lesson, to release her from solitary durance, in which she had been kept all the previous part of the day for some rebellious outbreak of passion. The door was opened, and out came the incipient Lola Montez, looking like a little tigress just escaped from one den to another!

Eliza's stay in Durham lasted only about a year. Captain Craigie (he had been promoted in late 1830), had served at Meerut under the command of Major General Sir Jasper Nicolls, who had distinguished himself by his leadership at the siege of Bhurtpore in 1825. Sir Jasper planned to return to England in the spring of 1831, and Craigie apparently saw the move as an opportunity to arrange for a more sophisticated education for his stepdaughter. A number of Sir Jasper's eight daughters were still of school age, and Craigie asked his former commander to place the girl where she would receive an education appropriate for a young gentlewoman.

Accordingly, Mrs. Rae and Eliza made the long coach journey from Durham and arrived on 14 September 1832 in Reading, in Berkshire, west of London, where Sir Jasper had his home. Sir Jasper was, Lola wrote, tall, with a high forehead and receding hairline above a stern face with two black, bushy eyebrows. Accustomed to command and obedience, the general, though fine and educated in his manners, allowed a certain military rigor to govern his relations, including those within the family circle. Lola characterized him as believing silence was dignity and coldness was seriousness. The twelve-year-old Eliza made an equally unfavorable impression on Sir Jasper, who early formed the opinion that the girl would come to no good. Having two self-willed egotists in the same household would have inevitably meant conflict, but the girl was not meant to remain in the Nicolls household but merely, as Sir Jasper phrased it in his journal, to be "put to school." Eliza was enrolled at a boarding school run by the Misses Aldridge in Bath, in Somerset.

Bath, a fashionable spa for the British upper class, was yet another new world for Eliza. Its architecture, including that of the famous abbey, the Pump House, and the Assembly Rooms, was far more impressive than anything Montrose or Monkwearmouth had displayed, and the sophistication and wealth of the inhabitants were far greater as well. But for the most part, Eliza would have been able to get only occasional glimpses of the fashionable life in Bath. Like any good girls' boarding school of the day, the Aldridge Academy kept a tight hold on its residents, letting them out only rarely and under close supervision. Most of Eliza's time was spent at 20 Camden Place (now Camden Crescent), where several years earlier the Aldridge sisters and their mother had rented a fashionable row house in which to open their school.

Camden Place had been planned as a sweeping arc of three-story town-houses to rival the Royal Crescent and the Lansdown Crescent, the elegant, curving housing developments that remain some of Bath's most coveted addresses. But the soil of the steep hillside on the right end of the arc proved unsuitable for building, so the crescent of townhouses has a slightly trun-cated look, with the imposing central pavilion located off center. Eliza's school was the next to last townhouse on the north end of the arc, and the great Corinthian pilasters ornamenting the classic facade gave it a most imposing aspect for a young ladies' boarding school. Above the entrance, in the honey-colored limestone that adorned the whole building, was carved an elephant, part of the arms of Lord Camden, for whom the development was named.

If Camden Place was not as fashionable as the other two townhouse cres-cents, it far surpassed them in the grandeur of its views. The street in front of the Aldridge Academy commanded a sweeping view of the lush, narrow, and winding Avon river valley. Down the slope in front of the school was the tower of the Walcott Church and Chapel, to which the girls were probably marched each Sunday. To the right the view swept over the gardens and houses along the London road toward the jumbled rooftops of central Bath, dominated by the gray eminence of the venerable abbey.

The Aldridge Academy had a boarding enrollment of about fifteen girls who ranged in age from ten to seventeen or eighteen. The curriculum included the usual feminine arts—dancing, sewing, drawing, and piano—but there was also an unusual emphasis on languages, including Latin and French. According to Lola, French was the normal mode of communication within the school, with English allowed only on Sundays. Girls who spoke English during the week had a fine deducted from their pocket money. The French she learned in Bath would serve Lola well, although she never spoke or wrote it idiomatically, even after years in Paris. Dancing was to become her profession, and needlepoint and playing the piano would remain favorite diversions her whole life.

How much contact young Eliza had with anyone outside the school is hard to say. She claimed to have spent school holidays with the Nicolls family in London and Paris and at "their castle near Bath," but Sir Jasper's journals make clear that these are Lola's fantasies. In fact, she was probably more or less abandoned at the school, like many boarding children of the age, to be reclaimed when marriageable.

The years at Bath seem nevertheless to have been happy ones for her. She remembered herself as having been the chief agitator against adult authority among the students and said she never tired of organizing tricks and pranks on the teachers. The education she received was outstanding for a girl of her class and station; at the time, many daughters of the middle class were simply taught by their mothers the skills deemed necessary to perform as a wife and mother. Sir Jasper estimated that Craigie invested more than £1,000 in his stepdaughter's education, a sum well over a full year's income for a captain; and Lola later gratefully remembered the sacrifice her mother and stepfather had made to develop her intellect. Those who came to know Lola Montez were often surprised at the breadth, if not always the depth, of her acquaintance with literature, art, and philosophy. The foundation of that knowledge probably was laid on Camden Place.

In Bath, Eliza grew into a young woman, her body filling out into a beautiful figure. She would spend nearly five years in Bath, the longest continuous period she would remain anywhere in her life. Like many teenage girls, she began to construct her own romantic persona, styling herself "Eliza Rosana Gilbert" now, adopting a more romantic name to fit the new life she longed to begin.

Sir Jasper did not approve of Eliza, nor, as much as he valued Captain Craigie as an officer, was he much taken with Mrs. Craigie. Simply attempting to get the mother to communicate with him about Eliza's education had proved frustrating. "At last we have heard from Mrs. Craigie," he wrote in his journal on 14 February 1834, "who was I supposed constrained to answer our numerous letters tho' she heard from us 6 times before this effect was produced—I felt greatly surprised—not a little vexed—and in some degree repented of having so easily undertaken an unpleasant and apparently thankless task. I likened her to a tortoise who buries her eggs lightly in the sand, and leaves them to sun, and to chance."

Eventually Mrs. Craigie realized that Eliza soon would have to be removed from school and prepared for married life, the most respectable and desirable course—and practically the only one—open to a young woman of her station. This was something that Mrs. Craigie could not expect the Nicolls to do for her; and with Eliza approaching seventeen, there could be no further delay. So on 2 November 1836, Mrs. Craigie left Calcutta on the steamer *Orient* to take Eliza from school and bring her back to India.

One of her fellow passengers was Thomas James, a lieutenant in the service of the East India Company, a member of the Twenty-first Native Infantry. He was good-looking and twenty-nine, about two years younger than Mrs. Craigie. He was returning to his native Ireland on convalescent leave, which, under the liberal policies of the Honorable Company, meant he might be gone for several years.

James came from County Wexford, where his family was part of the Protestant landed gentry but had no distinction nor great wealth. Mrs. Craigie told him of her plans to take her daughter from school and urged him, once he had visited his family, to come to Bath, perhaps take the waters for his health, and to call on her.

It is impossible to know how Mrs. Craigie and her daughter felt on that day in May 1837 when the mother stepped through the doorway of the school. They had parted when Eliza was six, and her memories of her mother must have grown vague and confused. And the child that Mrs. Craigie had sent off so many years before no longer existed. According to Lola's account, which may be colored by later events, the meeting got off to a bad start. The daughter, Lola wrote, threw her arms around her mother's neck and kissed her, and Mrs. Craigie reacted by crying out, "Oh! My dear child, how badly your hair is dressed!"

The relationship seems to have gone downhill from there. We have only Lola's accounts of what went on at Bath, and she never told the story the same way twice, but it appears that Mrs. Craigie moved her daughter from Camden Place into rooms that she had rented. Eliza continued to attend the academy while she and her mother lived together and, apparently, learned to dislike each other rather intensely.

At some point the handsome shipboard companion, Lieutenant James, arrived in Bath and visited the mother and daughter. To Eliza, who had been allowed limited contact with men, the thirty-year-old officer seemed old. She described him as of average height, with blue eyes and rather attractive brown hair, sparkling white teeth (rare in those days), a low brow, and searching eyes. He seems to have impressed her with how little he said. Lola referred to him as her mother's "cavalier," and she said that she and her teachers were struck by the protective manner he appeared to adopt with Mrs. Craigie.

At some point that spring Eliza's mother apparently raised the subject of marriage with her daughter. According to Lola, her mother told her that she was to return to India to marry a man named Lumley who was in his sixties. In Lola's account, he was a judge of the Supreme Court of India. At that time, however, there was neither a judge in India named Lumley nor was there a Supreme Court of India. So it seems most likely that Mrs. Craigie raised the possibility of Eliza's marriage to Major General Sir James Rutherford Lumley, a 64-year-old widower, who, as adjutant general of Bengal, was Captain Craigie's commanding officer. Marrying Eliza to the adjutant general might have been a shrewdly callous move for the Craigies, but it is impossible to know whether Mrs. Craigie seriously suggested it to her daughter. The general also had two bachelor sons in India; they, rather than their father, may have been the prospects she had in mind for her daughter. But we have only Lola's account, and she never allowed facts to interfere with a story designed to justify her conduct.

Whatever the facts, Lola recounted that as Lieutenant James escorted her daily between her lodgings and the academy, she took him into her confidence and shared her distress over what awaited her in India. As a man of thirty dealing with a girl from boarding school, James could not have had any great difficulties manipulating her emotions, providing her with sympathy and advice to gain her trust and finally her affection. At some point he decided that he wanted the schoolgirl, not the mother. Lust may have left him unclear himself as to what his intentions were, but he proposed to Eliza Rosana that they run off to Ireland. Lola would have us believe that the seventeen-year-old was so innocent that she expected the officer to "love her like her Papa"; it is unlikely that either of them truly realized what they were about to undertake. In any case, one evening at an appointed time James arrived with a carriage before Mrs. Craigie's lodgings, Eliza slipped out, and the horses pulled the conspirators slowly up the steep Bristol road. And the next day, only thirty miles from Bath, he was, wrote Lola, "no longer 'my Papa.'"

3

The Joys of Married Life

Whatever James intended, it must have become clear rather quickly that he would have to marry his Rosana. There were possible legal consequences for seducing a minor, and James probably realized that he would be committing social and professional suicide were he to seduce and abandon the stepdaughter of one of the Honorable Company's well-regarded officers. And perhaps he felt that it was time for him to settle down. He could certainly do worse than return to India with a beautiful young wife.

The couple sailed to Ireland and sought out James's older brother, the Reverend John James, who was vicar of the Church of Ireland parish of Rathbeggen, a few miles outside of Dublin. On 23 July 1837, Eliza Rosana Gilbert, as she now called herself, and Lt. Thomas James stood together in the little stone church of Rathbeggen and were married by the bridegroom's brother according to the service of the Book of Common Prayer. The only other people present were the vicar's wife and nephew, who signed the parish register as witnesses to the marriage. After the ceremony the couple left for Dublin, where they took lodgings in the heart of the city, on Westmoreland Street.

News of the runaway match reached Sir Jasper Nicolls back in England. "I am not a bad prophet as to the figure which young people will make in life," he wrote in his journal under the heading "Wretch Gilbert." "I always predicted the 'vanity and lies' of EG would bring her to shame—She has started very badly, if not worse, for, leaving school in June, she married a Company Officer without a penny, in 2 or 3 weeks—Her mother I fear cannot be blameless—at all events the 1800 or 2000 £ expended on her education and her mother's voyages is lost."

A few weeks later he added, "We have now heard of EGilbert from 3 quarters—all very, very, unsatisfactory both regarding herself and her husband—however Mrs. Craigie introduced the Gentl, and must bear the results as well as she can—She asked Lady N's advice thro' Mrs. Rae, and we have told her to let her daughter write, but not to return her to confidence imm'—nor to see her—They are full of contrition already—but I fear that they want to draw on Craigie's funds by that means, which we have warned her against." A few months later he summed up the matter: "Mrs. Craigie having lost all her spirit's comfort by the frauds of her silly child, & encouraged by Craigie, means to return to Calcutta in a few days. Hers has been a lot such to be pitied—a kind step-father has lavished £1000 on her child's education & the dirty ungracious whelp has thrown it all away on the first man she met—The day of punishment surely awaits from some source—her husband's fraud & falsehood, and her own."

If we are to believe Lola—and in this case we probably can—the punishment had already begun. First she discovered that James harbored something baser than fatherly affection for her, and now she was realizing that he was someone other than the romantic husband of her schoolgirl dreams. "The child had sought only a protector," Lola wrote, "but she found a master."

Shortly after the marriage the couple traveled south to visit the family seat, Ballycrystal, on the slopes of twenty-five-hundred-foot Mount Leinster, whose dark form dominated the rolling patchwork of fields stitched together by ancient hedgerows. Ballycrystal was simply a large house built from the abundant local stones and set on a gentle slope amid the rural poverty. Eliza's father-in-law, a widower also named Thomas James, was part of the Protestant gentry who governed the Catholic farmers. He had lived in Dublin but had retired to Ballycrystal to play the squire.

Many members of the squire's large family came to Ballycrystal to meet the bride. In spite of the company, Eliza soon found that she had traded the monotony of boarding school for the monotony of life in the Irish countryside. She described the daily routine in the household as hunting, followed by eating, followed by more hunting, followed by tea. The ceremonial tea drinking drove her to distraction. "These endless cups of tea, drunk with methodical conscientiousness in the same quantity, in the same rooms, these medicinal ablutions taken with unshakable solemnity at fixed times got on my nerves and made the whole business, whose pleasures I had never been able to understand, repellent to me."

Lola never was known for having a placid, even temperament, and confinement in a manor house certainly would not have brought out the best in her. Her new husband became moody, too, she says, and began to strike her when he was feeling sullen. And the great difference in their ages became troublesome. Though Eliza found some of her sisters-in-law congenial, life for her at Ballycrystal was unbearably joyless and depressing: "I wished for nothing more intensely than to be abducted once more, but this time not by a potential husband but by anything or anyone who would rescue me from the deadly monotony of this eternally repetitive life, from these cold English faces . . . no smiles, no friendly glances, no kind words."

Their return to Dublin came none too soon, and the bustle and activity must have seemed exhilarating to her. In their lodgings in Westmoreland Street she could finally play the mistress of her own household and entertain guests. The vicar of Rathbeggen came to dinner a number of times, and Lieutenant James and his wife frequently entertained and went out.

But as the spring of 1838 faded, it was time for James to think of returning to India. In the fall it would be two years since he had left India, and an overlong absence would endanger his prospects with the Honorable Company. Before leaving for India, the Jameses traveled through Scotland and England so that Eliza could visit her childhood friends as a married lady. They spent the summer traveling and preparing for the voyage to Calcutta. On 18 September they set sail from Liverpool aboard the *Bland*.

If life in Dublin had disguised the incompatibility of the couple, the summer tour and the four-month voyage seem to have made it all too clear. "A long trip together suffocates love," Lola wrote, "even on the honeymoon. Travel by coach makes one weary and sleepy. You go to sleep from boredom and awake bored. The spirit and the feet lose their patience.

"The sea," she continued, "makes women sick and men extraordinarily unpleasant. In the marital cabin you are constantly bumping into one another. You can't turn around without unwillingly embracing one another."

While not as confining as life at Ballycrystal, the shipboard routine had its limitations. James, according to his wife, drank porter and slept like a boa constrictor. She spent her time chatting with the other passengers during the day and attending dances in the salon at night.

Long before land came into sight, there were signs that the voyage was ending. The drainage of the Ganges extended well into the ocean, filling the sea with brown silt and broken branches. The passengers of the *Bland* disembarked at Diamond Harbor below Calcutta on 25 January 1839, and Eliza was back in the land of her childhood.

Eliza, now a young matron, experienced Calcutta very differently than she had as a six-year-old. She had been in Great Britain for eleven years, and the great city had to seem far more exotic to the woman than it had to the child. She could appreciate with new eyes the lush plant life and the spectacle of daily life on the streets and along the river. But now she was an officer's wife, and it was unthinkable that she wander about alone or with natives in the fascinating Indian part of the city. Her sphere was confined to British Calcutta, the residents of which did their best to bring the Mother Country to the tropics. On the day of the *Bland*'s arrival, the Jameses could have spent the evening at the Town Hall attending a performance of Haydn's "The Creation," hardly the sort of entertainment associated with the exotic East.

It is doubtful that Eliza had much chance to shine in the ballrooms of Calcutta. Lieutenant James may have taken a few weeks to visit old friends in the capital and arrange passage upriver, but the Twenty-first Native Infantry was now stationed at Karnal, north of Delhi, more than a thousand miles away.

The trip began in boats that traveled at just a few miles per hour. Eliza had made the same journey with her parents nearly sixteen years earlier. Her only recollection of the first part of this journey seems to have been of constant bickering with her husband. She claimed that he had begun carrying a pocket notebook in which he would record her transgressions against wifely duty and then preach to her from it about her shortcomings. The boats passed Patna and then Dinapore, where Lola's father was buried. In the holy city of Benares she was impressed by the great stone terraces leading down to the sacred river, by the mass of Indians streaming up and down them, and by the worshipers standing in the water, praying and making their ablutions.

Beyond Benares the Ganges was unreliable for navigation, and the roads were too primitive for wheeled vehicles. The passengers continued the journey in enclosed litters carried by natives. This had the virtue of separating the feuding couple during the day. The bearers were changed like post horses at regular intervals. Lola compared the rhythm of the march to the slow trot of a Parisian cab horse, and she never forgot the rhythmic, monotonous chants sung by the bearers.

The lieutenant and his bride probably reached the garrison in the spring of 1839. Karnal lies on the upper edge of the north Indian plain, a landscape broken only by the enticing but distant view of the Himalayan foothills. The post was hot and dusty and undistinguished, though Karnal was a bit greener than most of the surroundings because of some nearby wetlands. But the wetlands bred malarial mosquitoes that plagued the garrison. A few years later the depredations of the mosquitoes would force the army out of Karnal, but for now the garrison was home to the Jameses. It is likely that Eliza contracted malaria here. In her later years she suffered extended attacks of severe chills and fever with headaches, which were successfully treated with large doses of quinine. Her persistently fragile health in later life could well have been the result of chronic malaria.

Life in the closed society of only a few score officers and their wives must have been monotonous. Social convention restricted the wives' freedom severely, and the women were expected to absent themselves from all social events when their husbands were not in camp.

Eliza made friends with the women and enjoyed the household of servants that even a junior officer could easily afford to keep. The endless movement of the punkhas made the heat endurable inside the bungalows, but the slow, steady rhythm must have emphasized the monotony.

Mrs. Craigie and her daughter had been in correspondence, and when the mother went to the fashionable resort of Simla, in the Himalayan foothills, for the hot season, Eliza joined her. The grande dame of Simla's summer society was Emily Eden, the spinster sister of Bengal's governor-general, Lord Auckland, and in her letters home she left a remarkable first-hand account of Eliza and her mother at Simla:

Sunday, Sept. 8 [1839]
Simla is much moved just now by the arrival of a Mrs. J[ames], who has been talked of as a great beauty all the year, and that drives every other woman, with any pretensions in that line, quite distracted.... Mrs. J[ames] is the daughter of a Mrs. C[raigie], who is still very handsome herself, and whose husband is deputy-adjutant-general, or some military authority of that kind. She sent this only child to be educated at home, and went home herself two years ago to see her. In the same ship was Mr. J[ames], a poor ensign, going home on sick leave. Mrs. C[raigie] nursed him and took care of him, and took him to see her daughter, who was a girl of fifteen at school. He told her he was engaged to be married, consulted her about his prospects, and in the meantime privately married this child at school. It was enough to provoke any mother, but as it cannot be helped, we have all

been trying to persuade her for the last year to make it up, as she frets dreadfully about her only child. She has withstood until now, but at last consented to ask them for a month, and they arrived three days ago. . . . Mrs. J[ames] looked lovely, and Mrs. C[raigie] had set up for her a very grand jonpaun, with bearers in fine orange and brown liveries, and the same for herself; and J[ames] is a sort of smart-looking man, with bright waistcoats and bright teeth, with a showy horse, and he rode along in an attitude of respectful attention to "ma belle mere." Altogether it was an imposing sight, and I cannot see any way out of it but magnanimous admiration.

Tuesday, Sept. 10
We had a dinner yesterday. Mrs. J[ames] is undoubtedly very pretty, and such a merry unaffected girl. She is only seventeen now [*sic*], and does not look so old, and when one thinks that she is married to a junior lieutenant in the Indian army, fifteen years older than herself, and that they have 160 rupees a month, and are to pass their whole lives in India, I do not wonder at Mrs. C[raigie]'s resentment at her having run away from school.

Simla must have seemed a paradise to Eliza after months in the swelter of Karnal. Here, at an altitude of more than seven thousand feet, the air was cool and fresh in the pine forests that sloped down steeply from the hill station. Rhododendrons grew thirty or forty feet tall on their spindly trunks, and great gray apes jumped and swung through the trees and clambered over the rooftops.

To the north, the snows on the majestic Himalayan range glistened, making the air seem even cooler. Simla was among the first of many hill stations that the British would develop for their comfort and amusement in India. Although conditions were still relatively primitive, a great succession of balls and races and charity auctions and masquerades made for a busy summer season.

The return to Karnal must have been painful for Eliza, and life there probably was even more monotonous and unendurable after the cool and carefree month in Simla. When the season ended, the governor-general and his party, including his sister Emily, descended from the hills to begin their trek to their winter seat. On 12 November they were greeted on their arrival at Karnal by a parade of the garrison. "We were at home in the evening," Emily Eden wrote, "and it was an immense party, but except that pretty Mrs. J[ames] who was at Simla, and who looked like a star amongst the others, the women were all plain." The visitors camped at Karnal for five days, and a round of entertainments was produced, including a dinner for the gentlemen alone, pony races, and a ball. On the morning of 17 November the governor's party continued its progress, and Miss Eden wrote

> Little Mrs. J[ames] was so unhappy at our going, that we asked her to come and pass the day here, and brought her with us. She went from tent to tent, and chattered all day, and visited her friend Mrs. ———, who is with the camp. I gave her a pink silk gown, and it was altogether a very happy day for her, evidently. It ended in her going back to Karnal on my elephant with E. N. by her side, and Mr. J[ames] sitting behind, and she had never been on an elephant before, and thought it delightful. She is very pretty, and a good little thing, apparently, but they are very poor, and she is very young and lively, and if she falls into bad hands, she would soon laugh herself into foolish scrapes. At present the husband and wife are very fond of each other, but a girl who marries at fifteen hardly knows what she likes.

Miss Eden was under the impression that Eliza was seventeen, but she was in fact almost certainly nineteen at the time. The most logical explanation seems to be that Miss Eden learned Eliza's age from Mrs. Craigie, who may have made herself a few years younger than she was and didn't want to explain how she could have a nineteen-year-old child. Or perhaps she was not eager to admit that she had been only fourteen when her daughter was born.

In February 1840 the Twenty-first Native Infantry was transferred to Moradabad, about one hundred fifty miles southeast of Karnal. Perhaps through the influence of Major Craigie, Lieutenant James was appointed adjutant of the recruit depot at Bareilly, about sixty miles farther southeast. The recruit depot was responsible for the enlistment and training of the Indians who made up the rank and file of the Honorable Company's armies, and as adjutant, James would be an administrative officer, like his father-in-law.

The garrison at Bareilly was substantially smaller than the one at Karnal, and the climate was just as bad. Though the surroundings were not malarial, they offered scarcely greater attractions for a young officer's wife than what she had known before. And there was probably less opportunity for the couple to escape each other than there had been at Karnal. "Days become centuries," Lola wrote, "when you're trapped in an unhappy marriage."

Lola later claimed that her husband ran off with another officer's wife, but that story conflicts not only with the facts but with other accounts that she herself gave. She apparently left him, possibly because he was physically abusing her, and went to her mother and stepfather in Calcutta. But Mrs. Craigie had no sympathy for her only child; first Eliza had destroyed her chances for an advantageous marriage by eloping with James, and now she was abandoning the very match for which she had sacrificed her future. The mother refused to have the scandal come to rest under her roof, and she gave Eliza the choice of returning to her husband or going back to Great Britain. Eliza chose Britain.

On 5 August, Lieutenant James took three months' leave from his post at Bareilly to visit Calcutta, where he and Major Craigie made arrangements for Eliza's return to England. Craigie wrote to his sister, Mrs. Rae, and to friends in London to arrange for her reception there until she could catch a steamer to Scotland, where she would stay with his brother, Dr. Thomas Craigie, in Leith. All were told that Mrs. James had never recovered from a back injury sustained by falling from a horse at Meerut and that she was returning to a healthier climate to convalesce. Even if there was still hope of a reconciliation, it would be years before the couple saw each other again, and James arranged for a separate income for his wife in Great Britain.

Passage was secured for Mrs. James on the *Larkins*, and Lieutenant James and his brother-in-law, John Thornhill, a civil servant in Calcutta, came out to the ship to inspect her cabin. Thornhill discovered that an American couple he knew, Henry P. Sturgis and his wife, Mary, of Boston, would be traveling on the same ship, and he and the lieutenant asked them to take Eliza under their care during the voyage.

Major Craigie and Thomas James took Eliza to the ship on 3 October 1840. Craigie said his farewell there, and Lola remembered that great tears ran down his cheeks as he took his leave. He also, she claimed, put into her hand a bank draft for £1000, a sum that, carefully used, would initially give her a fair amount of independence back home. James sailed part way down the Ganges before he said farewell to his wife and took a boat to shore. He had asked the ship's captain, Charles Ingram, and his wife, Ann, to do all they could to make the voyage easy for Eliza, and it seems likely that James felt real affection for his wife and regretted how things had turned out. That would help explain his reaction to the news of her that would reach him from England.

Although she was only twenty, Eliza's name was blotched with the scandal of elopement with an older man and now with the scandal of a failed marriage. An honest relationship with another man was out of the question as long as her husband was alive. She could live with her stepfather's relatives and try to survive on the income James had established for her, but she was far too young and spirited to start sitting by the fire and counting pennies. On her own, there was little that she could respectably undertake. Her education was particularly good for a woman, and she might be able to find a position as a governess. With the proper recommendations, perhaps she could become a female companion to a lady of rank. Her prospects must have seemed few and somber.

About ten days into the voyage, the ship stopped at Madras, capital of another of the three presidencies of the East India Company. One of the passengers boarding at Madras, George Lennox, quickly caught her attention, and she must have caught his. Lennox, not yet twenty, was a lieutenant in the Fourth Madras Cavalry, but he held the prestigious position of aide de camp to the governor-general, Lord Elphinstone. He was a nephew of the Duke of Richmond, one of the richest and most influential members of the British nobility; but the Lennox family was large , and the power and wealth were rather dilute by the time they reached his level. He had been in Madras for more than three years and was returning home for the first time.

The *Larkins* cast off from Madras, and within a few days Captain Ingram and his wife began to notice that Mrs. James was acting "unguarded and flighty" around Lieutenant Lennox, who seemed more than a little disposed to flirt with her. The dalliance developed quickly, and it wasn't long before all on board were aware Mrs. James and Lennox were behaving in a shameless manner. Mary Sturgis, who had been charged by Lieutenant James with the protection of his wife, felt that she had to call Eliza to her senses, but the young woman's response was a vehement demand that the American mind her own business.

The ladies on board were expected to leave the passengers' promenade on the poop deck and retire below at an appropriate hour, but Mrs. James and Lieutenant Lennox remained together on the poop after all the ladies were gone. And late at night as they sat by the rail, Lennox was seen to slip his arm around her waist, and she made no objection.

The disapproving stares and their desire for privacy led them to begin visiting each other in their cabins. The doors were closed, but everyone knew that the sofa on which they sat together became a bed by night. When it was pointed out to Mrs. James that it was not proper for a woman to visit a gentleman in his cabin alone, she replied that, because Lennox's cabin had a window and hers did not, it was much cooler that hers during the day, and she dismissed any objection. The captain's wife kept an eye on that window; and when the venetian blind was open, she saw them time and again sitting on his sofa with his arm around her waist.

In the evenings the lieutenant would come to Mrs. James' windowless cabin and remain until late into the night. Morality aside, Captain Ingram felt it his duty to point out that she was creating a fire hazard by receiving a visitor and keeping a lamp on long after lights-out; Eliza coolly told the captain that she would do as she liked and would not be under the control of anybody.

The *Larkins* plowed across the Indian Ocean toward the Cape of Good Hope, and the shipboard scandal grew daily. Never, fumed Captain Ingram, in all his years in the service of the East India Company, had he seen such improper conduct in a married woman. One Sunday morning as the passengers and crew assembled on deck for the divine service conducted by the captain, Mrs. James and Lieutenant Lennox quietly retired to her cabin and closed the door as the prayers of the others rose up to God.

Every society must find a way to enforce its norms of decent behavior, and the ultimate sanction aboard the *Larkins* was exclusion from the captain's cabin. The Ingrams agreed that they could no longer receive Mrs. James, who was therefore excluded from the celebration of Christmas and New Year's at the captain's table. But the sanction does not seem to have moderated her behavior in the least.

Indeed, it was whispered about the ship that not just impropriety but actual immoral conduct was taking place. Caroline Marden, the Ingrams' maid, kept an eye on the door to Mrs. James's cabin, knowing that sometimes the rolling of the ship threw the door open. Her patience was rewarded a number of times, giving her glimpses of Lennox and Eliza kissing and of the two together, with Mrs. James dressed only in her stays and petticoats; more than once he was actually lacing up her stays. And after the door swung open to reveal Mrs. James putting on her stockings in front of Lennox, there could be no doubt about the nature of the relationship.

Major Craigie had written via the overland mail, which arrived in England two months earlier than the *Larkins*, to arrange as carefully as possible for his stepdaughter's transfer to Leith. "We are very anxious that Mrs. James should not be delivered for any time in London but that she should proceed at once to Scotland," he wrote, perhaps sensing the snares awaiting his stepdaughter on her own. Sarah Watson, a widowed sister of Lieutenant James, lived at Blackheath in Kent outside of London, and Craigie's sister, Catherine Rae, came down from Edinburgh and stayed with Mrs. Watson to await Eliza's arrival and accompany her to Scotland.

On Saturday, 20 February 1841, the *Larkins* landed its passengers at Portsmouth, and Captain Ingram watched with disapproval as Lieutenant

Lennox and Mrs. James walked off together, arm in arm. After their luggage had cleared customs, it was too late to get up to London. So they went to the Star and Garter Inn, where Lennox got them a suite of two bedrooms with a common sitting room. But by the time they arrived in London the next night, apparently even that concession to propriety seemed pointless, and when they got to the Imperial Hotel on Tavistock Row in Covent Garden, they agreed that they needed a sitting room with just one bedroom and a large bed. They had a dinner of cutlets and tea sent up and then retired for the night together.

The next morning Lennox collected his luggage, paid the bill, and went to catch the coach to Chicester. His parents, at their home in Bognor, would certainly hear soon of his arrival on the *Larkins*, and he would have a hard time explaining why he had been in London instead of coming straight home after three years away. Eliza caught a hansom cab in front of the hotel and went to look for lodgings. Lennox would be back and she would be there for him, not on her way to Scotland.

Two days later Eliza moved into a first-floor suite at 7 Great Ryder Street. Lennox was back from Bognor before the end of the week, and he came to see her every day, arriving as early as nine and often staying the whole day, sometimes taking her to the theater but leaving before midnight. Although Eliza had made no effort to contact the relatives who were to meet her, they tracked her down, and early one afternoon she returned to find her sister-in-law, Sarah Watson, waiting for her in her drawing room. Mrs. Watson, who knew what was going on between her sister-in-law and Lennox, was not a scold or a prude, but she saw that Eliza was destroying whatever future remained to her by persisting in this connection.

Eliza knew Mrs. Watson from her visit to Ballycrystal and liked her; but the more Mrs. Watson argued, the more unyielding Eliza's defense became. Eliza even swore an oath that she would never go to any friend of her stepfather's, including Catherine Rae, his sister.

Mrs. Watson was discouraged, but in a few days she was back in Great Ryder Street with Mrs. Rae, who joined in the effort to persuade Eliza to go to Scotland. When the young woman refused to go, Mrs. Rae offered to take her in herself at her home in Edinburgh. There was affection between Eliza and the older woman, who had been the girl's surrogate mother in Monkwearmouth, but it was difficult for Mrs. Rae to convince Eliza that the excitement of being her own woman for the first time—of being young and pretty and in love in London—was something she would regret. Eliza wavered, but in the end Mrs. Rae left, defeated, and returned to Scotland. Mrs. Watson also gave up her efforts, and letters went off to India reporting the sad facts concerning the life Mrs. James had adopted.

Eliza left the rooms on Great Ryder Street and moved to the more fashionable Half Moon Street in Mayfair. The affair with Lennox continued, and Mrs. James grew into a minor figure in London society. Her large deep-blue eyes and jet-black hair impressed all who saw her. She regularly rode the fashionable carriage paths in Hyde Park, driven in an elegant phaeton behind a pair of matched gray ponies.

But toward the end of July, something changed for Eliza. She moved from Half Moon Street to a less fashionable address, then a week later moved once more. After another week she moved yet again. Finally, toward the end of August 1841 she moved to a cottage on Hornsey Road in suburban Islington. The affair with Lennox seems to have run its course. Perhaps his family and friends were able to convince him that the affair had no future and that he could only damage himself by continuing it. Or perhaps the passion born in the close confines of a ship couldn't survive in the distractions and temptations of London.

By the end of the summer Lennox wasn't calling any longer, and Mrs. James was a woman with a past. With the intoxication of romance over, Eliza must have been faced with some sober realities. The funds she had when she arrived were disappearing, she later wrote, "by a sort of insensible perspiration, which is a disease very common to the purses of ladies who have never been taught the value of money." She had never had to manage money, and it did not come naturally. Her impulse was always that money was there to be spent.

Eliza certainly met other men as she was squired about London by Lennox, and there were probably some who were willing to take the lieutenant's place and help out a pretty woman with her expenses. But the affair with Lennox had been passion and romance; Eliza had actually thought that she would divorce Lieutenant James and become Mrs. Lennox. Moving from that fairy tale to being just another of London's high-priced courtesans was even worse for the proud, rebellious young woman than admitting she had been wrong. Eliza stayed on in Islington, considering her situation and probably receiving letters from India filled with outrage, recriminations, and sorrow. In October she at last packed her things and caught the coach to Edinburgh, to live with Mrs. Rae.

But it was too late. Word had reached Lieutenant James of his wife's betrayal. Whether he was driven by a sense of offended honor, wounded love, or simply relief at having a reason to rid himself of his responsibility for Eliza, James had promptly decided that his wife and her lover would not be allowed to sin with impunity. But even express mail took at least two months to travel between Britain and India, so it was some time before the necessary signatures could be obtained to put the ponderous wheels of justice into motion.

In the meantime, Eliza James had moved in with Catherine Rae at 15 Nelson Street in Edinburgh and was living a life of quiet respectability through the cold, gray Scottish winter. That came to an end on a Friday in the middle of March when an unknown gentleman called for Eliza Rosana James. When she received him, he served her with a summons to appear to defend herself against the accusation of adultery before the Court of Arches in London.

Thomas James had sued her for divorce. He would subject her to the public shame of being branded with adultery, virtually the only ground for divorce. If Eliza had been considering a conventional life, that of a governess or lady's companion who would retire into quiet obscurity, those thoughts disappeared now. She would stay no longer with Mrs. Rae. She would make her own way in the world, suiting herself and no one else.

4

L O L A   M O N T E Z   I S   B O R N

Lola never really explained her decision to go on the stage. She would claim it was a matter of need, not choice; and with all prospect of financial support from her husband cut off, that was probably true, at least in part. But for a woman whose will was as great as her charm and whose ego was as impressive as her beauty, the stage must have seemed an obvious choice. Eliza Gilbert James decided that she would not be content counting out her days in respectable poverty. She wanted to live, to see the world, to be her own woman, and she would make the stage her springboard to all she desired.

The British theater world revolved around London, to which Eliza returned early in 1842. An acquaintance suggested that she meet as many young men of good society as possible in order to establish her career. Her affair with Lennox had brought her into contact with the better circles in London, and as a vivacious and beautiful woman of intelligence, she would have no trouble meeting the right men. From them she probably received not only the introductions necessary to establish herself in a new career but also enough money to maintain herself elegantly until she had her own income.

According to her own account, Lola first intended to become an actress, so she went to study with Fanny Kelly at the academy she had opened behind her home on Dean Street in Soho. Miss Kelly, a famous actress who had recently retired, formed the school for young actresses with the avowed intention of counteracting the social and artistic prejudice against women on the stage. But the new student was found wanting, perhaps because her accent was too unorthodox or because her small voice could not carry well in London's large theaters. If she truly wanted a life in the theater, it was suggested to Mrs. James, dance might be the art form she should pursue.

At twenty-two, Eliza was far too old to begin to study classical ballet, which required training and practice from an early age. Her only hope was to specialize in something less technically demanding, such as character or national dance. Spain and Spanish culture were then much in fashion. Even the greatest ballerinas of the age—including Fanny Elssler, Marie Taglioni, and Fanny Cerito—introduced Spanish boleros and chacuchas and fandangos into their repertoires, albeit in refined versions that exploited their classical training and the taste of their audiences. Lola wrote that she engaged a Spanish dancing master in London for four months to teach her the dances of his homeland, and then she took a trip to Spain.

Although the trip allowed her to learn the dances at their source, it may also have been a means of escaping London as *James v. James* was about to be tried in Consistory Court and *James v. Lennox*, for damages for adultery, was about to come to issue in Queen's Bench. And the trip may have been designed to effect the disappearance of Eliza Gilbert James and the emergence of an exotic, unknown beauty: Lola Montez.

There is no way of knowing just when and why she abandoned her identity and created her new persona, a woman with a different past and with decidedly different prospects for the future. Perhaps she realized that as Eliza Gilbert James, a native of Limerick with questionable morals, her credibility as a Spanish dancer would be limited at best. But as Maria Dolores de Porris y Montez, the proud and beautiful daughter of a noble Spanish family impoverished and exiled by the cruel Carlist civil war, she would be a figure of romance and fascination.

Mrs. James sailed to Cádiz, known for its traditional dances, and she may have also visited Seville. She would later claim to have been the principal soloist of the Teatro Real de Sevillia, but, as for so many of her stories, there is no evidence to support her claim. She did, however, learn something of Spanish dancing, Spanish dress and customs, and the Spanish language. And she also acquired an addiction to tobacco in the form of cigarettes, which she learned to roll deftly, or potent little cigars.

Back in London, James's action against Lieutenant Lennox for "criminal conversation" with Mrs. James came before Lord Denman in the Court of Queen's Bench on the chill and foggy morning of 6 December 1842. Opening arguments were interrupted by a whispered conference as the white wigs of the opposing counsel bobbed together before the bench, and then the barristers announced to the judge that the defendant had offered to consent to entry of judgment against him in the amount of £100, which counsel for Lieutenant James was willing to accept for his client. A public discussion of the nature of Mrs. James's and Lieutenant Lennox's "conversation" was delicately avoided as Lord Denman entered judgment for the plaintiff in the stipulated amount.

A little more than a week later, in the old courtroom of the Doctors Commons near St. Paul's Wharf, Dr. Stephen Lushington of the Court of Arches sat to hear the case of *James v. James*. The Court of Arches was not a royal court but a Consistory Court—an ecclesiastical court—for divorce was still under the jurisdiction of the Church of England; the court acted not in the name of the young queen but in that of the archbishop of Canterbury. Lushington had already heard testimony in the case on several occasions. In previous hearings Eliza Rosana James had three times been called in open court and had each time failed to respond in person or through counsel. Now, as the court prepared to rise at the end of its Michaelmas term, the matter was ripe for judgment.

Lushington was completely satisfied that the evidence proved Mrs. James's adultery, and he ordered entry of the standard sentence in divorce actions. It decreed "divorce or separation from bed, board, and mutual cohabitation," and it also provided that "neither of them in the life time of the other shall in any way attempt or presume to contract another marriage." A divorce by the Consistory Court gave no right of remarriage, even though King Henry VIII had created the Church of England to free himself from Catherine of Aragon so that he could marry Ann Boleyn. To obtain a divorce absolute with a right to remarry, Lieutenant James would have had to obtain a special act of Parliament, which would cost more than £1000 and might require political influence, too. Such bills were passed only once or twice a year. Remarriage in Great Britain obviously was reserved for the rich and powerful, something that Lola Montez would forget at her peril.

At that moment, Lola Montez was still being born. By spring Lola had decided that it was time to return to England to launch her career. She took passage on a ship and arrived in Southampton on about 14 April. The trip from the harbor to London seems to have been most fortuitous for her. The Earl of Malmesbury, a prominent nobleman and a politician of some importance, recorded in his memoirs that he happened on that same day to be returning to London on the train from Heron Court, his country seat in Hampshire. The earl was thirty-six, married, wealthy, and influential. There were contemporary accounts that he had in fact known Eliza James before she became Lola Montez and had actually arranged and financed her expedition to Spain. But according to the earl himself, he first met the raven-haired siren when the Spanish consul at Southampton asked him to look after a young Spanish woman who had just landed.

As they rode together on the train to London, the earl wrote, she told him of herself and her life. She was the widow of Don Diego Leon, whose execution had recently received much publicity in Europe. Diego Leon had been involved in an attempted putsch against Queen Isabella II and the regent Christina and was the lone rebel who refused to flee when the conspiracy collapsed; he had been promptly shot for his steadfastness, posthumously winning hearts all over Europe.

Now, the blue-eyed beauty said, she had been forced to flee her homeland in order to sell some property in London and give singing lessons, for she had lost everything. The earl wrote that he took pity on the hero's widow and invited her to perform her native ballads at a benefit concert at his home, where she sold Spanish veils and fans to his guests. And because she expressed a desire to go on the stage, he introduced her to Benjamin Lumley, the powerful impresario of London's famous Her Majesty's Theatre.

Whether we can believe the earl's assertion that he was one of the first dupes of the beautiful and wily Lola Montez, there were certainly men of rank and wealth who quietly worked to promote the newborn Spaniard. Someone had to provide the money for her dancing lessons, for her Spanish sojourn, for her theatrical costumes, for copying the orchestra parts of the music to which she performed. What her benefactors received for their generosity is as difficult to specify as their identities, but it would have been unusual had Lola not been trading sexual favors. In most theaters, the corps de ballet was paid less than a living wage on the theory that each dancer would find one gentleman or more from the audience who would provide for her maintenance in exchange for private performances of a special nature.

Lola deftly skirts the problem in her memoirs:

Should I have rejected such friendly offers of help? I certainly recognized the dangers that could thereby arise for me, the gossip it had to cause; but we poor women are such helpless creatures that we do not always have a choice of means. Often we are forced to achieve our goals by whatever is available to us, even when we recognize that we are thus put in an unflattering light.

Besides, I had already seen and experienced enough of the artistic world to know that an artiste, even with the best effort, cannot always avoid bad appearances. Should I, at the cost of tremendous sacrifice, perhaps even renunciation of a brilliant career, try to be an exception from the general rule? That would have been laughably foolish. The purity of my conscience would have to be enough for me, and with my natural carefree spirit I decided to place no importance upon attention to appearances.

Whoever was paying the bills, Lola was living well and being seen on the edges of the finer circles of society. Malmesbury's lobbying of Lumley on Lola's behalf was another turning point in her life. The earl was an important patron of Her Majesty's Theatre, and Lumley, an astute judge of talent, sensed that Lola had a combination of beauty, stage presence, and "something *piquant* and provocative" that could mean a hit; so the impresario let himself be "taken in" by the beautiful novice.

Lumley demonstrated his confidence in the young woman's theatrical abilities by scheduling her stage debut for 3 June, when she would dance "El Oleano" between the acts of a gala performance of Rossini's *Barber of Seville*. The gala nature of the evening was due to the presence of the queen's uncle, the aged King of Hanover, who was on a state visit to his niece and would occupy the box of his sister-in-law, the Dowager Queen Adelaide. The glittering elite of the capital's nobility were expected to attend, and anyone with any pretension to being someone would be scrambling for tickets.

From his office under the colonnaded portico on the Haymarket Street side of the theater, the wily Lumley began a small publicity campaign to ensure his debutante's immediate success. Malmesbury and the opera house clique behind Lola could be counted on to spread the word among their friends, and Lumley called in one of his own friends in the press, the critic of the *Morning Post*, to prepare the journalistic field for Lola's triumph. He invited the critic to one of Lola's rehearsals, introduced him to the beautiful Spaniard, and left them together to let the woman work her charms on him. "Her figure was even more attractive than her face, lovely as the latter was. . . . Her foot and ankle were almost faultless." It was clear to the critic that the woman was not a finished dancer, yet there was something about her beauty, her fascination, that disposed him to give her "the support of my influence and pen."

After the rehearsal they sat and talked, and the critic discovered that Lola's fascination was far more than physical. "Now, who is there, you will let me ask," he wrote afterward, "that has ever had half an hour's conversation with the Donna Lola, that can, for an instant doubt, but he has spoken with a sparklingly brilliant creature. I at any rate certainly do not. She is, probably enough, of that genius, which in England is invariably called 'fast,' but her speed is most indubitably that of talent.

"She conversed with me of almost everything—Nay! I had almost said, of a good deal more—told me anecdote after anecdote of Spanish life, many of them very 'fast' ones indeed, with a *verve* and *entrain*, which were irresistible."

The critic of the *Post* was ready to do whatever was necessary to ensure Lola's success. But, like Lumley, he could see that her performance would be found badly wanting if judged by the standards of the classical French-Italian school of ballet that dominated the dance taste in London. The key to Lola's success was to discourage viewers from comparing Lola with the ballerinas they knew and to encourage them to see her in a class by herself and let her fire and panache overcome any resistance.

On 3 June 1843, the morning of the performance, a long article prepared the ground for the debut:

> Donna Lolah Montes, who makes her debut to-night upon this stage, will for the first time introduce the Spanish dance to the English public.... The French danseuse executes her pas with the feet, the legs, and the hips alone. The Spaniard dances with the body, the lips, the eyes, the head, the neck, and with the heart. Her dance is the history of a passion . . . Lolah Montes is a purely Spanish dancer. . . . In person she is truly the Spanish woman—in style, she is emphatically the Spanish dancer. . . . El Olano is, like the Cachuca—not the Cachuca of Duvernay, Elssler, or Cerito—an intensely national dance, and will be as new to the generality of English eyes as we believe it to be beautiful. The variety of passion which it embodies—the languor, the abandon, the love, the pride, the scorn—one of the steps which is called *death to the tarantula* and is a favorite pas of the country, is the very poetry of avenging contempt—cannot be surpassed. The head lifted and thrown back, the flashing eye, the fierce and protruded foot which crushed the insect, make a subject for the painter which would scarcely be easy to forget.

With interest thus provoked, the audience began to arrive at Her Majesty's on that cool spring evening to witnesses the stage debut of Lola

Montez. The house was sold out, but the lobby was crowded with those who were eager to see what all the excitement was about. On the stage, Rossini's sparkling opera began; because the lights in the auditorium were not dimmed during the performance in those days, there was also a sparkle from the bejeweled audience. As the first act ended with its rollicking, syncopated finale, Lola saw the glittering assemblage through the peephole. In the mirror she checked her costume; the tight velvet bodice echoed the jet black of her hair and accentuated the curves of her bust and waist, and the skirt of dark red, blue, and violet would swirl to reveal glimpses of her finely formed foot and ankle.

There was a bustle backstage as the crew removed the opera set, brought on a backdrop of a Moorish chamber in the Alhambra, and set up a folding screen in the doorway at the upstage center of the set. The stage manager called out "Places!" and several girls from the corps de ballet rushed on and took their positions against the back of the set. As the first bars of the slow Spanish music came from beyond the curtain, Lola wrapped herself in a long black lace mantilla, made sure her castanets were tight in her hands, and took her place behind the closed door. The stage manager signaled for the curtain, which rose to reveal the ballet girls staring with anticipation at the closed door.

The door opened slowly, and the lace-draped figure stepped deliberately into the stage lights. She paused a moment to allow the effect to work on the audience's curiosity, then suddenly stripped off the mantilla, threw up her arms, and began slowly to move them with the rhythm of her castanets as she paced with stately grace about the stage. She didn't smile, not once, but displayed the proud haughtiness of a flamenco dancer. Swaying her body and arms, Lola embodied all the moods of her dance: passion, languor, pride, anger. Her movements were fluid, vigorous, and controlled, and the castanets punctuated each episode of the dance. At first the audience seemed stunned into silence; they had been warned that this was a different school of dance from what they had known, but it was so different that they simply looked on, not seeing any of the feats of virtuosity that they were used to applauding. This woman didn't even keep her toes turned out, as all dancers did, but moved about the stage with her feet parallel and pointed forward.

But gradually, with assistance from Lola's supporters in the house, the audience began to applaud certain dramatic movements or a sudden pose; and as Lola mimed the crushing of the tarantula and as the dance reached its climax, the auditorium began to be swept up in a wave of enthusiasm for this Spanish novelty.

The curtain finally fell, and Lola could hear the muffled storm of applause behind it. When the stage manager signaled the curtain up for calls, she stepped forward to the footlights in a shower of bouquets. Her admirers had come well prepared, and flowers blanketed the stage about her; but in her role as a proud Andalusian—or perhaps simply as a woman overwhelmed by her reception—Lola Montez did not deign to pick them up, and one of the liveried stage attendants had to scamper out and collect them. The applause and cheering went on unabated, and finally the curtain was lowered. The stage manager then hustled everyone into position again, and with a signal to the conductor, her entire performance was repeated.

As Lumley watched the encore, he marveled at the spectacular enthusiasm Lola had generated. He had had doubts not only about her story of being a Spanish refugee but also about her abilities on the stage. True, she was immoderately beautiful, but there was no way she could be called a "danseuse"; it was clear to his experienced eye that, despite her electric stage presence, Lola was an absolute novice. But Lumley knew audiences as well as dancers, and he could tell from this response that Lola Montez would bring in substantial amounts of money at the box office for some time to come.

After the encore there were more flowers, and this time Lola actually stooped to pick some up; but as she did, someone backstage lowered the curtain, and, much to the amusement of the audience, Lola found herself trapped at the footlights. After some charming embarrassment and more cheers, she made her way along the footlights and slipped backstage, where the stagehands were preparing the set for the second act of *The Barber*. She knew she had scored a hit and that her success was assured, and she hurried to change out of her costume to begin celebrating with her admirers. Eliza Gilbert James was now dead and buried. Long live Lola Montez!

As her friends clamored about her and conducted her in triumph out the stage door, the elated Lola may not have noticed Lumley standing surrounded by a group of gentlemen in evening clothes. They were expressing themselves with some vehemence, and the impresario's face darkened as he listened. He did not like was he was hearing.

The newspapers on Monday were almost unanimous in their praise, even if they expressed certain reservations. The *Morning Post*, of course, led the chorus of approval:

Her wonderfully supple form assumed attitudes that were not dreamt of—the line of beauty being still preserved, in spite of the boldness of her movement. At one moment she bent down to the ground, moving her arms as if she were gathering roses in a parterre—and at the next moment starting to her feet, and raising her arms playfully in the air, as if she were showering the flowers on a lover's head. At one moment, her dancing represented seduction and entreaty—and next, she suddenly stamped her feet on the ground, placing her hand on her hip with a look of pride and defiance, like a fencer bidding his antagonist to come on if he dare and meet his doom.

The *Morning Herald* summarized, "The young lady came, saw, and conquered." And its critic even dared to compare Lola's skills with those of the classical ballerinas.

She is evidently a superior pantomimist, and understands the expression which may be evolved by bodily action and the gesticulation of the limbs. Her play with her arms is quite beautiful, and the inflection of her wrists is free and graceful in the extreme. There is nothing angular in her posturing; her frame seems subservient to an artist-like will, and a suggestion is embodied with an immediate definition of elegance. Such an exhibition as El Oleano of course does not develop the qualities of exhibitory dancing; it is essentially a *pas de charactere*, and its requisitions are of the body rather than of the feet; but it may be presumed that the dona has accomplishments even in this direction worth looking at. She has not quite the refinement of Fanny Elssler in her mode of executing character steps, but she has an equal buoyancy of manner, and can present phrases of satire and frolic to the eye just as happily.

The *Times* was grateful at last to have seen "a Spanish dance by a Spaniard, executed after the Spanish fashion." Its critic wrote, "Her dance is not characterized by buoyancy, by remarkable grace, but it may be said to have much intensity," and concluded,

Dona Montez is quite *sui generis* as a *danseuse*, and that the whole basis and purport of her dancing are so totally different from those of the other artists of the ballet, that a legitimate rivalry can no more exist between her and them than between her and one of the singers. It is the more necessary to bear this distinctly in mind, as Dona Montez will most assuredly be underrated by many judges of the ballet, who, setting up the French and Italian standard, will refuse to acknowledge those peculiarities of her dancing which are really striking, and blame her for the absence of those qualities she has not even attempted to acquire.

The critic of the *Evening Chronicle* analyzed the reason for the sensation in some detail:

Donna Montez is not a *dancer*, in the general acceptation of the word. She has (or at least displays) none of the *execution* of the art—no pirouettes, no entrechats, no wonderful displays of agility. Her dancing is little more than a gesture and attitude, but every gesture and attitude seems to be the impulse of passion acting on the proud and haughty mind of a beautiful Spaniard; for she is exquisitely beautiful, in form and feature, realizing the images called up by a perusal of Spanish romance. Her dancing is what we have always understood Spanish dancing to be—a kind of *monodrama*—a representation of various emotions succeeding each other with great rapidity, but with coherence and consistency.

The Era was a weekly, and its critic had more time for judicious consideration of the debut before filing his report, but he reported the success in terms just as glowing, concluding, "The only fault found with the donna's dance was that it was far too short."

Unfortunately for Lola, the critic of *The Era* was wrong, for some important spectators had found serious fault with the donna's dance. The men surrounding Lumley after Lola's debut had been gentlemen of society, some of whom had deep knowledge of and admiration for things Spanish. Others in the group may have had less knowledge of Spain, but they were well acquainted with a Mrs. James, who had become moderately well known in certain social circles two years earlier and who had disappeared with what was left of her reputation. Together they upbraided the impresario for presenting a woman who was not only a publicly declared adulteress but also a fraud as a Spanish dancer.

Lumley was embarrassed. Few of his artists were models of morality, but none of them had been divorced for adultery. Far more damaging, however, was the testimony of these men that Lola was not Spanish at all and could by no stretch of the imagination be deemed to represent the authentic school of Spanish dance. An impresario might chance presenting a known adulteress to the public—who knows, it might even help the box office. But no man of the theater could survive public knowledge that he had consciously foisted a fraud on the ticketbuyers. Because so much of the puffery concerning his new star had been based on the "true Spanish character" of her dancing, there was no hope of salvaging anything once word was out that Dona Lola was as British as her audience. Glumly, Lumley assured the protesting gentlemen that, if their assertions were confirmed, Lola Montez would never again appear on the stage of Her Majesty's Theatre.

We know from Lumley's memoirs that the Earl of Malmesbury and others protested to the impresario that Lola was who she claimed to be. And even if she wasn't, she still was a wonder on the stage. But Lumley, convinced that she was no Spaniard, was unwilling to risk his credibility for a short-term profit.

Within a week a concerted attack on Lola Montez began with an article in the *Age*. Its theater critic began by referring to "nauseating articles" in the *Morning Post* and that paper's "perpetual deviation from the strict line of veracity." As a prime example of the *Morning Post*'s "false and fulsome system," the *Age* cited the coverage of the debut of Lola Montez by a critic who praised the danseuse not only *after* she appeared but even before. "It is really a duty to inquire upon what principle he has founded and published such a mass of falsehood. The 'Senorita' whom he seeks to palm off on the credulity of Opera subscribers, is a personage who has received for some time past in the nomenclature of Mrs. James, and who, though a remarkably pretty woman, knows more of many other things than she knows of dancing and more of the locality of Clarges-street, or thereabouts, than she does of the Teatro Real, Seville."

The salvo in the *Age* could not remain unanswered, and it led Lola to a free public forum that she would frequently use in the future: a letter to the editor. Of course, any letter to the editor of the *Age* might well end up in the dust bin—at the very least it would be accompanied by a biting rebuttal—so she directed her reply to publications likely to print it without mocking commentary. The letter first appeared in the *Morning Post* on 12 June, the day after the appearance of the *Age*, and subsequent versions appeared in the *Times*, the *Era*, and elsewhere. It ran, with some small variations, thus:

Sir:

Since I have had the honor of dancing at Her Majesty's Theatre on Saturday, 3 inst., when I was received by the English public in so kind and flattering a manner, I have been cruelly annoyed by reports that I am not really the person I pretend to be, but that I have been long known in London as a disreputable character. I entreat you, sir, to allow me, through the medium of your respected journal, to assure you and the public in the most positive and unqualified manner, that there is not one word of truth in such a statement. I am a native of Seville and in the year 1833, when I was ten years old, was sent to a Catholic lady at Bath, where I remained seven months and was then taken back to my parents in Spain. From that period until the 14th of April last, when I landed in England, *I never set foot in this country and I never saw London before in my life.* The imperfect English I speak I learned at Bath, and from an Irish nurse, who has been many years in my family. The misfortunes caused by the political events of my country, obliged me to seek a livelihood elsewhere, and I hoped that my native dances might be appreciated here, especially those that are new to the English. . . .

Believe me to be your obedient and humble servant,
Lola Montez

Of course it was practically all a lie (Sir Jasper Nicolls had observed that Eliza was quite a liar as a child), but Lola had little to gain by telling the truth. So she simply repeated her lies with as much show of outrage as possible.

"All this 'controversial fuss' about an opera-dancer!" exclaimed the *Court Journal* in exasperation. But the *Spectator* wrote, "Judging of Donna Montez as an amateur—which we presume her to be—her performance is sufficiently remarkable for novelty and character to entitle her to another opportunity of propitiating public favor. The English spirit of fair play is opposed to the condemnation of any one on insufficient grounds, especially when the person is a woman and a refugee from her native country; therefore we shall be glad to see Donna Montez once more on the boards of the Italian Opera."

The *Age* was not about to let the matter drop, particularly after Lola attempted an unorthodox appeal to the editor himself:

The lady perched herself in our office on Tuesday, for the space of four hours, with the view of impressing upon us the identity of her person—she presented herself subsequently at our private residence, and in the evening we saw her at the Opera. Having had opportunities of hearing her dialect, we certainly think that, considering the only English she speaks she learnt at Bath in seven months, from an Irish nurse, it is anything but "imperfect," and while slightly tinged with a foreign accent (which *might* be assumed) her pronunciation is excellent. . . . [P]resenting herself at our office in worn-out apparel on the morning of the evening when she occupied an opera box dressed in velvets and satin goes a very little way towards a proof *who* a lady is!

We can assure the Donna that, at this very moment, despite her public denial, we could name some noblemen and gentlemen who *will* insist upon it that she is no other than Mrs. James; but as there is more than *one* Mrs. James on the *tapis*, they now choose to be cautious as to which Mrs. James she is. . . .

If it were worthwhile for the present, to go on any farther with this foolish matter, we could give the names of the Noble parties herein referred to—and if the Senorita should give us any additional trouble, we undoubtedly shall do so, and state many more things, by no means agreeable either to read or to write.

Whether this threat to drag members of the nobility into a worse scandal ruined Lola's chances for reinstatement, or whether she at last realized that Lumley was determined not to associate himself further with her fraud, Lola finally gave up her hope of further success on the stage of Her Majesty's. She had debuted on Britain's most prestigious stage, so an engagement at another theater, were she even able to get one, would be a step backward in her new profession; the only reasonable course was to go abroad to continue her career. She loved the excitement of new countries and new cities, and now her London friends were introducing her to foreign aristocrats who were liberal in their promises of assistance.

In late June or early July she was introduced to a German relative of Queen Victoria's. He was a 46-year-old prince of the tiny domain of Reuß-Lobenstein-Ebersdorf and had the unlikely title of Prince Heinrich LXXII. Prince Heinrich seems to have enjoyed flirting in French with the pretty young Spaniard and was gracious enough to pay a few of her pressing debts and to invite her to visit him in Ebersdorf to see the life of a bachelor prince.

At about the same time someone suggested to Lola that she dance in St. Petersburg. After conceiving a vague plan to tour eastward through Europe, arriving in Russia for the fall theater season, she began to make arrangements to leave the country.

Before she could embark on her next adventure, Lola received a call at her apartment from Edward Fitzball, a young playwright and lyricist. A performance at the Covent Garden Theater for his benefit was scheduled for 10 July, and he hoped to fuel ticket sales by obtaining the services of the most talked-of dancer in London. Lola agreed to dance, insisting that she would accept no compensation; it was perhaps the first of her countless acts of generosity to fellow artists.

Years later Fitzball recalled the night of the benefit:

> Lola Montez arrived on the evening, in a splendid carriage, accompanied by her maid, and without the slightest affectation, entered the dressing room prepared for her reception. When she was dressed to appear on the stage, she sent for me, to inquire whether I thought the costume she had chosen for the occasion would be approved of by my friends. I have seen sylphs appear, and female forms of the most dazzling beauty, in ballets and fairy

dramas, but the most dazzling and perfect form I ever did gaze upon, was Lola Montez, in her splendid white and gold attire, studded with diamonds, that night. Her bounding before the public, was the signal of general applause and general admiration of her beauty—and general admiration of her dancing, which was quite unlike anything the public had ever seen; so original, so flexible, so graceful, so indescribable. At the conclusion of her performance, I need scarcely add, how rapturous and universal was the call for her re-appearance; after which, when I advanced with delighted thanks, again holding up her hand, in graceful remonstrance, she refused to hear me, and in half-an-hour, in the same carriage, had quitted the Theatre; from that time I have never again had the pleasure of seeing the *generous*, the beautiful Madame Lola Montez. Singular as are the various reports respecting her, which have reached us in different papers, to me, at least, as I have here set down, and everyone must allow it, she was all that was generous, ladylike, and gentle.

At Fitzball's benefit Lola again danced "El Oleano" and also introduced "La Sevilliana." Shortly afterward she completed her preparations for going abroad, and with no public notice she left London in mid-July, sailing off in search of adventure. She probably didn't know exactly where she was going and certainly knew there was no telling where she would end up.

5

GERMANY CONQUERED
WITH A WHIP

In her memoirs Lola Montez wrote that she sailed from her troubles in England to Hamburg, which she found to be small, empty, and lifeless in comparison with London. But she did not intend to linger in Hamburg. Her immediate destination was the tiny realm of her new friend Prince Heinrich.

Heinrich was one of those feudal lords of pre-Bismarck Germany who are remembered fondly by composers of comic operettas but hardly even rate footnotes in European history. He was a member of the Reuß dynasty, which controlled several small regions in Thuringia in southeastern Germany. Over the centuries the family had divided, consolidated, and redivided its estates in a thoroughly confusing manner, so that Heinrich LXXII was now lord and master of a principality of 165 square miles of wooded hills and modest farmland harboring about twenty thousand subjects.

His capital was Ebersdorf on the Saale, a town of about twelve hundred, where he spent most of his time hunting, inspecting his woodlands, and begetting bastards. Serenissimus, as he was styled, did have partial control of the bustling town of Gera, which had more than ten thousand inhabitants, but he shared sovereignty there with his cousin, the prince of Reuß-Schleitz, who was also named Heinrich.

Actually, *every* male child in all branches of the Reuß family had to be named Heinrich, so each was distinguished by a number designating his sequence of birth. Thus, Prince Heinrich LXXII's father had not been Heinrich LXXI but Heinrich LI; twenty other male Reußes had been born between the father's birth and his son's.

Prince Heinrich had just returned to his little palace from his trip to London when one day in late July the 3 o'clock post wagon delivered to him a letter addressed in French. It was from Señorita Montez, who fondly recalled their pleasant hours together in London and announced that she would be in Leipzig the next day and was looking forward to paying him a visit.

The prince did not receive many visitors who were not named Heinrich, so his court was set to work preparing Ebersdorf to welcome the fair Spaniard. Everything was cleaned and polished, and the gardens were weeded and replanted to display the prince's prized flowers to best advantage. All the members of the prince's civil service pressed and brushed their gala uniforms, and horses were dispatched from the prince's stables to establish relays from Leipzig to Ebersdorf for the great six-horse ceremonial coach that would bring the visitor.

The servants arriving in Leipzig to escort the lady noticed that she was a bit out of the ordinary. She communicated with them in bursts of French, first insisting that her large trunk be strapped to the opulent coach, not carried on the separate luggage wagon; then she insisted that everyone not busy with driving the carriage ride in the coach with her so she would have someone to talk to. When everything was ready for departure, she stopped in front of a beggar and dumped a handful of thalers into his hat, then stepped up into the coach, and they were off.

Between rolling cigarettes and puffing clouds of blue smoke, Lola tried to engage the servants in conversation, but their reticence and their French didn't make for much animation. Even so, she seemed to be enjoying herself immensely. At one of the relays, when the horses had been changed, she climbed up onto the box to tell the coachman that she wanted to drive herself. When at last he understood, he replied that the horses were too inexperienced and that he couldn't allow it; she gave him a hard blow in the face with her fan and climbed back into the coach to roll another cigarette and try to get her companions to laugh at one of her stories.

Finally the coach pulled into the square before the palace in Ebersdorf, where the prince, resplendent in his uniform of white with light blue lapels and cuffs, signaled for the coach to halt as a drum roll alerted the honor guard to present arms. Lola emerged from the coach, offered her hand for a kiss, and took the prince's arm as he introduced the members of his tiny court. He was about to lead her into his palace when she dropped his arm and walked over to inspect the dozen members of the honor guard with the precision of an old sergeant. She knew how these things were done.

That evening, at the prince's reception for his guest, Lola impressed everyone, particularly the ladies, with how modest and considerate she was. As she chatted with the guests in French she candidly admitted that she knew that the prince's invitation to her had not been serious but that she was far too curious to miss the chance to visit. Now that she was here, Lola observed, Heinrich would just have to put a good face on it.

Lola wrote that she was at first pleasantly surprised by the court of Ebersdorf, finding even its modest charms more than she had expected and expressing surprise at how graciously the prince had welcomed his essentially self-invited guest. But the sameness of each day soon bored her, and within days she and Heinrich got on each other's nerves. She found the Lord of Reuß-Lobenstein-Ebersdorf more than a bit ridiculous in his vanities, and she was frustrated that no one at the tiny court could hear her jokes about him without being shocked.

During her stay Lola got to know more of Ebersdorf's inhabitants, all of whom would not have filled one of London's better theaters. She had liked dogs all her life, particularly large ones, and she and the prince's St. Bernard, Turk, were soon friends. Together they strolled through Heinrich's beds of rare plants, and Lola deftly decapitated the flowers with a switch. She wove the fallen blossoms into a chain that she hung around the neck of the prince's stallion, telling the grooms not to remove it until the master had a chance to see how fine his horse looked.

Heinrich was not used to this sort of behavior in his princely residence; if he had ever forgotten, he probably began to remember why he was still a bachelor. But he could not be faulted as a host, and on the fourth day of his guest's sojourn he arranged for a visit to one of his favorite spots: his hunting lodge of Weidmannsheil, where a rustic breakfast would be served and entertainment provided. In the prince's new phaeton it was a half-hour drive to the lodge, where Heinrich proudly gave his guest a tour of every nook and cranny of the structure. In a clearing under the great oak and linden trees, a table had been set for them and twenty guests.

The prince seated Lola at his right, and as the meal began, the Combined Band of the Foresters and Miners of Weidmannsheil began a serenade from behind a screen of branches. The players really *were* foresters and miners and left something to be desired as musicians, and the guest of honor began to grimace whenever a particularly sour tone split the air. Noticing that this annoyed her host, Lola teased him by pantomiming even more acute pain with every cracked note.

The climax came when a chorus, made up mostly of children who had climbed into the trees, began performing the "Reußian Folksong." Lola sprang up, threw her hands over her ears, and screamed, "Oh, that's horrible! Get rid of that rabble!" The prince, about to lose his temper, rose from his place, told the chorus to get out, and grasped Lola by the left wrist to lead her back to the table. She seemed to misunderstand his intention, and her right hand went to the dagger she kept in her belt; but then she realized her overreaction, smiled, and sat down.

Repeatedly in her life Lola Montez would react to offended authority with outrageous provocation, and this day was no exception. Seeing one of boys of the chorus scrambling down from a tree, she turned to her new friend Turk and, with a gesture, said, "Get him!" In two leaps the St. Bernard had knocked down the boy and pinned him with its front paws on his chest. The boy screamed with fright, and the prince himself leaped up from the table, grabbed Turk's collar, and pulled him off his victim. He turned with rage to Lola and yelled, "That won't happen again, Madame! I am the master here!"

"And I," replied Lola sarcastically, "am the mistress!"

That did it. Heinrich excused himself and strode toward the stables. The men rose and followed, but the prince ordered all but one trusted aide back to the table and commanded that the program go forward as planned. The prince and his aide drove back together to Ebersdorf.

There was a great stir among the prince's guests until Lola, after an original and funny apology for her role in the incident, began to reestablish the festive mood. Under the spell of Lola's easy charm, the prince's angry departure no longer seemed a matter of great concern, and all embarked on the planned excursion to points of interest in the surrounding forest. At a beautiful overlook above the sea of trees, Lola entertained the group by persuading the youngest officer to be her partner in a Spanish folk dance as she sang the accompaniment. Afterward, they all returned for a grand banquet in the dining room of the hunting lodge.

Back at the palace, Prince Heinrich and his aide conferred on an appropriate and swift means of relieving Serenissimus from the annoyance of his houseguest. Perhaps, the aide suggested, a dancer might be lured away by the promise of a good engagement. He was acquainted with Herr Kapellmeister Karl Reissinger at the Court Theater of the King of Saxony in nearby Dresden. With a letter of introduction to the kapellmeister in her hand, she might be inclined to accept a coach ride to the Saxon capital.

The aide drafted a letter to Kapellmeister Reissinger while Serenissimus wrote a note to Lola, pointedly addressing it to "Mrs. James." With the two letters, the aide drove back to the hunting lodge, where the banquet was coming to an end. After asking to speak privately to the prince's guest, he gave her the letters and told her, as diplomatically as he could, that Serenissimus wished her out of his realm that day. At that Lola smiled mockingly and observed, "That's not such a long trip!"

The dancer graciously took her leave of the other guests, climbed into the carriage with the aide, and told the coachman, "Drive!" remarking to the aide, "You see, I'm carrying *you* off!" On the trip back to Ebersdorf she regaled the officer with witty stories and observations, and when they arrived, she insisted that he come with her to her room. Going to her trunk, she rummaged through her things, finally pulling out a pair of castanets and saying, as she handed them to the aide, "Here, a souvenir of my visit to your corner of the world." Then she climbed into the waiting coach, waved with her fan, and with far less pomp and circumstance than when she had arrived four days before, Lola Montez departed Ebersdorf for Dresden.

Lola arrived at Dresden's Hotel de Wien on 7 August and went to present her letter to Kapellmeister Reissinger. Although it was summer, Reissinger was in the Saxon capital, and the Court Theater was open. He agreed to engage her. A novelty like this Spanish dancer could be worked in easily between the acts on almost any evening; and on Wednesday, 9 August, Donna Lola Montez of the Italian Opera in London made her Dresden debut dancing "El Oleano."

The response in Dresden must have been a disappointing after the wild enthusiasm in London. Opera was the favorite entertainment locally. The Dresden Kapellmeister Karl Maria von Weber had won international fame with his operas and orchestral works, and now Reissinger's colleague Richard Wagner was making a name for himself, particularly with his new operas *Rienzi* and *The Flying Dutchman*. But the Dresden public did not get terribly excited about dancers, and Lola was no exception.

"Donna Montez had an opportunity today only to display her lovely theatrical figure, her expressive, obviously Spanish face, and the delicacy and sweep of her movements," was the most praise the critics managed. But Lola had learned in London that it pays to get to know journalists. Though in

47

Dresden she had not had time to introduce herself before her debut, she went to work making contacts and admirers.

It wasn't long before the Dresden correspondent of the *Deutsche Allgemeine Zeitung* was filing the following report: "At the moment we are seeing a curious and strangely lovely vision on our stage. Donna Dolores Montez, premiere Spanish dancer of the Italian Opera in London, en route to Petersburg, is giving us guest performances of her national dances. . . . In London, as the most prominent newspapers there reported, she had the greatest success and was feted there not only by the cream of society but was received with many marks of distinction by Queen Victoria herself; indeed, she was allowed to demonstrate before that august personage her second and not inferior talent, the playing of native Spanish songs on the guitar, something she does not perform in public."

Lola apparently knew that good publicity doesn't necessarily trouble itself with the truth.

On the evening after her debut, Lola introduced "La Sevilliana" to Dresden. The critic of the *Abend Zeitung* was less kind than he might have been: "In the matter of the dance divertissement (?) this evening, as yesterday, we found in Donna Montez little grace in her poses or movements, too little finish in what dancing in the manner of a Taglioni, Elssler, etc., demands. The dancer's friends could have spared her the demonstration of the wreath tossing from the third gallery before the start of the dance (apparently by someone paid for his effort!) as well as the contrived cheering at the end, which was punctuated with hisses from many quarters; such things do only harm."

On Friday the 13th, Lola Montez made her third and final appearance in Dresden, performing for the first time "Los Boleros de Cadix," together with a repetition of "El Oleano." "Los Boleros" had been prepared in London, but the brevity of her English stage career kept her from performing it. Though she had been in Dresden only a week, she already had charmed a coterie of young gentlemen, who occupied the proscenium boxes and tossed flowers when she appeared, applauded "until their hands were bloody," one critic said, and loudly called the dancer to the footlights at the end of her performances. Again there was a distinct division of opinion in the auditorium, and the flower tossing was greeted with hissing and boos.

Having danced her entire repertoire, Lola prepared to move on. She had made friends with enough of the right people in Dresden that she could travel on to Berlin with impressive letters of introduction. Lola herself claimed that the Queen of Saxony (a sister of King Ludwig of Bavaria) was so charmed by her that she gave her a letter of introduction to her sister, the Queen of Prussia; that seems be one of Lola's innumerable improvements on the truth, but the dancer definitely arrived in the Prussian capital with influential letters.

Lola attracted many gentlemen admirers in Berlin, and a few who were less than gentlemen. One evening two boorish Berliners were attempting to force their company on the beautiful dancer when a thirteen-year-old boy stepped forward to shame the men into retreat and to offer Lola temporary refuge in the hotel where he was staying with his father. Lola accepted the invitation and met the boy's father, the writer and translator Eduard von Bülow, who was visiting from Dresden. The father would see quite a bit of Lola in Berlin, and he would use his observations as the basis for a short story entitled "Die neue Melusine." The few events of the story are largely fiction, but the bulk of "Die neue Melusine" is a portrayal of a dancer, Imagina, who is clearly based on Lola.

According to Bülow's account, Lola came down each morning at ten to the dining room of her hotel, where she was greeted by men of many nationalities, all enchanted by her. Lola ate little as she held court, speaking uninhibitedly in faulty schoolgirl French. Her extraordinarily plastic and animated face would flush or grow pale constantly during the conversations, usually with no apparent relation to what was being said.

The naïve Montez charm and graciousness was such, wrote Bülow, that she was idolized even by those who felt the brunt of her capricious temper; although when she became truly angry she said exactly what she thought, and that made enemies for her. Despite her moods, Lola maintained an air of propriety, an implicit demand for respect that allowed her to preside at her breakfast levees and at late-night smoking parties without the conversation turning masculine and raw. The writer said that whenever a guest said something crude or insulting to her, she would pointedly act as if she had heard nothing.

Lola arrived just as a major disaster struck Berlin's theatrical life. The Royal Opera House on Unter der Linden, an architectural jewel built at the command of Frederick the Great, was gutted by fire on the night of 18 August 1843. But performances were quickly rescheduled at the Schauspielhaus in the Gendarmenmarkt and at other venues, and entertainment in the Prussian capital went on remarkably smoothly.

Lola was able to use her letters of introduction to secure an engagement at the royal theater. According to Bülow, she used a letter to an assistant director of the royal theaters, who immediately engaged her for a series of performances at a good fee. She clearly had other contacts, for she was noticeably favored by someone within the royal circle; and there were rumors that she had had an affair with King Friedrich Wilhelm IV's brother, Prince Albrecht, whose wife had left on a trip to Italy just about the time Lola arrived in Berlin.

Whatever the circumstances, she was engaged as a guest soloist, and by 26 August, the day of her debut, there was a stir of anticipation, thanks in part to articles by her journalist friends. Interest was so great that the management of the royal theaters suspended the use of free passes for her performances.

Her debut was once again "El Oleano," but newspaper criticism was scanty and mixed. She seems to have been well received; one newspaper noted loud applause for her performance, and another felt that, although she made a fine impression on the stage, her dancing was a trifle too lively and lacking in subtlety. Another critic was less impressed and made the first explicit references to the sensuality of Lola's dancing: "The guest appearance of the dancer Donna Lola Montez, from Seville, set Berlin to wondering how such a substantial reputation could have preceded this lady. Her beauty, of rare, voluptuous fullness, is beyond any criticism. Her dancing, however, was no dancing at all but a physical invitation. If it is said of Taglioni that she writes world history with her feet, so can it be said of Donna Montez that she writes Casanova's Memoirs with her whole body."

In Bülow's short story, "El Olano" was only about ten minutes long and accompanied by a monotonous melody. It depicted the pursuit of a young girl by a poisonous spider, which she finally turns on, pursues, and kills. Lola wore the tight black velvet bodice, a skirt of blue, red, and white satin squares, a black hat on the back of her head, and red and white camellias in her hair. Her castanet playing was masterful, he wrote, and the greatest impact of her appearance came from her expression of total involvement and joy in her dancing.

She appeared again two nights later in "La Sevilliana" and was again received with applause. On 2 September, in what was already billed as her next to last performance, the Berlin public got to know the remainder of her repertoire, the "Boleros de Cadix," and Bülow claimed that she was so dazzling at this performance in her costume of silver and white that he overheard departing spectators exclaiming, "The girl is a wonder. She's an art work of Nature!" But whatever enthusiasm the public might have had for Lola soon appeared to wane, and there were complaints that every dance she did was essentially the same one under a different name.

To give the public something new, Lola rehearsed a pas de deux called "La Gitana" with a dancer from the Berlin company, and she danced it as her "last performance" on a bill with Scribe's play "A Glass of Water" at the Schauspielhaus on 5 September. Although her admirers showered the stage with flowers, the applause was feeble and mixed with hisses.

But declining enthusiasm among the press and public had no effect on Lola's popularity in court circles, and on the following night she danced "El Oleano" before King Friedrich Wilhelm IV himself at the City Theater in Potsdam. While at the theater the king received word that his expected state guest, Czar Nicholas I of Russia, had finally arrived in Berlin, and he rushed off to welcome his brother-in-law to the capital.

The czar's visit was a major event, and preparations had been under way for some time. The Prussian army had been drilling for a series of grand maneuvers to be executed before His Imperial Majesty on the great parade grounds surrounding the city. The two rulers started their full program the next day by arriving on the field at 11 A.M. to observe troop maneuvers. Even though it was a workday and stormy weather was blowing great clouds of dust about, an estimated fifty thousand people came out to see the troops perform and to catch a glimpse of the emperor and their king.

At 2 P.M. the czar and his host boarded a special train for the short trip to Potsdam, where at the rococo palace of Sans Souci a luncheon was held for the czar and other distinguished guests. There was a serenade of trumpet music at the gala table, which was set for sixty.

After the meal the brilliant party—the men resplendent in their uniforms and their ladies in their finest early-evening attire—was driven the length of the Great Park to Friedrich the Great's massive Neues Palais. The guests repaired to the private theater in the south wing of the palace, where the curtain rose on a special performance of Donizetti's opera *The Daughter of the Regiment* (quite appropriate for the military theme of the czar's visit).

When the first act ended the stage was cleared, the orchestra retuned, and the curtain went up on Lola Montez, who three months earlier had been denounced as a fraud and only days before had been hissed at Berlin's Schauspielhaus. She now danced a command performance of "Los Boleros de Cadix" before the Emperor of Russia, the King of Prussia, and the cream of central Europe's nobility. The noble ladies had been given the front row, and the gentlemen sat behind in their gold- and silver-adorned regimental uniforms. There were no critics present for the performance and Lola herself left no account, so we have no way of knowing how she was received or how she felt looking out into the eyes of the czar and king.

But Lola did later tell a story of dancing at a grand reception for the czar, though it sounds like one of her "improvements on fact."

> During the entertainment of the evening she [Lola Montez] became very thirsty and asked for some water—and, on being told that it was impossible for her to have any, as it was a rule of Court etiquette that no artists should eat or drink in the presence of Royalty, she began to storm not a little, and flatly declared that she would not go on with the dance, until she had some water. Duke Michael, brother of the Emperor Nicholas, on hearing of the difficulty, went to the king and told him that little Lola Montez declared she was dying of thirst and insisted that she would have some water. Whereupon the amiable king sent for a goblet of water, and after putting it to his own lips, presented it to her with his own hand, which brought the demand of Lola for something to drink within the rule of the etiquette of the court.

The incident probably never happened, but the story is a good example of how Lola often portrayed herself as a bit unreasonable—perhaps a little childish—and unimpressed with rules. It seems to have been a fairly accurate self-assessment. Bülow wrote, however, that Lola was well received at the Court not only by the men but also by the ladies because she demonstrated a natural tact and propriety that belied her being something so common as a dancer.

Even though her performance of the pas de deux had been billed as her last, Lola was scheduled for yet another appearance at the Schauspielhaus, on Sunday, 10 September. The main feature of the evening's program had been Beethoven's opera *Fidelio*, and its performance was not entirely well received by the audience, as some of the singers were particularly weak.

As Lola stepped onto the stage, she was greeted by scattered applause along with loud hissing. She performed "Los Boleros," which one critic described as "waltzing widely about the stage," and at its conclusion received more applause mixed with hisses; one very loud voice demanded an encore. The defiant Lola danced again, to the outrage of a loud portion of the audience, who accompanied her with hissing, whistling, and stamping. Her admirers unsuccessfully tried to counter with applause. The evening ended in a general uproar among those who had remained in the auditorium, and Lola Montez's career on the Berlin stage had found its definitive conclusion.

Whether she had hopes of further performances, was enjoying Berlin (or someone in it), or was uncertain what the next stop on her road to St. Petersburg should be, Lola stayed on in Berlin, taking in life from her hotel on Unter der Linden, between the blackened ruins of the opera house and the impressive Brandenburg Gate.

The main attraction in Berlin continued to be the military maneuvers and parades in honor of the czar, and each event attracted thirty thousand to sixty thousand viewers. On the Sunday following Lola's last performance came the climax of the military festivities, an event that seems to have been the occasion of one of the legendary encounters of Lola's career. The czar and the king were to take the salute of a parade of thirty thousand troops in the Friedrichfelde, on the eastern edge of Berlin, and the Prussian troops would publicly wear their newly designed uniforms for the first time. The city became a ghost town as people streamed out to enjoy the spectacle. For more than a week it had been impossible to rent a carriage for the day of the Grand Parade. The viewers began arriving on the field at 5 A.M., when dusty fog still obscured the grounds. As the sun rose, it was soon apparent that the day would be hot, and even without the huge crowd and the masses of marching and galloping troops, huge clouds of dust swirled about.

The police tried to hold back the crowd from the parade ground and from the area reserved for the royal party, but they were simply undermanned. It wasn't long before individual riders and carriages began breaking the line into restricted areas and actually interfering with the parade of the troops.

Lola had spent a good deal of money to hire herself a fine saddle horse for her stay in Berlin. She was an excellent rider and enjoyed appearing on spirited horses in fashionably cut "amazon" outfits, as riding dresses were then called. It appears that Lola rode to the parade alone; at least none of the accounts mentions any companions, who would have been likely to intervene in what subsequently occurred. She may have been alone because she was romantically involved with someone at court and was hoping to join him, and perhaps that was why she tried to ride into the area reserved for the nobility who accompanied the emperor and the king. According to a newspaper account very likely attributable to Lola herself, she inadvertently found herself in the royal suite when her horse shied at the sound of an artillery salute and bolted into the restricted area.

Much more likely is that Lola, seeing that the gendarmes were incapable of maintaining order, attempted to place herself in the VIP section. A harried gendarme galloped over, grabbed the bridle of Lola's horse, and began to lead her out of the restricted area. (One report, possibly Lola-inspired, claimed that the policeman hit her horse with the flat of his sword.) The outraged Spaniard lashed out at the officer with her riding whip. He was incensed by the attack, but he had his hands full with trying to keep the crowd in order, so he left Lola in the spectator section.

The full significance of this incident becomes clear when one recognizes that sex roles in Western society were then much more sharply defined and universally observed than they are today. Women were expected to be physically passive, weak, and dependent on men for protection of their persons and their honor. Exceptions to this norm were rare and disdained. Little had changed in Europe in the sixty years since Mary Wollstonecraft had written that society forced women into sanctioned prostitution by making marriage and motherhood not only the sole honorable course for women but the sole course economically possible. Even in relatively liberal England, a woman frequently spent her entire life without social and legal rights, except through the man responsible for her: first her father, then her husband, and finally her son.

A woman's dependent role was underpinned by social norms that discouraged her from doing anything alone. Even on shopping trips a woman was expected to be accompanied by another woman, a servant, or a child. To some extent this was a means of declaring her status, since prostitution was so common in some European capitals that a woman on the street alone might be assumed to be a street walker. But in another sense it reflected the societal definition of a woman as someone who could not exist except as an adjunct to someone else, usually a man.

So Lola was something of a social outlaw simply by being a woman on her own. Women of the theater generally had exceptional status in society, but it was frequently that of the half-caste, of someone who did not deserve to be shunned by all decent persons but at the same time could not be received freely in their homes. Women like Jenny Lind, who managed to achieve status both as an artistic idol and as an icon of middle-class morality, were rare.

Another subtext to the story of Lola and the gendarme is the concept of honor. This concept, as it was then applied, was perhaps akin to the Oriental concept of "face." Its precepts were enforced with the type of sanctions that today promote conformity in Japan and other countries, where "the nail that stands above the others gets hammered down."

Among the social sanctions perpetuating this system was shunning, a social device that survives in the Western world only in such places as military boarding schools and separatist religious sects. No one would speak to a dishonored man or his family or allow them to call. Worse, shunning could mean economic ruin: a lawyer would find that he no longer had any clients, a journalist would find that no editor wanted his work, a merchant would see his sales drop to nothing. This living burial by society was extremely hard for women, who had no real retreat from constant snubs on the streets and in the shops.

The code of honor declared it a disgrace for a gentleman to be struck publicly without prompt redress. If the blow came from another gentleman, it could be returned in kind or could lead to a duel. If the blow came from an inferior, the punishment would be a sound beating at an appropriate time. Inferiors included all nongentlemen—that is, servants, the working class, and women. A woman who publicly struck a man, unless she was the victim of outrageous offense to her dignity (raising the question of how she had allowed herself to be in a position to be insulted without a man to protect her honor), made herself unwomanly in the eyes of society and lost any claim to its protection.

Finally, it is important to remember that we live in a much more violent age today. For example, at the time of the incident between Lola and the gendarme there had not been a single murder registered in Munich over a two-year period. And cases of battery and theft averaged slightly over one per day for the whole city, which had a population of more than 100,000. The police, occupied primarily with hustling beggars, vagabonds, unemployed servants, and illegal aliens off the street, solved nearly 100 percent of the crimes reported to them.

The first repercussion of Lola's attack was not long in coming. According to the newspapers, an officer of the lower criminal courts called on the dancer at her hotel to serve her with a summons to answer a charge of assault on a gendarme. Lola, the story goes, flew into a rage, ripped up the summons and stamped on the pieces. As a result of this rampage, Lola was charged with contempt of the judicial process, a more serious charge. Lola herself later claimed that the only result of her encounter was an apology from the captain of the Berlin gendarmerie for the rudeness of the officer she had assaulted.

The newspaper account, given Lola's regularly displayed temper and contempt for authority, rings a good deal truer than her story of the apology. But just how the matter was resolved is unclear. The newspapers reported that

Lola Montez had already been convicted and sentenced and that only a pardon from the king himself could save her from months, if not years, in prison. In fact, the matter seems never to have gotten to trial; in all likelihood, it was quietly dropped after a strong hint from above. After all the discussion in the press of Lola's sad future at the hands of Prussian justice, and Lola's reply that she had received an apology, one newspaper admitted that although she had not been prosecuted, this forbearance was merely proof of the gallantry of the police even toward ladies whose outrageous behavior gave them no right to the deference normally accorded their sex.

The incident ultimately came to nothing, but it turned into a gold mine of publicity for Lola. The story of her whipping of the Prussian officer was picked up eagerly by the foreign press, and it made the rounds of the capitals of Europe, transmuting itself into stories of whole regiments of Prussian officers fleeing her singing whip. Almost all the early prints of Lola show her holding a riding crop, and the story followed her the rest of her life.

Strangely, Lola herself preferred to forget the incident on the parade field; in her memoirs she claimed that her unpleasantness with the Berlin police arose from her smoking on the street, something forbidden even to men in those days. Whatever the facts, Lola recognized that the time had come to continue her tour to St. Petersburg. After the fiasco following *Fidelio*, the theater no longer was open to her, and any noble protector she may have had likely turned cool after the spectacle she had created on the Friedrichfelde. So she shook the dust of Berlin's sandy plain from her hems and departed for Warsaw.

News of the transformation of Eliza Gilbert James into Lola Montez would have reached her mother and stepfather at about this time. Major Craigie, who was now the acting adjutant general of the army, had been ordered from Calcutta to assist in establishing a new headquarters at Allahabad, up the Ganges. He and Mrs. Craigie set out, but the major's health began to fail, and he was finally persuaded to stop at Dinapore.

Eliza Craigie must have felt that Dinapore carried a fatal curse for her happiness. Exactly twenty years before she had arrived at Dinapore only to watch her first husband die in agony, and he lay buried here. Once again she would watch her husband die in Dinapore.

Craigie was only forty-four, but he knew his time had come. He wrote his will, directing that his extensive property at Simla not be sold until summer arrived, when it would bring a good price. He could not enumerate his debts but thought they were few. "My sole wish is that the property I leave behind me may cover my debts and should there be any residue, I bequeath it to my beloved wife, Eliza Craigie."

On 8 October, he died. Those who knew him seem to have remembered him as a good and conscientious officer. His one legacy to the lore of British India was the creation of Craigie toast, a savory compound of tomatoes, eggs, Worcestershire sauce, and other condiments, which became well known in Anglo-India during the nineteenth century.

The funeral took place in St. Luke's Church, on the edge of the great parade ground at Dinapore, and afterward the widow followed the coffin of Patrick Craigie to the very cemetery where twenty years and two weeks before she had buried Edward Gilbert. Lola claimed that when news of her stage debut reached her mother, Mrs. Craigie sent out notices of her daughter's death and put on mourning; the black crepe her mother wore would seem to have been not for her daughter but for her husband. Not yet forty and twice a widow, she may have also mourned her own happiness.

6

The Road to Russia
—And Back ·

On arriving in Warsaw, Lola took rooms at the best hotel in the city, as she always did; in this case at the Rzymski, or Hotel de Rome. She had letters of introduction to several important men, and in a few days she had established a circle of Warsaw admirers, including the banker and industrialist Piotr Steinkeller and the publisher and critic Antoni Lesznowski.

Poland at that time was governed from Warsaw, with the Russian emperor as its king. In 1830–31 there had been a violent, brutally suppressed revolt against Russian rule that led many young Poles to emigrate to the West. When Lola arrived in October 1843, Poland was ruled by the czar's viceroy, Prince Ivan Feodorovitch Paskievitch, who was, at sixty-one, a distinguished general quite capable of carrying out the harsh policies of surveillance and suppression favored by Nicholas I.

With the help of her Polish friends, Lola obtained a contract for a series of performances at the enormous Grand Theater, which dominated a large square in central Warsaw. The director of the theater was Colonel Ignacy Abramowicz, a fifty-year-old former adjutant of the viceroy who also was chief of the city's gendarmerie. Despite his military background, Abramowicz had a taste for culture, and the colonel's favorite art was the ballet—he was a connoisseur of both the dance and pretty women.

As usual, Lola used her charm and beauty to win over the press. On Saturday, 21 October, the newspapers published anticipatory eulogies to their new darling, who would debut that evening. As in London, Lola danced "El Oleano" in the intermission of Rossini's *Barber of Seville*. The reaction of the public apparently was mixed. The ballet of the Grand Theater was extremely good, and some observers considered Lola's appearance as a guest artist an insult to the company; but her beauty, stage presence, and the enthusiasm of her admirers in the auditorium was sufficient to allow the debut to be termed a success.

A second performance, of "Los Boleros de Cádiz," took place the following Tuesday, and the reaction, led by Lola's loyal claque, continued to be largely favorable. Then came a break of two weeks before her next appearance.

The facts around Lola's stay in Warsaw are difficult to establish, because virtually everyone who wrote of her visit had a different version of events. According to some, she alienated Abramowicz by refusing to perform because the audience was too small. Others say she held up a performance by arriving at the theater more than an hour late. Another wrote that Abramowicz turned against her because she threw him out of his own carriage in a rainstorm after he made indecent advances to her. Others, including Lola herself, claimed that Paskievitch ordered the director to get rid of her after she mocked the viceroy's unsubtle advances.

Whatever the cause, the consensus is that Abramowicz wanted to break Lola's contract to be rid of her. Perhaps it was in his role as chief of the gendarmes rather than as theater director that he felt she had to go, because it was reported that Lola was talking a lot of politics with her new Polish friends, expressing her astonishment that they could tolerate the Russian oppression and saying that, were up to her, she would dispose of the tyrants with a secret poison she knew.

At the end of October, Lola wrote a letter to the *Journal des Débats* in Paris to correct what she claimed was its faulty account of her encounter with the gendarme in Berlin. She took the opportunity to add a few lies to dignify her public image: "Before I left Berlin to come to Warsaw for a few days, Her Majesty the Queen of Prussia, to whom I had had the honor of presenting a letter conceived in the kindest terms from Her Majesty the Queen of Saxony, deigned to accord me another for Her Majesty the Empress of Russia. . . . I also hope, after the St. Petersburg season, to appear on the Parisian stage and to obtain there the approbation which every artist so justifiably covets, and it would pain me to arrive in France preceded by an undeserved reputation."

On Tuesday, 7 November, Lola renewed her run at the Grand Theater with performances of "La Sevilliana" and "Los Boleros de Cádiz" on a bill with Donizetti's opera *L'Elisir d'Amore.* The audiences seem to have been growing restless, perhaps with Abramowicz's encouragement but very possibly out of a feeling that they were seeing nothing new. On the following Saturday Lola did give them something completely new: "La Saragossa," which she danced with "El Oleano" between acts of Auber's *Fra Diavolo.*

Abramowicz received secret police reports about the claque that Lola's friends were maintaining in the theater. Steinkeller was regularly sending about two dozen workers from one of his factories, and Lesznowski would send a half-dozen or so typesetters from his newspaper, all with orders to demonstrate enthusiasm for Lola's art.

The director decided to create his own counter-claque. On Tuesday the 14th, when Lola was scheduled to dance "La Sevilliana" and "Los Boleros de Cádiz," Abramowicz stationed his men in plain clothes throughout the auditorium. As the dance began, hisses rose up toward the stage and then were mingled with whistles. Lola's supporters responded with applause and cheers, and soon the music of the orchestra threatened to disappear beneath the din.

Lola danced on, defiantly oblivious to the growing tumult, until the curtain fell; but the hisses and cheers faded in surprise as the curtain was violently thrust aside and Lola strode to the footlights, her face transfigured with rage and indignation. Speaking in French, she thanked those who had applauded her performance and made her welcome in Warsaw. Then, thrusting a finger up toward Abramowicz, sitting in the director's box, she cried out, "Messieurs et mesdames, I owe this unworthy insult to that gentleman! There is the rascal who thus attempts to revenge himself on a feeble woman, who would not submit to his infamous proposals!"

The mass of the audience, who had endured the war of the factions during the dance, were surprised by Lola's dramatic declaration and burst out enthusiastically, "Bis, bis—again, again—brava, Lola, brava!" What was supposed to be a well-organized demonstration against the Spaniard was threatening to turn into an anti-Russian, or at least anti-Abramowicz, uprising.

Word flew throughout Warsaw of Lola's denunciation of Colonel Abramowicz before the audience at the Grand Theater. As it circulated, the story mutated, perhaps with some assistance from the colonel's minions. One version had it that Lola had turned her posterior to the audience in response to the hisses and jeers. Abramowicz saw that he needed to get the woman out of town before she could become a rallying point for young nationalistic troublemakers—and before she could do anything more to make him look like a fool.

But Prince Paskievitch was at the viceregal estate of Skierniewice for the autumn hunt, and Abramowicz hesitated to expel a prominent foreigner in the absence of his superior. A guard was put on Lola's hotel room, where she was under house arrest until Paskievitch's expected return. Lola's initial reaction to the restrictions on her movement seems to have been increased outrage, and she got into an affray with one of the policemen on duty at her door. According to some accounts, the hot-blooded Spaniard pulled her dagger on the hapless constable and was subdued, but it is possible that she simply slapped him a time or two. That was sufficient, however, to add to her reputation as a fiery and fearless Andalusian.

When the prince regent returned to Warsaw from the hunt, he had no hesitation about expelling Lola. He ordered her escorted back to the Prussian frontier at Posen by an officer of the gendarmerie, tactfully adding that he thought that Colonel Abramowicz need not take this assignment himself. "But remember," the viceroy said, "she's a Spanish woman; they've always got a dagger stuck in their garter."

With the dancer's fate resolved, the problem became getting her to submit to it. She had decided to turn her arrest into a siege by refusing to come out of her hotel room. Abramowicz was not eager to create a spectacle by dragging her from her hotel and throwing her into a carriage, and no one was forgetting the viceroy's remark about the dagger. So the colonel called in Lola's protector, Steinkeller, to tell him that unless he wanted to go to jail for contributing to the disturbance of public order at the Grand Theater, he should devise a way to get Lola Montez quietly out of her hotel room and into a carriage within twenty-four hours.

Steinkeller and his wife decided to invite Lola to come with them to visit their estate in the country. By this time Lola may have realized that she had nothing to gain by remaining in Warsaw and that she ought to get on with her trip to St. Petersburg. Whether or not she believed the ruse of the Steinkellers, Lola packed her trunks and went quietly down to the carriage waiting for her outside the Hotel Rzymski on 22 November.

Word spread quickly that Lola was leaving, and a number of young men for whom she had become a symbol of revolt, or at least of romantic recklessness, tried to accompany the carriage as a guard of honor. But they were stopped on Abramowicz's orders at the barriers of Warsaw, and Lola continued her journey without her admirers.

Or at least without most of them, for she seems to have charmed Officer Rospopov, the gendarme assigned to accompany her to the frontier. Her escort rhapsodized about her in his memoirs: "Lola Montez was beauty itself, perfection incarnate. She had blue eyes, thick black lashes, finely arched eyebrows, abundant, thick, black hair with bluish highlights, a supple figure. In addition, she was full of charm, gay, amiable, seductive, and at the same time naïve as a child."

Back in Warsaw, Abramowicz taught a lesson to Lola's supporters, including Steinkeller and Lesznowski, by having them rounded up and thrown in jail just long enough to discourage them from challenging him again. Lola was left at the cold, bleak frontier of Prussia to continue her journey, but she always retained an affection for Poland, and for the rest of her life she would feel drawn to the Poles she met in her travels around the world.

The dancer took the train from Posen to Stettin, near where the Oder River flows into the Baltic, and registered at Hartwig's Hotel on 24 November. Having been checked on her triumphal progress toward St. Petersburg, she needed time to plan her next move.

After being ejected from the czar's kingdom of Poland, a normal person might have abandoned hope of traveling on to his imperial residence. But Lola seems to have been confident that her contacts in high places (even if we decline to believe her claim that the Queen of Prussia had written her a letter of introduction to the czarina) would get her into Russia. Since the route across Poland was closed to her, she would have to travel along the Baltic coast through Pomerania and East Prussia.

For the moment, however, Lola got herself booked for two performances in Stettin, on 30 November and 1 December. She may have returned to Berlin, which was just four and a half hours from Stettin by train, to shop for fashionable winter clothing. Temperatures were now regularly below freezing, and Berlin would offer better shopping than any other city she would see before arriving in St. Petersburg.

After about two weeks in Stettin, she set out in a post coach traveling eastward, and she arrived in the bustling Baltic port of Danzig on 9 December. Lola set to work getting herself an engagement at the local theater and winning over the gentlemen of the press. She succeeded on both counts, arranging to debut on Wednesday, 13 December, and receiving a flattering notice in the Danzig *Dampfboot*.

She performed three times in Danzig, where subscriptions were suspended as people paid higher prices to see the famous guest artist. The houses were crowded, but much of the public seems to have gone away disappointed. "We want art, we want character, we want delicacy, we want fine taste; this Atalanta hunt, these antelope leaps seem far too Spanish to us," the *Dampfboot* reported some of the viewers as saying. "Well, what did you expect?" replied the newspaper's enchanted critic. "It's *supposed* to be Spanish!" "But," added the journalist, "the enthusiast and opponent alike agree that Señora Montez is a charming vision and her performance extremely tasteful." The audiences' reaction was generally less than exuberant, however, and by the final performance Lola was not in the best mood, acknowledging the applause in an offhand and abrupt manner.

Lola Montez began 1844 by continuing her tour toward St. Petersburg, appearing on 4 and 6 January Königsberg, the coronation city of the Prussian kings. Her reputation had preceded her again, and the theater manager demanded premium prices from the crowds that pressed to get tickets to her two performances. A review of her first performance gives some idea of the pantomime in Lola's dance and the deep impression she was able to make on at least some in her audience:

> At the instant of her appearance she fills the whole, numberless assembly with vibrant life; every eye fixes itself on her charming form, every glance follows her slightest motion, marvels at the rapid changes of her movements, and reflects the easy grace of her floating steps. Bending low, almost to the ground, to escape the passionate *majo*, she suddenly rises, stands majestic as a goddess before whom mortals must sink in the dust; then she rages at the rascal, stamping her foot; but won over by his longing glance, she taunts him jokingly, swings with her flexible body left and right, and is not to be captured by the swiftest hand until she appears to give up the struggle, but remains ever the idolized victor. The storm of applause that sweeps over her is resounding evidence, and we gladly confess it, Donna Lola Montez has conquered us. Königsberg need not be ashamed that it pays homage to the beautiful dancer from the fiery South, that Northern eyes glowed brighter at the sight of her and offered her the flowery wreath of full approbation, which such a favorite child of agile Terpsichor deserves.

From Königsberg Lola traveled by coach through the cold and snowy Baltic winter, through Tilsit on the Memel River and to the border that Prussia shared with the Russian Empire. At last she entered the country that had been her destination since the previous summer. She journeyed to Riga, whose culture was shaped by Latvian, Swedish, German, and Russian influences; the theater was remarkable for a city of its size. Lola danced here, too, and then turned toward St. Petersburg.

For the story of Lola's visit to St. Petersburg, we have only her own unreliable accounts. In her autobiographical lectures in 1858 she recounted that she was well received by the czarina and that the czar and his ministers "appeared from the first anxious to test her skill and sagacity in the routine of secret diplomacy and politics," all of which is obvious nonsense.

It appears that she did reach St. Petersburg but that her letters of introduction, courting of journalists, and highly placed friends failed her. The czar himself had heard of her adventures in Warsaw and written Prince Paskievitch a teasing letter about them. Nicholas I, notorious for his oppressive regulation and surveillance of his empire, very likely let it be known that the beautiful and fascinating Lola Montez, whom he himself had met, would not be allowed to further disturb the peace of his empire. Not only would no theater engage her, it also appears that none of the heavily censored newspapers even mentioned her. Her 1851 memoirs claim only a single performance in the Russian capital, which supposedly was a success, after which she was forced to flee because of a scandal.

There may well have been scandal and hasty departure. The weather was miserable—snow had been so heavy that wild animals were coming into the towns to look for food—but Lola made a lightning dash with post coaches around the snow-covered Baltic coast, traveling day and night toward Berlin. As she passed back through Tilsit on the evening of 15 February, the local paper reported the rumor that she was leaving Russia in such haste because of an unpleasant occurrence in Riga. But she had been in Riga a month earlier, so it is possible that whatever unpleasantness occurred actually took place in St. Petersburg, as she claimed in her memoirs.

"If the journey to St. Petersburg had been boring, the trip back was far more so," she remembered. "Nature had spread her white winding sheet over the countryside through which I traveled, giving it a stifling monotony." Lola probably had a great deal of time in the chill of the lumbering coach to reflect on where she had been and where she might be going. Since the collapse of her London career after a single night of triumph, St. Petersburg had been her goal. Now she needed a new direction, a new destination.

In Warsaw, nearly four months before, she had written that she was looking forward to appearing in Paris, the mecca of the dance world and Europe's cultural capital. But she probably had no contacts in Paris, no letters to the men who could get theatrical engagements for her and induce journalists to allow her to charm them. But if not Paris, where then?

According to Lola, the answer came by chance. "A coincidence was to resolve my doubts, as it so often happened that suddenly, without warning, totally unpredictable events turned the course of my life and drove me in a new direction, led me to a new country that a quarter-hour before it would never have occurred to me to visit."

In this case, she said that the event that changed her life came when she descended from the coach while the horses were being changed. In the post house, Lola eagerly picked a newspaper left on a table. She loved reading generally, and she was an avid devourer of newspapers, another trait that her contemporaries regarded as unladylike. One of the articles reported that Franz Liszt, the idol of the concert hall, had begun another series of performances, and the item noted some of the scheduled dates and venues. Then and there she decided she had to meet Franz Liszt.

Everything Lola Montez ever said or wrote must be weighed with caution to determine whether it contains any factual content at all. But in this case, it may well be that she decided on the spur of the moment to seek out Liszt in order use him to advance her career.

If she passed through Tilsit on the evening of 15 February, Lola's dash back across East Prussia and Pomerania could have brought her to Berlin no earlier than 20 February. Liszt interrupted a series of three concerts in Dresden and took the train north to play a concert at Dessau on Saturday, 24 February, and another at Köthen the following day. Both cities were only a few hours by train from Berlin, but Lola would have had no more than a day or two to recover from her exhausting trip before taking the train to intercept Liszt in Dessau or Köthen. She hardly would have been likely to leave Berlin almost immediately without a goal in mind. In this case, Lola may indeed have been telling the truth when she wrote that her encounter with Franz Liszt was no accident.

7

T H E   C O N Q U E S T   O F   A   G E N I U S

Lola Montez was aiming high, for Liszt was an international celebrity of unparalleled renown. The Hungarian with the flowing hair and classic profile had begun as a child piano prodigy and risen to a height of virtuosity that had made him a legend. His concert tours attracted hysterically enthusiastic audiences, and the royalty of Europe vied to honor him.

Now, at age thirty-two, Liszt was nearing the zenith of his career as a performer but had begun to shift his attention away from concertizing to composing and to promoting music he admired. He had recently become director of court music for the Duke of Weimar; as kapellmeister for the duke, he would be able to pursue these other interests, and in a few years he would abandon the concert platform altogether.

Liszt's personal life was in troubled transition, however. His liaison of more than a decade with Marie, Comtesse d'Agoult, was foundering painfully. They had had three children together, but they were growing apart. Marie resented the beautiful women with whom Liszt's name was linked in his travels, and she had begun to find a new life of her own, drafting the first of the novels that would bring her fame under the pen name Daniel Stern.

Lola wrote that she attended Liszt's concert and was overwhelmed by his virtuosity. Their eyes met for one electric instant. Afterward, she sent him a note asking him to call. Liszt had always admired feminine beauty, particularly when combined with sharp intelligence, so it is not surprising that the virtuoso was attracted by the Spaniard.

According to Lola, she proposed to Liszt almost at once that they "unite their artistic paths" and travel together. He agreed, she wrote, and the same day she moved into adjoining rooms at his hotel. It is hard to judge how much truth there is in this. What is clear is that Lola did succeed in attaching herself to Liszt and that she returned with him to Dresden, first stopping in Leipzig at the Hotel de Bavière and then checking in the next day with Liszt at his favorite hotel in Dresden, the Hotel de Saxe.

On Tuesday, 27 February, Liszt had an 11 A.M. rehearsal for a concert that evening in the Opera House, and Lola probably attended the rehearsal. The newspapers remarked that the two of them were seen together a great deal in Dresden, and it is likely that she went everywhere she could with him.

While in Dresden, Liszt wanted to see a performance of Richard Wagner's grandiose opera *Rienzi, Last of the Tribunes*. He had met the composer a few times, admired his music, and had heard the opera praised by friends who had attended its premier production in Dresden. *Rienzi* was not scheduled at the Court Opera during Liszt's stay, but at his urging the management pulled together a cast and announced a special performance for 29 February.

In the meantime, there were a thousand invitations for Liszt. Not being the center of attention was a new and not entirely pleasant sensation for Lola. "I had been reduced," she wrote, "to a pale, lightless satellite of a great star, I, who had otherwise been spoiled by the accustomed feeling that I was the sole and unchallenged source of light and warmth in my part of the artistic firmament."

Liszt's Tuesday performance, featuring Beethoven's Fifth Piano Concerto, went off well. At the close of the concert Liszt was congratulated by his admirers, and Lola probably had her first opportunity to meet Wagner, who was impatient with and disgusted by the dilettantes and courtiers who fluttered about Liszt. Wagner had been out of town working on *Tannhäuser* when Lola danced in Dresden, but the reports of her adventures surely convinced him that the woman had no conception of art as he understood it.

Lola continued to play the role of satellite, and on Thursday night she accompanied Liszt to the special performance of *Rienzi*. The music was powerful, but Lola couldn't understand German and probably would have had difficulty comprehending the complex plot about feuding nobles in fourteenth-century Rome. It must have been with relief that she went backstage with

Liszt at intermission to congratulate the tenor, Joseph Tichatschek, on his fine performance of the title role.

In Tichatschek's dressing room they ran into Wagner, and Liszt was so sincere and enthusiastic in his admiration for the opera that Wagner was touched and encouraged. But Lola's presence soured the occasion for Wagner. It is almost certainly to her that Wagner referred in his autobiography when he wrote that "Liszt's curious lifestyle at the time, which constantly surrounded him with distracting and annoying elements, kept us on this occasion from achieving any productive rapport." Liszt seems to have made the situation worse by telling Wagner, in an aside, that Lola fancied him because he was the only man not paying court to her. "I didn't even notice her," Wagner replied. But he had noticed her and would brand her a "heartless, demonic being."

Lola, who was not a great admirer of opera generally, probably rejoiced when, after about five hours, the Roman Capitol went up in flames and almost everyone who had had anything to sing was incinerated.

Lola had not forgotten the young man from Dresden, Eduard von Bülow's son, who had come to her aid in Berlin six months before. Now that she was back in Dresden, Lola had invited Hans to come to Room 17 at the Hotel de Saxe after the opera to meet the great Franz Liszt. She knew that Hans' passion was music, and she had entertained him by singing her repertoire of Spanish songs. Liszt received the fourteen-year-old graciously and invited him to demonstrate his abilities on the piano. Hans sat down and, in honor of his patroness, began to play his arrangement of the songs he had heard from her. Lola must have been delighted, and Liszt, after listening attentively to the performance, sat down and began to improvise on the same Spanish themes. Hans was astounded as the melodies he had played were transformed through a series of incredible variations and ornamentations. The young man immediately decided to devote himself to becoming a musician.

Lola's introduction of Hans von Bülow to Franz Liszt sparked a remarkable chain of events. Hans became a brilliant pianist and one of the great conductors of the nineteenth century. He was Liszt's student and friend, and thirteen years later he married Liszt's daughter Cosima. Like Liszt, Bülow became a proponent of Wagner's music, conducting the first performances of *Tristan und Isolde* and *Die Meistersinger von Nürnberg*. But Wagner would humiliate Hans von Bülow by stealing Cosima and marrying her himself. So on the same evening that Lola's distracting presence delayed the rapprochement between Liszt and Wagner, her introduction of

Hans von Bülow to Liszt set in motion a drama central to the lives of all three musicians.

Liszt's last concert in Dresden was a benefit for an Italian tenor, Pantaleoni, who performed with the pianist in the salon of the Hotel de Saxe. (Liszt was nearly as famous for his generosity as for his virtuosity, and he performed in a great number of benefit concerts.) It is uncertain why Liszt decided to help Pantaleoni, but, according to Lola, the singer was grateful for the assistance and was a jovial companion to the couple on their expeditions in and around Dresden. The concert went well, although some complained that Pantaleoni had a poor voice and used too much falsetto.

Difficulties arose, however, at a dinner for Liszt held by a group of prominent men of Dresden. Lola is the only witness who left a full account, but central elements of her story are probably true. Lola asserts that the meal actually was a breakfast at one of the city's finest delicatessens. Though she had not been invited, she by now considered herself welcome wherever Liszt went, and she persuaded him to take her along even though no other women would be there. By the standards of the time, no lady would have consented to being the sole female at a private party, but Lola was famous for doing things no lady would do.

According to Lola's account, she discovered when they arrived that Pantaleoni had not been invited, and she insisted that their boon companion be sent for. When the tenor finally arrived, he was so indignant that his invitation had been an afterthought that he was insulting to the entire company and actually exchanged blows with Gottfried Semper, the architect who had designed the Opera House in Dresden. Lola says that she was so outraged by Pantaleoni's behavior that she berated him at length and with great vehemence. Pantaleoni, she writes, looked at her coolly and said, "Madame, I am not a gendarme." This remark played so cruelly on her unfortunate encounters with men in uniform that Lola slapped him. He responded with a gesture so rude that, if we can believe her account, she fell into a faint. The assembly rose in an uproar and scattered.

This version of events may contain more than a little of Lola's heightened reality. There are only two newspaper accounts with which to compare it. A report from the paper in faraway Königsberg states, "At a dinner held in Liszt's honor in Dresden an unpleasantness arose, as a result of which the Spanish dancer Lola Montez, all too well known for her artistic performances in Berlin and Warsaw, was expelled from the city." The only reference to the event in the surviving Dresden newspapers is cryptically ironic: "A number of artists and friends of art gave Liszt a dinner, which was particularly interesting for the national contrasts of the debates of the agitated Italian (Pantaleoni), the fiercely defensive Spaniard (the dancer Lola Montez, in whose company Herr Liszt frequently showed himself here), and the not always hesitant Germans, and which will give the great artist a pleasant souvenir of Dresden."

Clearly, something quite unpleasant happened; whether it was anything like Lola's account is impossible to say. But Liszt had to travel north to fulfill engagements, and if he had considered taking Lola along, she was no longer part of his plans.

A story that seems to have first appeared in print in the twentieth century describes how Liszt, having seen what a terror the dancer could be, quietly locked the door of their hotel room on the sleeping Lola and paid the manager for the entire furnishings of the room on the condition that he not unlock the door for twelve hours, giving him time to get a safe distance from his fair friend. This rumor may, in fact, have been in circulation at that time, because Lola remarked in her memoirs on an unflattering account of her parting from Liszt.

Their parting at the end of that week in Dresden was likely with some relief, perhaps on both sides, but it was not bitter or vituperative. Lola's account of Liszt in her memoirs is not unflattering; and, according to one report, Liszt several years later rhapsodized to friends about Lola, calling her "the most perfect, the most enchanting creature I have ever known! . . . Oh, you must see her! She's continually new, continually changing, constantly creative! She is truly a poet! The genius of charm and love! All other women pale beside her!"

The best evidence indicates that Liszt gave Lola letters introducing her to his influential journalistic and theatrical friends in Paris and promised to arrange her debut at the Opéra when he returned to Paris in April. That may have been exactly what Lola had hoped for when she left Berlin to present herself to Liszt.

8

THE JUDGMENT OF PARIS

Paris in 1844 was the cultural capital of Europe. In the city of three-quarters of a million people, eleven thousand made their living as artists—about 50 percent more than worked as lawyers. The city of the Bourbon kings and the imperial capital of Napoleon still spread out from the Cathedral of Notre Dame, but it was growing and changing rapidly. Now nearly half of the city's population was made up of new immigrants from the provinces; under Louis Philippe, the "citizen king," the middle class was on the ascent, and everyone was out to make a fortune. Honoré Daumier did not need to look far to gather material for his *Charivari* caricatures, which skewered the pretensions of the nouveaux riches, and Henri Murger was chronicling the lives of nonconformists who called themselves bohemians. At the Conservatoire concerts Hector Berlioz was producing unprecedented new orchestral sonorities, and the week she arrived in Paris, Lola would have seen that *Le Siècle* was beginning the serialization of *The Three Musketeers*, a new novel by the wildly popular Alexandre Dumas.

It was a society of ferment, in which social conventions were breaking down, and of self-indulgence. Lola took to it immediately and quickly went about presenting Liszt's letters of introduction to journalists and men of the theater. She soon discovered that it was easy for a beautiful woman of wit and intelligence to make friends in this town. On 18 March, Lola Montez was introduced to the Parisian public in the newspaper column written by Jules

Janin, the powerful and feared critic of the *Journal des Débats*, and a good friend of Liszt's.

Through the letters and her beauty she rapidly got to know men of influence, including members of the famous—or perhaps notorious—Jockey Club, an exclusive organization of wealthy connoisseurs of horses and women. Besides appearing prominently at race tracks surrounding Paris, they were nightly patrons of the theaters and music halls, expressing their enthusiasm for their favorite ballerinas, many of whom were their very intimate friends.

Lola had begun to take coaching from Hippolyte Barrez, a choreographer at the Opéra, while her friends lobbied its director, Leon Pillet, to allow her make her debut. Pillet was reluctant. The Opéra was the most prestigious ballet stage in the world, and he was convinced that Lola, for all her beauty, stage presence, and spirit, wasn't up to the standard of his house.

Lola's new friends in the press began a campaign to pressure Pillet. On 24 March, *Le Corsaire* complained that, although Lola Montez "dances the most voluptuous boleros and is perhaps the only woman who can perform this dance of the gypsies in all its romantic energy," she was being denied a chance to appear. On the same day, the *Journal des Théâtres* stated, "There is no hope that we will see Lola Montez dance at the Opéra; is this then the only stage in Paris where Europe's most enlightened public may applaud a talent worthy of its praise?"

The campaign worked, and on Wednesday, 27 March, the bills went up around the Opéra in the rue Lepeletier announcing that following the evening's performance of *Der Freischütz* there would be a choreographic pastiche entitled "Le Bal de Don Juan," in which Mlle. Lola Montez would make her first appearance on the stage of the Académie Royale de Musique, dancing "l'Olia" (apparently the same dance she had called "El Olano" and "El Oleano" and would later call "El Olé" and "El Olle") and "Les Boleros de Cadix." Lola Montez, whose entire career consisted of barely two dozen performances over the previous nine months, was about to make her debut on the hallowed boards of the Paris Opéra.

The house was packed with balletomanes, members of the Jockey Club, and the simply curious, who had heard of Lola's beauty and fire. One paper reported, "There was no stall, no stool, nothing to be had. Happy was he who managed to squeeze as a seventh into a six-seat box!" The tension was broken by the applause greeting Lola's appearance on the stage, and then, if we can believe the account that appeared a few days later in *Le Siècle*, Lola made a singular entrance in the history of the Opéra: "After the first leap, she stopped on the point of her foot, and with a movement of prodigious agility, she detached one of her garters. The lorgnettes were riveted to the sight. Mlle. Lola moved once more towards the footlights, waving between her fingers the ribbon which had just encircled her leg, and, fortifying herself with her most rebellious graces, she threw this ribbon to the spectators. Mlle. Fanny Elssler is content to throw kisses to the public when she dances the cachucha; but Mlle. Elssler is only a Spaniard from Berlin; Mlle. Lola Montez, who is a Spaniard by blood, throws her garter to her admirers, which is quite another Andalusian style."

Although the garter tossing produced a stir, the audience grew restless as "l'Olia" continued. Lola's dancing was simply too unorthodox to meet with approval from a very critical audience in the temple of dancing orthodoxy. She seemed determined to ignore every rule of the French-Italian school of dance, and her beauty could not excuse everything.

The applause after "l'Olia" was less than thunderous, and the audience's attention shifted quickly to the other sensation in the "Bal de Don Juan," the polka to be danced by M. Coballi and Mlle. Maria. The polka was the rage in Paris and had first appeared on the stage of the Opéra only two days before. Whether the polka was indecent was a matter of great controversy, and the Sixth Court of the Correctional Police of the Seine had recently sentenced a young woman to six months in prison for performing in a public dance hall what the presiding judge called "this manifestation of a profound corruption, which threatens to penetrate into all classes of the society."

The performance of the polka seems to have gone off without scandal, and after dances by MM. Petipa and Mabille and Mlle. Dumilatre, Lola returned for "Les Boleros de Cadix." This time the audience reaction was distinctly negative—in fact, the word immediately spread that Lola Montez would never again be seen on the boards of the Opéra.

That was the report in some of the newspapers the next morning, although *Le Corsaire*, whose critic Pier-Angelo Fiorentino became one of Lola's good friends in Paris, claimed, "The debut of Mlle. Lola Montez was worthy of her brilliant and multiple reputation, which preceded this remarkable dancer here. She astonished and charmed the public." But the general tenor of the criticism was expressed in another newspaper: "The beautifully agile woman with the flashing eye was warmly welcomed, but the dancer was rejected, and Lola Montez will no longer appear at the Opéra." Lola won a reprieve from Pillet, however, and was kept on the bill for the repetition of

"Le Bal de Don Juan" on Friday evening after the world premiere of Halévy's *Il Lazzarone*, which would be attended by prominent critics. She wrote to the editor of *La Presse* to make sure that he mentioned her scheduled appearance.

It appears that she did not repeat the garter incident at her second performance, but she had as little success as two nights before. The audience grew even more impatient than before, and some wag is said to have cried out that "l'Olia" looked awfully like a cancan. This time the criticism was unreservedly negative, even mocking:

> Mlle. Lola Montez is a very beautiful person, who is endowed with a lovely figure and the most beautiful eyes in the world. If that sufficed, her success would have been complete. Unfortunately, that's merely an initial advantage; it has to be justified with talent. Mlle. Lola Montez doesn't know how to dance; she doesn't know the first elements of choreography. Her figure and her eyes, which she paraded before the auditorium with martial assurance, did not disarm the spectators, who welcomed her with indulgence at her first dance, but who at her second hissed her with such vehemence that it determined the withdrawal of her name from the bills. Mlle. Lola Montez still has her beauty as a consolation. She can combine it with good study, and then, since we won't prejudge the future, we would hope to be able to confirm at some later date the success that has eluded her today.

The *Journal des Théâtres*, which a week earlier had bemoaned Pillet's initial refusal to let her appear, now wrote: "It's perfectly excusable for the young Spanish dancer to have dared to mount the boards of the foremost French theater; but it is far less so that the management could have convinced itself she belonged there."

The greatest dance critic of the Parisian press was Théophile Gautier, who knew not only dance but also was well acquainted with Spain. He wrote in *La Presse:* "Mlle. Lola Montez has nothing Andalusian about her except a pair of magnificent black eyes. She *habla*s very mediocre Spanish, barely speaks French, English passably.—What country is she really from? That is the question.—We could say that Mlle. Lola has a small foot and pretty legs.—As for the way she uses them, that's another matter. It must be admitted that the curiosity excited by Mlle. Lola's various run-ins with the police of the North, her horsewhip conversations with Prussian gendarmes, was not satisfied. . . . Having heard of her equine exploits, we suspect Mlle. Lola is more at home on a horse than on the boards."

After two performances, Lola's failure was obvious. By the time Liszt arrived in Paris on 5 April, he could do little to repair the damage. But he may have decided to avoid Lola altogether, for his liaison with her had set off a destructive explosion in his relationship with the Comtesse d'Agoult. Certainly Marie, who was living in Paris, had heard that this woman of dubious credentials had arrived in the city with letters of introduction from Liszt after traveling with him in Germany. The comtesse and Liszt had a final, violent quarrel in which she cried that she did not object to being his mistress but that she did object to being *one* of his mistresses.

Lola had quickly made friends in Paris, where the truth of her origins and identity was much less important than elsewhere. In this mobile society she was accepted on the basis of her beauty, wit, and charm.

She made friends, particularly among journalists. One of them, Fiorentino of the *Corsaire-Satan*, sometimes worked in the famous "novel factory" of Alexandre Dumas, writing parts of the massive output published under Dumas's name. Lola also got to know Dumas, the playwright, gourmet, and social lion who dominated the fashionable salons. His energy, talent, vanity, and genius for self-promotion—which were as impressive as his massive physique—gave him a unique status among the lions, climbers, nobility, and ambitious provincials who made up high society.

How Lola lived in Paris is uncertain. It is unlikely that she had saved much from her dancing income; throughout her life she spent liberally on herself, and she gave generously to anyone in need. Lola was probably the mistress of a number of men, but there is little evidence that she ever traded sexual favors for money.

Throughout much of her life, Lola's best friends were men, and some of those friends certainly became her lovers. It would have seemed appropriate and normal to her for men to give her money for the things she needed, just as she would have given them money had they needed it. It was simply that usually she was the one in need.

Although her debut at the Opéra had been a fiasco, Lola did not abandon the idea of dancing again in Paris. She continued to take lessons and waited for the furor to die. She seems to have devoted herself to having a good time, and these first years in Paris must have been some of her happiest. She went to the races, to the Opéra, to the music festival organized by Hector Berlioz. In July 1844 she was in the papers again, this time on account of her skill with pistols: "Mlle. Lola Montez . . . has left a card at the Shooting Gallery of Lepage . . . entirely perforated with pistol balls, in firing rapid double *coups*.

The most famous Parisian shots avow themselves vanquished by the prowess of the fair Andalusian."

In late summer rumors began to circulate that Lola would reappear at the Opéra or that the Theater of the Porte St. Martin would stage a work for her. In September she had actually begun training for a debut at the Theater of the Porte St. Martin, but nothing immediately came from her efforts.

Lola ran with the lions of Parisian society until the fall of 1844, when she met Alexandre Henri Dujarier, the young co-owner and cultural editor of *La Presse*. Dujarier was the epitome of the "new man" in Paris. Born on 20 June 1815, just two days after Napoleon's empire finally crumbled at Waterloo, he was a child of the modest provincial bourgeoisie that was transforming society in the 1840s. He had gone into business at an early age, apparently establishing himself as a private banker, and through his shrewdness he had become extremely wealthy before he turned twenty-five. In 1839, Dujarier became the partner of one of the great figures in nineteenth-century French journalism, Emile de Girardin, by using most of his fortune to help Girardin buy up his own bankrupt newspaper, *La Presse*. With Girardin responsible for the news and politics and Dujarier managing the business and editing the cultural side of the paper, *La Presse* caused a revolution in journalism. Dujarier was the first journalist to realize that if circulation increased, advertisers would be willing to pay higher rates, giving the paper greater net income even if the subscription price was lowered. In November 1844 he introduced a series of dramatic changes at *La Presse*, cutting the price of an annual subscription in half, adopting a larger format, and announcing that some of the best-known authors of the day, including Dumas, had been signed to exclusive contracts to serialize their new works in *La Presse*.

It was said that Dujarier was swept away by Lola Montez the first time he saw her. Lola must have found the tall, thin young man with the receding black hair and bushy side whiskers attractive, too, for she soon was established as his mistress, moving into an apartment next to his at 39 rue Laffitte, in the elegant neighborhood near the cafes favored by the fashionable elite. She acted as his hostess at home and his companion when he went out, and in the meantime she went forward with the resumption of her dance career, possibly with assistance from Dujarier. Her debut at the Theater of the Porte St. Martin, set for 6 March, was to be a performance of "La Dansomanie"; she also was rehearsing a role in a grand fairy spectacle entitled "La Biche aux Bois."

It had been nearly a year since her unfortunate appearances at the

Opéra—her last public performances—and she must have been nervous about confronting a Parisian audience again. Circumstances were different now, however; not only had she charmed many of the critics, she also had many more fashionable friends, including Dujarier, who could exert his influence to ensure her success. The day before her debut the newspapers were announcing that "all of fashionable Paris has made a date for the evening in order to make the success of this pretty artist more brilliant and complete."

The Porte St. Martin was not particularly stylish, but on the cold Thursday evening of Lola's debut it was overflowing with the dandies of Paris, the ballet girls from the Opéra with their lovers from the Jockey Club, the fashionable clientele of the Café de Paris, and the leading critics. They had come prepared, and when Lola appeared, in a Spanish costume of black silk, with a black lace mantilla flowing down from a high comb in her black hair, the audience went wild throwing flowers on the stage. One critic wrote that the flowers seemed to be the full harvest of fifty greenhouses, and another swore that an entire tree landed on the boards. The stage was so completely covered with flowers that Lola hardly had room to dance.

Lola displayed two other costumes for her polka and mazurka; they were of sequins and lace, and everyone agreed that they were elegant and striking and in perfect taste. Unfortunately, the critics were not so appreciative of her dancing. They were more indulgent than they had been a year before, and many were obviously trying to tell the truth yet not be critical. Her friend Pier-Angelo Fiorentino dealt with the problem in his positive review in the *Corsaire-Satan* by discussing the crowd, the flowers, and her costumes; he never commented on her dancing. The review of Dujarier's close friend Charle de Boigne in *Le Constitutionnel* tried to put the performance in a hopeful light: "With a few more well placed *battements*, Lola Montez's talent will be admired as much as her beautiful eyes."

The critic of *Rabelais* was positive but hardly flattering: "There is something lasciviously attractive, voluptuously enticing in the poses she takes; and then, she's a pretty, very pretty, extremely pretty person, and she throws you kisses so complete that you applaud at once, only to ask yourself afterwards if it was right or wrong to applaud. . . . Go see her: it's singular, it's funny, it's entertaining."

The critic of the widely read *Le Siècle* regretted ironically that Lola had spoiled the flower-bedecked triumph of her entrance by attempting to dance. Dujarier's own critic in *La Presse*, Théophile Gautier—who a year earlier had questioned her origins and suggested she stick to riding horses—now not only was willing to accept at face value Lola's claim to being Spanish but wrote with enthusiasm of her fiery cachuchas: "She dances them with an unbridled audacity, a mad ardor and a wild verve that must shock the classical lovers of pirouettes and ronds de jambes; but is dance so serious an art that it allows no invention, no caprice? Must it be constrained by invariable correctness, and isn't it enough that a woman is beautiful, young, lithe, and graceful? . . . The rigorous will say she lacks study, that she allows herself things prohibited by the rules.—So what!"

It was not an unalloyed triumph, but it was certainly a success, and her role in "La Biche aux Bois" promised a long run that would give her stage experience and exposure. For the first time since her London debut, Lola must have felt that she was on the way to establishing herself professionally. That might have happened had it not been for the sudden tragedy that would change her life.

9

AN APPOINTMENT IN
THE BOIS

Lola had noticed that for the past several months Henri Dujarier had been socializing increasingly with less respectable members of the theatrical and artistic world—with music hall dancers and dandies of no particular merit—and she worried that trouble would come from it. On Friday, 7 March, the evening after Lola's debut at the Porte St. Martin, Dujarier was invited to a party at the restaurant Les Trois Frères Provençaux in the Palais Royal. He was reluctant to go, but when his friends insisted, he agreed to be there. Lola wanted to go with him, but he felt that the company was unsuitable for her. She asked him to stop going places that he was not willing to take her, and he promised that this would be the last time. As a consolation, he gave her a ticket to the Vaudeville and told her that he would be back by midnight.

After the dinner at Les Trois Frères, the guests adjourned to the gambling table to play lansquenet, an old German card game that had come back into favor in Paris. One of the other guests at the party was a tall twenty-four-year-old with long chestnut hair and whiskers and the sonorous name Jean-Baptiste Rosemond de Beaupin de Beauvallon. He was a native of the Caribbean island of Guadeloupe and the critic of the rival newspaper *Le Globe*, whose editor was his brother-in-law. Dujarier lost heavily but kept gambling into the early morning hours in an effort to recover his losses. When he stumbled out to his coach at dawn, any satisfaction he may have felt at having won back part of his money was dampened by his suspicion that an angry exchange he had had with Beauvallon would bring him further trouble.

That afternoon, when he awoke and dragged himself to his desk at *La Presse,* Dujarier learned how true his premonition had been. Two gentleman called on him on behalf of Beauvallon, stating that their friend had felt that Dujarier had behaved rudely the evening before. They wished to know whether that had been his intention.

Dujarier was curt. He would not offer apologies or explanations to Beauvallon, and he told the gentlemen that two of his own friends would contact them the next day. Dujarier saw that he was being drawn into a duel, and although the prospect troubled him, it came as no surprise. What was surprising was that it had not come to this before. Parisian journalism was a battlefield of politics and polemics, and affairs of honor were common outlets for the constant ill feeling generated by freewheeling members of the fourth estate. Dujarier was in a particularly vulnerable position. Not only was he, as an extremely wealthy self-made man, an object of envy, but he also owned *La Presse* with a man who had placed himself outside the code of honor, leaving Dujarier all the more exposed. Emile de Girardin had been involved in a number of duels before he killed a prominent opponent. The battle aroused great public feeling, and a sickened Girardin announced that he had done all a man of honor was required to do and would never fight again.

Dujarier had known that dueling was inevitable, but he had never been trained in fencing and shooting. Lola, a crack shot, had encouraged him to go with her to the shooting galleries, but he had said, "Why should a woman be shooting pistols? I don't know how to shoot and I hope never to have to use a pistol." And yet he must have known that he would one day be challenged to a duel. And now that the challenge had come, he felt he would just as soon get it over with, acquit himself honorably, and perhaps discourage future challenges. Even if he found a way to reconcile with Beauvallon, he thought, there would be twenty more waiting to challenge him. Better to get it over with.

Dujarier tried to hide from Lola that he was going to fight a duel, but she guessed what was afoot and demanded the details. He refused to tell her anything but assured her that everything would turn out all right.

Lola had another performance of "La Dansomanie" on Monday, 10 March, but Dujarier begged off accompanying her, saying that he had important paperwork to finish. Alone in his study, Dujarier took out his will. He read it over and added some bequests, including one leaving Lola Montez seventeen shares in the Palais Royal Theater. He asked to be buried beside his sister. As the evening wore on, his doom seemed increasingly inevitable to him. He wrote a last letter to his mother, saying that he regretted more than anything the pain his death would cause her and that he hoped she would rather weep for a man of honor than for a coward.

When Lola returned from the applause and flowers and whistles at the Theater of the Porte St. Martin, she again pressed Dujarier to tell her about the duel. He became exasperated, saying that he was busy and needed to be alone, and they began to argue. Finally, the dancer contented herself with his promise to come see her in the morning at nine, and she left him and went to sleep in her apartment.

It was a restless night for Lola. She knew something was wrong. At seven she told her maid to ask Dujarier to come see her. The servant found Dujarier dressed and eating soup. He told her that he would come to see her mistress shortly. Then he took up a quill and wrote a final note:

> My dear Lola,
>   I am leaving to fight with pistols. This explains why I wanted to sleep alone and also why I didn't come to see you this morning. I need all my composure and I must avoid the emotions that seeing you would have caused me. At ten, it will all be over and I'll run to embrace you, unless . . .
>   A thousand tendernesses, my dear Lola, my good little woman whom I love and who will be in my thoughts.
>   D   Tuesday morning

Dujarier poured himself a glass of Madeira. He was dressed in black, as the code of the duel required, and he had put on warm flannel so he wouldn't shiver in the cold. It had snowed during the night, and a few flakes were still falling. He put on his black overcoat, stuck the bottle of Madeira in the pocket, and went down to where his coachman and valet were sitting ready on the box. Charle de Boigne, one of Dujarier's seconds, would ride with him, and Arthur Bertrand, the other second, was coming with a doctor. Just before they departed for the Bois de Boulogne, the usual venue for Parisian duels, Dujarier gave his valet, Gabriel, the note to take up to Lola, and they were off.

Early that morning the seconds had arranged the details of the duel. It was to take place at ten in a clearing in the woods known as the *chemin de la Favorite*. In his ignorance and inexperience, Dujarier had chosen pistols, the most deadly dueling weapon and one with which he was totally incompetent. The adversaries would be placed facing each other thirty paces apart, and at the signal, three handclaps, each could advance five paces and fire. After one party fired, the other must stop and return the fire immediately.

The journalist's nerves were showing the strain after the long night, and when the two carriages arrived at the cold, bleak clearing, Dujarier offered Boigne a glass of Madeira and then quickly downed one himself. The clock of the church at Neuilly struck ten, but there was no sign of Beauvallon and his party. The men paced, trying to keep warm in the bitter cold. Ten-thirty came, and then eleven. They sent the servants out searching in the vicinity to see whether there had been some confusion as to the site, but no one was found. His seconds advised him that since the other party had not arrived, he could honorably return to town, but Dujarier said that he would simply have to waste some other morning out here; he would wait until noon. He paced back and forth with the doctor, murmuring, "How strange it is, to be fighting and not to know why."

It was eleven thirty-five when Beauvallon and his party finally arrived. They were deeply apologetic, offering a string of excuses, but Beauvallon and his seconds all rejected Boigne's final effort to effect a reconciliation. A pocket notebook and a glove marked the places where the men were to take up their positions. The tension was becoming too much for Dujarier, who hardly seemed to understand as Boigne put the pistol in his hand and showed him how to hold it. Dujarier gripped it, accidentally pulling the trigger, but the charge failed to ignite, saving the life of Boigne, who stood at the end of the muzzle. Boigne recocked the gun and told Dujarier to fire at once when the signal was given, thus forcing Beauvallon to return his fire without advancing or taking careful aim. Then he stepped back, saw that both men were in position and prepared to give the signal.

Boigne brought his hands together in three measured claps that sounded across the frozen air among the trees. Dujarier remembered what he had been told and fired at once, the ball passing some twenty feet above and to the right of Beauvallon. At this point a practiced duelist would have turned sideways to present the smallest possible target and have held his empty pistol before his face for some small protection, but Dujarier stood frozen, the gun at his side, awaiting his opponent's shot. The journalist's seconds swore Beauvallon did not return fire instantly, as required, but instead stood forty or fifty seconds taking careful aim. It may have seemed that long to them as they stood anxious over their friend's fate, but people who heard the shots said there were three or four seconds between them. To Dujarier it must have seemed an eternity as he stared at the pistol leveled at him.

At the end of his extended left arm, Beauvallon could see his adversary's pale features framed by the blackness of his side whiskers, a perfect target. Finally Boigne cried out, "Well, fire then! Fire!" and Beauvallon's shot rang out. Dujarier didn't move at all. For an instant it seemed the ball had missed him. A troubled look came over his face, then his legs melted beneath him and he slumped and fell backward like a sack. The doctor and Boigne ran to him, lifting him and opening his tie and coat. He was conscious, but the half-inch lead ball had left a bloody round hole at the lower right corner of his nose. The doctor saw at once that the wound was mortal, but he told Dujarier, "Courage now, we'll have you better in no time," and the man's mangled features took on a look of serenity.

Boigne asked him whether he was in much pain, and Dujarier managed a slight movement of his head to signal he was. His mouth was filling with blood, and the doctor told him to try to cough, but the paralyzed man couldn't breathe, much less cough. The end came with merciful swiftness; the wounded face convulsed in a sudden agony, the eyes clouded over, and Dujarier squeezed the doctor's hand and died.

Beauvallon and his men had already perfunctorily offered their services, collected the pistols, and left in their fiacre. Boigne thought that he could carry Dujarier's long, thin form by himself, but the limp body was awkward, so he and the doctor together carried the slumping, bloody corpse to the coach, which raced off at full speed to evade the guards in the Bois, who would have heard the shots and could arrest them for abetting a duel.

When Lola Montez received her lover's note, she set out at once to find out where the duel was to take place. She went first to find Boigne or Bertrand, but both of them were gone. Then it occurred to her that her lover's close friend, Alexandre Dumas, must know what was happening, and she rushed to his home in the Chaussée d'Antin. When Dumas told her that Henri's opponent was Rosemond de Beauvallon, Lola was aghast. "He's lost!" she exclaimed, for she knew how helpless her lover was with a pistol, and Dumas confirmed what she had heard of Beauvallon's prowess with weapons. Despite her pleading and raging, Dumas could not or would not tell her where the duel was to take place. There was nothing she could do but return to Dujarier's apartment and wait, just as he was waiting, pacing in a clearing in the Bois de Boulogne.

It was after midday when she saw his coach returning. As it came to a halt, she rushed forward and pulled open the door herself. Dujarier's bloody corpse slumped into her arms. The doctor and the seconds hastened out of the carriage to take the body from the stunned woman to carry it upstairs to the bed Dujarier had told his servants to prepare. Lola took to her own bed, and a doctor was called to attend her. At a little after 2 P.M., the bell at 39 rue Laffitte rang, and the officers of the king were admitted to begin their investigation into the murder of Alexandre-Honoré, known as Alexandre-Henri, Dujarier.

The funeral took place on Thursday afternoon, 13 March, at the church of Notre Dame de la Lorette, and Honoré de Balzac and Alexandre Dumas were among the pallbearers. After the service a crowd of family members and friends walked behind the four white horses drawing the hearse to the Montmartre Cemetery, where Emile de Girardin delivered the eulogy.

As surely as Beauvallon's bullet had killed Dujarier, it had also destroyed Lola's chance of building a career on the Parisian stage. In the wake of the murder of her lover and protector, she was in no condition to fulfill her contract in "La Dansomanie," nor was she able to attend the rehearsals for "La Biche aux Bois." And perhaps without Dujarier's influence and financial support, the Theater of the Porte St. Martin had less interest in her services. Whatever the reason, Dujarier had been buried only ten days when the *Corsaire-Satan* announced that Lola Montez no longer belonged to the company of the Porte St. Martin.

10

SEEKING DISTRACTIONS AT HOME AND ABROAD

In the midst of her mourning, Lola's most immediate problem was money. Dujarier had been a ready and an almost limitless source of money, but now Lola had to pay her own rent and satisfy her creditors. Dujarier had left his major asset, his share of *La Presse*, to his mother and his infant nephew, and had left most of his personal property, including his horses and the opulent furnishings of his apartment, to Alexandre Dumas. To Lola he had left only the seventeen shares in the Palais Royal Theater, which were worth less than 1,000 francs. Nevertheless, that was better than nothing, and early in April she went to court to force Dujarier's executors to deliver her legacy; but the court ruled that the law allowed M. François, Dujarier's brother-in-law and executor, more time to distribute the estate. Lola moved back into a hotel just off the Boulevard des Italiens and seems to have returned to the life she led before meeting Dujarier, living off gifts and loans from friends and lovers, floating in the demimonde. Although she swore that she had been deeply in love with the journalist and that they were to be married, life had to go on, and wealthy admirers distracted her from gloomy thoughts.

Then as now, most Parisians of means abandoned the city in August for the resorts, and Lola was determined to follow the fashionable world. Her plan was to start a tour at Spa, the Belgian resort whose name became generic for Europe's elegant retreats with healing waters, gambling, and intrigue. Before she departed, Lola asked her friend Fiorentino to include an item in his newspaper about her departure; at that time she probably learned of his own plans for August, which included attending a music festival in Bonn.

Lola found much of the elegant world assembled in Spa, where conversation often turned to the coming festival in Bonn. Lola made quite an impression with her bold beauty, her wit, and her charm, and she ran into people she knew, including Jules Janin, the powerful critic and friend of Liszt who had introduced her to the Parisian public in his column. Janin now regarded Lola with bemused disdain; he, too, would be in Bonn for the festival. By the end of the week in Spa, and particularly after she was turned away from a fashionable ball for lack of an invitation, Lola decided that she, too, was going to Bonn.

Bonn, then only a sleepy little university town on the Rhine, was overwhelmed by the influx of distinguished and not-so-distinguished visitors from all over Europe. Franz Liszt had promoted a fund to erect a statue of Beethoven in honor of the composer's seventy-fifth birthday—Bonn was Beethoven's birthplace—and had proposed a great music festival for the unveiling. Despite much initial enthusiasm and many promises of help, the financial and artistic responsibility for the project had fallen largely on Liszt. All the difficulties were overcome, however, and the festival and unveiling were scheduled for the middle of August, in the presence of King Friedrich Wilhelm of Prussia and his cousin Queen Victoria.

The unofficial festival headquarters was the hotel Zum goldenen Stern, whose resourceful owner, Herr Joseph Schmitz, had erected temporary accommodations beside his hotel and converted some rooms into modified barracks. The city was so inundated with visitors that many, including Liszt, lodged in nearby Cologne. Lola arrived at the Stern and insisted that she be put up there because she was a guest of Liszt himself. She might have succeeded had not one of the soloists at the festival, a tenor from Berlin, recognized her and informed the manager that it was unlikely that Liszt had sent her a personal invitation.

Lola finally found lodging in one of the many private homes that were taking in guests for the festival. She attended her first concert on the evening of her arrival and certainly joined the multitude in the market square before the town hall for the official unveiling of Beethoven's statute before the assembled royalty and dignitaries. Lola was also seen "in a suite of ladies and gentlemen in attendance on" Liszt at the grand banquet afterward in the huge hall that had been erected at the Stern to feed 450 at a time.

On Wednesday, 13 August, the final day of the festival, Liszt conducted a cantata that he had written for the occasion and then played Beethoven's E flat major concerto, which Lola had heard him play in Dresden a year and a half earlier. Afterward everyone adjourned to the great temporary dining hall for a final gala banquet. Admission was by ticket only, but hundreds who had no tickets surrounded the entrances to the hall trying to get in. The ticket holders had to fight through the mob to the entrance, and many then found that their seats at the tables were already occupied by interlopers.

Among the crowd of the ticketless swarming around the rear entrance was Lola Montez, who was trying to charm or plead her way in. She had been grabbing arms and making her plea for some time before a kindhearted local resident took pity on her and escorted her into the banquet hall as his companion. Women made up a small minority of the people attending the festival, and at the banquet they were naturally seated near one another. Propriety required that a lady not be seated alone among gentlemen. Hence the good burghers of Bonn were astonished and moderately scandalized to see their fellow citizen not only enter with Lola Montez on his arm but also to lead her to his table near the center of the hall, where she was the only woman in a sea of men.

After the banquet, the gentlemen broke out their cigars and the ladies retired from the hall—except for Lola, who may well have lit up herself. Now began a series of seemingly endless toasts: to the King of Prussia, to Queen Victoria, to Beethoven, to the sculptor, to the organizers of the festival. When most of the guests were awash in champagne, Professor Oscar Wolff from the University of Jena introduced the moving force behind the festival, Franz Liszt, to say a few words. Liszt spoke in German, a language with which he was never completely at ease, rambling awkwardly before concluding with another toast, "Here all nations are met to pay honor to the master. May they live and prosper, the English, the Dutch, and the Austrians who have made the pilgrimage here!" At this a Frenchman rose and screamed in French, "You've forgotten the French!" and an uproar broke out among the banqueters. Another Frenchman arose and objected to the fact that toasts had been drunk to the King of Prussia and the Queen of England but no toast had honored the King of the French. An Englishman yelled back, "Why not the Emperor of China and the Shah of Persia? They didn't come to the festival either and certainly have just as much right as your 'Citizen King' to be forgotten!"

Liszt was trying desperately to make himself heard—to explain that he had lived among the French for fifteen years and could never have intended to slight them—but emotions and the general din were running too high. Professor Wolff tried to calm the guests with reason, finally climbing onto a table to gain attention, but he was shouted down. Lola then took it upon herself to intervene, climbing onto her table amid the glasses and shouting in French, "Speak, Professor Wolff, speak, I pray you!" The situation threatened to turn ugly, and Schmitz, the proprietor, ordered the brass band in the hall to play its loudest to silence the angry voices. This succeeded in driving many of the combatants outside, where a sudden thunderstorm finally dispersed the contentious babblers of a dozen languages.

With the festival over, Bonn was quickly slipping into summer somnolence, so Lola journeyed up the Rhine to elegant Baden-Baden, a scene of far greater excitement. Baden-Baden was one of the most fashionable resorts in Europe at the time, and its elite clientele, including royal vacationers from every ruling family on the continent, was drawn as much by its famous gaming tables as by the curative powers of its waters. Lola said that although gambling was never a passion with her, she enjoyed trying her luck at the tables. The casinos were probably also a good place to meet men with money to spare.

But whatever luck Lola may have been having at the gaming tables, her eccentric behavior attracted the disapprobation of Baden-Baden's official guardians of public morality. Cries of outrage rose after the dancer one evening gave a public demonstration of her agility by throwing a leg over the shoulder of a gentleman standing next to her. But when, in the great hall of the spa, she dazzled an admirer sitting beside her by raising her skirt up to her thigh, the resulting outcry led the police to order the shameless beauty to leave town. Baden-Baden joined Ebersdorf, Berlin, and Warsaw on the list of cities that had expelled Lola Montez. Lola returned to Paris and the life she enjoyed.

At some time during her sojourn in the French capital Lola developed a fixation that would color her thoughts and actions forever: she believed that the Jesuits were her sworn enemies and would do everything in their power to slander and destroy her. She had arrived in Paris at a time when agitation against the Society of Jesus was particularly passionate. The historian Jules Michelet was denouncing the Jesuits in his lectures at the Collège de France, and in Eugène Sue's wildly popular new novel, *Le Juif Errant*, the two principal villains were Jesuits. European newspapers of the period were full of long articles on the Jesuits' alleged efforts to undermine governments, influence kings and legislators, and destroy all opposition to their power.

It is difficult to recapture the image that the Jesuits often had in the nineteenth century. Religion was a political issue, particularly in countries with populations divided between Catholics and Protestants, and held an importance far closer to what we today associate with the Reformation rather than with the nineteenth century. Political rights and power were frequently tied to religion, informally and by law. Even in relatively liberal Great Britain, Catholics had no real political rights until passage of the Catholic Emancipation Act in 1829. The question of ultramontanism—whether Catholics' first loyalty was to their national sovereign or to the pope "beyond the mountains"—was a burning issue in France, Spain, and many of the German states. It was no wonder that the Jesuits were widely seen as a "fifth column" working for the power of Rome against the forces of nationalism and liberalism. In many countries, including nominally Catholic ones, the Society of Jesus was banned.

Although Lola had been raised a Protestant, her masquerade as a Spanish noblewoman required her to pretend to be a devout Catholic. According to a contemporary story, which must have originated with Lola herself, her war with the Jesuits arose in Paris when she was secretly approached by members of the Society who wished her to help them convert a Russian nobleman, one of her intimate friends. According to the tale, Lola not only refused to be part of the plot, she also informed Guizot, the French foreign minister. The Jesuits were briefly banned from France for their attempt to interfere in Franco-Russian affairs, and the Society of Jesus swore eternal vengeance on Lola. She heartily reciprocated their animosity. There is no way to prove this tale completely false, but the story of Guizot expelling the Jesuits from France for interfering in affairs with Russia is demonstrably false, and the rest probably is, too.

Whatever the real reason, Lola became convinced that the Jesuits were her enemies, and from that conclusion she frequently leaped to the converse proposition, that anyone who was her enemy was a Jesuit. These convictions waned somewhat as she grew older but never disappeared, even long after she had given up pretending to be Catholic.

In Paris, Lola was troubled more by anxious creditors than by anyone with dark political motives, but she still managed to occupy a series of fashionable apartments and lead a life filled with parties, the theater, and wealthy, titled friends. In February 1846 Lola danced once more, this time a cachucha at a benefit at the Gaité Theater. At the end of March she made one of her most famous public appearances, not on a stage, but in a courtroom. The trial of Beauvallon for the murder of Dujarier was about to begin in Rouen. Dujarier's death had caused a sensation a year before, and now the trial was exciting even greater interest. Everyone wanted to see the celebrity witnesses, including Lola, Alexandre Dumas, and the music hall stars who had attended the dinner at Les Trois Frères Provençaux. Public interest was further inflamed by rumors that Beauvallon had somehow rigged the duel so that the hapless and inexperienced Dujarier was doomed from the start by a murderous conspiracy.

On her arrival at the Palace of Justice on the morning of 26 March, Lola was very much the center of attention, though Alexandre Dumas, who arrived in an open carriage like some potentate, did manage to create quite a stir. The courtroom was the medieval hall of the parliament of Normandy, an imposing chamber with a gilded ceiling and lined with statues, but it was far too small to accommodate the crowd of local citizens and Parisians who wanted to take in the judicial drama. Even the counsel tables were taken over by spectators, forcing the attorneys to move toward the temporary bench erected for the judges. People were packed so closely that it was almost impossible to move in or out, and even though it was not yet April, the heat in the chamber became so oppressive that the windows had to be opened.

The Paris newspapers had arranged for private stenographers to take down the testimony so that it could be rushed to the train and printed in special expanded editions as the trial went on. When the judges first entered in their red velvet robes, the mass of humanity crammed into the chamber struggled to its feet with difficulty. The president of the court promptly ruled that in the future this act of respect could be dispensed with.

The trial began with the reading of the act of accusation, which detailed the story of Dujarier's slide down the conventions of honor to his death. After the reading, the advocat-general, who was officially prosecuting the case, made an opening statement; but much of the prosecution's work at the trial would be done by Léon Duval, who represented Dujarier's mother and brother-in-law in their action for damages against Beauvallon, which was being tried along with the criminal action. Beauvallon was being defended by Pierre Antoine Berryer, a brilliant bulldog of a defender who was already a legend and would become one of the most famous French advocates of the century.

The president of the court interrogated Beauvallon, who acquitted himself well under questioning and made a favorable impression on the crowd. Then came the first of the dozens of witnesses, the doctor who had performed the autopsy on Dujarier's body. His testimony must have been especially painful for Lola, particularly when he opened a parcel he had brought with him and pulled out her lover's bloodstained clothes, the pistols used in the duel, and the lead ball that killed Dujarier, flattened from passing through his face and slamming against the inside of his skull.

The parade of witnesses covered every detail of the events that led to the duel in the Bois de Boulogne. The day's session came to an end at 6 P.M., nearly eight hours after the crowd had surged into the courtroom.

The next morning's session began promptly at ten, and one of the first witnesses called was Alexandre Dumas. The crowd stirred as the flamboyant author and playwright strode forward to take the oath. The president asked him his name, then his age, and then his profession. To the last question Dumas replied with a flourish of uncharacteristic and calculated modesty: "I would say 'dramatist' were I not in the birthplace of Corneille." "There are degrees, in accordance with the centuries," responded the judge dryly.

After Dumas stepped down, his son, also named Alexandre, testified briefly, and then the court called Dolores Montez to the stand. The reporters noted a stir of curiosity in the crowd as she came forward, elegantly dressed in a black silk dress, a black veil, and wrapped from head to foot in an elegant cashmere shawl. Lola raised her veil and removed the glove from her right hand to take the oath. She gave her age as twenty-one, subtracting five years, and her profession as "artiste of the dance." Her face showed the sadness that the testimony had reawakened, and the emotion in her voice made it even harder to understand her heavily accented French, for which she apologized more than once.

Had she known the duel was with Beauvallon, she testified, she would have stopped it. The president asked her how she would have done that. "I would have told the police, or if I had to, I would have gone there myself." This remark produced a sensation in the audience, including some laughter, over which Lola added emphatically, "I would rather have sacrificed myself." One reporter wrote that it was clear from her tone, her attitude, and her arms, firmly crossed under her shawl, that she meant what she said.

When she came to the point of describing Dujarier's note to her on the morning of the duel, she reached into her bosom, pulled out the paper itself, and passed it to the president of the court, who read it into the record. As

Lola listened to her lover's final words to her, tears streamed down her face. Léon Duval wished to put a few questions to the witness, and he began by asking why Lola hadn't mentioned certain matters a year earlier, at the time of her initial deposition.

"I don't know anything about it," she cried. "I couldn't talk about it. It's always the same questions. I'll always repeat the same things. I was sick . . . in bed . . . surrounded by doctors and the law. A woman would have to be nearly heartless. . . . It was I who received his dead body . . . I opened the door of the carriage. . . . I'd had a presentiment for two months that there would be a duel, since he'd begun mixing in company where he didn't fit in."

"You know nothing more?" ventured Léon Duval.

"My God! Monsieur, I opened the carriage, he fell stiffly into my arms. . . . He was quite dead."

Lola was allowed to lower her veil and return to her place.

The parade of witnesses continued for two more days. If the matter were being decided simply in accordance with the law, Beauvallon had no hope of escaping conviction for murder. But he and everyone else in the courtroom knew that French juries never applied the murder statute to a duel unless the combat had somehow deviated from the traditional code of dueling, unless some unfair advantage clearly had been taken.

So, even though Beauvallon clearly was determined to provoke Dujarier to fight, and even though Beauvallon had taken aim and shot a disarmed Dujarier full in the face, there was little doubt that an acquittal was at hand. Léon Duval conceded as much when he concluded his argument to the jury by saying that even the best and holiest causes have often lost, but they have been strengthened by their defeats because they have shamed their opponents. "If M. de Beauvallon leaves this courtroom absolved," he declared, "the bloody principle of dueling will have won nothing: the fraudulent duel, the motiveless duel will have won the match, but the cause of dueling will be thereby dishonored."

The final arguments were on Sunday evening, and thousands swarmed around the Palace of Justice, held back by squads of soldiers and gendarmes. The president of the court repeatedly called for reinforcements to drive back the mob outside so that the arguments in the courtroom could be heard. Berryer, who was renowned for his eloquence, did not deliver one of his finest pleas on behalf of Beauvallon, but it didn't really matter. It was approaching midnight when the jury was finally given the case. They took ten minutes to acquit Beauvallon.

Lola must have felt that Beauvallon had murdered her lover with impunity, and that bitterness may have contributed to her resolution to leave France. Dujarier's executor continued to find reasons to delay handing over the stock she had inherited, but it was worth only 775 francs. Her creditors were becoming a nagging problem, too. If one theme runs through Lola's whole life, it is a longing for new adventures, new challenges, new faces, and new horizons; and during the spring of 1846 she decided to abandon her life in Paris. She may have been encouraged to leave by her new lover, Francis Leigh, a young, blond Englishman who had served briefly as an officer in the Queen's Tenth Hussars before resigning his commission to amuse himself in Paris. Leigh was buying her the clothes she would need for the summer season because they planned to make a circuit of fashionable spas and resorts together. Along with her fashionable clothes, Lola packed her costumes and her music and made no plans to return.

In June the railway opened from Paris to Brussels, and Lola and her lover may well have been among the first passengers, traveling as Mr. and Mrs. Leigh. They went on to Ostend, where the summer was hot and the sea was calm along the great, sandy North Sea beaches. Lola traveled in style with a number of trunks, including one filled with her capital, the jewels she had managed to accumulate from her gentlemen admirers. Also in the party were a chambermaid and Lola's dog. All her life Lola loved animals, particularly dogs and birds, and she frequently took dogs along when she traveled.

In August they left Belgium, traveling to the fashionable resorts in Germany. Lola and Leigh seem to have parted there. For a few days she was seen in Heidelberg in the company of a Russian nobleman from Latvia, probably Baron Georges Meller-Zakomelsky, whose path would cross hers again. It may have been Count Meller who introduced her to a new and influential admirer, Robert Peel, the twenty-four-year-old secretary to the British ambassador to Switzerland and eldest son of Sir Robert Peel, who just three months earlier had retired as British prime minister.

The intelligent young diplomat was small, dark, good-looking, and vivacious, but he lacked his father's sobriety, integrity, and sense of purpose. Peel had just been transferred to Bern after two years in Madrid, and he was already bored. After his experience in Spain he must have realized that there was something dubious about Lola's alleged origins, but he wasn't about to trouble himself about the provenance of a pretty woman. Lola seems to have left her Russian friend and Peel behind when she returned to Heidelberg to try to intercept Leigh.

Lola found him there and took a room in his hotel. If she was attempting a reconciliation, it didn't work, because after a few days Leigh was reportedly refusing to let her into his room. According to one story, the definitive end of the relationship came when she took a shot at him. But given her proven marksmanship, the incident must have been simply an expression of her feelings for him, not a serious assault.

Mid-August found Lola in Homburg, a popular spa north of Frankfurt, where she was reportedly attracting the glances of all the men. Homburg, like most of the resorts, put on a program of summer entertainments, and it was announced that Lola Montez would dance there in the performance of 29 August, the last of the summer season. But to everyone's surprise, she packed and left just before the performance. Only a few close friends knew that Peel had invited her to join him in Stuttgart for what promised to be a wonderful month-long party. A huge celebration was being staged by the King of Württemburg in his capital to welcome Crown Prince Karl, who was returning from Russia with his new bride, Grandduchess Olga.

Lola spent September partying in Stuttgart, but the first chill hint of fall was in the air, and it may have been reflected in a change in her relations with Peel. The young aristocrat was reported to be complaining that Lola's extravagances were costing him far too much. With the summer over, the major theaters would be looking for attractions for the fall season; Lola would strike out again, as she had three years before, seeking employment on the stages of Europe. According to one story, she decided to try her luck in Vienna. The route from Stuttgart to the Austrian capital would take her across the Kingdom of Bavaria. Perhaps she could pick up a guest engagement at the court theater in the Bavarian capital. Now that the festivities in Stuttgart were drawing to a close, Munich's Oktoberfest would be like a continuation of the party.

11

A King in Autumn

It was not yet 5 o'clock on an October morning in 1846, but King Ludwig I of Bavaria was already hard at work in the royal palace. His apartments overlooked the monument he had erected to his father, King Max Joseph, in the center of Munich. The king was proud to declare that his was the first lamp to be lit each morning in Munich, and although he was now sixty, his early-morning routine had changed little since he had become king twenty-one years before. He rose before five—sometimes before four—said his morning prayers, put on the simple green housecoat he had worn every morning for the past forty years, and plunged into the mass of state papers and memoranda awaiting his attention. His gray-blue eyes scanned each document; then he would take up one of the white goose-quill pens prepared for him and, in his characteristic black, bold handwriting telegraphically scrawl, in the wide margin on state documents, his comments, demands, inquiries, encouragement, and outrage.

If a document or letter was blank on one side and did not need to be returned or filed, King Ludwig would set it aside to use for scratch paper. He saw no need to waste good paper, or anything else for that matter. In his years on the throne he had taken Bavaria from the financial disorder left by his father and made it into one of the most fiscally sound kingdoms in Europe, largely through his merciless attention to every florin flowing out of the treasury.

With many of those carefully hoarded florins he had commissioned Germany's finest architects, sculptors, and painters to build and decorate Munich, transforming the city of one hundred thousand into a center of European art and design. His neo-Renaissance addition to the royal palace dominated Max-Josephplatz, and at the other side of the royal residence lay the mile-long Ludwigstraße, one of the great urban creations of the century. The broad ceremonial thoroughfare was lined with an architecturally harmonious ensemble of buildings, creating a splendid vista from the Italianate portico of his Feldherrenhalle, honoring great generals, to his classical Siegestor, the triumphal arch going up just beyond the university.

Along the street stood other monuments to Ludwig's vision and generosity. The commercial arcades of the bazaar, the massive brick facade of the Royal Library, the twin gray towers of St. Ludwig's Church, and finally the great courtyard of the university. King Ludwig transferred the university to Munich from Landshut; the school had become one of the outstanding centers of learning in central Europe.

Outside the king's window were the sounds of the city coming to life, but he couldn't hear them. Like his mother and eldest sister, he had been born hard of hearing, and his deafness increased as he grew older. His speech was loud, uninflected, and sometimes difficult to understand, and he accompanied it with erratic, vehement gestures that could startle new acquaintances. All his life he had struggled to compensate—to read lips, to guess at unheard words—but he never could easily follow conversations in a group, and when he had to preside at the Council of State, he always studied the agenda carefully beforehand to anticipate the course of the discussion.

His deafness separated him from other men as much as his kingship did, and it reinforced his native mistrust of those around him. They felt his suspicions—and they felt his wrath on the not infrequent occasions when he flew into a rage over a perceived disloyalty, incompetence, or treachery. King Ludwig could be rude, abrupt, and thoughtless, but he was just as capable of great kindness, benevolent good humor, and sensitivity that would have been remarkable in a ruler without his handicap. He was inordinately concerned for the well-being of his servants and subjects, always anxious that his civil servants not endanger their health by overwork. He might pay their starvation wages grudgingly, but he was quick to tell them to safeguard their health.

His poor hearing meant that his command of languages (he knew several) was never idiomatic. His German often wandered far from accepted rules of grammar and syntax, his most characteristic idiosyncrasy being an easily parodied tendency to omit subjects and overuse participles: "Always having had German spirit, and it repeatedly having demonstrated."

In spite of, or perhaps in part because of his difficulties with language, Ludwig was an enthusiastic poet, producing a stream of sonnets, odes, and poetic meditations. His poetry reflected his deepest interests, including classical Greece and Rome, the German character, the beauty of art and nature; but Ludwig also wrote of his own nature, struggles, and sorrows. Most remarkable of all, he published his poems, giving anyone who cared to read them a window into the soul of the king. It was not considered great poetry, but much of it was not bad, and all of it was interesting to the extent that it embodied the thoughts and feelings of an extraordinary figure.

Ludwig perhaps saw himself more as a poet than a king, for he was a poet long before he became a king. It was with his poetic nature that he justified a part of his life that did not harmonize with his strict Catholic faith: his need for women other than his devoted queen, Therese. She was a good wife for him, a wonderful mother to their eight children, and dedicated to making her husband happy. But she had received only a limited formal education in her native Saxe-Hildburghausen and could do little to satisfy Ludwig's need for a muse, for a bright and witty feminine companion whose mind had the fire and restlessness of his own. Nor could she do much to meet Ludwig's romantic and erotic needs. Ludwig had told her before their marriage that he required freedom in his personal life, and Therese, however reluctantly, had conceded him that freedom and remained devoted to him. Thirty-six years ago this week they had married; it was impossible for Ludwig to forget his anniversary because it had become the custom to repeat the wedding celebrations on Munich's Theresien Meadow every October. Oktoberfest, as the celebration was called now, was no longer a commemoration of the wedding but a weeklong celebration of Bavarian nationhood.

Ludwig rarely failed to appear at Oktoberfest to mingle with his subjects. This afternoon horse races were scheduled, and he intended to be there. He might see some pretty faces in the crowd, perhaps one pretty enough to occupy one of the few places still unfilled in the Gallery of Beauties. Some wags called the gallery a "harem," but to Ludwig his collection of nearly three dozen commissioned portraits of the most beautiful women he had ever seen was a monument to his taste in art and feminine beauty, and a group that included his own daughter and daughter-in-law could hardly be a trophy gallery of his conquests. He had actually slept with only a few of the women pictured. Court portraitist Joseph Karl Stieler, one of the finest of the age, had captured each of the king's selections on canvas, and the new north wing of the palace by the Hofgarten contained a room designed for the Gallery of Beauties, to which the public was admitted on a regular schedule. The king's selections showed no bias of nationality or rank; alongside members of his own family hung an Englishwoman, a Greek, a banker's daughter, even a humble miller's daughter. It had been a long time since he had commissioned Stieler to add another portrait to the gallery. And it had been a long time since he had been in love.

The king longed for the joy of falling in love, for the admiring devotion of a beautiful woman, for the excitement of pursuit and the thrill of conquest. But his last birthday, his sixtieth, had seemed to him a mournful turning point, the depressing borderland between manhood's prime and inevitable decline; now he was trying to reconcile himself to never again seeing a woman's face light with joy and excitement, never again feeling her heart race as he held her. Queen Therese had recently announced her desire to sleep alone, but his life wouldn't be sexless; he still had a number of friends among the actresses at the court theater, and the king would always be welcome on his discreet visits to Munich's finest establishments for gentlemen's entertainment. But Ludwig wanted to be in love again and be loved as a man, not as a king.

He knew he was not handsome; he had always been the ugly duckling of the Wittelsbach dynasty, with his long, pointed nose on an angular face scarred by smallpox, and recently a cyst-like swelling had appeared on his forehead. But he knew that he could be loved for himself, that he could win a beautiful woman's heart, and he felt something dying within him as the realization grew that he would never experience that again.

King Ludwig was a rare royal phenomenon, an autocrat who took his responsibilities with utmost seriousness, and there was no aspect of policy-making, no detail of administration in the kingdom too minor to receive his attention. The mass of documents he reviewed each morning was one of his principal means of keeping a tight rein on Bavarian bureaucracy and seeing to it that his guiding hand reached to every level of his government.

Bavaria did indeed have a written constitution, one of the first in Europe, and to Ludwig his promise to abide by it was, like every other promise a king makes, holy and unbreakable. But the constitution, although it provided for a parliament, the Landtag, left the king's authority largely unchecked in most matters. Within the forms of the constitution, Ludwig was one of the last of the true Western European autocrats, absolutely aware of his royal rights and prerogatives and determined to use all of them to govern his kingdom as he saw fit. Even his ministers of state were nothing but errand boys if that was how he chose to treat them. They had no authority other than what the king gave them, and he could dismiss them at any time.

Even in his deafness, the king could hear the church bells outside announcing morning mass. Munich was a Catholic city; half a century earlier a Protestant would not have been allowed to reside there. But the changes in its borders during and after the Napoleonic wars left Bavaria one-third Protestant; even Ludwig's queen remained true to her Protestant upbringing, despite his hopes and repeated urging that she convert. The king himself was devout, but he vigorously resisted any attempts by Bavaria's Catholic hierarchy to extend church authority at royal expense, and he regarded some of the bishops, including Karl August Graf von Reisach, the archbishop of Munich and Freysing, as scheming allies of the power-hungry Jesuits and ultramontanes.

And yet Bavaria had gained a reputation in Western Europe as a conservative and rabidly Catholic kingdom, largely through the influence of Ludwig's principal minister, Karl von Abel. For nearly ten years, Abel, who had been a liberal in his youth but had become committed to the conservative Catholic cause, had been entrusted by Ludwig with leading his government. Abel was a brilliant politician and the nemesis of the liberals and Protestants in the kingdom; but he knew that the achievement of his political program depended on his ability to convince the king that his goals were the king's own. At this he had succeeded masterfully, carefully cultivating Ludwig's own conservative instincts and steering Bavaria on a course that was distinctly conservative and Catholic. The Catholic character of Bavaria was promoted at every opportunity, even to the point of allowing the Catholic hierarchy quasi-institutional control over certain aspects of local administration. While there was no active oppression of Protestants, the rights of existing congregations were tightly restricted, and the establishment of new congregations was almost impossible.

Abel's one major failure had been his inability to persuade the king to readmit the Jesuits to Bavaria, from which they had been expelled many years before. On this point Ludwig was immovable, to the relief of Queen Therese, who had a deep fear of the Society of Jesus. In fact, although the king continued to consider Abel the finest statesman in Bavaria, his own feelings were turning more and more against the most conservative Catholic elements, causing him to place less confidence in Abel where religious affairs were concerned. Ludwig's move toward the religious center had begun five years earlier, at the funeral of his stepmother, who had been a Protestant. As the state funeral procession approached Munich's Theatriner Church, where the Queen Mother was to be entombed beside King Max Joseph and other members of the Wittelsbach royal family, Ludwig was aghast to see that none of the Catholic clergy standing before the church had put on ceremonial vestments; his shock became outrage when he learned that they refused to perform any sort of memorial service for a dead Protestant and only reluctantly would allow one to be buried in the church. Although their behavior may have conformed to church doctrine, the king took it as a personal insult from men who owed much to him, and he was deeply embarrassed that it took place in the presence of his brother-in-law, King Friedrich Wilhelm IV of Prussia, the principal royal patron of German Protestants. Since that time Ludwig had grown more suspicious and skeptical of the Catholic establishment in Bavaria, and he sensed that Abel was no longer the man to speak for him in religious matters.

Deliberately, but with an efficiency grown from long experience, the king worked his way through the petitions, reports, and memoranda of the day. Among them was a memorandum from Colonel Baron von Frays, the director of the Royal Court Theater. Ludwig loved the theater, particularly Schiller, and attended the great columned theater across Max-Josephplatz quite often. He gauged his popularity by the enthusiasm of the public demonstrations that greeted his appearance there. He usually tried to study the text of the plays or the libretti of the operas beforehand so that he could follow the performance.

But the court theater also had fallen victim to Ludwig's frugality. He had abolished the Italian opera company that his father had maintained, and he limited efforts to bring in high-priced guest stars, who usually didn't pay their way at the box office. "The well known Spanish dancer Lola Montez has arrived here," wrote Frays, "and requested to dance on this stage during intermissions."

Spain and the Spanish language were among King Ludwig's passions. With typical energy he had taught himself Spanish, even though there were no native speakers of the language in Munich. He knew Italy and the Italian language well and loved them both, traveling to his villa at the Garden of Malta in Rome nearly every other year. But Spain remained for him a romantic dream, a land of poetry, guitar serenades, and hot-blooded women.

As crown prince during the Napoleonic wars he had even considered volunteering to fight in Spain to help drive out Napoleon's occupying army; but his longed-for trip never materialized, and the king had to satisfy himself with reading Cervantes and Calderon and looking at prints of the Alhambra.

A Spanish dancer. "She wishes either half the net receipts or 50 louis d'or for each evening," Frays continued. "Because, on the one hand, this type of guest performance presents no particular prospect of advantage for the box office, and, on the other hand, police intervention was necessary due to the public offense given by said dancer at a number of locations where she guested, Your Majesty's most obedient and devoted servant requests . . ." A fiery Spanish dancer, it would seem. Ludwig picked up his quill and wrote in the wide margin, "How did the dancer in question give public offense?" and put the memorandum in the pile of documents requiring a reply. A real Spanish dancer.

12

THE ENCHANTED PRINCE

Lola had arrived in Munich with her lapdog, Zampa, on 5 October 1846 and taken rooms at one of the best and most visible hotels, the Bayerischer Hof on Promenadenplatz. Visitors to Oktoberfest crowded the streets and hotels. The fall weather was fine for sightseeing, but Lola made it a point to stop by the Court Theater and make her bid for guest appearances. Baron Frays knew that decisions on guest artists, particularly on one who was asking for half of the net box office or fifty louis d'or, would have to be made by the king, so Lola received no immediate answer. But she probably learned that Frays was not favorably inclined toward guest artists and must have considered how she might go over his head.

Back at the hotel she ran into one of the few Bavarians she knew, Heinrich Baron von Maltzahn, a fifty-three-year-old playboy of some renown who had residences in Baden-Baden and on the rue de la Madelaine in Paris, where Lola had known him. Maltzahn did not spend much time in Bavaria; he had married well three times and succeeded in being widowed each time, which had left him with enough money to indulge his tastes in environments less morally stringent than his native country. By a happy coincidence for Lola, Maltzahn was making a rare visit to Munich to enter his elder son at the university and was also staying at the Bayerischer Hof. Ludwig liked Maltzahn and had appointed him long ago to the honorary position of chamberlain, although they had rarely seen each other in recent years because of the baron's expatriate life. Lola must have recognized Maltzahn as a way to circumvent Frays, and he almost certainly wrote her a letter of introduction to Ludwig so that she could obtain a private audience with the king.

One day after Lola arrived in Munich, Robert Peel also checked in to the Bayerischer Hof. He may have followed her from Stuttgart, either by prior arrangement or in an effort to mend some quarrel that had caused her to leave. Or perhaps he merely had business in Munich or wanted to attend Oktoberfest. Whatever the reason for his arrival, if he had hoped to amuse himself with Lola, he soon found that she was developing new interests.

King Ludwig usually granted private audiences in the late morning. On the morning of Thursday, 8 October 1846, Lola put on a black velvet dress, which emphasized the beauty of her hair, the perfect curves of her figure, and made her skin appear even more fashionably pale. She could have walked the few blocks from the hotel to the palace, but since one did not arrive on foot to see the king, she almost certainly took a fiacre from the Promenadenplatz to the massive doors opening onto Max-Josephplatz. From the entryway, a great staircase led up to the royal apartments and the king's audience chamber. The military adjutant on duty that day was Count Ludwig Lerchenfeld, and he probably took Maltzahn's letter of introduction from Lola and laid it before the king. Perhaps a letter was not even necessary, given Ludwig's interest in beautiful women and things Spanish; Lola was admitted, and outside Lerchenfeld could hear the king greet her loudly in Spanish. The conversation continued for quite some time, longer than a normal audience, and the king's loud Spanish reverberated into the antechamber.

A rumor about this audience began to circulate in Munich not long afterward. According to the story, Ludwig pointed inquiringly toward Lola's well-formed bosom and said, "Nature or art?" Lola is said to have answered by simply stepping to the king's desk, taking up a pair of scissors, and cutting open the front of her dress to reveal Nature's endowment. The story neglects to explain how Lola left the audience chamber and returned to her hotel with her dress cut up the front, and all evidence indicates it is completely false. But while the rumor tells nothing about what actually went on during the interview, it reveals a great deal about the public conception of the relationship between the king and the dancer.

In fact, it appears that the king wasn't swept away by her at this first encounter. He did not even bother to send Baron Frays a special order to engage Lola but simply noted, along with other matters on a document he was returning to the theater director, "I told Lola Montez in Spanish to speak with the theater director. I reserve the final decision for myself." This paper seems to have crossed with Frays's reply to the king's question about how Lola had gotten involved with the police elsewhere.

Frays said that, according to newspaper reports, she had smashed a champagne glass over the head of an officer who troubled her with unwelcome attentions at a restaurant in Berlin, spent fourteen days in jail for striking a gendarme with her riding whip at a review there, and in Warsaw responded to the audience's unenthusiastic reception of her art with certain immodest gestures and the turning of the rear portion of her body toward the auditorium. But, added Frays, perhaps sensing the direction the king's interest was taking, if the dancer were permitted to appear on the stage of court theater, "the box office would not suffer because the reputation she has acquired would draw the curious into the theater." That seems to have been sufficient for the king, who ordered Frays to talk to Lola Montez that very day—to discuss her wishes, her fee, and the number of performances—and indicated that he wanted her to dance only in the intermissions and in Spanish costume.

The messengers sped across the square, carrying the correspondence between the king and his theater director. Frays proposed that the dancer be engaged for a single performance with the option for more, should the king be pleased. Knowing the king's desire to save a kreutzer whenever possible, Frays also suggested that she could be talked into settling for a third of the net box office receipts rather than half. Her dances would fit best in the intermission of Johann von Plötz's comedy *Der Verwunschene Prinz* (The Enchanted Prince), which was scheduled for performance on Wednesday, 14 October. But in the first of a long series of acts of generosity to Lola, Ludwig wrote in the margin, "I authorize Lola Montez to dance in the intermissions next Saturday for half of the net income." Then as an afterthought he added, "Further decisions I will make at that time." And then another thought came to him: "The response should be made yet today and should state that I am looking forward to seeing her dance."

The notice to Lola that she would make her debut in two days failed to indicate the king's special interest; perhaps Frays was too busy and annoyed to include it because he was scrambling to assemble the cast of *The Enchanted Prince;* a comedy by Nestroy had originally been on the program. Ludwig went on with his official duties and visits to Oktoberfest, but he could not get the Spaniard out of his mind. Stieler should add her to the Gallery of Beauties, he thought.

In light of the events to follow, the theatrical setting of Lola's debut in Munich could hardly have been more ironic; not only was the play titled *The Enchanted Prince*, but as Lola waited backstage at the end of the first act she could hear (but not understand), the actress in the part of Evchen recounting how at a masquerade she had convinced a roomful of noblemen that she was a countess. The curtain went down, and the stagehands bustled about, removing the shoemaker's shop set and preparing the stage for Lola's first dance. After the set was readied and the orchestra tuned, Lola slipped on her castanets. The king was waiting expectantly in the second tier of boxes, the level occupied by the court and the nobility. The royal box dominated the auditorium from the center of the horseshoe of boxes, but Ludwig usually preferred to leave it empty to sit with family and friends in one of the side boxes.

The orchestra struck up the slow introduction for "Los Boleros de Cadix," and the curtain rose on Lola standing alone on the stage. In the illuminated theater she could clearly see the king in his box, and she made him a gracious bow. Then she began her dance languidly, swaying to the staccato of her castanets. Gradually the tempo increased, and she began to move about the stage, leaping and weaving her arms together over her head. The king's eyes followed her every movement and watched how her costume revealed the suppleness of her figure and the smallness of her feet. He had never seen a real Spaniard dance before, and the exotic beauty of the woman and her movements left him as thoroughly enchanted as the prince in the play.

The dance grew faster, finally ending with a climactic flourish, and applause burst forth. The dance connoisseurs in the audience were skeptical of the woman's abilities as a dancer and of the authenticity of her dances. The skepticism increased during the second intermission, when she danced the "Cachucha," the "Oleano" under a different name. Here the pantomime with the spider impressed some of the critics, who felt she might be good in the mute role of Fenella in Auber's opera *La Muette de Portici*. The applause was warm but not overwhelming, and Lola was called to the curtain twice in order to acknowledge the audience's homage.

One of the critics noted that opinions were divided about her dancing abilities but that everyone was taken by Lola's "fiery eye, the beautifully formed nose, her profile, and her beautifully arched eyebrows." Ludwig was unconcerned with questions of dancing refinement, authenticity, or tastefulness. He was completely enthralled by Lola's fire, spirit, beautiful face, and magnificent body. He must have her for his Gallery of Beauties. The next day he wrote impatiently to Stieler, "How do things stand? Will the portrait be painted? If it will be, give me the day and time of the first sitting. As quickly as possible." If Stieler were to paint her portrait, it would be a perfect opportunity for the two of them to talk, away from the officers and young gentlemen who had begun to swarm around her. Already she was driving all other thoughts from Ludwig's mind.

The king began to visit Lola at the Bayerischer Hof, sometimes in the afternoon, sometimes in the evening, often twice a day. The young men who had begun to keep company with her avoided the king's visits, both because he did not like to socialize with people who had not been formally presented to him and because his hearing problem made him prefer talking in very small groups. Maltzahn was welcome, however, and they could all speak together in French; when the king and Lola wanted to speak privately to each other, they spoke Spanish.

Ludwig was eager to see Lola perform again, and she danced a second time on Wednesday, the 14th, after the one-act *Der Weiberfeind* (The Womanhater) and between the two acts of *Müller und Miller*. Lola repeated her cachucha and in the second intermission danced a fandango with a member of the court theater's ballet company. The critics remained as skeptical about her dancing and as impressed with her beauty as before, but now audience reaction was both more vehement and more divided. As before, Lola had two curtain calls, and this time a pair of wreaths and other flowers were thrown at her feet.

But an unimpressed section of the audience expressed its feelings in hissing so loud that some observers said that it was louder than the applause. The king was angered at this rudeness to the beautiful guest, and an investigation was made to find the leaders among the hissers. A gendarme named as one of the guilty parties was promptly transferred to Regensburg.

Now there was no question in Ludwig's heart; he was in love again, and at his age! In the pocket notebook he carried with him he began to compose his first poem in Spanish: "Yo te quiero con mi vida . . ." "I love you with my life, my eyes, my soul, my body, my heart, all of me. Black hair, blue eyes, graceful form . . ." The portrait sittings at Stieler's studio in the Barerstraße had begun, and as the painter worked, the king and the dancer sat together on the painter's red sofa and conversed in Spanish. She sometimes played the guitar and sang Spanish songs.

Ludwig could not spend enough time with Lola, but the dancer, used to noblemen who merely mouthed romance, had not yet grasped how fully she had conquered the king's heart. She went ahead with her tour plans, nearly arranging a guest appearance at the Augsburg theater before the afternoon of 22 October at Stieler's, when Ludwig pressed her about her plans. Did she really intend to leave? Lola realized how much he wanted her to stay with him, and whether she was sincerely touched or simply an adept actress, tears welled as she murmured to him, "No puedo dejar Munic, I cannot leave Munich." An attachment kept her here, she said, looking knowingly into the king's eyes. Never, she confessed, had she felt what she felt for him.

Ludwig's heart leaped at the thought that not only was Lola going to stay but that she might also be feeling something of the passion he was feeling. He had to give her a gift, something of himself, and he presented her with a magnificently bound edition of his three published volumes of poetry. She could not read them, but he would make French translations of some of the poems for her, and if she would be staying in Munich, she would certainly learn German.

Lola began to see herself not as an itinerant dancer but as the official mistress of the king of Bavaria. Not that there was anything physical to their relationship. But if she was not his mistress, what was she? Lola's own feelings for Ludwig at this point seem to have been ambiguous: her admiration—perhaps akin to a daughter's affection—was dominated by a willingness, even a need, to manipulate him for her own purposes.

Munich was becoming more aware of the king's new passion and its object. One night Ludwig stayed so long in conversation with her at the Bayerischer Hof that the street door was locked for the night when he came down, and there was a bit of embarrassed bustle as the staff let the king out of the hotel. On 19 October Lola presented the king with a rose during the sitting at Stieler's studio; back at the palace Ludwig realized that he had forgotten the flower and asked Stieler to have a messenger bring it to him, sealed in a bag, but the bag did little to prevent talk around town.

Word got around that Lola was encouraging the king to become a Freemason (Lola had developed a great admiration for Freemasons), and the story began to circulate that the Spanish woman was a secret agent of the British foreign secretary, Lord Palmerston, sent to lure the king into the camp of the liberals. Although his father had been both a Catholic and a Freemason, Ludwig had no intention of joining the society, and he paid attention to Lola's political opinions only when they coincided with his own. But in some quarters there was real concern that this foreign woman was manipulating the king for her own or someone else's political purposes.

Within weeks, public dubiousness over the king's new favorite was exacerbated by her growing imperiousness. Lola began to display an arrogance grown of self-satisfaction in the power she felt over the king. The first skirmish, an argument with the manager of the Bayerischer Hof, resulted in Lola and Zampa moving into new quarters: an apartment in an annex of the Goldener Hirsch, another of the fine hotels of Munich. This hotel was closer to the palace, and Ludwig continued to make no attempt to conceal his visits to Lola. Her position was becoming more and more established. She was granted a seat in the lower boxes at the court theater for every performance, and a series of special guest appearances by the famous Jenny Lind at the end of October allowed Lola to display herself before the curious eyes of Munich's elite. But she resented having the court and nobility literally looking down on her in the theater, and she soon persuaded Ludwig to give her a permanent seat, in Loge One on the far right-hand side of the privileged second tier, which she promptly had reupholstered in red velvet.

Ludwig was aware of the resistance Lola was beginning to encounter in Munich, but he put it down to jealousy, xenophobia, and Lola's somewhat abrupt manner. He was too entranced to see what was happening. He wrote to one of his closest, oldest friends, Heinrich von der Tann, to tell him of the transformation:

> More than twelve years ago you said to me, what a joy it would be at 48 (my age then) to have conquered a heart. What does my dear Tann have to say when I tell him that the sixty-year old has awakened a passion in a beautiful, intelligent, spirited, good-hearted twenty-two year old nobly-born woman of the South, her very first! . . . Admiration (it's immodest to repeat it, but she said it) of all that I had accomplished filled her at first, and then came love. And I can compare myself to Vesuvius, which seemed burned out until it suddenly erupted once again. . . . I thought I could no longer feel the passion of love, thought my heart was burned out, thought I was no longer what I had been; that was a troubling feeling. Now I'm not like a man of forty or even a youth twenty, no, like an amorous boy of twenty; I'm in the grip of passion like never before. Sometimes I couldn't eat, couldn't sleep, my blood boiled feverishly, I was lifted to heaven's heights, my thoughts became purer, I became a better person. I was happy, I am happy. My life has a new vitality, I'm young again, the world smiles on me.

13

THE KING'S MISTRESS

Lola Montez began to assemble a court befitting a king's mistress, most of it gathered from Munich's middle class. Crescentia Ganser, a language teacher and the wife of one of the sculptors employed on Ludwig's buildings, was hired to be her companion and interpreter. Berta Thierry, a member of the ballet company at the court theater, and her sister, Mathilde, an actress, were Lola's frequent companions. The sisters lived with their father, were desperate for money, and were among the first to see the direction the royal largess was flowing. By 21 October, Lola had persuaded Ludwig to grant the Thierrys 200 florins. Baron Maltzahn, who stayed on in Munich until November and was already becoming known as "the man who brought the Spanish woman to Munich," was frequently seen in her company.

One day early in Lola's stay a twenty-six-year-old artillery second lieutenant, Friedrich Nußbammer, came to her assistance when she was being insulted by some Munichers; he was rewarded with an invitation to call on her. He soon became her favorite companion in her daily expeditions around the city. The rumor began to circulate that Ludwig intended to marry Lola to Nußbammer to regularize her status in Bavaria.

But Lola's most faithful companion was a large black dog that resembled a cross between a boxer and a mastiff. She named it Turk, perhaps recalling the dog of Heinrich LXXII; and the sight of Lola sweeping along the streets with Turk became familiar to residents of the capital.

If Lola was to settle in Munich, she needed a house of her own. She decided on a small but elegant mansion, No. 7 in the Barerstraße, near Stieler's studio. It was a two-story structure with a nearly square facade displaying two rows of five tall windows directly on the street. A large lot extended on each side of the house and well behind it.

The king had quickly discovered that Lola possessed no ability to deal with money other than to spend it as rapidly as it came into her hands. Lola herself admitted that she could not budget her money, so someone was going to have to manage her finances. Ludwig found what he thought was a perfect solution. Carl Wilhelm Baron von Heideck was a widower and retired general who was nearly the same age as Ludwig and one of his old friends. They had gone through a period of estrangement, but now they were friends once more, and the king had Lola invite Heideck to join them for tea in her rooms at the Goldener Hirsch. Although the general felt that he was a little old for the society of young ladies, the king insisted, and the three of them sat drinking tea and conversing in French, since Heideck, although he had spent time in Spain in his youth, had forgotten his Spanish entirely.

The course of the conversation turned to Lola's inability to deal with florins and kreutzers: "Yes," said the king, "my good Lola can't deal with money and I'm afraid that she'll be most thoroughly swindled when she remodels her house. You ought to do her the favor of checking over the bills that come in so that she doesn't get completely fleeced." "Gladly," said Heideck, only too willing to take on a little task that might help him remain in the king's good graces. And so General Heideck became Lola's business manager.

On 1 November, less than a month after Lola had checked into the Bayerischer Hof, the king secretly began paying her a stipend of 10,000 florins per year, in monthly installments. A Bavarian cabinet minister received a basic salary of only 6,000 florins per year, the highest paid professors at the University of Munich drew no more than 2,000 florins per year, and a dancer at the court theater might get 200 a year. An English visitor to Munich at the time declared that a man could live there on £50 a year, or about 500 florins, and that with £100 a year a gentleman could really enjoy life. In addition to the monthly stipend, Ludwig promised Lola her own coach and the house in the Barerstraße, and he budgeted about 20,000 florins to remodel the house.

Lola soon became a familiar sight in Munich's best fashion salons and jewelry stores. Much to his distress, General Heideck discovered that Lola was telling everyone to send their bills to him, though Lola had the money. Heideck found that Lola was taking over more and more of his quiet retirement.

When it was not more bills landing on his desk, it was a request that he decide how much she should pay her new servants, notes about the negotiations over the house, or a request from the king that Heideck hold a little tea party at his apartment in the Briennerstraße so Ludwig and Lola could get together without exciting the gossip caused by his visits to her hotel.

Other old friends of the king's asked the general for advice on how to get Ludwig out of the grasp of the Spanish woman, whose arrogance was becoming intolerable and whose influence was unpredictable. Heideck, on the basis of his decades of association with Ludwig, warned against open opposition to the relationship. Opposition simply stiffened the king's resistance; Ludwig even boasted of his unyielding hardheadedness whenever he was challenged. If left alone, the king would recover from this infatuation, Heideck said. But if he were opposed he would make an issue of defending Lola, the general warned.

Although Heideck and others attempted to school Lola in the manners of good society, it was little more than a month before she precipitated the first of many incidents that would make her a pariah in Munich. Lieutenant Nußbammer, who was already being spoken of as her lover, was advised by his fellow officers to shun a woman with a reputation like Lola's. Nußbammer seems to have been inclined to defy his brother officers, but Lola obviously had doubts about his loyalty. On the night of 15 November, something, perhaps his failure to appear at her rooms in response to an invitation, sent her into a rage. She went looking for him shortly before midnight, marching with her maid past the dark and shuttered houses in Munich's barely illuminated streets to his apartment in the Frühlingstraße.

When she found No. 9 she was in no mood to strain to read the nameplates, so she simply pulled the bells for the entire building, quickly rousing the formidable landlady. Nußbammer was not at home, the landlady angrily informed Lola in French. Lola replied that he had to be at home and proceeded once more to ring all the bells. At this point, Lola uncharacteristically fainted, and her maid was unable to take the stricken woman back to the Goldener Hirsch by herself. A glazier who lived across the street at No. 19 graciously invited the women into his home, where Lola was treated with eau de cologne and a drink of wine. The glazier could not have suspected how many broken windows he would be replacing over the next year and a half thanks to the woman lying in his parlor. Finally she recovered enough to manage the walk back to the hotel, and peace returned to the Frühlingstraße.

The next day the scandal of Lola's night wanderings was already flying about Munich when she returned to the scene and again rang the bells. Once more the landlady answered, and Lola asked her if she were the woman who had earlier refused to open the door. When she admitted that she was, Lola began screaming abuse at her, to which the landlady retorted in French, "Don't scream, miss, I'm not deaf!" Lola yelled back, "I am no 'miss,' I am 'Madame'; I am the king's mistress!"

Waking an entire apartment house in the middle of the night while looking for a man would have been more than enough to destroy a woman's reputation in Munich. But to return and scream that she was the king's mistress— that was shamelessly audacious, and the woman appeared either completely mad or oblivious to normal standards of human behavior.

But the story was not over. Lola was still angry at Nußbammer, and when the king came to call on her that day she accused the lieutenant of insulting behavior. She got Ludwig's promise that the soldier would immediately be transferred out of Munich. Back at his desk in the palace, the king took a moment before he dressed for the evening concert at the Odeon to write an order to the War Ministry. Nußbammer was to be informed at 7 the next morning that he was being transferred to Würzburg and that he must be gone by 7 P.M. the day after. He was not to return to the vicinity of Munich without the king's express permission. Ludwig, who was a jealous man, must have been relieved to see the lieutenant out of town.

The concert that evening was performed by a singing group, and the king and queen attended with some of their grown children and with royal visitors from Holland and Sweden. Lola, in a green satin dress covered with black lace, was easy to pick out in the half-empty auditorium. Word had gotten out that she would be there, and most of the seats around her, in the section behind that reserved for the court and nobility, remained unoccupied. During the intermission the king abandoned the queen, his children, and their guests to come back to talk to Lola. Every eye in the hall was on Ludwig and Lola as he addressed her in his Italianate Spanish, and everyone was aghast to see that the Spanish woman remained seated as the king addressed her. Finally, through gestures, he let her understand that one rose when speaking with the king, and she stood to receive his report that Nußbammer would soon be on his way to Würzburg and would trouble her no more. Then he returned to his family, where Therese had been unable to conceal her embarrassment at being abandoned for Lola before the public and the royal visitors.

Nußbammer must have been stunned to receive notice of his transfer. If he had any doubt what the source of his difficulty was, he had no doubt where the solution lay, and he turned to Lola. Apparently it was all a misunderstanding; at least he managed to convince Lola of that, and as he packed his things to move to Würzburg she decided to have the king annul the transfer she had urged upon him the day before. The king ordered the War Ministry to cancel the previous instructions, to treat the matter as if it had never happened, and to send a messenger with the next train to try to catch the lieutenant before he could report to the artillery regiment in Würzburg.

Ludwig chose to see this incident not as an example of Lola's capriciousness but of her goodheartedness, for once she realized that her accusations were untrue she had immediately done everything possible to rectify the injustice. All the same, the king was not unaware of the scandal that resulted from this nor was he oblivious to the fact that Nußbammer was handsome and young. He asked Lola to promise not to see the lieutenant again without the king's knowledge.

Lola had another matter to lay before the king. A policeman investigating the disturbance in the Frühlingstraße had called and had interrogated one of her servants. Lola was outraged over the stories about her that were being spread throughout Munich. Someone had impersonated her on Sunday night in the Frühlingstraße in an effort to blacken her reputation, she claimed. Lola wanted the police to quit bothering her and instead work on silencing the people who were slandering her.

The king wrote a note for her to take to Baron Pechmann, the new acting police director, expressing his outrage at the shameless slander and persecution being visited on Señora Lola Montez and calling for an end to it. Ludwig told her to pay a call on Baron Pechmann tomorrow after the police director had made his regular Friday morning report to the king. And, he added, he looked forward to seeing her in the theater that evening.

Johann Nepomuk Baron von Pechmann arrived promptly the next morning for his weekly report to the sovereign on the security of the capital. He was a thirty-seven-year-old career jurist of a long, noble Catholic lineage; and though he had been acting police director only since the first of October, the baron was regarded as an upright and even-handed man. The Spanish woman had bothered him from the first. Only after repeated demands had she come to police headquarters in the Weinstraße to complete the obligatory registration for foreigners, and even then she had been able to provide nothing indicating her identity or status. She had not even taken the matter seriously, filling in the blank after "Accompanied By" with the words *un chien*, a dog.

The baron's investigators had quickly turned up the stories of her expulsion from Berlin, Warsaw, and Baden-Baden. They knew about the note that disclosed she had been sleeping with Dujarier before he was murdered. His spies had even heard gossip that she had been openly whoring after her arrival at the Bayerischer Hof, offering her services to anyone with two florins. Unlikely as the story may have sounded, the police director was willing to believe the worst of this woman who had turned his king's head so completely. He was positive that she was responsible for the uproar in the Frühlingstraße, but no one was willing to admit having had a good look at the woman except the glazier, and now he was saying that he couldn't identify Lola Montez as the woman he helped. Pechmann had a report that Lola had bought the man's silence with 40 florins and a note promising that her friends would be further rewarded, but there was no way he could prove it. How was he going to explain all this to His Majesty?

The police director discovered that he did not need to explain the incident to the king. Ludwig already knew all about it and had his own definite opinion: "As sure as I'm standing here, she wasn't the one responsible for the business in the Frühlingstraße! But that's the way they are, my Munichers, I know them! And the most respectable are the worst!" The king lectured Pechmann about how lies and slander about himself and the royal family regularly made the rounds in Munich. Now there were people trying to destroy the reputation of his foreign friend. "I know my people! But they shouldn't think they can squeeze me or force me into anything. Here they're coming right up against me, and I have a head and a heart—I've said it before—like the rocky cliffs at the Königssee!"

The baron could see that his report on the incident would not change anything, so he simply asked the king whether the investigation should continue. "You'll be getting a lovely visitor," Ludwig told him. "I've sent her to you, and she can talk to you about it herself. I gave her a note that will tell you the rest."

That midday, while the police director was at his home in the Sommerstraße, the Spanish woman arrived with Ambros Havard, the owner of the Goldener Hirsch, who would act as her interpreter. She angrily demanded that the investigator who had interrogated her maid be transferred out of Munich; the glazier could confirm that she had nothing to do with the affair in the Frühlingstraße, and it was a personal insult to the king to continue to investigate his good friend once it was clear that she was not involved. The baron used his best diplomatic skills to explain to her that the officer had simply been doing his duty, but he added that he would do his best to follow the royal order to suppress slander concerning her. Pechmann was amazed at how rapidly her face could change from a mask of angry passion to one of seductive charm. She gave him her hand to kiss, told him that she would be honored to have him call on her, and left him to consider what course he could pursue in good conscience.

That very day, the king had decided to revise his will. "I would not be a man of honor, would be unfeeling if I made no provision for her who gave up everything for me, who has no parents, no brothers or sisters, who has no one in the wide world except me; nonetheless she has made no effort to have me remember her in my last wishes, and I do so totally on my own initiative. Knowing her has made me purer, better. Therese, my dear, good, noble wife, do not condemn me unjustly." Ludwig directed his executor and heir to give Lola the last oil portrait painted of him before his death and 100,000 florins, as long as she had never married, and to provide her with an annual income of 2,400 florins for life, or until she married.

"Lolitta (that's what I call her) is slandered terribly, has been and will be," the king wrote to his friend Tann. "A foreign woman who wants to settle in Munich, who's pretty, whom the king loves, who's spirited, what more does it take to arouse hatred, lies, and persecution. All that will be defeated, too, firmness will triumph in the end. She is not simply someone who loves me, she is my friend, too. She's told me that she'll always speak the truth to me, and she's already told me a number of things I didn't enjoy hearing. . . . She loves me so much. I'm providing for her, but she's not my kept woman."

The first signs of the king's stubbornness in the face of resistance, exactly what Heideck had dreaded, were beginning to appear. The king could not understand why people would not leave him and Lolitta alone. As a ruler he devoted most of his time, his thoughts, and his energies to ruling his country well; and it baffled him then that no one seemed willing to allow him any peace in an innocent, private relationship, which, as he saw it, made him a happier man and a better ruler, and which, if he were Ludwig von Wittelsbach, private citizen, no one would even think twice about.

The negotiation to purchase No. 7 Barerstraße for Lola were nearly complete, and the papers would be signed on 1 December. The house was being purchased in Lola's name, not only to conceal how much the king was spending on her, but also because once she owned a home, Lola would be eligible to apply for Bavarian citizenship. It was important to Ludwig that her status be formalized, and Lola insisted that once she was a Bavarian he make her a member of the nobility because she had been born into a noble Spanish family. Ludwig could not have seriously considered the ramifications of his promise to make her a Bavarian countess. The king considered his word a holy bond, and this would be one promise Lola would never let him forget.

General Heideck remarked to King Ludwig that many people of not particularly severe moral standards felt that it was scandalous for the king to associate with a woman who been branded as unchaste at the Dujarier trial. "I know everything," the king replied. "She told me everything; she doesn't pretend to be an angel. When she was tossed so young, beautiful, and helpless into the world, the wonder was not that she was seduced but that she didn't sink deeper. Which of these haughty women would have managed better than poor Lola under the same circumstances? . . . I know all of them and don't set much store by their untested virtue." In matters not as well documented as the Dujarier trial, Lola found that her constant avowals of love for Ludwig and his passion for her meant that the king would always believe her version of events and listen skeptically to anyone else's account. Lola's oath always to tell him the truth, no matter how painful, suspended his native mistrust, and his affection for Lola gave anyone speaking against her a heavy burden of proof.

Lola's new friends could sense the resentment and anger that were boiling up against her in all classes of society, and they counseled her to use her influence over Ludwig to promote a popular public cause. The schoolteachers, they told her, had repeatedly petitioned the king for a wage increase, and their economic distress was becoming a matter of public concern. If she could persuade Ludwig to grant the teachers more money, she would gain a reputation for benevolence throughout the country.

Lola did intercede with King Ludwig on behalf of the schoolteachers, and he agreed to make 120,000 florins immediately available to increase their salaries. But any favorable public reaction was outweighed by the confirmation this gave to the fears that Lola could and would intervene in political matters; and she further undermined royal authority by announcing that she had persuaded the king to increase the salaries a full week before Ludwig issued the order. It heightened the conviction among Bavarians that the Spanish woman posed an unpredictable threat to the established order, and those who had anything to lose now joined their efforts against Lola with those who opposed her because of her arrogant, aggressive, and eccentric behavior.

At Baron Pechmann's weekly audience on 27 November, the king questioned the police director about stories concerning an insult to the king in the Frühlingstraße incident. The baron explained that the insult lay in the claim of the woman that she was the king's mistress. "That Lola did *not* say," responded the king. "She's too sharp for that, she has intelligence and a good education. I think a great deal of her, a great deal, but honorably. Yes, I love her, I won't deny it at all, but to have a mistress, that's something else. One raises a man up, the other drags him down. But the whole thing is a disgusting intrigue; she's beautiful, she's young, she's not from here, so jealousy and frustration are playing their game with her."

Ludwig told Pechmann that he had personally interviewed the glazier, who had confirmed Lola's denials. "The respectable people persecute her the most," exclaimed the king. "I can't understand what they have against her. They're trying to get *me* to abandon her, but that's exactly the right way, just pure slander, to force me—ha! I have a head that no one is going to break so easily, it's like iron, no, like steel. I've shown that often enough." The king directed Pechmann to drop further investigation of the Frühlingstraße incident, saying that Lola did not want to embarrass publicly the woman who had impersonated her.

Pechmann left the palace deeply troubled. He felt that no one was telling the king the truth about Lola. The police had a spy in Lola's household, Frau Ganser. Perhaps Ganser's reports could open the king's eyes to what Lola really was. But first he would discuss the matter with his superior, Minister Abel.

Winter was coming on, and the cold, wet weather and the chill insolence of the Munichers made the capital an uncongenial place for Lola. On 25 November, during one of the king's daily visits, she urged him to abdicate, to come away with her to live peacefully under the sunny skies of Spain. The king didn't seriously consider it, but it flattered him that this beautiful young woman wanted to run away with him. She was inspiring him to more poems:

> Let the poet sing raptures anew,
> Without love the blood grows cold;
> Let it warm itself once more
> In the eternal glow of love!
> . . . .
> In the ether's brilliant heights,
> The transfigured soul soars
> When I am near you,
> Where bliss surrounds me.

14

A BATTLE WON

Minister Karl von Abel was troubled. Up to now he had held himself aloof from the Lola affair. He had served his king nearly ten years as principal minister and had seen many favorites come and go, but he sensed the danger of this one, not only because of her extraordinary audacity and unpredictability but even more because of the intensity of the king's passion for her. King Ludwig remarked that Abel was the only man around him who did not speak against Lola; that pleased the king, but Abel's silence came not from conviction but from caution. Now Baron Pechmann stood before the minister, asking whether it was his duty to continue his efforts to reveal to the king the real nature of Lola Montez or whether he could avoid irritating His Majesty further by letting the matter drop.

Abel's advice may not have been entirely without self-interest. Speak to the king, he told Pechmann, tell him everything you have discovered about the Spanish woman. "He'll hit the ceiling," the minister told the police director, "but afterwards he'll be calmer and will thank you for your frankness. That much I know about the king. When he sees that your frankness comes from a devoted heart, he'll never hold it against you."

At his weekly audience, Baron Pechmann told the king that he felt he must make use of his obligation to speak with utmost frankness in all matters concerning the king. The general ill feeling against Lola Montez, he said, was growing disturbingly fast in all classes of society, and those aligning themselves against the Spanish woman included not only evil-minded people but also the king's most loyal and devoted followers.

"Listen," said the king, "that doesn't bother me a bit. It'll all blow over. There's pure maliciousness behind it."

"I see it as my duty not to remain silent about this ill-feeling," Pechmann continued, "because some of its sources affect Your Majesty directly. The fact is that everyone believes that Lola Montez, in disregard of all feminine decency, speaks openly of Your Majesty's favors to her."

"Oh, no, that's empty talk. So what can she say about me? I'm not even on those kind of terms with her. That's envy and jealousy," said Ludwig.

"It is further charged," continued the police director, "that she boasts of particular influence in affairs of state and has let it be known that she wishes to introduce a government à la Maintenon in Bavaria."

"A lot of chance that has with me. I know very well who reigns in Bavaria. No one is going to talk me into anything."

"This opinion is supported by the fact that a full eight days before Your Majesty decreed your most gracious salary increase for the teaching personnel and sent the implementing directive to the ministry, Lola Montez had publicly let it be known that she had convinced Your Majesty to effect this most gracious measure."

"Listen, *that* is true, but none of the rest. That's true, I don't deny it. But when she or anyone else recommends something to me and I approve it, is there something wrong with that—can you charge them with a crime for that? Oh, no, certainly not. That's true. She had spoken to me about it first. But she could have kept her trap shut, she didn't need to talk about it. That wasn't smart. But we *did* something, something important. I can believe she likes to make a show of my favor, wants to make a little display, show off a bit and sometimes bites off a bit too much in the process. But she has her good qualities, and no one is talking about those."

The baron felt that now that he had begun, he had to carry on to the end. "If Your Majesty will not take it harshly that I make further use of your grant of total frankness, I must further note that the entire city"—and here, in order to be as confidential as the king's poor hearing allowed, the police chief nearly pressed his mouth against the royal ear to say—"is full of talk that Lola Montez constantly allows various men to visit her at night and specifically that she is still visited by Lieutenant Nußbammer."

"Now look—my God—that's nothing, I know that. How Nußbammer had the gall and would have used violence against her, I came to her afterwards and found her in tears. Take this state of things, no, no, there's nothing there. Lola isn't that type of person. But I know my Munichers."

Pechmann admitted that he could not prove Lola Montez's immoral behavior, but he implored the king to question older and wiser servants as to the truth of his report and not to doubt his loyalty or his motives in bringing the matter before the king.

"No, good fellow, I don't hold it against you that you've told it to me. It was right of you, I want to hear the truth, and it hasn't always reached me— but there's nothing to this—that's not how she is, Lola. But it's right that you've spoken to me about it. It was the honorable thing, and I thank you for it." The king stood silent before Pechmann, lost in deep and troubled thought. Then without a word of dismissal he turned and walked from the audience chamber.

That evening Pechmann had Frau Ganser's daily surveillance reports brought to him, with their details of the comings and goings in Lola's apartment and of her conversational indiscretions. Meanwhile, the king was confronting Lola with all that Pechmann had said, and the dancer let Ludwig feel the full violence of her offended honor, of her despair at being abandoned by her only friend in the world; Lola and Ludwig shared a romantic, self-dramatizing nature, and she instinctively knew how to touch the king's heart. Ludwig was moved to tears, but the reconciliation that followed did not really dispel the suspicions that had been planted in his mind. The king walked back to the palace still deeply disturbed.

Lola, on the other hand, seems to have felt confident that she had won the battle for the king's mind, if not the war; and the next morning she sat down to write her first letter to her friend Pier-Angelo Fiorentino, the Parisian journalist, since leaving France.

Well, dear Fiorentino, I left Paris at the beginning of June as a lady errant and raced about the world and *today* I'm on the point of receiving the title of *countess*! I have a lovely property, horses, servants, in sum, everything that could surround the official mistress of the king of Bavaria.

Here I am, surrounded by the homage of great ladies, I go everywhere, all of Munich waits upon me, ministers of state, generals, great ladies, and I no longer recognize myself as Lola Montez. The king loves me passionately; he's given me an income of 50,000 francs for life and has already spent more than 300,000 francs on my property, etc., etc.

I do everything here. The king publicly shows his great love for me. He walks with me, goes out with me. Every week I have a great party for ministers, etc., etc., which he attends and where he can't do me enough homage.

I know, dear Fiorentino, you always wished me well and that this news will please you. That's why I'm writing, because, although surrounded by all the glories and homage of my most ambitious hopes, alas, sometimes I dream, I think of Paris.

Dear Paris!

In truth, there isn't real happiness in grandeur. There is so much envy, so many intrigues. You always have to play the great lady and weigh your words to each individual. Alas! my joyful life in Paris!

But I'm resolved. I won't leave this world to which I find myself elevated as if by a miracle. The king has a passion of true love for me. He's never had mistresses before. But my character pleased him. He is a man of remarkable talent. A true genius and one of the most elegant poets currently existing in Europe. My slightest whim is a duty for him, and all of Munich is bewildered. They don't know what to say any more. He loves me so much that everyone I like is immediately in favor. . . .

Give my regards to all my acquaintances. Oh! Paris! There it was I suffered so, but there I was also so happy.

Farewell, dear friend. I send you a kiss. Thank God you aren't here because I can have neither friend nor . . . . . . [ellipsis in original] Grandeur is so difficult!

Your ever affectionate,

Lola

But Lola's resolve to remain in this new world was being undermined that very morning. Frau Ganser had gone to see Baron Pechmann. She could not stand it any longer, she told him. Last night's wildly emotional scene between the king and her mistress had shaken her badly, and she did not want to be part of intrigues any longer. What should she do? The police director told her to go directly to the king and to tell him everything she knew about the behavior of Lola Montez. As additional evidence to lay before the king, he gave Frau Ganser copies of her daily espionage reports.

The king was in his private study when Lola's companion was announced on a matter of urgency.

"What are you bringing me, my dear Ganser?" the king inquired.

"Your Majesty is betrayed!" cried the woman dramatically, throwing herself on her knees before the king.

"By whom? Not by my Lola?" asked Ludwig as he took the reports Frau Ganser held out to him. After the last night's tumultuous scene, his emotions were still taut, and this dramatic entrance and declaration by Lola's companion strained him to the breaking point. He glanced through the secret reports and fell on his knees beside the woman, tears streaming from his eyes. Frau Ganser told him that he must never see Lola again, but Ludwig could not face the prospect, so he went to his desk and wrote an agitated note to General Heideck:

> Happiness is not for this earth. I was happy here, but now I am thrown down from my heaven. *The unbelievable has happened.* The years I have yet to live I had hoped to pass in exalted love. It was a dream.... *It is over now.* But no undue haste. The bearer of this, the wife of the sculptor Ganser, will show you the evidence. You are calm, I am not. Leaving myself time for reflection, I intend to come to your home about 1:30 today. I think it would be best for Lolitta to meet me there. If I must break with her forever (I fear nothing else is possible), still I want to see her one more time. No violence is to be feared from me. The king is ashamed, but the 60-year-old man is not, that tears fill his eyes as he writes this.
>
> Just one hour ago, happy yet was
> Ludwig

The king told Frau Ganser to take the note and her reports to General Heideck's home in the Briennerstraße. The general was still at breakfast when the woman handed him the king's despairing note and her espionage dossier. Heideck briefly interrogated Frau Ganser, then dismissed her and began to leaf through the notes. There were notations of the visits of Lieutenant Nußbammer and others at hours when no respectable lady would have received gentlemen callers alone; Ganser did not know what had gone on, but the mere fact that the dancer repeatedly allowed herself to be alone with men in her rooms at night was sufficient under contemporary standards to brand her as immoral.

Ganser had also been assiduous about noting any comments Lola had made about prominent people during her parties: "The king promised me on his honor as a gentleman and as a king that Hörmann [the president of the provincial government of Oberbayern] will never be a minister of state." Frau Ganser's notes quoted Lola, "President Hörmann is not popular, no one likes him, no one can stand him; I know everything they're saying about him. He'll have to go because he has interfered in my affairs."

"The king wants me to write to his friend von der Tann," Lola had declared, according to Frau Ganser. "That I can do; friends far away are no problem, but the king shall have no friends close to him."

And when someone had remarked to Lola that the king's friend and former mistress, the actress Constanze Dahn, was a woman of spirit, the spy had recorded Lola's response as, "If she were, she wouldn't still be on the stage." Such a comment was a bit insolent for a dancer whose fortuitous retirement was of such recent date, but it was not exactly the stuff of high treason. Nevertheless, the reports showed that Lola flouted prevailing views of what was proper, feminine, and moral and that she was arrogant, petty, and eager to make use of her influence over the king.

Heideck was still leafing through the report when he was surprised by the arrival of Ludwig himself, who had been unable to wait any longer to pour his heart out to his old friend. Ludwig threw his arms around the general's shoulders and cried bitterly: "So there is no more joy for me. I thought I had found a woman to be a friend to me for the rest of my days, someone to fill the empty hours with intimate, spiritual joy and make me forget the troubles of state with quiet inspiration and companionship. I honor and love the queen, but her conversation is simply not adequate for my spirit, and my heart needs feminine society. I'm used to it. I had hoped that I'd found such a woman in Lola, and she betrayed me."

Heideck was shocked at the king's condition—and at his pale face and red-rimmed eyes—and he told the king to pull himself together, to think of his health and of his obligations as king, and to stop torturing himself. The general told Ludwig that he must avoid the stress that seeing Lola again would cause him, that she deserved only his scorn, and that he should refuse to see her ever again.

"No, Heideck, I can't do that," replied the king, "can't condemn her without a hearing. I couldn't live with myself if I did that. But I won't see her until you've spoken with her. Don't worry, I can pull myself together."

Heideck knew that the king's unwavering sense of justice would never have allowed him to deny Lola the right to answer the charges against her. And, as Heideck could tell, the king was already hoping that Lola could refute the charges.

"She may be innocent," he told Heideck, "or at least not so guilty as this woman claims. I've encountered that before. Think how persecuted she is, how she and I have already been slandered. No, I will not condemn her unheard; her faithlessness has caused enough pain in the depths of my soul that I don't want to compound it with self-recrimination because I was unjust to her."

The king and his friend agreed that Heideck would confront Lola with Ganser's reports and that Ludwig would come to see her afterward, at about

2 P.M. The general dreaded this interview. He already knew how quickly Lola's moods could change, and he had no idea how she might react to these espionage reports. It was said that she always carried a dagger and a miniature pistol with her, and Heideck made a mental note to keep an eye on her hands so that she would not surprise him.

It was already nearly two when Lola and her maid arrived at the general's home. The general told her that he had something confidential to discuss with her and asked her to dismiss the maid. Lola sat down on one end of the general's sofa, and he sat opposite her and began to speak. Heideck told her the purpose of their meeting, outlined the substance of Frau Ganser's reports, and then reproached her bitterly for her conduct.

Lola erupted into a towering rage. She swore by her father's grave, by everything she held sacred that she was innocent, that it was all a web of lies and distortions, and burst out angrily against a weak king who was willing to believe such falsehoods. She sprang up off the sofa and flung away her shawl, then her hat, and cursed the day she had met the king, swearing that she would go back to Paris at once and leave this pit of scoundrels forever. Heideck, stunned by her fury, watched as her eyes seemed to darken and bulge and foam appeared on her lips as she ranted. With the rage of an Old Testament prophet Lola began tearing at her clothes, and Heideck was afraid she would rip open her dress. He was trying to calm her and was urging her to go home just as King Ludwig walked in, as pale and shaken as he had been during his earlier visit. Lola immediately directed her rage at the king, berating him for having spied on her, for having so little faith in her, for betraying her trust and devotion; she would leave Munich and everything she had here and never come back. Heideck accused her of gross lack of respect for His Majesty, telling her she should throw herself at his feet and beg forgiveness. Lola spat back that an innocent woman has no need to beg forgiveness, and as she threw herself around Heideck's parlor she slammed into the étagère, knocking the general's teacups to the floor.

Ludwig's heart was torn by the bitterness of Lola's words, but he did his best to calm her while his old friend silently hoped that seeing this furious incarnation of his *querida* would reveal to the king Lola's true nature. Lola demanded that Heideck leave them alone, and the king ordered him to leave; the general, feeling that the king was in no physical danger from the woman, retired to the next room. Now they spoke in the bizarre, garbled Spanish that was their private language. Lola's rage dissolved into tears, and Ludwig sat comforting her and assuring her of his love. After about a quarter of an hour, Heideck stuck his head in the door, pointing to his pocket watch to remind the king that it was nearly three, the hour at which Ludwig usually ate his principal meal of the day at the palace. The king waved him away wordlessly.

At last they were reconciled. The king was convinced once more that Lola's love for him was real, and she agreed not to leave Munich. "If all the accusations had been true and she had contritely confessed them to me," Ludwig later wrote, "such a great, passionate love filled me that I would have forgiven all of them."

Lola rushed out past the general, followed by the king. Heideck helped Ludwig into his overcoat, remarking, "Well, now Your Majesty has seen the fury; I confess, she's turned everything here upside down. I've never seen such a demon. Your Majesty won't being seeing her again." "On the contrary," responded the king as he walked to the door, "I promised to call on her this evening." "But Your Majesty," blurted the general as he tried to explain again why the king should abandon the Spanish woman. Ludwig cut him short with sharp impatience: "I gave her my promise, and I won't let anyone dictate to me." The king left feeling much better, and Heideck was left feeling much worse.

Back at the palace, one of Ludwig's old friends made an ill-advised effort to get the king to break with Lola, using Frau Ganser's reports, the Dujarier trial, and all other evidence he could muster. The intent was apparently to reinforce Frau Ganser's dramatic presentation, but the effect was just the opposite of what had been intended. The king now regarded the arguments as fully answered, and this second assault by Lola's enemies so soon after Frau Ganser's revelations prompted the king to suspect that there was a conspiracy against Lola and that a concerted effort was being made to manipulate him. Ludwig was naturally prone to seeing plots swirling around the throne, not always without justification; and in this case his suspicions were probably well grounded. Abel certainly knew of the efforts to separate the king from the dancer, but he limited his involvement to giving confidential encouragement and advice. As Heideck had predicted, the campaign to turn Ludwig against Lola was moving the king unshakably to her side.

When he called on her that evening, Lola convinced the king that Frau Ganser's reports were all lies. Ludwig himself recalled that Frau Ganser had once reported to him that the crown prince was having an affair with a countess, a story that had proved completely false. He even asked Heideck to return the heart-stricken note he had written that morning after receiving

Frau Ganser's report so that he could show Lola just how deep his feelings for her were. More than ever the king regarded Lola's enemies as his enemies and her friends as his friends. It became a matter of honor to him to demonstrate that the whole world could not separate them.

The next day Ludwig wrote Baron Maltzahn in Paris, asking him to return to Munich as soon as possible because it was clear that Lola needed a loyal and understanding friend, particularly one who was respected and influential in Munich's better social circles. Maltzahn replied that he would like to be named one of the king's aides-de-camp and to be allowed to spend his summers at his estate in Baden-Baden, which the king at once approved. "Love, honor, and duty bind me to Lolitta," he wrote Maltzahn. "A conspiracy was formed here to separate me from her, but it has merely bound me all the stronger to her."

Although the bonds between the king and his favorite had been strengthened by the assault, Ludwig was often far from comfortable with Lola's behavior. Just after the Ganser affair, the king noted in his diary, "She is meddling in personal matters of state. . . . concessions made to her, she wants more. . . . Where will it lead?" He was also aware of the ill feeling Lola was arousing among the nobility by her unrestrained and premature use of the emblem of the nine-pointed crown, the symbol of a countess. It appeared on the buttons of her servants' uniforms and was part of the pattern on the expensive silverware she had ordered. In more than two decades on the throne Ludwig had elevated relatively few commoners to the nobility, almost none to the level of a countess, and the aristocracy was scandalized at the thought of a former dancer of dubious talent and more dubious reputation joining their ranks. The king had indeed promised to make her a countess, but he now tried to suggest to her that perhaps it would be better if she were simply a baroness. That title, said Lola confidently, was unacceptable; either she became a countess or she would remain simply Lola Montez.

But only a few days after the Ganser incident the would-be countess provoked a full-scale police investigation by storming the sensitive security areas of the Central Post Office trying to retrieve a package she had mailed to Nußbammer, assaulting at least one postal worker in the process. The king's exasperated response when he received the detailed police report on the incident may have contained as much frustration with Lola's continued antics as it did with the obvious relish of those reporting them. "If I don't ask about her myself," he wrote Baron Pechmann, "I don't want any mention from my police director of my dear Lola Montez." The baron, who took both obedience and duty most seriously, felt that the king's command did not and could not constitutionally prevent him from continuing his investigation of the invasion of the post office, and on the following Monday morning one of his agents interrogated Lola's maid Jeanette and Berta Thierry, who were suspected of being Lola's accomplices in the incident.

Within the hour Baron Pechmann had received a note from Lola telling him to leave her alone or she would complain to the king. Pechmann responded with a summons demanding that Lola appear within one week to answer for her "excessive behavior in the postal building." It was a war of wills that he probably realized he could not win.

The next morning one of Lola's liveried servants returned the summons to the police chief with his mistress's compliments and her response that because she could not read German she had no idea what the paper said; she felt it would be best if he let the matter drop. Pechmann responded that government servants in Bavaria were to issue documents only in German and that she should have someone translate the summons for her; in any case, he could not drop the investigation without authorization.

The servant returned to Lola, who was in bed with severe menstrual cramps that had kept her awake most of the night. In fifteen minutes the servant was back to deliver the summons, ripped to pieces, to Pechmann. The director coolly noted the fact in the investigation file and had the servant sign the entry as a witness. Ulrich Thierry, the father of Lola's female companions, appeared almost immediately to apologize for the terrible misunderstanding, saying he had just explained to Mlle. Montez that the destruction of the summons constituted contempt of the judicial process, and Mlle. Montez begged the baron to forget it ever happened. The baron declined to forget.

Now Lola played her king. At 1:30 a messenger arrived with a note for Pechmann: "To the Acting Police Director Baron von Pechmann: *Most earnestly* I inform the aforesaid to leave my dear Lola Montez in peace. Unacquainted as she is with our local usages, she should not be dealt with so punctiliously. Baron Pechmann, let it not be forgotten, is only acting director, and even if he were definitively police president, his tenure in office is at the king's pleasure. *I am weary of these machinations. . . . No response, but obedience.* Ludwig"

Pechmann was not ready to concede the game. He went before Abel and argued that because the destruction of the summons came under the criminal code he was required to investigate it further and that, under the constitution, the king had no right to suspend a criminal investigation. Abel was sympathetic to the zealous police director, but it must have been clear to him that not only had Pechmann let himself become emotionally involved in the matter but also, much more importantly, that the king himself was emotionally involved. As much as the minister would have rejoiced at the Spanish woman's expulsion from Munich, he could see quite clearly that Pechmann was piloting his ship of office straight for the immovable rock of the king's granite will, and Abel had no interest in signing on for the voyage.

Although he received only feeble moral support from his superiors, the police director held his course and ordered the interrogation of everyone with knowledge of the destruction of the summons. The king responded with a swift order that Abel immediately transfer Baron Pechmann to some small town in the provinces. The matter of the shredded summons was dropped after a physician certified that at the time of the incident Mlle. Montez was in a "temporary, interesting condition" and was not responsible for her actions. A new joke began to make the rounds in Munich: What's the difference between Prussia and Bavaria? In Prussia the police kicked Lola Montez out, in Bavaria Lola Montez kicked the police out.

Ludwig was becoming exasperated by the resistance he met in everything concerning his dear Lolitta; Pechmann was the worst offender but far from the only one. The city authorities were arguing over permits for the work being done on Lola's new house in the Barerstraße. The Art Association, which with three thousand members was hardly an exclusive organization, voted to refuse Lola membership even though the king was the group's principal patron and despite the fact that Stieler's portrait of her was drawing crowds to its exhibition hall in the arcades on the Hofgarten. The Museum Society, the foremost social club in Munich, each of whose members owed something to the king, had unanimously rejected her application. The city of Munich had rejected her application for citizenship, and now the provincial government was refusing her. The few Munichers who let themselves be seen in her company were finding themselves socially and economically shunned by nearly all their fellow citizens.

But far more annoying to King Ludwig than the petty snubs and the passive resistance of the citizens were the efforts of members of his own family to meddle in his affairs. His sister Charlotte Auguste, the widow of the Austrian Emperor Franz, had just written him: "What about the example you're setting? The world forgives this type of thing in young men, but in old men. . . . think of your subjects. . . . Brother, have mercy on your soul, your country, and on me for writing this to you. But I want to be able to look at you with pride—release her hand from you, fill it, give her money, lots of it if necessary, as long as she leaves. Each word of this letter pains me. . . . Use your mind, use your will! I pray to God to help you. . . . Your *true* friend, your tender loving sister." Ludwig gave her the briefest of replies: "May everyone mind his own business, and people ought to know me well enough to be convinced I tolerate no interference in mine."

Amid this emotional turmoil the king carried on with his royal duties as usual, rising well before dawn and poring over mountains of state papers, awarding honors, and closely supervising the work of his ministers. On 15 December he announced that an important administrative change would take effect on 1 January; the departments of religious affairs and of education were to be made independent of the Ministry of the Interior, where Abel had been responsible for them, and would be given to the less conservative minister of justice. Ludwig wrote to his old friend Tann that he had been planning such a move for nearly a year but had waited until liberal agitation for reform had died down so that the change would clearly be seen as an act of royal will, not as a surrender to pressure. The king wrote that he had long ago let the minister know that in religious matters he felt him too tied to the extreme conservative wing of the Catholic party; nevertheless, he told Tann, Abel "is a statesman like no other in Bavaria and one I value greatly."

Taking religion and education out of the principal minister's hands might have no immediate effect, but it would hearten the Protestants and the liberals and signal to the ultramontanes that they were not in charge. "I wouldn't be surprised if they lay the blame at poor Lola's door," the king wrote, and to some extent, that is exactly what happened. Although the inner circles of government knew that this change had been coming, the public perception was that Lola Montez, who railed against the Jesuits and urged Freemasonry on the king, was influencing the course of the ship of state. Everyone who had been content with the previous direction had new reason to hate and fear the Spanish woman.

Just before Christmas, Lieutenant Nußbammer returned from Ansbach, where he had been sent on leave—partly to get him away from his fellow officers, who felt that his behavior with Lola brought dishonor on the regiment, and partly because Ludwig must have sensed that Lola's interest in the young man was more than casual.

The surviving direct evidence tells us little about Lola and Nußbammer (though in her letter to Fiorentino she implied that it was impossible for her to have lovers); but if we look at her behavior in the Frühlingstraße, at the post office, and subsequently, it is appears that during her early months in Munich she was more emotionally involved with the lieutenant than with the king. The king may have been unable to admit to himself the sexual jealousy behind his attitude toward the lieutenant, but Lola was very much aware of it; and when Nußbammer visited her on his return to Munich, she decided not to mention it to the king, as she had promised.

The year was coming to an end, and Ludwig wrote a status report to Tann. "In 48 years in Munich I've never experienced this, and to tell the truth, it doesn't make a very good impression on me.... My family here behaves itself very well, particularly in the case of the queen; I appreciate it very much, I love her. But the Jesuit party, at least a part of it, ... are angry with Lolitta, who is Catholic but a *sworn enemy of the Jesuits;* that's obviously an unforgivable crime. Who knows, if she were doing the opposite and introducing the Jesuits into Bavaria, along with the holy Ignatius Loyola we might get a half-holy Lola.... All their machinations have produced exactly the opposite of what they intended, and they'll recognize my character in that."

On the last day of 1846, two correspondents were each drafting notes for Ludwig's eyes only. In his room at the Hotel Maulik, Baron Maltzahn, just arrived from Paris, was drafting an agitated message begging the king not to nominate him as his aide-de-camp. "*My life* is Your Royal Majesty's to command," he declared, "*but not my honor.*" In the short time since his arrival, Maltzahn had had a rude awakening. "The situation here is completely different from what I thought; *unfortunately* during my absence Lolita has insulted all classes of society, offended everyone, and the city and the nation are so up in arms that with the best will it is *too late, impossible,* to improve her position, at least I'm too feeble to manage it.... I ask Your Royal Majesty most humbly to grant me one hour in which I can speak with you without interruption to consider what can yet be done."

In her rooms in the Goldener Hirsch, Lola had asked one of her German friends to lightly pencil a New Year's wish in German to her royal friend and protector, and she was laboriously tracing in ink the outlines of the strange characters so that she could tell him she had written it with her own hand. "May the New Year grant much joy to the man for whom I would like to sacrifice my life, may our hearts be ever new in the holy bliss of the purest love," she traced. Her wish for the new year, Lola wrote, was to bind herself to Ludwig, with "strong, tender bands, in sweet innocence."

15

Mistress versus Minister and Mob

When Ludwig granted Maltzahn the requested audience on the bright, chilly morning of New Year's Day, the baron, one of the few men the king thought could be numbered among Lola's solid supporters, painted a devastating picture of the outrage, scorn, and even hatred that she had provoked throughout Bavaria. As a king, Ludwig might be able to weather this public resistance, said Maltzahn, but he, a private person who had not lived in Munich for thirty years, would be ground down by the daily slander, snubs, and hostility. He also implied that while he considered himself a friend of Lola's, her reputation in Paris and elsewhere was such that she might not be an entirely appropriate choice as the king's favorite. Ludwig was stunned; he had hoped that Maltzahn would be able to reverse public sentiment on Lola. "But how shall I help myself?" exclaimed the king. "I am bound to her."

Later that day Baron Maltzahn paid a call on Lola, and Ludwig's bewilderment after his interview with Maltzahn turned to anger when Lola told him what the baron had said to her. She said he had first upbraided her for her behavior and then offered her a life pension of 50,000 francs a year if she would leave Bavaria at once and not return. The king could not believe that Maltzahn was willing or able to offer such a sum on his own initiative and from his own funds. When he heard that Maltzahn had had a long interview with Archbishop Reisach, Ludwig surmised the real source of the bribe. After trying to convince the king of the purity of his motives, Maltzahn decided that family business required his presence elsewhere, and he quickly left town. There seems to have been at least an element of truth in Lola's account of the proffered bribe, and Ludwig believed it completely. From that day forward he felt certain that Lola did not love him for his wealth, since she had rejected so much to remain at his side.

Lola had become a celebrity and a target for the scorn of street urchins. Crowds would follow her when she went out, and boys would whistle, yell, and sometimes toss horse manure from the street. Things got so bad that Ludwig assigned gendarmes to guard her at all times, and she rarely went out walking now. With the brown brougham purchased for her in Paris and the two superb black horses from the royal stables, she and her mounted gendarmes made an impressive parade.

Ludwig had ordered another of his distinguished court painters, Wilhelm von Kaulbach, to paint a portrait of Lola. When Lola first arrived in Munich, Kaulbach had done a pencil sketch of her that captured her fresh, exotic beauty. But the artist grew to despise the Spanish woman as much as anyone in Munich, and when the king asked him to do a preliminary sketch for a portrait of Lola in Renaissance costume—she would resemble Mary, Queen of Scots, probably both because of the king's enthusiasm for Schiller's play about the ill-fated queen and to portray Lola in the role of persecuted Catholic—the painter produced a charcoal sketch of a grim-looking Lola with funereal flowers in her hair, a belt of snakes, a headsman's block and ax in the background, and a newspaper report of the Dujarier trial lying open on a table beside her. Ludwig rubbed out the Dujarier headline on the newspaper and, showing his blackened finger to the artist, said, "This is a black fantasy." But he insisted that Kaulbach paint the portrait.

The portrait was to be full-length and life-size, in late Renaissance costume and style but without any direct references to Mary of Scotland. The sittings began in Kaulbach's unheated studio between the great rolling English garden and the river Isar. Ludwig came each time, conversing animatedly with the unwilling Kaulbach and with Lola, railing against the ingratitude and treachery of the nobility and ultramontanes and keeping the chill from Lola with a charcoal warming pan. At one of the sittings, Zampa, Lola's white lapdog, got into the adjoining garden, where Kaulbach kept a large collection of animals as pets and models, and began a full-throated chase after the painter's six white peacocks. Lola charged out to rescue her dog, followed quickly by Kaulbach, eager to protect his birds, and the king, who was not willing to be left behind. Any passerby that winter morning would have been bewildered to see a winding procession of six white peacocks, a yapping dog, the notorious Lola Montez in Renaissance costume, the famous painter Kaulbach, and the King of Bavaria himself.

Ludwig was not pleased with Kaulbach's portrayal of his dear friend, and he let the artist know it. The painter insisted on depicting Lola with a grim, even menacing expression, though he dropped the more sensational attributes of his original sketch. The king respected the artist's independence and did not order him to change the painting. But he refused to buy it, and it would remain unfinished in the artist's studio for decades.

The police were now frequently ripping down posted copies of an anonymous and much-repeated bit of doggerel beginning "Montez, you great whore / Your time will come soon," and concluding "To the devil with the royal house / Our loyalty is at an end / It brings us only shame and ridicule / God help us." The king was looking ill and haggard, and he was said to have fainted several times in January 1847. Priests began to urge their congregations to "pray for the redemption of the great, gray man," and there were stories that priests in the confessionals were ordering prayers that the king would abandon the Spanish woman.

The king was probably less troubled by the public criticism of his relationship with Lola than by his inability to control her relationship with Lieutenant Nußbammer, who was almost universally regarded as her lover. Ludwig had tried to get Lola to promise not to see the officer without royal approval, and he had made clear to Nußbammer that he was not to be around Lola without the king's knowledge. But both of them seemed content to ignore the royal wishes, and on 17 January the tense triangle erupted in a repetition of the comedy of November, with Nußbammer once again being transferred out of Munich by the king's personal order and then being ordered back again the same day.

Two days later the king created a scene when he arrived for tea at Lola's rooms and found the lieutenant there. The king was angry at Nußbammer, and he was angry and disappointed that Lola had ignored his command not to see the young man without his permission. But Lola convinced him that it was only out of the goodness of her heart that she let Nußbammer come around, since the poor fellow was hopelessly in love with her and it would have been cruel to refuse even to see him after he had suffered so much for her sake.

Ludwig could not remain angry with Lola; and even in the moments when his ardor cooled a little, he felt committed by his honor and his word to this woman who told him she had no one else in the world, had given up every-thing for him, and loved him with a passion—an awe, she said—that she had never felt for any man. Aside from his moral commitment to her, there was the question of his authority as king if he appeared to back down from the public position he had occupied in her defense.

In spite of his misgivings, the king still found the Spanish woman fasci-nating; as much as she tormented him with her whims and impertinences, she knew how to maintain his interest. On 26 January Lola surprised him with an alabaster model of her foot on a yellow marble pillow, modeled by Johannes Leeb, a sculptor in Ludwig's stable of artists who had become part of her circle. "Heart of my heart, my Lolitta," the king wrote to her. "You gave me great pleasure with the lovely surprise of sending me your foot in marble—your foot has no equal—it appears to be an antique ideal—when Leeb had left, I covered it with fervent kisses." He would use it as a paperweight in his private apartments, kissing it often, and eventually it would become sym-bolic of the troubling depths of his obsession with her. In return for her pre-sent, Ludwig commissioned Leeb to create a marble replica of his hand holding a pencil and writing poetry.

Ludwig continued to receive admonitions about his relationship with the dancer. Most of them he ignored, but one, from Melchior Cardinal von Diepenbrock, the prince-bishop of Breslau, evoked an extraordinary re-sponse. The king respected Cardinal Diepenbrock and did not consider him an extremist like Archbishop Reisach. Diepenbrock wrote the king that he had called upon the spirit of the late Bishop Johann von Sailer, who had been Ludwig's religious mentor, to assist him in what he felt he must tell the king. The spirit of the dead bishop had spoken to him, wrote the cardinal: "Tell the king this—King Ludwig, a poisonous tree grows above you whose deadly perfume numbs you, robs your eyes of vision, intoxicates your senses and wholly beguiles you so that you see not the chasm before you, the open chasm that threatens to swallow up your honor, your reputation, the happiness of your family, of your land, of your life, as well as the salvation of your soul. . . . King Ludwig, awake from your dream! . . . Do not sully your name, 'til now so noble, as did the French Ludwig [Louis XV], whose offensive life itself dug the pit of the Revolution."

Only after more than a week did the king prepare a reply to the prince-bishop's letter. He took time first to draft what he wanted to say and then he wrote:

My lord prince-bishop, I make it a practice not to reply to letters on the subject discussed in yours of January 29, but out of respect for *Diepenbrock*, whose good opinion I value, I will make an exception. Appearances deceive. I've never kept mistresses and I don't like the practice. I always had acquaintances to stimulate my fantasy and these were precisely my best protection against sensuality. I have a poetic nature that cannot be measured by normal standards. I will tell you how appearances deceive by giving you my *word of honor* that I am now in the fourth month since I was intimate with the queen or any other woman and before that I had abstained for almost five months. I am an autocrat within the limits of the constitution, that is well known, and that I will remain. . . . Dearly do I wish to know of some means by which I could instantly make the world understand that. I cannot break, I would no longer be able to respect myself, people want the impossible from me.

The king gave a copy of his reply to the dean of the Munich cathedral and told him to send it out to all the bishops in the kingdom. Perhaps a circular letter with the king's sworn statement on his sex life would be extraordinary enough to stop the gossip.

On Wednesday, 3 February, the Council of State held a preliminary discussion of the king's intention to grant Bavarian citizenship to Lola Montez. The councilors declared that because they had no documents establishing Lola's age, religion, national origin, or education, they were unable to act.

Late that night, Lola and a group of her friends were returning to her apartments at the Goldener Hirsch. From the corridor of the hotel they stopped to look through the windows into the assembly rooms, where Ambros Havard, the hotel's owner, was holding a Carnival party for his suppliers and some of his friends. He had sent Lola Montez an invitation to the party, which she had accepted but then changed her mind. Most of Lola's companions decided to join the party but Lola herself remained in the corridor watching the revelers. One of Lola's friends, a former croupier at the casino in Baden-Baden, began to annoy the other guests, and they complained to the host, who told the interloper that if he did not know how to behave he would have to leave.

At this point Lola entered from corridor and began arguing with Ambros Havard. She apparently threatened to move out of his hotel if he was going to treat her friends this way, to which he responded, "The sooner the better," or something similar. Lola answered by delivering a solid slap to his face.

One of Havard's guests, Master Tailor Ignaz Riehle, rushed to his host's assistance, telling Lola that she didn't belong at the party, and a hefty slap from Lola smashed the tailor's glasses. Riehle was enraged, and he and Lola began a shoving match as he tried to eject her. Havard's son Philip rushed to defend his father, and a free-for-all would have erupted had members of Lola's party not pulled her out of the fray and retreated. Lola's bodyguards arrived during the angry uproar and began to calm the crowd and investigate what had led to this breach of the peace. Lola's first thought was to call in her patron, and she had a note sent to the palace informing the king that an unpleasantness had occurred and asking him to come as soon as possible.

Ludwig was given the message when he awoke, just after five, and in the cold darkness he hurried over to the Goldener Hirsch. The gendarmes were still interviewing witnesses, and Lola recounted to the king her version of the brutal assault on her by Havard and his guests. The king was moved to tears—whether of compassion, anger, shame, or frustration, no one could say—but he declined to intervene in the police investigation and took measures to see that all the facts were gathered and weighed impartially. In the course of the day he made two more visits to Lola to see how she was recovering from the events of the night.

The immediate result of the fight was that Havard refused to provide Lola with anything more from the hotel kitchen—not even a glass of water—so that it became imperative that she find other lodgings until she could move into her house in the Barerstraße. She found an apartment on the third floor of Theresienstraße 8a, just off the Ludwigstraße near the Royal Library.

The Wednesday night fight was still the talk of the taverns and drawing rooms of Munich on Saturday afternoon, when Lola was on a shopping expedition near the Frauenkirche, Munich's cathedral. She was accompanied by a young English sailor, Mathilde Thierry, and her dog Turk. On the Frauenplatz a deliveryman was loading his wagon, and for reasons unknown, Turk lunged and bit the man on the foot. The deliveryman was more stunned and angry than hurt, and he reached for a club to hit the animal when Lola intervened to protect her pet and slapped the man four or five times across the face. The man was even more stunned now, but he probably felt it beneath his dignity to exchange blows with a woman, so he threatened the sailor with his club.

Lola and her friends hustled off down the street, but a number of people had witnessed the incident, and word began to spread quickly of the Spanish woman's latest outrageous attack on a good burgher of Munich. An angry crowd began to form, and as Lola and her companions came back through the Frauenplatz, it became a mob. They fled into the store of the silversmith

Bartholomä Meyerhofer, where they were besieged by a crowd that grew rapidly to several hundred persons. The gendarmes in Lola's bodyguard called for reinforcements from the nearby police headquarters in the Weinstraße, but the mood of the mob was growing ugly, and they were not about to disperse without getting their hands on Lola. After the incident at the Goldener Hirsch, word had spread that the Spanish woman had said she would die in Munich before she would let herself be driven out, and the crowd seemed eager to oblige her. Fortunately, the silver shop was built solidly, and a direct assault by the mob seemed unlikely.

Toward 5 P.M. the early winter darkness began to settle over Munich, helping to conceal the ladder that appeared at the rear of the shop. As about four hundred people yelled for her at the front, Lola Montez escaped into the courtyard behind the shop and used the ladder to climb over a wall and into a window at the rear of the Weißes Lamm Guesthouse. From there she escaped unnoticed down the Weinstraße.

When she was safely home, the gendarmes announced to the crowd that Lola was gone, but they refused to believe them, maintaining their siege and erupting every now and then into waves of catcalls and whistles. Finally, at about 8 P.M., more than four hours after the incident began, mounted gendarmes were ordered in, and the mob was dispersed with only a few arrests. Turk, who was not as good at climbing ladders as Lola's other companions, had to be left in the shop and rescued later.

Lola complained loudly to Ludwig and demanded an investigation. He told friends that he found the incidents amusing, but the ill feeling against his favorite in Munich was now not only nearly unanimous, it was turning vicious. As always, Lola met opposition boldly, even insolently, and on the day after being trapped in the silver shop she pointedly took a Sunday promenade on the crowded streets with her British friend. That evening she timed her arrival at the opera so that she appeared in the auditorium at exactly the moment the audience rose to greet the entrance of King Ludwig. During the performance, of Meyerbeer's *Robert le Diable*, she surveyed the boxes with what some spectators took as brazen impudence.

The next day the Council of State was again scheduled to consider the question of the naturalization of Lola Montez, this time under the chairmanship of the king himself. New developments made Ludwig secretly anxious for swift action to make Lola a citizen. The police investigation of the incident at the Goldener Hirsch was nearly complete and would be presented to a court soon, perhaps within forty-eight hours. There was a possibility that

Lola would be charged with attacking Havard and Riehle and ordered to stand trial. As a foreigner, she ran the risk that the judge would refuse to grant bail for her and order her jailed immediately; if she were a Bavarian citizen, however, jail was a remote possibility. Ludwig would have been distraught to see his beloved jailed under any circumstances, but at this moment it would represent a triumph of those opposed to her and a direct insult to the king's authority. It was important that she become a Bavarian as quickly as possible.

The meeting was frustrating for the king. Not a single councilor was prepared to support the naturalization of Lola Montez. Again they used the woman's undocumented status as an excuse to take no position. The king ordered the council to convene again the next day and to vote, telling them he would regard refusal to render an opinion as open disobedience. The constitution did not require the king to obtain the council's consent before he granted citizenship, he simply needed its opinion, and he was determined to have it.

The king had taken into his confidence a member of the Council of State whom he felt sure was not a member of "the Party," as he called the ultramontanes. He was Georg von Maurer, the only Protestant member of the council and a distinguished legal historian and jurist. Ludwig had told Maurer of his fear that Lola might be arrested once the court considered the Goldener Hirsch incident, and he wanted the councilor's advice on avoiding the worst. Maurer took on responsibility for tactical planning and for discreet inquiries with the court.

That night a great torchlight procession was organized to cheer beneath the windows of Archbishop Reisach, the rallying point of the ultramontane and anti-Lola factions in Munich. The march was diverted from the most direct course so that it could pass in emphatic silence beneath the king's windows in the royal palace. Ludwig pronounced himself amused and told everyone he spoke with that he could think of nothing more appropriate than a torchlight procession to the archbishop's palace. "Let them take light to where there is darkness!"

The Council of State meeting held on Tuesday went as expected. Maurer, playing a bit of a double game, said that he felt the king would be ill advised to declare Lola Montez a Bavarian, that given the state of public opinion, "it would be the greatest calamity that could befall Bavaria"; yet he felt the king had the constitutional right to naturalize her even in the absence of all documentation of her status, and he voted yes. All the other members voted no, both on the basis of her lack of documents and, as they diplomatically put it, "on other very important grounds."

The following morning, when the official protocol of the council meeting reached his desk, the king wrote Maurer asking what course he should take to protect Lola from imprisonment after the court hearing. Maurer advised that "the lady in question should undertake a little trip (this morning yet) or should conceal herself. If the court orders no arrest at noon, then she can reappear. If, however, as is quite possible, the court orders her arrest, then she will be nowhere to be found." Maurer further advised the king to decree Lola's naturalization at once and to have the document immediately countersigned by a minister so that it would have legal effect. Then if the court ordered her arrest, the document would be sufficient to quash the order.

In the margin of the protocol of the council's session Ludwig wrote, "Having heard the Council of State, I hereby grant Bavarian citizenship to Señora Lola Montez (Maria de los Dolores Porris y Montez), free of tax and seal, with retention of her current citizenship. Munich, February 10, 1847 at a quarter to eleven in the morning." The minister for the royal household, who normally would have countersigned the naturalization decree, returned it unsigned to King Ludwig, respectfully stating that he preferred to give up his office rather than put his signature on the document.

The new problem of finding a cabinet minister willing to countersign the decree lost most of its urgency with the arrival of a second message from Maurer. According to one of the officers of the court that would hear the Goldener Hirsch case, the matter would be delayed until the next day; and even then, it seemed almost certain that the court would accept bail for Lola Montez.

Minister Abel, who for months had evaded a direct confrontation over the "unspeakable female," as he called her, now faced the inevitable. He announced to his ministerial colleagues that in view of the king's decision on the naturalization question, he was going to tender his resignation. The others told him that they would not stay on in the cabinet without him, and Abel began to draft a memorandum to the king to announce the resignation of his government en masse. Although Abel was probably acting primarily on principle and wished to end his political career unsullied by Lola's scandal, he seems to have harbored some hope that the mass resignation would cause the king to reconsider.

In his memorandum Abel told the king that all of his ministers shared

Maurer's opinion, expressed in the Council of State, that the naturalization of Lola Montez was the greatest calamity that could befall Bavaria.

> Since October of last year the eyes of the whole country have been upon Munich, and in all parts of Bavaria opinions have been formed about what is going on here, which is practically the only subject of conversation in family circles and in public places; and from these opinions a mood had arisen that is most troubling.
>
> Respect for the monarch is more and more being eradicated in the minds of men because only expressions of bitter reproach and loud disapproval are heard.
>
> At the same time, national pride is deeply offended because Bavaria believes itself governed by a foreigner, whom the public regards as a branded woman, and any number of opposing facts could not shake this belief.

Abel went on to speak of the bitter tears of the prince-bishop of Breslau, of the laughter and scorn directed at Bavaria throughout Germany and all of Europe, from the huts of the poor to the palaces of the rich. Slowly but surely all the pillars of the kingdom were being weakened by the poison working upon the nation, and soon even the loyalty of the armed forces would be open to question. There was no telling, he wrote, what could be expected from the next meeting of the Landtag if things continued this way.

Abel collected the signatures of his colleagues in the cabinet and sent the memorandum of resignation to King Ludwig on 11 February. The king was surprised and gave Abel until noon on 13 February to reconsider, but the minister held fast to his resolution, and the government was dissolved. Ludwig wrote to his friend Tann on 13 February, "Abel remained adamant. He is getting his dismissal, the rule of the Jesuits is broken. . . . I'm pleased with the calm and cheerfulness I've felt yesterday and today. Up to this moment, Lolitta knows nothing. . . . I'm glad Abel came in to resign and that people know that; nice, that he's stepped down, I recognize his great services, think he's an upright man. . . . Things have come a long way here; the question, whether the king or the Jesuit party would rule: *I have answered it.*"

Lola had told Ludwig that she would turn twenty-two on 14 February and that she wanted him to be the last thing she saw in her twenty-second year and the first thing she saw in her twenty-third. (In fact, Lola turned twenty-seven in 1847.) He came to her apartments in the Theresienstraße on the evening of the 13th, and it must have seemed a special birthday present when he told her that he had accepted the resignation of the entire cabinet.

He was the last person she saw as she retired for the night, and so that he could wake her early on her birthday morning, she gave him the key to let himself in.

As soon as Lola heard that her arch enemy had resigned, she moved to take over. She presented the king with her own list of candidates for ministerial posts and told him that she wanted to confer with the appointees or to take part in their audiences with the king. Ludwig was not about to abandon his role as autocrat, no matter how much he was taken by this woman, and he ignored Lola's efforts to gain political control. Rumors began to circulate that the king, having toppled a government for Lola's sake, was beginning to weary of the Spanish woman.

Forming a new government turned out to be more complicated than the king had expected. Although he saw the fall of Abel as the end of ultramontane control in Bavaria and as his own triumph over the Jesuits, Ludwig initially considered forming a government with men politically allied with Abel. Only when these politicians declined to take up ministerial posts—either because they saw conflict with the king as inevitable or because, as Ludwig suspected, there was a conspiracy to embarrass him by making it impossible for him to find new ministers—did King Ludwig turn to men closer to the middle of the political spectrum. He chose Maurer to be the minister of justice and of foreign affairs. Authority over finance and religious affairs and education went to Baron Friedrich von Zu Rhein, an old opponent of Abel's and a foe of the Catholic hierarchy. Johann Zenetti, a career bureaucrat and devout Catholic, became the new minister of the interior. All of them were named acting ministers.

Although the king himself loudly proclaimed the new system in Bavaria as a major change of direction and authorized Maurer to send a circular letter to all foreign governments announcing it, the only real change was a change of attitude by Ludwig himself, for it was he and not his ministers who set policy and direction. As before, the king's ministers had little more than a convenient position from which they could attempt to persuade the king to follow their counsel; even after the "change of system" Ludwig himself held the political reins tightly.

In the process of forming a new government the king found himself distracted by other events. He was infuriated to discover that the resignation memorandum presented to him by his cabinet had been leaked and that copies were being circulated, particularly by the Catholic party, and that the full text was appearing in foreign newspapers. The leak seems to have been an accident rather than a political calculation by Abel, but the king was outraged to see the ministers' remonstrances to him over his devotion to Lolitta read and discussed in every tavern in Europe.

If the ultramontane party had hoped to gain public support by distributing the memorandum, they were badly disappointed. Public opinion seems generally to have turned against the ministers rather than against Ludwig. If the ministers thought the Lola affair was such a calamity, people asked, why had they waited until they were prepared to resign before they said anything to the monarch? The image of a bitterly weeping bishop was not one most people thought added dignity to a ministerial petition, and the military was insulted by the implication, signed by the minister of war, that the troops were becoming unreliable.

In addition to the general opinion that the memorandum was a feeble, even shameful document, the public welcomed a change from above. After nearly a decade in power, the conservative Catholic regime was no longer as attuned to the realities in Bavaria as it should have been. The press began referring to the new cabinet hopefully as the "ministry of the dawn," and Bavarians were willing to give the Maurer–Zu Rhein government a chance.

At the same time, another surprising document began circulating in Munich, this one purportedly a letter from the pope to King Ludwig earnestly beseeching him to abandon his sinful ways and return to the path of virtue. The few persons in Munich who were acquainted with papal correspondence immediately recognized the letter as a forgery, but for most of the readers it must have seemed yet more evidence that Lola would be the king's damnation.

At the university, the faculty and student body had become increasingly identified with the conservative Catholic cause during Abel's tenure. The faculty senate meeting of 18 February was coming to a close when Ernst von Lasaulx, professor of philosophy and aesthetics, rose to make a proposal. Lasaulx, the son-in-law of Joseph Görres, another faculty member and the "grand old man" of conservative Catholicism, suggested that the senate, as the highest moral body of the capital, formally call on Herr Abel to express its admiration for what he had done in the past week to maintain the dignity of the crown.

There was silence in the senate. The rector finally objected, saying that such a thing had never been done. After heated debate, senate members passed a motion to send a delegation to thank Abel instead for what he had done for the university during his term.

All of this confirmed for Ludwig that the ultramontanes were loyal to him only so long as they believed they could control him and that they would stop at nothing to regain power. Now he would show them who really ruled in Bavaria. He began by firing Lasaulx, and his purge of the faculty over the coming months would sweep away almost all of the conservative Catholic professors.

The students at the University of Munich, particularly those studying philosophy, were generally conservative in their sentiments, and Lasaulx was a favorite of many. When a notice from the professor announcing his dismissal and bidding farewell to his students appeared on the university bulletin board early on the morning of 1 March, a number of students decided to march to Lasaulx's home and cheer him with the traditional *vivat* to show their support. At about 10 A.M. several hundred students stood before the professor's house in the Ober Gartenstraße and cheered and sang student songs in his honor.

The group broke up, but at about noon notices were posted on street corners announcing that there would be a march to Lola's apartments in the Theresienstraße at 4 P.M. to bring her a *pereat*, the traditional student expression of antipathy. Word of the planned demonstration reached the king, who dispatched a note to Xavier Mark, the newly appointed police director, asking him personally to assure Lola's safety. The king had reason to be concerned. The report of a provincial officer forwarded to Ludwig that morning by Minister Zu Rhein implied that the mood in the countryside was becoming worse and concentrating more and more on Lola, and there had been repeated threats that she would be kidnapped or murdered.

Lola waited at her window with four friends to see what would happen, and a gendarme patrol watched the street. At a little after 4 o'clock a dull rumbling could be heard, and then the Ludwigstraße end of the street filled with an immense mob of men—according to one estimate, nearly six thousand (the university had an enrollment a little over fifteen hundred)—marching to whistle and shout beneath Lola's windows. A woman watching from a house across the street saw what Lola did:

> She had a plate in her hand and a knife; as the noise got out of control she took the knife and brandished it repeatedly with enraged gestures at the people below; then she shook her fist and anger contorted her features. I had often heard of a fury, but yesterday I saw one for the first time. She was lovely despite her rage; I won't forget the sight. Then she had a glass

of champagne brought and mockingly toasted the crowd. Suddenly a stone flew upwards, and a thunderous "bravo!" rang out. Two men, one of them the ever-faithful Lt. Nußbammer, wanted to pull her away from the window, naturally fearing the worst from the outraged crowd; but she flailed about herself like a madwoman and hit Nußbammer so that he staggered backwards. Now several platoons of infantry arrived and attempted unsuccessfully to push the people back. The students had left after they had done their pereat; the rest of the human mass remained and was constantly enlarged by new arrivals.

The king had finished his afternoon meal and was preparing to make his regular visit to Lola when he noticed from his windows that the streets were unusually crowded. Zenetti, the new interior minister, arrived to warn the king that there was a mob in the Theresienstraße and that he shouldn't think of going to visit Lola Montez. That, of course, made the king determined to go. He got his hat, his coat, and his cane, and started out with Zenetti in his wake, cutting over from the Ludwigstraße to the Amalienstraße to avoid the bulk of the crowd.

The military trying to clear the street in front of Lola's house was exasperated; if the woman would simply shut the window and stay inside there was a chance the mob would disperse. But the mocking, outrageous show she was putting on kept the crowd angry and determined to remain, attracting more troublemakers. Just as the troops had finally succeeded in posting pickets at the entrances to the street, they and everyone else were astounded to see the king and the interior minister striding into the crowded Theresienstraße in the early winter twilight. Zenetti was not about to risk social death by setting foot in the Spanish woman's house, so the king walked alone through the crowd, holding himself as erect as he could. The stunned men stood dumbly aside until Ludwig shouted, "Hats off before the king!" and most of them removed their hats; some cries of "vivat Ludwig" resounded, mixed with whistling and laughter.

In the house, Ludwig was greeted by his beloved, who sent someone down to the street to bring up some of the stones thrown by the mob, to show him how large they were. The king could not have been pleased to find Lieutenant Nußbammer once again part of the company. Outside, reinforcements enabled soldiers with lowered bayonets to clear the street in front of the house, but the mob pressed against the line of soldiers, still screaming and whistling. As the men were driven back, Lola's neighbor across the street heard her "ringing, mocking laughter that cut right through me. It was truly mocking laughter from hell." The object of the mob's fury stood in the window yelling insults and making scornful gestures.

Toward 6 o'clock, mounted troops cleared the street entirely, and the mob appeared to begin drifting apart; but, as was quickly reported to the king, it was simply moving on. Six was the hour when many more men got off work, and the newcomers joined the mass as it began to move down the Ludwigstraße toward the royal palace. There the mob surged out onto the Max-Josephplatz, and some of them began throwing rocks at the palace windows. Queen Therese, who was visiting a friend across the street, wanted to return to the greater security of the palace but feared that her carriage might be attacked, so she sent it back empty and had a servant bring her a large hat and cloak with which she disguised herself for the short walk to safety in the Residenz.

When the king was told that the mob was assaulting his palace, he left at once to take command of the situation. This time as he strode down the street the mob had lost nearly all respect for the royal person. A few men took off their hats to the king, but they were threatened with stoning by the rioters if they did not put them on again at once. King Ludwig was pursued down the main street of his capital by a whistling, catcalling mob that mocked his attachment to Lola and pointedly cheered Queen Therese.

Police Director Mark rushed to the king's side to give him his arm, but there was nothing he could do to ward off the jeers and scorn of the pursuing mob. The king strode on toward the palace, angry and silent. Now the entire military garrison of the capital was on the streets, and the Civil Guard had been called out, too, though relatively few guardsmen appeared to defend the Spanish woman. Those who did refused either to serve in the Theresienstraße or to guard her new home in the Barerstraße. The mob disintegrated, streaming off down side streets, randomly smashing street lanterns and the windows of unsuspecting burghers. By 10 all was quiet; the king finished the evening with his usual game of cards with the queen and even asked her why she was looking troubled. But Ludwig's show of indifference was just that; inside he was angry, vengeful, and troubled: "My nobles, the Jesuit party, the priests have incited the demagogues to abuse me, to wound me, but I'll show them."

The next day everything seemed normal once more, though stories of the events of Monday circulated around town. Lola was said to have tried to fire on the mob with a pistol only to be pulled back at the last second by Nußbammer. According to another story, she had caught the stones thrown up at her, juggled them, and then thrown them back.

The turbulent course of events was taking its toll on King Ludwig. Never in nearly fifty years in Munich, almost half of it as king, had he been subjected to such scorn from his people. It left him angry, shaken, and confused. And although he was impressed with the great physical courage Lola had shown, he saw for the first time something of the wild, demonic side of her nature; he began to believe that perhaps not everything he had heard about her had been lies.

In the wake of the riot, another letter arrived from Ludwig's sister Charlotte Auguste, the dowager empress of Austria. Her last letter, full of tearful concern about his relationship with Lola, had brought the gruff response that she mind her own business. This time she tried to appeal to his pride: "Ludwig, the otherwise so independent strong Ludwig . . . , ruled by a charming girl!" But she could not sustain a mocking tone, and her words told him of the terrible pain she felt over everything she heard. "I wanted to say this to you most earnestly, without any hope of success, but so that you at least understand what I feel, I, who love you and am your ever-faithful sister, C." As a postscript she wrote, "The thought that you might not even read my letter cuts me to the heart."

This time Charlotte Auguste received not an angry rebuff from her older brother but a confession. His love for Lola was over, he told his sister, but he was bound to her by his honor. "The intoxication of my soul is over," he wrote. "Submission will come, but it is difficult!"

16

THE COUNTESS AND HER COURT

King Ludwig had thought that Lola's spell over him was broken, but fate conspired to pull him deeper into his obsessive passion. The king had been looking ill, despite his boasts of extraordinary good health; and on 9 March the strain finally manifested itself, as it had before during times of stress, in an outbreak of disfiguring red blotches on his face. Ludwig retired to his private apartments and refused to be seen until the eruption disappeared. That meant, of course, that he could no longer call on Lola. But she insisted on seeing him at least once every day, so the king allowed her to come to the palace and make her way up a private stairway to his sickroom.

Ludwig was amazed that she was not, like the queen, repulsed by his disease, and he was touched by her visits. For the first time, they were alone together regularly, and that pleased the king very much. Sometimes passersby in Max-Josephplatz would see them sitting by the window reading together from *Don Quixote*. As the weeks passed, their intimacy slowly grew, and the king's joy and gratitude at Lola's compassion, together with an increasingly explicit erotic undercurrent to their relationship, made Ludwig forget his resolution to put her out of his heart. Not that Ludwig stopped hearing unpleasant stories about Lola. Tann kept him apprised of the rumors about her, including the story that the king kissed the Spanish woman's feet.

Work progressed on the remodeling of the house in the Barerstraße, but General Heideck was nearly at wit's end trying to control Lola's spending. In

147

December he had carefully devised a budget for the 833 florins and 40 kreutzers that Lola received monthly from Ludwig's privy purse, but she had subverted the budget from the beginning, simply sending Heideck the bills for anything she could not afford on her allowance. The general retained supervision of the budget for the new house, but a ruby-and-pearl bracelet costing nearly 500 florins was typical of the sort of thing Lola tried to get him to pay for out of the household furnishings allotment. When she did buy something for the house, it was never what he recommended but always something several times more expensive, including a porcelain service from Paris, a silver tea service for twelve, a punch bowl with glasses for eighteen, and a dinner service for seven.

Heideck had to act. When the 20,000 florins the king had allotted for furnishing the house was paid out, the general notified Ludwig that he was telling all the tradesmen Lola frequented that he would no longer be responsible for her debts. She first felt the effect of the policy when she was in Meyerhofer's shop trying to order more silver. When Herr Meyerhofer explained to her that the terms of payment might have to be changed, Lola flew into a rage and put her fist through the glass door of a cabinet beside her, cutting her hand. The startled silversmith had to stop the bleeding with a handkerchief until a doctor could treat the cut. When Heideck tried to explain to the king that this type of hysterical, uncivilized behavior was making Lola a social pariah, Ludwig responded simply, "This time she punished herself, and it served her right."

Lola actually was trying to improve her public image. The Austrian chargé d'affaires in Munich wrote back to Vienna that she was in fact beginning to become rather popular. Since the riots on the first of March she had been maintaining a low profile, and now she attempted something of a propaganda effort. She always had been an avid newspaper reader, and she had seen accounts of her adventures in Munich in the French and British press. (The Bavarian newspapers had been forbidden to mention her name since December, and she could not read German anyway.) With Ludwig's approval, she sent letters to *The Times* of London and *Le National* in Paris protesting their coverage and explaining that she had been the victim of a vicious Jesuit conspiracy. She disclaimed any personal responsibility for the change of government, as much as she approved of the king's action, and closed her letter to *Le National* by saying that if she had expended her efforts in the cause of the Jesuits, whose motto was "the end sanctifies the means," they would now have not only a St. Ignatius Loyola but also a Sancta Lola. This little bon mot, which the king himself had passed along to Tann months before, struck many Catholics as blasphemous impudence.

More unwelcome press coverage caused her to undertake a major public relations effort. On 20 March the *Pictorial Times* of London published an article about Lola that was largely accurate, saying she was twenty-six or twenty-seven, had been married to a Lieutenant James of the East India Company's army, had spent time in India, and was known for her temper. Accompanying the article was a print of her holding a riding whip.

Lola's relationship with the king clearly would not survive her being unmasked, so she promptly denied the story and presented her own version of her biography. On 31 March she sent nearly identical letters to all the major newspapers in London, Paris, and parts of Germany. Lola's brazen lie read as follows:

Sir,

In consequence of the numerous reports circulated in various papers regarding myself and my family utterly void of foundation or truth, I beg of you through the medium of your widely circulated Journal to insert the following:

I was born at Seville in the year 1823. My father was a Spanish officer in the service of Don Carlos, my mother a lady of Irish extraction, born at the Havannah, and married for the second time to an Irish gentleman, which I suppose is the cause of my being called Irish and sometimes English, "Betsy Watson, Mrs. James, &, &."

I beg leave to say that my name is Maria Dolores Porris Montez and I have never changed that name.

As for my theatrical qualifications, I never had the presumption to think I had any, circumstances obliged me to adopt the Stage as a profession—which profession I have now renounced forever—having become a naturalized Bavarian and intending in future making Munich my residence.

Ludwig was using his convalescence to write more poetry and to prepare the fourth volume of his published poems. One of the sonnets he chose to include for publication, which was reprinted in Bavaria's most prominent newspaper, was an undisguised attack on the ultramontane party:

You have driven me out of paradise,
Forever have you barred it to me,
You who have embittered the days of my life,
But you have not caused me to hate rather than love.
Steadfastness is not yet splintered;

Although my years of youth have drained away,
My youthful strength remains unabated.
Tremble, you who wished me your slave!
You, who oppose me, have no equal.
Your own deeds have condemned you
For ingratitude, the whole catalog of slander.
The clouds disperse, the heavens are aglow.
I hail that decisive moment
That destroyed your power forever.

Lola's house in the Barerstraße was finally ready for her to move in, and it truly was a little palace. The cost of purchase and redecoration had come to nearly 40,000 florins, exceeding the king's original budget by about 20 percent. The house was the first in Munich to have large plate-glass windows, which could be protected by moveable iron shutters. It had a fountain with four carved dolphins, gilded bronze doorknobs for all the rooms, and a doorknob set with turquoise crystal for the front door. Some of the rooms were decorated in Pompeian style, and the whole house was furnished in the height of elegance. There were white marble mantelpieces, a carved piano with inlays of brass, a salon, a dining room, a ladies' room, a "Don Quixote" room, a yellow room, and a green room. Most impressive of all was the crystal staircase leading to the boudoir, dressing room, and bedroom on the upper floor. Ludwig let Lola have an Etruscan vase from the Royal Collections to decorate her house, as well as an outstanding old copy of a Raphael Madonna and a selection of books from the Royal Library.

At last, on 26 April, King Ludwig was well enough to leave his apartments. His reappearance in the theater was greeted with an enthusiastic demonstration by the audience, with the exception of Lola, who remained seated. Perhaps this was meant to demonstrate her intimacy with the monarch, but her impertinence only scandalized the public once more. At the suggestion of Tann, Lola wrote yet another letter to a newspaper, this time to the widely circulated *Allgemeine Zeitung* in Augsburg. She appealed to the public's sense of justice and fair play by branding as a dishonorable slanderer anyone who spread stories about her without being able to furnish proof.

In spite of the continuing discord sown by Lola, this was one of the happiest times for the king and his favorite. Spring had finally arrived after a long, cold winter, and the two spent many afternoons walking together in the magnificent gardens of the Nymphenburg Palace, on the edge of Munich. Lola's new house gave them more privacy than they had had either in her rented rooms or in the palace, and they could spend their evenings alone together in seclusion.

The new ministry was making efforts at formulating new political initiatives, particularly in the area of legal reform, but it was dogged by what was generally seen as its unholy origin. Maurer had at least obtained the king's promise that no minister would be required to visit the Spanish woman. The new ministers' careful avoidance of any contact with her annoyed Lola, particularly because she had been responsible for getting them into office, and her hostility to Maurer and his colleges grew.

Ludwig kept abreast of all governmental business, but now his free time was increasingly devoted to Lola. He had ordered Stieler to paint a second portrait of Lola for the Gallery of Beauties, and, as before, the king attended all of the sittings at the artist's studio. This time the former dancer was portrayed in a black velvet dress, as the king had first seen her, with a collar of white lace and with black lace over her hair. Stieler's portraits were fine likenesses, but their poses often had a classical repose that sometimes bordered on lifelessness; this portrait, however, masterfully suggested the energy of Lola Montez with a subtle offset of her shoulders and left arm, which gave the figure a springlike tension. She appeared almost to be preparing to lunge at something off the left side of the frame. Stieler was a good colorist, and here he expertly modulated what could almost be a study in black and white with the red of the sofa (whose form emphasized the shift of the figure to the right), of the flowers above Lola's right ear, and of her lips. The portrait is justifiably one of his most famous.

The royal family usually left Munich for the summer and returned before Oktoberfest. This year the queen had announced that she would take the waters at Franzenbad, and the king was making plans to go first to Bad Brückenau and then on to Aschaffenburg, two of his favorite retreats. And he wanted to spend the summer with Lola, away from the gossips and spies. His advisers had gotten him to agree to wait until fall to try to penetrate the social resistance to Lola in Munich, but he would not be convinced that he should not spend the summer with her. A riding accident early in May had seriously injured Friedrich Nußbammer, and the absence of the young lieutenant from Lola's circle probably facilitated the growing intimacy between the king and Lola. There was no longer any talk between them of "purest love" and "sweet innocence," as there had been at New Year's.

Although she caused enough outrageous incidents to keep the gossips busy and herself ostracized, Lola was not the object of public anger and bitterness that she had been in February and March. Her behavior certainly was less provocative than it had been, but it also seems likely that the agitation against her by the conservative forces had abated. They appeared willing to bide their time, waiting for Lola and the new ministry to commit the blunders they felt sure would come.

The abatement of agitation against the Spanish woman caused new seekers of the king's favor to flutter about Lola's flame. Among them were a minor official in the War Ministry, Johann von Mussinan, and his son Oscar, who had a job in the Topographical Office. The son worshipped at Lola's feet, and the father was a gossip and intriguer of limited intelligence and imagination. A more substantial recruit to Lola's cause was Franz von Berks, the 54-year-old director of the provincial government of Niederbayern. Ten years earlier Berks had been a valued aide to the principal minister who had preceded Abel, Prince Ludwig von Öttingen-Wallerstein. After the fall of Wallerstein's government in 1837 and the advent of the conservative Catholic regime, Berks had been relegated to the provincial government at Landshut. Interior Minister Zenetti had been one of his colleagues there and thought him a superficial windbag, an ambitious charlatan, and a shifty intriguer. Now Berks decided to lash his hopes to Lola's rising star. Although the social boycott of Lola was far from ended, she began to seem almost popular.

King Ludwig was riding a wave of popularity himself. Some of the measures of the new cabinet, such as the separation of the courts from the administrative apparatus and the reform of some of the university regulations, had met with widespread public approval; and because the people knew that the king had the final word on any change, they were grateful to him as well as to the "ministry of the dawn."

The partial dissipation of the atmosphere of hostility around them must have contributed to the increasing harmony between Lola and Ludwig, which in turn seems to have emboldened the king finally to press his now overtly sexual interest in his beloved. On 15 June Ludwig bid farewell to Queen Therese as she departed for Franzenbad via Eger. They would see each other again in about ten weeks. Two days later, Ludwig spent the night with Lola. It was the only time they were ever able to spend an entire night together, and, because of Lola's constant complaints of ill health and the danger of pregnancy, it was one of the few times they had sex. What Ludwig had been certain was his spiritual communion with a new muse had degenerated into what nearly everyone had always thought it was: the familiar obsession of an aging man to posses both the affection and the body of a beautiful young woman.

More than ever the king must have wanted to believe that Lola belonged to him alone, but Lola made no effort to conceal the handsome young men around her, and the king was jealous. Ludwig and Lola were about to travel to Bad Brückenau, separately, to keep scandal at a minimum; but Lola insisted on delaying her departure to visit Lieutenant Nußbammer, who had just undergone abdominal surgery, an ordeal that in those days—before anesthesia, asepsis, and antibiotics—was not only tremendously painful but also often fatal. She even persuaded Ludwig to accompany her to the young man's bedside and to spend an hour and a half there, which the king must have done with some reluctance.

And on 18 June, after the king had spent the night with her, Lola had some visitors from the university. Members of one the student fraternities, the Palatia, called at the Barerstraße that evening and were enchanted by Lola's beauty, wit, and charm. One of them was the senior, the highest officer of the Palatia, a twenty-one-year-old law student named Elias Peißner—Fritz, to his friends. Although his impulses seem to have been more liberal than those of the majority of students at the University of Munich, Peißner's initial feelings for the Spanish woman appear to have been nothing more than the awe of a naïve young man for a beautiful, sophisticated woman rather than any interest in her possible liberal influence on the politics of Bavaria.

The encounter was to have immediate and serious consequences for Peißner and his companions because some students walking past Lola's house as she was entertaining her guests observed through the tall parlor windows not only that the senior of the Palatia and his friends had crossed Lola's threshold but also that they had, in a playful gesture, put one of their Palatia caps on her thick, black hair.

The report was carried back to the other members of Palatia, and Peißner and his fellows were accused before an assembly of the corps not only of consorting with the Spanish woman but of allowing her to dishonor the Palatia cap. The accused either were expelled or resigned in disgust, depending on whose account you read. The elder Mussinan suggested to them that they form their own fraternity, which would serve as a guard of honor for Lola Montez and be under her patronage. This was the origin of the Alemannia, a fraternity that would be ostracized by all other students but which would play a more important role in Bavarian history than any other student organization.

The development of the new fraternity was delayed by its patroness's departure for Bad Brückenau. Early on 22 June she took the train to Nürnberg, where she received a friendly reception from city officials and was given a tour of the scenic high points of the old town. According to one report, the city fathers were eager to please her in the hope that she could influence the king to build a direct rail line between their city and Würzburg.

Her itinerary called for her to travel on to Bamberg and spend the night there; but she arrived in Bamberg later than planned, and the welcome by the municipal officials seems to have been much less impressive than what she had received in Nürnberg. It had been a long day (the train journey from Munich to Nürnberg took seven and a half hours, and it was a further two hours to Bamberg), and Lola is reported to have made some intemperate remarks about Bamberg and its hospitality. Whether or not this was a precipitating cause, the crowd at the station grew hostile, and the air was filled with whistling, insults, and flying stones and horse manure.

Lola asked one of her hosts whether there were monasteries in Bamberg. After being told that there were two, she is reported to have remarked that she should have known this was so, because it was clear that the Jesuits were in control. This remark further enraged the crowd, which pursued her carriage to the Bamberger Hof, where she was to spend the night. The mob became so unruly that the Bamberger Hof was forced to close and fortify its doors. When it became clear that the unrest was not about to abate, Lola decided not to spend the night after all. A carriage was prepared to take her to Würzburg and then on through the night to Bad Brückenau, and she departed amid catcalls and jeers.

Ludwig was so angered when he heard Lola's account of how she had been insulted in Bamberg that he ordered the city fathers to send a delegation to her to beg her pardon for the treatment she had been accorded. The king was looking forward to a summer idyll with his love, but many circumstances, including Lola's mood, served to frustrate his hopes. Crown Prince Maximilian and his wife were also visiting Bad Brückenau during the early days of the king's stay, but the crown prince refused to meet Lola, so the king had to divide his time between them. Ludwig's old friend Heinrich von der Tann was there, too, and the king let him escort Lola about and introduce her to the other visitors at the resort while he was himself busy with Maximilian. To compensate for their inability to have much intimate time together, Lola sent Ludwig pieces of flannel that she had worn under her clothes, next to her body.

When the king did have time with Lola, she was high-handed, demanding, and irritable. It was not enough for her that he had just named her friend Berks to the Council of State. She was angered by the continuing social boycott directed against her, and she insisted that Ludwig carry out his promise to her to make her a countess. The nobility must learn that she was one of them; her noble Spanish pride demanded it. The king's advisers had urged him to wait until the fall, when things might have calmed down, to try to bring Lola into society, and Ludwig had told Maurer that he had no intention of making Lola a countess any time soon; but now she was pressuring him, and his reluctance aroused her indignation. She began to treat him with less and less affection and respect, practically ordering him about before the horrified Tann.

On the evening of 20 July her behavior finally became too much even for the lovestruck king. He burst out at her in a fit of anger and then turned and walked out of her apartments. Tann, who witnessed the scene, immediately remonstrated with Lola for provoking the king, but she went into a screaming rage against him that was heard all over the neighborhood. The king, already regretting his anger, sent a servant to inquire whether Lola was suffering from nerve fever, and then he wrote a note to Tann, in French, obviously so that he could show it to Lola.

> My dear Tann,
> The brusque tone I used to my beloved Lola was indeed crude, I confess it, tell her so. My feelings had been hurt by the tone she adopted yesterday, and not just yesterday, a tone that was the opposite of a loving being. That explains but it doesn't justify. I hope she will forgive me, but also that she will treat me differently, not like one of her servants but like someone who deeply loves her and is her true friend. If I would be welcome to her, she should let me know.

Lola made no reply, allowing Ludwig to spend an anxious night. The next day she had a carriage loaded with her luggage (empty, according to one account), ordered post horses, and let it be known that she was leaving Bad Brückenau and Bavaria, too. When word reached Ludwig, he panicked, racing first to Tann, who saw that the king was likely to follow Lola Montez to the end of the earth. Then the king flew to Lola herself, pleading with her not to abandon him. But Lola announced that she could not remain amid spies and enemies, so if she were to stay, Tann would have to go. She had no trouble convincing Ludwig that Tann's remonstrance to her had prevented their reconciliation, and that was enough for the king to order his old friend to leave.

Once Lola had her way, her mood changed dramatically, and she was warmer and more affectionate to Ludwig than she had been for some time. The next morning Tann left for Aschaffenburg, and Lola appeared triumphantly at the king's luncheon table. That afternoon the king himself took the reins of one of his carriages and drove with Lola into the countryside. Their reconciliation was complete.

There were many stolen kisses—on her mouth, on her hands, and on her feet. The king had developed an erotic fascination with the dancer's feet, and it baffled him because never before had he been excited by a woman's feet. Perhaps it was because Lola usually denied him her body, warning of her frailty and the danger of pregnancy, that Ludwig's erotic impulses were directed to her feet; it excited him to kiss them and take them into his mouth. Now his Lolitta was truly his once more, and he would keep his promise to make her a countess.

Back in Munich the public was marveling at Stieler's new portrait of Lola, which was on display at the Art Association. The general feeling was that he had surpassed himself, though the work did nothing to change public opinion about the sitter. Josephine von Kaulbach, wife of the painter Wilhelm, wrote to her husband in Berlin that Stieler's portrait of Lola was the past and that his own grim portrayal was the future. Considering her husband's portrait of Lola prompted Josephine to reevaluate the oil portrait sketch of the king that he had done four years earlier and which, like the portrait of Lola, remained in the artist's studio:

> You know I was never happy with your portrait of the king, it never appeared worthy enough to me; . . . But I tell you, you have a sharp eye that sees into the human soul; this man could not have been more truly and better captured. . . . I have to confess, I'm so impressed by the spiritual likeness; the whole movement expresses a wobbling, an insecurity, the tremendous flutteriness of his nature; . . . Hasn't he shown now how changeable, unsteady, insecure, and vacillating he is in his disposition. . . . This striking portrait will have great meaning for posterity, the whole biography of this curious man is contained in this picture. Don't laugh at me. And the portrait of the Spanish woman, after frequent, long contemplation, has great meaning; it is impossible to stand before this picture and joke about the person, you really can't laugh; it makes you serious and sad, and this mood, this seriousness permeates the picture; another destiny, but an incredibly sober, tragic destiny; . . . you probe into the innermost depths of a person, and that makes your portraits classics.

Munich was also talking about the publication of the fourth volume of the king's poetry. Not only did it contain the sonnet obviously directed against the Catholic conservatives, but it also contained an undisguised hymn of allegiance to Lola Montez that seemed to be anything but vacillating and unsteady:

> To L***
> I believe thee, and when appearances deceive,
> Thou art faithful and ever true,
> The inner voice betrays me not,
> It says: Your loving feeling is right.
> . . . .
> The iron hardens beneath the hammer's blows,
> It becomes the hardest steel.
> When they array themselves to tear thee from me,
> They simply chain me all the firmer to my choice.

In Bad Brückenau the idyll suffered another interruption, this time when Lola fell seriously ill with fever and chills. The illness was probably a recurrence of malaria she had contracted in India, and Ludwig's personal physician successfully treated her with large doses of quinine. The plan was for Lola to travel first to Würzburg and then back to Munich, while the king went on to Aschaffenburg, where he would be joined by the queen in the fall.

The king and Lola went their separate ways from Bad Brückenau on 4 August, and after his arrival in Aschaffenburg the king wrote to Maurer, "Señora Lola Montez is to be created a countess. I want to hear no objections whatsoever because I have a royal promise to fulfill." To Lola he wrote, "This morning I wrote the order to Maurer to prepare your nomination as countess so it can be ready on my birthday (the 25th of this month). Until the day of publication, until the 25th, it has to be a secret. . . . I can do without the sun above, but not without Lolitta shining in my soul."

The minister was stunned when the king's message arrived in his office. He was still struggling to establish a new direction with his government and to build its credibility with the public and other governments. He had reluctantly signed the woman's naturalization at the end of February, but that fact had never been made public, though there were rumors that he had done what no minister in the previous government was willing to do. If he signed Lola's countess diploma, he would be publicly branded and politically crippled.

Maurer replied to the king that he would make no objections; a man's word, particularly a king's word, should be holy. But he told Ludwig that he was stunned because the king had assured him only a few months ago that he was not contemplating making Mlle. Montez a countess. Maurer had heard that Lola was saying that the king would make her a countess at either Bad Brückenau or Aschaffenburg, that the ministers would be forced to call on her, and that she would rule in Bavaria. He had not believed it, but now that the first part had come true, he feared that the other assertions would follow.

The minister reminded the king that any cabinet member who called on Lola Montez would be shunned by the members of the Landtag, which would make it impossible for him to perform his ministerial functions. He suggested that the king was preparing to squeeze him like a lemon and then cast him aside. Perhaps the best solution would be to form an entirely new government. He would make up the diploma for Mlle. Montez, Maurer told the king, and hold it until Ludwig named a minister willing to countersign it. Maurer warned the king that although he had rescued Ludwig from an abyss in February, the king had for some time been heading for a second, deeper one. The minister thought it would be best if Ludwig began looking for someone to replace him.

The king replied defensively that what he was doing was completely constitutional and that he expected a devoted servant like Maurer to cooperate and not force him to find a new minister. Above all, Ludwig wrote, the king must keep his word; everything else was secondary to that. "I have no intention of forcing any of my acting ministers to visit L. M. Baron von der Tann is here with me, and L. M., who repeatedly expressed a strong desire to visit Aschaffenburg with me, is not here, a proof that she does not rule. The king reigns and rules, and I hope that Maurer will not think me so ignoble that I would wish to treat him like a lemon (that I never did), and I don't believe that he will disobey me."

Maurer saw that the king was determined to make Lola a countess and that his signature on the diploma could effectively end his political career. But if he were going to be driven from public service, it would be only prudent to take something with him. The minister wrote the king that he would, reluctantly, prepare the diploma, but warned that it would be taken as an insult by the nobility and ought to be delayed until after the next meeting of the Landtag. The king would still be keeping his word. Providing the signature, Maurer pleaded, would have serious personal consequences. The ultramontanes had already used every opportunity to persecute him, and now he could view his future only with great apprehension, he wrote. After Maurer's many sacrifices for Ludwig, it would be simple justice if the king named him to the heredity nobility in the Reichsrat and gave him an estate commensurate with that rank. Bestowing that honor would only be a paying back of faithful service and the losses the minister had suffered. The king would be setting himself a monument, Maurer wrote. The minister further suggested that it would be appropriate, in light of the great sacrifice his signature on the diploma would mean, if the king made Maurer's son, a distinguished legal scholar, an extraordinary professor at the university with a salary of 800 or 1,000 florins per year.

The king was enraged not only by Maurer's barely disguised extortion attempt but also by his delaying tactics. Ludwig was determined to make Lola a countess on his birthday. "I demand obedience," he wrote, "especially from my ministers." He wanted the diploma with Maurer's signature. "If you don't do it, it will happen anyway, which you don't seem to realize, even if it is to my own detriment. *I shall not yield.* If you nevertheless refuse to sign, *I command* that the diploma, with everything else in order, be sent to me at once." Maurer signed the diploma and dispatched it to Aschaffenburg. The king did ultimately name the minister's son to a professorship, though not at the elevated salary his father had suggested, but the rest of the extortionate demands were ignored.

In the meantime, Lola had stirred up another hornet's nest. Her reception in Würzburg had been reasonably civil. Curious crowds followed her, but they were not openly hostile; some citizens called on her, and a dinner was planned in her honor at the house of Baron Ziegler, a local notable. Mussinan had accompanied her from Bad Brückenau, Berks had arrived from Munich to serve as her escort, and a local attorney, Karl von Günther, and his wife, Fanny, had been attempting to ingratiate themselves with Lola. On the afternoon of 6 August, Lola, Berks, Günther, and some others, followed by a crowd of about two hundred curious Würzburgers, headed for a promenade in the Court Garden. A military sentry was posted at the gate to the garden, and as Lola and her entourage approached, the guard noticed that they were leading Lola's lapdog Zampa. The sentry stopped the group at the gate and pointed to a sign that forbade smoking, walking on the grass, and dogs in the garden. One of the men picked up the dog to carry it, as he had on an earlier visit to the garden, but that did not satisfy this sentry; no dogs meant no dogs, carried or walking. Lola objected, and the exasperated soldier, who probably didn't understand Lola's French, reached for the dog or for her—or for both, depending on which witness told the story. Lola drew back and delivered a solid blow to the side of the sentry's face, which first surprised him and then left him angry. As he was about to react, Günther grabbed him from behind and pinned his arms, and the party pushed by into the garden. Part of the curious crowd began to jeer and whistle as the rattled little group tried to promenade casually about the garden, and the sentry went for assistance. Lola and her party soon decided to return to her hotel, and they left the Court Garden by another gate.

In no time the word spread all around Würzburg of Lola's attack on the sentry, and now the crowds following her became hostile. Her carriage was pursued by a whistling, shouting mob as she drove that evening from her hotel to Baron von Ziegler's house on the Domplatz, where dinner was being held in her honor. The howling continued during the meal, and finally Lola's empty carriage was sent back to her hotel in a successful effort to decoy the crowd away from the house. But the noisemakers roamed the streets into the evening, and the police and gendarmes patrolled to try to restore order. Lola finally slipped back to her hotel and wrote the king a letter, telling him that five thousand people had been in the streets whistling and yelling, and that "it doesn't surprise me at all because you must know the number of Jesuits there are here, and the archbishop [sic] is their leader." She continued, "Everyone begged me not to say anything to you about this, but it's my duty to you that you know what the others know and that the king isn't more ignorant than anyone else of what is going on in his own country. Farewell, my much and ever beloved Louis. Love me always as I love you, which is with all my heart and soul, for life, your faithful Lolitta." The next day she returned to Munich.

Ludwig replied, "It's a pity what happened at Würzburg—you did well to tell me about it. . . . I reread your letter and at the last words, 'Louis . . . always as I love you,' I kissed it and kissed it—*The world doesn't have the power to separate me from you.*" And he reminded her to wear the flannel in the two places next to her body as he had asked and then send it to him.

Although her fevers were recurring, Lola received a visit in the Barerstraße from Elias Peißner, now the senior of the Alemannia, the fraternity formed to support her. They had chosen their colors: red, gold, and blue; and Lola promised to see to it not only that they received the king's special protection but also that each of them would have a cap and fraternity insignia of the finest tailoring. Peißner was in awe of this beautiful woman, and as she sat between him and Mussinan on the sofa in her parlor, he was careful not to brush her skirts with his knees. At the end of his short visit, she offered him her hand and said, "Don't forget me altogether," because he was returning home for vacation. He would not forget her, and she would not forget him.

The king wrote something to Lola every day they were apart. He wrote on fine gilt-edged paper in sheets folded over to make four pages. Each day he wrote something more to her, and when the four pages were full, he mailed the letter and began the next. He wanted Lola to write a little to him each day, but she never did. He wanted her to number her letters consecutively, the way he did, and to tell him each time she wrote which letters of his she had received, but she never did. He wanted her to answer each of his questions, which he frequently numbered for her, but she never did. Ludwig struggled continually to bring into Lola's life a little of his own obsession with order, system, and budgeting, but he never succeeded.

Ludwig was generous to his favorite, but the rumors of his expenditures on her far surpassed reality and contributed to the impression that the king was bleeding dry the royal coffers for Lola. Only weeks after the dancer arrived in Munich, gossip was declaring that Ludwig had already given her 180,000 florins, which was more than he would spend on her over the next two years. In February gossip had whispered that the king had given Lola 40,000 florins to console her for the government's opposition to her naturalization; now when she returned from Bad Brückenau, the story circulated in Munich that she had come back with 70,000 florins worth of new jewelry from her royal friend.

King Ludwig's birthday was approaching, and Lola finally would be elevated to the Bavarian nobility. The diploma, a multipage masterpiece of the calligraphic art, was already mounted in a blue velvet cover with a blue and white braided cord leading to the round metal box containing the wax impression of the great seal of King Ludwig I. Opposite the page with the king's signature was a handpainted representation of Lola's arms as the Countess of Landsfeld. The four quarters of the shield had a sword on a red field, a rampant crowned lion on a blue field, a silver dolphin on a blue field, and a pale red rose on a white field. Above the shield was the nine-pointed crown of a countess. Ludwig gave it to a courier to be delivered to Lola on the morning of 25 August along with a note to her: "Countess of Landsfeld, for me, my ever dear Lolitta, on my birthday I give myself the gift of giving you your diploma as a countess. I hope it has a good effect on your social situation, but it can't change the government. Lolitta can't love, much less esteem a king who doesn't himself govern, and your Luis wants to be loved by his Lolitta. Enemies, especially your female enemies, will be furious to see you a countess, and it will be that much more *necessary* for you to be modest and prudent and to avoid all occasions for tumult, to avoid places where there are a lot of people. It's possible enemies will try to cause disturbances in order to make attempts on your life. Be careful!"

The king's birthday, the Bavarian national holiday, was a day of triumph for the new Countess of Landsfeld. She drove to church in the morning to offer thanks for her elevation, and that evening she had a dinner for two dozen guests, with her diploma displayed on the sideboard. Afterward the party gathered around a bust of King Ludwig in her garden as a band played and fireworks lit the scene.

There were rumors not only that the king had obtained Queen Therese's permission to make Lola a countess but also that the queen would herself invest the countess the Order of Therese, the highest Bavarian distinction for women of the nobility. Astonishingly, the story was generally believed in Munich, reported by the ambassadors there to their respective capitals, and repeated in the foreign press. Only when it filtered back to the queen at her summer residence was the rumor denied, but the denial did not always reach as far as the rumor had.

Ludwig wrote to the new countess that both the last thing he had done in his sixty-first year and the first thing he had done in his sixty-second year was to kiss her portrait. "Except when I am sleeping, breathing and thinking of you are the same for me," he told her. "It's true, absence destroys a passion if it is weak, but it increases a strong one. *The whole world has not the ability to separate Luis from his Lolitta.*"

But Ludwig's devotion was no protection from the wrath of his favorite. A week after the king's birthday, someone in Lola's circle brought to her attention that her elevation to the nobility, like all royal decrees, had no legal effect until it was published in the official gazette. Lola was livid to learn that she wasn't a countess at all, and her anger crackled through the letter she dashed off to "Luis":

> You should know me well enough to realize that above everything else, I am proud and that I am not like the people who have no spirit—You have given me a *title* of your country, which was very well and nice of you—but if this title is not *announced officially* in the papers in accordance and in regularity with and conforming to the order of all your other acts, you should not be surprised if I for my part don't want to accept this *title*, which you have given me as if you were ashamed of your own act—and which you

and your ministers have been afraid to publish, as is done with each title
that you are gracious enough to grant—

You have humiliated me in this as I have never have been. . . . You have
caused me great pain and it is the greatest triumph for my enemies.

I hope you will rectify this error if you love me as I love you.

Your faithful Lolitta Montez

The king promptly sent an order to Berks, who was rapidly making himself indispensable to both Lola and Ludwig, for the publication of the enno-
blement in the official gazette.

Lola had more attacks of fever, but when she was well enough to write,
she peppered Ludwig with advice about matters of state or complaints about
the conspiracies being hatched against her. She and Berks saw to it that her
followers received royal favors, and both of them interceded with the king on
royal appointments in the army and bureaucracy. None of these matters was
of great importance, and the king was too jealous of his own prerogatives to
allow Lola to govern him in significant decisions, but altogether they created
the appearance that the Countess of Landsfeld was manipulating the king.
Perhaps even worse, they fostered resentment and undermined morale
within both the uniformed services and the bureaucracy, where promotions
and pay increases under King Ludwig had been notoriously difficult to obtain
because of his indefatigable budget-cutting.

As she did her best to reward her friends, so Lola worked to punish her
enemies. She repeatedly warned the king that the interior minister, Zenetti,
was in league with the Jesuits. According to one report, the countess informed
Zenetti that his days as a minister were numbered after he had grown impatient with her constant visits to his office with extraordinary requests and
had told her that he had no time for her personal affairs. More than once she
let Ludwig know that she thought Maurer was incompetent; his supreme
political sacrifice in signing her naturalization document and her diploma did
not compensate in her mind for his insistence that no member of the cabinet
should call on the new countess.

The ambitious Prince Wallerstein had been given a summer leave from his
post as ambassador in Paris. He would remain in Munich because the king
had been forced to call a special meeting of the Landtag for September, and
the prince was a member of the Reichsrat, the upper house. Wallerstein
sensed that his opportunity to return to power might at last be coming, and
he was moving with caution and cunning. He knew that any open contact
with the Countess of Landsfeld meant political and social ostracism, but he

must also have recognized that a minister without at least her tacit allegiance would see his royal support undermined, as Maurer was learning. Berks had been a valuable assistant to Wallerstein during the prince's service as principal minister ten years before, and Wallerstein probably used his former protégé to assure the countess of his favorable attitude toward her aspirations. There were even rumors that the prince was secretly visiting the Barerstraße house.

Lola apparently knew Wallerstein, at least by reputation, and she neither liked nor trusted him. But she came to see that there was no hope of increasing her power or acceptance in Munich as long as the Maurer cabinet was in power. The Maurer government was already generally regarded as moribund, except by the most ardent liberals. The minister's signature on the countess's diploma had buried the last hope for the ministry of the dawn, and Zenetti and Zu Rhein both attempted to resign. The king rejected their resignations because there was no time before the Landtag session to reorganize the government, but it became evident that the government could not long survive the end of the legislative session.

Ludwig himself tried to avoid discussing matters of state with Lola. His letters to her mentioned the little events of his daily life, how he avoided kissing any of his in-laws good-bye on the lips so that his would remain true to her, his walks, the weather, how often he thought of her, the rare occasions when he dreamed of her, how he wore the flannel she had sent him under his clothes and turned it so that he would be sure to have the side that had touched her body against his. Repeatedly he asked if she had worn the flannel "in both places."

Lola's letters, on the other hand, were increasingly political, filled with praise of Berks and other protégés and with criticism of the director of the royal theater, of Maurer, of Zenetti, of Wallerstein, and even of Prince Karl, the king's brother. She forwarded reports of cabals and treason. Berks and Mussinan industriously wrote the king letters filled with the gossip of Munich, reports of plots against him and Lola, of petty insults and calculated snubs.

As the king's return to Munich approached, he seems to have been torn by conflicting emotions. His health began to suffer, his chronic migraine headaches returned, and he kept to his bed. He was receiving anonymous obscene letters about his relationship with the Countess of Landsfeld, and they troubled him. He knew that back in Munich, with the Landtag in session, he could again be in a political and social cauldron, and he must have regretted the passing of the last idyllic days in Aschaffenburg. At the same time, he longed to be with Lola; he was already planning their reunion. He and the queen would meet and return together to the capital on 7 October, and the next day would be the anniversary of the morning when he had first received Lola Montez. He wanted to come to her early in the morning in the Barerstraße and to see her again completely alone, "without man or dog" present, he wrote. He asked her to tell him just when she went to sleep and when she awoke. They could continue reading *Don Quixote* together. In their two months apart he had written her twenty letters, with entries for every day.

As much as he loved Lola, Ludwig knew that life with her was not always easy. In his last letter from Aschaffenburg he tried to anticipate trouble by telling her what he did *not* want from her. He wrote a draft first to make sure he put it as gently as he could: "My very dear Lolitta, you can make me happy and unhappy. Unhappy if you presume to govern, that I must obey your will. I want to listen to you, and I'm capable of supporting ideas, if they are good ones, that aren't my own with the same fervor as if they came from me. You make me unhappy if every day you talk to me of business, so that instead of relaxing after having worked so much, it all continues with the people around you, who make one request of you after another. I don't speak of the worst of all, of unfaithfulness; the noble character of Lolitta isn't capable of that. Make happy the one who wishes to see you happy."

On the first of October, the beginning of his fiscal year, the king compiled his personal accounts. This year his calculations showed him that in the twelve months since her arrival he had expended exactly 100,992 florins and 53 kreutzers on his beloved blue-eyed Spaniard. That apparently did not seem excessive, and he ordered his private secretary to double the Countess of Landsfeld's annual stipend, effective 1 October, to 20,000 florins a year. Now that she was a countess, she would need to maintain an appropriate household. And perhaps the king hoped that with double the income Lola would be able to keep within a budget.

On the evening of the king's return to Munich, Lola preempted the planned early-morning anniversary reunion at her house by secretly making her way into the royal apartments to surprise Ludwig. He was touched and overjoyed. The king soon found, however, that his new Countess of Landsfeld was not only far more demanding and imperious than Lola Montez had been, but she rarely had time for him except when she wanted something. He could not admit it to himself, but his dream of love began to become an almost hallucinatory nightmare.

If Ludwig had ever sincerely harbored the hope that with patience and persistence he could win over his queen so that Lola could obtain her cherished goal—presentation at court and social acceptance—his illusion was ended by a letter he received from Therese a week after they returned to Munich. Although they saw each other daily, the queen chose to put this matter in writing, perhaps because she wanted her thoughts to be absolutely clear, perhaps because she could not bring herself to speak the words:

> What a loving duty it is to me, under all circumstances of life, to maintain for you, *untroubled*, your domestic happiness must have been proven to you during the final weeks of our stay at Aschaffenburg *because at that time I* found a notice in the official gazette of an event that I, with my knowledge of your character, had thought impossible, and by which I was deeply pained. Far be it from me to let you hear a reproach over this matter here. The purpose of these lines is nevertheless by means of a word candidly spoken in *the present moment* to prevent a further possible indulgence through which the peace of our family circle would be forever disrupted. I owe it to my honor as a woman—which is dearer to me than life itself—she whom you have raised in rank never—under no circumstances, to see face to face;—should she seek to gain admission at court through a promise of yours, you can tell her, you know it for a fact—yes, from my mouth: the queen, the mother of your children, would never receive her.
>
> In this confusion, in order to prevent any future trouble, I see it as my *duty* to tell you openly now of my absolutely unshakable resolve. And now, not one word more, either written or spoken, of this difficult matter. You will find me, as before, cheerful, grateful for every joy you give me, and ever watchfully endeavoring to maintain for you, my Ludwig, the untroubled tranquillity of our home.
>
> Your Therese

Now the king was in the unpleasant situation of knowing that Lola's greatest ambition was, for the foreseeable future, impossible for him to fulfill and that he would eventually have to tell her so.

Ludwig's hopes for tenderness and quiet hours reading Cervantes with Lola were dashed by the realization that his beloved was a very busy woman. The fraternity that Mussinan had called into being, the Alemannia, had recruited about fifteen students at the university, and they had become something like a uniformed bodyguard for the countess (in addition to the nine gendarmes who were now assigned to guard her and her house). Lieutenant Nußbammer was finally gone, transferred to Bamberg; Lola had been seen abusing him in public again, and gossip said it was because his injuries made it physically impossible for him to satisfy the Spanish woman.

The intensely jealous Ludwig probably was relieved at the departure of his rival Nußbammer, but the Alemannen more than took the lieutenant's place. They paraded everywhere with Lola, spent evenings in her parlor or at their pub, Rottmann's in the bazaar, and made day excursions with her into the country. The countess rarely was seen without at least a couple of good-looking young men at her side. In local parlance, they were "Lola's harem" or the "Lolianer"; and under the mores of the time, any young woman, countess or not, who spent her time constantly in the company of single young men who were not her blood relatives was hardly more than a whore.

In Munich, as elsewhere, Lola flouted standards of moral conduct while at the same time raging over the lack of respect she was shown. Perhaps her struggle against society's constraints could be seen as a revolt against the injustice and hypocrisy inherent in a social order where women had relatively little right of self-determination and where the appearance of morality was far more important than its actual practice. But Lola's contemporaries recognized her as not so much an idealistic rebel out to reform society as a willful and unconventional egotist who aspired to be the idol of the very society she mocked and scandalized. The Austrian ambassador to Paris had privately sent a harshly one-sided yet perceptive assessment to Prince Metternich in Vienna: "Lola Montez is a person without education, ill-mannered, without fixed ideas, whose capricious game can't last. She is more unrestrained and sensation-addicted than depraved and ambitious." But now she had discovered ambition.

Lola's self-esteem was enhanced by the arrival in early October of George Henry Francis, a London journalist and acquaintance of hers, who had come to see whether there was a good story in what she was up to in Munich. The result of his visit was a long article, "The King of Bavaria, Munich, and Lola Montez," which appeared in *Fraser's Magazine* in London and which, though Francis expressed reservations about the propriety of her relationship with the king, helped to establish the legend of Lola Montez as a liberal thinker who introduced an enlightened regime to benighted Bavaria, where, Francis noted, "the customs and manners of the people are much more primitive than among us." Although the article contains many gross inaccuracies, its portrait of Lola in October 1847 rings true in many respects:

As is usual with women of an active mind, she is a great talker; but, although an egotist, and with her full share of the vanity of her sex, she understands the art of conversation sufficiently never to be wearisome. Indeed, although capable of violent, but evanescent passions,—of deep, but not revengeful animosities, and occasionally of trivialities and weaknesses often found in persons suddenly raised to great power,—she can be, and almost always is, a very charming person, and a delightful companion. Her manners are distinguished, she is a graceful and hospitable hostess, and she understands the art of dressing to perfection.

The fair despot is passionately fond of homage. She is merciless in her man-killing propensities. . . . On the other hand, Lola Montez has many faults, which history has recorded of others in like situations. She loves power for its own sake; she is too hasty, and too steadfast in her dislikes; she has not sufficiently learnt to curb the passion which seems natural to her Spanish blood; she is capricious, and quite capable, when her temper is inflamed, of rudeness, which, however, she is the first to regret and to apologize for. . . . Everyone whom she does not like, her prejudice transforms into a Jesuit . . . but these restless suspicions are a weakness quite incompatible with the strength of mind, the force of character, and determination of purpose, she exhibits in other respects.

Maurer's ministry of the dawn was stumbling through the Landtag session, but its fate was already sealed through the despair of its ministers, the king's discontent, and Lola's persistent sniping. On 15 October, Lola convinced Ludwig that it was time to act on his resolve to dismiss Maurer, and the next day Prince Wallerstein and Berks (who was now unquestionably Lola's chief political adviser and emissary) met privately to discuss formation of a new cabinet when the Landtag adjourned.

At the end of October, word spread of the arrival at the Goldener Hahn Hotel of a distinguished visitor for the Countess of Landsfeld. He was the Baron de los Valles, famous as a comrade in arms of Don Carlos, the pretender to the throne of Spain. The baron was a French royalist who had attached himself to the pretender's cause and gained a rather hollow title as a reward. Despite the baronage, Los Valles had fallen on hard times and now survived by acting discreetly as an itinerant wine merchant. His arrival in Munich was occasioned by the hope that his old friend Lola might help him get an order from the king and other noble customers in the Bavarian capital.

The presence of the baron at Lola's dinners and soirées imparted a distinguished air to her salon, at least until word got around that Los Valles was now a tradesman. Then the baron himself grew troubled by Lola's behavior. He was shocked to see Lola flirting outrageously with a young Pole in her entourage named Eustache Karwowski, first encouraging him with signs of affection, then evading him and even demeaning him before her other admirers. Matters grew worse when appeals from Lola and Mussinan brought the senior of the Alemannen, Fritz Peißner, back to Munich from a long stay at home. The countess pointedly seated Peißner at her right on every occasion and made him her obvious favorite, much to the distress of the baron, who was both insulted that he was denied the place of honor himself and concerned that she was so obviously provoking Karwowski to jealous violence. Lola made the baron's conservatism an object of humor, though Los Valles was not at all amused, particularly when Peißner saw fit to share in the fun.

In spite of his slightly ridiculous self-importance and his all too evident self-interest, the baron was sincerely concerned about Lola. He was appalled that she used her influence with the police to have Archbishop Reisach put under surveillance, and he tried to warn her that she would never win over her enemies in Munich by using scorn, ridicule, and intrigue. She was going to undermine not only her position but also her health, he told her; her chronic chest disease would be aggravated by the life she was living. And it simply would not do for a lady to be escorted about by a gang of students. Lola blew up at the baron; she had encouraged him to come to Munich in order to give prestige to her salons, not to preach to her, and she wouldn't tolerate it.

The baron realized that he had gone too far, and he had not yet managed to speak to the king about ordering wine. Ludwig, in fact, was annoyed by Lola's visitor and could not wait for him to leave. The trip appeared to have been completely in vain for the baron, who left Munich troubled both by his failure to make a sale and by what he had seen in the Barerstraße. In a long letter he made one last effort to bring Lola to her senses; he did not blame her for her frivolous, abandoned behavior, he wrote, it was the fault of her parents, who had neglected her, and of the constant adulation she had received from early childhood. But, he warned, "recognize the abyss that you are digging beneath your feet, an abyss that will swallow you up together with the monarchy if you persist in the direction you have taken and if you obstinately refuse to conform yourself to the laws and customs of the country you have adopted." Lola did not reply.

The Duke of Leuchtenberg, the king's nephew and the czar's son-in-law, visited Munich early in November and attempted to separate Ludwig from Lola. At the dinner arranged for the duke's farewell, the queen signaled for all the courtiers to leave the members of the royal family alone together, and the duke begged Ludwig to allow him to take the czar the happy news that the Countess of Landsfeld was no longer in Munich. The other members of the family added their pleas and tears to no avail; Ludwig was shaken by the assault but resolute and could only reply, "You don't know her; she's so kind."

The object of the king's devotion was, at just about this time, expressing the same sentiments about him to Fritz Peißner. "I really love His Majesty the King," she told the student, "because he is so noble, my good old man." She had introduced Peißner to the king at her house, and the young man had been received graciously in audiences at the palace. While Lola repeatedly assured Peißner that the king was merely her dear friend—like a father to her—she quickly made clear to Fritz that her interest in him was of quite a different nature. "You have my heart," she told him, "but don't ask for my body until we are married." Peißner was dazzled to find himself the beloved of a beautiful countess, and he let himself believe that the king's repeated expressions of confidence in him meant that the marriage plan had royal approval.

Gossip in Munich already told of the beer-drinking and smoking parties that Lola held with the Alemannen at her house (they were commonly referred to as orgies), sometimes with the king present, but the senior stayed on after everyone else left. Fritz and Lola would retire to her boudoir and passionately embrace and caress and kiss until she sent him home. Then one night as they lay together in her bedroom the countess decided that he wouldn't have to wait after all. "What's the matter with you?" she asked with feigned surprise. "What do you want? You're so red." Then her hand slipped down, moved aside encumbering clothing, and guided him to the ecstatic loss of his virginity.

Peißner was overwhelmed, hopelessly in love, ready to die for this woman. Afterward Lola made him kneel with her, and they swore by the Holy Crucifix never to be unfaithful to each other. For him it was an awesome, solemn moment. From now on everything else in life became secondary to him, and he made love to her whenever she would let him. By the end of the month, without saying anything to the king, Lola had given him his own room in one of the outbuildings used by her servants.

The session of the Landtag at last drew to an end, and the king and Wallerstein prepared to announce the new government. The prince knew that he was staking his political future on the unlikely chance that he could either separate Ludwig from Lola or quell the rising tide of outrage and disgust she was creating, but Wallerstein was nothing if not self-confident. He had been out of power for a decade, and now the excitement of feeling the levers of government once more under his hands may have blinded him to the enormous difficulty of the task.

Self-confidence did not rule out caution, however, and all the new ministers, except Berks, requested not only that they be named only acting ministers but also that their current positions be held open for them so that they could leave the government at any time. The cabinet was not a stellar one. Wallerstein was the only figure of international stature. He would hold the portfolios of the foreign ministry and of education and religious affairs. Filling the important post of interior minister was Lola's confidant, Franz von Berks. Wallerstein had resisted Berks's appointment, but the king told him that he had promised the Countess of Landsfeld that Berks would be in the new government, so the prince had to accept this pariah as a colleague or remain outside the government.

Wallerstein privately spread the word that his cabinet, with the obvious exception of Berks, had the king's promise that they would not be required to visit the house in the Barerstraße. But insistent rumors had been circulating for more than a month that Wallerstein was secretly conferring with the countess at her home, and Maurer told friends that Wallerstein had not only pledged himself to visit the countess but promised to lure other guests of stature there, too.

In his dispatch to Lord Palmerston, the British ambassador expressed the consensus of the diplomatic corps and informed opinion in Munich:

It is impossible, my Lord, not to perceive that feelings of discontent are taking deep root in this country, & I cannot but apprehend that unless a change of System calculated to allay them is speedily entered upon, very unpleasant consequences may in the end ensue.—The democratic party favored by these circumstances is indubitably gaining ground, & I really do not see on what the Sovereign can lean for support. I am using a mild expression when I say that the King is most unpopular with the mass of People;—the nobles are dissatisfied beyond measure with what is going on, & judging from the language in the Chamber & the accounts which reach the Capital from the provinces, the clergy, whether catholic or Protestant, are alike making use of the Power they possess to unite the Public Mind against him. In any other Country such a State of things could not long endure without a crisis, but the patience of this people does not seem to admit of estimation by the ordinary rules.

17

THE ROAD TO REVOLUTION

Even before the Wallerstein cabinet took office, Lola and her friends were preparing its first crisis with an incident on the evening of Sunday, 28 November, that would develop into a minor diplomatic imbroglio and a major conflict between the king and Lolitta. During performances at the Royal Theater, the Alemannen and the countess's other admirers stationed themselves throughout the auditorium in order to eavesdrop for any information that might prove useful to the countess's cause and to discover any slanders that might be circulating about her or them. On this particular evening, some of the Alemannen overheard Count Eduard de Richemont, a well-connected young French aristocrat living in Munich, saying something to two of the king's nieces about Karwowski, who was seated in a box opposite them. Fifteen minutes later Karwowski appeared with three companions at the door of the box, demanding that Richemont explain his insulting remarks. Richemont replied that he must have been misunderstood by the eavesdroppers since he had said nothing insulting about anyone. Karwowski withdrew, but exchanges between the parties continued, and it became clear that a duel could result.

Richemont seems to have been generally well liked in Munich's young social circle, and Karwowski, as part of Lola's circle, was generally despised; so to protect the Frenchman, about thirty of the most prominent young men of the capital held an extraordinary convocation in the middle of the night to declare that anyone who crossed the threshold of the Countess of Landsfeld was dishonored and incapable of giving satisfaction, that is, someone no man of honor could meet on the dueling field. This decision was communicated to Richemont and to Karwowski.

At 6 o'clock the next morning the French ambassador called on Wallerstein, who was about to become foreign minister, asking him to do whatever he could to avoid trouble, for if something happened to Richemont, there would almost certainly be repercussions for relations between the two countries. Wallerstein was sympathetic, particularly because Karwowski had been saying publicly that the eavesdroppers had declared Richemont a liar in Lola's salon in the presence of Berks and Wallerstein. If people became convinced he had indeed been in Lola's house, the new principal minister would probably be shunned and his ministry doomed before it began. Wallerstein saw to it that Richemont got a police guard, and he allayed the king's anger at the declaration of public contempt that the midnight convocation had laid upon Lola's circle by telling him that Karwowski had been running up gambling debts and using the king's name freely, claiming to be a royal intimate.

Ludwig, who kept few secrets from Lola, told her that the Russian ambassador had called on Wallerstein on the first day of the new government and had presented him with an affidavit from Prince Paskievitch, the viceroy of Poland and Lola's old nemesis, stating that Karwowski was a dangerous character and demanding his immediate return to Poland. Maybe she saw that he was inclined, even eager, to be rid of the handsome young Pole. Perhaps it was in an effort to win the king to her will that, for the first time since June, she consented to sexual intercourse with him on the afternoon of 1 December. It would be the very last time.

Even though Lola yielded to his desires, Ludwig secretly gave Wallerstein permission to deport her Polish gallant. Jealousy almost certainly played a role in his decision. The king resented the Alemannen and all the other young men Lola gathered about her, just as he had been resentful and angry at the attention she had shown Nußbammer. He wanted her to himself, and he was frustrated and hurt to see that she increasingly preferred the company of young and handsome men.

Wallerstein would have been as happy as the king himself to find a way to replace the Alemannen and the rest of the disreputable circle around the countess with at least marginally acceptable companions. The Alemannen, he warned the king, were a great danger to the countess, for they could provoke irremediable scandal and riot at any moment. If the Countess of Landsfeld could manage to live quietly for four or five months, the prince told Ludwig, it would change the complexion of things greatly.

Whether because she was worried that the Russian diplomatic effort would succeed or because she felt secure in her apparent triumph, at the Royal Theater on Friday, 3 December, the Countess of Landsfeld pointedly lorgnetted Count Severine, the Russian ambassador, and made threatening gestures at him from her box. If Lola was feeling confident of the king's support, this time she was mistaken, for at 4 A.M. the next morning the police rousted Eustache Karwowski and told him to dress and get his things together because he was being deported. Wallerstein was merciful, directing that the young man not be deported to Austria, which was ready to turn him over to the Russians, but instead be allowed to make his way to Paris, home of the Polish exile community.

To the man on the street it looked as if the king had at last stood up to the Spanish woman, had finally set a limit on her whims, and was beginning to show some backbone. Perhaps a few of the more perceptive citizens recognized that the king's action was not a sign that he was freeing himself from Lola's power but was, on the contrary, ridding himself of a rival.

Mussinan was assigned to give Lola the news of Karwowski's deportation, since he was the only official in her entourage with too little authority to force someone else to confront her. She flew into a rage, and it was some time before Mussinan was able to report to the king that she had calmed down.

But Lola's rages were like a volcano in eruption, seeming to subside only to explode again without warning. She dressed and drove to the Interior Ministry, where she burst into the office of her satellite, Berks, and ranted at him for an hour and a half before he could calm her. She had, he reported to the king, gone home satisfied.

Berks was wrong, too. The king had urged Maria Denker, an actress who had become a member of Lola's entourage, to speak to the countess, woman to woman, of the inappropriateness of surrounding herself with young men and to urge her to consider distancing herself from the Alemannen. When Denker arrived Lola was with Ernestine Opitz, the proprietress of Munich's finest jewelry store, discussing acquisitions the countess wished to make. The actress was exactly the wrong person to arrive at this moment because she had recently remonstrated with the countess about showing herself so openly with Karwowski, even asking Lola to promise not to see him again. Lola now raged wildly at Fräulein Denker, screaming epithets and accusing her of being a party to the deportation; the actress was appalled and embarrassed that Frau Opitz was witnessing such a degrading spectacle. Denker, who must have seen some scenery-chewing rages in her career, had never experienced anything like it. The countess screamed that for this betrayal, the week-old government would have to go; she had made them all, and she would destroy them. Denker tried to calm her as she blushed at the gutter French being heaped upon her. Finally, she retreated in confusion and wrote a troubled note to the king reporting on the utter failure of her mission.

After the reports of Mussinan, Berks, and Denker, the king must have had little doubt what awaited him on his visit to the Barerstraße that night, but the vehemence of Lola's attack may have surprised even him. The screaming match between the two of them over the deportation was so loud that it awoke the countess's neighbors. Someone would have called a gendarme had there not already been two of them on duty in front of her house, both assiduously pretending to hear nothing. When Ludwig at last fled Lola's fury, she pursued him out of the house, and the evening reached its screaming conclusion in the street.

But, as the king knew, Lola's moods were as transitory as they were extreme. The next morning he sent Mussinan to get a storm report and perhaps to calm the countess. He arrived at about 11 A.M. and found that the countess was holding a levee, dressing as she was waited upon by six supplicants and admirers. It was two hours before the crowd cleared and Mussinan felt he could raise the question of the departed Pole. To his surprise and relief, he found Lola deeply apologetic about her behavior the day before, and she told the courtier that she had heard such terrible things about Karwowski since his precipitous departure that if he returned, she would *ask* the king to deport him.

The dust settled on the Karwowski affair, but more than enough problems remained. The queen was adamant in her resolve never to meet the Countess of Landsfeld, and she also refused to receive anyone who frequented the house in the Barerstraße. At the same time, the Countess of Landsfeld was becoming more aggressively self-important, perhaps out of frustration at the ostracism directed at her and her adherents or perhaps out of native combativeness. Munichers were forbidden to say the name Lola in conversation, and the gendarmes had orders to warn citizens that they should speak of Marie, Countess of Landsfeld, as she now styled herself. The countess showed herself on the streets of Munich these days accompanied by two liveried lackeys, something only the queen and the crown princess had hitherto done, and she was not above loudly calling the noblest ladies of Munich canaille when they failed to acknowledge her.

As all this was taking place on the streets of the capital, the king had Berks tell Wallerstein of one of his special duties. Berks reported back to Ludwig that the prince was surprised and after an hour's discussion was shaken and weary. "He said he should go back to Paris while it was still possible," Berks told the king. The task imposed on the discouraged prince was, apparently, to break the nobility's boycott of Lola and accomplish her acceptance into Munich's best society so that the queen would be more likely to allow the countess's presentation at court. Only two days before, on 10 December, Wallerstein had endorsed the idea of Lola's starting a literary salon but had specifically warned Ludwig that the nobility and the other members of the royal family should not be involved at this point. The king, he had suggested, should appear at the salon not as a private man but as king, to provide official sanction and dignity.

Wallerstein sent the king a memorandum outlining the obstacles to aristocratic acceptance of the Countess of Landsfeld. A primary problem, he wrote, was the Alemannen. Until these rowdy, arrogant, provocative young men ceased to be Lola's boon companions, there was little hope of change. And any change would have to be gradual and steady. If things did not improve before the middle of the next year, the prince wrote, there will be a terrible explosion.

Wallerstein also composed what he saw as a diplomatic but instructive essay on how the new countess could best conduct herself, which he sent to Lola through one of her sycophants. Lola's reaction was bitter rage that this man, whom she had made a minister and who still refused to call on her, should presume to tell her how to run her affairs and conduct herself, and she swore that she would see Wallerstein stripped of his office by the first of March.

In mid-December the new government instituted its first liberal reform. A revised censorship law was decreed for press coverage of domestic affairs, ostensibly abolishing the strictures imposed under Abel's government and returning to the greater freedom that had existed under Prince Wallerstein's prior administration. In fact, the manner in which the new law was interpreted and applied resulted in little change.

One explicit change had been made: an exception was included allowing prior censorship of "personal attacks," a policy that editors quickly recognized as an effort to prevent the publication of any negative report about the

Countess of Landsfeld. Stories about her in foreign newspapers coming into Bavaria were already being obliterated with black paint. Despite the exception, Lola was angry with Ludwig for issuing the decree without consulting her; it was too much freedom, the countess complained, and the ultramontanes would take it advantage of it. She told him that instead of liberalizing the censorship, he should be building a large and efficient secret police force to spy on his citizens.

In the week before New Year's, plans went forward to create a salon for Lola. The cabinet member deemed most likely to follow Interior Minister Berks across the threshold of Barerstraße 7 was the vain and ambitious new minister of war, Baron von Hohenhausen. The team planning Lola's social metamorphosis felt that he would join the salon if he were approached properly.

The concerted effort to form a new, respectable, and ever-widening social circle about the countess was set to begin, but the manner in which 1848 was rung in on the Barerstraße was in itself a setback for the endeavor. Lola threw a party for her Alemannen, and a good deal of drinking went on, though Lola herself was rarely seen to drink much alcohol. According to some sources, the inebriated Alemannen had removed their trousers and were carousing in their long shirts when the accident happened. The students had hoisted their patroness upon their shoulders and were parading her in triumph around the drawing room, which had a rather low crystal chandelier. The Countess of Landsfeld was carried straight into her chandelier and knocked bloody and unconscious to the floor.

Two gendarmes ran to fetch the nearest doctor, who bound up Lola's wound and was soon joined by her personal physician. The doctors determined that she had suffered no serious injury, but her already battered reputation had been further damaged. Even a woman as infamous as the Countess of Landsfeld could still be harmed by gossip about how she had been knocked cold by a chandelier in the midst of a drunken orgy while being carried on the shoulders of a crowd of half-naked young men. It was not an auspicious beginning to the new year.

Word reached the king that the Countess of Landsfeld had had an accident during the night, and he sent at once to inquire after her condition. He was assured that the matter was not serious, but when Ludwig heard that the Alemannen had been half naked at the party, he ordered a secret investigation. If the story were true, it might present him with an opportunity to banish the students from Lola's presence. The inquiry established that neither of the doctors had seen the students half naked when they arrived. Other evidence was not forthcoming.

But the issue became secondary to the king when he encountered Peißner in the street early on the morning of the 3rd and was startled to learn in the course of their conversation that the student seemed to have access to the Countess of Landsfeld at all hours. He wrote an angry and troubled note to Berks, asking him to find out what was going on, and that evening he lost his temper with the countess over her relationship with the young man. As soon as he was back at the palace, he wrote asking her forgiveness, and she was quick to grant it. But he still was extremely unhappy and was troubled by his own relationship with Lola and by her relationship with the Alemannen.

The king's worst suspicions were fueled when someone secretly told him that Lola was sleeping with Peißner. Ludwig did not want to believe the story, and Lola vehemently denied it when he confronted her. It would have been no consolation to the king to have known that Peißner himself would soon grow suspicious and jealous because he believed that Lola, despite her protestations of eternal fidelity, was also sleeping with Ludwig Leibinger, another of the students in the Alemannia.

Gossip in Munich supported Peißner's belief that the king was planning to marry him to the countess. The rumor even generated a sense of relief among the people because it meant that the king was not in the grip of a guilty obsession with the woman. The king's feelings, the story went, were platonic admiration for the countess's character, he felt no jealousy of the Alemannen, and he even warned some of them against her.

The painful truth was almost the opposite. Ludwig sought some way to defend his wounded pride as a man and as king, and he began drafting a statement for her in Spanish, which he titled "My Situation":

> I come after everyone else, in all situations. If there is no one else to talk with or nothing else to do, then I may remain, otherwise I'm driven away. Everyone has more influence than I do; if Turk the dog could talk, he would be heard with greater attentiveness. I'm good for paying and obeying, for fulfilling wishes. If I fail to do everything I've been told to do, I am told that I have done nothing. When I do fulfill wishes, I hardly ever hear an expression of thanks, much less an expression of happiness, it's as if I've merely done my duty. Conversation consists of listening to . . . requests, requests pronounced not with sweetness, but in an imperative manner; the mistress of the house orders her servant about. Never has a *querida* had more independence and never has a *querido* had fewer rights. She likes to live in her style, with students and without the least regard for my heart and my rep-

utation, humiliating me in the opinion of the public. *She doesn't want to live
as a querida* but she wants the power of a *querida*.

King Ludwig apparently never gave Lola his complaint. Despite the pain
and humiliation she caused him, he felt bound to her by his honor even more
than he was erotically obsessed by her. So the effort to break her out of social
quarantine continued. Berks and Wallerstein prepared a joint memorandum
to the king on how Baron Hohenhausen should be invited to the Barerstraße.
First, the minister was flattered with personal presentation by the king of
the knight's cross of the Order of Civil Service. Two days later, when he was
at the palace to dine, the king tried to invite him casually to join him that
afternoon for tea at the Countess of Landsfeld's house. Hohenhausen was
startled and seems not to have known what to say; he chose to interpret the
king's invitation as a military order and appeared for tea, then announced the
next day that he wished to resign as minister.

The king was angry about this newest complication, but Wallerstein
immediately moved in to smooth over matters with his practiced diplomacy.
Hohenhausen was persuaded to submit a letter to the king explaining his
understanding of the matter. Wallerstein then allowed the letter to be leaked
to the public in an effort to convince the general he had nothing more to lose
by continuing in office. He knew that the general was heavily in debt and
needed the income of a minister. But Wallerstein had miscalculated; the social
disgrace that resulted from calling on Lola was greater than the baron's
financial need, and Hohenhausen submitted his formal and irrevocable resignation as minister of war. It was a serious embarrassment for the king and
the government, and it demonstrated just how completely Lola had become
a matter of state importance.

The support of the military, which would be crucial in event of a crisis, was
being eroded daily by the king's own indiscretions. Early in January he told
a local commander that it was a disgrace that his officers refused to greet the
Countess of Landsfeld when they passed her on the street. The colonel
replied that only with a written royal order would he even try to get his officers to greet the countess. Ludwig was stunned and angry.

In the street a few days later the king stopped a young officer who, he had
heard, was particularly vociferous in his complaints about the countess.
Ludwig humiliated him with a tongue-lashing in front of all the curious
onlookers. A Bavarian general had already told the Prussian ambassador privately that the obedience of the officers and men was anything but certain if

they were called to duty in the defense of the Countess of Landsfeld, and now morale had been so damaged by Ludwig himself that it was uncertain whether the troops would follow royal commands at all. There were rumors that at the next Landtag a delegation of officers would request that the armed forces be required to take an oath of allegiance not to the king but to the constitution, a proposal that had previously been espoused only by radical liberals.

Berks was having at least as much trouble as Prince Wallerstein. His social ostracism was nearly complete in Munich, and any official dignity to which he might have aspired was destroyed by Lola's regular visits to his office, where she arrived with a lackey carrying a large portfolio containing all the matters she wished the minister to handle for her. It was said that Fritz Peißner was operating a regular employment bureau out of the Barerstraße, negotiating government positions and salaries with petitioners based on their degree of allegiance to Lola and what they might be able to do for her.

The prince and Berks were conferring on the afternoon of 12 January—trying to find a way to divert enough scholarship funds to the Alemannen so they would be financially independent, something the countess had insisted upon before she would consent to abandon the society of her notorious admirers—when a delegation of the red-capped paladins appeared to speak to the prince. He was aghast to hear from them that they wished to invite him to their official *commers*, or formal banquet, which they would be holding, thanks to a substantial monetary gift from the Countess of Landsfeld, in the large hall of the Bayrischer Hof on Saturday night. Wallerstein, ever the diplomat, deftly explained that it was constitutionally inadvisable for ministers to have relations with student societies, and the seemingly satisfied Alemannen went to report back to their patroness.

The prince realized that his repeated admonitions to this woman to use savoir faire, to act with discretion and thought for the consequences, were so much wasted ink. He had written to her, "If you wish to be a countess and the friend of a monarch by the grace of God, then you must adhere to convention and avoid compromising situations," but it was now clear she didn't understand what he telling her.

If he still had any doubts, they were answered as an enraged Lola herself suddenly appeared before him with her toady Mussinan in tow. She knew very well that Minister Zu Rhein had addressed the initial commers of the Isaria fraternity the previous spring, and she told Wallerstein that his constitutional prattle could not deceive her. She declared that the struggle he had unleashed would be one of life or death, and she would have the king behind her. The countess overwhelmed him with a torrent of unidiomatic French, telling Wallerstein that what she decided should happen, would happen, even if it meant a revolution that would bring down both her and the king. Now you will see, she trumpeted, what a spirited woman can accomplish when she sets all the levers of intrigue in motion. And she swept out of his office with Mussinan behind her.

Wallerstein, left alone with his gloomy thoughts, wrote the king a memorandum. The countess lacked knowledge of Bavaria, he wrote. The Alemannen commers was a stupid idea that would succeed only in stirring up the other fifteen hundred students at the university. The king and his principal minister were playing on an undermined field, he warned. Savoir faire, Wallerstein's approach to every difficulty, just might turn out to be useless. This had taken matters back a few steps, he concluded.

Minister Berks saw no obstacles, constitutional or otherwise, to associating with the Alemannen, and he was the keynote speaker at the banquet. The hall was decorated with a large portrait of His Majesty and, opposite it, the arms of the society together with its motto: *Virtus omnium vincet quodque malum!* (Manly virtue triumphs over every evil!) It was said that the countess, whose attendance at this traditionally all-male event would have been deemed in very poor taste, could not resist showing herself on the balcony of the hall to greet her faithful companions on their night of celebration. The administrators and faculty of the university had been invited, but nearly all of them seemed to have been unavoidably detained elsewhere. Berks, Mussinan, the police chief, and more than fifty other male members of Lola's circle, together with about eighteen Alemannen, made up the company filling the hall. The interior minister's address could not have been better calculated to infuriate the student body against the Alemannen. You are, he declared to Lola's loyalists, a model of manly virtue, an example much needed among the degenerate youth of the age, and he called upon them to continue to demonstrate the freedom from vice that had been their hallmark. Peißner responded on behalf of the Alemannen, and toasts with beer and general drinking continued until nearly 4 o'clock in the morning.

Prince Wallerstein proved to be a prophet. The rest of the university students were outraged by the Alemannen's commers, particularly by the implication in Berks's speech that these shunned outcasts who had sold themselves to a foreign whore were models they should strive to emulate. Now whenever an Alemann in his distinctive red cap appeared at the university or even on the street, he was greeted with a chorus of catcalls and whistles.

Matters were made worse when Rector Friedrich von Thiersch chose this moment to remind all students of their obligation to attend lectures, causing the Alemannen, who had been more than lax in attendance, to begin appearing regularly for classes. When an Alemann appeared in a lecture hall, all the other students would rise and leave, and professors usually refused to lecture when most of the class was absent. Lola, too, was treated with contempt by students, and she took to declaring to all within earshot that if things didn't change, she would have the king close the university. By 27 January the constant noise and harassment were so serious a problem that Peißner drafted a petition for intervention by the king, which Lola forwarded.

In response to the petition, harsh punishments were decreed for students who were found harassing other students or participating in disorders. The new rules seemed to have some effect, and the persecution of the Alemannen began to subside until fate intervened to renew student outrage against Lola and her supporters. Joseph von Görres, perhaps the most respected professor at the university and the intellectual leader of the conservative Catholic cause that had found expression in Abel's politics, died on 29 January. Even those Bavarians who were not fully in sympathy with Görres's thinking respected him as a man of unquestioned integrity who had been a leader in the resistance against Napoleon's repression in Germany. The university went into mourning, and the Alemannen were temporarily forgotten.

The funeral was on 31 January, and as the long procession of mourners solemnly accompanied the coffin down the Ludwigstraße toward the cemetery, they were shocked to encounter the Countess of Landsfeld, apparently out for her regular noonday promenade on Munich's most fashionable thoroughfare. For Görres's followers, Lola was close to being a female antichrist, and some of the students in the procession began whistling at her and grumbling threats. Lola was brazen and fearless in the face of the hostility, yelling at the mourners to clear a path for her on the sidewalk, and the situation threatened to get out of control, particularly after the countess declared that she would have the university closed if the students couldn't show her appropriate respect. Eventually the gendarmes moved in to separate the parties and escort the countess to safety, but the students would not forget the insult to Görres's memory by the patroness of the Alemannen.

The harassment of the Alemannen resumed with even greater vehemence

The Misses Aldridge's Ladies Boarding Academy—where Lola lived and studied from age twelve until age seventeen, when she eloped to Ireland with Lt. Thomas James—was on Bath's fashionable Camden Circle. The school occupied the next-to-last townhouse at the far end of the crescent. From Bath & Bristol, *by John Britton, 1829.*

In September 1839, Lola and her husband escaped the torrid heat of his garrison to join her mother on holiday in the idyllic Indian hill station of Simla, seen here in a photograph taken some fifteen years later. Collection of Dr. Reinhold Rauh.

Wilhelm von Kaulbach's perceptive 1843 oil sketch of King Ludwig I of Bavaria. The encounter between Lola Montez and the king, who met on 8 October 1846, would change their lives and alter the course of Bavarian history. Bayerische Staatsgemäldesammlungen.

Almost immediately after meeting Lola, King Ludwig commissioned Joseph Stieler, his court painter, to paint Lola's portrait for the king's Gallery of Beauties. The painter's first effort, now lost, was replaced by this version, painted in the spring of 1847. This image still attracts the most attention from tourists visiting Munich's Nymphenburg Palace, where Ludwig's gallery is now displayed. Schloß Nymphenburg, Schönheitsgalerie.

This woodcut, the earliest representation of Lola Montez, portrays her in the dancing costume in which she made her debut in London on 3 June 1843, and as she later appeared before King Ludwig I on the stage of the Bavarian Court Theater in October 1846. From the Pictorial Times, 15 July 1843.

In addition to sitting for her portrait by Stieler, Lola was sketched by King Ludwig's other outstanding court painter, Wilhelm von Kaulbach. The artist's initial attempt at portraying the dancer was far more benign than the full-scale oil portrait that the king ultimately commanded him to undertake. From Wilhelm von Kaulbach, by Fritz Ostini (Bielefeld: Velhagen & Klasing, 1906).

Early in 1847 the king ordered Kaulbach to paint a full-length life-size oil portrait of his "Lolitta." By this time the painter was anything but an admirer of Lola, and the malicious cast he gave to the features of the "Spaniard" caused Ludwig to reject the work. Münchner Stadtmuseum.

Lola's diploma as a Bavarian countess—the focus of endless intrigue, strife, and political crisis—lies open to show the signatures of the king and his principal minister together with Lola's coat of arms as Countess of Landsfeld. Geheimes Hausarchiv Urkunde 54/4/32,1; Bayerisches Hauptstaatsarchiv.

Shortly after becoming a countess, Lola seduced twenty-two-year-old Elias Peißner, the leader of the Alemannia. His affair with Lola would change his life. From Die illustrierte Zeitung, *February 1848.*

A contemporary caricature of Ludwig's abdication lays the blame on the king's unwillingness to be separated from Lola's lovely legs, an interpretation with more than a grain of truth to it. From Ein vormärzliches Tanzidyll, *by Eduard Fuchs (Berlin: Ernst Frensdorff, 1904).*

PAS DE FASCINATION:

OR,

CATCHING A GOVERNOR!

A FARCE,

In One Act,

ORIGINALLY LICENSED BY THE LORD CHAMBERLAIN, AND
PERFORMED AT THE

THEATRE ROYAL, HAYMARKET,

UNDER THE TITLE OF

LOLA MONTES:

OR,

A COUNTESS FOR AN HOUR.

BY J. STIRLING COYNE.

CORRECTLY PRINTED FROM THE PROMPTER'S COPY,
WITH THE CAST OF CHARACTERS, COSTUME, SCENIC ARRANGEMENT
SIDES OF ENTRANCE AND EXIT, AND RELATIVE POSITIONS
OF THE DRAMATIS PERSONÆ.

ILLUSTRATED WITH AN ENGRAVING BY MR. SLY.

LONDON:

PUBLISHED AT THE NATIONAL ACTING DRAMA OFFICE,
19, SUFFOLK STREET, PALL MALL EAST; "NASSAU STEAM
PRESS," 60, ST. MARTIN'S LANE, CHARING CROSS; TO BE
HAD OF STRANGE, PATERNOSTER ROW; WISEHEART, SUFFOLK
STREET, DUBLIN; AND ALL RESPECTABLE BOOKSELLERS.

PAS DE FASCINATION.

In April 1848 a farce entitled Lola Montes *appeared on the London boards. Briefly banned, the play spread its caricature of Lola throughout the English-speaking world for the rest of her life. From the first edition of the play.*

This 1847 lithographic portrait of Lola was probably the one she sent to Ludwig from London, calling it a "very good likeness." The king felt that although it captured a bit of her "peerless expression," it made her face too fat. San Francisco Performing Arts Library and Museum.

A French humor magazine took this satirical view of Lola's escape from a bigamy prosecution by portraying her fleeing across the English Channel with her new husband, George Trafford Heald. From Ein vormärzliches Tanzidyll, by Eduard Fuchs (Berlin: Ernst Frensdorff, 1904).

The earliest surviving photograph that is indisputably of Lola Montez is this portrait made by Meade Brothers in New York City on 22 December 1851, one week before her American debut. Pennsylvania State University Libraries.

When Lola Montez visited the Philadelphia daguerreotype studio of Marcus Root on 2 February 1852, she met a delegation of Indian chiefs who were having their portraits taken following a visit to the "Great White Father" in Washington, D.C. Besides having Root make a conventional portrait of her, Lola, with her delight in defying convention, insisted on being photographed with the Arapaho chief Light in the Clouds, certainly the first photograph of a white woman sitting arm in arm with an Indian. Harvard Theatre Collection (left); Collection of Gail Dane Gomberg Propp (below).

Not long after being photographed with the Indian, Lola chose staid Boston as the scene of another photographic outrage when she posed holding a cigarette, probably another photographic first for a woman. Although not particularly flattering, it is perhaps her best-known photograph. Metropolitan Museum of Art, gift of I. N. Phelps Stokes, Edward S. Hawes, Alice Mary Hawes, and Marion Augusta Hawes.

San Francisco's historic Mission Dolores church, seen here in a photograph taken in the mid-1850s, was the venue for Lola's last wedding, held early on the morning of 2 July 1853. This alliance, to the journalist Patrick Purdy Hull, was the least durable of all Lola's marriages, lasting barely two months. Bancroft Library, University of California, Berkeley.

SPIDER DANCE.

This sketch, one of the few depictions of Lola's dancing drawn from life, shows her performing her notorious "Spider Dance" in Adelaide during her Australian tour of 1855–56. The modesty of her costume and the unprovocative pose support claims that the alleged indecency of the "Spider Dance" was wildly exaggerated, possibly with help from Lola herself, who was always her own best press agent. Mortlock Library of South Australiana, Adelaide (B9422/2).

In this photograph, probably taken after Lola's return to New York from California late in 1856, the dowdiness of the enveloping lace shawl and the expression of sad resignation give her a matronly air that comports with her mourning for her drowned lover, Frank Folland, and her growing piety. The lapdog, which sat patiently motionless during the long exposure for the photo, is probably Gip, Lola's constant companion in the years following her return from Australia. Harvard Theatre Collection.

Less than two years later, the sparkle in her eye, the firm jaw, the new swept-back hair style, and the elegant dress show that Lola has re-created herself once more. The book in her hand is probably a reference to her flourishing career as a lecturer and to her own successful books, which would date the photograph to between July and October 1858. Museum of the City of New York, gift of Elwin M. Eldridge.

This Meade Brothers photograph is probably the last taken of Lola Montez and may date from the spring of 1860, following her return to New York from her final lecture tour. There is a weariness about her now, and her forty years have made clear inroads on her legendary beauty. There is still life in the dark blue eyes, but the hint of a droop in her left eyelid may indicate that she had already been suffering small strokes prior to the massive one that struck her on 30 June 1860, crippling her left side and nearly killing her. Harvard Theatre Collection.

one thousand eight hundred and sixty

Lola *Montez*,
Countess of Landsfeldt

The obvious effort taken to make this signature testifies to the tremendous struggle Lola waged to overcome the effects of her devastating stroke. By Christmas she had fought her way to hope of full recovery, but within three weeks she died of pneumonia. This document assigned to Isaac Buchanan any claim Lola had on property in Bavaria and was probably signed late in July 1860, at the time she executed her last will. Bayerische Staatsbibliothek.

This nineteenth-century photograph of the grave of Lola Montez in Brooklyn's Green-Wood Cemetery shows it much as it appears today, except that the headstone is no longer legible. After all she had done to create her own legend and obscure the truth about herself, it is perhaps no surprise that her tombstone was inscribed with a name she never bore—her maiden name preceded by "Mrs."—and that her age was given as older than she could possibly have been. Lola might well have appreciated the irony. Theatre Arts Collection, Harry Ransom Humanities Research Center, University of Texas at Austin.

than before. Thiersch spoke to the student body, urging calm and appealing for order, but the pursuit of the crimson-capped "Lolianer" continued. By the early days of February, incidents at the university were becoming more serious, most of them involving the *Obscuranten,* students who were not members of any of the fraternities, and Alemannen.

Hohenhausen's replacement in the War Ministry, General Heinrich von der Mark, took office and promptly went to tea at Lola's house, though he was said to have been less than congenial company, treating his visit as a military duty. When they were introduced, Lola tried to obtain a favor for an officer she knew, and the general was said to have told her the officer was undeserving and that she should not meddle in military affairs. No one expected von der Mark to remain in the cabinet for long.

On the night of Sunday, 6 February, there were gasps from the audience at the royal theater as the Countess of Landsfeld arrived in her box at the far right of the second tier. She was wearing a dazzling ensemble of tiara, necklace, and bracelet of incredible size and beauty, all in glittering diamonds. Gesturing across the theater, Lola called the king's attention to the stir her jewels were making, and no one had any doubts about where her adornment had come from. It was whispered that the jewelry was fabulously expensive, worth 60,000 florins or more. In fact Ludwig had acquired it for only 13,000 florins, but that sum was nonetheless more than twice the annual salary of a cabinet minister. In his misery and dejection, the king was still trying to win Lola's attention and affection in any way he could, but his efforts simply fueled public resentment of her arrogance and of his indulgence of it. Lola gave the audience yet another display of her impudent imperiousness by stroking the extended forefinger of one hand across the forefinger of the other at hapless General Hohenhausen in a childish and triumphant gesture of "shame on you!"

As Rector Thiersch arrived at the university for his 11 o'clock lecture on the morning of Monday, 7 February, he could hear that the tumult around the Alemannen had begun again in earnest. The whistling and catcalling would subside as Thiersch passed, but he could hear it start up again behind him. The gendarme post at the Triumphal Arch near the university had been reinforced, but the rector didn't want to consider police intervention. He was relieved to see the carriage of Prince Wallerstein, who as minister of religion and education was ultimately responsible for the university, pull up in the great courtyard.

The prince enjoyed the respect of the students, and he had come to make his own effort to calm them. He knew how irritated the king was growing, and he hoped that a collision of wills could be avoided. Wallerstein began to address the students assembled before the main entrance of the university, telling them he had no desire to interfere with their freedom or to command their opinions but that the order and respect that were traditions of German universities must be maintained. Up to now only measures of university discipline had been applied to deal with the disorder within the university, but further disregard for the wishes of the king, who had always been a father and patron to the university, was likely to result in intervention by the civil authorities. In closing his remarks, he led the students in three cheers for King Ludwig.

At the end of the speech the rector asked the students whether they would pledge not to disrupt the peace of the university, and he was answered with an echoing "Yes!" from the assembly. But the echo had hardly died away before the pledge was broken. Two Alemannen who had listened to the speech off at one side were spotted as they hurried away from the dissolving crowd, and a chorus of whistles and insults sprang up behind them as they were pursued into the Ludwigstraße. The two Alemannen were hounded by a howling group of perhaps four hundred the whole length of the street—all the way to Rottmann's Cafe, at the north end of the bazaar, where they found refuge. The crowd gradually dispersed, but feelings continued to run high throughout the afternoon. As students gathered later to watch the changing of the guard in the Hofgarten, one of the Alemannen, Count Eduard von Hirschberg, slapped another student in the face, either for some perceived insult or out of a desire to provoke a hostile response. The student did not strike back, and the other students dispersed to avoid conflict; but the first blow had been struck in the Alemannen's confrontation with the rest of the student body, and matters had taken a serious turn.

That night all of the student corps except Alemannia met to draft an appeal to Prince Wallerstein and to the academic senate complaining that the Alemannen were guilty of insulting and provocative behavior but were protected by the gendarmes. They pleaded for the dissolution of Alemannia. They agreed among themselves to disband and cease wearing their colors "until a better time" if, as they expected, their petition was denied. If the struggle with the Alemannen were to provoke official sanctions, the fraternities could better survive if they could not be assessed collective guilt. The government was taking its measures, too. Infantry and cavalry patrols began making regular rounds in the streets of Munich, leaves were canceled, and the garrison strength was augmented.

Tuesday, 8 February, was quieter, though another lecture was canceled because three Alemannen sat alone in the hall. Berks sent the king a draft proclamation closing the university until the fall semester; the proclamation would be implemented if any further disorder arose. Ludwig had already had enough, however, and seems to have decided that the only solution was to shut the university down. Thiersch, visiting Prince Wallerstein that Tuesday afternoon before the meeting of the academic senate, was told in confidence that the question of the closing of the university was no longer one of "if" but simply of "when."

Ludwig certainly had a strong motive to close the university: suppressing what he saw as incorrigible disrespect and disorder by the students. He was a monarch who dealt harshly with such behavior. Eighteen years earlier a similar closure had quickly brought the desired result. But it is possible, even likely, that in the back of Ludwig's mind another motive played a role this time. For months his ministers had struggled to disengage the Countess of Landsfeld from her notorious companions, the Alemannen. Ludwig himself was eaten by jealousy and suspicion, particularly over the senior, Peißner, who the king feared might indeed be the countess's lover. By closing the university, the king, without appearing to will it, could effectively disband the Alemannen and banish Peißner. Lolitta could not blame him because he would be acting in defense of the Alemannen. She might at last have some time for him again; and with the students gone, there would be some hope of making her socially acceptable.

Wednesday, 9 February, was a brilliant winter day in Munich, and the fine weather brought people into the streets. Things had been quiet at the university in the morning, and Thiersch had begun his 11 o'clock lecture when he was interrupted by whistles and cries in the Ludwigstraße. Students at the windows told the rector they could see three Alemannen walking toward the university, and Thiersch suspended his lecture to go down to meet them. Peißner and two companions told the rector that they had come to make a formal complaint concerning the abuse and assaults to which the Alemannen had been subjected; they had already, he said, informed the king of their complaints. The Alemannen went with Thiersch to his office, and a protocol was drawn up for their signatures. Then Thiersch escorted them to the main entrance of the university, saying at the threshold, "This is the limit of my authority," and gave them into the protection of waiting gendarmes. Monday's screaming, scornful procession down the Ludwigstraße was repeated, but this time the crowd was augmented by many nonstudents who were out enjoying the weather.

The Alemannen again sought refuge in Rottmann's Cafe, which now was besieged by unruly students and citizens. The belligerent young Count Hirschberg was coming through the nearby arcades of the Hofgarten when he was surrounded by a whistling, mocking crowd. Reaching into his coat, he pulled out a long dagger and struck out at one of his tormentors. The knife cut only the sleeve of the young man's coat, but the surprise and outrage of the crowd was greater than the injury. The young count struck out once more, without serious effect, before a gendarme grabbed his arm and wrenched the dagger free; the Alemann broke and ran for Rottmann's Cafe, where he sought sanctuary with the others.

The crowd cried for the gendarmes to arrest Hirschberg, but the police commissioner on the scene declined to try to extract the student from the cafe and bring him through the angry mob, saying that carrying a dagger was only a minor offense. This apparent unwillingness to bring an Alemann to justice further incensed the mob. They stood—loud, hostile, and threatening—outside the line of gendarmes, who were now reinforced by mounted police.

All this was taking place almost under the windows of the palace, where a buffet luncheon and dance was going on. When King Ludwig was told that the Alemannen were besieged in Rottmann's Cafe, his first concern was that Lola might appear and be attacked by the mob. Without bothering to change from his formal clothes, the king threw a light green hunting jacket over his black dress suit and rushed out of the palace toward the Barerstraße. He had no illusions about the state of his popularity, and it crossed his mind as he entered the street where an angry mob howled that he might never come back. But he still had other illusions: "What does it matter whether you return?" he said to himself. "You're going to Lolitta!"

He encountered Lola on the street, coming from her house, and he led her back to the Barerstraße. She must promise not to leave her house, he told her. Her presence on the street not only would put her in danger but could inflame emotions. She must promise. Lola promised. Ludwig would have stayed with her, but his guests awaited him at the dance, and he had to get back. He left deeply troubled, knowing from experience how little he could rely on her promises and not knowing what to expect from the mob. As King Ludwig hurried back to the palace his face reflected turmoil: his deathly pale features were contorted, there was foam on his lips, and his eyes darted about wildly.

Promise or not, Lola was not about to abandon her Alemannen in danger, and she put a simple dark blue bonnet on her head, wrapped herself in one of her elegant cashmere shawls, and was driven to see Police Director Mark. But the director was not in. Lola then decided to leave her carriage and walk the five hundred yards down the Theatrinerstraße to Rottmann's Cafe, where the Alemannen were besieged by the mob and the gendarmes. It was about 12:45, and the crowd had quieted down; the situation seemed calm enough that a number of the better citizens were enjoying their usual midday promenade on the Ludwigstraße.

A jeering crowd had followed Lola's carriage to police headquarters, and now, with reinforcements of the curious, they formed a great wake behind her as she strode toward trouble. Oscar Mussinan, the young son of her faithful adherent, struggled to keep pace as he pleaded with her not to go into the square, where between the Odeonplatz and the Feldherrnhalle perhaps three thousand people were now gathered. The countess was not listening. As she came past the yellow baroque facade of the Theatriner Church and into the great square, an angry cry of recognition went up from those closest to her, and the crowd surged toward her, yelling insults and threats. Lola traded insult for insult and threat for threat until horse manure began flying in her direction and some of the men in the mob began to crowd and jostle her. She retreated to the nearby Austrian Embassy, then to the palace of the Arco family, but at both places the porters shut the door on her.

There are several accounts of what happened next. According to one, she was knocked down into a pile of manure. Another says a man grabbed her by the throat and slammed her against an iron fence, and yet another claims that she began striking out left and right. It was also reported that she drew one of her small pistols to drive the mob back, and Oscar Mussinan, in trying to wrest the gun from her, stepped on her skirt and she fell to the ground. Perhaps all the stories are true. She was now clearly in danger of being torn to pieces, and her situation was so desperate that it aroused the pity of two young apprentices in the crowd, who stepped forward and defied the men pressing in, giving her an opportunity to escape into the Theatriner Church.

She was not safe in the church, however, because the crowd streamed in after her. The priests rushed forward, telling everyone to respect the sanctity of the church and protecting Lola from immediate attack; but the crowd watched her carefully to be sure she didn't escape. She threw herself on her knees and cried out loudly, "God protect my best, my only friend!" The priests were urging everyone, particularly the Countess of Landsfeld, to leave the church, and the mob began to move around her, waiting until she stepped outside the tall doors to renew its attack. But the mounted gendarmes who had been guarding Rottmann's Cafe had seen the commotion on the other side of the square, and now they maneuvered their horses in front of the church, clearing the crowd from the doors. Lola emerged and was surrounded by a wedge of eight or ten gendarmes on foot, who escorted her down the Residenzstraße through the surging, cursing crowd. To some onlookers, her exotic beauty appeared more striking than ever as she strode, shaken and enraged, past the sea of threatening faces. At Max-Josephplatz she passed through the sentries into the sanctuary of Ludwig's palace, and the mob was robbed of its prey. All entrances to the palace were closed, and troops were called out to surround it.

The king was upset and angry. He blamed the students for Lola's near-fatal encounter, and he took the draft order for the closing of the university, extended the closure from the fall semester to the winter semester, and dispatched it to Prince Wallerstein with orders to countersign the decree and post it immediately without plea or protest. Under its provisions, all students who were not not permanent residents of Munich would have to be out of town by noon Friday, less than forty-eight hours away. In the street, the crowd gradually dispersed. Just as darkness was setting in, a carriage raced out of the palace to carry the Countess of Landsfeld home. Another carriage took Count Hirschberg from Rottmann's Cafe to police headquarters, where he was charged with carrying a knife and released.

The military were patrolling the streets and guarding the palace and Lola's house. Any chance of street disturbances disappeared by about 9 P.M., when a heavy, cold rain began to fall. Ludwig called at the Barerstraße that evening as usual, where he found Lola and the Alemannen celebrating, and after he left, the countess and the Alemannen continued the party. At about 11 P.M. she came out to the drenched troops, who had the street sealed and under watch, to offer them beer, wine, and food, but she was told that they did not want anything that came from her. Count Bassenheim, whose house was just south of Lola's, also offered food and drink, which the troops gratefully accepted.

By the next morning the rain had stopped, and the dispirited students assembled early at the university. They had brought a horse for Rector Thiersch and persuaded him to ride at the head of the long and solemn procession of the student body from the university, down the Ludwigstraße, and then up the Briennerstraße to Thiersch's home at the corner of Karlstraße and Arcisstraße, only about two blocks from the house of the hated countess. The rector put on his academic robes and regalia and stood on the balcony of his house to address the hundreds of students gathered below.

Speaking eloquently and with emotion, Thiersch tried to reconcile the students to the harsh measure the king had invoked and promised that he and the university senate would do all they could to effect mitigation of the decree and to find financial assistance for the students who had no money available to return home on such short notice. The students cheered the rector, sang "*Gaudeamus igatur*" and other university songs, and then marched off in straight rows back over the Dultplatz (now Maximiliansplatz) and through the Karlstor to pay their respects to Prince Wallerstein at his ministerial office next to the St. Michael's Church. Passing the end of the Barerstraße, they shouted their pereat toward the house of the countess but made no move toward the troops on guard. The king, who was visiting the countess that morning, may have heard them as they marched past.

As they arrived before the ministry, the marchers were surprised to see about two dozen gendarmes led by Captain Baur-Breitenfeld, one of Lola's minions, appear out of the Weitegasse (now Ettstraße), behind the church. The five hundred or so students were augmented now by increasing numbers of curious spectators, and the street was well filled. After the students had raised a cheer for the prince, Captain Baur ordered four mounted gendarmes to move the crowd back and disperse it. Some of the students retreated inside the gate of the ministry building, where they shouted insults and taunts at the gendarmes. Gendarmes on foot rushed the gate to drive out the students, who quickly swung the great doors shut against the charging policeman, knocking two of them to the ground.

The gendarmes forced the doors open and began clubbing the students with their batons. Captain Baur was said to have hit one young man, a pharmacy student from Lübeck, across the back of the head, and he fell to the ground unconscious. The incident was over quickly, but the story spread like wildfire that the unarmed students had been charged from ambush by gendarmes with bayonets fixed and that a student had been struck from behind and killed by Captain Baur. In fact, the student was not even seriously injured, but the story of his death was widely repeated and believed, giving the cause a martyr and yet another villain.

Early in the afternoon Munich's highest civic officials and the city council gathered privately in the ancient Rathaus, the city hall, to discuss the king's closing of the university. At the same time more than a thousand of the city's most respected citizens crowded into the medieval assembly hall of the Rathaus to protest. The university had major economic significance to Munich, bringing more than half a million florins into the city annually. Although the closing of the university would create financial hardship for many, the consensus of Munichers was that the king's decree was wrong because it was unfair to the students, insulting to the city, and manifestly unjust. All had seen Lola Montez parading around insolently with her Alemannen, and no one doubted where the real origin of this decree lay. Beyond insistence that the university remain open, the most universal points of agreement in the Rathaus that afternoon were that Lola's influence over the king was an abomination and that she had to go.

The acting burgermeister, Kaspar von Steinsdorf, told the crowd that its assembly was probably illegal, since it had not been officially sanctioned, but a thousand voices shouted down any idea of dispersing, and the meeting began to consider the situation. It was decided that a delegation would ask the king to revoke the decree, and the citizens crammed into the hall insisted that they wished to follow the delegation to the palace and assemble in the Max-Josephplatz in orderly rows to await the king's decision. Steinsdorf and the other officials advised strongly against such a demonstration, saying the king would surely regard a large mass of men before the palace, no matter how orderly, as an attempt to intimidate him. But the burghers said they had a right to peacefully and respectfully petition their king. A delegation was quickly sent to request that the king receive the burgermeister and representatives and to inform him that the citizens assembled in the Rathaus would gather in respectful silence before the palace to await the result of the audience.

The delegation was told that the king would not return to the palace until 3:30. In fact, he was probably in his apartments with Lola, who visited him there secretly that afternoon. Lola's visit was not a happy one; the king would not exempt the Alemannen from his decree. The countess was not pleased, and she told Ludwig that since this would be the last night she had with them, she would hold a farewell party for Alemannia, and he need not make his usual call that evening.

As 3:30 approached, Burgermeister Steinsdorf and the rest of the delegation arrived at the palace in a carriage, and the thousand and more citizens who had gathered in the Rathaus marched silently, four abreast, from the

Rathaus to the square before the palace, where they arranged themselves in rows. The gates of the palace swung closed, and unarmed cavalry and infantry took up posts between the silent burghers and the palace. The crowd in the Max-Josephplatz grew as the curious arrived, and soon more than two thousand men spilled onto the steps of the royal theater and stood under the arcades of the post office.

When the delegation was finally announced to the king, he sent word that he would not receive them. When the burgermeister humbly insisted, the king responded that he would receive no delegation so long as two thousand men were arrayed before his palace. Steinsdorf asked the king's aide to explain that he and the rest of the delegation had tried to dissuade the others from appearing; but, in any case, the respectful silence of his subjects, loyally awaiting his response to their petition, was in no way a threat to the king. Word came back that the king had made a written reply to their petition and that they would receive it through normal ministerial channels. They were told that the king was at dinner now and could not be disturbed.

Steinsdorf asked to speak with Prince Luitpold, who was not at dinner and quickly received the delegation. He listened sympathetically to the explanation of their mission and promised to intercede with his father on their behalf. He was joined by his wife, Augusta, called Princess Luitpold, and the two of them led the delegation through the reception rooms of the palace to the anteroom of the throne room. The prince and princess left the delegation and went in to make their intercession. From the throne room the delegates heard the king's voice, loud and clearly angry, followed by the tearful voice of Princess Luitpold. The exchange continued for some time, punctuated by the rattle of the king's scabbard against the floor.

At last the doors opened, and Prince and Princess Luitpold, both of in tears, came out. "The king will see you," she told the delegation, "but do not expect a friendly reception." The grand marshal of the court led the burgermeister and his companions, who were self-conscious because they had not had time to don their official robes and regalia, through the corridors to the king's audience chamber, overlooking Max-Josephplatz.

They were admitted to the royal presence, and the king, in a general's uniform and pacing back and forth across the chamber, at once attacked. "Does a deputation come petitioning with 2,000 men at its back? My response to your written petition has been made, and you'll receive it through my minister. I have denied the petition, and I stand by my decision. I carefully considered my order to close the university, and I'm not going to let you talk me out of it."

Whenever the king paused in abusing the Munichers for their greed and ingratitude, punctuating his points by slamming the end of his saber scabbard into the floor, the delegates tried to reassure him of their motives and recognition of his beneficence, but Ludwig was not to be moved. "I'm standing by it, I'm not going to be frightened out of it; my life you can take from me, but not my will." As the delegation was shown out, he took their petition and wrote on it, "I'm sorry for the burghers that the tumult has forced me to adopt this measure. To give in would be weakness. If the burghers do not behave peacefully, they will force me to move my court elsewhere. That is to let them know. Munich, February 10, 1848, facing the thousands on the Max-Josephplatz."

The delegation drove back to the Rathaus, and the burghers, who had stood silently for more than two hours in the February chill, returned to hear the results of the audience. When Steinsdorf announced that the king's response would come through the ministry, perhaps not until the morning, those assembled declared that they would not leave the Rathaus until then.

Dusk was closing in, and in the Barerstraße things were turning violent. A mob of some fifty or more had gathered in the Karolinenplatz in front of the troops blocking the entrance to the Barerstraße. The Countess of Landsfeld could be seen standing on her balcony above the street, chatting with the gendarmes on guard below. The mob at first contented itself with screaming and whistling, but members of the crowd shortly discovered that Count Bassenheim (Lola's neighbor but definitely not her friend) had left his garden gate open, allowing them to pass behind the military picket. The soldiers saw this flanking action but made no move to counter it. One of the gendarmes appealed to the officer in charge of the soldiers to stop the flood of rioters, but the officer replied that his orders were to block the street and that unless the gendarme could present him with a written order from an appropriate officer, that was all he intended to do. The soldiers actually pointed out the route around the end of their line to late-coming rioters who hadn't noticed it.

The rioters, armed with slats ripped from a picket fence, now advanced on the ring of gendarmes guarding Lola's house. The gendarmes charged with bayonet, driving the invaders back in a panic, as Lola stood on the balcony clapping and shouting, *"Très bien, très bien!"* While the attackers were being driven back into the Karolinenplatz, a squadron of cuirassiers arrived and scattered the crowd. There were several serious injuries on both sides of the

192

encounter. Lola went back into the house and prepared the champagne for the Alemannen.

Down at police headquarters in the Weinstraße, a crowd was screaming for Captain Baur. Berks, conceding to public outrage at the rumor of Baur's killing of a student, had already arranged to replace him. But the mob was there to vent its feelings, and rioters overturned beer wagons to block the streets so they would not be disturbed as they tore up the paving stones and proceeded to smash every window in the police headquarters. The damage was substantial; even the ceramic heating ovens were smashed, and eight glaziers were put to work replacing all the windows.

At the Rathaus, Minister Berks, looking incongruous in a blue suit (black was expected for all official occasions), appeared with a message from the king. The shouted insults of the assembly left the minister no doubt how thoroughly unpopular he was, and he might not have been allowed to speak at all had he not been the king's messenger. The vaulted hall, never intended for night assemblies, was gloomy in the light of a few candles; lanterns were placed beside the minister so he could read the royal decree. In the flickering shadows everyone strained to hear that King Ludwig intended, because the citizens had peacefully withdrawn from the Max-Josephplatz, to allow the university to reopen for the summer semester—as long as the Munichers behaved themselves in the meantime: "I have the good of the burghers at heart, I've demonstrated that for more that twenty-three years."

A chorus of angry voices declared that that was not enough. "We want Lola Montez out of Munich!" "And Captain Baur, too!" Berks, whose face was now pale and covered with sweat, withdrew to the small council chamber, where he told the magistrates that he had already ordered Baur's suspension and that the Alemannen were included in the king's order for all nonresident students to leave Munich. Steinsdorf went out to announce this to the shouting multitude. He was repeatedly interrupted by cries of "We'll have no peace until Lola Montez is out of town" and "Let's get weapons and burn down the house in the Barerstraße!" Steinsdorf was finally able to get agreement that the burghers should assemble again the next morning at 8 o'clock, when they would address the problem once more, and the assembly hall emptied.

The king, in an effort to act as if all was normal in Munich, went to the theater, which was nearly empty, stayed for only the first act of Auber's *La Sirène*, and returned to find a note from Lola: "I heard of the infamous conduct of your son and daughter Luitpold—but remain ever as *noble* and *great* as you are, it's your duty to demonstrate that now. Yours ever faithful unto death, Lolitta"

Just before 9:30 a note came in from Berks, who summarized the events of the last few hours and speculated on what the morning would bring. Ludwig took up one of his white goosequill pens and wrote to Lola:

> Just now a letter has come from Berks telling me of the enormous unrest in the city and that without the arrival of a squadron of cuirassiers and the firmness of the police, there could have been an assault on your house. "Tomorrow will be a hot day," he writes me and that it would be good for your health not to stay around here. *I implore you* if you ever loved me and if you love me now, leave for *one day*. It seems best, without saying anything, to go early in the morning to Lake Starnberg, and I repeat, say *nothing* to *anyone*, If it suits you, tell me a time when I can come and see you at your house before you go. You can come back the next day. Better that you leave tonight. You're not afraid, you've given me proof of that, and yesterday gave me new proofs. Not for me, but I'm afraid for you, and if blood is shed on your behalf, the hatred will increase enormously and your situation will become worse. *This must be avoided. The world, you know, is not capable of separating you from me.* I *implore* you once more to take this advice. Lolitta will always love
>
>   Her faithful Luis

The messenger came back from the Barerstraße with Lola's response. She wasn't leaving.

There was a good deal of sleep lost that night in Munich. The members of the noble upper house of the Landtag, the Reichsrat, consulted and called a meeting of all members for 9 A.M. in the ballroom of the Bayrischer Hof. They planned to draft a petition to join their plea with the burghers' that the students be allowed to remain. The students themselves were up debating whether to comply with the order to leave Munich. The general staff of the Civil Guard was trying to decide what to do if the guard were called up to restore order in the streets; it was very possible that no one would respond to a call to defend the Countess of Landsfeld, and even those who appeared might refuse orders and become an armed mob.

The countess herself dispatched a note to Ludwig in the middle of the night urging him to have the light cavalry embark at once by train from Augsburg for Munich. The cuirassiers here are worthless, she told him. The king did order the troops from Augsburg to Munich, but they could not reach the capital in time. No more than two thousand troops could be mustered from the local garrison, and they might have to face ten thousand in the streets.

Ludwig began drafting an appeal to the citizens of Munich. "Look at what Munich was and at what it is, that says enough, also that the university is here," he wrote, reminding them of all he had done for their city. And after all this, how could they rise up against him? Would they force him to move his residence to another city? "Munichers, do you want to break your father's heart!" he wrote, but he never finished the draft.

Friday, 11 February, dawned with the promise of being another bright midwinter day. Perhaps off in Turin, where he was in political exile as ambassador to the Kingdom of Sardinia, Karl von Abel remembered that exactly one year ago he had submitted his now famous resignation memorandum to King Ludwig. In Munich, however, few people could have had time to think about the past; the city was tense and anxious over the day that was just beginning. Before 7 A.M. hundreds of burghers had already gathered in the Rathaus, and their mood was determined and uncompromising. If they didn't get the decision they wanted from the king they would go to the Barerstraße to take care of things themselves. Burgermeister Steinsdorf reminded the burghers that last evening everyone had agreed to meet at 8 A.M., and he persuaded them to give him at least until 9 before they took matters into their own hands. Then he rushed off to find someone to avert the violence and murder that looked imminent.

At Berks's office he ran into Joseph von Maffei, one of Munich's major industrialists and the commanding colonel of the Civil Guard. Maffei was telling Berks that calling up the Civil Guard could be disastrous, for even he had no idea what the civilian volunteers might do once they were assembled. Steinsdorf told Berks and Maffei that if the burghers were not informed by 9 A.M. that the students could stay and that Lola must go, there would be an attack on the Barerstraße. And once blood began to flow, there was no telling where it might end.

Berks left hurriedly for the palace, and Steinsdorf returned to try to buy time with the hundreds of burghers who were pouring into the Rathaus. Their mood was distinctly more hostile and impatient than it had been the day before. The king's reply will come before 10, he told them; the interior minister is at this moment in the palace to request that the students stay and the countess leave. Someone asked whether she would be leaving only the city or be forced to leave the country, and the men began chanting, "Out of the country! Out of the country!" Shortly before 9, a message came from Berks, who wrote that at 10 the council of ministers would consider letting the students remain and that the king had decided on appropriate action in the case of the Countess of Landsfeld. The crowd wanted to know what the appropriate action was going to be, but they were willing to wait until after the council meeting before taking any action of their own.

At the palace, the Duchess of Leuchtenberg, the king's oldest sister, had arrived at 6:30 to beg him to give in to the demands of the people, but he wasn't ready to yield. The reports coming in to him were distressing. The burghers at the Rathaus were threatening violence against Lola, the Reichsrat was plotting at the Bayrischer Hof to place the crown prince on the throne, the Civil Guard refused to report for duty, and the city commandant said his soldiers could not be relied on to resist armed citizens. Most dramatic of all was the king's interview with the new minister of war, von der Mark, who announced that if King Ludwig intended to order him to use the army to defend Lola Montez against the citizens of Munich, he would take the pistol he had brought with him, step into the antechamber, and blow his brains out.

The king sent Mussinan to plead with Lola to leave the city at once and then prepared to preside over the meeting of the council of ministers. A note arrived from Mussinan saying that Lola refused to be moved, that she was still in bed and would not speak with him. The excitement in the streets, he wrote the king, is frightful. The only way to avoid disaster might be to let the students stay. The Civil Guard has failed in its duty. The military cannot be relied on. It is total betrayal.

At the council meeting, Berks confirmed Mussinan's observations on the precarious state of public order, telling the king that if the mob attacked the house in the Barerstraße, the countess could be a corpse within the hour. But, he pointed out, the closing of the university had been an act to punish the students, and the king had a constitutional right to mitigate or pardon; because the students and the burghers had petitioned in a loyal and peaceful manner, it would be appropriate for the king to exercise his pardon power in this case. Ludwig knew very well that what he was going to do was no free exercise of his pardon power but a concession coerced by the threat to Lolitta's life and to his own crown, but he appreciated the opportunity to frame it as something other than complete and ignominious surrender. He agreed to allow the university to reopen at once.

The king refused to order the Countess of Landsfeld out of Munich, but he said that he would do everything he could to see that she left for her own safety. He would go himself to the Barerstraße to convince her that she must leave, and as soon as the council adjourned, Ludwig put on his coat and, ignoring attempts to stop him, began walking alone to see Lola.

The city commandant, General von Kunft, had appeared at the Rathaus at about 9:30 and announced that the Countess of Landsfeld was to leave the city within an hour and that Police Director Mark was on his way to inform her that he was empowered to enforce the order. The general was cheered, and some members of the crowd, not waiting to hear the result of the meeting of the council of ministers, headed for the Barerstraße to see the Spanish woman's departure. Kunft's announcement was false, since Ludwig had insisted that he had no constitutional authority to order her out of Munich. Why the general made his announcement and on whose authority is a mystery, but it did defuse the tension in the Rathaus and throughout the city.

Word of the countess's impending departure spread quickly, and Munichers of all classes and ages hurried, laughing, into the Barerstraße, where the troops and gendarmes stood passively aside. Lola showed herself on the balcony and was greeted with a tumult of scornful laughter, screams, and whistling. She went back into the house and ordered her servants to close the great iron shutters that protected the lower windows facing the street.

A few loyal friends and some of the Alemannen had made their way into the besieged house to plead with her to leave at once. She argued, she threatened, she made demands, but her ultimate resolve was to "stay and die!" Some of her friends continued to try to convince her while others looked for a secure avenue of escape. The mob had filled the Barerstraße, so exit in that direction looked dangerous. A ladder was set up against the rear garden wall to prepare an escape there, but the crowd was warned by neighbors who could see into the courtyard of Lola's property, and scores of the rioters surged over the field behind the wall to block that exit.

The multitude was an astonishing mixture of Munich society, and some of the most distinguished members of the nobility, male and female alike, were seen in what was almost like a great Carnival party, with a bit of blood lust thrown in. The wall and shutters on the Barerstraße made that side of the house relatively secure, but now the mob began to climb the rear fences and the garden wall, and fist-sized stones started smashing into the courtyard windows of the mansion.

Suddenly, to everyone's astonishment, Lola swept out of the house with a pistol in her hand, planted her feet on a small rise in the garden, and shouted in broken German to the mob streaming over the wall, "Here I am! Kill me if you dare!" Frozen for a moment by her wild challenge, the mob watched Lola rage at them, and then the shower of stones was directed at her. "Bad shot!" she screamed. "If you want to kill me, here's where you have to hit!" and she pointed to her heart. It was too much for her friends and servants, who rushed out to overpower her and drag her, screaming and kicking, back into the house. Lieutenant Theodor Weber, an officer whom Lola had gotten transferred from Würzburg to Munich the summer before, helped George Humpelmeyer, Lola's coachman, harness her two pitch-black horses to the carriage. George got up on the box and whipped the animals into a frenzy as her friends and servants dragged the countess, still kicking and screaming, from the house and threw her into the carriage. Weber leaped in beside her, the gates were slammed open, and George drove wildly out into the surprised crowd in the Barerstraße, turned left, and raced north. The mob was stunned for an instant, and then jubilation broke out. Lola was gone!

Back at the Rathaus, the cry had gone up, "The ministers are coming!" as Wallerstein, Berks, and other cabinet ministers were seen arriving from the council meeting. Wallerstein strode into the great hall waving above his head a piece of paper covered with King Ludwig's bold, black handwriting. "Gentlemen!" he said. "The king in his council of ministers has commanded that the lectures at the university should continue. The royal decision was made after the acting minister of the interior in his capacity as police minister had most strenuously emphasized that the demonstration of the citizens did not have the character of a rejection or a threat but was simply an appeal to the heart and to the mercy of the king."

Then, turning to the other subject of immediate interest, he told them, "The father of the nation gave yet another proof of his benevolence through a free decision; I need not say more; everyone knows what is meant. Nothing any longer stands between the king and his people!"

Voices shouted, "Is she really gone?" The minister said yes. "Is she leaving just the city or the whole country?" "Doubtless the country," said Wallerstein, who called on the assemblage to march, as it had the day before, to the Max-Josephplatz, this time to express gratitude to monarch.

But the king was not at home. At that moment he was trying to get to Lola, who he thought was still in her house in the Barerstraße. But the crush of bodies was too much even for a king to make his way through, and he was forced to circle around behind and climb over the garden fence. The scene that greeted him was an orgy of destruction. With Lola gone, the mob occupied the courtyard and began to try to demolish the building. The windows on the courtyard side had been smashed, including those in the wintergarden off the drawing room. Since the servants had secured most of the house, the rioters were busy looting the remains of the Alemannen's farewell banquet from the kitchen in the outbuilding. One looter charged about brandishing a calf's leg as if it were a sword, and others were emptying the champagne bottles.

As the king walked alone across the courtyard a large stone aimed at the house struck him solidly on the arm. Some of the soldiers, who had been observing the pillage, recognized the monarch, and drawing their sabers, they moved in to protect him from further injury. The cry went up, "The king! The king!" and the mob froze before King Ludwig. He placed himself on the steps before the door of the house, and his loud, uninflected voice quavered with emotion. Without receiving any delegation, without an uproar before my palace, I have today given the order to reopen the university, he told them. The crowd cheered and cried "vivat!" I expect, he continued, that this, our house, will be spared, and that those who love me will return to their homes. There were more cheers and the crowd broke into the national anthem, "Hail to Our King, Hail!"

As the rioters began to disperse, Ludwig walked out into the Barerstraße to post a military guard on the house. No one seemed to be in charge, and the soldiers were milling about with the crowd. The king called them to order and gave instructions for the posting of a watch on the house to prevent further damage. Commanding the troops distracted him from the storm of emotions he was feeling. From one of Lola's servants he learned the details of her departure, but no one had any idea where she had gone. She had insisted that she would not leave, so no plans had ever been made for a refuge.

With the guard in place and the mob dispersing, the king, looking bowed and broken to onlookers, began to walk back alone to the palace, followed by a large part of the crowd. As he reached the Karolinenplatz, he saw a screaming group gathered around something lying in the street. They stepped aside as Ludwig approached, and he saw one of Lola's friends, Gregor Mayrhofer, a chocolate maker, crouched terrified in the gutter, covered with horse manure and bleeding from the beating he had received as he tried to escape from Lola's house. Ludwig put the man under his protection, and Mayrhofer struggled along behind the king, fearing for his life, as the mob followed, yelling insults and threats at the beaten man. The grim-faced king saw Mayrhofer safely home and then walked back to his palace.

In the square before the palace, the crowd from the Rathaus awaited the king's return. At one point they saw the figure of Queen Therese at the windows of her apartment, and in response to calls from the square below, she came forward and was greeted with enthusiastic vivats and cheering. The burghers continued waiting patiently for the king until the part of the crowd that could see beyond the eastern end of the palace noticed a familiar brown brougham with its pitch-black horses racing down the far side of the palace from the direction of the English Garden. The carriage came to a halt in front of the palace gate opposite the riding school, apparently attempting to gain admission. But the gate was locked, as all of the gates of the palace had been since the previous afternoon. From the square excited cries went up; "It's Lola! She's here! She's trying to get into the palace!" George whipped up the horses again, turned their heads toward the old part of the city, and raced off into the warren of twisting, small lanes.

At last, a little after noon, the windows of the king's apartment opened, and Ludwig appeared, looking terribly shaken. In the square below, Burgermeister Steinsdorf led the multitude in three cheers, and the king disappeared from the window. A delegation of the Reichsrat was waiting to express its gratitude to him, but the king had a servant tell them the injury from the stone was causing him too much pain to see anyone right now. Instead, he received Minister Berks, because with Berks he could talk about Lola. Ludwig told the minister about confronting the angry mob, about being hit with the stone, about how he had saved her house from destruction, about how he had no idea where she had gone. And as he spoke, the king wept.

18

THE FUGITIVE

After the futile effort to find refuge in the palace, Lola's coachman had twisted and turned through old Munich and finally raced out the Sendling Gate, heading south. At Großhesselohe, about five miles up the Isar River from Munich, they stopped at the beer garden and small hotel near the Trinity Chapel, a popular place for pilgrimage and day excursions in spring and summer but quiet and isolated in the middle of February. Herr Pfaner, the owner, and his family did not share the general hatred of the Countess of Landsfeld, and she, Lieutenant Weber, and George were taken in. Horsemen had set out from Munich to ensure that Lola Montez did not try to return to the city, but they lost her trail.

Lola was indeed determined to return to Munich, but her first concern was to reestablish communication with the king. She scribbled a note telling him that she was safe at Großhesselohe with Weber and begging him to hold to his resolve. She would wait for him there, she told him, until everything was quiet. George changed from his livery into farmer's clothes and set out with Lola's message.

Back in Munich, the afternoon was an occasion of general rejoicing. Strangers smiled and greeted one another and exchanged stories of the events of the morning. After appearing at the Rathaus to express their gratitude to the burghers for their support, the students of the university returned to the courtyard in front of the school, where a barrel of beer was opened in celebration. The gendarmes, who had been all too zealous in their defense of Lola, were the objects of public scorn and sometimes actual assaults, and soon they were rarely to be seen on the streets. Patrols of the Civil Guard and private citizens were established to ensure peace, and by dusk most of the military units that had been ordered into service had returned to their barracks. After a week of disturbances, the city began to return to normal.

Lola's coachman cautiously made his way into Munich. Somehow he put Lola's message into the hands of someone who could get it to the king. Then, having grown too confident in his disguise, he decided to join the celebrating crowds in a tavern in the Barerstraße. He was recognized and was being handled roughly by the denizens of the bar when a patrol intervened to take him into protective custody.

In Großhesselohe, Lola was getting restless. Lieutenant Weber tried to convince her that returning to Munich now was madness, but inactivity under these circumstances was impossible for her. She asked Frau Pfaner to prepare a disguise for her, and together they found some peasant clothing and then powdered her hair white. The tavern owner hitched his horses to a wagon, and with his seventeen-year-old daughter, Caroline, sitting beside the disguised Countess of Landsfeld, they drove back toward Munich.

Once back in the city, Lola reportedly made an effort to get into the palace but was unable to get past the sentries. She visited the home of her friends the Gunthers and heard that most of the Alemannen had taken refuge at Blutenburg, an ancient fortified hunting lodge a few miles west of Munich. The students knew the landlord, who leased the property from the crown as a site for excursions from the city.

Arriving at the lodge late on that bitterly cold night, Lola must have found the fire in the main hall almost as welcome as the sight of her astonished Alemannen. About ten of them had gathered there; she rushed to Fritz Peißner and begged him to return with her to Munich to reestablish her power. Peißner was not eager to link his fate to hers again. Not only did he regard a return to Munich as insane, but his faith in the countess was badly shaken. Although she swore the holiest oaths of fidelity to him, Peißner had watched her lavish her attentions increasingly on his fellow Alemann Ludwig Leibinger, and now he suspected that she was sleeping with him, too. He told her he wouldn't return with her. Lola pleaded with him, but when he remained adamant, she slapped him and yelled at him, asking him if this was how he intended to pay back all she had done for him. Hadn't she gotten his father a high-paying job as a ministry messenger? Hadn't she given him that 1,500-florin pocket watch he was wearing?

After the tension and terror of the day, Peißner, who really believed himself in love with the countess, charged out into the darkness of the courtyard, threatening to kill himself. Lola rushed out after him, begging him to relent and to be hers once more. She finally won him over, and they went back into the hall to prepare for the return to Munich. The portly proprietor, Joseph Schäfer, strongly objected to any further travel at this late hour. Without his help, they couldn't return, so it was decided that everyone would try to sleep for the few hours before the dawn. There were no beds available this time of year, so most of the Alemannen bedded down on straw in the main hall while Peißner and Lola retired alone together to an unheated upper room where she slept on a sofa, covered with coats for warmth, and Peißner stretched out on chairs nearby.

In the meantime, Ludwig, who had received Lola's note, took Berks with him in the early morning to Großhesselohe, expecting to find Lola there. The king had concluded that it was simply too dangerous for her to remain in Bavaria. Together with Berks he decided she should travel first to Lindau on Lake Constance, then cross over to Switzerland, where he would meet her in Lausanne in two months and spend at least several weeks alone with her at last. But Lola was no longer at Großhesselohe, and all the king could learn was that she had gone back to Munich in disguise. Ludwig returned to his palace, dejected.

But news of Lola's whereabouts was not long in coming. Herr Schäfer had slipped off to report his unexpected guests as they slept. He went first to Berks, who told him that the Countess of Landsfeld was simply awaiting her effects before traveling on and that her presence at Blutenburg should not alarm him. Schäfer was not satisfied that Berks took the matter seriously enough, and he went to see Prince Wallerstein, who told him to go to the police. The landlord, apparently weary of wandering about Munich in the light of dawn, instead headed back to Blutenburg but stopped on the way at Nymphenburg Palace, where he persuaded the commander of the cuirassiers to send a squad of cavalry back with him to Blutenburg.

But Berks—who was now well aware that Lola was a danger to the state, even if she had put him where he was—did indeed take her presence at Blutenburg seriously, and he had taken his own measures to see that she was rendered harmless. As Schäfer and the cuirassiers arrived at Blutenburg at about 8 o'clock, two policemen appeared; they had orders from Minister

Berks to see the Countess of Landsfeld safely to the steamboat at Lindau. The two officers entered the main hall of the lodge and found Lola sitting on a bench with several of the Alemannen. She had written a letter urging the king to move the royal residence to Nürnberg as a well-deserved punishment for the way the Munichers had behaved. And, according to Schäfer's wife, Lola had repeated to herself that morning as she dressed, "Now I want the crown!" When the police officers announced the reason for their presence and displayed their orders, Lola sprang up enraged, shouting *"Raus! Raus!"* and the officers retreated into the courtyard.

Eventually some of the Alemannen came out to read the orders and then went back inside to try to reason with the countess. After about half an hour Lola emerged with Peißner, Leibinger, and Jacob Härteiß, who had been selected as her Alemannen escort, but she was not about to go quietly. She threatened the policemen with her miniature pistol, and when they presented her again with their orders to escort her to Lindau, she tore the paper to pieces and threw them on the ground. Peißner, with a bit more sense of convention, carefully picked up the pieces. After boasting that she had been in a cafe in Munich last evening but not a fool recognized her, and warning the officer in charge of the cavalry detachment that the king would move his residence to Nürnberg, Lola finally submitted, and she, the three Alemannen, and the two policemen packed themselves into a waiting carriage to drive to Passing, the nearest train station on the route to Augsburg. The cuirassiers provided a mounted escort just to be sure that no detours were attempted.

The trip to Lindau involved changing trains and transferring to carriages, and it was 10 P.M. Saturday before the party pulled into the picturesque town on Lake Constance. Along the way, Lola had written a letter to Ludwig:

> My very ever beloved Louis
> These lines are from the train from Augsburg—I am very unhappy—my poor heart is broken—I have no clothes with me, nothing, nothing—I had to put on a pair of pajamas. This democracy has won a great victory but I hope it is not forever. . . . I haven't stopped loving you, dear, dear Louis. . . . Please don't make me wait long before you come to me—I'm so unhappy—but I'm not afraid—I have a little pistol and a dagger with me—and note—place no further confidence in Berks—*caution* and *prudence*—I have my reasons for this. Yours ever faithful unto death,
> Lolitta

Poor Baur—he did his duty—and dear Louis, be careful of influences—this is all a *plan* to separate me from you so that you will more readily listen to your enemies who are determined to succeed, but dear Louis
FIRMNESS

A steamboat was waiting to ferry the countess across the lake to Switzerland, but Lola refused to leave without her clothes and personal effects, and she and the students checked into the town's best hostelry, the Hotel de la Couronne. The policemen turned over their duties to a local magistrate, who received secret orders from Berks to arrest the Countess of Landsfeld if she attempted to return to Munich.

The mood of the public was festive in Munich, but the king was torn by feelings of loss, anger, and revenge. Ludwig was isolating himself from those around him. Prince Wallerstein, who had never really had the king's full confidence, had seriously undermined his position by the stance he had taken during the crisis, particularly his remark at the Rathaus that "nothing any longer stands between the king and his people." The king resented the implication that Lola had separated him from his subjects. Now the principal minister compounded matters by writing the king a gratuitous memorandum attacking the Countess of Landsfeld for her arrogant and immoderate behavior, reminding the king of his repeated warnings that Lola had to change her ways, use savoir faire. She was her own worst enemy, Wallerstein wrote, and she told me that she would have me out by 1 March, that she had already convinced the king. But I'm not angry with her, he concluded, because I regard her as having absolutely no responsibility for her own acts.

Wallerstein had sealed his fate; the king secretly resolved to dismiss him as soon as the students left town on holidays. Berks was the only minister who now enjoyed the king's confidence, though Lola had warned the king against trusting him, apparently because of his role in arranging her exile. At the same time, public resentment focused more and more on Berks; proscription lists were circulating in Munich with the names of anyone who had connections to Lola, and Berks was high on all the lists. But the king was determined to show the world that although Lola had been forced to leave by an ungrateful and disorderly citizenry, his loyalty and affection for her remained unchanged. On the very day that Lola left Munich, Ludwig bluntly told Queen Therese that the catastrophe had attached him more firmly than ever to the Countess of Landsfeld. While the gendarmes were being pursued and attacked because of their defense of Lola, Ludwig ordered that they be paid a bonus for that defense. And now Berks, the most hated man in Munich, became his closest adviser.

Across Europe, conservatives and radicals alike avidly read the telegraphic reports of the uprising in Munich, and an astute observer in Berlin commented, "Don't they see that the people can do anything, when they want to? That the power of princes disappears in the face of the determined might of the people?" The lesson of Lola's departure and of the reopening of the university had certainly not been lost on Munichers, and petitions began to circulate privately with new demands to be made upon the king concerning civil rights and liberties.

In Lindau, Lola was understandably miserable, and she sat down to write Ludwig a long letter that probably reflects the way she spoke to the king:

I seem to myself like a criminal in flight, even more so because, probably on Berks's advice, you mixed the police up in this scandal, and you'll see in the papers that *I* was forced to leave by *you yourself* and that the police escorted me; I hadn't expected that from you, my dear Louis, and I'm *very certain* that this *cruel* idea was not yours—but I am resigned to *everything* now. . . . I'm in a deplorable state physically, and even more spiritually, because who knows now that I have been separated from you whether enemies and false friends will tell you lies about me—Now I know why that person unknown to me told you that infamous lie about the student Peißner, and you, my poor dear Louis, believed it! . . . I beg of you not to forget what I have suffered for my Louis, because I didn't want to deceive you like the others, but always told you the truth about others even against my own best interest; that is enough to assure you that I love you infinitely; but I am so unhappy now—although everyone here is very nice to me, I think that only in the tomb will I find rest. . . don't confide in anyone, neither man nor woman—*no one is completely sincere* [text is double underscored in manuscript]—to pass my time in exile, I want to study German, and in a little while I hope to be able to write to you in your own language. But, my dear Louis, in truth I can't wait the whole time in Switzerland—in truth, *it's not possible*, this country is so sad in winter and cold. . . . I think with fear and *horror* of living in Switzerland—it's a terrible punishment— send me another passport with an English name—and I'll leave with it on the instant for Palermo—I got my period yesterday and I am very indisposed. While I'm here I don't intend to go out in order to avoid public curiosity—farewell, my Louis, until I get a letter from you, and my *dogs*, servants, and things arrive, I'll wait here, and from my heart I give you thousands of kisses from your faithful

Lolitta

Don't forget me and don't be unfaithful to me.

At this crucial moment in his reign, when Ludwig was inclined to withdraw, hurt and angry, into himself despite his desperate need for sound political advice, Lola urged him to trust no one. The public euphoria that followed Lola's flight and the reopening of the university quickly ebbed as people realized that Ludwig was deeply resentful of what had happened and was simply biding his time until he could reassert himself and bring Lola back. Ludwig was like a wounded lion, and everyone around him grew cautious and silent.

While the whole nation was aware of the public humiliation the king had suffered, no one realized that his heart was breaking over what he believed was Lola's betrayal. For weeks Ludwig had suspected that Lola was having an affair with Fritz Peißner. Now an illustrated broadside entitled "The Night in Blutenburg" detailed the stay of Lola and the Alemannen at the lodge, including the fact that she and Peißner had retired to a private room for the night, or at least for the few hours of it remaining before the dawn.

Although Ludwig was no longer publicly denying the sexual nature of his feelings for Lola, he still maintained the pose of platonic lover so effectively that even Peißner, who often saw the king and Lola together, could believe that Ludwig was planning to marry him to the countess. In fact, Ludwig was tortured by fear that Lola's heart did not belong to him alone, and discovering that Peißner and Lola had spent the night together at Blutenburg was as devastating to him as a man as the coerced reopening of the university had been to him as a monarch. That she could casually retire in front of the proprietor, his family, and all the Alemannen to sleep with Peißner appeared to indicate that her relationship with the student was just what rumor had told him.

When Mussinan took the king's letters to Lola at Lindau, Ludwig instructed him to persuade the countess to get rid of the students and to tell her that under no circumstances would any of them be allowed to travel to Switzerland with her. Mussinan also received orders to see whether the Alemannen were sleeping in their own beds, and he carried a message from Ludwig to the three that any of them who left German territory to follow the countess would lose all hope of the king's help.

Torn between missing her desperately and despising her for what she had done, the king poured out his agony in a letter to Lola: "I was desperate, almost mad in this separation from you; if only you had been a faithful lover to me; and even during the time you were here I was convinced you weren't; the separation from you has made me so, so unhappy! Luis is not subtle like Lolitta or Prince Wallerstein, but he is no fool. I don't speak of the Jesuits or the nobles, they felt other motives, but you have betrayed my love in public and made an enemy of it. Your infidelities have betrayed my heart, but it forgives you, and I repeat: the world is not capable of making me break with you, you alone can do that. Do you want that, Lolitta? Oh, if only it were possible for you to be faithful to me in all things, or at least sincere, a limitless sincerity!"

But he never sent that letter. Instead, the reproach that Lola actually received was almost casual: "You are my faithful friend," he wrote her, "but a faithless lover. . . . You can't imagine the effect produced on the public that on the very night of the catastrophe Peißner, of all people, went to bed with you at Blutenburg. . . . Always concerned with his *faithful friend* Lolitta is Your faithful Luis."

Lola's reply treated the Peißner matter as secondary. First she wrote Ludwig that the ultramontanes had achieved their goals by freely distributing money in the right places. She had always told Ludwig he shouldn't be so tightfisted, particularly with the army officers, "but you didn't do anything and now look at the consequences." "As for Peißner, the student," she wrote:

> You must think I am very mean spirited and that my heart is quite miserable to occupy myself with a lover—when all my ideas, all my thoughts have to be first to defend you and then my friends—I come last of all—no, my dear Louis, I have *other things* to do with these students than the bestiality of sleeping with them—don't you think I haven't had a better reason, all this time? Do you really believe that this Peißner or some other student is my lover? To have *all of them* fall in love with me, yes, that was my intention, a man can do a lot for love. . . . These things they say about the students are laughable—I'm so far above such common lies—but later you will discover why I have been so much their friend—but one thing I *swear* to you is that *not one of them is or will be my lover.* . . . If you could read my heart, you would see that love without you is no love at all—it's animal bestiality, and all my life I've been known as a *cold* woman because most people have no idea of the *ideal* love I have only for you—dear Louis—in front of everyone here I'm happy so they don't have the satisfaction of seeing me sad—I'm too proud for that, but alone, sometimes in the night, when no one sees me, I have *cried* so much, far from *you*, my only protector, who has done so much for love of me—I'm crying right now—I can no longer see the paper through my tears—it seems to me the world wants to slowly break my heart—It would be better to kill me quickly, that would be better than the constant pain in my heart.

And as the king read of Lola's tears, he could see the faint stains on the page in his hand. He was not completely convinced, though he desperately wanted to believe. But the students must leave. The same day Lolitta had written him her tearstained letter, he had written one to her:

Very dear Lolitta,

You know it: the whole world does not have the power to separate you from me, you alone have it. *The decisive moment has arrived.* If a student travels with you, or joins you, *you will never see me again, you have broken with me.* Lolitta, you inspire a love in me as no one ever has before in my life. Never have I done for another what I have done for you. With your love, it would mean nothing to me to break with everything. Much beloved, think of the past 16 months, how your Luis has conducted himself in this time we have known each other. You will never find a heart like mine. Lolitta has the decision.

But it was another letter he never sent. Instead, when he dispatched Mussinan to Lindau again, this time with orders to escort the countess to Switzerland, the king told him to press the matter of the students' departure with the countess as soon as their passports arrived. That was just what Mussinan did, and Lola burst out screaming and sobbing. Her agitation increased when the messenger reminded her it was the king's will, that she herself had promised Mussinan that the students would be sent back in a few days. I told you that, she said, simply to keep you quiet; I never had any intention of sending them away. Mussinan became persona non grata at the Hotel de la Couronne, and Lola wrote Ludwig that "to make you happy, I'm separating myself from all my friends. I'm ready to travel alone. Because of the strange ideas you have about those students, I made them leave to satisfy your ideas."

When Augusta Masson, Lola's maid, arrived in Lindau, Lola accused her of stealing a valuable prayer book that had been a present from Ludwig, as well as some expensive cashmere shawls. She fired Augusta during a violent scene and then wrote Ludwig four rambling, repetitive pages of invective and hysteria, accusing the maid of being a thief and a whore, insisting that all of Augusta's effects be searched and that her mother's house be searched, and demanding that no effort be spared in recovering the items and bringing the maid to justice.

Lola then suggested that the actress Maria Denker provide her with feminine companionship on the trip to Switzerland. Ludwig had passports to Palermo prepared for both of them under false names, but when Lola realized that such a journey would involve a winter sea voyage of two weeks, something she dreaded, and that Ludwig was determined to meet her in Lausanne on 11 April, she reconciled herself to staying in Switzerland.

Waiting in Lindau, Lola continued to read the foreign press assiduously and had the German press translated to her. "Read the *free* newspapers of your country," she wrote to Ludwig, "and see the evil that *Wallerstein* has created with his free press—and remember my words—if you had formed a *secret police*, this terrible thing never would have happened."

When Maria Denker finally arrived, more trouble was brewing at the Hotel de la Couronne. Lola had once again shifted her affections from Peißner to Ludwig Leibinger. Mussinan reported to Ludwig that the other student, Härteiß, told him that he had seen the countess similarly transfer her affections before the final days in Munich. The countess treated Peißner with obvious indifference, even anger, and grew more and more affectionate with Leibinger. Peißner was sick at heart and sure that if she had not been having sexual relations with his rival before they left Munich, she certainly was now, for Leibinger stayed alone with her in her hotel room long after everyone else had said good night. Peißner finally provoked an angry scene with Lola in which she threw herself at his feet, crying, "Forgive me, your bad woman!" She sobbed that she hadn't really wanted Leibinger, that she didn't love him, that it was a silly caprice, and they had a reconciliation of sorts. Frau Denker was appalled by what was going on and told Lola that she should avoid creating such obvious scandal. The countess's response was to slap the actress and shove her out the door of the hotel room, and Denker angrily returned to Munich, leaving Mussinan alone to act as Lola's escort into exile.

At 9 A.M. on 24 February, a few days after the three students had left to join their fellow Alemannen at Plauen in Saxony, the countess and Mussinan descended to the dock at Lindau, where about a hundred curious citizens were waiting to see her depart. There was no jeering, and the men respectfully removed their hats as Lola boarded the steamship *Ludwig* to cross Lake Constance to Romersholm in Switzerland. Once on the Swiss side, she took a coach to Zurich and checked in that evening at the Hotel Baur. There she found a letter to "My dear Lola" from her old friend Robert Peel, the British chargé d'affaires in Bern. It would be a pleasure, he wrote, to see her again. The chargé wished to offer her any assistance he might be able to provide in her new Swiss home.

19

BOLDNESS AND BETRAYAL

In response to Peel's invitation, Lola traveled on with Mussinan to Bern, where she met her old friend and other members of the diplomatic community. Politics was the topic of the day, but before Lola could grow weary of recounting her adventures in Munich, news arrived that shocked everyone and monopolized discussions: a revolution had broken out in Paris, King Louis Philippe and his family had fled across the channel with little more than what they had on their backs, and the Second French Republic had been declared. Europe's year of revolution, 1848, was now in full swing, and memories of the first French revolution, terrible for some, glorious for others, preoccupied everyone. Lola, surrounded by political rumors and diplomatic gossip much richer than what she had usually heard in Munich, was more fickle in her convictions than ever. On 27 February she wrote Ludwig: "Things in France are very bad—I'm worried about Munich. . . . above all else, keep Wallerstein. . . . If you love me, prove it and be very politic with Wallerstein—although he's a bad man, he's the only one who can hold things together—above all, give *him some public attention.* If he leaves, your Lolitta will never be back in Munich."

The next day she wrote the king: "This man [Wallerstein] is the most dangerous in the world for you. . . . don't leave Wallerstein *any power* or influence on you—he is your perdition."

The king had probably never taken Lola's political advice very seriously, though he did listen to it and even asked for it, but now he must have realized that she was useless as an independent voice to guide him. Unfortunately, the only man he seemed willing to listen to was Lola's toady Berks.

Ludwig continued to undermine his own position by making no secret of his simmering rage at the exile of the countess, and no one, from Wallerstein to the lowest apprentice in the streets of Munich, trusted him to act rationally. As a consequence, the natural desire to force more concessions from King Ludwig took on even greater urgency.

The general unrest in Munich was so evident that Berks finally tendered his resignation on 2 March, but the king persuaded him to take merely a leave of absence. It came none too soon, because that night a mob attacked Berks's apartment in the Ludwigstraße, forcing him to flee Munich in disguise with his family. The rioters raced from Berks's home through the dark streets of Munich, causing serious damage to a number of public buildings, including the Interior Ministry and, once again, the police headquarters.

Before the riot, groups of citizens in Munich and other cities in Bavaria had begun drafting petitions asking the king for major liberalizations, among them ministerial responsibility to the Landtag, abolition of press censorship, institution of public trials with testimony by witnesses, representation of German citizens in addition to governmental representation at the German Assembly in Frankfurt, a new voting law, a new police law, and a military oath to the constitution instead of to the king personally.

After the night of rioting, a petition to the king circulated in the capital and soon was reported to have the signatures of ten thousand people, or 10 percent of the population. When presented with the petition, Ludwig, to whom all the proposed liberalizations were offensive, tried to play for time by dissolving the Landtag and calling for new elections. But public restlessness and distrust of the king's motives grew, and on 6 March the city armory was stormed, and a full-scale revolution threatened to break out. Ludwig was told that unless he yielded, the mob would burn his palace to the ground. He capitulated and signed what became known as the March Proclamation, granting virtually everything requested by the petitioners.

The king was angry, depressed, and bitter at the concessions that had been forced from him and at the degradation he felt, but he did not lose sight of his hope of seeing Lola in Switzerland in April. He was afraid that he would not be able to leave the country if the Landtag was in session, but he was assured that after an initial convocation, only the principal committees of the two houses would remain sitting, leaving him free to, as he wrote Lola, "fly to your arms."

For the moment, King Ludwig was once again the father of his country. On the night of 6 March the city was illuminated in honor of the king, who was tortured by one of his migraine headaches. Now he was the hero of the nation, but he was disgusted at himself for having allowed his royal will to be broken. Jubilant citizens thronged the Max-Josephplatz, and at last the grim-faced King Ludwig appeared with Queen Therese above the wildly cheering multitude. As the thousands below shouted their loyalty and devotion, Ludwig muttered the single word "humiliated!" and turned away.

In spite of his feeling of self-contempt, Ludwig, thanks to the constitutional concessions he had been forced to grant, now appeared more secure on his throne than he had been since the day Lola Montez arrived in Munich. If no new storms swept trouble into Bavaria, he had a better chance of navigating the political reefs and shoals of this year of revolutions than perhaps any other of the German princes. He might even have a crucial role to play in guiding the German nation through a dangerous moment in its history. But trouble was once again on its way to Munich, in a coach traveling from Switzerland.

The Countess of Landsfeld was an unhappy exile. Granted, her reception in Bern had been a reasonably pleasant one—so pleasant that she gave no thought to traveling on to Lausanne, which had been her original destination. In Bern Robert Peel called on her, introduced her into the diplomatic circle, and promenaded with her about town, where they were followed by bands of the curious. Lola had also renewed an acquaintance with a nobleman from Latvia, Baron Georges Meller-Zakomelsky; he was probably the Russian nobleman with whom she had traveled around Germany in the summer of 1846.

But what she was hearing, and not hearing, troubled her. The news of the revolution in Paris and the flight of King Louis Philippe had shaken her; she wrote an agitated letter to Ludwig quoting the Book of Proverbs—"Boast not thyself of tomorrow, for thou knowst not what a day may bring forth"— and warning him to get all of his money and valuables out of the country to some place beyond political turmoil. Come to me, she wrote to the troubled king, come and live with me in tranquility. I will devote my whole life to you; you'll see how much I've changed. In the midst of Europe's political panic, she told him, I am the most afflicted of all. Even the first days after I was driven from Munich were not as horrible as the present, and each day I feel more miserable. Now that I am gone, my enemies will tell you lies about me and poison your mind against me, but whatever happens, dear Louis, you will always remain for me what you are.

Most troubling to Lola was the fact that she had not heard from Ludwig since she left Lindau. She feared that the king had begun to hear more stories of her behavior while she was in Munich, and she convinced herself that her friends were abandoning her. She wrote to Fritz Peißner at Plauen where he and the other Alemannen had found temporary refuge, and told him she must see him; and if he would not agree to meet her secretly at Frankfurt am Main, she would come to Plauen herself (the type of threat she typically used to get her way). Peißner was still bitter about her affair with Leibinger, but he noticed that no letters from the countess were arriving in Plauen for Leibinger, and he decided to travel to Frankfurt.

In the meantime, news reached Bern of the renewed turmoil in Munich. Her friends in Bern had been asking Lola troubling questions about what sort of guaranty she had for her annual income of 20,000 florins from King Ludwig, and she realized that her financial well-being was dependent on the continuing goodwill of a sixty-one-year-old king on a shaky throne. Had he abandoned her? Could she win him back?

With only bad news arriving and not a word from Ludwig, Lola decided on a desperate measure, one that not only would put her in mortal danger but also would have dramatic repercussions in the life of King Ludwig and for the fate of the Bavarian crown. She decided to disguise herself as a young man and, with Baron Meller as a traveling companion, secretly return to Munich to try to speak to Ludwig, to win him back.

The Countess of Landsfeld and Baron Meller left Bern by coach, traveling north across Baden and Württemberg into Bavaria. Heavy snow fell that day, and the two of them arrived at the Bayerischer Hof in Munich late on 8 March. They hurried to Wurzerstraße 12, where Caroline Wegner lived upstairs. Caroline's father had worked on the upholstery in Lola's Barerstraße house, and the countess had befriended the daughter and got her new husband a job as a government messenger. Now Lola and Meller stood in the darkness insistently pulling the bell on the Wegner apartment.

The noise caught the attention of an officer who occupied the ground-floor apartment, and he opened his door in time to see two figures, wrapped in cloaks, being admitted and led upstairs. He noticed that the smaller of them was wearing a false beard and was speaking excitedly in French; his suspicions were immediately aroused because there had been rumors that agitators were planning to set fire to the royal hay depot, located just up the Wurzerstraße. The officer pulled on a coat and hurried off to police head-quarters, returning with two gendarmes who insisted on searching the Wegner apartment. The occupants said the two strangers had already departed, but then the one with the false beard was discovered hiding under a sofa and was led off to police headquarters in the Weinstraße.

There the astonished officers of the law found that the young man in their custody was none other than the much-hated Countess of Landsfeld. A mes-senger was sent to wake Police Director Mark, who quickly dressed and, at about 1 A.M., made his way to the palace. The police director was perplexed; if it became known that Lola Montez was back in Munich, there was no telling what the consequences would be. But he knew that the king would not forgive him if he expelled the woman without informing him first. Roused from his sleep, Ludwig could hardly believe what Mark was saying to him. The police director urged him not to see the countess and to give the order for her immediate deportation, but Ludwig would not hear of it. He dressed quickly and hurried with Mark to the police headquarters, where he was admitted to the room where the countess was being held.

It was an emotional reunion. Lola told him she had been frantic and had risked being torn to pieces by a mob because she had not heard a word from him since leaving Bavaria. The king assured her that he had written some-thing every day, but of course until 7 March he had been sending all his let-ters to Lausanne. For three hours they talked alone together, and Lola reproached him for his faithlessness, saying that he had forgotten her and was transferring his affections to another, probably to Maria Denker, who was a schemer. Ludwig assured her that she was constantly in his thoughts, that he was faithful to her as he never had been to a woman. Her jealousy bothered him; it seemed so irrational, and yet it was flattering. It made him feel that she loved him as a man, not simply as a powerful and wealthy king.

We have to be together, Lola insisted; I can't endure this separation. The king ruefully explained that it was clear she could never live in Munich again. Then come away with me, she said. Leave Bavaria. Your people don't love you any longer; they don't appreciate all you have done for them. Leave them, come live with me. Abandon the thankless burden of your crown, and when we are together in tranquility and love, then your people will realize all they have lost. Ludwig was tempted, but what Lola suggested was too much. Abandoning the throne, his wife, his family, and his nation was more than he was prepared to do, even for his obsessive love.

Lola had practical considerations to discuss, too. Somehow Ludwig must guaranty her income; as there was no telling what chaos might be ahead, Peel thought he should put her money safely in Belgium. Ludwig assured her that her lifetime financial security was his constant concern and that he would make sure she would not want for money, though he needed to work out the details carefully.

More than that, she told him, she wanted to sell her house and have all of her beautiful things sent to her. That needed to be done as soon as possible. And he should dismiss Wallerstein. The minister was plotting against him and wanted to put the crown prince, whom he could control, on the throne. His hand had been behind the mob that drove her from Munich.

Ludwig was overwhelmed to think that this woman had risked her life to come to him, but for her own safety, she had to leave. Lola and the king said their farewells there at the police station. He fully expected to see her again in a few weeks in Switzerland. Gendarmes escorted her and Baron Meller back to the Promenadenplatz and put them on the westbound post coach leaving at dawn.

Standing in her masculine disguise looking up at the starry late winter sky, Lola knew she was seeing the dark shadows of Munich's turrets and spires for the last time. She thought of her sixteen months of astonishing glory in the city, of the proud ambition that had seized her, of her violent and sudden fall. Then she climbed into the waiting coach and headed to new adventures.

The news of Lola's return spread rapidly through Munich. With the newly declared press freedom, it even was fully reported in the newspapers, though her interview with the king was tactfully omitted. But everyone heard that she had spent three hours alone with Ludwig, and new rumors and suspicions of the king's real motives and intentions sprang up not only in Munich but also across Bavaria. The situation was aggravated by the fact that no official escort out of the country had been placed on the Countess of Landsfeld, and even the police were unable to track her movements beyond Landsberg, where she had eaten lunch on the day of her expulsion. Bavarians began to doubt that the Spanish woman had really left the country.

Ludwig, meanwhile, was doing his best to accept being hailed as the father of the nation's liberties, which he viewed as public degradation. In his mind, the revolutionaries had beaten him and now they had the incredible presumption to expect him to smile and rejoice with them. The king took satisfaction on 11 March , exactly one month after his beloved Lolitta had been driven away, in suddenly dismissing Prince Wallerstein, whom he held responsible for most of the unpleasant events of the last four weeks. Ludwig was gratified by the prince's surprise and shock. Wallerstein's last sin in the king's eyes had been failing to get Ludwig's formal permission before informing Gottlieb von Thon-Dittmer, a liberal Protestant politician, that he would take Berks's place as interior minister. The king accepted Thon-Dittmer as minister but fired Wallerstein, who, he told the new interior minister, was the "prince of lies."

The city celebrated on 13 March, an official day of thanksgiving to mark the king's 6 March proclamation. Ludwig could barely contain his disgust as he was paraded in triumph about the city. The students tried to unhitch the horses from the royal carriage and draw it themselves, but he ordered them to desist. As he rode down the Ludwigstraße with Queen Therese, past the flag-draped buildings and the cheering crowds, Ludwig remarked bitterly that in the space of a few days Jesus Christ heard the hosannas of the multitudes and then was crucified by the same people.

In spite of the prevailing enthusiasm for the king, Lola's visit had poisoned the public's mind, undermining Ludwig's authority. Rumors circulated that Lola Montez was hiding somewhere within Bavaria, awaiting the right moment to emerge and lead the king into reactionary repression. Mobs appeared before purported hiding places and demanded to be allowed to search for the fugitive countess. The king received letters from Lola's few remaining friends telling him that if he knew where in Bavaria she was hiding, he should tell her to flee for her own safety. Ludwig was baffled, for he believed that she had returned to Switzerland, but no one completely trusted his denials of knowledge.

On 15 March a mob attempted to storm the royal palace at Fürstenried, outside of Munich, because of a rumor Lola was hiding there. Others were sure that she was in the royal palace in Munich. The disturbances became so serious that the interior minister felt obliged to ask the king what he knew of the countess's whereabouts, and Ludwig again swore he knew nothing.

Ludwig himself may have unknowingly set off the most serious incident by paying a call the morning of 16 March on Caroline Wegner, whom Lola had visited on the 8th. In addition to thanking Caroline for her loyalty to the countess, Ludwig wanted to ask the young woman whether she knew where Lola was. But the king was seen entering and leaving the building, and word spread that Lola Montez was again hiding in the Wurzerstraße. A mob surrounded the building to prevent any escape until a team of gendarmes arrived to search the building thoroughly. They even built a fire to make sure the countess wasn't hiding in the chimney. The mob was angry that the Spanish woman had escaped, and it grew suspicious when the gendarmes, her personal guards when she lived in Munich, were incapable of finding her.

That evening, while the king was at a performance of Mozart's *Abduction from the Seraglio*, a mob again gathered around the police headquarters in response to a rumor that Lola was hiding there. Again the paving stones were torn up, and every new window in the building was shattered. But this time the mob actually attempted to demolish the building. The window frames were destroyed by stones, the drainpipes were ripped down, shutters were torn off, and the walls themselves damaged. Finally the main door was beaten down, and rioters rushed into the building. They beat gendarmes in the corridors and tossed files out into the gutter.

Interior Minister Thon-Dittmer, who enjoyed great popularity, rushed to the scene and was attempting to calm the mob when a rock hit him in the head, sending a stream of blood down his face and onto his coat. King Ludwig was called from his box at the theater, and drumrolls signaling the mobilization of all troops and of the Civil Guard were heard. The mob swarmed around the city, trying to break into the armory and harassing the troops stationed at major public buildings. The ministry issued a declaration that a member of the Landtag had just returned from a trip to Karlsruhe, where he had seen the Countess of Landsfeld on the 14th taking the train to Heidelberg. It was a long, restless night in Munich, but the patience and discipline of the ill-paid troops prevented bloodshed.

The next morning there was another angry assembly at the Rathaus. This time people demanded the immediate dismissal of Police Director Mark, for his handling of the recent return to Munich of the Countess of Landsfeld, and the reinstatement of Lola's first victim, Baron Pechmann. In addition, the petitioners insisted that the king ban the countess from Bavaria and order her arrest if she were found in the country.

A delegation presented the petition to Thon-Dittmer, who had recovered from his injury of the evening before; he and the other ministers went to the palace to beg the king to grant the requests. Disturbances in Vienna had just forced Prince Metternich, the wiliest of statesmen, to tender his resignation, and the specter of continental revolution was rising. The ministers counseled total concession.

Ludwig was stunned by these humiliating demands. It was constitutionally impossible for him to exile a Bavarian citizen, he told them. A month earlier he had merely asked the Countess of Landsfeld to leave Munich for her own safety; he had no right to tell her to leave, even if he had wished to. The ministers told the king that the demands of the petition had to be granted in some manner, perhaps by revoking the countess's citizenship; otherwise, the ministers said they could not answer for the reaction of the burghers. Ludwig denied that he had the right to revoke her citizenship, but the ministers insisted that some formula had to be found, and ultimately the king decided to implicitly renounce Lola's citizenship on her behalf by issuing a decree stating merely that she had "ceased to possess Bavarian citizenship."

For him this was a betrayal not only of his dignity as a king but also of his loyalty to Lolitta. He sat down and wrote her a sad, bewildered letter:

My very beloved Lolitta
The love of your heart for your Luis makes me certain that you want me to make the sacrifice of renouncing your Bavarian citizenship. The revolution is at Vienna, and in Munich something terrible will happen this afternoon, if not before; your citizenship ceases, *in consequence and in conviction of your love for me.* I pronounced that you no longer have it, at the insistence of the heads of the ministries, who came to me. I did it in the certain anticipation that your love will make this sacrifice for me. But the truth is that my beloved Lolitta was right, that Luis is no longer loved, only your heart remains to love me. You yourself told me you felt you could not come back to Munich. You would be murdered if you came. Even without citizenship, you remain Countess of Landsfeld, it makes no difference. . . .
It is possible, but I cannot say for certain now, that I will renounce the crown; in this critical situation it seems to me a lack of courage to do so. My so beloved Lolitta, always love
Your faithful Luis

Ludwig was beginning to struggle with the idea that he should abdicate. With all of his failings, he most certainly had the character of a sovereign, a man who imposed his will on others; that made the concessions that had been wrung from him excruciating, but it also meant that he could hardly be happy as anything less than a king. Now, however, he had been so demeaned in his own eyes, had been forced to make so many reprehensible concessions that the king began to wonder whether there was any point going on. Only Lolitta truly loved him, and as long as he remained king, there would be no telling when he could be with her. If he were a private citizen, no one could object to his seeing her whenever he wished.

As King Ludwig wrestled with this dilemma, Lola was in Frankfurt with Fritz Peißner. She had indeed passed through Karlsruhe on 14 March, on her way to a rendezvous with her lover. She had been recognized while changing trains in Heidelberg, and the university students, in solidarity with their fellows in Munich, had jeered and shouted insults for the two hours she had to wait there. The purported purpose of her trip was to confer on business with a friend in Mannheim, but its real goal was reunion with Peißner.

Apparently on the theory that the best defense is a good offense, Lola had written Ludwig after her return to Bern from her secret trip to Munich, hysterically accusing him of taking Maria Denker as his lover. She told Ludwig that Denker had been sleeping with one of the students, that she was also the lover of Minister Berks, that she had engineered Peißner's recent expulsion from Alemania—which, Lola had heard, had driven the poor young man to seek solitude in Besançon. Denker has doubtless told you that Peißner was my lover, she said, but that was all a lie. "I tell you once again," Lola wrote, "that he was never more than a *brother* to me . . . You know very well that I'm an orphan, without father, mother, brother, or sister—isn't it natural in that position that I would seek out some people . . . to confide in more than others. . . . You have to believe me, Louis, that your Lolitta never saw in poor Peißner more than a man who had a pure love for her like the love for the Virgin Mary. . . . But for the world, it is all evil, all impure. Oh, life, when I think of it, I long for death—but your noble image always appears to me and inspires me with the confidence that a few good men still exist. . . . I can say with François I, 'All is lost except honor!'"

Lola also advised Ludwig to ally himself strongly with the conservatives in Austria and sweep the "republican canaille" from Bavaria by calling in Russian troops, whose notorious brutality could restore order in no time. Confide in no one, she warned him, because all those around you are traitors. And to make matters as confusing as possible, she now, only days after pleading for the opposite during their interview in Munich, again begged the king to hold on to Wallerstein, even though the prince was not well disposed to her. "Your lover Denker will be furious with you," Lola wrote, "but for your sake, for my sake, for your family's sake, you must make peace with Wallerstein." She did not know that the king had dismissed the prince the day before.

In Frankfurt, Peißner took a room at the Hotel de Paris and Lola at the Hotel Landsberg. Although neither knew it, it was to be their last untroubled meeting. Again she spoke of their marrying, swearing to him that she would be his wife, but Peißner told her to be sparing with her oaths, that she might regret them one day. Both of them felt isolated and abandoned.

Peißner's fellows had expelled him from the Alemania. His chances of completing the final semester of his legal education were dim, and his prospects gave him little reason for hope. Lola complained to him that she was abandoned by everyone and wept bitter tears during their evenings together.

From her hotel in Frankfurt she wrote Ludwig, accusing him again of notoriously carrying on an affair with Denker, "a woman without beauty or spirit, who is nothing more than a common actress."

> After all I've suffered for you, chased from Munich for my devotion to you, and having at this moment no more than what I have on my back—your conduct appears strange and *heartless* to me. . . . My *conscience* is *clear, pure,* may others be the same—My affliction, caused more than anything by your conduct, is very great—it hurts me less to be deprived of all my luxuries, to which I have become so accustomed, than to read in foreign newspapers of your conduct.—Oh Louis, Louis, how you have betrayed me! You are *truly weak;* now it is clear. Farewell, later you will see your error. You have made me unhappy forever. What a difference between your conduct and mine, for I am forever, in the midst of your total abandonment of me,
>
> Your faithful and once beloved Lolitta

It is possible that Lola had convinced herself, in the absence of all evidence, that Ludwig was having an affair with Maria Denker, but even if she had, this letter to Ludwig, written when she was spending her nights in Frankfurt with Peißner, is incredibly duplicitous, hypocritical, and permeated with self-righteous mendacity. Perhaps the strains of the preceding months had induced a temporary psychosis that relieved her of moral responsibility for what she was now doing and writing, but in fact it appears that this moment in her life marked an absolute low point of egomania and self-deception.

It was probably just as well that Lola's accusatory letters had not yet reached King Ludwig as he struggled with the most difficult decision of his life. On the 16th, he had told Queen Therese that abdication now would be cowardice, and he wrote the same thing to Lola the next day, but over the following days abdication occupied his thoughts more and more. He began to discuss the idea with Crown Prince Maximilian and with a leader of the liberal Protestant opposition, Baron Hermann von Rotenhan. On the 17th the king mentioned a possible later abdication to his ministers, but they wanted to hear nothing of abdication, now or later.

Rotenhan suggested to King Ludwig that perhaps the only way to avoid further demeaning concessions, perhaps the sole means of rescuing the dynasty, was to appoint a cabinet of ministers responsible to the Landtag and to govern as a constitutional monarch with limited powers, much after the English fashion. If the king could not reconcile himself to such a system and be loyal to it, the honorable and chivalrous thing to do would be to step aside and allow his son to usher in a new era. This formulation of his dilemma appealed to Ludwig.

On the 18th a proposal was made in another assembly in the Rathaus that the king should be asked to establish the crown prince as a co-regent. The motion received little support, but that same day the king told Baron Rotenhan, "For 23 years I have ruled as a true king and now I'm supposed to be reduced to signing my name, bound and chained on both hands; no, I can't do that. Perhaps someone just starting out could deal with that, but after 23 years, it can't be done."

On the afternoon of Sunday, 19 March, Ludwig, so full of emotion that he most uncharacteristically forget to number his letter, sat in his private apartments and wrote again to Lola: "Very dear Lolitta, to whom I am so, so devoted, within this hour *I have abdicated the crown*, freely, without its ever having been suggested to me. My plan is to come to your arms in the month of April to Vevey, and to live there some time, at your side. Afterwards I will meet my family at Aschaffenburg. Without the knowledge of a single head of ministry, I made my declaration in the presence of all the princes of my house. My son Max knelt and asked for my blessing. All five of us broke down in tears. . . . Today I'm feeling well. Once I had made my declaration that I wanted to abdicate, I became happy. . . . Happy if he is with his Lolitta will be, Your faithful Luis"

The complex motivation for King Ludwig's abdication was not completely clear even to the king himself, but one of the strongest factors leading him to give up the throne was reflected in a second letter to his Lolitta that same day: "God knows when I would have been able to see my Lolitta without this." And three days later he wrote her, "I put down the crown, but Lola I could not leave. Your last conversation had a great influence on me in my decision to abdicate."

Whatever had motivated him, Ludwig had made his irrevocable decision, and now he drafted his own farewell as king to his citizens: "Bavarians! A new direction has begun, one other than that contained in the constitution under which I have ruled now for 23 years. I lay down the crown in favor of my beloved son, the Crown Prince Maximilian. True to the constitution did I rule; to my people's welfare was my life dedicated; as conscientiously as a loyal civil servant did I handle the properties and money of the State. I can look every man in the eye. And my deeply felt thanks to all who were devoted to me. Even though descended from the throne, my heart beats ardently for Bavaria, for Germany!"

20

A Countess in Exile

When King Ludwig's farewell note appeared on the streets of Munich, the citizens were stunned. There was no celebration, no happy faces were seen; some people were seen to weep. The British ambassador remarked, "It is somewhat singular that His Majesty should have chosen the moment when evidences of a reaction in his favor were beginning to manifest themselves among the more moderate burghers." Like all aspects of his reign, the abdication of King Ludwig received his close attention to detail. A decree signed by himself and the new King Maximilian II provided that Ludwig would retain title to major properties in the kingdom, receive an annual income of 500,000 florins, have the right to choose his residence and move about freely, and be addressed as "His Majesty, King Ludwig of Bavaria."

In Frankfurt Lola had been heard saying publicly that Ludwig would abdicate and join her in Switzerland, but no one had believed her. The newspapers carried the story that she had come to Frankfurt to cash a 500,000 florin bank draft given her by Ludwig during her lightning return to Munich. As usual, the rumors of Ludwig's largess far exceeded the considerable sums he did give Lola.

At the same time, Lola continued to pepper the king with letters of reproach for his faithlessness, declaring herself alone, lost, and abandoned now that he had transferred his affections to Maria Denker. "What ingratitude for a life sacrificed for you!" she wrote him. Ludwig was pained by

Lola's groundless accusations, but he felt flattered by the effect his presumed faithlessness seemed to have on her. He wrote assuring her vehemently of his unswerving faithfulness to her.

Back in Bern, Lola caught up on the latest gossip and rumors in the diplomatic circles, and then she was stunned but pleased when the news of Ludwig's abdication reached her. "I have just heard that you have abdicated your crown—I hope with all my heart that this is the truth because then you have preserved your dignity and have retired from public life with honor and *much spirit.*"

She continued by imploring Ludwig to give the new king a letter she enclosed in which she warned him in the strongest terms that the radicals would declare a republic of all the German-speaking nations in Frankfurt on 30 March, that their victory was certain, resistance futile, and that he should immediately send all of his family's valuables and cash out of Germany to a place of safety and prepare to flee. "One last time," her letter to King Max concluded, "do not scorn this news, which is certain, all too certain. The force against you is too powerful. You must succumb. *Do not lose a moment.*" Although Ludwig told her he had passed along her warning, the evidence seems to suggest he was wise enough to keep it to himself.

Lola also told him that she felt he handled the question of revoking her citizenship very well, and she sent him her naturalization certificate, the root of so much trouble for Bavaria, to be presented with another letter to King Max saying that she wished never to return to his kingdom. Then the countess addressed a topic that would become a leitmotif of her correspondence with Ludwig: money. "Everyone thinks," she wrote, "you should put all your money with the Bank of England. You won't get interest and must pay a fee, but it will be safe." As for her own financial welfare, "many of my friends are worried, not that you will forget me because all know you have a noble heart, but if an accident were to happen to you (God forbid), I am lost—then I would have to beg in the streets—what a position for me and a triumph for all my enemies—for my part I would prefer the 'last refuge' to going without money."

The last refuge was presumably suicide, something she would more than once suggest to Ludwig was her only recourse if he couldn't give her the money she needed. But most of all, she told him, she was looking forwarding to being with him again, and this time she would do whatever pleased him. "I'm happy all these things have happened, my dear Louis, because now I'm more certain of having you than I was before.... How wonderful it will be to have you here with me, and these things must have proved to you that I will love you always and never leave you, and my greatest *pleasure* will be to do *your desires, more than in the past,* if *I can;* you will be happy, and I'm convinced now that you can live in peace and you will live longer and in better health. . . . I feel I can't love you enough after what you have done, but you'll see later that you have done *a very wise act* in stepping down from the throne."

Then she wrote to Peißner, telling him to come join her in Switzerland.

Ludwig had never been miserly when it came to Lolitta, but now his reduced resources made restraint imperative. Under the terms of his abdication, his annual income was only about 20 percent of his income as king. "I entreat you to keep order in your affairs . . . pay your debts every month . . . don't make superfluous expenditures, and don't run up debts. *My purse is no longer in a position to be able to pay for them.*" He would continue to pay her 20,000 florins a year, but he could no longer pick up the bills for her "incidentals," as he had in the past. As for guarantying her income by depositing a sum in a foreign bank, he would prefer to wait until the political situation stabilized a bit; having the money in Bavaria seemed as secure as anywhere else. The king gently pointed out to her that the declaration of the German republic and the suppression of all monarchies, which she had warned would occur on 30 March, showed no signs of coming to pass soon.

Ludwig was much more interested in anticipating the joy he would feel at their reunion, now only a few weeks off. He would see her in Vevey no later than 16 April, he wrote. But Lola had some changes to make in the plans. She had left Bern to find a place for herself and Ludwig at Vevey, but Vevey was far too small and melancholy, she told him. Lausanne, too, was not for her. Geneva, however, was lovely, and Peel and Meller were helping her look for a suitable house. The only problem was that everything was so expensive.

In the meantime, she had taken a sumptuous suite in the Hotel de Bergues, where she had magnificent views of the lake and Mont Blanc. The owner of the hotel was fifty-five-year-old Alexandre Emmanuel Rufenacht, an officious but well-meaning former officer in one of Napoleon's Swiss regiments. He was flattered that the Countess of Landsfeld had chosen his establishment, and he was proud to introduce his wife and children to her. By 5 April, Lola had found something in nearby Pregny that seemed suitably cozy to her, the Chateau de l'Impératrice, once the home of Empress Josephine; the villa, with sweeping views of the Alps, cost 140,000 Swiss francs (a Swiss franc was roughly half of a Bavarian florin, so the price would have been about three and a half times Lola's annual income from the king, probably well over a $1 million in modern terms). Peel recommended that she rent the villa until the king could see it and approve its purchase, so she leased it for six months at 500 francs a month, unfurnished. Of course, because it was unfurnished she could not move in until all of her furniture arrived from Munich. And she would need new curtains and carpets. And there were a number of substantial repairs to be made.

In the meantime, she returned to Bern to meet Peißner, who arrived on 8 April. What Peißner found was chaos. Peel and Meller had expected Lola to reimburse them for accompanying her to Geneva to find a home, but the countess refused. The gentlemen also insisted that the Countess of Landsfeld pay them the 2,500 francs she had lost to them playing cards. She was outraged and began calling Peel a scoundrel and a thief. She locked Baron Meller in her hotel room and then asked Peißner to stab him, which the young man declined to do.

In light of the goings-on in Bern, it was perhaps just as well that complications were developing in Munich surrounding Ludwig's planned visit. Newspapers quoted Lola as saying that the king would come to her in Switzerland, and the public was outraged. Again the burghers assembled in the Rathaus, and they were heard declaring that if King Ludwig left Bavaria to see that woman, he should be barred from returning and his 500,000 florin annual income should be terminated. Johann Mussinan, once loyal to Lola, told the king that a revolution could result if he left to see the countess. One of Ludwig's aides-de-camp declared that the trip would incite such public anger that it would threaten the throne itself, and he informed the king he would refuse to accompany him to Switzerland. Ludwig fired him.

Finally King Max himself spoke to his father, imploring him to delay any journey out of the country. There isn't a night I don't go to bed, he told the old man, wondering if I will still be king the next day. Ludwig was hurt, baffled, and desperately disappointed, but he agreed not to leave. The royal family was relieved, though having the old king leave Munich would have removed the awkwardness of having two kings living in the same capital.

Ludwig wondered why anyone should care what he did. He had no power. It wasn't fair to make him a prisoner like this. He wrote a sad letter to Lola, swearing that this was merely a postponement; he had told King Max and Therese that. To reassure Lola of his devotion and concern, he told her that he had revised his will to make her legacy the income from 400,000 florins, which, deposited in a Bavarian bank at 5 percent, would assure her income of

20,000 florins for life. He repeated to her, "I will be yours unto death, no slander can make me break with you."

Slander was on the way, however. Lola had had a bitter fight with one of her sycophants, who wrote to Ludwig telling him that the countess had behaved in a most reprehensible manner and was now en route to Geneva with Peißner. The news of the young man's presence with Lola in Switzerland must have torn the king's heart with suspicions, but all he wrote to her was, "Have the *same* faithfulness for me that I have for you." Not knowing the king had learned that Peißner was with her, Lola again lied to Ludwig, writing, "I got a letter from Peißner saying he wants to go to Schleswig Holstein and needed a saber and helmet. I sent him 100 francs and I hope it's the last of him and his letters—I think he's mad—but my Louis, I am still in love with you, to see you would be such a pleasure and to give you some years of my life because without you life is nothing. . . . I'm always unhappy. Sometimes I'm so depressed I think I'll die."

Lola's belongings were arriving from Munich—fifty-six crates weighing more than eight tons—and she asked Ludwig to pay the freight bill. Otherwise, she said, I won't be able to claim my furniture, the newspapers will pick up the story, and there will be a scandal. Frau Opitz, the jeweler in Munich, had already served her with papers establishing a lien against her house in the Barerstraße for unpaid bills of more than 5,000 florins. Her hotel bill in Bern was still unpaid because she had had just enough money left to pay for her trip to Geneva. Her suite and meals at the Hotel de Bergues in Geneva were terribly expensive, but she couldn't move into her villa, where she would be able to live so much more cheaply, unless she had her furniture, and she needed money for that. Ludwig made her a gift of 1,000 florins so she could claim her belongings but told her again to economize.

The affair with Peißner was losing momentum. The young man began to realize that there was no place in her future for him, and he was astonished at the countess's ability to spend money. She now had eight or nine servants, a carriage, horses, a suite at the hotel, an opulent rented villa, and she was buying quantities of jewelry and flowers and anything else she could get on credit. Lola was not pleased to see Peißner spending time with one of Rufenacht's daughters, and she pointedly let him know it. Toward the end of April, Peißner fled Switzerland for Giessen, where he hoped to enroll in the university.

Lola kept pressing Ludwig for more money, but he did his best to force her to live within the income he gave her. Money increasingly became a focus in their correspondence. Lola not only wanted her income assured to her, she hoped to be able to tap into the capital providing that income. She kept pressing the king to put on deposit the amount he had promised her so that she could draw on it as necessary. "Dear Louis, one more time I ask for an affirmative reply to my request that you give me a sum for my *signature*. I'm in such a disagreeable position. I don't have a cent. If you're sincere with me, the proof will be if you deposit for my instant use the money you promised— without it I'm lost—and I can only destroy myself—because I can't live in any other position than that to which I have become accustomed."

After a year and a half Ludwig knew that Lola's extravagance would exceed whatever amount was available to her, and he refused to make anything more than 20,000 florins a year available for her signature. He told her bluntly, "When it comes to money, you're terrible." The king laid out for her precisely how he was prepared to guaranty her income:

> Write me if you want me to send you a full legal gift of the interest and dividends on a sum of 400,000 florins in a bank here, which would earn about 20,000 florins a year. Such a gift would be independent of politics, independent even if I lose my own state pension. If I put the money in another bank, it would produce less than 20,000 florins because the interest would be below 5%. Another bank would not pay dividends, which I receive as a founding stockholder of the bank. . . . Write me if 400,000 florins at Geneva gives 3½% interest; that's 14,000 florins instead of about 20,000 here. If you'd rather have the 14,000 florins, I'll put it in Geneva. . . . If you get your money only once or twice a year, pretty soon you would find it gone. Experience has shown you spend your money at once.

If Lola had been a calculating adventuress, as she was often portrayed, she would have leaped on Ludwig's offer to irrevocably assign her the income from 400,000 florins. Despite the king's repeated requests for a reply, she was, characteristically, incapable of giving him an unequivocal answer. Instead, the king received reproachful, despairing pleas for money immediately: "It seems to me as if soon there won't be any Lolitta on earth any longer—I can't sleep or eat anymore—I don't know what I've done to deserve this terrible punishment from you that you refuse me a few thousand francs—I've promised and sworn to you not to ask again—if only you knew how hard it is to suffer for lack of money—if you don't help me, I will kill myself or go mad. . . . This is what I get for my sacrifices in Munich. I hope this letter will touch your heart."

After she had an infusion of cash and the bill collectors were no longer camped before her door, the issue of guarantying her income was usually dropped until the next emergency. Herr Rufenacht began writing King Ludwig privately concerning the business and personal affairs of the countess; and though Ludwig was normally unwilling to deal with strangers, he maintained a secret correspondence with the hotel owner in the hope that he could bring order to Lola's financial affairs and at the same time obtain information on her personal life.

Off in London, the notorious Countess of Landsfeld was appearing on stage for the first time—not as a performer, but as a character. J. Sterling Coyne, one of the most prolific playwrights of the London theater, had composed a one-act farce entitled *Lola Montes, or A Countess for an Hour* that was introduced with great success on 26 April at the Theatre Royal in the Haymarket, near Her Majesty's Theatre, where the countess had made her dancing debut five years earlier. To avoid the prohibition on depicting living royalty on stage, Lola's royal patron was not King Ludwig but Prince Greenasgras. The farce was heading the bill and showing signs of a long run when it was banned in its first week by the Lord Chamberlain. Rumor said that either the Bavarian ambassador or Sir Robert Peel, at his son's urging, had requested the ban.

But Coyne was not about to let a successful play die, and on 22 May it reappeared as *Pas de Fascination, or Catching a Governor.* Lola Montes became Zephirine Joliejambe and Prince Greenasgras was Count Muffenuff, Russian Governor of Neveraskwehr. In this guise the play was allowed to continue on the London boards, and it soon made its way around the English-speaking world as one of Coyne's most frequently played works. Throughout her life Lola would find *Pas de Fascination* (often under the title *Lola Montez*) appearing on the theatrical bill in cities she visited, and it continued to hold the stage for some time after her death.

Back in Geneva, Lola had finally moved into the magnificent Chateau de l'Impératrice. Not everything was completely ready—much of her furniture had been damaged in transit and would have to be repaired, and an architect would be making some modifications for her—but moving in on 24 May was for Lola a dream realized. Rufenacht, whom she constantly recommended to the king because he was a Freemason, found two lady companions to add respectability to the entourage the countess had assembled with Ludwig's money.

In less than three weeks, however, Lola was sick in bed again with the malarial fever she'd had at Bad Brückenau. "It's all the same for me, life or death—I'm afraid you'll be angry with me when you get this, but I have to tell you—you know everything was damaged en route from Munich, and I had to get carpets and curtains and I had to do it and chandeliers and crystal and porcelain—most were completely broken—and the stables . . . . with tears in my eyes and death in my heart, I see your angry face before me, but these were *indispensable things*. . . . I can't pay it all by myself—my monthly money just covers house, stables, and servants—I had to stop my harp lessons and send back the harp and piano I had rented. . . . Yesterday they sent a bailiff . . . and with all this the Jesuits are intriguing against me. . . . an American gentleman said to me the other day, I could earn a lot of money dancing because my name is well known there—dear Louis, to leave you would be death, but what can I do?"

Once again, Ludwig paid. From her letters, filled with her tales of financial woe, he picked out the loving words and phrases, which were sometimes nearly lost in the mass of monetary matters, and kissed those places over and over again as he read her letters in the English Garden or on the grounds of the Nymphenburg Palace. The king still desperately needed her love, and he was hoping for more than that. It was nearly a year now since the only night they had ever spent together; and only once since then had Lola consented to sexual intercourse with him. Despite the foiled rendezvous in April, he was planning to see her during the summer, and now he became bold enough to ask her what kind of reception he could expect.

Because King Ludwig was aware that his letters to Lola could fall into the wrong hands, he wrote his most intimate thoughts to her on little pink slips of paper that he inserted in his letters and on which he wrote, "Burn this at once after you have read it" or "Write your reply on the back and return this in your next letter." At the end of May he wrote a little pink slip asking Lola if when they met again she would like to have sex with him (using *besar*, adopting the Spanish equivalent of the French *baiser* in its vulgar form).

Lola, who had just received the king's promise to pay Rufenacht for all of her hotel bill, was unequivocal in her response: "[H]ow can you ask if I want to *besar* with you? You know that I'm devoted to you as much as it's possible, that I love you more and more for everything you've sacrificed for me—certainly I want to, and it pleases me when I think that my very beloved Louis can *besar* with his Lolitta, I'm more in love with you than ever and now my health is completely in order, much, much better than it was in Munich. . . . My dear Louis, I ask you to be faithful to me until you come to me, and then you can *besar* with great gusto and pleasure. My heart is yours, my *cuño* too, and all of me."

Her words were more than Ludwig could have hoped for, and he wrote her that each time he read her letter, he got an erection.

Lola kept encouraging the king to come visit her during the summer, while the weather was warm, but in the meantime, she had found herself some new playmates. With her beauty, vivacity, wit, and Ludwig's money, the countess had again attracted a circle of young men. They came from all classes of Geneva's society, but as a group they hovered on the outer edges of social respectability. The men began to frequent the Chateau de l'Impéra-trice, much as the Alemannen had made Barerstraße 7 their headquarters, and the many rooms of the villa provided ample accommodations when they wanted to sleep there. The countess was once again flouting propriety by allowing men to stay overnight under her roof. The villa had its own dock down on the shore of Lake Geneva, and Lola decided to buy a fair-sized boat, powered by oars and sails, along with several smaller boats, in which her admirers could take her out for excursions. They dubbed themselves the corsairs. Real pirates on Lake Geneva probably would have been viewed by the countess's neighbors with only slightly less approval than were these corsairs.

Insinuating himself into Lola's circle at about the same time was one of the most remarkable of the many strange people the countess would meet. Auguste Papon, who was about the same age as Lola, styled himself the "Marquis de Sard," telling everyone that his father had been adjunct prin-cipal of the Treasury of France and that his mother was from one of the oldest noble families of Provence. In fact, Monsieur Papon was a confidence man, but a curious one. His betrayals seem to have been effected at least as much to assert his superiority over his aristocratic victims as to separate them from their money.

Papon's grandfather had been a waiter in a Geneva coffeehouse, his father a swindler who fled Geneva for the South of France. Auguste grew up in Toulouse, where he studied with distinction at the Catholic seminary there and was said to have been a protégé of the archbishop. Deciding not to enter the priesthood, he became an attorney in Marseilles, where he gained a rep-utation for bad debts and bad conduct, which led to his disbarment. He fled to Switzerland, where his parents had set themselves up in Nyon on the north shore of Lake Geneva, and his small figure—with its dark, Mediterranean features and lively, malicious eyes—became well known in what passed for high society in Geneva. Papon missed no opportunity to be charming, but those around him sensed a calculation to his warmth. And he made no secret of his attachment to the goals of the Jesuits.

The pseudo-marquis and the pseudo-Spaniard became acquainted when the Countess of Landsfeld checked into the Hotel de Bergues, where Papon had been living for several months. After Lola moved into the villa, Papon invited her to visit him and his family at their Villa Mon Répos at Nyon; the corsairs rowed her to the villa, where she was received by the Papons and the curé of Nyon. By July, Ludwig began to notice that Lola's letters were coming less often. Finally, late in the month, Papon moved into the villa.

When Lola did write, she usually urged Ludwig to find a way to get her jewels to her. She missed being able to wear them, but arranging a secure shipment was a problem. The king decided that he would bring the jewels with him when he and Lola at last had their secret reunion, and he busied himself making the plans and ensuring that Lola was ready and willing to travel to a rendezvous where they would not be recognized. Among other things, he had her tell him exactly when she was expecting her next menstrual period and how long it would last.

The site Ludwig chose for the reunion was Malans, a small town in eastern Switzerland, south of Liechtenstein and roughly half-way between Geneva and Innsbruck, where Ludwig would begin his part of the trip. He was spending the summer at Berchtesgaden and would travel to Innsbruck to visit royal relatives. From there he could make a quick, incognito trip to Malans to spend a few days together with his beloved. Lola pleaded with him to come to her chateau, but the trip would simply have taken too much time, so Ludwig insisted on meeting in Malans.

Their reunion was set for the beginning of August but delayed until mid-August and then until early September. During this time Papon was assuming an ever greater role at the Chateau de l'Impératrice. Lola's two female companions were uncomfortable with what they saw going on and finally fled when Lola abused them for refusing to spend the night aboard the boat with her and the corsairs. Papon moved into the women's room, which was closer to the bedroom of the mistress of the house. The corsairs themselves were gradually marginalized by the marquis, assuming less the roles of boon companions and more those of servants, and Rufenacht was no longer welcome at the chateau.

Lola's increasingly infrequent letters told Ludwig how the passage of time was simply making her love for him grow, how she rejected invitations to come live with friends in Paris and London because she could not bear to be any farther from her Louis. In his letters to her he seemed preoccupied with the past, and he wrote ever more frequently of his desire to have her feet in his mouth. "I take your feet into my mouth, where I have never had any others, that would have been repugnant to me, but with you, it's just the opposite." He wanted her unwashed feet in his mouth as soon as she arrived at Malans, he wrote, so that he could show her his feelings.

King Ludwig found 25 August to be a difficult day. It was the first birthday he had celebrated in nearly a quarter of a century that had not also been a national holiday. And, more important, it was the first anniversary of his creating Lola the Countess of Landsfeld. Birthdays and anniversaries were of major importance to Ludwig, and he must have been hoping to receive tender birthday greetings from Lola and perhaps an expression of gratitude not only for her elevation to the nobility but also for all his sacrifices for her. Instead, the letter he received from her that day made no mention of his birthday nor of her elevation to countess but told him that she didn't have a cent and needed 1,000 francs in order to meet him in Malans.

Ludwig was frustrated and desperate. For Lola to meet him 2 September she had to leave no later than 29 August. Had she given the matter any thought she would have known that, with mail from Geneva to Berchtesgaden taking seven or eight days, it was impossible for her to write for money on 17 August and expect to receive it before the 29th. The king was frantic because now he had no way of knowing before he left whether she would actually come to Malans. He wrote her an agitated letter telling her that he would make the trip without knowing because it would be too painful to him to miss a chance to be with her.

There were two consolations for him in Lola's letter, however. She told him that he was the only man or woman in the world for whom she had any affection, that she not only loved him, but she also respected him. The second was a circle she had drawn in the margin by her signature. "I send you a kiss from my mouth," she wrote. "Please kiss it—it's the kiss of a tender and devoted heart for you." That was just the sort of sentiment Ludwig so often hoped to find in her letters but so seldom did. But it was not enough to dispel his suspicions, and he wrote to Rufenacht, requesting an immediate answer to a list questions about Papon, and then wrote again the following day to encourage a swift reply. Ludwig mentioned, perhaps suspecting what sort of man Papon was, that he was worried about his letters being stolen.

Lola borrowed the money for the trip from Rufenacht, who had made her sign a note for it, and departed at 7 P.M. on 25 August with her maid, two of her corsairs, and a little boy she had grown fond of. The trip was long and uncomfortable, and Lola was not at all pleased when she arrived in Malans to find not Ludwig but his valet, who gave her 2,000 francs, some poems, and a letter from His Majesty: "Tears come to my eyes because instead of holding you to my heart, to speak to you of my feelings, I must write. . . . Since my last letter I have learned the cause of the disturbances in Munich. . . . The revolutionaries had spread the story that I have presented you with diamonds belonging to the State (your Luis a thief!). The rumor started because the treasury will not allow them to be seen. . . . New bloody fighting is to be expected and the worst consequences if I go to the Tyrol. Persons very devoted to me, not your enemies, have told me this. *It's a terrible situation. . . . don't love me less*, it's not my fault. . . . I repeat, the whole world doesn't have the power to separate us."

Enclosed with the money was a little note: "The drawing in your letter that is meant to represent your mouth (each time I give it a kiss), I took at first to represent your *cuño*, and my *jarajo* began to get erect. As much pleasure as your mouth has given me, your *cuño* would have pleased me greatly. I give kisses to the one and to the other."

Lola's reply was not terribly sympathetic: "What great pain your letter caused me, I who for so many days had looked forward to seeing you—but you seem to have people around you who do everything possible to keep you from coming to see me—this revolution story is very overblown, probably to make you afraid—don't be afraid—I know your family is *doing everything possible* to keep you from me and all sorts of stories to make you afraid."

Equally disturbing to her was the fact that Ludwig had not sent her jewels with the valet. On her return to Geneva, she told him, she was going to move out of the villa and into a small house nearer the city, where rent was only about 110 francs a month. But please send her jewels, she wrote.

In fact, the reports of unrest in Munich were real, and the demonstrations had turned violent; newspapers reported that the king had left for Switzerland and again suggested that he be denied the right to reenter Bavaria and that his income be terminated. Now that Lola had mentioned Papon in her letters, Ludwig asked her a set of eight questions about him; Lola replied, "You know, you can't be sure about anyone, but he seems to me to be a gentleman and distinguished." He is not young or handsome she told him, but very serious, an author. He's an ultramontane, she mentioned casually. "But I'm not in love with him, Louis," Lola told him. "I love only you, and no one could love me the way you love me." She mentioned that she thought she would leave Switzerland and travel to Rome to live in his Villa Malta.

Ludwig was not satisfied. This woman, who had seen herself as the object of Jesuit persecution to a point that even Ludwig had become skeptical, had now taken an acknowledged ultramontane into her home and called him a distinguished gentleman. What is your motive in this relationship? he asked her. The king quickly disabused Lola of her idea of living in Villa Malta. He told her that he could not allow her to stay in the villa, because it would cause too great a scandal, and that he could not afford to give her money to travel to Rome.

Now troubling news arrived from Geneva almost daily, and the king's mood deteriorated. Rufenacht wrote the king that Peißner was back in the city, apparently invited by the countess to counterbalance Papon, who appeared to make her uneasy even as she gave him control over her affairs. Lola was telling everyone, Rufenacht wrote, that the king was going to give her a million francs in cash and another million in jewels and that she would take Papon and his parents to live with her in the king's villa in Rome. Lola herself wrote Ludwig to warn him again that the revolutionary storm was about to break and that he must get his wealth out of Bavaria at once.

The king finally sent Lola's jewels to her via his banker, but in the same letter in which he said that he kissed the tender words she wrote him, he told her, "It seems to me you want: Luis for love, Papon for conversation, and Peißner to *besar*, otherwise you wouldn't have called him from such a distance, which causes you new expenses."

Gloom pervaded Ludwig's private world. Every day now Ludwig felt acutely the bitterness of being a king without a crown, and he regretted his abdication. "Here I am back in my jail," he wrote to Lola after his return to Munich on 3 October. "It seems impossible that you haven't written in half a month." The only consolation was a letter from Rufenacht in which was enclosed a copy of an apologetic letter that the hotelier had received from Fritz Peißner. The student had been warned by Rufenacht not to respond to the summons to the Chateau de l'Impératrice because "the countess is playing Lola again," but Peißner had hoped to persuade her to pay his debts, and he borrowed money to make the journey. When he arrived he found the countess not only under the spell of Papon and surrounded by the corsairs and senseless extravagance, but on the verge of bankruptcy herself. He spent a week living in a back room at her villa, realizing how little was left of the eternal love she had sworn to him less than a year ago. Then he returned to Giessen without saying goodbye to her. He wrote Rufenacht only to apologize for being too ashamed to call on him.

On the second day after his return from Berchtesgaden, the king was surprised when his servant brought him a note from the Marquis de Sard, written that morning in Munich. Papon wrote explaining that he had arrived to give King Ludwig the enclosed letters from the Countess of Landsfeld: "I know you will save me from a disgrace worse than death—my God, where is my self-respect—the Countess of Landsfeld in such a sad position, without security, with nothing, and in an *infernal, infamous* country—Please receive this man who, in the moment of my misery, came to offer me his services— he's a man of heart—he's a Freemason—that says everything."

Lola seemed to have forgotten that Rufenacht was a Freemason, too. Two more short notes were enclosed, each repetitively pathetic, one saying that she was in bed coughing blood. It was good to have a letter from her after so long, but the king was not pleased. Lola's recommendation of this Marquis de Sard meant little in light of her history of misjudging people. Was the man her lover? Now Rufenacht had become a scoundrel in Lola's eyes, even though his secret correspondence with the king led Ludwig to believe that he was one of the few honorable, reliable people she had come across. And without hearing a word from Papon, Ludwig already knew what her problem was: money. Would this never end?

Ludwig received the Marquis de Sard. The king had been depressed, and now he was angry, but the experienced swindler Papon knew how to win the confidence of his victims—to listen to them, to discover their weaknesses and their dreams, and to use them for his own benefit. He allayed the king's suspicions and anger with a courtly obsequiousness designed to flatter a retired monarch. He laid out the latest financial crisis of the Countess of Landsfeld. Everything she had of value was pawned, he said, and her creditors were about to execute on the remaining contents of the villa, where Lola lay sick unto death.

Ludwig was reluctant to give Lola any more money, even after Papon told him of the passion she felt for her king. The marquis returned to Switzerland with a letter to Lola from the king promising the loan only if she gave him a lien on the Barerstraße house, even though he knew the liens already filed against the property exceeded its value. After Papon's departure, Ludwig received a letter from Lola replying to his accusation that she had "Ludwig for love, Papon for conversation, and Peißner for *besar*." "Some day all secrets of this world will be opened before God and then, my dear Louis, you will be persuaded of my faithfulness and the sincere love of your slandered Lolitta. Dear Louis, there is death in my soul—without you I am disgraced in this world, without friends in a country so terrible for strangers as it is at Geneva. . . . if you don't come to my aid, I will be the joke and ridicule of the world—my honor will be completely lost, what shall I do, it is too terrible and my health is always so fragile—but God is good, and you, my dear Louis, you are too devoted to me to abandon me."

Lola was right, and Ludwig sent her 20,000 francs without waiting for her to assign the lien to him. The king's personal fiscal year ended on 30 September, and he wrote to Lola that in the first two years he had known her, he had spent 158,084 florins and 16¼ kreutzers on her, and that did not include what he had given to her friends and allies, who had come begging for help after her fall. Changes in economies and lifestyles make it impossible to establish an exact equivalency for the Bavarian florin or gulden of 1848 and the American dollar at the end of the twentieth century, but a florin would have been roughly equal to $20 today, meaning that Ludwig had spent about $3 million on Lola in two years and that his allowance to her of 20,000 florins was equivalent to about $400,000 a year.

Lola moved out of the chateau late in October and into a house nearer the city, which she shared with the Papon family. Auguste Papon's influence over her now reached its peak, and in a letter to the king that would have left anyone who had known her in Munich incredulous, she lectured on the virtues of the Jesuits and ultramontanes in this year of revolutions: "It is the duty of every Apostolic Catholic to forget everything *personal* and with all his heart and love of God and hope for His mercy after death, to support in its peril our glorious church—better the Jesuits than those people who want to overturn everything—kings, religion, everything that is the best in nations. . . . [The ultramontanes] are a million times better than those base and ignoble people who do so many terrible things each day and so many assassinations. . . . How many times better the Jesuits who have always exalted religion—the power of kings—public order."

And Papon's influence was evident as she again berated the king for failing to establish an independent fund to guaranty her income: "What a terrible thing for me if something were to happen to you, my dear Louis, and if I were alone in the world without a cent—you know well I possess absolutely nothing. . . . What a terrible situation—today in affluence and tomorrow in the poorhouse—*procrastination* is our worst enemy. . . . this uncertain position is the same for me as if you gave me a slow-working poison. . . . just a little effort from you could fix everything—I think when you love someone you don't want to hold that person in *mortal fear* that nothing in this world can appease—by a terrible thought that devours every hour of the day—this can't be love—I swear to you by my feelings for you that I would not for my *life* put you in this same fear I suffer."

She even told him that she had recently refused an offer of marriage from of a wealthy London barrister because she could never leave her beloved Louis. But her beloved Louis must guaranty her income. Although months earlier he had asked her in vain where she wanted him to deposit 400,000 florins for her life income, now Ludwig wrote that it would be unwise to transfer so much money just before the Landtag met. As he had already told Papon in Munich, his annual income, though fixed by his abdication agreement, still had to be approved by the Landtag. Nothing should be done to give the legislators an excuse to withhold approval. Lola would have to be patient until the adjournment of the budget session.

Patience was not one of Lola's virtues. The experience of almost having everything she possessed sold out from under her appears to have impressed her, and she was troubled about her financial situation. More important, she was bored. The chill fall weather, the lack of money, and Papon's dominance of the household had put an end to the summer idyll with the corsairs. Peißner, who might have provided some diversion, had quickly come and gone. In her smaller house with the Papon family, Lola was at least closer to Geneva, so she could enjoy what the city had to offer in the way of social diversion.

At the theater she noticed the good-looking Julius, Lord of Schwandt, who had just turned twenty and was a cousin of the Count of Schließen. His parents had died some years before, and he was said to be in line for a fortune when he reached majority. Baron Meller, who was also in the audience, agreed to introduce the countess to the young man, and Julius was fascinated by Lola.

A serious flirtation began to develop between the lord and the countess (eight years his senior), and Lola's relationship with Papon simultaneously began to deteriorate. The marquis seems to have set his hopes on living off the fortune that he expected Lola to extract from the absent and married King Ludwig, but he was far less certain that he would share in the spoils if the countess took up with a marriageable aristocrat. It appears that Papon vigorously opposed the relationship with Lord Julius, and Lola reacted as she always did to opposition: by being as contrary as possible. When the

Papons made it impossible for her to receive her new friend at her rented house, she took to meeting him in Baron Meller's rooms at the Hotel de Bergues.

Only a month earlier Lola had urged King Ludwig to accept Papon into his confidence as a noble and trustworthy friend, and now she tried to protect her remaining credibility with the king by breaking the news of Papon's new status, as a cunning and deceitful enemy, slowly: "I don't have unlimited confidence in him, although he is (I believe) a worthy man, you know how rare it is to find a truly sincere friend without any self-interest—many people have told me not to put all my confidence in him because he's a man of great ambition and vanity, two things native to the generality of men—and it seems to me that he is not exempt—it seems to me, too, that he speculates that one day I can return to Munich and that you will compensate him for all the services he has performed, and because he's for the Jesuits, he seems to me at this moment a very necessary but very dangerous man. . . . My servants have said that he has taken papers addressed to me—one thing is certain, that he is not very sincere."

Papon had begun a correspondence with Ludwig, and the king does not seem to have taken the hint from Lola that the man was not to be trusted. When the marquis wrote Ludwig that the countess was desperately depressed at the king's failure to guaranty her income, but that she had declared her poverty would be the best proof of her disinterestedness, Ludwig at once wrote Papon a sympathetic reply. What did the countess prefer? the king asked. As he had often told her, she would get more interest if the capital were left in Bavaria, but if she were willing to accept a reduced income on a deposit overseas, he could scrape together about a million francs (roughly equivalent to the 400,000 florins Ludwig had always proposed as the capital to guaranty Lola's life income) and would deposit it wherever she wished. But since he had already been vociferously reproached in Bavaria for what he had done for her in the past, it would be far better if the matter were postponed until the budget session of the Landtag ended. Let sleeping dogs lie, he told Papon.

But as Ludwig was writing this, the final rupture came to pass, and the marquis and his parents were all ejected from the countess's house. Lord Julius was said to have proposed marriage to Lola, and then, at the urging of some of his worried friends, he escaped from her to Chambéry, France. Before pursuing her bolted prey, Lola wrote to the king of the break with Papon, who, she said, had been informing everyone that he was going to marry her himself:

He has sworn vengeance, these are his own words to my servants: *My vengeance will pursue her everywhere and I will make her die on a bed of straw*—what do you think of those words of a gentleman? . . . the Count of Schleissen (Lord of Mecklenburg) has been here for six weeks, a very very handsome young man with a great fortune—when he saw me, he got introduced to me and has had a great passion for me—three days ago he came to my house and declared his love and asked to marry me—the poor boy, it caused me great pain when I told him without hesitation that I love you forever—my *duty*, my honor would not permit me to love or marry anyone and, honorable or dishonorable, if I accepted the love of any person, my name in history would be forever sullied—this is the only true *temptation* I have felt, far from you, my dear Louis, and your memory made me strong. . . . it's much better if I make a little trip to break off these visits and think of you.

Just a week before, the king had passionately begun a letter, "I want to take your feet in my mouth, at once, without giving you time to wash them after you've arrived from a trip," but it was to be the final flame of his obsession for Lolitta. Now his letters took on a tone of sad resignation, as if he were awakening from a long and beautiful dream. His reaction to Lola's declaration of her steadfastness in the face of temptation showed how his mood was slowly changing: "How you love me! Loved by *Lolitta*. What proof you give me!! It is true love. But I must not put my interests above yours, I must not be egotistical; if you have *the conviction that you would be happy* married to Count Schließen (but not without making the most positive inquiries), I do not want to oppose myself to your happiness. I do not want you to reproach me with having caused you to lose true happiness. But to know that you were a kept woman, that would be unbearable for me. *Even if you should marry, I will never feel passion for another.*"

Lola returned triumphantly from Chambéry, bringing Lord Julius back with her, but at the request of the local representative of the lord's guardian the police intervened to verify whether undue influence was being exercised on the young man by his new friend. Although no charges were brought, the Countess of Landsfeld suddenly decided to take a trip to London, possibly at the suggestion of the Swiss authorities. As a noncitizen, she was subject to expulsion on twenty-four hours' notice; Ludwig, on Rufenacht's advice, had months before urged her to take up Swiss citizenship so that her right of residence would be secure, but Lola had protested that she would lose the right to call herself Countess of Landsfeld.

To make sure that the king would not heed anything Papon might be writing about her, Lola told Ludwig the false marquis had been caught performing sex acts with a young man in a public park and probably had been engaging in such behavior under her own roof. Papon had indeed been busy conveying his outrage and wounded pride to the king, along with details of the countess's pursuit of Lord Julius.

Lola and her maid, escorted by Baron Meller and his manservant, departed from Geneva on Monday morning, 27 November, leaving behind the chaos she had managed to create in her nine months in Switzerland and heading for new adventures in London.

21

"THIS CHANGES THINGS"

Ludwig was baffled. With almost no preparation, Lola, who only a few days earlier had been telling him how good she had become at making economies and staying within a budget, was undertaking a costly journey at the onset of winter to the most expensive capital in Europe—ostensibly to escape the attentions of Lord Julius, hear some good music, and take care of her health, which, she had often told him, suffered dreadfully in the fog.

En route to London, Lola began once more to bombard the king with reproachful, pleading, self-pitying letters begging him to guaranty her income with capital deposited in England. Revolution is coming to Germany within six months, she told him, and the guillotine will be at work. Get your money and my money out of the country, she pleaded. From her Leicester Square hotel she kept up the refrain:

> I like it that you tell me to marry, but you forget that a woman who isn't in her first youth, and with all the stories the newspapers in Munich wrote about me, and essentially without money, in the 19th century it would be a miraculous thing to find a *respectable* husband . . . and the most impossible of the impossible is after being the *beloved of a king, you cannot descend to the others*—and the cruelest of all is that you don't want to give me an independent and honest existence in my own name . . . dear Louis, if you love me still, which *I can't believe*, do this for me and then I will be able to *breathe*!!! It seems to me a punishment from God, what happened in Munich, as much as I now feel my unfortunate position in which I am left,

if I were a few years younger, I could dance, but I don't have the strength, my health is worse and worse, and it is your fault. . . . each time I look at your portrait, it hurts me greatly to think of the false position in which you have left me—Farewell, you were my only illusion.

Ludwig's reply indicated that Lola's spell over him was losing its effect: "Without lying, I cannot say I enjoy the contents of your letter. . . . I have to repeat that it is impossible to fix your income as you wish before the conclusion of the budget session of the Landtag, which hasn't yet begun."

As the first of December arrived, the king noted he had been celibate an entire year, which was unusual for him. He asked Lola what her reaction would be if he were to be unfaithful to her, and he asked her to tell him truthfully, with a promise of no reproach from him, whether she had also been celibate. His questions got no response.

The king's remaining affection for his Lolitta was further poisoned by a long letter dated 1 December that he received from Auguste Papon. The quondam marquis (he had dropped his title now) complained that his letters to the king were no longer being answered: "The position in which the Countess of Landsfeld has placed me is such that *I cannot, I will not, I should not accept it, even for a few more days.*

"The most terrible vengeance is simple for me.

"I prefer a reparation. But I will not demand this reparation, Sire, from the countess, incapable as she is of giving anything worthy of me."

Oozing oily self-righteousness, Papon announced to the king that rather than avenge himself for the countess's ingratitude by publishing an exposé of her life, together with Ludwig's letters to her, he would, as a gentleman, be content to return all the documents in his hands and publish nothing if King Ludwig would bestow on him the honorary title of chamberlain and pay him 10,000 francs.

The breathtaking arrogance and hypocrisy of Papon's extortion letter probably did not impress King Ludwig as much as the implication that Lola had given Papon his letters. He couldn't believe that was true, and he would not allow himself to be blackmailed. Ludwig did not answer Papon's letter, and at first he said nothing to Lola about it.

She, after one week in London, announced to him "Dear Louis, Geneva makes me so sick, since I've seen London, I don't want to live there but I want to settle in London. . . . it's the same price as France and Germany. . . . Believe me, Switzerland doesn't suit me at all—I think with terror that I must return there—it's so sad and the people so bad-hearted. . . . I've rented a little house, very small, for four guineas a week, which isn't much. . . . I'll possibly leave here in a few days for Paris and in four days I'll be in Geneva to put everything in order to settle here for some months—my cough is already almost gone—and now I'm much healthier and *stronger*—I like the English cooking with good beefsteaks and good porter—it does me good. . . . it's so lively here—it's not possible to be sad—and sadness did me so much harm in Geneva."

In the space of about ten days, a speed that astonished the king, she left London, packed up everything in Geneva, sent her coachman ahead with her carriage, gathered up Zampa and Turk, and departed again for London.

The first days of 1849 brought to Ludwig the final revelation of just how completely his beloved had betrayed him. Fritz Peißner had come to the king begging for financial assistance to finish his studies outside of Bavaria. Under repeated and insistent prodding by the king, the young man at last confessed the details of how Lola had seduced him, how she had sworn eternal love with him, begged his forgiveness when she betrayed him with Leibinger, and how the two of them were meeting secretly in Frankfurt as Ludwig agonized over whether to abdicate.

The king was crushed. He had long suspected that Lola had been unfaithful to him and had been ready to forgive her, but she had always protested her innocence, her inability to love anyone but him; and he had wanted so desperately to believe that this young, beautiful, vivacious woman truly loved him for what he was. He wrote, "I very much suspected that you were unfaithful to me last winter, and now I am *certain*. Peißner has *besado* with you many times." But then he decided to say nothing to her. Instead, as he so often did, he put his feelings into a poem for himself alone:

> Had I but never seen you!
> For you I gave my last blood,
> Torn apart by nameless agonies,
> For you, my life's brightest flame of love!
>
> I set myself defiantly against everyone,
> Trusting in your loving heart,
> Let nothing move me, unshaken
> In the restless storm breaking upon me.
>
> What I always refused to believe,
> That you were faithless, is really true;

Nothing could wrest from me my trust in you,
Yet now at last I clearly see your guilt.

A kingdom you wished to control
And boasted that you the ruler were.
You wanted to reign exalted over all,
And ever turned toward what was base.

With betrayal have you repaid my trust.
You wanted my money, you wanted my power.
What you achieved, that all raged against me,
Transformed my existence into night.

Deep within I was already broken,
Aggrieved, wounded, sickened by the world,
As villainous outrage revealed itself,
As faithlessness was added to ingratitude.

The years' long dream has now vanished,
I have awakened in a wasteland.
All that I sensed, all that I felt is no more,
And yet I am still bereft of my crown.

His letters became tedious news and weather reports, and Lola noticed the difference. "It seems to me that you don't love me so much," she complained. But his attention was partially distracted from his mourning for lost illusions by the realization that Papon was serious about his threatened publication. Just after the beginning of the year a prospectus appeared in Switzerland for a book that would include intimate letters of the king and Lola, some of them in facsimile. In the prospectus Papon announced that the book would not be a polemic nor a satire but a simple account written without hate or passion.

But there was no question that the book was going to be distinctly unflattering to King Ludwig.

> Louis of Bavaria, infatuated with an itinerant dancer, and fleeing Munich before the noble resistance of a proud ministry and general indignation avenging a public morality that had been outraged too long, is pitiful. . . . A single thought is mine: that of devotion to society as a whole, perhaps to His Majesty himself.

246

Indiscretion becomes a duty when the writer proposes, as I do, to give, without fear, disinterested, a history lesson to the people, a lesson in government to the kings.

The wise men of a rude folk of antiquity ordained that on certain days, in order that their sons might be inspired with a horror of drunkenness, an inebriated slave should be led forth.

Then the man was an enslaved menial.

Today it is a king.

Who will complain?

The person Papon hoped would complain obviously was the king himself, who no doubt would be eager to pay to prevent publication.

Lola read a copy of the prospectus sent to her by Rufenacht, and she wrote to him from London that she had friends there "with long arms, who won't allow insults to an old man who is incapable of defending himself." The hotelier, eager to show Ludwig how industriously he was pursuing the matter, passed along Lola's letter, which could only have been another arrow in the king's wounded heart. Just two days after writing her letter to Rufenacht, Lola wrote to Ludwig, that defenseless old man, telling him she would probably go mad if she really believed that he had no intention of guarantying her income and that "if you could read my open heart, you would see how much love and affection I have for you—if you were no more, I hope to die—there is nothing for me in this vile infamous world."

Ludwig was troubled at the prospect of Papon's publication, and he repeatedly asked Lola to tell him whether any of his letters to her were missing, whether Papon could have copied them, whether he could have any of his poems to her. Lola assured him that she still had all his letters, that Papon had never seen them. "It is most disagreeable to me," he wrote her, "to see everyone reading what I wrote to a man who you told me had your confidence." Ludwig finally offered to pay Papon for the return of the documents and a promise not to publish, but Papon had grown impatient, and the first installment had already gone to press. It appeared with no great fanfare on 1 February.

Papon adhered roughly to his proposed table of contents in this first installment, guessing at the facts of Lola's origin and early life based on the various and conflicting stories she had told. He added some of his own observations, noting that she could read and write Spanish and was even better at English, that her French was studded with English and Spanish expressions, and that she could sometimes understand German. Most offensive to King

Ludwig would have been a sarcastic and partially fictionalized account of Papon's meeting with the king in Munich. Claiming to have seen Lola's portrait hanging in the Gallery of Beauties next to that of Princess Alexandra, the king's daughter (from Papon's description, it seems unlikely that he ever saw the gallery), Papon concluded the first installment with an access of moral outrage: "After having so long soiled the conjugal bed, the throne, he dared to scourge with this impure contact the spotless beauty of a girl who weeps in her mother's bosom over the eternal disorders of her father! Is then nothing sacred for this man?"

As a man for whom anniversaries were very important, King Ludwig struggled through February 1849. A year earlier he had been miserable over Lola's treatment of him, and then he was cast into despair when she was driven from Munich. The memories, now further darkened by the knowledge of her deception, were excruciatingly painful. On the 11th, the anniversary of her departure, Ludwig walked to the Barerstraße house—at the same hour as he had the year before—and remembered how proud he had been that he had been struck by a rock from the mob, that he had suffered danger and physical pain for her. Finally, on 17 February, in his daily entry in his letter to Lola he wrote, "I had strongly suspected that you were unfaithful to me last winter, now I am certain. You were in love with Peißner, and you have *besado* many times, not just with him, but with L. Leibinger, too."

The next day he continued the letter as if he had written nothing out of the ordinary, thanking her for her letter of the 11th, discussing her gossip. Then his suddenly agitated writing betrayed his emotion as he wrote: "Please tell me sincerely if you have love affairs and if they are of the heart or purely physical; Lolitta cannot be long without one or the other."

During the following days he recounted the news of Munich until the sheet was nearly full, and then he wrote, "Because you have been unfaithful to me, I no longer sign myself 'Your faithful Luis,' but that doesn't mean I am not. Luis"

Lola, rarely prompt in her response to Ludwig's letters, lost no time in replying to his accusation: "I was never *besado* by anyone except you in Munich. . . . you can accuse me, this is the truth—everyone can say the opposite, *but it is false, as God is in heaven*—my conscience is pure—if I were to die today, my last words would be that you (since the death of Dujarier) are the only man I have really loved and cared for, today as before I would give my life and soul for you, my noble Louis. . . . listen to me, these are the words of the *purest blood from the bottom of my heart* and every person has some sacred feelings—all I have are mine for you—May the Holy Virgin Mary lead your heart to believe me—I need her and her divine assistance against the snares and intrigues of so many enemies—I don't believe I am forgotten by the Jesuits—once they are against you it is for life, everywhere, always."

Ludwig was not convinced, but his heart was still hers. He still sat thinking of her in front of her portrait and her bust, he still went walking where they had walked together, and at night he still dreamed of her. But he no longer trusted her. Now he signed his letters, "Your devoted Luis"; and though his devotion remained, his obsessive need to be loved by this woman was fading.

Lola had been in London scarcely a month before she began to discover that it was none of the things she had imagined it was. As Ludwig had warned her, her money did not go as far as she expected: "In London it is very expensive to live with the greatest modesty." The lively streets that had so delighted her on her arrival now had no charm: "London is like a great prison, everywhere you see walls." And the weather, which was to be so much better for her than Geneva's had been, was undermining her health: "The climate here is very bad, I never see the sun, never. . . . My cough is still very bad, and I see clearly the climate in London won't make it any better, and I'm losing all my strength, something very fatal for me." She even sent King Ludwig a doctor's certificate indicating "considerable tenderness, without marked disease, in her left lung," and supporting her decision to go to the south of Spain for some time to recuperate.

Ludwig had no objection to her making the trip, though he repeatedly and vainly asked her why she had so suddenly moved to London in the first place. But, the king warned her, he could not afford to give her anything more than her 20,000 florins a year (which was equivalent to about £2,000, a comfortable income, even in London).

To raise money for her trip and to dispose of the tons of possessions she had had carted from Munich to Geneva and from Geneva to London, she consigned most of what she had to Phillips's Auction Rooms in New Bond Street, where they were sold on 22 March. Lola had told Ludwig that she would like for him to have the paintings he had given to her—among them the fine copy of Raphael's "Madonna of the Veil" and Stieler's first portrait of her—if he was interested in buying them from her, but he let them be auctioned. The sale of the Barerstraße house at about the same time probably didn't bring Lola any cash, but the proceeds may have finally satisfied a few creditors.

Lola set the date of her departure from Southampton to Cádiz for 7 April, but she was grappling with the problem of obtaining a passport. Her masquerade as a Spaniard presented a serious problem, since there was no way she could convince anyone at the Spanish embassy that she really was Spanish. The Bavarian passport Ludwig had provided her in the name of Mrs. Bolton when she fled Munich had expired after one year. And she was unwilling to admit that she was Eliza Gilbert James in order to obtain a British passport.

She had repeatedly insisted to the king that he could simply ask King Maximilian II to have a new passport issued for her. Ludwig was just as insistent that nothing could be done for her. Even if she were in Munich it would have been impossible to obtain a passport, he told her. Why can't you just go to the Spanish embassy in London and get a passport there, he asked. Lola told him that by accepting Bavarian citizenship she had lost her Spanish citizenship and could regain it only by payment of a large sum of money. Because Ludwig himself had signed the legally questionable decree stating that Lola ceased to possess Bavarian citizenship, he really ought to get her a Bavarian passport, she suggested. But the king was adamant. He was well aware of the intense and nearly universal animosity toward her in Bavaria, even if she seemed incapable of grasping it.

So 7 April came and went without Lola obtaining any legal travel documents. She moved out of her rented house in Queen Street and took another, this time in Half Moon Street, the short but fashionable Mayfair street where she had lived briefly in 1841 when she was still Mrs. James. She continued her efforts to obtain a passport, but with the arrival of a warm spring, she seems to have become much less eager to leave England.

Lola was maintaining a fairly low public profile—a very low one by her standards—but was associating with an odd group. Most prominent among her acquaintances was Lord Henry Brougham, a leader of the Whig party and former Lord Chancellor of England, a man of intellect who was nearly as famous for his eccentricities as Lola Montez. Lord Brougham, a happily married man, reportedly was seen with the Countess of Landsfeld in public, but his relationship with her appears to have been a good deal more casual than she chose to portray it. In Half Moon Street she held receptions at which gentlemen of good and less good London society appeared, including earls, barristers, journalists, military officers, politicians, and men of uncertain profession.

The most extraordinary new figure in Lola's life was a five-year-old French girl named Nina, whom Lola first mentioned to Ludwig in April.

According to Lola, the girl's respectable parents had both died, and she had sent for Nina to come from Paris to live with her. "She's of good character and sweet and I want to adopt her—it's a great distraction and occupation for me. . . . every morning I teach her lessons myself—she has a lot of spirit and talent even though she's very young."

The sudden appearance of a child in Lola's household naturally leads to speculation that Nina was actually Lola's daughter, but for her to have been five in the spring of 1849, she would have been born between Lola's London debut and her debut in Paris, a period of frequent travel and theatrical appearances that would almost certainly rule out a concealed pregnancy.

Her realization that Ludwig's purse was no longer so freely open to her did not keep Lola from trying to get him to guaranty her allowance: "If something were to happen to you—as Papon says, I would die in the poor house—I have nothing, you know this very well, and I cannot believe you would leave me in misery—you know very well that I have no desire to marry—I couldn't for love because I don't believe in love—out of self-interest I couldn't because I have nothing of my own—who in this century would want to marry a woman who has nothing of her own? At the moment, my position is not the happiest in the world, it's as God wills, and one mustn't grumble against his will—Now all I want in the world is pure *friendship*, love I'll leave to others, to me it's nothing."

The reference to Auguste Papon must have irked Ludwig, who was still trying to contain the damage caused by Papon's memoirs and to resist his efforts at extortion. The second installment appeared in the second week of March, and in it Papon had abandoned his published outline, which had been mainly concerned with the story of Lola Montez. Instead, Papon gave his version of his conversations with the king in the palace at Munich and then ridiculed everything he reported the king had said to him. He even ridiculed his own courtly responses to the king with detached amusement at his own deceptions.

Most damaging for Ludwig, at the moment when the Landtag was considering not only his annual income but also his debts to the state, was Papon's accurate publication of the king's letter to him from the previous November concerning the guaranty of Lola's income. In it the king had not only declared himself ready to transfer a million francs to an English bank if Lola wished it, he had told Papon that any action must be deferred until after the Landtag session in order to "let sleeping dogs lie."

Docile and confident legislators of Bavaria, vote, vote once more!
The old man needs gold!
He was such a good, such a great king!
And then, it's such a noble use to which he has put all that wealth!
Have you read, deputies?
And you, Sire, have you read? . . .
Is it with *joyful confidence* that you see this document in everyone's hands, before everyone's eyes?
Patience, Sire, it is neither, thank God, the most important, nor the most glorious, nor the last. . . .
Your Majesty did me the honor of writing me a good many other things.

Papon's vitriolic taunting of King Ludwig concluded with a mocking challenge to the poet-king to respond to Papon's publication:

To work, Sire, write!
Your Majesty writes so well!
Recount, Sire!
Recount our long, intimate conversations, your interminable audiences, my notes, my words.
Courage, Sire! after having outraged Europe, now make it laugh!
In the arena, the defeated gladiators who could raise a laugh were spared.

Even Ludwig felt that the viciousness of the second installment was so exaggerated that it diminished the intended effect. The general reaction of the few people who saw Papon's publication may well have been that of the reviewer for the local newspaper near Papon's home in Nyon: "If the least literary merit were a counterweight to the impudence and shamelessness of thought that is the hallmark of these installments, one could make some allowances. But there is neither taste nor style here. What one finds here above all are the exorbitant pretensions of the author, an incomparable fatuity, an unparalleled affectation to make a personage of himself. . . . It is hard to understand how such a person dares in his publication to speak of virtue, of duty, of disinterest, of probity, when, on every page, if he is not lying or inventing, he is betraying secrets of intimacy and confidence."

The Swiss authorities had had enough of public extortion being carried on within their borders, and they deported Papon and his parents to their native France.

Back in London, Lola was trying her hand at writing, too. She told Ludwig that she was writing "Oriental Tales" and that she was considering writing her memoirs. She thought she might publish an account of her travels in Spain, she said, if she ever managed to get a passport so that she could make the trip. She sent the king a new lithographic portrait of herself that she thought was a good likeness. He responded that it caught something of her expression but made her face seem too fat.

It troubled Lola that the king's letters no longer had entries for each day, that they were shorter now and more wistful than passionate. On 15 June she wrote him bemoaning the change. In the light of subsequent events, her letter might seem to be a lie designed to rekindle Ludwig's affection and generosity, but the remarkable truth about Lola Montez is that the letter may have been sincere. Her inward vision, just as her outward vision, was strongly colored by what she wanted to see:

> [A] voice inside of me seems to say that you have other loves and that your Lolitta is forgotten—for several nights I have been tormented by unpleasant visions—I have a presentiment of something terrible— nothing else could affect me this way but the loss of your love, which was the impulse in my life that brought out the best in me and made me believe in God—because you were and are in my eyes the most noble and perfect that God has made in this world—If, after this life, the truth of things of this world is made known, you will see the best and purest feeling I have for you, and my heart has not failed you for a moment, either in your presence or in your absence—Many people here tell me I'm too young to live without a husband or lover, but there is no great merit in my conduct, for where in this world could I meet a being as noble in soul as you? For a few days I could love another, but when I would compare him to you, my love would fail. . . . may God protect you, Louis, you deserve it more than any other in the world—leave me a little place in your heart.

The king's reply showed clearly the perspective he had painfully achieved on their relationship: "The opinion you expressed in your letter of the 15th made me happy, but I don't deserve your reproaches; instead of having forgotten you, I am always thinking of you, Lolitta, and each day I write on my letter for you; you get more letters from me than I receive from you. *I can give you my word I'm not in love with anyone.* How differently you express yourself now compared to [last] winter when you were here, when it frequently seemed to me that my presence was an annoyance to you, that you preferred the company of students to mine, humiliated me in front of them, making me wait while they were with you."

Now Lola wrote that she wanted to see her Ludwig, and when he left Munich to summer in Berchtesgaden, she asked him whether he would let her pay a clandestine visit on him there. She seemed incapable of grasping the vehemence of the feeling against her in Bavaria.

Ludwig didn't respond to her suggestion. But he agreed without objection to her request for three months' allowance in advance. Since the previous October, when she had sent Papon to Munich, she had not troubled him for more than her allowance, and he may have believed that she was now able to budget her expenses. She wrote him that she was too poor to go to the theater and that her great distraction now was Nina's morning lessons. She was having migraines again and hoped to be able to take sea baths later in the summer on the Isle of Wight.

But Lola's summer plans changed early in July when a friend helped her to acquire a false passport. Once again she was making plans to sail to Cádiz. She wanted to leave before the end of July, particularly since the queen and persons of fashion had left London and because cases of cholera were being reported. The countess had begun to prepare to leave for Spain when something happened that would bring another abrupt change into her life.

Lola had taken up driving in nearby Hyde Park, the fashionable venue for displaying oneself to other people of good standing. On one of these excursions a young army officer with a dog attracted her attention. Just what role the dog played in forming the acquaintance is variously reported, but one way or another the man was given to understand that a visit from him would not be unwelcome, and he subsequently appeared at 27 Half Moon Street.

His name was George Trafford Heald. He was twenty-one, making Lola eight years his senior, and tall, slim, and a bit awkward in his movements. He had straight light-brown hair, a sparse mustache with whiskers, and a small upturned nose that gave him a decidedly juvenile air. Heald, a native Londoner, was the only son of the late George Heald, a barrister of Grey's Inn originally from Horncastle in Lincolnshire. His mother had died when he was quite young, and when his father died he was left under the guardianship of a spinster aunt, Susanna Heald. He had attended Eton and then Corpus Christi College at Cambridge, but he left without taking a degree and purchased a commission as coronet in the Second Life Guards, one of the most fashionable regiments in the British army. He was living at the barracks in Regent's Park, which gave him a great opportunity to sample the social life of the capital.

Heald was a commoner, but his father had left him far better off financially than many members of the nobility. His annual income was to become the subject of much speculation, but it was described in a court hearing as between £7,000 and £8,000 a year. A common British laborer of the age earned about £1 a week, a respectable house could be rented in London for £50 a year, and a young professional considered himself doing well at £250 a year. Although it is difficult to translate currencies over a century and a half, the coronet's annual income was roughly equivalent to $1 million in late-twentieth-century century America. Since he had attained his majority, all the money was his to use as he saw fit, and his income was likely to increase with the death of some of his relatives.

Heald was quite taken with the Countess of Landsfeld, and in his awkward, inexperienced manner he paid court to her. Lola does not seem to have taken him very seriously, and she went ahead with her plans to leave for Spain. Then, on 13 July, Heald surprised her by proposing marriage after having known her for just a few weeks. It was an unexpected but not unwelcome offer. Once she had made some inquiries concerning Heald's wealth (and it would have been in keeping with the manners of the age for him to have accompanied his declaration of love with a detailed declaration of his financial situation), Lola must have realized that the match might give her the financial independence she had sought for years.

Marrying Heald could also solve some other vexing problems in her life. First of all, there was the recurring annoyance of trying to get a passport. If she were Mrs. Heald, a British passport would be readily available to her. Second, there was the matter of her social status. Even with her title Lola remained distinctly on the periphery of respectable society in London. As the wife of a wealthy officer in the Life Guards she would have immediate status as a lady of rank and might eventually hope, once all the fuss about Ludwig and her stage career died down, to obtain the ultimate mark of social acceptability in Britain: presentation to Her Majesty Queen Victoria. And finally, it is possible that Lola was attracted to Heald and not averse to having a man in her life again.

Lola seems to have decided quickly that marriage was in her best interest, but first she wanted to let the king know and get him to promise to continue paying her annual allowance. Just four days after her previous letter, in which she had made no mention of Heald, she wrote Ludwig about a "very important matter," saying that she wanted "in everything to be guided by your opinion." She told him that Heald, a young officer of good family, had asked her to marry and that her friend Lord Brougham thought that it would be a good idea. It would solve her nationality problem, she wrote, and clarify her ambiguous status in society. The young man is not rich, she told the king; his annual income is only £800.

> Now, dear Louis, always cherished unto death—believe me, one thing I swear to you before God—I am not in love with this gentleman, it is a completely different sentiment—of good opinion and respect for his character and honorable position and so I won't be alone in the world without *protection,* open to every insult offered me—now it is for you, dear Louis, to say, if you do not wish it, I love you enough to renounce this marriage, *although it is very advantageous for me....* but if you permit me to marry, *our relations are still the same*—I could never never change to you, it's impossible—my life belongs to you exclusively—I am yours with all my soul—a husband can make no difference in the love I have for you and which will not leave me until death—Please don't lose time replying to me—without your permission that you promise me the income for life, the gentleman's family will not permit this marriage.... A thousand kisses and eternal love from *your* Lolitta

She sealed the letter, wrote on the envelope "to be given to His Majesty at once," and sent it off. It reached Ludwig at Berchtesgaden on 22 July, just one day after her previous letter, and he was more than a little surprised that she was considering marriage to a man she had not even mentioned when she last wrote. "What happened in four days?" he asked. But he had frequently written that he would not oppose her marrying if it were for her happiness, and now he repeated that. But before he gave his complete approval, he wanted to know a bit more about the man: his name, his age, his rank in the army.

By Ludwig's standards an annual income of £800 meant that Heald was quite well off, and he could not see why he should have to continue her pension if she married him. If his family was making it a *condition* of their consent, he did not wish to stand between her and happiness, but he did think that, in light of his greatly reduced income, 10,000 florins a year ought to be enough. He told her to get advice from Lord Brougham concerning a marriage contract and to consult a doctor to see whether her lungs were sufficiently strong for her to be engaging in sexual relations. The king said nothing about their relationship remaining the same. He signed himself "Your devoted Luis" and mailed the letter off promptly, expecting to hear more about Lola's intended spouse in her next letter.

Instead, the next news of Lola and her young man reached him through the newspapers, and he immediately wrote to her with unconcealed anger at what he saw as her series of lies to him: "You wrote me July 16 that you would follow my opinion in the matter of marrying an officer of the guards who had no more than £800 of income per year, and whose family would not consent if you did not continue to receive the same income you get now. I learn this officer is named George Trafford Heald, that he has an income little different from £4000, and that you married on the 20th, before I could receive your letter of the 16th, which arrived the 22nd. *This changes things.* Luis"

22

MISTRESS HEALD ON THE RUN

In fact, the marriage had taken place on 19 July. It is unclear why Lola rushed to the altar with Heald; according to one story, when Heald's commanding officer asked him to delay marrying for six months, the countess insisted that the marriage take place at once. Whatever the reason, the couple and their witnesses went early on that rainy Thursday morning to the French Roman Catholic chapel in King Street where, after formally promising that any children of the union would be raised in the Catholic Church, they were married in a French service. Then the wedding party moved to the fashionable St. George's Church in Hanover Square, where the couple was married a second time, this time in English and according to the rites of the Church of England in a service performed by the Reverend Albert Alston.

In the marriage registers Lola signed herself Maria de los Dolores de Landsfeld and stated that she was born in Seville as the daughter of Colonel Juan Porris and Maria Fernandez. She put herself down as a widow, acknowledging for the first time that Lola Montez had been married.

Unfortunately, Lola Montez's widowhood was wishful thinking. Susanna Heald, the coronet's aunt and former guardian, had heard stories that her nephew's bride, whom she regarded as a shameless gold digger, already had one living husband, which was all the law of England allowed any lady. Miss Heald had her solicitors begin making inquiries.

In the midst of her honeymoon, which seems to have been spent in Half Moon Street, Lola received Ludwig's suggestion concerning her pension and then his angry reaction to the news of her marriage. She replied immediately: "Dear Louis, for the love of God, leave me what you promised, without it, it's death for me. . . . because I'm married, this doesn't make me love you less—I love you as much. . . . We have a great need of money right now to buy furniture for a house, but I would have to do it with the money you give me each month. . . . Believe me, Louis, I know you better than you know yourself, and I'm certain that your are too much a king and a gentleman ever to take anything from me that you have promised me for life so many times—without this faith in your word, I wouldn't have married. . . . I repeat, I feel nothing for Mr. Heald—but he's a very amiable man and you are always the topic of conversation."

But securing her pension from the king would quickly become a minor problem for the Countess of Landsfeld.

On Monday, 6 August, 1849, Inspector John Whall was at his usual post— the St. James Police Station in Little Vine Street, Piccadilly—but that morning he had a most unusual assignment. He was to arrest a countess for bigamy, and not just any countess, but the famous Lola Montez. We have no way of knowing whether Inspector Whall knew of the countess's history of violent encounters with men, but he did take Sergeant Gray with him to assist in taking the lady into custody. They had an appointment at 8:30 in Half Moon Street with Susanah Heald, who was the party formally laying the information against the Countess of Landsfeld, and her solicitor, who wanted to ensure that the warrant was properly executed. Half-past eight came and went, and the policemen waited in vain for Miss Heald and her attorney. A traveling coach had pulled up in front of No. 27 and had been loaded with luggage when Inspector Whall finally saw a cab pull into the street with the complaining party and her legal adviser.

The four of them entered the Heald residence together, where they encountered the young coronet, with whom the policemen were already acquainted, having recently handled a case of theft involving one of his servants. They explained the purpose of their visit, and just then the countess herself came bustling into the corridor to enter the waiting carriage. Inspector Whall let his sergeant step forward, introduce himself, and explain to her that she must consider herself in his custody on a charge of bigamy because she had married Heald while her husband, Captain James, was still living. Although Lola seems to have refrained from attacking the officers themselves, she shoved her new husband about, pushed Miss Heald to one side, and kicked away a couple of the household dogs running about underfoot in the midst of the excitement.

Lola protested heatedly that she had been divorced by an act of parliament and added, "I don't know whether Captain James is alive or not, and I don't care. I was married in a wrong name, and it was not a legal marriage." When the officer insisted she accompany them to the police station, she exclaimed, "What will the king say?" and declared she had been granted a divorce from Captain James. The officers explained that everything would have to be determined in court and that her presence at the police station was absolutely necessary. Their quarry warned them that they would not have her alive, that she always carried means of self-destruction with her, pointing meaningfully to a small pocket on her dress, which presumably contained a vial of poison, but Whall and Gray exhibited only patient insistence.

Seeing that there was no way out, Lola sent Heald off to find legal assistance and mounted with the two officers into their carriage for the short ride to the Little Vine Street Police Station, where she was booked on a charge of bigamy. By this time the tempest had passed, and Lola was content to charm the members of the constabulary. She apologized for the trouble she had given the arresting officers and graciously allowed herself to be introduced to the other inspectors at the station and to the superintendent in charge, whom she asked if he wouldn't join her in a cigar. The superintendent informed her that smoking was forbidden on the premises, and Lola expressed her regret that he would not light up as she did so herself, contentedly defying the regulation.

A hearing was scheduled for early that afternoon before the magistrate sitting at the Greater Marlborough Police Court, Peregrine Bingham the younger, and by the time the session was to begin, the street in front of the court was crowded with people who had heard of Lola's arrest. Extra police had to be called in to control the throng, and the bailiffs were hard put to accommodate all those of rank and privilege who insisted on seats in the small courtroom. Lola appeared at half-past one, a picture of good taste in a black silk dress with a close-fitting black velvet jacket and a plain white straw bonnet trimmed with blue and a blue veil. She looked as much at ease on Heald's arm as if she were going to a luncheon in her honor rather than a criminal hearing. The defendant took a chair within the bar of the court, and Heald was allowed a chair beside her, where he showed himself to be unfailingly attentive, holding her hand in both of his, whispering into her ear, and exchanging smiles with her as he pressed her hand to his lips.

The police report stated her age as twenty-four; she was now consistently subtracting five years from her age. A reporter in the courtroom erred in the other direction by assessing her age as "at least 30" and described her as about middle height, rather plump, and with unusually large blue eyes with long lashes. Representing the countess was Sir William Henry Bodkin, a prominent member of the Temple who was described by a fellow barrister as "acute and clear-headed," but this afternoon would not be his finest hour. Since England had no office of public prosecutions and all criminal charges were, at least in theory, brought by private individuals, the barrister engaged by Miss Heald to prosecute the bigamy charge was William Clarkson, also of the Temple.

Although the case had been put together with great speed because of Lola's impending departure from England, Clarkson had impressive evidence to marshal against the Countess of Landsfeld. With a series of witnesses, the prosecution was able to establish that Lola Montez was Eliza Gilbert James, whose marriage to Captain James of the East India Company had been terminated by the Consistory Court in 1842 with the specific provision that neither party could remarry during the life of the other. The record of her marriage to Coronet Heald was presented, and finally the most recent return on the Company's personnel in India was offered in evidence, indicating that, as of 13 June, James was alive and with his unit. Clarkson rested his case.

Bodkin's task was not an enviable one, and he had had only a few hours to acquaint himself with the case. He decided that the best he could hope for was to try to get his client released on bail, and that was what he sought. He was willing to admit that enough proof had been laid before the court to justify further inquiry. But enough had also been stated to show, Bodkin claimed, that even if the imputed offense had been committed, it was committed under circumstances that certainly appeared to justify the act. The barrister asked the magistrate to allow the countess to leave the court after posting bail to guaranty her appearance at an inquiry on a day to be agreed upon.

Magistrate Bingham, noting that the law presumes innocence, pointed out that the prosecution was asking a presumption of guilt, for there was no proof that Captain James had survived the numerous casualties with which life is beset in a military profession and in a tropical climate for the six weeks between the official return of 13 June and the marriage on 19 July.

But because the advocate for the defendant had admitted that he judged sufficient ground had been laid for further inquiry and had offered to find sufficient bail, the magistrate ordered a remand and liberated the prisoner upon her presenting two sureties for £500 each and posting her own bond for £1,000 for her reappearance in court. It was a significant bail, equal to Lola's entire annual allowance from King Ludwig. Heald's solicitors provided the two sureties for £500 each, and Heald himself apparently paid Lola's personal bail of £1,000. The countess was free to walk out of court, but she and Heald remained inside until the curious crowd outside grew tired of waiting for her and drifted away.

Lola and her new husband continued with their interrupted departure for the Continent; but instead of sailing to Cádiz on 7 August, as they had planned, they headed for Paris, en route to Italy and perhaps Egypt to see the pyramids. They stopped at the Hotel Windsor in Paris, then continued by train, coach, and steamship to Marseilles, where they sailed on the *Marie Antoinette* for Rome. There Lola saw the famous sights of the city and went to visit Ludwig's Villa Malta. The caretaker let her in, and she saw everything Ludwig had described to her so many times: his bedroom, the garden, the terrace where he wrote his poetry. Lola had never lost her affection for Ludwig, even though she had deceived him; and it was bittersweet moment for her to feel his presence there in the villa.

From Rome they traveled overland to Naples, where they arrived on 27 August and checked into the Hotel Vittoria, quickly changing the modest rooms they had reserved for a sumptuous suite. Their stay was brief, however, for when Heald stopped by his bankers' office in Naples he found a letter waiting for him with disturbing news. Apparently it was from his solicitors, who explained that Miss Heald's barrister, Clarkson, had informed the magistrate that the countess had fled the court's jurisdiction. If she were not back in London by 10 September, when the next hearing was scheduled, the total bail of £2,000 was likely to be forfeited. Even for someone with an income of £7,000 a year, the bail was nothing to be tossed away, and Heald and Lola decided to return to London at once. There were no ships leaving Naples for Marseilles, so they chartered a steamer for a fee of several hundred pounds and sailed for France.

Meanwhile, Lola Montez had become more notorious than ever before. The news of the bigamy accusation was taken up by the world press as the latest and most outrageously eccentric caprice of an extraordinary woman. In England, the affair gave rise to journalistic commentary on the inexcusably confusing, difficult, and expensive process of obtaining a true divorce in Great Britain; the process would be changed dramatically by the Divorce Act of 1857. Other commentary focused on the blatant hypocrisy of Victorian morality, exemplified by the outraged insistence of the colonel of the Second Life Guards that Coronet Heald resign his commission because he had endeavored to make the Countess of Landsfeld his lawful wife, whereas everyone knew that the colonel would have taken no offense whatsoever had the young man simply kept her as his concubine.

The bigamy scandal gave every newspaper another opportunity to review the strange and adventurous life of this young woman, including stories of her girlhood in Scotland and Durham. Major excerpts from the divorce testimony concerning her shocking behavior with Lieutenant Lennox also found their way into a number of newspapers. Miss Heald had succeeded in making Lola an even greater celebrity than had all the Bavarian rebels.

Lola and Heald won their race against time, arriving in London at about 11 P.M. on Friday, 7 September. The next morning Lola set out to determine the status of her case. She learned that her dash from Naples to London might have saved the bail of £2,000 from forfeiture but that Miss Heald's attorneys likely had evidence now that Captain James was still alive in India on 19 July, which would mean that Lola could expect to be bound over for trial at the Old Bailey. There was even the possibility that she could be jailed until that trial.

This was not what Lola had bargained for. Perhaps she had believed that her solicitors had somehow convinced Miss Heald to call off her prosecution and that the trip back to London was necessary simply to ensure that the bail was not lost. Now, when it was clear to her that by appearing in court she might rescue the bail but lose her freedom—and would certainly face a trial for bigamy that could send her to prison—Lola had no hesitation about what she would do. The next day she left London for France and arrived in Boulogne on the Folkestone packet on the night of Monday, 10 September. Her bail was forfeited.

In Boulogne, Lola waited for Heald to join her once he had completed some business in London. At last, for the first time since 1 August, she wrote to King Ludwig. She had not received his last two letters, which had been mailed to Seville, according to the instructions she had given him before being arrested, so she did not know how angry the king was when he confirmed through newspaper stories and private inquiries that she had lied to him about the extent of Heald's fortune and about his family's insistence that her pension be continued. And he had finally voiced his bitterness about learning that she had been sleeping with Peißner in Frankfurt just after having returned to Munich to urge him to abdicate so he could be with her. Nevertheless, he said he would continue her pension at 10,000 florins a year, and he had wished her happiness in her marriage.

Ignorant of all this, she now wrote him trying to explain the bigamy action. It was an infamous act of revenge by Miss Heald, she told Ludwig, and it had galvanized public opinion in her favor. The old woman was doing it because she had not been able to squeeze more money out of her nephew, Lola claimed, and because she was insane. In the spring of 1847, newspaper reports had reached Munich that Lola had been married to an officer named James, and she had told everyone that it was a cousin of hers who had married Lieutenant James. Now she did not deny to Ludwig that she had indeed married James, but she told him that the "marriage with Mr. James was never legal—I was baptized Catholic [almost certainly a lie] and never was married in the Catholic Church, only in the Protestant Church, and for that reason, in my conscience it was not a legal marriage." She had to concede, however, that her conscience and British law did not coincide on this point and that she was not legally married to the young coronet. And since she had no marital rights against Heald, she wrote, it was imperative for Ludwig to continue to pay her at least 10,000 florins a year or simply to settle a sum of money on her sufficient for her to live. "But for me the greatest happiness is still to receive your letters," she told Ludwig. "Countless kisses to you, ever beloved Louis—I could never meet another like you, with your heart and noble sentiments—God keep you in his care—your devoted and tender Lolitta."

Ludwig no longer believed her. He replied that her not having written him for a month and a half contradicted the sentiments of devotion she expressed. He laid out her lies to him. And what had happened to the little girl, Nina? Now he simply signed himself "Luis," without fidelity or devotion. He cut her pension in half effective 1 October and began listing her in his accounts as "Mistress Heald."

Lola made no direct reply to any of his accusations or questions. Shortly after Heald arrived in Boulogne, the couple went to Paris, where they set themselves up with a secretary, two servants, and two maids in a luxurious suite of rooms in a fashionable hotel in the Rue de Rivoli. Lola had the secretary send out announcements of her arrival, and soon she was receiving calls from Parisian dandies, English noblemen, Russian princes, Bavarian barons, and many of her old theatrical friends. The Countess of Landsfeld, as she continued to call herself, gave a grand dinner for all of them, where she appeared wearing dazzling jewels, including a triple bracelet of emeralds containing a diamond-encircled portrait of King Ludwig, who, she told everyone, had always been just like a father to her, despite slanderous stories to the contrary.

Indeed, Lola announced to anyone within earshot that she had a duty to her new husband to refute all slander by asserting the purity of her life prior to her marriage to him. Now she transformed her parents once again, this time making her mother Irish (the *Cork Constitution* had recently reported that Lola's mother came from that city) and her father a Spanish nobleman. She had been raised in great austerity, and her first marriage, to Lieutenant James, had been a mere formality to save her virtue from a lecherous guardian. In fact, most of the notorious incidents in her life, including the attack on the gendarme in Berlin, her expulsion from Baden-Baden, and so on, had all been a result of her efforts to preserve the virtue and honor that she had succeeded in bringing intact to her marriage to Coronet Heald, the first man who had truly won her heart.

The newlyweds left Paris for Marseilles again and a boat to Barcelona, at last embarking on Lola's Spanish "homecoming." Heald was probably able to speak the language in France, but in Barcelona he and Lola were thrown more and more together, and squabbles and full-scale screaming arguments were the result. The story went around Barcelona that Lola had superficially wounded Heald with her ever-present dagger during one of their disputes. Finally the bridegroom fled, leaving Lola angry and disgusted. Three days later he returned, apparently incapable of breaking with her or of organizing his own return to England. Lola took him back, but she sat down and wrote Ludwig just what she thought of Heald: "What a pity you aren't near me to see for yourself the eternal punishment I've brought upon myself—This man not only is without spirit, foolish, brutal, but he is without heart, and he insults me before the whole world. . . . How, after knowing you, can I give my love to another, and this other man is without spirit, ignorant, a quasi-lunatic who is incapable of taking a step by himself."

Lola insisted that Heald had only £600 a year, not the £6,000 or £7,000 that Clarkson alleged, and she told Ludwig that she had not written for a month because she was ashamed to tell him what a terrible mess she had made of her life. "I beg you in your next letter to send me some of your hair," she implored the king. Once more she wrote the words of love that had meant so much to Ludwig in the past: "Oh, if you knew how much my thoughts travel to you—how much I think of you, you would be certain that I love you—my soul is with yours forever and ever—I can love no other but you—believe my words, they are written in misery and affliction far from you. . . . I love you more in my unhappiness than when I was happy—Adios, dear Louis, I am still the same Lolitta of heart and soul, loving you more than ever—Your Lolitta, yours unto death"

King Ludwig was now back in Munich, and he was getting over Lola. His morning routine no longer included writing at least a few lines to her. He still thought about her often, but he was reaching the conclusion that a great deal of what he had never wanted to believe about Lola had always been true.

Lola and Heald departed Barcelona via the coastal steamer *El Cid* on 5 December, arriving in Cádiz on 17 December. There were some in Cádiz who remembered Lola from her visit in 1842, when she was learning the Spanish language and Spanish dance, and they noted that her looks had deteriorated markedly in seven years while her temper had not improved at all. Relations between Heald and his bride had also deteriorated, and Lola's major delight seemed to be terrorizing her husband in public. On Christmas morning he left the Fonda Himenez, where they were staying, to take a walk. He never came back. Lola heard that he was headed for Algeciras, where the *Pacha* was about to sail for England, and she tried to stop him but without success.

Heald sent her a note of farewell from the ship, saying that though he really had nothing against her, he simply couldn't go on like this and wanted to return to England. The only bright spot in her dismal situation came in the form of a letter from King Ludwig that she received on 8 January. The letter itself was not encouraging. "I told you that the world does not have the power to separate me from you (it seems to me that I have given you great proofs of this) and that only you could do it. It is not your enemies who have made me change my feelings for you but your conduct. You always look outside for motives for what happens to you, but you must look inside. How could you be in a good situation when for some time nearly all your acquaintances have been betrayed by you. . . . Be happy and may you *convert*, for your good in this world and the other, I wish it very much. Luis"

In spite of his words of admonition, Ludwig included bank drafts for Lola's allowance for the first three months of 1850, and that made all the difference in the world to her. Now she could pay her bills in Cádiz and launch an effort to recapture Heald's affection.

Lola wrote to Ludwig thanking him for the money and suggesting that more would be very welcome. More than that, she asked Ludwig if he would send her a letter for Heald admonishing *him*. The man was so vain, Lola wrote, that she was sure that words from Ludwig recalling Heald to his better feelings would have a sobering effect. She also asked Ludwig to help her find Heald's hiding place. "You alone are for me the ideal of all that is great and noble of heart, of the soul," she wrote him. "That is why I love you so much—and why I am for life, Your Lolitta forever."

Late in January she sailed from Cádiz for France and again took up residence in Boulogne—as close as she could get to Heald and not be subject to arrest. Ludwig had replied to her outrage at Heald's abandonment and her complaints of poverty and ill health with a few terse lines concluding, "It was very disagreeable for me to hear that your husband has left you. I am sorry. Luis."

Now the Countess of Landsfeld hit upon an idea to renew the king's interest in her and cause him to supplement her income. On 25 February she wrote to him:

> The first thing I did was send to London for the package in which are all the letters you've written me—and very well that I did this without *wasting time*, for two days after the package with your letters was dispatched, Mr. Heald went to the attorney where they were and asked for them—when he learned I had called for them, he was furious—God knows what he would have done with your letters if he had gotten them in his hands— This man is very vicious and capable of everything base and dishonorable. . . . the gentleman wants to annul the marriage, but I will certainly resist because the other marriage was not *legal.* . . . I would like very much to confide all of your letters to me to you yourself, but how am I to send them?—I have no money to pay for someone to take them to you. . . . if Mr. Heald could steal them from me, they would certainly be published immediately. . . . I am thinking more of you than of me—although I don't have money to buy myself shoes. . . . This *monster* [Heald] has also taken poor *Turk* from me, my only consolation and *friend*. . . . I have nothing to do but cry, cry the whole day and night—it's terrible to be *alone—and unhappy and poor*—but in all this, thank God, your letters are safe. . . . For God's sake don't abandon me—my hope is in you—Your devoted, your unhappy Lolitta, once loved by you

King Ludwig replied instantly to Lola's letter: "At this hour your letter of February 25 has come into my hands. You offer to send me my letters, which I will receive with pleasure, and which you can have sent in security by means of any banker. When I have them in my hands, I will send you the drafts for April, May, and June, even if it is premature. . . . Luis"

If the king didn't know his Lolitta well enough already not to expect his letters to arrive any day soon, Lola's prompt reply disabused him of any illusions about her letting them go easily: "Why do you write me such cold letters?—it's very cruel of you—it's not my fault that I'm unhappy and poor. . . . As for your letters, now that I am calmer and people are not tormenting me so much, I would like to keep them—I will send them to you only if I'm going to be traveling, which isn't likely—to travel you need some money, something I don't have—please write me friendlier letters—you have *a very capricious heart and you forget very easily*—but I'm not like you, I'm still your devoted and tender Lolitta for life—Tonight I'm going *incognito* to London, something very dangerous but I have to see Mr. Heald so he will give me money and the things he took from me."

Ludwig had clearly taken the bait Lola had dangled in the form of his letters, and once again he answered her immediately, trying to separate her from the letters with the one thing he was sure appealed to her: money. "Enclosed are the drafts for April, May, and June. . . . I hope I will receive at once the letters you have offered to return to me. Luis. . . . *If my letters do not arrive beforehand, it is certain no draft will be sent for the month of July.*"

A long silence from Lola followed, both because she had her allowance through the middle of the year and because her secret expedition to London had been crowned with more success than she could have expected; she not only convinced Heald to open his purse to her once again, she managed to persuade this "vicious" and "dishonorable" young man to come set up a lavish household with her in Paris. The countess arrived in Paris late in March and soon moved into an impressive mansion known as the Chateau Beaujon just off the Champs Elysées, reportedly signing a fifteen-year lease at 15,000 francs a year. Heald arrived shortly thereafter with an array of servants, fifty trunks, five carriages, and seven horses.

The notorious couple at once began a 50,000 franc redecoration of their new abode, and an army of workmen descended on the chateau. Relations between Lola and Heald were still unstable, and on one occasion one of the painters working on the redecoration felt obliged to intervene to prevent violence between his employers.

The Healds did not entertain on a lavish scale, keeping mainly to a small circle of Lola's friends and parasites, but they were often seen driving up and down the Champs Elysées with the fashionable crowd, she leading in an elegant calèche and he following behind her in his phaeton. Lola was usually unmistakable wherever she went because she took to having her carriage drawn by four matched white horses.

There were rumors that she had deposited about £40,000 (certainly the equivalent of several million dollars today) with an American banker in Paris, but that was probably a story she planted herself to keep her creditors generous. It was a fact, however, that for the moment the workers redecorating the Chateau Beaujon were being paid in cash. The loving couple had also commissioned a portrait of themselves from a fashionable painter who lived near them. It was to represent the moment of their engagement, showing Lola seated on an elegant sofa, Heald standing beside her in his Guards uniform and holding her hands as he gazed into her eyes. On a malachite table nearby rested a sumptuous jewel box displaying the coronet's wedding gifts to his bride.

This life in Paris was costing an enormous amount of money, and Heald, wealthy as he was, began to get letters from his solicitor urgently requesting his presence back in London to discuss his income and make arrangements to deal with the bills that were coming in. When Heald finally did make the trip to London, Lola, obviously worried about what ideas the solicitor might be putting into her husband's head, sent two friends to bring him back to Paris before any arrangements could be made.

At the end of May, Lola wrote to Ludwig for the first time since he had sent the drafts for April, May, and June. She excused her extended silence by saying that she had been unable to leave her bed after suffering a severe recurrence of her malarial fever together with intestinal problems.

My life is unhappy, very unhappy—Mr. Heald is more than a tyrant to me in his conduct—and I positively can't leave him because I have nothing with which to live. . . . you ask me to send you your letters, but although you promised and swore to continue the little income you gave me during my whole life, now you want to take everything from me—the poorest man with any heart could not do that. . . . at every moment and in the presence of strangers I am insulted like a lost woman walking the streets. . . . some say I ought to sell your letters for publication, but that gives me a horror of betraying you—it pleases me much more to read your letters for myself and to think of that time that is forever lost—I beg you not to revoke my pension. . . . there is no other woman in the world who has suffered as I, who is persecuted as I am—and all of this because I was with you at Munich. . . . right now I live in a very nice house, but it's nothing—Mr. Heald has a lot (seven horses), but nothing is for my use. . . . I am as I was and as I will be forever in this life, she who loves you so very much, Lolitta

Ludwig decided that he needed a reliable source of information on what Lola's life was really like, and he asked the Bavarian ambassador in Paris, Baron August von Wendland, for a confidential report on the affairs of the Countess of Landsfeld. Wendland wrote back that she and Heald had rented an elegant house, had a large establishment of servants, horses, carriages, were seen in public places but lived quietly, and were said to be paying cash for all their extensive expenditures.

Ludwig wrote to Lola, telling her what he knew of her life in Paris, accusing her of lying to him, and repeating that she could expect no more money until he had his letters back. Lola could see that the only card she had left was Ludwig's letters, and she wasn't about to throw it away for nothing. "The pension you promised me for life is of the *greatest necessity*—you don't know what *necessity* means—it is a *terrible word*. . . . If you want, I would much prefer that you give me a sum on delivery of all the papers and letters of yours I have, and then we won't speak any more of money—if you want to do that, then you would not have to pay me the pension any longer—*I will be satisfied with the sum you choose to give me* because, in truth, you can see I have a great need of money—I know your letters are very valuable, and if something were to happen to me, others could do with them what I am incapable of doing, although many publishers here and in London have offered me money, a lot, for them, to publish them in English or French. . . . believe me, it is a terrible thing to be in *need*—a person is capable of a lot when *obliged* to do it." She no longer made any protestations of her undying affection.

Although Lola, with her ceaselessly shifting characterization of everything she did, might seem capable of convincing herself that this letter was simply a rough but necessary shove to get Ludwig to do the right thing, her remarkable concluding sentence made it clear that even *she* recognized she had written an extortion letter: "Nothing I have said here on the subject of your letters or the pension is my own idea, it is the advice of friends who want to manage the whole thing without scandal and in a manner to satisfy you. Lolitta"

Ludwig made no reply to Lola's letter. Instead, he peppered Wendland with more inquires into the details of Lola's life in Paris. Among other things, he wanted to know if Heald had guaranteed Lola a sum of money or a pension in the event he died before her. The ambassador replied that the consensus in Paris was that if Heald had done something like that, his life would be in danger.

Lola had not been lying to Ludwig that she and Heald were in serious financial trouble, but their problems were largely the result of the extravagance of the household they were attempting to maintain. Late in July, four of the horses were sent to be sold in London to cover expenses, and arrangements were being made to try to get the carriage maker to take back one of their carriages. Heald's attorney was about to come to Paris to discuss what measures would be necessary to confine their expenditures to their income when Heald once more decided that he had had enough and again abandoned his wife. Heald seems not to have been totally without blame in the manner of his parting, since the evidence is that he took with him not only all of his own portable possessions but also most of Lola's, including her diploma of nobility, her marble model of the king's hand, and all of the king's letters to her.

Lola was left with almost no cash to pay the army of creditors or even the rent on the Chateau de Beaujon. She attempted to have unpaid-for furniture sneaked out a back door, through the garden, and onto a waiting wagon but was reported to the upholsterer, and a bailiff halted the abduction of the security. The countess took off in pursuit of her husband, once more setting up a base of operation in Boulogne, but this time her efforts were in vain. Heald now was interested only in having his attorneys arrange a settlement that would free him from Lola Montez forever. The possessions that Heald had stolen were turned over to her solicitor in London, and negotiations began between the attorneys.

Heald finally agreed to pay the debts acquired while he was living with the countess and, reportedly, an allowance of £50 a month, but otherwise Lola was now on her own financially, and she returned to Paris as a much less flamboyant figure than before. Indeed, some members of the press refused to believe that she had actually returned when it was reported that she was one of several women of note being escorted around town by the exotic and wealthy ambassador of Nepal, who was making a tour of European capitals. In fact, she came back in mid-September and soon moved into a relatively modest apartment at 420 rue de St. Honoré, which was rented for her by a friend, Michel de Corail, who claimed to be a count. The lease on the apartment, which was in a fashionable section between the Place de la Concorde and the Church of the Madelaine, was not in her name, nor was the furniture rented in her name, so no creditors could pursue her personally if the bills went unpaid.

The previous four years had been harrowing for Lola, and she seems to have considered seeking spiritual support in religion. There were even stories that the Countess of Landsfeld would retire to a Carmelite convent in Spain. She had already shown an interest in spiritualism in London, but now Catholic ecclesiastics were seen calling on her in the rue St. Honoré, and she herself called on the priest of her local parish at the Church of the Madelaine. The curé reproached her for the extravagant and shameful manner of her life, but she replied that it was the result of the parental neglect she had suffered as a child. This was an excuse she had been using for years, and Ludwig's admonition that she look within for the causes of her sorrows seems to have had no effect.

Lola took to giving small parties at her apartment, and she was able to establish a multinational circle of figures from the worlds of politics, art, journalism, theater, and the idle rich. But now more than ever her primary concern was money; Ludwig had cut off her income in July, and the payments of £50 a month from Heald could not have been something she dared depend on.

To her credit, there is no evidence that Lola ever seriously considered publishing the king's letters to her, despite the veiled threats she made to him. Now she wrote to Ludwig once more, telling him that Heald's attorney had surrendered the king's letters to a solicitor in London but that she had no money to send for them or to return them to him in security. "You have forgotten me, me, your Lolitta, whom you swore so many times never to abandon—I have written you two letters and you have made no response— my God, what is my crime if it is not the love I *still* have for you. . . . if you will allow it, since the only way I have to live at the moment is to publish my memoirs, you can be sure that neither your name nor that of anyone near you will be compromised—it is the only proof of my affection for you that I can give, to let the world know of your great genius, your great spirit. . . . Oh, Louis, don't fail me now in my situation, which I can't describe for you, it's so miserable."

Ludwig had apparently decided that he had nothing to gain and much to lose by putting yet another letter into Lola's hands, and he may have been more than a little skeptical that she was living in abject misery on the fashionable rue St. Honoré. He did not reply.

Corail seems to have arranged for the serial publication of Lola's memoirs in the journal *Le Pays*, and he and an aging lesser light of the Académie française reportedly took on the task of putting her reminiscences into stylish and idiomatic French. Newspapers claimed that Lola sent extortion letters to everyone who might have reason to wish to influence their treatment in her memoirs.

Whether or not this was true, third parties did attempt to contact King Ludwig through Ambassador Wendland to suggest that in return for an annual pension of 25,000 francs the countess would be willing to return the king's letters and refrain from using them in her memoirs. Wendland told them to inform the countess that if she expected to receive any help from King Ludwig ever again she should return his letters at once and not mention anything about His Majesty in her autobiography. At the same time, the ambassador went privately to the French foreign minister and the interior minister to see what they could do about suppressing the publication of Lola's memoirs. The ministers called in the editor of *Le Pays* and informed him that if anything he published hurt France's relations with a foreign power he would be imprisoned immediately. The ministers also asked to review the manuscript of the memoirs so that they could suggest deletions. The editor, who was protected from censorship by laws of the new republic, refused to cooperate.

In a final effort to contact the king, a copy of the galley proofs of Lola's introduction, written as an open letter to Ludwig, was delivered to the Bavarian embassy in Paris with a request that it be sent to the king at once; the next morning, 8 January 1851, the first installment of Lola's autobiography appeared.

In spite of the assistance she had with writing, Lola Montez was clearly the mind behind the memoirs, which displayed the characteristic mixture of "lies and vanity" that Sir Jasper Nicolls had remarked in Lola so many years before. The introduction set the tone, addressing Ludwig personally and giving a preview of what the memoirs were to discuss: "It is your ideas as poet, as artist, as philosopher, your sometimes severe but always weighty judgments, the lofty ideas of a liberal, intelligent, and gracious king that I wish to lay before Europe, which has now sunk into such stupid materialism, which no longer believes, no longer thinks, no longer acts. . . . Society does all it can to make us women hypocrites. We are ceaselessly driven to say the opposite of what we think. . . . I will disclose many scandalous things that have been concealed up to now . . . . I will, nonetheless, remain ever within the confines of decency. When I must touch upon the private life of public figures, particularly when it is a woman, I will always do so with moderation and consideration."

The introduction wandered, changing subject abruptly and taking detours that led nowhere, characteristics of Lola's writing. It is surprising that Lola, who would develop the reputation of a reforming liberal, mocked the new French republic and its supporters, as well as political liberals generally.

She also managed to work some whopping lies into the introduction, among them the claim that the best rebuttal to the claims that she played the shameful role of a Dubarry or a Pompadour in Bavaria is that Queen Therese herself, as a token of her high esteem for the Countess of Landsfeld, invested her with the insignia of the Theresien Order. Lola topped this lie by declaring that the happiest day of her life was when King Ludwig took her by the hand and led her before the assembled nobles of his court, announcing, "Gentlemen, I present to you my best friend," royal words that were, Lola wrote, "sufficient to revenge a woman well."

As literature, the memoirs certainly attain no great stature, but they are entertaining, so it is difficult to account entirely for the general disappointment that greeted the publication of the early installments. It is likely that the readers who bought copies of *Le Pays* were hoping for the scandalous revelations that were hinted at in the introduction. But Lola stuck to a chronological scheme, regaling readers with stories of life in India that were neither scandalous nor particularly novel. Wendland was able to report to Ludwig that the public response had been resolutely tepid and that Lola was reportedly frustrated and angry that she was succeeding neither with the public nor with her efforts to sell her silence to Ludwig.

The installments of Lola's memoirs appeared irregularly in early 1851. She was said to be receiving 24,000 francs for the whole work, but only about a quarter of the memoirs had been published and 6,000 francs paid when *Le Pays* was sold, and the new owners, ardent supporters of the French republic that Lola treated with such scorn, refused any dealings with her. Lola reportedly tried to sell the remaining three-quarters to other Parisian journals, but she found no buyers at her price.

Toward the end of March 1851 an acquaintance of Lola's told her he would be going to Munich, and she used him as a courier for one last letter to Ludwig: "Oh, Louis, if you knew the miserable, but *honorable*, situation I am in—it is poor, very poor, but money got by ill means is always evil—I would prefer to live as I do than possess luxury in evil. . . . Oh, Louis, be charitable—remember it is Lolitta who begs—Lolitta who is the same for you. . . . For pity's sake, Louis, help me be dignified—Your letters, which Mr. Heald would not permit me to give you, are at your disposal—they are sacred to me—I am allowing a friend of mine to write what will be called my memoirs, but *nothing will be written of Munich.... Answer my letter*—some lines—what happiness for me if you write me a few lines—my heart is the same for you.... Your ever devoted Lolitta"

The king made no reply. This was the last of their hundreds of letters—letters filled with passion, anger, disillusionment, obsession, lies, recriminations, pleas for money, pleas for love. Although Lola had grievously deceived Ludwig, she could not, as the king had pointed out to her, bring herself to accept responsibility for her own acts. Even more inexplicably, her heart and mind were such that she seems to have been fully capable of feeling affection and respect for Ludwig at the same time she was trying to extort money from him. Whether for the sake of his honor or hers, she would always insist that their relationship had been purely platonic and intellectual; and for the rest of her life she would speak of him only in terms of the highest admiration.

Shortly after he received this final letter, Ludwig put into one last poem his thoughts on his Lolitta:

> Through you I lost the crown,
> But I do not rage against you for that,
> For you were born to be my misfortune,
> You were such a blinding, scorching light!
>
> Be happy! so my soul calls after you,
> Into the ever-receding distance;
> Now at last choose the path of salvation;
> Vice brings only ruin and shame.
>
> The best friend you ever had,
> You thrust faithlessly away,
> The gates of happiness were closed against you,
> You simply followed your lascivious longings.
>
> For life we remain divided,
> And never again will we meet face to face,
> Leave me my heart's so painfully won peace,
> Without it life is such a burden.

23

BEFORE THE FOOTLIGHTS AGAIN

What had brought Lolitta so strongly to Ludwig's mind was the arrival at Villa Malta of a courier, an Irishman named Patrick O'Brien who said he had served the king's son, King Otto of Greece, and that he was delivering a package from the Countess of Landsfeld. Ludwig refused to meet with O'Brien himself but deputized one of his courtiers, Count Franz Pocci, to deal with him. Pocci was aghast to discover that O'Brien had brought an unsealed package containing all of the king's letters to Lola Montez.

Ludwig was greatly surprised and relieved to have these hundreds of pages, full of his innermost secrets, back in his own hands. He sent O'Brien a note of thanks and 2,000 francs for the countess to show his appreciation for her act. O'Brien wrote the king that he was sure that the "weak and friendless woman, steeped to the chin in sorrow and distress," would be deeply grateful. He said Lola needed the money to redeem her silver from the pawnbroker who had lent her the money to send O'Brien to Rome.

When Lola got the news of the transfer she wrote to O'Brien that he should tell the king that she would die happy once assured of the king's goodwill. "Tell the king," she wrote her courier, "that his poor Lola is now morally dead and will never trouble him again. She will hide the pangs of her breaking heart from all the world and will try to end her days in peace with God and men."

Wendland reported to the king from Paris that the story of pawning the silver was said to have been invented to obtain more money from him and that O'Brien had gone to Rome on Lola's behalf because he had fallen in love with her. Although the Irishman received the impression that Ludwig would guaranty Lola an annuity, the king contented himself with sending her an additional 3,000 francs in appreciation of the unconditional return of his letters. It was the last money he would ever send her. Some weeks later Count Pocci received a letter from O'Brien saying that Lola had concealed from him her receipt of the additional 3,000 francs and had spread the story that O'Brien himself had tried to use the king's letters to extort money. He returned to Ireland feeling bitterly deceived, saying the countess was surrounding herself with low society.

The countess was certainly surrounding herself with a different society, for now, instead of trying to "end her days at peace with God and men," Lola was preparing to launch a new theatrical career. Her need for a substantial income and for a life full of incident in the public eye had driven her, following the failure of her marriage and of her memoirs, back to the stage. She had moved into a different apartment on the rue St. Honoré, at No. 362, and in the summer she began practicing four hours daily for the renewal of her life as a professional dancer, which had been interrupted after her second performance in Munich in October 1846, nearly five years earlier. Lola was sure to draw good houses, despite her long absence from the stage; after Queen Victoria, she was almost certainly the most famous, or infamous, woman on earth.

The countess put herself under the artistic guidance of Monsieur Mabille, the proprietor of the famous Jardin Mabille, an open-air dance hall on the Champs Elysées far more renowned among admirers of beautiful women than among connoisseurs of dance. Mabille choreographed several dances for the countess, among them a tarantella (probably related to the "Oleano" of her London debut), a Bavarian dance, a Hungarian dance, and a Tyrolean dance. The money from Ludwig probably helped pay for the lessons, the splendid costumes, and the copying of her music, but she was said still to be receiving her £600 a year from Heald, and contributions very likely came from male admirers.

Throughout the summer of 1851 Lola continued her dancing exercises and planned the resumption of her career as she carried on an active social life. Her new apartment seems to have been larger and better suited for entertaining, and the guests at her regular parties were a gathering of gentlemen from many nations and a variety of social classes. It was not unusual to find a few East Indians and Americans mixed in with representatives of the major European nationalities at the countess's soirées, and she would sometimes entertain her guests with a song or two in her small but attractive voice. Most of the evening she spent chain-smoking little cigarettes as she received the homage of the gentlemen, whom she fascinated with witty conversation in a variety of languages. One observer noted that she seemed not to speak any language perfectly but made the fewest mistakes in English. Her French, he noted, took on the accent of the person with whom she was speaking, and as she listened with a smile on her half-open mouth, there was a constant play of expression over her face.

Early in the spring of 1851 Lola had been introduced to Edward Payson Willis, an American who was the younger brother of a prominent editor and author, Nathaniel Parker Willis. The younger Willis became a confidant of the Countess of Landsfeld and encouraged her to revive her theatrical career by emulating the success that both Fanny Elssler and Jenny Lind had recently achieved in the United States. Another of Lola's American guests that summer was James Gordon Bennett, the editor and publisher of the *New York Herald*. Bennett sensed the editorial value of this intelligent, assertive, and resolutely unorthodox beauty, and for years his newspaper would provide her with priceless, if not invariably flattering, publicity.

By the end of the summer, newspapers in Europe and America were reporting that Lola would be coming to the United States in the fall, and the American press was quickly filled with expressions of outrage. The new American consul in Paris, Samuel Griswold Goodrich, who under the pen name Peter Parley was one of America's most prolific and widely read authors, wrote to a Boston paper: "Thousands of American ladies, it is expected, will rush to see one who possesses in a remarkable degree no artistic talent, and who has acquired notoriety—the only notoriety that makes her an object of attention—by her shameless dissoluteness of character. The exhibition, under such circumstance, of Lola Montez, I consider an immoral and demoralizing thing. It is an insult for American society; and if it succeeds as its projectors anticipate, it will afford the most painful and conclusive proof we have yet given of our growing corruption."

The New York Times solemnly intoned, "We shall be sadly disappointed if this creature has any degree of success in the United States. She has no special reputation as a dancer. She is known to the world only as a shameless and abandoned woman." The mere anticipation of her arrival was stirring up so much publicity that it looked as if Lola could hardly fail.

She signed a management contract on 26 August with Roux et cie. of the rue Lepeletier, covering performances given between 15 September 1851 and 15 March 1852 in France, America, Cuba, Brazil, Mexico, Chile, Peru, and Africa. Lola agreed to dance at least six performances a week, and Roux was to get 25 percent of her income in exchange for handling the business end of her tour.

As a final preparation for her reappearance on the public stage, the Countess of Landsfeld sent out several hundred invitations, to her many friends and to all members of the Parisian press, for a private preview of her act 12 September at the Jardin Mabille. About three hundred men attended, as well as a few women, who were described as being "of the elite of the ladies of high and of moderate fantasy." Lola kept them waiting two hours beyond the scheduled 8 P.M. performance time, and the guests entertained themselves with the punch, ice cream, and cigarettes their hostess had provided for them.

When at last she appeared, Lola was greeted with appropriately wild enthusiasm by her invited audience. She displayed three of the dances she had perfected under Mabille and three sumptuous costumes to go with them. According to one report, she reenacted the garter-tossing that had marked her Parisian debut at the Opéra more than seven years earlier. Théophile Gautier and others remarked that her dancing was actually far better than it had been then and gave the credit to Mabille. Gautier reported to his readers that she was still the svelte young woman they remembered—nervous, a little thin, with blazing eyes and sparkling teeth.

Four days later Lola Montez made her official return to the stage at Boulogne, where she had an enormous success before an audience that contained a high percentage of Britons. "The dance of Lola Montez is poetry in motion," wrote one critic of her debut, "sometimes fantastic, often lascivious, always attractive." The manager of the theater in Boulogne booked her for a third performance in addition to the two originally scheduled.

From Boulogne she traveled east to Arras, then into Belgium, playing in Ghent and performing three nights in Brussels, generally with less success than in Boulogne. Theaters raised prices for her performances, sometimes even tripling them, and many who attended simply out of curiosity about seeing a woman of such notoriety. The theater in Brussels was jammed the first night, but on the second the crowd was about normal; on the third night, attendance was disappointing. The press was not particularly complimentary.

She stayed at her favorite hotel in Brussels, the Hôtel de Suède, and one morning a gentleman representing Monsieur Arnaud, the proprietor of the Brussels Hippodrome, was announced at her rooms. Arnaud wished to propose to the Countess of Landsfeld that she, in exchange for 3,000 francs, perform six times at the Hippodrome, simply riding on horseback around the ring two or three times. Lola was outraged at the idea of appearing in a circus and informed the chagrined gentleman that "if I cultivate the art of dancing, it is from taste, and it is an insult to think me capable of taking wages from a director of mountebanks!" Her shouting brought Mabille into the room, and his arrival was sufficient distraction to allow the poor emissary to retreat before Lola could find the knife she had been looking for.

After a one-night-stand in Antwerp, the countess and her entourage entered Prussian territory, and on 1 October she opened in Aachen, dancing between the acts of a play. From Aachen she went on to Cologne, where she was to have first appeared on 5 October, but the police director banned her appearance. At a special meeting of the regional government, an appeal was rejected, indicating that the Countess of Landsfeld would not be welcome anywhere in Prussian territory because her presence might incite public demonstrations by liberals, socialists, and communists. Already there were reports that left-wing students in Aachen had escorted her with a guard of honor and that troops had to be called in to control the crowds at the theater there. Somehow Lola, whose political advice to King Ludwig had included withholding freedom of the press while establishing an efficient secret police and whose recent memoirs ridiculed republicans, was gaining a reputation as a wild-eyed liberal. In New York, Bennett wrote a long editorial in the *Herald*, possibly based on conversations with her during his summer visit in Paris, stating that Lola Montez was a socialist who had tried to introduce communal ownership of all property into Bavaria.

Lola's tour was seriously disrupted by the Prussian ban, for Roux had arranged engagements in Düsseldorf and Koblenz, followed by other appearances farther up the Rhine and perhaps as far away as Berlin. Now he was forced to find new bookings quickly, and as a consequence, Lola trekked to Bordeaux, where she opened at the Grand Théâtre with almost no advance publicity. The first performance, which sold out almost immediately, was before a sharply divided audience, and attendance at the second performance was substantially diminished.

Lola's dancing career was quickly falling into its earlier pattern—a pattern she cannily employed as long as she continued to dance. She knew that she was no great ballerina, that her attraction had always been her beauty and the novelty and fire of her dancing and, now more than ever, her notoriety. That meant that most people would not come to see her more than once or twice, so she made no effort to develop a large repertoire. Lola knew that she would be a traveling artist as long as she danced, since no city would be likely to support more than three or four of her performances before everyone had been accommodated. She had a shrewd instinct for managing her career, and if artistic verdicts on her were diverse, her financial rewards were almost always substantial.

From Bordeaux, the tour continued to Lyon, St. Etienne, and Dijon. Along the way Lola indulged in one of her most effective means of self-promotion, a letter to the editor. This one was directed against Louis Véron, the editor of the *Constitutionnel,* a prominent Paris newspaper, but since she knew that Véron himself would never publish it and probably because she guessed that potential ticket buyers were more likely to read a local paper, she sent it to the *Salut Public* in Lyon. In her letter, which was widely reprinted, Lola took Véron to task for a number of presumed slights and insults and then announced that if he persisted in insulting her, she would challenge him to a duel in which each of them would take one of two identical pills from a box and swallow it. One pill would be harmless, the other deadly poison. "You will not be able to refuse a duel with arms that are so familiar to you," she wrote, playing both on the allegedly poisonous nature of his editorial pen and on the fact that Véron had trained as a pharmacist.

The tour worked its way south, to Montpélier, Nîmes, and Marseilles. Although Lola's reception continued to be mixed (one report said she was greeted with a chorus of whistles in Marseilles), the box office receipts were more than adequate consolation. Roux had returned to Paris, banned from the tour by his temperamental star, and she herself was soon in the capital again, for she was booked on the steamer *Humboldt,* which was leaving Le Havre for New York City. Even though she had signed a contract with Roux, the countess decided to jettison him and take on her new friend Willis as her manager and secretary.

The *Humboldt* left Le Havre early on 20 November 1851 and crossed the Channel to Cowes, where it picked up more passengers, among them one whose presence on the voyage would totally overshadow that of the Countess of Landsfeld. He was Lajos Kossuth, the Hungarian patriot who had declared Hungary's independence from the Austrian Hapsburgs during the revolutions of 1848. When the Hungarian republic collapsed under Austrian assault, Kossuth fled to Turkey, where he was interned, regaining his liberty at about the time Lola resumed her dancing career. He had just finished a three-week triumphal tour of England, where he had been the toast of the liberals, and he was embarking on the *Humboldt* to reap the applause of the republicans in the United States. Willis had booked Lola's voyage long before there was any talk of Kossuth sailing to America, and the countess was not pleased to be sharing the ship with another celebrity, particularly one who seemed to have an ego as healthy as hers.

The voyage was not a pleasure cruise, as there were violent westerly gales and rough seas most of the way. During calmer days Lola would sit in the lee of the smokestack, wrapped in one of her cashmere shawls, and take her half dozen puffs on each of dozens of cigarettes as she watched the Hungarian stroll with his wife up and down the deck to the admiration of his fellow passengers. He was a humbug, she concluded.

Fortunately for Lola, Kossuth's seasickness was far worse than her own, and the hero spent most of the voyage in his cabin, leaving her alone to fascinate and amuse the passengers and crew. She was going to America because she needed the money, she told them frankly. Heald had stolen everything she had and King Max II had seized all of her Bavarian properties, so she had no choice but to return to the stage. But more than the money, she said, America offered artistic freedom; after the bitter cancellation of her appearances in Cologne by the repressive Prussian authorities, "the land of the free" looked more welcoming than Europe. She intended to try her hand at acting, and if success on the stage proved elusive, Lola felt that the lecture platform would offer her a forum for the exposition of her political and social theories.

Word that the great Kossuth would arrive on the *Humboldt* had preceded him, and when the ship slipped into the quarantine station in New York harbor at 1 A.M. on 5 December, the news went out quickly to all the political and fraternal organizations that had been preparing a huge welcome for the hero. Lola's first impression of the New World that morning included the thunder of saluting canon, the tumult of the cheering crowds, and the cacophony of the massed bands. Once the revolutionary and his party had been escorted from the ship to receive an official greeting before the thousands gathered at City Hall, only a few reporters were left behind to give an account of the arrival of the notorious Lola Montez.

24

THE CONQUEST OF THE
NEW WORLD

In 1851 the United States was still an object of fascination to Europeans. The class distinctions that were so evident in the dress and transport of the residents of the Old World were invisible in the New World. Nearly all the men, regardless of wealth or status, seemed to wear the same black suits, and there were no private carriages with coats of arms on the doors racing past humble pedestrians touching their caps. The nation was in the midst of an enormous wave of immigration, particularly from Ireland and the German states, that was reinforcing the essentially fluid nature of the American social system. The expansion into the Western territories, particularly Kansas and Nebraska, was exposing the festering issue of slavery, but despite the growing violence and agitation over the problem, few yet anticipated the terrible potential for crisis it held.

In Manhattan, Lola got in touch with Thomas Barry, the stage manager and impresario of the Broadway Theater, with whom she had been corresponding from Paris. Except for a couple of newspaper interviews, the countess kept largely to her room for the first few days after her arrival, recovering from the voyage. Reporters were surprised to discover that the notorious whip-wielder was not a formidable, muscular figure but even thinner than her lithographic portraits made her appear—almost fragile. And though she was no longer a stunning beauty, Lola's large, intense eyes and animated features still impressed the reporters, who thought she could almost pass for a teenager. She defended her reputation to them, saying, "If I was a woman of that description which I am presented, would I be compelled to go on the stage to earn a livelihood?"

Lola quickly attracted admirers in this society, where distinction came from wealth, achievement, and self-promotion. Sensing the mood in America, she now declared herself resolutely liberal, though her new American friends came largely from the more conservative ranks of the Democratic party. The republican Countess of Landsfeld, never at a loss for an opinion, charmed the Americans with her witty, flattering comments on their nation's politics and mores, and with her natural assertiveness, which seemed somehow native to the New World.

But it was to her dancing career that most of Lola's first month in America was devoted. She needed to get herself physically fit after weeks of inactivity, and Thomas Barry appears to have decided that the dances Lola had prepared under Mabille simply would not do for American audiences. Europeans might have been willing to pay elevated prices to see a solo dancer appear briefly between the acts of a play, but Americans would expect to see a star like the Countess of Landsfeld in a fully staged ballet.

To deal with the problem, Barry called in one of the first prominent American male dancers and choreographers, George Washington Smith. Smith, who was in his mid-thirties but still an excellent dancer, had enjoyed substantial success as a member of the company for the American tour of Fanny Elssler. It appears that he integrated the dances Lola had learned with Mabille into pieces of his own construction. One was entitled "Betly the Tyrolean," in which Lola had the title role of the mountain girl; the piece probably was based musically and dramatically on "Le Chalet," an 1834 work by Adolphe Adam.

Smith also prepared and rehearsed Lola and a corps de ballet in "Diana and her Nymphs" and "Un Jour de Carnaval à Seville," as well as devised a new solo work, "Pas de Matelot," for the star, which gave audiences the rare treat of seeing the Countess of Landsfeld in trousers impersonating a sailor in a series of dances meant to portray events of nautical life, including shipwreck and rescue. She would eventually supplement Smith's choreography of the concluding hornpipe by waving and kissing a small American flag, something that always brought a roar of approval from the audience. Finally, Lola's tarantella, or "Spider Dance," was reworked, sometimes being renamed a zapateado; according to one account, Smith also set it as a pas de deux so that he could dance it with her.

Lola found time before Christmas to stop in at Meade Brothers photographic studio to have her portrait made. The photo, from which a large lithograph was made, is the first one of Lola that can be definitely dated. Judging from the photo, the stories of Lola's striking beauty seem grossly exaggerated, but there are a number of factors to keep in mind. One is that she was certainly past her greatest beauty; she was nearly thirty-two, and the press had been remarking for years that she had lost her looks. Second, most accounts emphasize that much of Lola's beauty came from the mobility of her face, from the play of expression over her features (Stieler captured a hint of this in his famous portrait); because photographic exposures took several minutes, subjects had to remain still to be captured by the camera. Finally, criteria of beauty and its enhancement have changed in a century and a half; had Lola been subjected to modern hairstyling and makeup, her beauty might be more evident to modern eyes.

At last rehearsals had progressed to the point that the Broadway Theater could proudly announce on Christmas Day that Mlle. Lola Montez would make her American debut on its stage on Monday, 29 December, in the role of Betley the Tyrolean. In noting her coming debut, the *Courrier des Etats Unis*, one of the New York papers consistently hostile to her, observed approvingly that she had been commendably restrained in self-promotion, not exhibiting even the typical charlatanism that preceded a Broadway debut. Bennett, in the *New York Herald*, attempted to lower expectations by predicting that Lola's dancing would disappoint her audience because her greatest talent lay not in any ability as a dancer but in her intellect and "dashing powers of conversation, salient impulsive wit, and smart repartee." The editor urged Lola to give lectures instead, in which she could better demonstrate what made her so fascinating.

The Broadway Theater was packed with more than three thousand people that night. It was what was called a black house, because the universal black of the men's clothing was unrelieved by the color of women's dresses. Only about thirty women dared to present themselves at what was rumored would be an indecent and outrageous spectacle. The curtain rose on the corps de ballet arrayed across the stage in a tableau before the drop of the Tyrolean Alps. All eyes sought out the debutante, but it was several minutes into the ballet before Lola appeared at the top of a winding staircase meant to represent a mountain path. She was greeted with a roar of welcome and with applause that lasted several minutes, which she acknowledged with repeated curtsies. As the noise died, the music resumed and Lola descended to the stage, and another storm of applause arose and was acknowledged as before.

The audience was attentive as she finally began her opening "Tyrolienne," but it was soon evident that Bennett was right, that although she moved with grace and had a handsome face and neat, thin figure, Lola was not an extraordinary dancer. Her performance included no particular feats of control, strength, or agility, and even though the "Tyrolienne" was warmly applauded, at Lola's entrance for the pas de deux the crowd was silent; and Gaetano Neri, her partner, was actually applauded more enthusiastically than she at the conclusion of the dance.

Following a "mountain dance" by the corps de ballet, a lengthy costume change by the star left the audience restless and irritable. She finally reappeared, in a red and white striped satin skirt, a black velvet jacket with gold facings, and a jaunty red hat with feather. Lola performed a martial dance, probably a version of the cracovienne she had studied with Mabille, and concluded by leading the male chorus, attired as soldiers, around and off the stage with a little skip step. The audience was enthusiastic, and following a final gallop by the full company, the star of the evening was repeatedly called before the curtain to great cheering from the men and bouquets from some of the women. "Ladies and gentlemen," she said in a small voice with an odd foreign accent, "I thank you from de bottom of my heart for de very kind reception you have given me, a poor stranger in your noble land." Some in the audience noted that the entire ballet had lasted only forty minutes, and most acknowledged that Lola was not a great dancer. But she had a magnetic stage presence and a gracefulness that made it impossible to think she was anyone ordinary, and the crowd left feeling generally that it they had received its money's worth.

Even the critics who scorned Lola's dancing conceded that she knew how to hold an audience. The *Albion*'s critic, who stated flatly that she had "not the smallest chance in the world of achieving eminence as a dancer," conceded that she had "a marvelously handsome face, with an eye of exceeding beauty and force of expression; . . . she threw great spirit into her action and gave inklings to the curious of that latent fiery temper with which rumor has so generously endowed her." And he added that the published portraits of her "do not do her justice."

Her initial week-long engagement with the Broadway was quickly extended to a second week and then to a third week. As word got out that Lola's performance and attire were modest and decent, the percentage of ladies in the audience increased nightly, and as she introduced each of the new ballets Smith had prepared for her, business continued to be excellent. One report said that her first week at the Broadway produced the highest box office receipts that theater had ever taken in, and Lola's share of that was stated to be $3,400, supposedly more than any performer had ever cleared from a week in an American theater.

In the midst of her Broadway engagement Lola got into a financial dispute with Edward P. Willis that broke into the pages of the *New York Herald* in an exchange of indignant and accusatory letters. The dispute culminated with the publication by the *Herald* on 15 January, just as Lola was about to conclude her New York appearances, of a long apologia by the Countess of Landsfeld. The letter, widely reprinted in the American press, was remembered for years and appears to have had the effect of swinging public opinion in her favor:

Mr. Bennett—

I am sure you will not refuse a stranger, and that stranger a woman, a little space in your paper, for an appeal to an intelligent and generous community, against unjust and illiberal attacks upon her, intended to prejudice the people against her. . . . Since childhood, when I first came to know of America, my heart yearned to visit it. . . . I studied your institutions, and all my dreams of romance were connected with your happy country. . . . I have been wild and wayward, but, if I know myself, never wicked. . . . I have been traduced, and slandered, and vilified more, I think, than any human being, man or woman, that has lived for a century. If all that is said of me were true—nay, if half of it were true—I ought to be buried alive. . . . At the age of thirteen, injudicious, but well meaning friends, constrained me to an alliance with one much my senior in years, but who had not my affections, who did not seek to win them, and from whom I was obliged to part myself. No one ever accused me of falsehood to my vows of fidelity to him. We were divorced. . . . I went to England, and from thence to the Continent, and became, as the only resource for an honorable and virtuous livelihood, an *artiste*, an *actress*, a *danseuse*. . . . My enemies—made enemies because I was a proud woman—a self-willed woman—an ambitious woman, if you will, but an honorable woman, who would not become their instrument of wickedness—my enemies by falsehood, and forgery, and every species of crime, have assailed me, and hunted me throughout Europe and Great Britain, and now pursue me to America—but I defy—I proudly defy, the Jesuit band, and their tribes of tools and instruments, to instance a single act of mine, in the course of an eventful life, every day of which can be traced, that is coupled with dishonor. . . . The sweetest revenge I can take of all my enemies is to forgive them.

Lola recounts her version of her stay in Munich, saying that she opened the king's eyes to the perfidy and corruption of Abel and the other ministers.

> I entertained liberal views, and was the advocate of liberal measures then, as I am now; but I am no socialist, nor political revolutionary without cause. . . . [The population of Munich was] persuaded I was the enemy of the people, when, as Heaven knows, all my ambition was to promote their happiness and well-being, and make myself beloved for kind and good acts. A revolution was fomented by the Jesuits, and the good old King was dethroned and exiled. I sympathize with him in his misfortunes, and in his exile, and continue to correspond with him. . . . He is a poet, a painter, a sculptor, and as virtuous and kindhearted a gentleman as lives on earth. This venerable man was slandered with respect to me. I am a poor, weak, little woman. I love him as I would love a father. It is not a love any woman need be ashamed of. I am proud of it. He was my friend, and while I live I shall be his friend. . . . I hope that my simple story, told in my poor way, will be believed by the American gentlemen and ladies. It is true, as I live. I am not the wicked woman you have been told. I have never harmed any one knowingly. I am not the enemy of a single human being living. . . . Can I ask of my own sex to speak a gentle word for me, and be refused? I know I have erred in life, often and again—who has not? I have been vain, frivolous, ambitious—proud; but never vicious, never cruel, never unkind. I cannot help it if bad men approach me—if bad men scheme to become acquainted with me—if bad men seek to make me despise myself. . . . I appeal to a liberal press, and to the intelligent gentlemen who control it, to aid me in my exertions to regain the means of an honorable livelihood.

Most of the assertions in the letter are lies, though it is interesting to see Lola conceding her willfulness, pride, ambition, and frivolousness. Her self-deprecation seems to have been part of her charm in private, too, and it appears that she was more willing to laugh at herself and life's folly than the earnest tone of her letter might suggest. The wide republication of the letter had the desired effect of rehabilitating her reputation, and the Baltimore *Sun* concluded that the letter "appears to have shaken the established convictions of thousands respecting her life and moral character."

Her engagement at the Broadway Theater concluded with a benefit for the Firemen's Welfare Fund on Friday, 16 January. At the end of the performance, which raised $1,200 for disabled fireman, Lola was presented with a bouquet in a silver vase, which, she told the firefighters, was more gratifying to her than the $25,000 necklace that the Tsar of Russia had clasped about her throat.

Lola was thinking not only of how to improve her reputation in America but also of her theatrical career. From the beginning she had planned to make her debut as an actress in America, and before she took her dance troupe on tour she commissioned a playwright, Charles P. T. Ware, Jr., to dramatize the events of her life in Bavaria, as narrated by her to the author.

On the Monday following the close of her run on Broadway, Lola and her company opened at the Walnut Street Theater in Philadelphia. Her reception was much the same as it had been in New York, and the week-long engagement extended to a second week. Shortly after her arrival in Philadelphia, Lola went to the photographic studio of Marcus A. Root to have her picture taken. At the studio she happened to encounter a delegation of Cheyenne, Sioux, and Arapaho Indian chiefs who were returning to the Great Plains following an interview in Washington with the current "Great White Father," Millard Fillmore. Lola insisted on being photographed arm-in-arm with one of the "savages," Cheyenne Chief Light in the Clouds. The resulting likeness, together with another made at the same session, are the photographs of Lola that most resemble the young and spirited woman captured in Stieler's Munich portrait four years earlier.

She concluded her Philadelphia run with another benefit for injured firemen, this time receiving a portrait medallion of George Washington, for which she showed appropriate gratitude. Then Lola briefly returned to New York before taking the train to Washington to fulfill an engagement that had been delayed by the extension of her Philadelphia run. Newspapers reported appeared that she had cleared $10,000 from her New York and Philadelphia appearances, and her success continued during her week in the national capital. She visited the houses of Congress, and one of the gallant members of the House took her on a drive about the city.

She went on to Richmond for three successful performances attended by the governor of Virginia, the attorney general, and most of the legislators. She was extremely popular, particularly because she pronounced herself solidly in favor of states' rights and opposed to the Whig policy of intervention in states' affairs, explicitly endorsing the views of the late John C. Calhoun on the republic's constitution.

After a one-night-stand in Norfolk, the company turned back north for four appearances at the Holliday Street Theater in Baltimore, where her success continued and where one critic even wrote that her dancing showed real promise. There followed a two-week break before the whole company moved to the Howard Atheneum in Boston. An incident that occurred on the train to New England became one of the best-known Lola Montez anecdotes. It was reported in the Boston papers on her arrival: "Lola Montez, coming from Washington a few days ago, in the cars, is said by one of the Sunday papers to have indulged herself smoking a cigarette. One of the conductors is related to have remonstrated with her ladyship upon this infraction of the rules. 'Madame, you can't smoke here.' 'Eh?' said the piquant beauty, leisurely withdrawing the cigarette from her pretty mouth. 'You can't smoke here, Madame.' 'But you see I can,' and she puffed forth a volume of smoke into the very face of the mystified and abashed conductor, who was fain to leave the beauty to do as she pleased. So she finished her cigarette without further annoyance or interruptions."

Perhaps it was to capitalize on this story that Lola posed with one of her ubiquitous cigarettes when she was photographed in Boston by Southworth and Hawes. It probably is the first picture ever taken of a woman with a cigarette. Although it may be the best-known photograph of Lola Montez, it is one of the least flattering.

An incident during the second week of her Boston run made clear that not everyone welcomed the Countess of Landsfeld to the "Athens of America." Lola had met a number of prominent local figures, who took her to some of Boston's exclusive venues, including the Grand Lodge rooms of the Freemasons and the Atheneum. Among her new friends was a prominent merchant who offered to take her on a tour of Boston's highly regarded public schools. The merchant got in touch with a member of the Grammar School Committee, Frederick Emerson, and on Thursday, 25 March, the three of them and, reportedly, Emerson's wife, arrived at the Wells School for Girls in McLean Street. Mr. Emerson introduced the countess to the pupils in one class, and after observing the instruction for a while, the visitors took their leave and moved on to the English High School and the Latin School in Bedford Street. Here Lola managed to exchange a few sentences in French with a teacher during a French lesson, and in the Latin School she made a few comments to the teacher on a Latin phrase in the day's lesson. The foreign visitor and her escorts thanked the students and teachers and went on their way.

This apparently innocuous visit sparked almost ludicrous indignation in some sections of Boston society. The *Boston Daily Evening Transcript* led the editorial charge, publishing a letter exposing the introduction of a "notorious person into the public schools": "It is to be hoped that the individual who has inflicted so deep a stain upon our schools will have all the dishonor and shame of so infamous an outrage." At the meeting of the Grammar School

Committee on 30 March, poor Mr. Emerson was taken to task by a fellow member, Mr. Felt, who declared that the "introduction of such characters into our public schools had a very immoral tendency." Emerson defended Lola, saying that he had "not yet learned from any history entitled to confidence that she has forfeited her claims to the courtesies usually granted to those distinguished in her profession." Felt responded that he had "heard it stated" that she had been the mistress of the King of Bavaria and other prominent men, and he began to repeat the legends of Lola's immorality when Emerson interrupted to ask whether Felt was willing to have this gossip reported in the newspapers and spread among the schoolchildren. "The children," Felt replied, "know more about it than we are aware of. Ninety-nine out of every hundred of the misses of the school visited know more than we do about the character of the woman in question."

The *Transcript*, which had advocated a boycott of the rumored tour of Lola Montez long before she had even left Paris, now loudly beat its breast over the shame that had been brought upon Boston; and the issue became a major point of debate in the Boston papers, garnering even more attention than the debates in the legislature on adopting Maine's prohibition law (where Lola's name came up). The editorials were reprinted throughout the country, adding to Lola's wealth of free publicity. She herself waded into the fray with a letter to the *Transcript*, in which she took its editor, Epes Sargent, severely to task:

Believe me, sir, there is often more impurity in the mind of the critic than in the object of his criticism. There are men who stand before the Venus of Medici and the Apollo of Belvedere and see nothing in them but their nudity. . . . I speak of Jesuitical lies. . . . It was said, also, that I tamed wild horses, horsewhipped gendarmes, knocked flies with a pistol ball off the bald heads of aldermen, fought duels, threw people overboard to save them from drowning, and a multitude of other similar feats. Now, sir, do you see the sly, Jesuitical, infamous design of all this? It was simply to unsex me— to deprive me of that high, noble, chivalrous protection, which is so universally accorded to woman in this country by generous men. . . . I say my pilgrimage to America, for it was indeed a pilgrimage. . . . And as a lover at the feet of his adored mistress, a Mohammedan before the self-suspended coffin of the prophet—a travel-worn *pellegrino* prostrate before the *baldacchino* of St. Peter at Rome, so have I bowed, silent, content and happy before the only successful realization of a principle to which I have devoted my life. And now, when I, as a stranger, wish to pay a visit to those nurseries of your noble statesmen—your Websters, your Calhouns, your Clays—you cry out against me as an intruder! Fie on you, sir! . . . Above all, if you would have the character of an honest man, never give circulation to aspersions of the character of a lady of which you know nothing, which are false in themselves, and which, for my own part, I defy any man living to prove.

On the day of her last performance in Boston, Lola was given a tour of another of Boston's much-visited public institutions, the House of Correction, where, it was reported, she "instituted many inquiries relative to the mode of treatment and employment in the various sections of that institution, and exhibited no little judgment upon such matters." No voice was raised in the press that her presence might have a corrupting influence on the inmates.

She and her company left Boston for appearances in Lowell, Massachusetts, and in Portland, Maine, where she had crowded houses for three nights. Lola was back in Boston on 10 April to perform at a benefit for the victims of a recent fire, and she managed to get into a dispute backstage at the Howard Atheneum with the prompter, a Mr. Parsons, whom she apparently slapped and shoved when he tried to turn out the gaslights in a room she and some of her friends were occupying. One commentator observed that the language she used on the occasion settled the question of her origin: "The energy and expressiveness which she managed to infuse into her English on that occasion could never have been achieved by any but a native of the British Isles."

There was some talk that Lola might be arrested for battery, but the matter was allowed to drop, and Lola traveled on for performances in Salem, Massachusetts, and in Hartford and New Haven, Connecticut. The performances were financially successful, but the critic of the Hartford *Times* had the distinction of making the first recorded objection to the "indecency" of her "Spider Dance": "Lola Montez is not a good dancer. She makes a very bad work of it and does not even exercise good taste in selecting the 'spider dance' as one of her performances; for that makes her appear disgusting as well as a miserable danseuse. In it she flounces about like a stuck pig, and clenches her short clothes, raising them nearly to her waist, while with a thin, scrawny leg, she keeps up a constant thumping upon the stage, as if she was in a slight spasm."

Lola returned to New York City briefly and wrote an angry letter to the *Herald* protesting alleged Jesuit conspiracies against her forthcoming play on her adventures in Bavaria, thus providing some free publicity for her approaching debut as an actress. After getting involved at her hotel in another round of assaults and batteries with erstwhile friends, Lola left for an engagement in Albany, New York.

Back in Europe, King Ludwig was still receiving reports on Lola's adventures, including clippings from American newspapers, from Ambassador Wendland. The king replied to Wendland: "I see she's having squabbles in the New World as in the Old. She finds no peace in either. . . . Let me know if and when she's back in Paris. It would be better if she would stay in the fourth or fifth continent. . . . Not the art of her dancing but the memory of her stay in Bavaria brings her so much income, but I am afraid that unfortunately she won't be bringing much of it back across the sea with her, which would be, however, much to be desired since she must invest her profits well. Gold doesn't stay with her, and where she is there must be luxury and pomp."

Lola appeared before three large and enthusiastic houses in Albany and then moved on to Rochester and to Buffalo, where, the night after the troupe's first performance at the Eagle Theater, someone burned down the building. The dancers came over from their hotel to watch the fire, glad that they had taken their costumes back to the hotel with them. The next night their run continued at the Buffalo Theater with an even larger crowd than on the first night.

Then it was back to New York City for the rehearsals of *Lola Montez in Bavaria*. Lola continued to dance at the Broadway during rehearsals, and on 25 May 1852 she made her acting debut in the world premiere of *Lola Montez in Bavaria*, a precursor of today's docudrama and perhaps the first historical play in which the protagonist played herself.

The play was set in five "eras" entitled the Danseuse, the Politician, the Countess, the Revolutionist, and the Fugitive. Sets had been prepared for each era, and the set for the fourth era was announced to be a "correct view of the Lola Montez Palace in Munich." The role of King Louis, as he is called, was taken by Thomas Barry, the stage manager of the Broadway, who had written in January that he was thankful to be rid of her. Perhaps he had not changed his views, but he was astute enough to recognize box office appeal when he saw it. The archvillain of the piece, "D'Abel, the Prime Minister, a Jesuit," was played by H. J. Conway. Two imaginary characters, "Baron von Poppenheim, an exquisite, a patron of Lola and the Opera" and "Ludwig von Schootenbottom, an enthusiast in Lola and the Arts," were added for comic relief. In all, there were thirty-four characters in the play.

No copy of *Lola Montez in Bavaria* has survived, but the play was clearly based on Lola's version of what happened in Bavaria. She contended that the play reproduced the exact words spoken. The general plot line can be reconstructed from reviews of performances. At the rise of the curtain, habitués of the opera in Munich are seen discussing the magnificent new dancer Lola Montez. She appears in a dress of blue and white, the Bavarian colors, and receives the homage of her admirers. King Louis has also been captivated by her dancing, and he calls her to an audience in the royal study, where she speaks frankly to him, telling him that he is being duped by his Jesuit prime minister, who is an agent of Metternich and oppresses the Bavarian people.

The king, who is well meaning but old and easily misled, says he will act on her advice, and he decides to make her a countess. Lola tells him the artist Schootenbottom is unjustly imprisoned, but she allows "poor dear old Louis" to kiss her hand when he signs an order releasing the painter. The king wants Lola to move into the palace to be ever ready to advise him, but Lola, worried about appearances, consents only to allow Louis to build a small palace for her nearby.

D'Abel tries to bribe Lola through Baron Malthus (Baron von Maltzan) as the king listens in hiding, but when that fails the villain turns unsuccessfully to arsenic. Baron von Newsbaumer (Lieutenant Nußbammer) and Poppenheim fight a comic duel. Lola is presented at court, where the scandalous gossip of the ladies is that the "Moorish dancer" has bewitched the king. But after Lola comes to the aid of Queen Therese when she has a swooning spell, the dancer becomes the queen's dearest friend, and all doubt of the correctness of Lola's relations with the king is silenced.

D'Abel is dismissed and King Louis rules with Lola as de facto prime minister. Lola persuades the king to call upon the people to chose the new cabinet from among themselves. The liberal students rally to Lola's side as she causes the king to introduce enlightened government in Bavaria. The Jesuits conspire, and their bribes and lies bring about an uprising. Lola fights on the barricades with her loyal students, but at last her cause is lost and she flees into exile, disguised as Schootenbottom's mute sister. The piece concludes as the liberal students and the mercenaries of D'Abel clash in a final battle with great noise, fire, alarms and excursions, all to the strains of "La Marseillaise."

Unfortunately, no passages of Lola's part have survived, but there are a few examples of the language of the play. Here is D'Abel soliloquizing in the first era when King Louis has just left him: "Thus, in the humor as I find him, take I prompt advantage of its heat, so passing one more block the nearer to the keystone of my arch, reared by my acts of seeming honesty, to build our power. Thus man doth make of greater man his servile tool; thus mighty royalty sails onward o'er the deep of scheming purposes, unmindful of the little hand that wheels the helm; and thus good honest councilors make of their kings the pawns of their politics."

And here is a comic passage in which Schootenbottom discusses with his wife the possibility that all their possessions may be seized by officers of the law courts: "Law may walk in, as you say, and it may take my paints till all is blue; or it may conceive a relish for my palette—that proves its taste; or it may take my easel—that's easily taken. In that case I shall form an Art Union Association." Wife: "And what's that, I should like to know?" Schootenbottom: "What's that? Ask any free country. Why it's a kind of pitch and toss game between the public and the managers, as to whether the managers shall get your money for nothing, or whether you shall get nothing for your money."

It was clearly another age.

The initial run at the Broadway was enormously successful, but it lasted only four performances because Lola had already booked a road tour for the play. The critics felt that her acting was good—extremely natural and unhistrionic by the standards of the time—though her voice was small and she tended to force it. The play itself received praise, and it was suggested that Lola give up dancing to devote herself to the drama.

Two days after it closed in New York, *Lola Montez in Bavaria* opened at the Walnut Street Theater in Philadelphia with an entirely new cast except for the title character. It seems phenomenal today that the resident companies of American theaters could produce a five-act drama with thirty-four characters on two days' notice, but they did so frequently, if not always well. Lola toured to more than a dozen cities in *Lola Montez in Bavaria*, and nearly every time all the other cast members were new to their parts. The actors of the period were trained for prodigious feats of memory, and prompters were relied on much more than they are today. It is also probable that Lola sometimes used an edited version of the original to reduce the number of characters, as well as the length of the speeches and of the play itself.

The Philadelphia run seems to have been a great success, though at the last two performances Lola also danced, perhaps to increase the drawing power of the bill. One critic remarked that people were talking about Lola as much as they were talking about the race for the presidency, which was a topic of constant and heated conversation in that election year, as the passions that would lead to war were stirring.

Theatrical criticism was far less a profession then than it is today, and few journalists had the qualifications expected of modern critics. In Philadelphia, however, the anonymous critic of the *Sunday Dispatch* obviously had great knowledge of and experience in the theater, and his criticism of the play was devastating, though he scrupulously admitted that the neophyte star was a rather good actress:

> In this extraordinary piece Lola Montez the actress, endeavors to dissipate the supposed stains upon the character of Lola Montez, the woman, arguing as an actress in favour of the character represented, and asking general applause for her self-denying, liberal, and generous efforts in favor of liberty. The production is a windy current of unsubstantial puffs, which endeavors to invalidate the force of the old motto that "self praise is no recommendation," and to elevate the heroine to a dizzying height in public esteem. It is an acted autobiography, and the circumstances under which it is represented authorise the belief that it is a *lying* one. . . . As a dramatic production it is destitute of all merit, and presents various characters which are devoid of interest or originality. It is due to Lola Montez to say, that she appeared in this production with a dare-devil piquancy which, in any other character, would have been worthy of commendation. She was generally natural in her dialogue, though occasionally too extravagant in gesticulation.

Lola then took the train to Washington for a six-night run at the National Theater, and again the houses were packed and her notices were good. "There was no straining after stage effect—no mannerisms—all was natural and easy. Her voice is not agreeable, but her acting is good." By the end of the week, Lola's social stigma had disappeared to the point that ladies made up the majority of the audience, even for the "Spider Dance," billed as "La Zapateado."

Then Lola was off to Baltimore, where she played to huge houses at the Holliday Street Theater at the same time that Sterling Coyne's farce "Lola Montes, or Pas de Fascination" was playing nearby at the People's Theater on Front Street. The Baltimore run was to have lasted six nights, but on the fifth night Lola got into an argument backstage with George Washington Smith, who was still traveling with her as ballet master. According to one account, the countess accused Smith of saying that she did not fulfill her professional engagements, but reports of the cause of the confrontation differ. There had apparently been friction between the two for months, and now it erupted as Lola applied the flat of her practiced right hand to Smith's face. The star was preparing a follow-up blow for her stunned choreographer when the prompter and some other men restrained her. She went on with her performance that evening, possibly because it was a benefit for her, but the final scheduled performance the following evening, 19 June, was canceled, and Lola returned to New York City, where an entirely new production of *Lola Montez in Bavaria* was being prepared.

Tom Hamblin, who as an actor and impresario was a major figure in Manhattan theater in the first half of the nineteenth century, had just finished renovating his Bowery Theater, which with four thousand seats was the largest in the city. But the large and now elegantly appointed Bowery was not a fashionable Broadway theater, and Hamblin was looking for an attraction to reopen the house and set a new tone of respectability. It is evidence of Lola's new public image that he chose to book *Lola Montez in Bavaria*, and the fashionable audience that crowded the theater on 28 June fully justified his choice. As the run continued, it was clear that Lola was an unqualified success, and Hamblin was able to gross $500 to $600 per night, as opposed to previous averages of $120 or $130. Lola's share was more than $1,000 a week, a fantastic sum in a country where $500 a year was a good salary.

For the summer, when most of the theaters closed, Lola left Manhattan for the natural beauty of the Catskill Mountains, where she was reported "climbing precipices, fording the streams, and skipping about the rocks." By the end of August she was back in the city, taking part in a picnic in Yonkers organized by supporters of the Democratic Party and then dancing the hornpipe from her "Pas de Matelot" at a huge benefit performance held on 6 September at Castle Garden, at the tip of Manhattan Island, to mark the hundredth anniversary of drama in America.

Now began a period of preparation for another endeavor. Over the summer, H. J. Conway, who had played D'Abel in the first production of *Lola Montez in Bavaria*, had written two plays designed to show off Lola's dramatic talent and to perpetuate the image of her as a bold and liberal woman. One was *Charlotte Corday*, based freely on the story of the assassin of Marat, and the other was *Maritana, or the Maid of Saragossa*, a drama set during Napoleon's siege of Saragossa. Here Lola played a young Spanish woman who disguises herself and fights in her cowardly lover's place. This, of course, provided another opportunity for Lola's exquisite figure to be seen in men's clothes. She also doubled as a gypsy girl, demonstrating her versatility of characterization.

Lola chose to introduce her new repertory on tour, visiting first Boston and then Philadelphia. Despite—or perhaps because of—the controversy surrounding her first visit to Boston, she had no difficulty getting a booking at the Howard Atheneum for the opening of the fall season. The Howard was packed on opening night of the Boston premiere of *Lola Montez in Bavaria*, and the response was enthusiastic. The *Daily Mail* thought she was "masterly," "an original character, strongly mental, nervous and vivid as the lightning." It also remarked that she was leading a more quiet life than she had on her first visit to Boston, "having totally repudiated the crowd of suckers and bores that so constantly annoyed her on her last visit."

The world premiere of *Charlotte Corday*, on 27 September, was also a success with Bostonians. No one seems to have been troubled by the plot's liberties with history, through which Charlotte is loved and admired to distraction by practically every male in the cast, although she herself remains chastely devoted only to her heroic ideals. The play concluded with the executioner holding aloft the severed head of Charlotte (a rather unconvincing canvas effigy of Lola's head), leaving a number of subplots hanging unresolved. The *Herald* declared "Lola's impersonation is chaste and classic, evincing true force of character and womanly dignity. . . . Lola has not that range and depth of voice which give the most touching effects of pathos, her power is rather the electrical and propulsive, yet she always commands respect and touches very noble chords of feeling because she remains herself, and her acting has the gracefulness and truth of nature."

The *Daily Mail* sent two critics to see *Charlotte Corday*. One stated flatly, "We can conceive of no artiste who could look or feel the character with more effect than the accomplished Countess of Landsfeldt. . . . We promise for the lady a brilliant career, should she devote her energies to tragedy."

The *Daily Mail*'s other critic, however, wrote, "We think her talents better adapted to comedy than tragedy, her figure being too fragile and her voice lacking force and volume. . . . Certain it is, she is a woman of extraordinary capacity, possessing a keen perception and most active intellect, and considering the term of her novitiate in the profession, she succeeded in her delineations beyond our expectations."

Maritana was introduced at the very end of the Boston run. Initially, only the second and third acts were performed on a bill with *Charlotte Corday*, and then a full performance was given at the last matinee. Although Lola knew her part, the other actors seem to have been badly prepared, and the piece made no effect.

Lola opened in Philadelphia at the Chestnut Street Theater on 11 October, in *Lola Montez in Bavaria* and in the "Spider Dance." In the course of twelve days she also introduced her other two plays, along with a short farce called *Lola Montez in New York*, which Ware had written for her engagement at the Bowery Theater, where it was not performed because it was judged too weak. The characters of the play included the major New York newspaper editors, together with Kossuth and Lola, and it appeared only twice before disappearing into oblivion.

The *Daily Pennsylvanian* declared the engagement flattering for Lola and lucrative for the management, but thanks to the rigorous critic of the *Sunday Dispatch* it would not be a unanimous critical success. On the revival of *Lola Montez in Bavaria* the reviewer wrote, "The sublime impudence in which this play was conceived was well carried out by the artiste. . . . The stupidity of the piece would be insufferable were it not that the vagaries of Lola herself keep the audience up to the proper degree of attention."

Charlotte Corday, in which the popular actor John Drew played the comic role of Nero Wax, pleased the stern critic more as a play, but he was quick to point out Lola's faults. "Her style of elocution is very unnatural. She emphasizes every third or fourth word with energy, and slides over those which are intermediate with scarcely fair enunciation. This gives to her delivery a singsong monotony which is unnatural and affected. There was no spirit in her delineation. She was not near as interesting as in 'Lola Montez in Bavaria.' The latter role was rendered amusing by the abandon which characterizes it."

He called *Maritana* a "poor affair" but considered Lola's performance in it better than her performance in *Charlotte Corday*. The greatest eloquence of his critical wrath, however, was reserved for the "Spider Dance," which had him fairly foaming at the mouth:

> The manager of the Chestnut has during the week, been engaged in the experiment of endeavoring to ascertain how much indecency the public will stand without hissing a performer off the stage. The "Spider Dance" was performed by Mlle. Lola Montez on Monday and Tuesday evenings, to the ribald delight of sensual roués, and the disgust of all persons of refinement. In absolute obscenity, this dance exceeds anything with which an audience has yet been insulted in this city. All who witnessed it were astonished, not at the meretriciousness of the woman—because she is past all hope—but because it was almost incredible that the manager of any place of public amusement should allow such an exhibition to be brought before a respectable audience. There were several indications of a storm, which should have warned the management what was to be expected. On one or two evenings persons rose up in the parquet and denounced the woman and

her shamelessness. They were hurried away by the police. Gentlemen who had unfortunately brought ladies to the theater got up in the middle of the exhibition and hurried their fair charges from the building.

On Friday evening some persons *did* hiss in the upper part of the theater and the danseuse, with raised finger, defied them. There were not but few ladies in the house. The parquet was crowded by the same class of persons who would fill the front seats at an exhibition of model artists. Of course, *they* were gratified at the display, and a very unanimous encore was the consequence. Lola came out, bowed, picked up a bouquet, and retired. The applause continued in the most uproarious style. The artiste then appeared and made a speech in which she referred to the disapprobation which was expressed—said she had performed the dance "before all the courts of Europe" and that she "danced it to her Spanish nature," and "according to Spanish custom"—evidently supposing these assertions to be sufficient apology for any violation of modesty which she might indulge.

To put this moral outrage into perspective, it is worth noting that this was the era in which a lawsuit was filed in New York City against an operatic impresario, attempting to enjoin his further performances of Verdi's *Rigoletto* on the grounds that this masterpiece, "by its singing, its business, and its plot, was then and there such an exhibition of opera as no respectable member of the fair sex could patronize without then and there sacrificing both taste and modesty." It is possible that Lola performed the "Spider Dance" in versions of varying boldness, but it seems more likely that the occasional critics who thundered against its indecency (most critics generally treated it no differently from the rest of her morally unobjectionable repertory) were simply demonstrating their overdeveloped Victorian sensibility—a sensibility that provided Lola with an enormous amount of priceless publicity.

If Lola had planned on a New York engagement in which she could display her talents in *Charlotte Corday* and *Maritana*, it never materialized. Back in New York she turned her attention to planning a tour that reached into the South for the winter and then beyond. Since it seems that no manager traveled with her, she must have handled the engagements herself. Even at this point her goal may have been to reach California. The New York papers carried regular reports of the huge shipments of gold arriving from California, where the entertainment-hungry population was paying spectacular ticket prices and drawing the world's greatest performers to the already legendary Californian El Dorado. Lola, for whom money and adventure were powerful magnets, must have felt drawn to California. Whatever her ultimate destination, she seems to have left New York City this time without plans to return soon.

Her first engagement was in Charleston, South Carolina, where she opened in *Maritana* on 6 December. The play was repeated the next night, then she added the "Spider Dance" to the third performance. The fourth night she gave Charleston her view of history in *Lola Montez in Bavaria*, which she repeated on her last night, concluding with the "Spider Dance." If Charleston was scandalized, no record of it has survived.

She was to open on 20 December in Mobile, but the trip across South Carolina, Georgia, and Alabama took two days longer than she had planned. As she made her way through the South, Lola was impressed with the enormous fields of crops being tended by armies of slaves. Never had she seen cultivation on such a scale. Always observant and curious, she talked to the Southerners she met and reinforced the opinions she had formed on her visit to Virginia, and from her association with Northern Democrats, about the South's way of life and its "peculiar institution." The delayed Mobile engagement was a success, with full houses at premium prices and flattering reviews in the local papers.

Her tour had begun with critical and, more important, financial success, and Lola must have boarded the steamer to New Orleans with high spirits and a heavy strongbox. She arrived in the great port of the Mississippi on 30 December, checking into the Verandah Hotel to prepare for her engagement at Tom Placide's Varieties Theater and to welcome 1853.

New Orleans was a vibrant city that had retained much of its French and Spanish heritage. The tropical climate meant that the city was regularly devastated by yellow fever epidemics, but the natural advantages of its position near the mouth of the Mississippi River, the resiliency of its citizens, and the constant influx of new fortune-seekers allowed it to survive disease and flood. Here the curious American mixture of brashness, cupidity, and easy familiarity that Lola had met in the Eastern states was tempered with a Latin and Old World dignity and graciousness. The tremendous traffic of steamboats racing up and down the mighty waterway kept the city pulsing with activity and linked it not only with the cities of the interior but also with the ports of Europe.

The resident company at the Varieties was a good one, and its members learned their parts in *Lola Montez in Bavaria* quickly enough for it to be used as Lola's debut piece on 3 January. As for all of her American debuts, the theater was nearly filled, even though ticket prices were increased.

There were even a respectable number of ladies in the audience, who drew attention to their presence by showering the star with flowers.

On the second night New Orleans learned that Lola was not to be treated casually. A group in one of the boxes was talking and laughing among themselves so loudly and persistently that the audience was annoyed and the actors distracted. Lola stepped out of character (although it may be something of a metaphysical question whether you can step out of character when you are playing yourself) and addressed the audience. "Ladies and gentlemen," she said, "I am truly delighted to appear before you; but if there is a cabal against me I shall retire!" The alleged conspirators were shamed into decorous silence, and Lola's performance continued uninterrupted.

The reviews were favorable, remarking that Lola's acting style was free, easy, and offhand, unlike the histrionic style of most actresses. Many in the audience were disappointed that she did not dance, but the *New Orleans Daily Picayune* nonetheless advised "everyone to go and see Lola Montez, for she is certainly worth it," and subsequently called her "the most eminent actress who has appeared for many years." The critic of the *Courrier de la Louisiane* thought her enticingly androgynous, a battlefield of sweetness and energy. Like other critics, he found her high strung and full of nervous energy, but, he wrote, "as inexperienced as she is on stage, she forgets herself and moves with the ease of a woman circulating about a salon." She speaks English, he noted, "with a singular mixture of Spanish and Irish accents."

Lola played her own adventures for the first week of her initial two-week engagement, supplementing it at the fifth performance with the "Spider Dance," which packed even the standing room. New Orleans was not shocked by Lola's dancing, and an encore of the "Spider Dance" was customarily demanded by the enthusiastic audience at the Varieties.

In her second week Lola introduced *Charlotte Corday*, then, as was her pattern, added dancing in later performances. The 14 January bill included *Corday* and the "Spider Dance"; but after the play, an announcement was made before the curtain that the dance would not be performed. It is possible that Lola's partial indisposition was distress over a report that had appeared that day in the New Orleans papers saying George Trafford Heald had drowned at Lisbon when a yacht capsized. In fact, Heald was very much alive, and a correction was published a week later in some Eastern newspapers but apparently not in New Orleans.

Lola's attitude toward Heald, whom she had called an unfeeling brute and a thief, may have already softened with time and distance. She was still using his name, signing herself "Marie de Landsfeld Heald," and in later years she would consider "Mrs. Heald" her legal name as much as Lola Montez. The supposed widow may have been sincerely upset at the false report of the man's death.

But any effect the report of Heald's death may have had on Lola was transitory, and she was promptly engaged by Placide for a third week at the Varieties. Lola was taking her career seriously, and she had been using her time in New Orleans not only to charm the gentlemen of the city and be escorted by them to the points of interest, but also to increase her repertory. She opened her reengagement in the title role of a play new to her, *Clarissa Harlowe, or the Fatal Choice*, which Lola claimed was her own translation and adaptation of a French play based on Richardson's eighteenth-century novel. Again the critics viewed her efforts favorably. She also introduced *Maritana* and added her first purely comic role, Lady Teazle in Sheridan's classic *School for Scandal*. The critic of the *Picayune* said it was one of her best roles and that she had a good conception of the character. He remarked, "It was not such a Lady Teazle as we have seen but it was nevertheless very commendable."

Lola continued to draw large audiences to the Varieties, and Placide, despite the huge fee he had to pay her, engaged the countess for a fourth week, making her engagement in New Orleans by far the longest run of her stage career. When she took her last bow at the Varieties on 30 January she had played twenty-eight evenings in five plays and five dances. Her drawing power was great enough that after closing at the Varieties she was engaged for two purely dancing performances at the Orleans Theater. The Carnival season was approaching its climax, and though Lola clearly had plans to move on, she stayed to celebrate Mardi Gras in New Orleans.

The approaching departure from New Orleans precipitated a crisis between the Countess of Landsfeld and the lady's maid she had brought with her from New York. The girl had been engaged for six months with a promise of return fare to New York from wherever their travels might take them in that time. The extended stay in New Orleans had allowed the maid time to form an attachment to the city, or to someone in it, and she announced that she wished to have her wages, leave Lola's service, and settle there. That alone would have been enough to infuriate her volatile mistress, but the girl insisted on being paid the return fare to New York even though she had no intention of returning. That enraged Lola, who laid into her maid and sent the battered girl fleeing.

But American servants seemed less willing to accept beatings than their European counterparts, and Lola's maid promptly went to the New Orleans police and accused her mistress of assault and battery. Two police officers, who probably knew of Lola's turbulent relations with men in uniform, were dispatched to her rooms with a warrant for the arrest of the Countess of Landsfeld. Exactly what transpired when the officers attempted to execute their warrant is not clear, but according to one account, Lola defied them to touch her and drew her omnipresent dagger. One of the officers held her attention as the other slipped behind her and seized her by the arms so that the dagger could be wrenched from her grasp. Lola responded by kicking, flailing, and sinking her teeth into all accessible constabular flesh.

The row brought some of Lola's friends to the scene. They convinced the officers to release her, whereupon the prisoner dramatically seized a vial labeled "poison" from a sideboard and declared, "Now I shall be free from all further indignity!" After downing the contents, she sank to the floor. This heightened the drama of the scene as some ran to fetch antidotes while others tried to attend to the stricken woman and yet others berated the police for their brutality, which had driven a noble woman to this extremity.

Lola is said to have revived, smoked a cigar or two, and fainted again, as her friends, some of whom were distinguished citizens of the Crescent City, promised the officers that they would be responsible for the appearance of the accused at any hearing. The officers finally retired without their prey, and Lola miraculously survived the poison, though she took to her bed to recover from the brutal assault and had to cancel her appearance at a benefit scheduled for one of her fellow actors.

Within a week she was ready to depart for her next engagement, at the National Theater in Cincinnati. She took passage up the Mississippi, along with nearly four hundred others, on what was said to be the largest, most costly steamboat in the world, the *Eclipse*. This was the golden age of Mississippi steamboats, and the midwinter trip through the heart of the continent must have been impressive even to the well-traveled Countess of Landsfeld.

She arrived in Cincinnati on 26 February, and after only three days of rehearsal with the local company, Lola opened before a packed house in her signature piece, *Lola Montez in Bavaria*. Again she was a great success with both the public and the critics. "We visited the theatre much prejudiced against her in the capacity in which she was to appear; but before the close of her first act, prejudice gave way to conviction, and we detected ourselves in applauding the most *naive*, natural, and graceful actress that has ever adorned the boards of the National. Replete with life and animation, she threw such life and spirit into the play as none other but Lola Montez could impart. Her voice is feminine, and exquisitely musical; her reading is *sans reproche*, while her pronunciation of our mother tongue is strictly correct, having probably a slight tinge of foreign accent, but only sufficient, however, to make it the more bewitchingly fascinating. We can never regret having seen the actress Lola."

The Cincinnati *Gazette* declared, "The criticisms we had seen in the Eastern papers of her style of acting had not prepared us for the exhibition on her part of so much artistic excellence as she certainly displayed. . . . there was a degree of spirit and dramatic ability in her personification sufficient to deserve a decided reputation as an actress. There was nothing in the play to which the most fastidious could object."

Most interesting of all was the reaction of the critic of *Der Deutsche Republicaner*, a man with knowledge of European acting styles who wrote for Cincinnati's large German immigrant community and for whom the story of the play was contemporary history, not fantasy. He called the play itself a piece of ill-crafted foolishness, and he criticized the staging for giving Americans a bizarrely inaccurate depiction of the manners and dress of a German court. But when it came to Lola herself, his reaction was different:

> Up to now we could never fathom how it was possible for her to achieve such limitless influence over King Ludwig, who otherwise was never mild or malleable. Now, since she worked her witchery before us on the stage, we are fully convinced that poor Louis could not have mounted any resistance. Her expressions and gestures were completely admirable, she often reminded us of Rachel, who is accepted as an unattainable model in this area. Most interesting was the scene of her first encounter with Minister Abel, whom she meets with a glance of such a mixture of defiance and scorn, whose like we do not recall having seen before either in life or on the stage. Her later conversation with Abel, in which he attempts to entice her to join him, could also be called masterly. One problem with which Lola will have to deal in her career as an actress is a not particularly suitable organ, which may be inappropriate for many roles; but certainly she can partly overcome this problem through further practice. Her pronunciation is pure and correct, the audience misses not a syllable; that ugly modulation and vibration of the voice, that quaking and screeching that is constantly encountered with American actresses is totally alien to her, and in this respect she presented a most positive contrast with the other ladies in the cast.

The Cincinnati engagement was another unqualified success, with packed houses and an increasing number of ladies each night. Lola played thirteen performances in fifteen days and added yet another role—the title role in a play she may have seen in Munich, *Yelva, the Russian Orphan*, by Eugène Scribe. The role is completely mute, and except for the words "Edward, my brother!" at the conclusion of the play, Lola had to rely on her pantomimic abilities.

Joseph M. Field, who had been managing the theater in Mobile when Lola appeared there the prior December, had decided to return to St. Louis and open a season there at the Varieties Theater. Field had booked Lola into the Varieties, but the countess must have delayed her arrival in St. Louis by extending her successful run in Cincinnati; and the manager, who apparently was not told when to expect Lola, was exasperated when she finally arrived after he had repeatedly been forced to change his advertisements of her appearance at his theater. On 21 March, her opening night in *Yelva*, Field took the extraordinary step of inserting in the advertisements the statement that he "deems it proper to announce to the public that the increase of price from 75 cents to $1 . . . for tonight and the remaining nights of the appearance of Lola Montez is done at the imperative demand of that lady."

The manager's thirteen-year-old daughter, Kate, wrote to her aunt, "Well, Lola Montez appeared at father's theatre last night for the first time. The theatre was crowded from parquette to doors. She has the most beautiful eye I ever saw. I like her very much, but she performed a dumb girl, so I cannot say what she may do in speaking characters or as a danseuse. She is trying to trouble father as much as possible."

The St. Louis engagement was short (five performances) and tempestuous. Lola and Field were reportedly at one another's throats, and a newspaper reported that she "may be said to live in a perpetual storm," though it admitted that she completed her engagement "without, for a miracle, having whipped anybody while she remained here, as far as we have heard."

It seems to have been in St. Louis that Lola acquired a new manager, Jonathan Henning, a former telegrapher in his mid-twenties. Also at this time the first published references appear concerning her intention of traveling to California and perhaps to Cuba and Mexico, but first she and Henning took the steamboat *Reindeer* to Louisville, where she expected an engagement at the Bates Theater. But the booking fell through, and the two of them took passage on a steamboat back to New Orleans, en route to San Francisco.

They arrived back in New Orleans on 7 April, but before they could book passage to California, Lola added a bit more to her legend through another encounter with the Louisiana legal system. A gala benefit was given at Placide's Varieties on 8 April for the American Dramatic Fund Association, a welfare organization for actors. Lola was not on the bill, but she managed to charm her way past the man at the stage door (though she and Tom Placide were not on the best of terms at this point), and she and Henning watched the performances from the wings.

When a dancer whom Lola had befriended, Mlle. Ducy Barre, was about to begin her act, Lola crowded into the prompter's position to get a look. George T. Rowe, Placide's prompter and curtain-puller, a gray-haired fixture of theatrical life in New Orleans, told her that she had no business on the prompt side. Rowe's language, attitude, and perhaps his physical rudeness ignited Lola's short fuse, and a slapping, kicking, and shoving match erupted between the two. Lola called for reinforcement from Henning, telling him, "If you're a man, you'll whip him!" Henning then seized Rowe by the cravat and began to throttle him. Other parties intervened to pry the combatants apart, and peace was restored by the time the law arrived in the form of Officer Hard, who declined to haul either party to jail.

The next morning Rowe appeared in Recorder's Court and swore out an affidavit charging Lola and Henning with assault and battery. After being informed of the charges against her, the countess and her friends appeared at the court themselves, and Lola accused Rowe of assault and battery. The initial hearing was set before Recorder Winter on Thursday, 14 April. On that day, long before the hearing time, a crowd of men had gathered to see the show. As one reporter described it: "Standing there with dilated eyes and ears pricked up to catch every note of scandal that floated on the teeming atmosphere were citizens of every degree—sturdy yeomen and perfumed beaux, fiery gallants that love the smell of muslin, attorneys and counselors, and liquorish old gentlemen with standing shirt collars and double chins."

There was general disappointment when Henning told Recorder Winter that the countess was too ill to attend. The prosecutor objected that no medical certificate had been furnished, and, to the satisfaction of the crowd, Winter ruled that the the countess must appear and sent officers to bring her to court.

After some delay the defendant appeared:

At last she came, and escorted by her gentleman of business, tripped into the court room, light as a young gazelle, pale with agitation at the unusual scene, and with eyes flashing out the wild illumination of a poetic and tropical soul.

She was neatly and tastefully dressed in a skirt of straw-colored China glass linen, a black mantilla of Canton crepe, a Tuscan bonnet, smothered in the richest lace, and a white lace veil, star-besprent, that waved at her slightest breath, and like the mists of her own dear and purple Cyreness but half concealed while it adorned her finely chiseled and classic head.

Her appearance in court was signalized by a most refreshing excitement. All the unwashed republicans of the city were there and gazed at her as at some fierce and untamable beast, caged for their special entertainment. The target of a thousand eyes, and stared at worse than the zeuglodon, or any other monstrosity, her wit and self-possession did not forsake her. Seeing what a full house she was drawing, she naively remarked that the officers of the law had made a great mistake in not having tickets of admission at two dollars a head.

Indeed, the hearing turned into a classic Lola Montez performance. She took over most of the argument and cross-examination from her own attorney, and even Recorder Winter was unable to suppress a grin at Lola's impertinent wit. Matters began with the examination of Rowe, who gave his version of the encounter and denied that he had started the scuffle by kicking the lady. Lola countered that Rowe was a violent man, a Jesuit, and that she had called him that to his face. She produced a maid who swore that the countess had returned home with a red spot on her leg (below the knee) the size of a Mexican dollar, which she said had come from a kick by Rowe. Lola, from her place at the defense table, remarked in a stage whisper, "I could be content to be kicked by a horse, but by an ass . . . !" and laughter swept the court.

Lola went on to accuse Rowe of insulting her during her engagement at the Varieties by making indecent proposals, and she claimed that when she had reproached him for his shameful conduct he had begged, "At any rate, don't tell the old woman," meaning Mrs. Rowe. This brought gales of laughter from the spectators.

Thomas Placide was called. He had seen none of the struggle between his prompter and Lola, but when he was informed of the disturbance and told her that she must leave or be arrested, she refused and called him "a damned liar, a damned scoundrel, and a damned thief." "And so you are!" commented Lola in an undertone from her seat in court, and the spectators again roared with laughter.

Lola took over interrogating Placide:

Lola: Didn't you make a great deal of money out of Lola Montez, Mr. Placide?

Witness: You made $4 to every one I made. You go on the star system and get the lion's share.

Lola: Didn't you come behind the scenes in your shirt tail one night when I was playing in your theater, in a very immodest manner? And you know, Mr. Placide, you are far from being a handsome man! (The latter clause was spoken in parentheses, and the answer was lost in the excitement and applause which followed it.)

Lola: Didn't I offer to dance for that poor little Ducy Barre, and you would not permit of so generous an act?

Witness: I thought you would be no benefit to the house.

Lola: You know very well that I always draw good houses, and in proof I appeal to the audience now present. (This *ad captandem* was a signal for loud and long continuous applause, which the officers found great difficulty in quieting.)

A string of witnesses gave their accounts of what they saw backstage on the night of the benefit, and Winter ruled that the matter should be tried in First District Court, setting the countess's bail at $1,000. Lola's attorney pleaded that the charge was frivolous, that Rowe "had been injured neither in hair nor hide" and that a lesser bail was appropriate. The recorder reduced bail to $500, which was immediately furnished, and Lola rode home in triumph in a coach and four, taking with her the sympathies of most of the spectators. Whether the matter was somehow resolved or Lola simply jumped bail, she and Henning sailed down the Mississippi from Jackson Square wharf early on the morning of 22 April on the U.S. mail ship *Philadelphia*, bound for Aspinwall on the coast of Panama.

25

AT HOME IN THE GOLDEN WEST

In 1853 there were three sea routes to California from the eastern United States. Freight often made the long, stormy voyage around Cape Horn, but passengers and their luggage usually shortened the journey by crossing Central America overland at Panama or Nicaragua. Lola was taking the Panamanian route, which wound through hot, steamy, fever-infested jungles on a combination of narrow-gauge railway, poled boats, and mule track along the course of the present canal. The discovery of gold in California had transformed this tropical backwater into a world transportation artery, and it now boasted not only the most expensive railroad, per mile of track, in the world, but also several English-language newspapers. The trek across Panama had become far more civilized since 1849, but it was still a ghastly encounter, with mud, noxious insects, crushing heat, and limited creature comforts.

After a week on the Caribbean the *Philadelphia* deposited Lola, her maid, and her manager, with about two hundred fifty other passengers, at Aspinwall (now Colón), the terminus of the isthmus railway, on 1 May 1853. The tracks plunged off into the green wilderness of the Panamanian jungle, stopping abruptly at Barbacoas, about half-way across the fifty-mile-wide isthmus, where a trestle to carry the line across the Chagras River was under construction. The passengers and their luggage had to be transferred to shallow open boats and poled, at extortionate prices, up the river to the jungle village of Gorgona, where a few "hotels" provided overnight shelter from the mosquitoes and tropical rain.

When a ship had come in, the number of passengers staying in Gorgona always exceeded the supply of cots, so many were forced to pay well to sleep on the floor. Lola, of course, insisted not only on a private bedroom but demanded that the proprietor set up a cot in her room for her lapdog Flora. When the owner protested that all his cots were rented for the night and that he couldn't put one of his guests onto the floor, Lola responded, between puffs on her cigarette, "Sir, I don't care where or how your guests sleep, but I'd have you know my dog has slept in palaces. Get the cot, and say no more." The cowed hotelier complied, but when in the morning the countess was presented with a bill for $5 for Flora's accommodation, she was outraged. The bill was renegotiated at the end of Lola's pistol.

The remainder of the journey was made on saddle mules, which followed a narrow, mucky track up over the Continental Divide and then down into the little port town of Panama, where the ships for California anchored. Lola took a room at the Cocoa Grove Hotel on the edge of town. She sat before the door in the heat and blackness of the moonless night, holding court in a circle of gentlemen in the light shed by a lamp from the front hallway. Suddenly, from out the darkness they heard two clicks of a revolver hammer and then the voice of a Californian who was traveling with the group saying that someone was trying to shoot him. More clicks of the gun followed.

Lola cooly rose from her chair, ordered one of the men to get a light, and then strode into the blackness toward the man's voice. The men followed her, and in a few moments they had reached their friend and could see the figure of a man retreating into the jungle, but a gun fired after him also failed to go off. Lola questioned the shaken traveler closely, trying to determine whether he had made any enemies on the journey who might have been moved to attempt murder. Her investigation disclosed no suspects, but she told the near-victim that if she had been in his place, she would have grabbed the fellow by the hair and held him fast while she yelled for assistance. The gentlemen, who earlier had been impressed by Lola's intelligence and her feminine charm, had no doubt she would have dealt with the would-be murderer just that coolly and boldly.

Many of the gentlemen Lola met in Panama had just arrived from New York on the steamship *Illinois*, and some of them were distinguished citizens of California, including a U.S. senator and other federal and state officials who had attended the installation of the new Democratic administration of

President Franklin Pierce. Journalists were well represented in the group, too, among them the thirty-two-year-old editor of the *San Francisco Whig and Commercial Advertiser*, Patrick Purdy Hull. They all boarded the 1,600-ton side-wheel steamer *Northerner* and sailed for San Francisco on 5 May.

In the course of the two-week voyage Lola got to know Patrick Hull. His family had moved from New York state to Mansfield, Ohio, and he had become a lawyer in Cleveland. His contacts in the Whig administration had in 1850 gained him an appointment to help conduct the census in California, where he had stayed on as a journalist. Hull, according to the few descriptions of him, was good-looking, with a ruddy, chubby face, fine eyes, and curly hair. He was an active, extroverted man who was said by some to have no great intelligence, but he was reputed to be a great storyteller, and he may have kept Lola amused on the trip up the coast.

On 21 May, Captain Isham brought the *Northerner* through the Golden Gate, past the springtime green hills surrounding the bay, and by 6 A.M. the ship was secured at Long Wharf in San Francisco. A large crowd—alerted to the imminent arrival of a side-wheel steamer by the signal mast at the lookout atop Telegraph Hill—was there to meet the mail ship. The crowd was rewarded not only by delivery of an unprecedented 275 bags of precious letters but also the appearance of the Countess of Landsfeld herself, Lola Montez.

Although Lola's arrival caused a stir, San Francisco had grown used to celebrities and marvels. Far from being a primitive outpost populated by transient miners, the four-year-old city had developed into a substantial and sophisticated metropolis of fifty thousand, with buildings of brick and stone. Indeed, the gold rush effectively ended in 1853, when production fell dramatically, and the number of hopeful newcomers entering the goldfields was actually smaller than the number of the disillusioned who departed. Gold mining was becoming an industry, and the California economy was already beginning to diversify beyond precious metals.

Because hardly anyone had been in San Francisco for more than four years, there was no entrenched establishment. Although there was some racial discrimination, in many ways California was close to being a classless society, or a least a society in which an individual's status depended on little beyond demonstrated abilities and available cash. That must have appealed to Lola, who had always resented the power and prestige of the European nobility even as she strove to acquire them. Whether she arrived with the idea of becoming a part of this world—in which all men were equal and women were respected as partners and not playthings—she had been in California less than a month when the newspapers reported on her plans to settle in there.

But first there was gold to be earned. Lola arrived in San Francisco without having contacted any of the theater managers, but she quickly secured an engagement at the American Theater, one of the city's finest stages, recently renovated to hold about three thousand spectators. Henning quit as her manager just after their arrival, precipitating a scene in which Lola apparently informed him with some blows of her hand that he couldn't quit because he was fired. She then shredded before his eyes what was said to be $200 in checks to show her contempt for money.

Lola opened five days after her arrival in *The School for Scandal*, probably because it was a piece the resident company knew well. And putting the countess on stage while public interest in her was still high could only help the box office. As in any boom town remote from a central economy, everything in San Francisco was expensive, and the best seats for Lola's performances cost $5, five times the price of seats at her New York debut and ten times the price at some of her other engagements back East.

There was enough loose money in San Francisco to provide a packed house for her debut as Lady Teazle, and the box office took in $4,500 on opening night. The crowd was disappointed that she did not dance, but Lola doubtless knew she would have a full house the first night no matter what she did, and she was canny enough to hold her dances for evenings when they would help sell tickets. The first-night audience loved her, and critical reaction was favorable, as well, the *Alta California* saying, "Mdlle. Lola evinced all that grace and vitality which might be expected of one who had turned the heads of princes and unmercifully scored editors and assailants." Another journal expressed surprise that she had been acting only about a year, calling her Lady Teazle "entirely original and the rendering piquant and effective," though it did note that Lola was rather free with Sheridan's text.

While the company of the American learned *Lola Montez in Bavaria*, Lola's engagement continued with *Yelva* and the "Spider Dance." Once more the house was packed, despite the increased prices, and the audience was enthusiastic over Lola's pantomime as the Russian orphan. Her triumph in the notorious "Spider Dance" added yet another page to its legend, though the word went out that the dance was perhaps not for respectable ladies, because the danseuse was obliged to search for the spider in her skirts "rather higher than was proper in so public a place."

One editor, who had never seen the dance himself, wrote that the "'Spider Dance' cannot be witnessed by a virtuous-minded woman, in the presence of the opposite sex, without the blush of shame and offended modesty upon her cheek." But another critic, who had seen the dance, replied, "The 'Spider Dance' . . . is not a whit more indelicate than stage dancing generally. Indeed, it may be said with reference to Lola Montez, that her skirts are much longer than those of other *danseuses* we have seen upon the theatrical boards of California."

On Monday, 30 May, the company was finally ready with Lola's signature play, which was being produced in a grand manner, including the use of fifty supernumeraries for the crowd scenes. Rehearsals appear to have been insufficient, however, and the inadequacies of the play were emphasized by the company's poor initial performance. Nevertheless, as one critic wrote, "it is almost unnecessary to say that it was a complete triumph. . . . Lola was there with her energy and ready wit to compensate for the shortcomings of all the others." He went on to remark that the drama was not as flattering to its star as one might have expected: "The play represents Lola as a coquettish, wayward, reckless woman, intent on good, it is true; but not the wily diplomatist, the able leader which she is represented in history. She counsels the King with all the enthusiasm of a Red Republican sophomore, but with as much discreetness. History pays her a higher compliment than her own play."

Lola Montez in Bavaria improved in subsequent performances and continued to draw good houses. Lola worked her way through her repertory of plays and dances, astutely changing the combination of play and dances for almost every performance. And, as usual, her success was pecuniary as well as critical; she took in $16,000 in her first week at the American.

One of the new friends Lola made in San Francisco was a thirty-one-year-old Bohemian violin virtuoso, Michael (or "Miska," a name P. T. Barnum had invented to make him more exotic) Hauser, who had been touring Europe and North America since he was a teenager. Lola had been the only woman at a private matinee musicale Hauser had performed on 12 June, and she subsequently appeared on the same bill with him at a benefit. Hauser wrote letters describing his adventures (using a certain amount of poetic license), to his brother in Vienna, where they appeared in a local newspaper and were later published as a book. He wrote home describing Lola: "Has Lola drunk from the fountain of youth? There are still no traces to be found on her of an advanced season, only an eternal high summer with two incomparable stars of day, her two eyes on the glowing horizon. Naughty and frivolous as a little child, yet she can be impressive with a single glance, and woe to him who dares to call down her displeasure upon his head. But up to now she has always been very pleasant to me and never rude. She has a very excitable nature, and at the slightest cause her entire body trembles and her eyes flash like lightning. There is good reason to watch out for her because she is the bravest and most daring woman ever to trod the earth. At the same time, she has real intellect and an uncommon education."

Lola asked Hauser to join the troupe she was forming to tour of the cities in the interior. Outside of San Francisco there were no permanent acting companies, and taking supporting actors with her would be far too expensive and cumbersome. But with a couple of acts to fill out the bill, she could travel with her dances alone. The tour would begin in Sacramento, but first, she told Hauser, after swearing him to secrecy, she was going to marry Patrick Hull. Hauser wondered silently how many husbands this would make for her, but he kept his question to himself.

It is impossible to say why Lola married Hull. She may have deluded herself into believing that she was capable of retiring into rural domesticity in California with Hull and raising children. Marrying an American might also have been an attractive means of settling questions of her nationality, passport, and right of residency. And whatever other considerations she may have had, she probably found Hull a charming, attractive man with whom she would like to live. Lola had been spending time in the offices of the *San Francisco Whig and Commercial Advertiser* with Hull, who taught her to set type by hand, a skill she never forgot.

There had been rumors that Lola and Hull would wed, but the actual time and place of the ceremony were kept a great secret, and the majority of those who traveled out the plank road at dawn on Saturday, 2 July, to the old adobe church at the Mission Dolores were invited guests. The few dozen in attendance included a number of local dignitaries and friends of the groom. As the bride walked down the aisle she turned to motion for the double doors of the church to be closed to keep out any more of the curious.

Father Flavel Fontaine received two vases of artificial white roses at the altar as the bride's offering to the Virgin before conducting the brief Catholic ceremony. Lola's conscience may have been clear about remarrying, since she took the position that her marriage to James had never been valid and seems to have believed Heald was dead, because she had no reservations about telling the priest that her name was Maria Dolores Eliza Rosana Landsfeld Heald. Of course, she also told him that she was twenty-seven years old, shaving six years off her age and making herself five years younger than her bridegroom.

There was a brief reception with cake, wine, cigars, and cigarettes in the priest's apartments, after which the wedding party returned to the Gates House hotel on Bush Street, where the couple received the best wishes of their other friends. Then everything had to be packed and taken down to the wharf to be loaded on the steamboat *New World*, which would head up the river to Sacramento at 4 P.M. Lola and Hull waved good-bye and embarked on the sea of matrimony, in the form of San Francisco Bay.

Sacramento, not yet the state capital, had grown up around a fort and settlement founded under the previous Mexican government by a German Swiss, Johann Sutter, who was now struggling to maintain his massive Mexican land grants against the hordes of Argonauts, as the gold-hungry invaders called themselves. Sacramento had retained much of its character as a rugged frontier town, and audiences there were notorious for the vehemence with which they expressed their opinions. More than one thespian had been driven from the stage by showers of flying vegetables.

After spending their wedding night in a stateroom on the *New World*, Hull and his bride arrived in Sacramento and checked into the city's finest hotel, the Orleans. Opening night on 5 July at the Sacramento Theater went well, with Hauser carrying the weight of the program and Lola dancing "El Ole" and closing the bill with her "Spider Dance."

The second night was a different story. As Lola began "El Ole," raucous laughter came from some of the spectators down front, and Lola signaled to Charles Eigenschenk, her conductor, to stop the music. Hauser described what happened next in a letter to his brother:

> Boldly striding to the edge of the stage, with pride in her features and fire in her eyes, she looked out and delivered herself of the following address: "Ladies and Gentlemen! Lola Montez has too much respect for the people of California to view the stupid laughter of some simple-minded fools as of any consequence."—Renewed laughter—"I will speak!" she cried once more in a loud, impressive voice, and her eyes shot lightning—"Come up here," she continued, "Give me your trousers and take my skirts, you're not fit to be called men!"—Enormous laughter.—"Lola Montez is proud to be what she is, but you don't have the courage to fight with a woman who's not afraid of you, who scorns you—yes, this woman."—She wanted to speak further, but the uproar in the audience had reached its climax. Rotten apples and eggs whizzed through the air, and this bombardment, which was supposed to bring the female opponent to a better opinion of the male sex,

continued until the weaker vessel, on strategic grounds, executed a with-drawing motion and was out of the line of fire.

Lola's disappearance left the audience bewildered and divided; some hissed, some applauded, and some demanded their money back. The theater manager, Charles King, appeared before the curtain and announced that Lola would shortly conclude her dance; but as the minutes dragged by, the audience began to grow unruly again. King ran to Hauser and appealed to him to save the show, offering to double his fee if he could keep the audience from rioting. The violinist edged onto the stage with an eye out for flying comestibles and was surprised to be greeted by applause. He launched into a virtuoso display piece he had written, "The Bird on the Tree," and, according to Hauser's own account, so charmed the audience that the piece was encored. Then, he writes, the manager was called before the house and an audience spokesman said that Lola Montez was unworthy to appear before them but that they wanted more of Hauser.

If we can believe Hauser, Lola, on hearing this from the wings, dashed onto the stage and began to dance, but the crowd rose up against her, and she quickly retreated. "Everyone pressed toward the stage," Hauser writes. "Benches and chairs were smashed, and over the martial music of shattering window panes could be heard the battle cry, 'Scoundrel! We want our money back!'"

Once more Hauser was called out, and he worked his way through every piece that might distract the multitude, including variations on "Yankee Doodle." Lola consented to conclude the program with the "Spider Dance," as scheduled; but the audience was outraged when, in the midst of being pursued by the imaginary spider, Lola danced over to a bouquet that had been thrown on the stage by an admirer and repeatedly stamped on it. Her gesture was taken as arrogant defiance of all, friend and foe alike, and the crowd left in a decidedly bad humor.

An armed guard accompanied her back to the Orleans, but the evening was not yet over, for a crowd of several hundred arrived to serenade her with pots and pans, drums, and whistles. Lola appeared at her window with a lamp and, according to some witnesses, a pistol, curtsied to the crowd and endeavored to address them, but the racket drowned out her efforts. The musicians then gave three groans for Lola Montez and wandered off in an alcoholic haze, at which point the countess reappeared to have her say before the remaining crowd. She declared she could not believe that the good citizens of Sacramento would countenance such behavior; certainly no *man* would be guilty of such conduct toward a lady.

This sentiment was greeted by hoots, jeers, and groans, and the noise-making orchestra straggled back to renew its concert. Lola told them to bring their money to the Friday benefit she was dancing for the city's volunteer firemen; if they paid for their tickets, they could abuse her there all they wanted, she told them. The noisy assembly, which seems to have been motivated as much by a delight in rattling the lioness's cage as by any actual hostility provoked by her tantrum at the theater, finally dispersed.

The next day Lola was taking the incident no more seriously than were her serenaders. Hauser reports, "When I called on her shortly thereafter, she skipped up to me smiling and said naïvely, 'Believe me, dear Hauser, last night was worth more than $1000 to me. I was marvelously amused, and the catalog of my adventures has yet another entry!'" Nevertheless, Lola realized that there was some real ill-feeling against her, and rumors were circulating that the firemen would refuse to accept a benefit from her. And she knew that being hailed as a bold woman with an incisive tongue was a small step away from being condemned as a termagant. The countess had defied Sacramento to abuse her; now she would charm Sacramento into loving her.

That day everything was done to ensure that the disorder of the night before was not repeated. The city marshal and a full contingent of police announced that the first man who exhibited the slightest unruliness would be arrested. A good many complimentary tickets were passed out to people who could be counted on to enjoy the show; and it may have been Lola's own idea that her appearance be sanctioned by the presence of Johann A. Sutter himself, who entered the theater after everyone else was seated and was received with enthusiasm by the audience.

After the overture King appeared before the curtain and begged the audience to allow Lola Montez to address them, which it did with loud applause. Lola appeared before the crowd and began to speak: "Ladies and Gentlemen: Last evening there was an occurrence in this theater which I regret. It is a small theater; it is more like a drawing room. I am close to you; I am almost alongside of you; and the sound is not always distinctly understood. I am subject to a palpitation of the heart, and since I have been in Sacramento, I have suffered with it very much, which makes me at times feel very bad. While I was dancing I stamped my foot several times upon the stage, and someone laughed, as I supposed to insult me. I have many enemies, who have followed me from Europe and offered me insults, and I supposed it might be some of these who had followed me with that intention. I knew it was no American, for I have been loved and cherished by Americans, wherever I went."

It was a shameless speech that pushed every button: she was a misunderstood woman, a sick woman, a persecuted woman, a woman who loved Americans. She went on to explain that her stamping was part of the "world-renowned Spider Dance; and why should I not dance it in California?" Sometimes her friends threw a bouquet to her to represent the spider, she said, and that was why she had trod the flowers beneath her feet.

She concluded, "I will wipe out from my memory what occurred. It was unworthy of me, and I shall speak of it no more. Ladies and Gentlemen, if you wish me to go on with my dance, you have only to say the word." Her reply came as thunderous applause, and the evening was an unalloyed triumph. The audience, a critic wrote, "made the theater tremble to its deep foundations with the delirium of their applause.... The Countess entirely retrieved herself by the force of that genius which is justly an object of high admiration among all classes of intelligent men."

The remaining three performances in Lola's Sacramento engagement were well attended and successful, but another incident occurred to keep her name in the newspapers. The *Daily Californian*, in its report of the evening of Lola's rehabilitation, remarked that the house seemed heavily papered; Lola promptly replied with an open letter in which she challenged the editor to a duel, either with pistols or, as she had proposed to the editor of *Le Constitutionnel*, by selecting from two pills, one of which would be deadly poison. The editor made no reply, but the story was reprinted everywhere and added the "Pistols or Pizen" anecdote to the Lola legend.

After the final performance, Hull and Lola made a quick steamer trip back to San Francisco, where Hull relinquished his interest in the *San Francisco Whig*, and they were back in Sacramento in time for Lola to dance in a benefit performance for Charles King on 14 July. Then the troupe took a steamer up the American and Feather Rivers to open in Marysville.

Lola's local debut on 16 July seems to have been a fiasco on the scale of her second Sacramento performance. This time she does not appear to have been inclined to take it philosophically, and back at the hotel the police nearly had to intervene in the screaming match she got into with Hull and the members of her troupe. Hauser was not prepared to submit to any more of her caprices and made plans to return to Sacramento the next morning. According to one account, Lola dumped all of Hull's belongings out of a second-story window of their hotel.

Nevertheless, a second performance took place on Monday, 18 July, with Eigenschenk doubling as violin soloist. This time the performance came off well, and in a curtain speech Lola apologized for the absence of Hauser, who, she said, "was so flattered by his reception that he had left." Lola seems to have charmed herself back into the good graces of her husband and the rest of the company, and they all left for Grass Valley, in the Sierra foothills.

The road from Marysville to Grass Valley was only about 40 miles long, but it ascended nearly 2,400 feet. By the time the company could hear the mills pulverizing the quartz gold ore pulled from beneath Grass Valley, the landscape had been transformed from flat valley into cool forest.

Although it was a community of only about 2,000 people, about 300 of them women, Grass Valley was the sixth largest population center in California. It represented the future of gold mining in the state, an industrial future that would be far different from the independent and adventurous life of the forty-niners. Most of the placer gold deposits, which could be exploited by individuals working gravel with pans or "cradles," had already been worked out; and the much larger deposits that remained were principally hard-rock ores that could be reached only through shaft mining and industrial processing of the recovered rock. The day of the lonely prospector was already giving way to that of the mining engineer, leaving the field to entrepreneurs able to set up the industrial complexes required to extract the gold.

As idyllic as the Grass Valley setting was, the incessant pounding of the great ore-crushing machines, driven day and night by waterwheels or steam engines, was a constant reminder that the community was industrial. Much of the capital to finance the mines and refineries came from Europe, and Lola herself soon had a stake in the Empire Mine, which was to become the richest mine in California history, producing nearly 6 million ounces of gold from its 367 miles of shafts. According to a contemporary report, her investment was $20,000, a good-sized fortune.

In 1853, Grass Valley was a collection of one- and two-story wooden buildings built of the rough boards cut from the local pine and fir trees in the new sawmills. The town's first restaurant, the Epicurean Saloon, had just opened, and civic diversions would soon increase with the inauguration of the first bowling alley, the first bookstore, and the first bordello. Lola and Hull did not check into Grass Valley's one real hotel, the Beatty House, which featured dormitory accommodations in bunk beds, but moved into a cottage on Mill Street, not far from the center of town, owned by one of Hull's friends. The dispute in Marysville seemed forgotten, and the residents of Grass Valley noticed the smiles and endearments exchanged by Hull and his countess, who won over the the locals with her affability and good nature. Lola gave two performances in Grass Valley, in a little theater above the Alta Saloon, and both met with unqualified success before packed houses.

After her second performance, Lola took her troupe to Nevada City, another major mining camp just a few miles from Grass Valley. Her series of appearances at the little Dramatic Hall, located over a store, were equally well received by houses crowded with people paying double the usual admission. Lola was in wonderful spirits in these unpretentious and democratic mountain communities of high-spirited, hard-working men, and now she particularly enjoyed closing her performances with short, witty curtain speeches.

By the beginning of August she was back in Grass Valley, very likely prepared to abandon the stage and certainly prepared to settle down in the mining town, where the scenery and mountain air probably reminded her of the Bavarian Alps and Simla in the Himalayan foothills. She purchased the cottage on Mill Street, but it was not to be a haven of matrimonial joy. Before the middle of August the word was out that Pat and Lola were getting a divorce. One story said Lola threw Hull out when it became evident that he intended to live a life of leisure on her money.

Hull left Grass Valley for San Francisco on the morning of 13 September, and she expressed the wish that he would "trouble me no more." Although there were repeated newspaper reports of an impending divorce, no paper ever reported the dissolution of the marriage. It seems likely that Lola, perhaps having heard that Heald was still alive, simply let the matter drop. She continued to call herself Marie de Landsfeld Heald and Mrs. Heald, never again mentioning or showing any interest in Hull.

The countess proceeded with her plans to make Grass Valley her permanent home. The white cottage, shaded by towering trees and surrounded by a low picket fence, was small but adequate to her needs. It had a single story with a peaked attic above. A narrow central hall extended from the front door, with the few rooms opening off each side. Outside, a covered porch called a piazza surrounded the house, and Lola would swing gracefully in a hammock strung between the posts. There were small outbuildings suitable for guests and servants, a horse, chickens, and general storage.

Lola left her retreat in October, before winter closed the roads, and steamed from Sacramento to San Francisco to pick up furnishings. Among the items she acquired was one that would delight Grass Valley: a player piano that could execute airs from Hérold's *Zampa* and Donizetti's *La Favorite*. For her personal entertainment she also brought back a parrot, two more dogs, and a grizzly bear cub.

For the first time Lola was able to indulge her love of animals without restriction. She had always had dogs, and in Munich and Paris she kept a number of birds. In Grass Valley she soon built a small menagerie that included four dogs, a goat, a horse, a ewe with a lamb, three canaries, and a wildcat.

The yard around the cottage became her garden, and shortly after moving in she wrote to a friend asking him to have Johann Sutter send her flower seeds and vine cuttings from his famous farm. Lola frequently worked in her garden or tended the flowering plants on the piazza, and it was reported that she was one of the first local gardeners to cultivate the native cactus plants.

Her cottage became a center of social activity in Grass Valley, and she had a ready circle of admirers. She took to holding Wednesday evening salons, at which there would be good food, fine brandy, excellent cigars, and animated conversation. Sometimes Lola would sing Spanish songs and, according to one memorialist, occasionally she favored the company with a dance, though the cottage was too small to allow much room for her vigorous routines.

Traveling performers were always welcome at her house, sometimes even being invited to stay there during their visit. Ole Bull, the famous violinist, played in her parlor, and she drove to Nevada City to see the Monplaisir Ballet Company, which had once shared a benefit bill with her in New York City. Years later Charles Warwick, an actor who arrived in Grass Valley with a letter of introduction to Lola, recalled his first encounter with the Countess of Landsfeld on Mill Street:

> I found the gentle Lola in the back garden, having a little game with a couple of pet bears, with whom she seemed to be on terms of playful and endearing familiarity. She was bareheaded, sunburnt almost to the color of a Mexican, and with her hair hanging in rich profusion over her graceful shoulders. Her dress was of the simplest make and of the coarsest material, a common frock, short in the skirt and sleeves, leaving the shapely arms bare almost to the shoulder. . . . I was prepared to find a *blasée* woman of the world, an artful, speculative adventuress, who, after capturing the heart of the old King of Bavaria, and flitting from one European court to another like an erratic comet, had come among us from sheer *ennui*, not unmingled with a kind of cynical disgust for mankind on the average. . . . I can only aver that as I found her she was a generous, charitable, whole-souled woman. . . . During my short sojourn in Grass Valley I made the

acquaintance of all the principal people in the place, as acquaintance with Lola was a passport to the best society in the wild mining town. The Countess was a general favorite with all classes, from the rude, uneducated miner to the richest and most influential people in the rural El Dorado, and was looked upon as a sort of *fille du régiment* in that semi-civilized community.

Among her admirers in Grass Valley was one of the pillars of the community, John E. Southwick, director and part owner of the Empire Mine. Johnny, as everyone called him, had arrived in Grass Valley in 1849 and had been one of the original investors in the Empire Mine. He was "a man of education, prepossessing appearance, and the son of a New York merchant of considerable wealth." Southwick became close enough to Lola that visitors to her cottage found him playing the role of host, though there is no evidence that he lived with her.

That winter in the Sierra, when storms sometimes dropped several feet of snow in a single night, was probably the most severe Lola had ever experienced, but she seemed to enjoy it. Lacking real sleighbells, she had a sleigh fitted up with cowbells, and a number of times she made a clanging trip over the snowy road to Nevada City. "She flashed like a meteor through the snow flakes and wanton snowballs," reported the local paper, "and, after a thorough tour of the thoroughfares, disappeared in the direction of Grass Valley."

At Christmas, Lola held a party for the few little girls of Grass Valley, greeting each one at the door and ushering them in to see the decorated Christmas tree. They played games, had good things to eat, and each received a present from the hostess. Lola was especially fond of children and was often heard to say that one of her great regrets was that she had none of her own.

Two Grass Valley girls who probably attended that Christmas party had their own careers on the stage. Sue Robinson, born into a theatrical family, was performing by age ten and would continue to act until her sudden death at the age of twenty-six. Legend says that six-year-old Lotta Crabtree learned her first dancing steps from Lola, her neighbor on Mill Street, but there is no evidence for the story, and it appears more likely Lotta actually had her early training under Sue Robinson's parents, who opened a dancing school in Grass Valley. Lotta, however, who went on to become a sort of nineteenth-century Shirley Temple, knew the value of linking her name with that of a legend, and her publicity repeated the story of her studies with Lola.

Lola's grizzly cub, who lived chained in a corner of her front yard, was an object of fascination for children and adults.Perhaps it was simply growing too big to be a pet, or perhaps it was ill-tempered because it wasn't hibernating, but one day early in February 1854 the bear sank its teeth into Lola's hand as she was feeding it sugar, and then it attempted to maul her with its claws. A nearby man rushed to release Lola's hand by clubbing the bear over the head, but her affection for the bear was at an end. A notice shortly appeared in the *Grass Valley Telegraph* announcing "Grizzly for Sale."

With the coming of spring, Lola was once more able to get out and about, riding and exploring in the Sierras, but her luck had improved only slightly since her dispute with the bear. In May she was nearly crushed by her horse in an accident caused not by her tenderness for animals but by her love of flowers. The *Grass Valley Telegraph* recorded it all: "Madame Lola Montez came very near closing her eventful career on Sunday last. While riding for exercise, along a steep ridge, a little distance from her cottage, she observed a cluster of flowers on the opposite side of a wide ditch. Anxious to obtain the flowers, she reined her horse for the leap without sufficiently stopping to heed the ground. The horse cleared the ditch, but so steep was the ascent of the ground upon which he alighted, that he instantly fell backward, precipitating his fearless rider into the ditch below. Fortunately, the water was shallow, but more fortunate still, the horse struck some timbers lying across, beneath which lay the fair lady safely ensconced, and coolly watching the motions of the struggling animal directly above her. Assistance was at hand, and the Madame was speedily relieved from her dangerous position. It was truly a most fortunate and narrow escape."

Shortly after her narrow escape Lola made another excursion to San Francisco, but she was back to depart in July with a group of gentlemen friends from Grass Valley on a camping trip across the summit of the Sierra Nevada to visit the Truckee meadows and the Donner cabins. This was the site where the ill-fated immigrants of the Donner party had been trapped during the awful winter of 1846–47, when the survivors had been forced to eat the corpses of their companions in order to live. Lola's expedition through this majestic mountain landscape was also a bit of a disaster, if not of the same magnitude.

One member of the group turned back after getting into an argument with Lola that went on most of one night. He was, he reported, "prepared to face the tumult of a howling wilderness—nothing more." To everyone's surprise, Lola and most of the others in the party were also soon back in Grass Valley, for the man who was leading the pack mule with all their provisions had become separated from the group, leaving them with nothing to eat. They had been two days without food by the time they returned, but no thought seems to have been given to cannibalism.

As summer passed into fall, the Countess of Landsfeld continued to appear delighted in her rustic retirement, apparently giving no thought of returning to the stage and the world she had known. There had been a rumor in the spring that Lola would make a tour of the southern mines, but the story turned out to be without foundation.

There is, however, a possibility that Lola's thoughts were not all on retirement. A letter was published in 1914 that purportedly was written to Lola at Grass Valley from Washington, D.C., discussing a conspiracy in which southerners would finance the secession of California from the Union, and Lola would become Empress of California. According to newspaper reports in 1914, the letter, signed only with the initials "J. C.," was discovered in the lining of a sampler said to have been worked by Lola, but the document has since disappeared, and there is no way of determining whether it was a hoax. In Munich, even Lola's friends had despaired of getting her to keep political secrets; anything she knew would turn up in conversation. She had certainly matured since her Munich days, but given her volatility and unpredictability, it appears unlikely that a conspirator with any sense would have made her a part of a treasonous plot, much less propose to crown her empress.

In November 1854, Lola was involved in a fracas—not a general revolt but another example of Lola trying to exercise summary justice on behalf of her offended honor. The culprit was the hard-drinking editor of the *Grass Valley Telegraph,* a young blond graduate of Amherst named Henry Shipley. According to Lola's account, she had found Shipley a vain and pretentious windbag since he first called on her to introduce himself. His personal offense to her had begun when three singers visited Grass Valley to perform a pair of concerts. Lola had not even attended the concerts, being ill in bed, but having heard Shipley declare that he would write a review to "give these artists fits," Lola said she had "begged him to reflect," and he promised that he would write neither praise nor censure of the singers. Lola's concern for three performers she apparently hardly knew was not only an indication of a waning of the egoism that had ruled her life but a part of her natural empathy for those who earned their bread on the public stage, as her commentary on the encounter with Shipley makes clear: "Oh, readers, have consideration and kindness to the artist. I who write, since 1843, have roamed the world in many a clime, and in almost every theater in Europe I have been successful, though many as good, if not better, have failed, because destiny and fate opposed them and smiled on me. Oh, how many have I seen ill-requited for real talent—disappointed, sensitive to a degree, working hard, year by year, and not a step of the ladder yet reached. How many have I watched with smiling, radiant looks, whose very hearts were broke within them. A mother might be lying dead, a husband dying—what matters that to the manager or the public. 'Smile, smile,' say they, 'we want no dark looks here; sad faces don't pack the house.' If I were to write volumes I could never end with those sad realities behind the scenes, of which I was a daily witness."

Lola made no secret of her disgust with Shipley when his paper published a commentary suggesting that the singing troupe had banded together "for the purpose of inflicting misery upon all who will place themselves within hearing distance." The editor confronted her at her house, where she was sick in bed, and the only point on which their accounts of the encounter agree is that Lola threatened Shipley with a revolver. She claimed she drove him from her house at gunpoint after he threatened to cut her throat, though he declared that he retreated calmly in the face of unprovoked violence.

The last straw came in Shipley's commentary on Queen Christina of Spain on 21 November. The editor attacked the queen's journalistic efforts, saying, "There is such a Lola Montez-like insolence and barefaced hypocrisy in her lines that the ex-King of Bavaria might be delightfully mystified with them." Lola read it and exploded. "Insolence and hypocrisy indeed!" she thought. "Europe, hear this; have you not found me but too truthful, too bold, to say this? Has not the hypocrisy been on the other side? What were you thinking of, oh! Alexander Dumas, Beranger, Mery, and all of my friends, when you told me that my fault lay in my too great frankness? Oh, my friends, you knew not that Shipley lived and breathed—that his fiat had gone forth to the four parts of the world, and he had judged me at last to be a hypocrite!"

Lola was out of her cottage in an instant, the offending paper in one hand and a horsewhip in the other. She found Shipley drinking his morning refreshment at the Golden Gate Saloon on Main Street. In the editor's own third-person account in the *Grass Valley Telegraph* of what ensued, Lola entered the bar "using language which our devil says he will not set up. She struck at him, when he instantly caught the whip from her hand, she meanwhile using her nails with some effect." All bystanders, according to Shipley, refused the disarmed woman's appeals for support, even refusing her offer to buy a round of drinks. The editor claimed that he stood immovable and that he "treated her throughout with the most imperturbable coolness," until, after getting no response to his request for anyone wishing to take up Madame Lola's fight with him, he withdrew "in disgust and regret that a woman could so far forget her position. *Sic transit gloria mundi.*"

Lola remembered the encounter a little differently, and because Shipley had the only newspaper in Grass Valley, she drove the four miles to Nevada City to turn over her account to the rival newspaper there:

> I recollected the Women's Rights Convention, took the benefit of Lucy Stone's principles—bonnet on head and whip in hand; that whip which never was used but on a horse, this time was to be disgraced by falling on the back of an ASS. I went forth, strong in the principles as I have said of Miss Lucy Stone, and other strong-minded females—found this redoubtable man and as quick as a flash of lightning laid the said whip on his shoulder and head four times, on my word of honor, before my enemy could remember that he was sitting on a chair. The lady of the Golden Gate was sitting on one side, a gentleman on the other; after having given him four good whippings he got up and squared himself on the most approved Yankee Sullivan [a brutal prizefighter] principles, and was prepared to give me a stunner in the eye. The spirit of my Irish ancestors (I being a kind of three-quarters breed of Irish, Spanish and Scotch) took possession of my left hand and on the most approved Tom Hyer [an admired pugilist] principles, before he could attain my eye I took his, on which, thanks to some rings I had on at the time, I made a cutting impression. As usual this would-be great shoulder striker ended the combat with certain abuse, of which, to do him justice, he is perfect master of. *Sic transit gloria Shipley.* Alas! poor Yorick.

The whole encounter seems to have been quickly forgotten, except by the world's press, which passed along the story until it had filtered to every corner of the globe and embellished her legend a bit more.

For most of those who knew her in Grass Valley, however, the countess was anything but a harridan. She was accepted as an important person in the community, which, as in all the gold rush towns, had a cosmopolitan range of individualists and eccentrics, among whom Lola seemed far less bizarre than she had back in the "more civilized world." The residents of Grass Valley would remember her fondly. Just after she left her mountain home, a resident wrote, "Madam Lola (as she chose to be called while a resident of this town), although eccentric in some respects, did many acts indicative of a kind and benevolent disposition. We recall her riding many miles over the hills to carry food and medicine to a poor miner. More than once she watched all night at the bedside of a child whose mother could not afford to hire a nurse. Repeated instances of a similar kind are currently known here. . . . Lola was one of the lions of our town; and visitors from below, clerical as well as lay, while taking a look at our quartz mills, invariably sought an introduction to her, and always returned delighted from an hour's chat at her hospitable cottage."

In Grass Valley, where she was freed for the first time in twelve years from her assumed role as exotic Spaniard, and from flattery as well as scorn, Lola may have begun to sort the innate elements of her personality from those that she had created. There in Grass Valley she first read the books of Andrew Jackson Davis, a popular spiritualist and mystic of that period whose theories prompted her to begin reading the Bible seriously.

But the idyll of nearly two years was coming to an end; Lola was going to leave Grass Valley. The cause was probably her irrepressible need to see new places and peoples, to meet new challenges. The mining country was changing, too, becoming more civilized, and the California economy was faltering. Many of Lola's friends from the California stage had crossed the Pacific to tour Australia, and she must have heard about the rewards waiting Down Under. By spring 1855, Lola was making plans to produce her own tour to Australia and beyond.

The tour was to begin in Australia, where the Colony of Victoria was in the midst of its own gold rush and where newly wealthy miners were willing to pay well for good entertainment. Lola also had vague plans to take her troupe on to Hong Kong and possibly to the Philippines, to voyage back to the scenes of her childhood and youth in Calcutta, and to then travel on to Egypt and finally Europe.

In May she began assembling a small company of California stage veterans. She was able to reengage music director Charles Eigenschenk, who had supervised her California performances. The company included a tall, handsome actor for comic and romantic parts, the twenty-seven-year-old Augustus Noel Follin, who used the stage name Frank Folland. He had met Lola in Grass Valley a year before, and the rusticating countess had fascinated him with her beauty and charm, chatting with him in French and Spanish. Folland had showed her a daguerreotype of Miriam, his beloved half-sister, and Lola thought the girl so beautiful that she insisted on keeping the photo for two days before returning it. "She is in love with you," he wrote Miriam.

Folland had an estranged wife and two children in Cincinnati whom he continued to support, though he had been in California more than two years. In his last letter to his mother and half-sister before what he thought could be a profitable two-year tour of the world, the actor's tone was more distressed than jubilant, hinting at his self-dramatizing nature. He asked them to tell his wife that he was leaving, because he couldn't bring himself to write the news to her. And his cryptic closing, "I dare, dare not trust myself to say more. I should die if I did," raises the suspicion that his emotional turmoil may have already focused on Lola Montez.

By June 1855 the company was assembled. Lola left a will with Southwick, for she was now a woman of some property, as one newspaper noted in its farewell article:

> Mme. Lola has made many friends in California. Grass Valley which has been her residence the past few years loses one of its chiefest distinctions in the public eye. A kind nature and many courtesies and charities have made her a favorite with those who knew her well enough to reconcile not a few eccentricities and erratic indications. It will be remembered that the first and only engagement played by the Countess in this city was extremely successful and there certainly was in this country an ample fortune within her reach by a continuance of her professional effects. Choosing a different course and adapting herself to the circumstances of a mining life, she has still been fortunate and is numbered among the few who have made money in quartz operations. She retains her residence in Nevada County and likewise her interest in the mining business, proposing to return to California at the close of her projected campaign which we hope will prove both pleasant and prosperous.

The night before the company sailed from San Francisco, the actress Laura Keene, who had just returned from a tour of Australia, and a number of Lola's other theatrical friends gathered in the countess's rooms at the International Hotel to drink a glass of wine with her and say good-bye. One of those present that evening later wrote, "Lola was in the highest spirits, and full of pleasant and gracious farewell words for all. I think that even as early as that time, she had begun to abate something of the imperious and reckless manner for which she was so notorious."

A large crowd assembled at the wharf the next afternoon, 6 June, to see off Lola and her company. At age thirty-five, Lola had a long and difficult journey ahead of her, and she probably took this farewell more seriously than her countless previous departures. Many of her friends had come down from

Grass Valley to see her off, but she felt certain that she never would see one friend again, her poodle Flora, which had disappeared the week before.

The tide began to move out of the Golden Gate, and Captain Hays gave the command for the *Fanny Major* to cast off. Cries of "Godspeed!" and a disorganized effort at three cheers came from the wharf as the tall bark moved out across the bay, taking Lola Montez to new adventures.

26

To the Antipodes

The *Fanny Major* was not a large ship, and the more than two months it took to reach Sydney could not have been particularly pleasant; but the long voyage at least gave Lola's company time to rehearse. For *Lola Montez in Bavaria* the troupe would have to fill out the cast with locals, but otherwise the actors prepared small plays to perform with their own forces.

The *Fanny Major* stopped for provisions at the Navigators' Islands (now Samoa) on 17 July; and it was 16 August 1855, amid the stormy weather of the Australian winter, when the ship at last made its way up the Port Jackson channel and dropped anchor in Sydney's Darling Harbor. The sight probably reminded Lola and her companions of San Francisco, with its hills and islands around a stretch of water. The city itself was as much a city of immigrants as the California metropolis but was twice its size and had a distinctly British air to it, much more of London than of the frontier. The wandering aborigines, gangs of prisoners, and flocks of wild parrots that had once been features of Sydney were now largely memories, and it was said that one stretch of George Street resembled Bond Street in London as much as one street could resemble another.

Lola's arrival came as a surprise to the Australians, for she had organized her tour and departed before the news could precede her. But she was as famous in Australia as elsewhere, and she quickly secured an engagement for six performances at the Victoria Theatre on Pitt Street. The star took up lodgings at one of the city's finer establishments, Petty's Hotel, and rehearsals began for her debut in *Lola Montez in Bavaria*.

She opened to a crowded, expectant, and mostly male house on Thursday, 23 August, but the *Sydney Morning Herald*, the city's most prominent newspaper, pointedly ignored the event, just as it had ignored her arrival and would continue to ignore the presence of this scandalous woman in its city. *Bell's Life in Sydney and Sporting Reviewer* explicitly refused to join in snubbing this "extraordinary and gifted being" because of her dubious reputation and proclaimed, "Her *entré* was modest and elegant, and throughout the long performance she played with a mingled fervor, grace, playfulness, and pathos that fully gained the favor of all." *The Empire* solemnly reassured its readers that there was no truth to the rumors that the play could have a deleterious effect on public morals.

After the first performance Lola spoke to the audience from the stage, as she would after most of her Australian performances. She thanked the crowd for its welcome and appealed to the ladies of Sydney to show themselves in the theater, which they did in increasing numbers as the engagement continued.

The Sydney correspondent of the *Argus* of Melbourne saw the Bavarian play at the second performance and seems to have written what the *Sydney Morning Herald* was thinking:

> I am compelled to say that I differ entirely from those who think that Lola has any talent for histrionic art. Her appearance is good; her voice is, if not bad, deficient altogether in flexibility and sweetness, at least when raised to the pitch calculated for the stage. She is sometimes graceful for a moment or two, but coarseness and vulgarity is sure to follow hard upon such glimpses of a better spirit. Her grand effect is as a "postures." The manner in which she can conceal the exquisite proportions of her figure, and even to some extent deform them and then suddenly reveal them, in a burst of passion or an attempt at tenderness, in all their magnificence, is doubtless a study for the artist. She dresses her parts well—rather showily, but in taste; and takes very good care that no part of her beautiful figure shall be exhibited more than necessary. From one solitary glance of her foot during the whole piece, I should say it must have been some strong effort of female resolution which could induce her to keep it so studiously concealed. Her features are interesting, but not regularly beautiful, and, to my taste, not pleasantly expressive. The piece she played in . . . is about the greatest piece of trash and humbug ever introduced before an English audience. There is no indecency in the acting, but the whole tenor of it, socially, politically, and religiously, is profligate and immoral in the

extreme. Lola Montes, if I mistake not, will find her visit to Sydney turn out a failure.

An air of Victorian hypocrisy rises from this review, in which the critic describes an actress as coarse and vulgar in a profligate and immoral play and yet marvels at her resolution in concealing the "magnificence" of the "exquisite proportions of her figure," apparently excited and yet disappointed to catch but "one solitary glance of her foot during the whole piece." The critic was mistaken in his prediction, for Lola continued to draw packed houses for all six performances of her initial engagement, as well as during an extension of five nights.

During that first week in Sydney, Lola was already being troubled by the ill health that would plague her tour. This initial instance may have been lingering effects of the voyage, but she would continue to be troubled by fatigue, faintness, and headaches. On the fourth night of her engagement in Sydney she fainted and had to be revived by a doctor, and on the sixth night she canceled her appearance in one of the two comedies she was scheduled to play with Folland.

Lola was adding plays to her repertory, all of them light one- or two-act romantic comedies. *The Morning Call* was a two-character piece that she played with Folland, as was *Antony and Cleopatra*, a burletta having nothing to do with the figures from history but with a Parisian grisette and the handsome neighbor in the adjoining apartment. *Follies of a Night* and *Maidens Beware* were the other works she added in Sydney.

Only at the eighth performance did she finally appear as a dancer, in the "Spider Dance," which the bill claimed she had danced in New York for two hundred consecutive performances, something no one in Australia was likely to know was a lie. The belief that Lola Montez was a shameless, indecent woman had raised expectations that the dance would be scandalous and obscene, and the house was packed. There was some disappointment that Lola did not even twirl about to raise her skirt to her waist, as many respectable dancers did, and the search up her skirt for the spider seems to have been relatively restrained on this occasion. But the "Spider Dance" was nevertheless a great success, and she continued to dance each night for the rest of the engagement.

The full houses and the income they were bringing were gratifying, but they could not solve the problems developing within Lola's troupe. Professional and personality conflicts were causing dissension, and some members of the company began refusing to play the roles assigned them. By the end of the Sydney run, only Folland was still appearing on the bill with Lola. Working with the star was not always easy, but the recalcitrant players might have made a greater effort to get along with her had they had known that she was concluding that it had been a mistake to hire them in the first place.

Stage veterans in Sydney had already persuaded Lola to abandon her plans to play Hong Kong, India, and points beyond. There simply was not enough money to be made from the limited English-speaking populations in those outposts of the British Empire to justify the expense and risk of shipping an entire company over the enormous distances. If her tour was going to be limited to Australia, it was pointless for her to support her imported group of malcontents because there were plenty of better actors available locally who would work for less.

Lola was engaged to open in Melbourne the following week, and the members of her company grew restless as the date approached and no provision had yet been made for their departure for the Victoria Colony. On Friday, 7 September, the company asked for a meeting with Lola at noon in the Victoria Theatre. Lola didn't appear, but her manager was there to announce that the company was being disbanded and that she was taking only Folland and Eigenschenk to Melbourne. There was anger and consternation, because each had signed contracts and a promise of return fare to California, but the manager, who was himself being discharged, told them that Lola's attitude was that "they might all go to hell." They went looking for attorneys to assert their rights against Lola's efforts to abandon them.

Lola had taken her benefit the night before and had fainted in the wings once again. On the final night of the Sydney engagement she rewarded Folland, who had found great favor with the critics and public, with his own benefit. Early the next afternoon she was down at the wharf of the Australian Steam Navigation Company in Darling Harbor to board the steamer *Waratah*, which was to leave at 3 P.M. for Melbourne. One of the discharged actors had managed to see her that morning to ask whether she had anything to say to the company; her reply—"I am a married woman and you may do your best"—had indicated that she was going to try to evade responsibility by relying on the British legal doctrine that a married woman had no legal identity apart from her husband and so could neither enter into valid contracts without her husband's permission nor be sued separately from him. It was never clear just whom Lola at this point claimed as her lawful husband.

The attorneys for the members of Lola's troupe were scrambling to get their actions filed, declarations made, and writs issued before Lola slipped out of the legal grasp of the courts of New South Wales. Only the firm of Johnson and Johnson managed to get its paperwork to the sheriff in time to have a writ of *capias* issued for the arrest of the famous defendant. As the great paddles on the *Waratah* were about to begin turning, the idlers on the wharf saw Thomas Brown, the well-known bailiff of the Supreme Court of New South Wales, push his way through the crowd and heave his bulk into the mail launch taking the last bags to the ship.

Bailiff Brown hauled himself up the side of the ship and immediately sought out "Marie de Landsfeldt Heald, sued as Lola Montez," announcing to her that he was placing her under arrest on a suit for £100 and costs. Lola's attorney was on board to see her off and told Brown that he would provide bail for his client. Brown replied that even if the attorney provided bail on the £100 suit, the lady would still have to accompany the bailiff to the sheriff's office since there were said to be other writs requiring substantial bail. Other gentlemen came forward and told the bailiff they would provide bail, but now the ship was slipping down Jackson Harbor to sea, and no one seemed to have any cash they were willing to provide to the bailiff as bail for the prisoner.

Lola ignored what was going on and descended to the captain's salon, where she sat chatting with a couple of ladies. The bailiff grew more and more distressed. When the *Waratah* passed Dawes Point, it was intercepted by a boat carrying the clerk of another law firm bearing a handful of additional writs for Brown. If the bailiff noticed that none of the writs had actually been lawfully issued by the sheriff, he chose to ignore the fact.

Brown went down to the salon and, taking Lola by the hand, informed her that she would have to return to shore with him. She replied sharply, "I will not; I am a married woman and that is not my name." This was supported by a considerable number of people in the salon, and Brown, sensing that he could hope for no success there, went to read his warrant to Captain Warner and to the agent of the steamship company. The bailiff told them that he wanted the ship put in at Watson's Bay so that he could take the countess off, but the officers had no interest in getting into the dispute and told him that unless he had written authority to prevent the ship from proceeding, they would not put in.

Brown's desperation increased as he saw the *Waratah* approach South Head and the open sea. Lola had already gone to bed. The bailiff asked that a signal flag be hoisted to summon the water police, but the captain refused to cooperate and pointed out to Brown that he was demanding £7,000 pounds bail when he had only a single valid writ for £100. Brown at last gave up and went to James Crosby, the acting manager of the Victoria Theatre, whom Lola had just engaged as her new agent, telling him that he had to see Madame Montez to serve her with the additional writs. Crosby, described as looking Mephistophelian, with a long, white face and black beard, unlocked Lola's stateroom, and Brown was allowed to enter and lay the unissued writs on her bed. Then he clambered into the launch he had tied to the *Waratah's* stern and rowed in defeat to shore as Lola steamed on to Melbourne.

The *Sydney Morning Herald,* which had not deigned to even mention Lola Montez, now was pleased to carry two articles about her on the same page. One was a letter signed "One of Lola Montez' Company," which gave the embittered actors' side of their dispute with Lola. The other article was an account of Brown's effort to arrest Lola, which stated that "directly [after] she was arrested, it is said, she made for her cabin, undressed, and went to bed, telling Mr. Brown that she would not go with him, but that he might take her as she was if he chose." Even though the *Herald* subsequently published Brown's own unsensational account of the incident, it was the initial false story that was reprinted around the world. In some versions Lola invites Brown to enter when he knocks at her stateroom, and the bailiff walks in to find her standing before him wearing nothing but a smile. It appears that the abandoned players eventually were paid off by Lola's attorneys; the cases were not pursued, and Lola remained unmolested when she later returned to Sydney.

On the morning of 11 September the *Waratah* entered Port Philip Bay and steamed to Melbourne. Although the relatively flat site was not as dramatic as Sydney's, the town was bustling with activity created by the wealth generated from the nearby gold mines, where frontier towns like Bendigo and Ballarat were mushrooming. Then, as now, the capital of Victoria had a character distinctly different from that of its rival, Sydney. Although it did not lack representatives of Victorian morality, as Lola would soon discover, the city's proximity to the goldfields gave it a frontier character, with an accompanying tolerance of diversity and eccentricity.

Lola checked into the Grand Imperial Hotel and soon discovered that she had some old friends in Melbourne. One of them was Miska Hauser, whom she had last seen when he abandoned her in Marysville during their California tour. Hauser was afraid that Lola harbored a grudge, but when she heard he was in town she wrote him a friendly note inviting him to come visit her, and he called on her at the Imperial.

He found her stretched out on a sofa rolling cigarettes, with tarot cards laid out on the table in front of her. Lola had always been superstitious, and now anything related to spiritualism and the occult interested her. The room was filled with her half-unpacked trunks and cases. "I thought you'd come, you German bear," she greeted him. "I knew you couldn't be seriously peeved." Hauser reported that Lola was overflowing with stories and jokes and prattled on for an hour. Her dancing, he said, had improved, becoming both more sensuous and more refined.

Lola opened in *Lola Montez in Bavaria* to the usual crammed house at the usual increased prices just two days after her arrival, with Folland taking the role of the vain and ridiculous Baron von Poppenheim and the rest of the roles performed by resident members of the local company. The underrehearsed play does not seem to have made much of an impression on the critics, though they and the public were willing to acknowledge that the play was not what the evening was all about.

As Lola's successful engagement progressed, houses began to fall off, so even though she was sick with "eye-blight" (possibly migraine headaches), the "Spider Dance" was added to the bill for her benefit on Wednesday, 19 September. Lola seems on this occasion to have had to look long and hard for the spider in her skirts, and she was so exhausted at the conclusion that she had to be supported by two members of the company at her curtain call. The spider had once more worked its magic for her. The critic of the *Argus* denounced her the next morning: "Why the stage of the Theatre Royal should have been selected for a public exhibition of the kind which took place last evening we cannot imagine. . . . We feel called upon to denounce, in terms of unmeasured reprobation, the performances in which that lady figured last night. . . . If the management of the Theatre Royal aim at securing public patronage by such performances, they have no right to insult respectable ladies by inviting their attendance; and, if scenes of the kind are ever to be repeated, we consider that the interference of the authorities is imperatively called for to put them down as a nuisance, and as utterly subversive of all ideas of public morality."

The critic of the *Geelong Advertiser* had not attended, but what he heard, he wrote, confirmed the opinion expressed in the *Argus*, and he repeated the rumor that she had been supported at her curtain call because she was drunk. He added that the Theatre Royal had extended her engagement three more nights and had announced that she would dance the "Spider Dance" every night.

The *Age*, however, saw the "Spider Dance" differently: "Indeed the dance requires that peculiar kind of 'exhibition' which would be perfectly intolerable if not executed with the greatest elegance and unmisgiving precision. Her pantomime action was so perfect that, notwithstanding all the skill of the imaginary spider to secret himself in her dress, everybody saw the moment when she fairly shook him down, and stamped upon him with what has been called 'the prettiest little foot in the world.' The house came down with a storm of applause, and persevered in this till Madame Lola was led on, now evidently very giddy and ill from the gyrations and efforts of this extraordinary dance and scarcely able to thank the audience."

As might have been predicted, Lola herself fueled the controversy, replying to the *Argus* with a letter to the editor of the *Herald:* "I throw back with scorn the insinuation of the *Argus* that I in this dance come forward to pander to a morbid taste for indelicate representations. Theirs is the indelicacy who look at any work of art with an *arrière pensée* in their minds; let them remember that the symbol of innocence is the statue of Eve, and that since the days when Eve surveyed herself in the fountain, works of art, however portrayed, have by their very character been sacred from the ribaldry of the licentious or uninitiated; *par exemple*, the Venus de Medici, and Powers' Greek Slave.

"I shall be at my post tomorrow night, and shall there take a course which will test the value of the opinion advanced in the paragraph of the *Argus* above alluded to."

If any further publicity was necessary, it was more than adequately supplied by the Reverend John Lawrence Milton, a little old man with a long gray beard, who frequented the City Court sessions to fill the derelicts and drunks appearing there with a sense of repentance and righteousness. At the conclusion of the court session on 21 September, Milton rose with a copy of the *Herald* in his hand and solemnly advanced to the witness box, where he asked the magistrates to hear him out. As the voice of an outraged community and a protector of decency and morality, Milton asked for a warrant for the arrest of Lola Montez to prevent a repetition of the outrages she had committed on Wednesday night and which she publicly threatened, in her letter to the *Herald*, to repeat that evening. The magistrates advised him to prepare and submit his evidence and application in the usual form.

Naturally the house that night was crowded with men eager to see the

"Spider Dance." After patiently sitting through the comedies, they had begun to chant "Spider, Spider, Spider" when Folland appeared before the curtain to read an address from Lola in which she proclaimed that she was merely reproducing the guileless folk art of Spain in the "Spider Dance" and asked the audience whether they would see it. The audience of course responded loudly in the affirmative, though a few hisses were reported.

This time the spider seems not to have made its way quite so far up into her skirts. At least none of the newspapers, including the *Argus*, could find anything remotely objectionable in the dance. The *Age* sent a different critic to this performance, and he was not as impressed as his colleague had been, finding it "simply ridiculous—a hard, rigid, inflexible piece of pantomime."

Lola closed her first Melbourne engagement on 24 September and the next day took a steamer across Port Philip Bay to Geelong, where she opened that night in the newly refurbished theater. The Theatre Royal in Geelong was small, apparently holding only about five hundred people, but it gave Lola an opportunity to divide her Melbourne run into two engagements while continuing to make money.

Lola had begun adding a scenario of the "Spider Dance" to the bills: "A young Spanish Girl while amusing herself by dancing is stung by a Spider or Tarantula, which fastens itself upon her person, and as the poison gradually disperses itself through her frame, she becomes faint and exhausted, falls upon the stage, or reels off distracted."

This was apparently an effort to quiet rumors assigning a less benign storyline to the dance, though press reports indicate Lola seldom acted faint or exhausted, or fell on the stage, or reeled off distracted. Usually she mimed finding the spider, throwing it to the ground, and crushing it triumphantly before dancing a coda of celebration.

After concluding a successful run in Geelong, the company began appearing in Melbourne again, but the house was being shared with an opera company, and Lola managed only ten performances over twenty-seven days. She danced "El Ole" for the first time in Melbourne and learned yet another comedy, *Asmodeus, or The Little Devil.* Her first local appearance as Lady Teazle in *The School for Scandal* brought forth a perceptive review from the *Herald:* "Lola Montez's best points are the natural apparent readiness of her repartee and satire, which come from her with all the sparkle and acidity of real relish, and we more than suspect that she is naturally rather good at 'skinning alive.' Fun and gaiety however are decidedly her nature, and where these can be indulged, she is perfectly at home. As soon as she becomes serious or pathetic, the mask is seen through; and a pair of sparkling eyes, and a laughing mouth refuse to be subdued to seriousness."

Now she was given the dubious compliment of being targeted for satire, this time by George Coppin, a popular comedian and entrepreneur. Coppin produced a piece at his Olympic Theatre, where he appeared dressed as Cupid with his skirts hiked up like a butcher's apron. The printed program contained a parody of Lola's description of her "Spider Dance," which began, "The young and buxom god, while amusing himself by dancing, swallows a Brandy Spider, which takes immediate effect upon him."

Coppin had apparently obtained Lola's music for the "Spider Dance" to make his parody as close as possible to the original. Indeed, one complaint was that the dance was far too close to its model. The climax of Coppin's dance came when he pulled an enormous stuffed tarantula from under his skirts and jumped upon it with both feet. After the dance he came before the curtain and delivered a brief address, mimicking both Lola's voice and her mannerisms.

In spite of taunts that she had no talent and that no one wanted to see her more than once, Lola was doing extremely well. In two months she had given more than thirty performances in Melbourne and Geelong, even though she had been ill for more than a week and had had to share the Theatre Royal with the opera company during her second run.

The Lola Montez troupe left Melbourne on Tuesday, 20 November, for South Australia on the steamer *Havilah* and arrived at Adelaide three days later. Adelaide, the capital of South Australia, was far less cosmopolitan than Melbourne or Sydney. In 1855 it had just under 20,000 residents. Its single theater of significance, the Victoria, was proud to advertise the debut of "the world renowned Artiste, Lola Montes, Countess of Landsfeldt, Princess of Bavaria" on 26 November. Ticket prices were, of course, raised; the best seats went for seven and a half shillings, nearly an entire day's wage for the average skilled worker. But there was a full house to greet the star with vociferous applause as the curtain rose on *The Morning Call*.

The critic for the *South Australian Register* declared "Madame Montes is doubtless a first-rate *artiste,* and will assuredly command overflowing audiences if her performances are marked with the same taste and skill as those of last night." The *Adelaide Times* called her "the most natural and graceful actress we have seen out of England." Although on the second night the house was not full and ladies were still few, critical and public enthusiasm grew quickly, reaching its climax on 30 November when, with a rendition of the "Spider Dance," Lola became the first professional dancer ever to perform in Adelaide.

Called before the curtain by tumultuous applause, Lola expressed her thanks for the audience's approval, saying, "I am very happy that such an opinion has been expressed in Adelaide, because it will convince Dr. Milton, of Melbourne, that he was not quite correct when he asserted it would be attended here with a dreadful disturbance." It is a bit difficult to believe that Dr. Milton had expressed any opinion at all about the reception of the "Spider Dance" in Adelaide, but Lola always managed to make her opposition personal and omnipresent, whether as Jesuits or as poor Reverend Milton.

During Lola's performances in Adelaide, a local artist named J. M. Skipper was allowed backstage, and the pencil and wash sketches he produced, while clearly the work of an amateur, provide us a unique view of Lola in action. One sketch shows her performing the "Spider Dance," another "El Olle," both with castanets. The drawings emphasize Lola's figure, often mentioned by critics but less evident in her photographs. The sketches of her dancing also provide us with a glimpse of her costumes and an impression of her dancing style. Another sketch shows Lola and Folland performing *Follies of a Night*, and a fourth catches the dancer backstage in her costume for "El Olle," smoking a cigarette.

The late spring weather in South Australia was turning sultry, but Lola continued to draw full houses. The company had intended to leave Adelaide on 8 December with a benefit; but when the news arrived of the fall of Sebastopol to the allied troops in the Crimea, the local Freemasons persuaded Lola to remain to perform at a benefit for the widows and orphans of the heroes of Sebastopol. It was a suitably spectacular finale to two weeks of unalloyed success; the governor-in-chief and his lady occupied the state box, the Freemasons appeared in full regalia, and the performances were applauded enthusiastically.

The troupe was back in Melbourne on 18 December, and Lola and her company agreed to donate their services to a Christmas Eve benefit at Coppin's Olympic for the Backus Minstrels, an American show touring Australia. She contributed the comedy *The Eton Boy* together with "El Olle" and the "Spider Dance," and two nights later she and the other members of her troupe were back at the Olympic in the audience to watch a Christmas pantomime. It was during this stay in Melbourne that she met George Coppin, who had burlesqued the "Spider Dance."

On the 28th the troupe sailed to Sydney for another engagement, arriving there just in time to bring in 1856. Lola set herself up in Hart's Hotel on Church Hill, where she was surrounded by admirers, although members of Sydney's fashionable society remained more aloof than their counterparts in Melbourne and Adelaide. Smoking was one of the amusements at Lola's parties, and she showed her guests the "Spanish mode of *enjoying* tobacco instead of puffing out its fumes before they were tasted, in the absurd English style." She would take a long pull on her cigarette, then take a slow drink of water before exhaling a billowy cloud of smoke from her mouth and nose and, according to one report, from her ears.

Among the entertainments Lola provided at her soirees were efforts to communicate with the spirits of the dead by table rapping, spinning furniture, and the like. In Melbourne Lola had borrowed *The Night Side of Nature*, Catherine Crowe's two-volume exposition on spirits, poltergeists, doppelgängers, and things that go bump in the night. She now considered herself an expert on the occult and was becoming preoccupied with the spirit world.

The company opened on 7 January for a two-week engagement, and again the critical and public response was enthusiastic. On the first occasion that the *Morning Herald* deigned to notice Lola, it took her to task because during the scene in *School for Scandal* when Lady Teazle hides behind a screen, Lola had availed herself of this moment to light up a cigarette. This comment provoked a response from the footlights by the star. *Bell's Life* declared, "Such deadly sin, however, if sin it were, was the custom of her countrywomen; and she was perfectly indifferent to any unprovoked assaults on the part of an ungenerous press, fully relying upon the continued indulgence of the numerous unprejudiced friends who welcomed her nightly."

After completing her second Sydney engagement, Lola, Folland, and Eigenschenk sailed back to Melbourne on the *Telegraph* on 6 February. Crosby and his wife were to join them shortly for the long-planned inauguration of the largest theater in the Gold Country, the new Victoria in Ballarat.

On the Monday following her successful opening in the new theater, Lola's wrath was aroused when she read a letter signed "Civis" in that day's *Ballarat Times*. The author objected to the fuss being made over Lola's appearance and said, "The press should be a moral guide to the people. How can it discharge that duty when it fosters an unhealthy excitement about one who, to say the least, has no claim on our respect and whose notoriety is of an unenviable kind."

The editor of the *Ballarat Times*, Henry Erle Seekamp, was something of a local hero, having used his newspaper to stir up the miners against the political forces that would exploit and oppress them. He had been imprisoned for three months in the wake of the Eureka Stockade incident, Australia's only armed rebellion against state power. Whether or not Seekamp had written the "Civis" letter, he was not the type to back down when Lola denounced him from the stage following that evening's performance at the Victoria and accused him of libeling her after accepting her hospitality and consuming a very large quantity of her liquor, all the while boasting of his power and importance.

On Tuesday afternoon, 19 February, Lola attended a charity lottery at the Star Concert Hall in Ballarat and, on her second or third ticket, won a lady's riding whip. Since Lola's propensity with whips was well known even in Ballarat, it is hard to believe that mere chance put the prize into her hand. Lola soon began to suggest that her new acquisition would be just the thing to try on Seekamp.

It wasn't long before word got back to the editor, who grabbed his own heavy whip, strode down Ballarat's Main Road to the United States Hotel, where Lola and her company were staying, and ordered a drink at the bar. Lola, according to one memorialist, had been observing life on the main street from the balcony of the hotel and had asked someone who the little man with the glasses was. On being told it was Seekamp, Lola grabbed her whip, rushed down to the bar, and laid into the editor's head and shoulders. Seekamp responded in kind, and as the two tried to land blows without being hit themselves, Lola peppered her opponent with rhetorical questions like, "How dare you attack me in your paper?" and "Will you abuse me again?"

Seekamp had the much heavier weapon, and when he finally tried to use his fist on her face, a bystander felt the match unequal and put the newspaperman into a headlock. Someone disarmed Lola, too, but when Seekamp was released he charged at his opponent, grabbing her black curls and her dress, and then the two whirled in a hair-pulling match until they were again separated by members of the large crowd that now filled the bar.

Folland, who had been rehearsing at the adjoining Victoria Theatre, appeared on the scene shouting, "Where is he?" Seekamp had just struggled out of the hotel, and as Folland approached him he drew something from his coat. "Oh, if that's your game, I am ready for you, come on," said the actor as he pulled a gun from his pocket, and the farce threatened to become tragedy; but when Seekamp's weapon proved to be only a blackjack or small bludgeon, Folland pocketed his pistol again.

A crowd of jeering miners had filled the street around the men and begun to pelt Seekamp with oranges and apples and anything else at hand. Seekamp replied with a number of rude gestures involving his posterior before escaping to the safety of the Charlie Napier Hotel across the road as Lola defiantly flourished her whip at him from a window of the United States Hotel.

The news of the latest whip-wielding exploit of Lola Montez spread around the globe. *Melbourne Punch* devoted an entire page to a twenty-eight quatrain mock epic of "The Battle of Ballarat." At her performance the night of the incident, Lola said in her speech from the footlights, "He says he will drive me off the diggings, but I will change the tables and make Seekamp *de*camp." One observer regretted that she had in a moment destroyed the popularity of a man who had been a tribune of the people, but the actual damage to Seekamp's reputation does not appear to have been all that serious.

Lola continued to draw good houses during her second week and had an opportunity to visit the miners at their diggings, where she was received with enthusiasm. Thanks to her experiences in California she could discuss local mining techniques, which differed from those in use in Grass Valley. The claims worked by the miners were small: in some areas, the law restricted a miner to a plot no larger than twenty feet by twenty feet. As a consequence, the ore crushing mills also were far smaller than those Lola had helped finance in California. The star scrambled up and down the ladders into the pits and was liberal in "shouting," which was what the miners called buying drinks all around.

Lola's run in Ballarat came to a sudden end with another whipping incident, but this time she did not wield the whip. Lola and her manager James Crosby apparently had exchanged words over what Lola thought were suspiciously small net receipts for the house, of which she was entitled to a percentage. On Saturday, 1 March, Lola repeated her accusations of peculation to Crosby in front of his wife, who was prepared for just such a moment; Mrs. Crosby pulled out a heavy whip and began beating Lola so severely that the weapon soon broke. Mrs. Crosby, who was said to be solidly built, then grabbed Lola by the hair and beat her with her fist as Mr. Crosby looked on. By the time Lola escaped she was too severely bruised to perform that evening.

Lola's injuries were not severe, though her ego may have sustained a blow with long-term consequences. Throughout her life she reacted to adversity by taking bold action, and this time she was assisted by the theatrical acumen of George Coppin. Even though he had burlesqued her "Spider Dance," Lola seems to have been on good terms with him since playing the benefit at his Olympic. Coppin, whatever his judgment of Lola's talent or character, knew that the publicity emanating from Ballarat could sell a great many tickets, and on Saturday, 8 March, the newspapers announced that on that very evening at Coppin's Royal Amphitheatre, "In direct opposition to the advice of her Medical Attendants, MADAME LOLA MONTEZ (who is still suffering from the injuries received at Ballarat) has been prevailed upon to remain in Melbourne FOR SIX NIGHTS, previous to her engagement at Bendigo, after which she leaves immediately for California, and will make her first appearance before the public since the late outrageous attacks (both Moral and Physical) upon her."

On opening night the enormous amphitheater was sold out, including the standing room, and Lola was visibly stunned by the applause that swept up from the sea of faces. The reviewer for the *Herald* said, "It would be difficult to imagine a more triumphant ovation than that accorded Lola Montez on Saturday evening." He also stated that Lola was even more vivacious than usual, and that "it was quite clear that there was nothing at all the matter with her." The entertainment went off well, and at the close of the performance Lola told the audience that she regretted what had happened in Ballarat, though she "felt sure that her enemies would find that they had injured themselves more than they had her."

Her enemies certainly had not hurt her at the box office, and Lola drew full houses to the Amphitheatre every night. The engagement was extended three performances beyond the original six and might have gone longer but for the engagement in Bendigo. She continued to draw full houses without incident, until the night of Lola's farewell to Melbourne, which was a benefit for Folland. Lola had just begun the final number, her "Spider Dance," when one or two hisses were heard. She waved the orchestra, doubled in size for this grand occasion, into silence, and walked to the footlights. She declared that those who had hissed were no gentlemen and that where she was going, she would not be hissed. The audience, fearing that she meant her suite at the Grand Imperial, began shouting, "All right!" "They're no gentlemen!" and "Go on!" She responded by walking through the dance with no spirit at all.

Then, for her real farewell to Melbourne, she walked once more to the footlights and said with a laugh, "So much for the hissing community." She gave the cue to the conductor and again killed the spider, this time with her usual fire, as the audience cheered. In a short speech she expressed her thanks to Melbourne and to Coppin.

Lola closed in Melbourne on a Tuesday and was scheduled to open at the Criterion Theatre in Bendigo, another of the major gold mining towns, about eighty-five miles to the north, on Friday. In spite of her illness and the stormy weather, Lola's engagement in Bendigo went well, and at one point early in the run she even announced that she had acquired a cottage and would settle in Bendigo. The dramatic high point of the engagement came on the evening of 2 April, when the star again demonstrated her courage and self-possession.

The troupe was performing *Asmodeus, or The Little Devil* during a thunderstorm when a blazing flash followed by an explosion within the theater stunned everyone. A ball of lightning had entered the building through its metal roof, descended to the stage, split in two, and, passing close to Lola, Folland, and another actor, blasted about ten feet of the wooden outer wall of the theater to splinters, set gauze scenery on fire, and smashed an exit hole through the roof. The *Bendigo Advertiser* carried this report:

> From the front the flash was quite visible passing across the stage, and an odor remained like that from the combustion of gunpowder. The scene on the stage was almost indescribable. The performances were suddenly arrested by the flash and explosion, and the tearing of the wood, and scattering of the splinters, together with the igniting of the scenery, the screaming of the ladies, and the actors, scene shifters, &c., running across the stage in wild confusion, formed a scene of real interest, not often paralleled on the stage. Fear seemed to have taken possession of everybody, when, in the midst of all this, Lola Montez, who had been all the time on the stage, came forward and said—That she hoped the ladies and gentlemen would not be afraid. She was not. "The 'little devil' was used to powder and ball." With the greatest *sang froid* she then proceeded to give directions for the continuance of the piece. The curtain fell, and in a few minutes rose, and the performance went off very well.

At the end of the play, Lola was called before the curtain, and she said it was the first time she had played *The Little Devil* with real thunder and lightning. After concluding the evening with her "Spider Dance" she declined to perform an encore, saying that "after having thunder and lightning knocking about the stage," they should not expect the "Spider" again. "Speaking seriously and from her heart, she had to thank Providence for His divine dispensation, no one being injured. She hoped all present, when they went home, would thank the Almighty for their miraculous escape. She hoped when 'Asmodeus, or The Little Devil' was played again, he would not bring his thunder and lightning along with him.'"

Less celestial disturbances also marked the initial Bendigo engagement. On the day of their last performance before moving to Castlemaine, in the second week of April, Folland and Lola argued and he refused to appear that evening. Lola pointedly remarked from the footlights that she had never allowed private quarrels to interfere with her duties to the public. It was not the first time they had argued. In Melbourne, a friend had been forced to intervene at a dinner party when Lola went at Folland with her dagger.

The hall in the mining town of Castlemaine was not much of a theater. Planks had just been installed over part of its dirt floor, and it held no more than about four hundred people crammed to the walls. There was no room for an orchestra, so music was supplied on a piano by Mrs. Gill, who also acted in *Eton Boy*. (Eigenschenk had left the tour, probably in Melbourne.) But the miners were hungry for entertainment, and reserved seats were sold at ten shillings. The high ticket price was further justified by Lola's introducing the "Spider" on opening night, 10 April.

The performance went well, but Lola got into a shouting match with some of the miners during her curtain speech. She lost her temper and told them that she was as rich as any man in the room, that she was worth £70,000 and "didn't care a pin for anyone." Rather than begrudge her their ten shillings, she told them, they should be grateful she was dancing there at all.

Two performances had been scheduled in Castlemaine, but response was great enough to support a third, at which Lola and her audience again squared off during her curtain call. Someone hissed when she mentioned that *Lola Montez in Bavaria* was being prepared for her reengagement in Bendigo. "Lola indignantly condemned the 'hisser'; she had had five millions of lives in her hands in Bavaria; it was because she had not sacrificed them that she was dancing there that evening. She did not come there to be judged—she was judged long ago, at Her Majesty's Theatre in 1842 [1843]. She was the maker of her own fortune, and she would recommend the man who had hissed her, to go to school, and learn not to hiss what he did not understand."

The Castlemaine performances were not without their rewards, however, grossing more than £450. After Lola completed a second Bendigo engagement, the newspapers reported with some astonishment that she had been paid more than £1,500 for her performances there.

April had been cold and wet in Victoria, and Lola and Folland probably had no regrets about leaving the mining country for Melbourne, where they took passage on the *Wonga Wonga* for Sydney. With plans for an Asian tour abandoned and Australia offering little in the way of further conquests, they were ready to return to California. Lola and Folland made the short journey up the coast to Newcastle, where the three-masted American schooner *Jane A. Falkenberg* lay at anchor receiving passengers for San Francisco.

On 22 May the coast of Australia receded as they began their homeward voyage, but the prospect of returning to California must have been as unsettling as it was reassuring. Life at home would hold fewer certainties than touring Australia had. They needed to decide whether to continue their theatrical careers; Lola could retire again to Grass Valley, and Folland could rejoin his parents and half-sister in New York City or try to reconcile with his wife in Cincinnati. More immediately, they needed to decide whether they would continue together or go their separate ways.

Their affair had been stormy during the year together, but at least they had had the stable context of their professional relationship and its obligations. Folland's petulant refusal to perform in Bendigo showed that the glue holding their volatile temperaments together was beginning to fail. They were both given to mood swings and self-dramatization, and being trapped together on the ship for weeks could not have been easy for them. Lola seems to have been in the midst of a spiritual crisis at this time. Years later she would write, "Once I lived for and from the world, was carried away to commit *all* its fearful sins and deceptions. I then loved that world. It was my all. I kissed and worshipped its chains that fettered me. And why was this? Because I lived out of myself depending on it for my happiness, then for my very bread from it vices. Oh, it took me years and years to rise out of its degradations. I loathed myself, loathed sin. I from myself tried to reform, not in outward show, for I never was a hypocrite, but from an inward drawing toward the *light* which is *truth*. . . . My state was a wretched one, oh fearfully wretched. I began to see what a monster in spirit I was."

Her spiritual quest was probably given impetus by what her mirror and her body were telling her. She was thirty-six years old, and her beauty could not compare with that of younger women. And in Australia, exhaustion had repeatedly forced her to reject cries for encores. She tired more readily, and her body recovered more slowly from exertion. Death before middle age was not uncommon in the mid-nineteenth century, and Lola was confronted not simply with vanity betrayed by time but with her own mortality. This voyage would be a turning point for her.

348

On 7 July the *Jane A. Falkenberg* made an emergency call at Honolulu to drop off the second officer, whose right hand had been mangled in an accident during the shipboard celebration of the Fourth of July. Lola took the opportunity to spend a few hours on shore, promenading in the little town. To observers she seemed careworn and prematurely aged.

The ship was soon under way again, and that night a dinner was held on the *Falkenberg* in honor of Folland's twenty-ninth birthday. Much champagne was drunk, and the celebration went on into the early morning hours of 8 July. According to one of the few contemporary accounts, Lola's lover left the party and went up on deck to clear his head.

The waxing crescent of the moon had disappeared into the sea, and the blackness of the water must have seemed to blend seamlessly into the sky. As it was told when the *Falkenberg* arrived in San Francisco, a lurch of the ship pitched Folland overboard, and he disappeared. Another report said that he had chosen to sleep on deck and had vanished in the night. Later there were rumors that he had jumped overboard in despair over his endless quarrels with Lola.

Whatever the circumstances of Folland's death, Lola was devastated and held herself responsible. Later she would write that she had cried aloud in agony to God to be taken, too. When death would not come, she resolved to change her life, to try to find some purpose for her existence.

As Lola's meeting with King Ludwig had transformed her life outwardly, Folland's death began a transformation of her inner life. Eliza Gilbert could never entirely forsake Lola Montez, however, and she would always remain a proud and impetuous woman with a rather lax approach to the truth and an abiding love of the spotlight. But as her arrogance and anger began to disappear, the kindness and the charity that had always been an unheralded part of her character began to overshadow the more spectacular elements of her nature.

27

S O R R O W   A N D   S U C C E S S

After her lover disappeared into the waters of the Pacific Ocean, Lola was doomed to spend the next eighteen days trapped amid reminders of him. Each day she would see his possessions, the bed where he slept, his empty place at the table, the place at the rail where he would stand. And after two months at sea Lola had to wait two more days until the gray wall of summer fog cleared enough for the captain to find the Golden Gate. By the time she arrived back in San Francisco on 26 July 1856, Lola probably had decided that she should devote herself to caring for Folland's family. The newspapers reported that Lola was calling Folland the only man she had ever loved, was refusing to be comforted, and was grief-stricken to distraction on her arrival. Now she had settled into a persistent gloom.

Lola certainly wrote to Folland's widow in Cincinnati, notifying her of his death and offering to help her and Folland's two children financially. She also wrote the sad news to Folland's father and stepmother, Charles Follin and Susan Danforth Follin, in New York City, and probably offered to help them and Folland's beloved half-sister Miriam, whose photo Lola had so admired. If she had not already decided to abandon California to return to the East Coast, it had become her determination by late August, when she wrote that she hoped soon to perform the "Spider Dance" once more "in every city and town of the United States."

In the meantime, she rented a small house and set up a household with a maid, a lapdog named Gip and several companion canines, and a collection of exotic birds she had brought from Australia, including a large, talking, white cockatoo and a lyre bird.

Earlier that year lawlessness and political strife had led to the formation of a Vigilance Committee in San Francisco. Now the sober Vigilantes were keeping an eye on the city, creating more need than ever for amusement during the foggy days of summer. Lola was engaged at the American Theater, the successor to the house of the same name where she had made her local debut three years before. Lola wanted more money for Folland's family, and she may have felt that being back on stage would help take her mind off his death.

Her opening on 7 August in *Morning Call* and *Eton Boy* packed the theater, and the engagement extended successfully over two weeks; she mixed pieces she had previously played in San Francisco with plays she had learned for Australia. In the second week she performed one of her dances each evening, too. The critics generally praised her acting, one saying that her performance in *Follies of a Night* "could not have been excelled by any of the actresses who have visited us" and later declaring, "It is astonishing how this lady has improved as an actress since she first came to California."

The critic of the *True Californian,* who was seeing Lola for the first time, was pleasantly surprised: "We have heard a great many ill-sounding stories about her, heard her acting ridiculed, and her personal charms disputed. But we confess that

> If to her lot some trivial errors fall,
> Look on her face, and you'll forget them all.

"Her talents as an actress have been very greatly underrated in this community, and her appearance no less systematically disputed. We have witnessed her rendition of two by no means easily personated characters, and we are quite sure that but few of the boasted stars, who have crossed the continent for our enlightenment, could excel her in either of them."

After a performance of *Lola Montez in Bavaria,* which she now was claiming as her own composition, Lola told the audience from the stage that she had played the piece frequently in Australia, where "it had done very much towards dissemination of liberal principles." And the "Spider Dance" continued to attract overflowing houses. For the two weeks she took away more than $4,000, and one paper remarked with surprise that the engagement had been marked by no violence on the part of the star except for a slap she administered to a young man for an unstated cause.

Lola had a theatrical engagement in Sacramento, but before she steamed upriver she consigned her jewelry to the auction firm Duncan & Co. (operated by the uncle of another dancer and eccentric, Isadora Duncan), to be sold in her absence for the benefit of Folland's children.

The auction was a symbol of Lola's changing values. Jewelry represented a secure retirement fund for a single woman, but beyond its financial value, jewelry had always been part of Lola's vanity. The lithograph of herself she sent to Ludwig from London showed her wearing at least three rings on her right hand alone, in addition to a jeweled cross pendant. The amount of the bill she had left unpaid at Frau Opitz's jewelry store in Munich would have been sufficient to support several dozen Bavarian families for a year or more. Now she was putting that sort of vanity behind her for the benefit of others.

Her collection, which one newspaper declared was "probably not surpassed by any possessed by a single individual in the United States," was expected to bring $20,000 to $30,000, and more than five thousand people visited the Duncan showrooms to see the diamonds, rubies, and finely worked gold. But the eighty-nine lots were probably too many in a city the size of San Francisco, and the proceeds of the auction were under $10,000—a disappointment, but still a royal sum for Folland's children.

Lola opened at the Forrest Theater in Sacramento on 9 September, and on each of the five days she appeared, the evening's performance was sold out by 2 P.M. The first night of the "Spider Dance" brought in the highest receipts in the history of the Forrest, and Lola was clearly as great a draw as she had ever been.

From Sacramento Lola made a final trip to Grass Valley. The house and the garden had been allowed to deteriorate in her absence, but Lola may nevertheless have found it difficult to say good-bye to her mountain retreat. Much had changed; most of the town had been destroyed in a fire while she was in Australia, but it was rising from the ashes, more impressive than before.

Lola sold her cottage and took her final leave of Grass Valley. More than a decade later a newspaper reported that both her rose bushes and her memory still survived in the mountains. In Grass Valley she was remembered as a "creature of generous impulses. She beggared herself by her extravagances and her charities. The wretched and the poor think kindly of her memory. She was frequently found giving consolation to the one and substantial aid to the other."

Lola was scheduled to reappear at the Forrest Theater in Sacramento on 20 September, but she sent word from Grass Valley that she was ill, and her reappearance at the Forrest finally took place on the 29th. In the course of the run she appeared in *Antony and Cleopatra* with the brother of Edwin and John Wilkes Booth, Junius Booth, who was the stage manager of the Metropolitan Theater in San Francisco. Booth may have asked to her to open the Metropolitan's season the following week. On her return to San Francisco, Lola's California farewell engagement at the Metropolitan was announced, and she opened on 13 October in *Follies of a Night.*

The second night she made a speech from the stage, telling her audience that she was returning to the Eastern states not for herself but out of duty to others. The public and the newspapers were preoccupied with the impending general election, and the rallies, meetings, and marches held in the evenings cut into Lola's audiences for her final California appearances. On the day of her last performance, the critic of the *Daily Evening Bulletin* wrote: "It is very plain, however, to all but herself, that properly 'her dancing days are over.' Though yet rather graceful in her posturing, she does not display, nor is it to be expected at her age, that degree of elasticity and life which is required to maintain a high position as a danseuse. . . . It is vain to endeavor to oppose nature. But in some of her late performances, in such pieces as *The Follies of a Night,* and other light comedies, she has shown that she is one of the most graceful and lively actresses upon the stage, and it is a pity she does not confine herself to such parts."

Her final California performance on 17 October was in *Yelva,* followed by a valedictory "Spider Dance."

By now she must have heard from Folland's widow and his stepmother and learned that although the widow wanted nothing to do with her, the stepmother seemed willing to accept anything she wanted to give. Lola made out a will giving all she possessed to Folland's stepmother in trust for the actor's children, asking that they be schooled in the Spiritualist faith.

The California newspapers now reported that George Trafford Heald had died in June at Folkestone in a resort hotel. Only twenty-eight years old, Heald had gone to a slow, agonized end from the "white death," tuberculosis, and a chronic ulcerative disease of the bowel. The only distinction in his brief life seems to have been marrying Lola Montez. Lola appears to have considered herself his widow, and she would continue to use his name whenever she wished to be someone other than Lola Montez.

She boarded the Pacific Mail Steamship *Orizaba* at San Francisco's Washington Street wharf on 20 November, Thanksgiving Day. The morning paper carried a brief tribute to Lola, declaring that both before and after her trip to Australia she had drawn houses "such as few artists who have visited us have done." According to one report, she was returning to the East Coast with $23,000 from her theatrical ventures. The ship was headed for Nicaragua, and a number of Lola's fellow passengers were soldiers of fortune supporting Tennessee filibusterer William Walker, the "gray-eyed man of destiny," in his efforts to take over that country. At noon the great side wheel of the *Orizaba* began to churn, and soon Lola's well-wishers lost sight of her as the ship turned behind Telegraph Hill.

From San Juan del Sur on Nicaragua's Pacific coast, Lola and the other New York–bound passengers took a coach up to Lake Nicaragua, then a steamer across the lake, and finally boats down the San Juan River to the Caribbean coast, where the steamship *Tennessee* was waiting at San Juan del Norte to take them to New York City. There Lola arrived on 16 December, after being absent more than four years. She still had friends in the city, however, including a father and son named Heman and Charles Chauncey Burr.

The son, Chauncey, was a journalist who was active in the Fillmore wing of the Democratic Party. In 1856 he was forty-one years old, a broad-shouldered, fine-looking man with a florid face and a long, light beard. He had practiced law in Pennsylvania, then was a minister of the Universalist church before devoting himself to journalism.

Burr was convinced that "the Negro . . . belonged to an inferior race and was destined for servitude," and he devoted his eloquence as a speaker and author to opposing the abolitionists. He had edited and written a range of publications, including one that became the *New York Daily News*. Under the administration of President Franklin Pierce, which was just about to yield to the Buchanan presidency, Burr had declined an offer to be named ambassador to Berlin.

With her new religious consciousness, it was natural that Lola should renew her friendship with Burr rather than with companions who were more representative of the hedonism that had marked her life to that point. Another Universalist, Thomas Lake Harris, had edited with Burr a publication called *The Gavel*. Harris had become interested in spiritualism, and in

1850 he began conversing with spirits, who told him the secrets of the universe and all about civilizations on the planets and on the moon. Harris then founded the New Church in New York City.

It was probably through Chauncey Burr that Lola came to know Harris and his version of Christianity. She became quite enthusiastic about the seer and his teaching, though for Lola the central Christian doctrine—the sinner's redemption through the sacrifice of Christ—remained the essence of her faith; spirit messages and life on other planets played a secondary role.

But at the time of her return to New York, Lola's priority was meeting Folland's stepmother. This probably occurred before the end of December, and it is reported that when Susan Danforth Follin came to meet Lola at her hotel, Lola threw herself on her knees before Noel's stepmother, crying, "I have killed your son! I have killed your son!" Mrs. Follin seems to have reassured Lola she did not blame her for Noel's death, but Lola's attention was soon drawn to the dead man's half-sister Miriam, whose photo had so fascinated Lola.

Miriam was twenty years old, but because she could so marvelously affect the innocence and naïveté she no longer possessed, the family was able to pass her off as sixteen. In fact, she had gotten married when she was seventeen after her mother had discovered that she was being sexually initiated by a jewelry clerk who was plying her with diamonds. The clerk was given the alternative of marrying Miriam or going to jail for seduction. The wedding took place, but Susan Follin immediately took Miriam home and forbid her to see her reluctant husband, who procured an annulment two years later.

Miriam and Lola had much in common: both were intelligent, ambitious, strong-willed, and aware of their power over men. Miriam would go on to lead a life almost as colorful as Lola's, accumulating a string of husbands and lovers, a fortune, a title of nobility, and a major role in nineteenth-century American publishing as Mrs. Frank Leslie. But at this point in her life, Miriam was content to play the ingénue, and Lola was completely won over, imagining this grown woman as her little sister.

An undated letter of Lola's was probably written to Miriam shortly after they met, and it gives an idea of the degree to which the older woman was captivated: "Sweetest, . . . You know, dear pet, how I love you and what pleasure your society affords me. I could take you to my heart and give you a true sister's love, pure and devoted. I do not wish you to go if possible, for you have made me love you—you *little witch*. . . . Bless you, *sweetest*, Your Lola"

By the third week of January 1857 Lola had moved into the Follin home at

13 Stuyvesant Place, and preparations were nearly complete for Miriam to accompany Lola on a theatrical tour as her younger sister, "Minnie Montez." Susan Follin appears to have had no objection to the plan, and the tour began on 2 February at the Green Theater in Albany. They played there from Monday through Saturday, and Minnie Montez made her stage debut opposite Lola in *The Cabin Boy*. No reviews survive beyond a single reference to a crowded house on opening night.

Montez and Sister were booked into Forbes Theater in Providence on Wednesday, 11 February, but a flood sweeping huge blocks of ice down the Hudson had interrupted transportation to the eastern bank, where Lola and Miriam had to catch the train. They gave up trying to get across on Monday, but when matters had not improved by Tuesday afternoon, the actresses paid boatmen to ferry them across the perilous stretch of water.

They caught the 3 P.M. train, but their passage across the swollen, ice-clogged river had been so spectacular that a news article with a woodcut showing the daring women in the boat appeared in *Frank Leslie's Illustrated Weekly Magazine*, marking Miriam's first appearance in the publication she would later own and edit.

On opening night in Providence, hundreds were turned away from the packed theater. *Lola Montez in Bavaria* was performed on opening night and on the following two nights, and Minnie did not appear until the fourth night, once more acting in *The Cabin Boy*. A critic wrote, "The younger sister is quite as attractive a personality as she was represented to be, and acquits herself well on the stage, for a novice." The entire engagement was a huge success, "one of the most successful of its length ever performed here by any person," said the *Providence Journal*. "Now a man is lucky if he can get a chance to stand in the entry and obtain a glimpse of the stage occasionally by looking over the heads of the people."

Charles Blake in his *History of the Providence Stage* devoted several pages to this five-performance run, and some of it is very revealing of the person Lola had become:

> She remained one week, drawing full houses to the last, living during the day in retirement, reading religious works, and steadily, calmly, hopefully preparing for death, having full persuasion that consumption had sapped the pillars of her life. . . .
> The company at the theatre did not then contain many actors of talent. Among those whose personations were least successful was the "second old man," who, though of excellent character, had never been designed by

nature for the stage. . . . He soon became a mark for the boys in the gallery, who found a pleasure in ridiculing and mocking him. . . . Poor Duffy (this was the name of the actor) became grievously depressed, but redoubled his exertions to please. His increased activity was so ludicrous that the boys were frantic with delight, and their joy culminated one night during the engagement of Lola Montez, whose indignation was aroused at the brutality of their behavior. After a successful *coup* on her benefit night, she was called before the curtain, and instead of delivering the conventional speech tendering thanks, she broke at once into invective, uttering those short, sharp, and ringing upbraidings, which can never be forgotten by those who have heard them. She told the audience, now still from curiosity and shame, how she had observed the effect of their cruelty on an inoffensive man, whose simplicity of character and singleness of aim had endeared him to those who knew him best. At first, she said, he thought that some remissness on his part had incurred their displeasure, and he gave his whole time and all his thoughts to perfecting himself in his duty, but with so little avail that greater insults had been heaped upon him, and he had that evening announced his intention of forsaking the stage and leaving Providence. "Boys," said she, "his heart is broken—and by you! I have tried to persuade him to remain, and have assured him that you have no malice towards him; but he says he shall go. Boys, would you ruin the old man! Let me tell him that it is your wish that he remain; may I?" Such plaudits as broke from the throng, now sensible of the wickedness of their conduct, that theatre never heard before.

Blake also writes that when Lola discovered that the husband of one of the actresses appearing in *Lola Montez in Bavaria* was on his deathbed with consumption, she called at their home every day, relieving the wife at the sickbed, trying to bring the consolation of her faith to him, and contributing generously to their material needs. "When she left Providence, grateful hearts remembered her, and blessings followed her," the chronicle concludes.

When Lola left Providence she also apparently parted from Miriam, according to one later report because Lola "had ocular demonstration that Miriam was not an innocent miss." What is certain is that two months after Miriam played in Providence, a married man who was also a bank president and former congressman bought a house in Miriam's name on Seventh Street in Manhattan, presumably so they would have a place to meet privately.

Minnie Montez tried to resume her stage career in June, playing Albany once more in a work entitled *Plot and Passion*, but Miriam was meant for things other than traveling from one drafty theater to the next. Three months later she was engaged to marry an archaeologist who was a distinguished scholar and former diplomat. It is not difficult to image why Lola, at this point in her life, might have become disillusioned with her "little witch."

Lola's tour continued immediately to Pittsburgh, where she performed seven times, usually to full houses. Then Lola took the train to St. Louis, but her opening was delayed when she fell ill. She recovered in about a week, however, and crowds fought for admission to her opening at the St. Louis Theatre on 12 March. Midway through her engagement the *Missouri Democrat* declared that "her first audience was the largest ever within a theater in the city; and every succeeding night she has drawn greater crowds than have ever been drawn by any stars that have preceded her. . . . Lola is a genius, and is a kind-hearted, good woman, notwithstanding her little eccentricities."

After her engagement at the St. Louis Theater, an entrepreneur serving the interests of the city's large population of German immigrants talked Lola into the audacious plan of appearing at the Varieties Theater performing *Lola Montez in Bavaria* in German. Since Lola had spoken only fragmentary German even when she was living in Bavaria, she could not have given a terribly comprehensible performance, but she got through two evenings of *Lola Montez in Baiern* before packed houses. The sole critic to notice the event was discreetly silent about her performance.

Five days after her last appearance in St. Louis she opened in Louisville, Kentucky, to the applause of a large and fashionable audience. Her week-long engagement was extended, and one newspaper said, "Had she been heralded by the loudest praises and noticed daily in the most enthusiastic manner, her triumph could not have been greater."

The tour continued at the National Theater in Cincinnati, where she had performed four years earlier. The spring storms kept some of the audiences below capacity, but her engagement was extended to two weeks.

Then she debuted at Rice's Chicago Theater. Outside of noting that her opening night brought an overflowing house, the few newspapers that have survived carry no notices of her only engagement on a Chicago stage. Perhaps she had no success with Chicago audiences, or perhaps she was simply weary after nearly three months on the road, but Lola ended her tour after five performances in Chicago and returned to New York City, even though additional engagements in Detroit, Cleveland, and Buffalo seem to have been planned. It was reported that she returned with $7,000 for her efforts.

In New York she not only rested from the tour, but she also prepared for a major change in her performing life. Lola seems to have found Miriam unworthy and Follin's widow unwilling to be the object of her charity, so that left her free to reevaluate her professional life for her own purposes. Dancing was becoming an ever-greater effort, and she knew that she must give it up soon. Acting was less physically demanding, but it would become increasingly difficult to remain credible playing young women, and few starring roles in light comedy were written for middle-aged women.

Back in 1851, as she was sailing with Kossuth to America, she had told a reporter that she might take to the lecture platform. Now her age and the influence of Chauncey Burr, who was a noted "elocutionist," probably were jointly responsible for transforming Lola Montez into a lecturer. Once she began, she must have regretted not having tried public speaking before; the platform was superior to the stage in almost every respect except glamour, something she was now more willing to give up.

She would no longer have to rehearse with an orchestra or with colleagues, or deal with their temperaments. She would not have to travel with expensive costumes or sets, and towns with halls suitable for a lecture were far more common than those with theaters. Once she had paid for the rental of the hall, which was much cheaper than for a theater, she would not have to split the net box office with anyone except her manager. If she were successful, she might very well net more money lecturing than she had made performing on the stage at much higher fees.

In May and June 1857, Lola and Chauncey Burr worked to prepare her first lectures and polish her platform manner. Although Burr was then and still is frequently credited with writing Lola's lectures, it is clear from Lola's numerous published letters to editors and her surviving manuscript letters in English that she had a marvelous command of her native language and certainly had the wit and style to write everything she spoke from the platform. The manuscripts of her lectures are nearly all in her own hand, with many of her own editorial corrections. Even in her first lectures, when Burr was helping her, most of the ideas appear to be her own; moreover, the style of the lectures resembles Lola's other writings but is dramatically different from Burr's published works. Lola's statements must always be examined with healthy skepticism, but the best evidence is that she was indeed the author she claimed to be.

The plan was to prepare six lectures and tour with them, but only two appear to have been completed in that summer. On 13 July, Lola opened an acting and dancing engagement at the Metropolitan Theater in Buffalo, possibly meant to make up for a spring engagement she had canceled. The Buffalo engagement closed on 17 July, when Lola performed *The Cabin Boy*, the sailor's hornpipe, and the "Spider Dance." "It was," the *Morning Express* wrote, "a triumphant affair. The Metropolitan was crowded to suffocation by admirers of her dancing," and they may well have seen the last performance Lola Montez ever danced as she closed a career that had begun in London almost exactly thirteen years earlier.

In the last week of July Lola appeared briefly in Toronto, but no record survives except a copy of a program for *The School for Scandal*, billed as her "last night," from 25 July. Then, probably on Wednesday, 29 July, Lola picked Hamilton, Ontario, as the site of her debut as a lecturer. Her topic was "Beautiful Women."

It was not a profound lecture, but it was witty, informative, and offered advice that would be generally regarded as good even today. Lola began by discussing the subjectivity of beauty, that what one culture prizes another finds ugly. However beauty may be defined, she said, it is certain to fade with time. She went on to discuss famous women of beauty she had seen herself and their relative merits, and then she considered some of the national traits of beauty and the relation of fashion to beauty. Here she discussed her visit to the sultan's harem in Istanbul, a typical bit of Lola Montez improvement on the truth.

In her recommendations, Lola advocated light, unencumbered dress, particularly for girls and young women, whose bodies are developing. Most cosmetics she decried as countereffective and often dangerous. To Lola the three requisites for feminine beauty were temperance, exercise, and cleanliness. Temperance meant not only abstention from alcohol but also from strong coffee and heavy foods (no mention, however, of tobacco). Exercise should be gentle but taken daily in the open air. And a regular tepid bath with bran renewed the skin and the body. In an age when bathtubs were something of a rarity, Lola recommended that every woman make sure her house contained one.

But, in conclusion, Lola said, "I know of no art which can atone for the defect of an unpolished mind and an unlovely heart. That charming activity of soul, that spiritual energy, which gives animation, grace, and living light to the animal frame, is, after all, the real source of Woman's Beauty."

Lola drew a crowd to that first lecture, and a critic wrote she had "acquitted herself credibly." He thought her voice sweet and sufficiently strong but suggested that she vary her rate of speaking somewhat.

Two days later she repeated "Beautiful Women" at the American Hall in Buffalo, where the newspaper reported, "Rarely if ever was a Buffalo audience better pleased, we may almost say more fascinated, with a lecture than it was with that of Lola Montez." The next night she introduced a new lecture entitled "The Origin and Power of Rome," which was her tribute to and attack on the Roman Catholic Church.

"I know not that history has anything more wonderful to show than the part which the Catholic Church has borne in the various civilizations of the world," Lola began. But she quickly made clear that the greatness of the church lay in the past and that it had become an abomination. It was not "a lie and cheat" from the beginning. "We cannot deny it the merit of having worked well during those terrible [dark] ages." But since the Renaissance, the struggle of the Catholic Church "has been to drag the heart and brain of men backward into the night out of which it came."

Her thesis was illustrated by a comparison of Catholic Austria with Protestant Prussia, and of the Catholic cantons of Switzerland with the Protestant cantons, to show the insidious influence of Catholic doctrine on a population. Lola concluded by praising what she believed was the Protestant principle of the United States. "It is that principle," she said, "which has given the world the four greatest facts of modern times—steamboats, railroads, telegraphs, and the American republic!"

With the beginning of her lecturing career, Lola all but abandoned the pretense that she was Spanish. The last traces of the foreign accent she had affected disappeared, and critics remarked on the wonderful clarity and distinctness of her enunciation. She continued to pretend that her mother was of Spanish descent, but this lecture made clear that her masquerade as a Catholic was definitely over.

With Chauncey Burr probably accompanying her as manager, Lola began to tour New York and New England. Her initial audiences were not always large, but the reaction to her charming platform manner and her witty lectures was always extremely positive, like that of the correspondent of the *Boston Post* who wrote from Burlington, Vermont, "I cannot help thinking that she talks vastly better than she dances, and in my opinion that is her opinion. Her lecture was a decidedly pleasant and profitable entertainment."

If Lola had needed any additional publicity to launch her new career, she obtained it when she decided to lecture in Montreal at the end of August. A squabble broke out in the Montreal press over her character and the appropriateness of any decent person being seen at her lectures. It surpassed any journalistic ruckus she had stirred up in the past, and amusing highlights of the exchanges were reprinted everywhere.

The first salvo was launched on 26 August in the *Witness*, which declared, "The notorious Lola Montez is about to lecture in this city. It is to be hoped that respectable people will not degrade themselves by forming part of her audience." Lola responded with one of her famous letters to the editor, which was published in the *Pilot* on 29 August.

> A feeling of justice to myself impels me to ask you what motive any fair-minded man can have for assaulting me in the pursuit of an honorable and blameless calling?
>
> Is it not, sir, from the depravity of your own bad nature that this attack has sprung? Am I not earning my bread as respectably as you are yours?— and I rejoice in knowing that in the midst of all the malice and falsehood which have been heaped upon me, I have never yet, to my knowledge, been thus assailed by any man who was himself of a faultless life. My assailants have been from the ranks of men like yourself, who have no visible means of getting a character, but by shouting at the top of their voices against vice—men who, having worn themselves out in the service of sin, set up to be especial enemies of sinners....
>
> That my life has not been without errors, I do not deny; but that I ever deserved the abuse which such as you would heap upon me, I do deny, and history will one day vindicate my right to say this of myself....
>
> How will you meet him who has said, "Let him who is without sin cast the first stone"? Practice upon the precept of the "Master," and you will never more throw stones at me or any other human being....
>
> Sir, I pity you, and I forgive you, and it is with the hope that I may be the means of making a better-mannered and a better-principled man of you that I address this note.

This letter, reprinted widely, may have contributed to her further rehabilitation in the public mind. The *Witness* retreated into silence, but *Le Minèrve* took up the battle, weighing in with the declaration, "We write to avenge public morality.... We believe ourselves obliged to protest in the name of decency, in the name of public morality and of the fine society of Montreal against the scandal which has just broken upon this city.... What mother who has gone to hear this could return to her family and expect esteem and authority? ... The best thing we can do for Lola Montez is not to conceal from her the deplorable and tragic path she is treading."

The editor of *Le Minèrve* seems to have become positively obsessed with Lola; even after she left Canada he devoted nearly half a page to refuting the praise that rival journal *Le Pays* had heaped upon this shameless courtesan.

The effect of this attention was, of course, to ensure sellouts for Lola's lectures, with hundreds turned away. She had the wisdom not to deliver her analysis of the Catholic Church in Montreal, but she introduced a new lecture, particularly appropriate for French Canada, entitled "Wits and Women of Paris." This lecture was a string of portraits of the celebrities of Paris, together with a bit of commentary on Parisian mores. The portraits were said to be based on Lola's personal knowledge of each of the celebrities, but some of them show signs of having been assembled from other sources.

Demand for tickets was so great that "Beautiful Women" was repeated. The *Daily Argus* called Lola a "perfect elocutionist." "Her voice is of liquid sweetness; and her intonation, and the point she gave to passages of a lecture abounding in brilliant hits and happy pieces of playful satire were delivered with anything other than a foreign accent. . . . She is considerably thinner than represented in the plates we have seen, but the expression on her face and the luster of her eye no artist can do justice to. Her deportment is easy and ladylike, and she delivered the lecture with a grace and beauty of diction we have very seldom heard equaled by the most finished actress."

The *Pilot* was just as enthusiastic, printing long summaries of both lectures. Finding that demand for the summaries was "universal," the *Pilot* republished them together in a particularly large edition on 1 September. The *Transcript* and the *Gazette* also joined in the chorus of praise.

Lola continued her tour of New England and New York throughout the fall, receiving virtually unanimous acclaim. Her platform attire was always modest but elegant, usually a simple dress of rich fabric, and she wore no jewelry. Her lectures lasted about an hour, which was shorter than many others of the time and led to a few complaints, but her delivery was universally praised, and critics often alluded to the "high moral tone" of her lectures.

Lola finally reached Boston early in October and scored another success. The *Boston Bee* declared her the "unquestioned queen of the lecture room," and the *Herald* thought "in point of good delivery, clear enunciation and impressive style, we seldom, or never heard a lecturer that excelled the eccentric Lola." She now was able to produce a publicity bill with favorable quotes from newspapers in Buffalo, Montreal, New Haven, Hartford, Boston, and many other cities in the Northeast.

In November, Lola went to Philadelphia, where the aisles were full of standees at her lectures, leading one critic to remark that "she must find it very profitable." Here she added to her repertory "Gallantry," a lecture that showed unmistakable signs of her authorship. In her review of the history of gallantry through the ages, she highlighted the remark of King François I after the battle of Pavia—"All is lost, except honor"—a remark that Lola had quoted in a letter to King Ludwig nearly a decade before.

King Ludwig himself was one of the principal examples of contemporary gallantry discussed in Lola's lecture, and she had nothing but praise for him. Although the portrait of Ludwig that Lola had been purveying on two continents in *Lola Montez in Bavaria* was not completely flattering, in her lecture she said, "He is not only one of the most refined and high-toned gentlemen of the old school of manners, but he is also one of the most learned men, and one of the cleverest men of genius in all Europe." She avoided any comment on the nature of her relationship with the king, but she neatly followed remarks on Ludwig's troubadour-like worship of feminine beauty with a discussion of the inability of coarse natures to understand idealized, platonic love.

A Philadelphia critic commented on this renewed effort to alter her public image: "That her lectures have had the effect of vindicating her former self in this community can hardly be denied: for certainly the number and respectability of her repeated audiences could hardly be tortured into anything else than a voluntary tribute to merit of some sort; and if the almost unanimous commendation of her hearers of the style and of the matter of these lectures may be taken as a just criterion, their merit is such as the proudest need not be ashamed of. That much of her present success is attributable to the notoriety which preceded her to this country may well be admitted; yet, at the same time, it must also be admitted that if curiosity has contributed to the popularity of these lecture board performances, surprise and agreeable disappointment have been no less the result."

The same critic went on to discuss the fact that Lola's success seemed to rely not so much on *what* she said as on *how* she said it: "Indeed, her power of expressing thought and emotion through the medium of her facial lineaments is most extraordinary; adding to this the silvery sweetness of her liquid voice, and an exquisite correctness of articulation that lends a new enchantment to the language itself, and we have some clue to the capabilities of Lola Montez being attractive in a lecture, no matter what may be her theme."

The tour continued on to Baltimore and Washington, then back to Philadelphia, where she introduced "Heroines of History and Strong-Minded Women." Lola certainly felt that she was a strong-minded woman with a place among the heroines of history, and this lecture was her most personal statement yet.

Deeds, not words, were the measure of a strong-minded woman, she said, pointedly excluding the new feminists of Lucy Stone's Seneca Falls women's rights convention, whom Lola classified as hardly better than scolds. "One woman going forth in the independence and power of self-reliant strength to assert her own individuality, and to defend, with whatever means God has given her, her right to a just portion of the earth's privileges, will do more than a million of convention-women to make herself known and felt in the world." She even included a comic proposed agenda for a men's rights convention, which should complain of shirts on which all the buttons were missing, of socks with a hole at each toe, and similar masculine hardships caused by feminine neglect of domestic duties.

Lola had high praise for the pure heroism shown in the "private homes of the world" where Woman "in the midst of poverty, neglect, and crushing despair, holds on most bravely through the terrible struggle, and never yields even to the fearful demands of necessity, until death wrests the last weapon of defense from her hands!" But most of her lecture was devoted to anecdotes of prominent women of world history, from Cleopatra to Catherine the Great. She did not deny their faults: "I only demand that a great woman should be judged by the same rules by which a great man is judged. If the lords of creation demur to this, I shall challenge them to show me by what divine right they are justified in a career of pleasure which should be forbidden to woman!"

Although she defended the right of extraordinary women to take a prominent role in public affairs, Lola originally concluded her lecture by saying, "But still she is far the happiest, and, ordinarily the most useful woman, who has no ambition beyond the sphere that completes the duties of a 'happy and virtuous home.'" This she later deleted, perhaps because of what was about to occur in her personal life. A commentator on her new lecture added a personal note to his review: "We have to state, with much gratification, that this is the close of Madame Lola Montez's career as a public lecturer. We break no confidence and do not intrude on the secrecy of private life by mentioning that this fair and gifted woman is on the eve of a very brilliant matrimonial alliance. She proposes in ten days from this time to be en route to Paris. Her return to this country for a short visit may be expected in the spring."

On 12 December 1857, Lola left New York City on the *Fulton*, traveling to Le Havre and to what she apparently believed would be a final, safe harbor in her life. Lola had become reacquainted with Prince Ludwig Johann Sulkowski, a forty-three-year-old Austrian nobleman she had met in Berlin in 1843. Sulkowski had fled Austria in 1848 after siding with the rebels; his younger brother was killed on the barricades in Vienna. Fleeing first to Switzerland, the prince had eventually come to the United States, settled in upstate New York, and become a wealthy farmer.

The evidence is sketchy, but Sulkowski apparently convinced Lola that he wanted to marry her and take her to live on his Silesian estates, to which, he told her, he was being allowed to return after ten years in exile. He seems to have talked her into meeting him in Paris at Christmas.

What Sulkowski did not tell her was that he had a wife and five children on his farm in New York. Apparently his entire courtship of Lola was simply a hoax, as he had no intention of marrying her. Lola arrived in Paris on Christmas Day and immediately realized that something was wrong. Sulkowski was not there, and Lola probably discovered no one there knew anything about their impending marriage or about a ten-year amnesty, and she may have heard that the prince already had a wife.

The next day, "disappointed and feverish," she booked passage back to America on the first ship available, the Cunard steamer *America*, leaving Liverpool for Boston on 2 January. Lola was upset, and that evening on the Left Bank, a man who was incautious enough to step on her skirt received a solid slap to the face.

The wait to depart must have been agonizing because Lola seems not to have been certain what had gone wrong, though she certainly must have suspected that she had been played for a fool. When she returned, after a rugged crossing, the American press would report that she had married the prince in Paris.

It apparently was some weeks before Lola was certain that she had been deceived, for early in February she was still saying that she was about to marry. But she put the best face on it by telling her own lie, saying that *she* had broken off the engagement because the prince was traveling about with a celebrated singer as man and wife. If Lola had merely pretended to be cynical about romance and men before this incident, she no longer had to pretend.

28

GOING HOME

It was a beautiful, sunny day in Boston on 18 January when the *America* sailed into the harbor with Mrs. Heald on board. But Lola, who probably had disposed of most of her belongings and spent and given away her earnings in anticipation of marrying a prince, was in a less than sunny situation. She moved into a small room at 25 Bayard Street in New York City, where a friend, Otto von Hoym, the manager of the German Stadttheater, lived with his family. And she now rode crowded public streetcars instead of taking cabs, probably out of economic necessity.

But Lola had a ready means of making money, and within two weeks of her return she had debuted in New York City as a lecturer at Hope Chapel. Her first appearance, on 3 February, drew "one of the largest audiences ever to have assembled within the walls of that building," and the *Herald* declared that "she promises to be one of the most successful of female lecturers." The *Times*, which had been attacking her since before she arrived in America, devoted twenty-four column inches to a flattering review and summary of "Beautiful Women." She had planned to present "Wits and Women of Paris" the next week, but the response to the first lecture was so great that she repeated it two nights later.

During February and March she delivered all of her lectures, except the one on "Romanism," at Hope Chapel and at the Atheneum in Brooklyn. During the lecture series, Lola's name was splashed across the newspapers in a new rumpus. She was called as a character witness in a complicated action for an alleged debt of $390, a lawsuit that had been dragging on for a year. The claimant was the shady David Wemyss Jobson.

Jobson was a Scotsman who had stood for Parliament for Montrose, Lola's old home, in 1842 as a liberal and received no votes. He claimed to have been dentist to Queen Victoria, and he had written a number of medical, dental, and veterinary books, as well political treatises and a metrical version of the Sermon on the Mount. In New York City his principal occupations seem to have been dentistry, journalism, and litigation, but he succeeded at none of them and was known as something of a public nuisance. He was also suing James Bennett, the editor of the *Herald*, and was about to file a second suit against him; at the same time he was himself being sued by another dentist for malicious libel.

Lola, who had known Jobson in London in 1849, was called to give her opinion of his reputation for truthfulness. She testified before Referee John N. Whiting that Jobson had come to her at her home in Half Moon Street, introduced himself as an attorney, and offered to help write her memoirs. Later, she said, he had tried to blackmail her, and he was known in London as a liar and jailbird.

C. B. Schermerhorn, counsel for the plaintiff, began his cross-examination of Lola intending to discredit her. The newspapers published a partial transcript that offers some sense, albeit somewhat garbled by the transcription, of Lola's repartee:

Lola: My name is Lola Montez; my family name was Maria Rosanna Gilbert.
Schermerhorn: Where were you born?
Lola: In the beautiful town of Limerick.
Schermerhorn: How old are you?
Lola: Thirty-three.
Schermerhorn: When were you born?
Lola: Count; I cannot tell; I wasn't present when I was born; I have had two husbands and I am on the point of having a third; my first husband was Captain James.
Schermerhorn: Were you married to James?
Lola: The ring was put on my finger by a clergyman, but my spirit was never united to him.
Schermerhorn: What other husbands have you had?
Lola: Now, wait a moment; I'd never have you, be sure.

. . . .

Lola: I remained in Spain a few months, learning to dance; I was traveling perfectly alone, as I travel now; there was a charming little girl named Dolores in Spain, whose husband had deserted her.

Schermerhorn: For you?

Lola: No, I never did any of that sort of thing.

Schermerhorn: How many intrigues have you had?

Lola: How many have you? Well, come listen—None; I resided at the Court of Bavaria two years.

Schermerhorn: Who did you know there?

Lola: Everybody but yourself; I knew all about several millions of persons; I knew the King of Bavaria, Mr. Wittelbacher, he was called—that was his family name.

Schermerhorn: Were you the mistress of the king?

Lola: [*Rising*] What! [*Emphatically*] *No*, Sir. You are a villain, Sir; I'll take my oath on that book [the Bible], which I read every night, I had no intrigue with the old man; I knew the king and molded the mind of the king to the love of freedom; he took me before the whole court with his wife, and presented me as his best friend.

. . . .

Schermerhorn: Didn't Mr. Jobson subscribe a guinea to prevent you from being taken to the watchhouse?

Lola: He hadn't a guinea.

Schermerhorn: Did he not give you a guinea to keep you from taking to the streets for a livelihood?

Lola: [*Indignantly rising*] Am I to be insulted? Gentlemen, will you not protect me? [*The referee quieted her*]

Referee: Mr. Schermerhorn should not have asked the question.

Lola: Schermerhorn! Is that his name? Oh, ho! I shall have some questions to ask of *him*.

When the hearing reconvened, the spectators were so numerous that admission was by ticket only. Referee Whiting had taken the wise precaution of having two plainclothes policemen in attendance in his fourth-floor office when Lola's cross-examination resumed. But the cross-examination was mired in objections from Frederick L. Seely, counsel for the defendant, and from the witness herself:

Schermerhorn: Madame, was your name not originally Betsy Watson?

Lola: I don't choose to answer. I will answer no unimportant questions, or untrue questions. . . . I will answer, if you please, whatever is right; but when I don't answer a question, remember, it is one which is a falsehood in the minds of those men. [*Pointing to Jobson and Schermerhorn*]

. . . .

369

Schermerhorn: Were you not born in the town of Montrose, Scotland, and not in the town of Limerick, Ireland, as you have stated, and of one Mary or Molly Watson, and in the year 1815?

. . . .

Lola: [*Indignantly*] May I answer Yankee fashion one question with another back?

[*The referee endeavored in vain to induce the witness to keep silent*]

Lola: I have much to ask this Mr. Schermerhorn, or Skrekhorn, or whatever his name is. I have some little questions about a lady that you beat the other day, when you were brought before the Police Court.

Referee: [*In agony*] Madam! Madam!

. . . .

Lola: I only ask you whether you put your sweet little hand on that lady's neck so kindly.

Referee: I only ask you, as a personal favor, Madam, not to speak unless to answer a question.

Lola: I only answer, Yankee fashion, by asking another question.

. . . .

Schermerhorn: Were you not assistant chambermaid in the Star Inn of that town, Montrose?

Lola: [*Laughed ironically*] How can you expect anything better from such a rascal? [*Pointing to Jobson with her finger*] You must have dirt where dirt comes from. That man [Schermerhorn] is—

Referee: Oh! Madam, will you have the goodness to keep quiet?

Lola: I only called him a man.

. . . .

Referee: [*Imploringly*] Madam, won't you keep silent?

Lola: I was not born there; you cannot make me out a chambermaid; it is not a dishonest thing, either, if I was; I should have considered myself a far greater woman if I had been born a chambermaid than I am today. . . . Why, Sir, how do you know anything about me, or that I was a chambermaid?

Schermerhorn: I would say to this woman—this lady, I will call her—

Lola: Pray call me a woman—I am proud to be a woman. Your mother was a woman! [*Laughter*]

The testimony degenerated even further when Seely, in an objection, referred to Jobson as a "fellow." Jobson rose, shouting, "If you call me a fellow again, you vagabond shyster, I'll let you see!" Seely then informed Jobson that he would throw him out the window if he said another word. A wrestling match erupted between Jobson and Seely, and the *Times* reporter wrote, "The scene, had it not been somewhat tragical, would have been ludicrous in the extreme. The unfortunate referee kept running backwards and forwards, in a state of helpless terror. Madame Montez . . . exhibited her cus-

tomary coolness, but by the flashing of her eyes, and an involuntary movement toward Mr. Jobson's *caput*, when it was suffering sore infliction at the
hands of Mr. Seely, it was evident that she would have had no objection whatever to furnish herself with a *souvenir* snatched from that unfortunate peri-
cranium."

The plainclothesmen hauled Jobson off to jail, the referee declared that he
would have nothing more to do with the case, and Lola addressed the
reporters and everyone else in the room on the moral perfidy of Jobson and
Schermerhorn.

Both Seely and Jobson were sentenced to two days in jail for contempt of
court, and Lola visited Seely to demonstrate her support. When Jobson was
released from the Eldridge Street jail he rented Stuyvestant Hall to deliver
a lecture entitled "Lola Montez and Her Fancies" on the same night that Lola
herself was introducing a new lecture of her own, "Comic Aspects of Love,"
following a German-language performance of *Lola Montez in Bavaria* at the
Stadttheater. (Lola was portrayed by her friend, Mrs. Hoym.) Jobson's lecture drew fewer than forty persons, some of whom demanded their money
back when they heard what he had to say.

"Comic Aspects of Love" consisted largely of anecdotes taken from world
history. Lola distinguished between true love, which she said she would not
presume to satirize, and sentimental love, which she took as her target. She
made the point that monotony undermines a home as surely as discord can
set it afire, and she recommended that couples "part as often at least as is
necessary to give a little tinge of freshness to your reunion." She also
observed, "It is a great deal easier work to win a lover than to keep him. . . .
When husband and wife cease to court each other, the romantic passion will
soon fly the house."

She subsequently delivered "Wits and Women of Paris" and "Gallantry"
at the Stadttheater, but her praise of King Ludwig in the latter did not please
the German republicans in her audience. She also was working on a project
that probably resulted from public reaction to her testimony in the Jobson
case. The cross-examination on her origins and life history had aroused
public interest, and Lola decided to deliver a set of two autobiographical lectures. These were first presented on 5 and 13 April at Hope Chapel.

Lola told her story in the third person, referring to herself as "that 'eccentric' individual (as the newspapers call her)"; this softened the egocentricity
of an autobiographical lecture and also allowed her to adopt an occasionally
ironic attitude toward herself. Before beginning the narrative she pointed

out that a woman is usually allowed an "exceedingly narrow sphere of action" in the world: "She must be either the servant or the spoiled plaything of man; or she must take the responsibility of making herself a target to be shot at by the most corrupt and cowardly of her own sex, and by the ill-natured and depraved of the opposite sex."

A woman who is bold enough to defy convention but not strong enough to withstand the inevitable attacks on her is liable to be "swept down into the gulf of irredeemable sin." Lola declared herself if not the "best abused woman in the world" at least "pretty well abused at any rate," but she obviously felt she had proved she could take it.

"Perhaps the noblest courage, after all," she stated, "is to dare to meet one's self—to sit down face to face with one's own life, and confront all those deeds which may have influenced the mind or manners of society, for good or evil." If complete candor is the standard by which she wished to be judged, Lola did not quite measure up, for her lectures were filled with self-serving falsehoods. Many of them are petty: she shifted the year of her birth to 1824, claimed that her mother was related to the Montalvos of Spain, promoted her father to the rank of captain, claimed "Lola" was a childhood name. But the general outline of her early life was substantially more accurate than her memoirs for *Le Pays*.

She summed up in two sentences how much she came to regret her elopement with Lieutenant James: "Run-away matches, like run-away horses, are almost sure to end in a smash-up. My advice to all young girls who contemplate taking such a step is that they had better hang themselves just one hour before they start."

As she came to her adult life, the details grew less reliable. Lieutenant Lennox and her affair with him, which precipitated her divorce and drove her onto the stage, disappeared entirely from her narrative. In Warsaw, Lola's denunciation from the stage of the lecherous advances of Prince Paskevitch was, she said, applauded from a box by the prince's wife and nearly resulted in full-scale revolution against the Russians. Nevertheless, in St. Petersburg the dancer was consulted by the Czar and his interior minister about "vexatious matters with Caucasia."

Dujarier, she claimed, had left her more than $100,000, which she selflessly gave to his family. (This part of Lola's lecture, reported in the Parisian press, brought forth an angry rebuttal from Dujarier's brother-in-law.) As in her "Gallantry" lecture, King Ludwig received the highest praise. The immediate cause of the revolt against her in Munich was, Lola announced, Ludwig's impending introduction, at her suggestion, of the Code Napoleon, an anathema to the conservative forces. And she recounted her secret return to Munich was to obtain the king's promise to abdicate so that it would not be his hand destroying all the liberal reforms he had introduced at her urging.

Except for the distortion of her role and motives in Bavaria, this recounting of her career was probably more accurate than most that she had attempted. Toward the end of the lecture, Lola suggested that she would soon return to Europe, perhaps permanently, and plans were indeed afoot for a lecture tour of the British Isles.

The newspaper reports of Lola's testimony on her origins at the hearing had another surprising result. Mrs. Isaac Buchanan, the wife of one of Manhattan's prominent florists, had spent her childhood in Montrose. Mrs. Buchanan—Maria Elizabeth Thomson, as her name was then—had had a schoolmate named Eliza Gilbert, a spirited girl with black hair and dark blue eyes, whose stepfather had sent her to his parents in Montrose.

Mrs. Buchanan wrote to invite her old friend to call on her at her home on Seventeenth Street, just off Broadway, and she sent a floral arrangement to decorate the platform on the first night of Lola's autobiographical lectures.

Lola wrote to thank her for the flowers: "[A] thousand thanks for the splendid bouquet you sent me for my lecture last Monday. I do believe the flowers gave me an additional courage for the arduous task I had inflicted upon myself of telling my history to a thousand curious people who cared actually no more for me than the man in the moon."

She called on the Buchanans on the evening of 10 April, renewing the friendship after more than twenty-five years. The Buchanans would become important figures in her life.

The *New York Herald* now ranked Lola, along with Edward Everett and Horace Greeley, among the "principal lecturers of the day." "Some of them have faded a little lately, and the greatest of all seems to be Lola Montes, who alone is able to keep up the applause and excitement which she created when she first appeared behind the reading desk of Hope Chapel. In fact, Lola seems to have beaten all her illustrious rivals clear out of the field."

The autobiographical lectures were billed as being her last before her return to Europe, but because they continued to be so successful, and because any European lecture tour begun now would soon be interrupted by the summer holidays, Lola rented the Broadway Theater at the end of May and repeated her autobiographical lectures to good-sized audiences in the larger venue.

She was still drawing well, so she began a second series of lectures at the Broadway, and on three evenings she presented a double bill of a lecture together with a performance of *Morning Call*. These three performances were her farewell to the stage, where she had enjoyed much success in only five years.

Lola's run at the Broadway continued into the first week in June, when she delivered her lecture on Roman Catholicism for the first time in New York City. She had now lectured more than twenty-five times in New York and Brooklyn; but the summer season brought an intermission in most public amusements, so she rented a cottage well north of the city, at 90th Street and Third Avenue, in what was known as Yorkville, and began a career as an author.

Her first book, the text of her lectures, appeared before the end of June from a New York publisher. The *New York Herald* found the lectures "superficial," but other newspapers in New York, Philadelphia, New Orleans, Boston, and Nashville praised them for their brilliance, wit, and spirit, describing them as "among the *very best* things of the kind ever delivered in the country." A second edition quickly followed, from a Philadelphia publishing house, and shortly thereafter a London publisher came out with a pirated edition in three different versions, designed to appeal to all economic strata of the book market.

Again there were reports that Lola had not written the lectures herself, that they were purely the work of C. Chauncey Burr, and plagiarized at that. But Lola, in a letter to the *New York Herald,* denied the slur in her usual forthright manner: "I should not refer publicly to this matter but for the noise of some brainless snipper-snappers, who bear the same relation to literature and to literary people that sneaks, gossips, and backbiters do to respectable and well-bred people. One of them, probably the most starved and ragged of the demented crew, has ventured to attempt to levy blackmail upon me, as though it were possible for me to stand in any fear of twenty thousand such cowardly robbers."

Support for Lola's authorship came from an editor of the *Cleveland Plain Dealer,* who recounted the following story: "Lola Montez is a thoroughly cultivated and remarkably gifted woman, whatever her private faults may be; and to say that she is incapable of writing the lectures she delivers is alike absurd and mean. . . . The writer of this paragraph will make oath that once upon a time he saw the dashing countess take a composing stick, go to a case, and with no copy before her, set up a sharp and racy communication in which a certain editor was very handsomely used up. The only instruction she had was in emptying the sticks. The incident happened in Cincinnati. Lola Montez not write? Tell it to the marines. She can set type, too."

The success of the published lectures encouraged Lola to write more, and soon a second volume appeared under her name, *The Arts of Beauty, or, Secrets of a Lady's Toilet, with Hints to Gentlemen on the Art of Fascinating.* This volume contained Lola's practical hints on beauty care and hygiene, and the advice remains remarkably undated. Continuing with the principles she had espoused in her lecture on "Beauty," Lola recommended avoiding whatever is unnatural, including commercially prepared cosmetics, which she branded as dangerous, and we now know many were indeed poisonous. She provided her own formulas for skin creams, hair washes, waxes for hair removal, and the like, all made from natural products. Fresh air, exercise, moderation in all things, and scrupulous cleanliness were all elements of her beauty plan. She even included her own formula for tooth powder, advising that the teeth and gums be carefully cleaned after every meal.

The fifty "hints to gentlemen," all tongue in cheek, outlined exactly what a man should *not* do to win fair lady. Lola wrote that she includes them not only for the instruction of gentlemen but also for the amusement of ladies, because "the men have been laughing, I know not how many thousands of years, at the *vanity* of women, and if the women have not been able to return the compliment, and laugh at the *vanity* of the other side of the house, it is only because they have been wanting in a proper knowledge of the bearded gender."

The first New York edition of *The Arts of Beauty* supposedly sold sixty thousand copies in a few months. It was followed by a British edition, then a Canadian and French Canadian edition of forty-five thousand, a French edition, and several other translations. *The Arts of Beauty,* which has been reprinted in America twice since 1970, probably is the most widely distributed of Lola's works.

The final literary production bearing Lola's name is a book called *Anecdotes of Love,* which is a compendium of love stories from history, excerpted from unidentified sources. Lola's original contribution is a one-page introduction, and there is no way of knowing whether she actually had a hand in selecting the material in the book. It would appear to be an attempt to capitalize on the value her name is, and it contains little of interest.

The success of her lectures and books put Lola back on firm financial ground, and she could afford to enjoy the summer in Yorkville, with Gip, a menagerie of other pets, and a garden of flowering plants. After years of wearing her hair in shoulder-length finger curls, she adopted a new hairstyle, with her hair cut short and swept back in frizzy curls; it was a bit wild but quite attractive.

The diverse assemblage she entertained in Yorkville included a veteran or two of the spiritualist Stephen Pearl Andrews's sexual liberation movement, and word spread that Lola was organizing a free love commune in Yorkville. In fact, Lola's entertainments were devoted to her favorite diversion, conversation, of which she was an unquestioned master. Lola's guests were diverse because, as one of her friends noted, "She had a mania for meeting and knowing all kinds of peculiar people." She would preside over the gathering from an armchair in the archway between her front and back parlors, rolling cigarettes for everyone from a pouch of tobacco hanging off the chair, welcoming each newcomer with a "snappy" greeting, and talking about everything.

Lola was a legendary wit and raconteuse: "There was no chance to do anything but listen when Lola talked. That marvelous organ of language, which gave her thought vent, like the crater of a volcano in full blast, overwhelmed you with a lava of eloquent speech; and the mild suggestion of an idea which her one-sided conversation sometimes startled into activity tumbled back in a crushed and helpless state before it had fairly taken form." One of her more erudite friends wrote, "There was certainly no topic, within my range, at least, on which she could not converse with some substance of personal experience and reading."

Lola was not always the life of the party, however: "Indeed, she was unbearable at times, when it was quite evident that she was on the wrong side of a debate, and would fly into such a passion as no one could withstand, and I have frequently known her thus to break up a pleasant party. She never would confess to being in the wrong, and her friends were forced to charge her errors to the ebullitions of an uncontrollable temper, and no one ever asked her to apologize."

Toward the end of the summer, a cause attracted Lola's interest. The previous March a storm had destroyed the Church of the Good Shepherd, an Episcopal church led by the Reverend Ralph Hoyt. The church was still $5,000 short of the funds needed to rebuild, and Lola offered to deliver a benefit lecture on Roman Catholicism at Hope Chapel.

The minister gratefully accepted the offer, and the lecture was set for 13 October, but then criticism of the lecture and the lecturer began to appear in the religious press. The writers were outraged that any church could accept charity from someone as notorious as Lola Montez. Indignation became so great that the Episcopal bishop reportedly forbade Hoyt from accepting anything from Lola or even associating with her.

Lola responded in her usual manner, with a letter to the editor:

The idea of a clergyman in the selfish times we live in, giving food and clothes to the freezing and starving, instead of "feasting" them on "tracts," struck me as being most unheard of conduct in a minister, and I felt a strong desire to give my mite and help to rebuild a church which is to be used for a very novel but true Christian purpose. Nor did I for a moment imagine that there was to be found even in the benighted regions of clerical bigotry and intolerance, one so stupid and so shameless as to find fault with a truly philanthropic clergyman for his willingness to receive a donation from me to feed and instruct the poor. I did remember that it was the doctors of theology and the pious folks who crucified the Master. . . . But I am contented to leave it with thinking minds to say who is the better Christian, myself, or the cold heartless Pharisee who would crush me or anyone else for doing good. . . . And, to my lecture on Rome, I shall add a postscript in relation to anti-Christian and anti-American bigotry and intolerance, which may, also, as it appears, be used to rob the poor and divest man of his natural rights.

Lola gave the lecture as scheduled and then began to prepare for her trip to the British Isles. Although she had hinted that she might settle in Great Britain, her plan was to return to America when the tour ended in July 1859.

On Monday, 8 November at 3 P.M. the steamship *Pacific* chugged away from New York harbor to the cheers of thousands of Irish-Americans. They were there not to bid farewell to their compatriot, Lola Montez, but to celebrate the inauguration of rapid steam service to Galway, which was meant to strengthen links with Ireland and speed up mail between America and Europe. Lola was accompanied in first class by both C. Chauncey Burr and his father, who would manage her tour.

The trip from America was a rough one; the cold North Atlantic was whipped into heavy seas by the freezing headwinds, and icebergs, one of them more than three hundred feet high, drifted past. It had been more than twenty years since Lola had seen Ireland, when she left for India as Mrs. Eliza Rosana James. When the *Pacific* arrived at Galway on 23 November, Lola Montez returned as a celebrity, and the press was waiting to report that she had none of the new crinolines under her flounced black silk dress and that she wore a rich fur mantle over it. "She spoke in terms of very warm affection of Ireland, as her native land, and she said she was most anxious to visit Limerick, her birthplace, which she left when a mere child."

Lola and the Burrs took the train to Dublin, but before she could revisit the places she had known as a young bride, she left for Limerick and Cork. Lola's aunt Mary and her two children lived in Cork, and Lola apparently paid them a quiet and private visit. The newspaper in Limerick reported that she might also visit Lord Ashtown's family at Castle Oliver near Kilafiane. Lady Ashtown was Lola's second cousin, but it seems unlikely that she would have welcomed her relative to the stately halls of the newly rebuilt Castle Oliver, because Lola's descent was illegitimate and her reputation still dubious.

It was to defend her reputation that Lola, when she returned to Dublin on 5 December, wrote to the *Freeman's Journal*. The *Daily Express* had published a biographical article about Lola that included a translation of Dujarier's last note to Lola, in which he explained why he had chosen to sleep alone on his last night on earth. Lola alleged that the correct translation of the original French would be "This explains why I did not see you before going to bed," which is simply a lie. She also made the curious error of stating that Dujarier was killed in November, when the duel actually took place in March.

Lola went on to defend her position in Munich, demonstrating the blamelessness of her relations with King Ludwig by stating that "the Queen of Bavaria was my *firm friend* to the last" and that, when Lola was forced to flee the city, "the good queen was seen to weep at the window of the palace." This also was, of course, a lie.

The conclusion of Lola's recital of lies and half-truths is wonderfully audacious: "To the thousands of malicious and ridiculous falsehoods which have been published against me, I will not and do not reply, it being my determination to patiently leave the events of my life to history, while I leave my calumniators to that God who has ordained an especial act for the punishment of 'all liars,' and who will I fear, find the next world a good deal *hotter* than they have made this one to me. It is, however, a matter of pride to me that after being more than ten years a target for their intolerant malice, the only act of my whole life which they dare attempt to stigmatize with moral fault, they are compelled to locate far off under a cloud of revolutionary smoke and dust in Bavaria."

Some of her relatives had come to Dublin to see Lola lecture at the Round Room of the Rotundo on Wednesday, 8 December, when she spoke on

"America and Its People." The Burrs had done their work well, and the hall was packed with a fashionable audience. So many chairs were placed on the platform that the speaker hardly had space to stand in front of the reading desk draped with a crimson cloth. Her entrance was greeted with sustained applause, and many in the audience were struck by her enduring beauty, which was set off by her simple dark velvet dress.

The real subject of Lola's lecture was the role of the foreign-born in the United States. She began by stating that America was now incapable of stemming the flood of immigrants and that it would be best if the nation abandoned the xenophobia of the Know-Nothings and concentrated on assimilating the new population as rapidly as possible. Too many of the new-comers still identified themselves as German-Americans or Irish-Americans or the like, and Lola called their mutual animosities the "first muttering sound of a social and political war of races, which is inevitable in America."

She told her listeners, to their great satisfaction, that America was edging toward anarchy, with the Vigilance Committees and Bloody Kansas as prime examples of the trend. Applause greeted Lola's statement that "many men of eminence" had admitted to her that some form of monarchy was the only remedy for the inevitable catastrophe. Equally gratifying to the Dubliners was her assertion that "few monarchies in Europe dare to assume powers more dictatorial" than those the American government exercises and that England was actually the freer of the two nations. American democracy was an illusion because only a sixth of the population had the vote, and the caucus system of nomination for office by party elites made suffrage meaningless, she said.

The uniformity of American dress impressed Europeans as expressive of equality, she said, but political equality did not mean social equality, and no people are "so much afraid of being soiled by coming into social contact with vulgarity as the American people." "Wealth—the almighty dollar—is the greatest respectability in America. Without that there is hardly the smallest chance for any emigrant to achieve a respectable position."

But a hard-working immigrant who went west, away from the crowded cities, could still make a fortune in America. "He must work for what he earns; idleness, prodigality, and intemperance will pay him off only with poverty, misery, and disgrace." Lola concluded her lecture with examples, some of them humorous, of Irishmen who had achieved success in the New World.

Public and critical reaction was favorable. "The lecture was pleasing, instructive, and piquant," said the *Freeman's Journal.* "Her elocution, without being dramatic, is finely expressive, and her voice, which is particularly sweet and richly toned, is always clear and audible, though never loud." Another newspaper declared, "In the attributes of elocution, the Countess of Landsfeld is not excelled by any of her sex throughout the world."

Two nights later Lola gave another crowded and even more fashionable audience her views on "Comic Aspects of Fashion." This lecture contained little serious social commentary. It dealt with the power of fashion since its origin, which Lola traced to fig leaves in the Garden of Eden, to control all aspects of life. Men were ridiculed no less than women, though she reserved special comment for the controversy over the trend toward skirts supported by hoops or crinolines. Lola called them no worse than their predecessor, starched petticoats, and stated her belief that many women could be said to have "died of starched petticoats."

The third and final lecture of the Round Room series was "English and American Character Compared," which contained a perceptive and rather positive exposition of the American character. Although the population west of the Atlantic seaboard "is now rough, turbulent, and little blended with the more refined graces of civilization, yet it is nevertheless the beginning and the foundation of what is to be the character of a really original and new nationality in America."

American religion, she said, is dominated by sects characterized by fervor, even frenzy, and great mutual intolerance. "In America you soon learn to draw a distinction between liberty and tolerance—for their social meaning is very different. There is no part of the world where public opinion is more powerful or more completely a tyrant than in America." And yet, Lola admitted, moral courage is a distinguishing characteristic of the American.

Americans as a people are constantly reading and philosophizing, she said, with the multiplicity of sects and theories as the natural result, and nothing is ever done without a reason. "You may deplore such a result, you may mourn over the extravagance and follies into which men's minds fall, but that is precisely like deploring the establishment of steamboats and railroads because people sometimes get smashed to pieces by them."

On the eve of the Civil War, Lola once again predicted that America was headed for war and anarchy, nevertheless she concluded by holding out hope, too: "But those stirring and embattled times which must shortly come to pass will call into the field new and stronger men to wield the destinies of the Government. Then politicians will have to give place to statesmen. . . . Men will appear who will be equal to the great task—men whose minds will grow great and strong under the pressure of the mighty circumstances which will demand their patriotism and their genius. So that whatever form government may assume there, whether it continue a republic, or take some form like a representative monarchy, it can never be other than the home of freedom."

The Countess of Landsfeld had begun a tour more extensive and more demanding than anything she had yet undertaken. From Dublin she went back to Cork, where she lectured twice, then to her birthplace, Limerick, for a single lecture. She had originally spoken of plans to appear in Belfast and Waterford, but after the holidays she crossed to England and began 1859 with a lecture in Manchester.

The Burrs kept her extremely busy; she rarely went more than a few days between lectures. At the end of January she spoke in Glasgow twice, and then went to Edinburgh. It would be interesting to know whether she visited Montrose or looked up old friends in Edinburgh or Sunderland, where she spoke on what may have been her thirty-ninth birthday, 14 February. In the Scottish capital one of the newspapers fulminated at the effrontery of the woman, calling her appearance an "offense against that decency and decorum in which the inhabitants of this city have hitherto professed to believe," but Lola drew standing-room audiences of "distinguished" citizens.

A typical week had her speaking in Sheffield, Nottingham, Leicester, Wolverhampton, and Worcester. Lola's managers did their publicity work well, and she lectured consistently to packed auditoriums. Her reception appears, from the newspaper reviews, to have been almost invariably enthusiastic, although some said that her lectures were too short—sometimes only forty-five minutes—for the high ticket prices. The best seats to Lola's lectures often cost more than three shillings, while comparable seats at readings given by the popular Charles Dickens were only two shillings. Lola was taking in a great deal of money.

She presented "Comic Aspects of Fashion" more often than her less frivolous lectures. "English and American Character Compared" also appeared frequently, but she lightened it with more comments about American social habits and fewer about politics. On a few occasions she also delivered "Strong-Minded Women."

In York's Concert Room on 16 February, Lola was halfway through "Comic Aspects of Fashion" when she noticed that a well-dressed man in the reserved seats was quite pointedly thumbing his nose at her, a gesture that was far more offensive in 1859 than it is today. She interrupted her remarks and, with a withering glance at the offending party, exclaimed her surprise that here in York she should for the first time in all of her lectures be insulted by a "fashionable man." The nose-thumber was actually a a man of some rank and importance, and the policeman on duty at the door deemed it impolitic to intervene. Lola concluded her lecture without further interruption and was lustily cheered.

At the beginning of April, after four months of almost constant travel, Lola arrived in London for the conclusion of her tour. She still had quite a few friends in London, and she stayed with one of them on Weymouth Street, off Portland Place. A letter she wrote just after her arrival in London has survived, and it portrays the deep spiritual concerns of this celebrity who spent her evenings giving witty lectures: "Oh blessed be God's *holy* name forever. *I have found,* found what nothing else can be compared to, what nothing else, what no one can give either by sympathetic advice or kinds words. That the love of God was so great to the most depraved of sinners that he gave his Son, His divine Humanity, that He might come into the world to take all sin from the world and die for us, that through his death we may have eternal life. . . . Think what a sinner I was, how impossible it once seemed to me to become even better, and it is only by his constant care and love and by my fervor and sincerity of heart that he has accomplished this *miracle.* . . . I am a frail sinner in myself. I only breathe truth and peace because I prayed Jesus to come and dwell in my heart. I feel very *humble.* I have myself renounced much money and am poor as far as money goes. I did the right thing for love of my God."

Her convictions, however, could not keep her from lying, a trait that had marked her from childhood. The *British Spiritual Telegraph* published the following report, which must have been based on information from its subject:

> The Countess of Landsfeld too, who is now lecturing with such success in London, whilst in America, made careful inquiry into the whole range of Spiritual phenomena, and having satisfied herself of their reality, had the honesty and strong sense to avow her convictions. She delivered several public lectures on Spiritualism, giving the proceeds to charitable purposes, and showing those generous sympathies, which have never been strange to her. Whilst in America, she was engaged to be married to a gentleman there, who was unfortunately killed, and it was found that he had left her the whole of his fortune, amounting to £20,000. She refused to receive any

of it, and gave it up to her lover's relations; a noble spiritual act, which may well be counted in estimating her character, and contrasts with doings of others who have more pretensions.

One of her friends wrote later, "She ... was quite regardless of the truth; even in these last years, when her ardent desire was to be a good Christian, her lax native character was stronger than her new resolves, and she would utter the most absurd untruths."

The Burrs rented fashionable St. James Hall near Piccadilly Circus for Lola's first public appearances in London since she had danced there in the summer of 1843 (unless her involuntary appearance at Great Marlborough Street Police Court in 1849 is included). She spoke first on "English and American Character" on 7 April and continued over the following rainy week with "Europeans in the New World," "Comic Aspects of Fashion," and "Strong-Minded Women." Although the press treated her lectures without much seriousness, the reporters admitted that her "large and fashionable audiences" went away entertained and satisfied. Whatever the value of her lecture, one critic wrote, "within three minutes of its commencement the Countess had complete possession of her audience," and another declared that it "appeared to give unanimous satisfaction."

But the *Evening Journal* was outraged that, whatever the truth of Lola's life and whatever the merit of her lectures, the audiences came because of her notoriety: "It is a fact that, whether justly or unjustly, she is not believed in popular estimation to have any claim to be [a perfect pattern of propriety], that causes her lectures to be given and the audience expected. It is really high time that, in the interest of morality and propriety, some protest should be made against this class of exhibition."

Following her final lecture on 15 April, the Burrs apparently returned to America and Lola stayed on in London, even though she had originally planned to return to America at the end of her tour. She renewed friendships, and some of her acquaintances induced her to buy the leasehold of a fashionable furnished house in Mayfair on the eastern edge of Hyde Park—26 Park Lane West, which she made her residence. She imagined that she could create a steady income by renting out part of the house to fashionable boarders while she lived in comfortable retirement.

The plan soon went seriously awry. No fashionable boarders rushed to occupy rooms, and Lola was hopeless as a manager, quarreling with the servants as debts piled up. It was perhaps in an effort to raise money that Lola announced two more lectures at St. James Hall in June. For the first of these evenings, 10 June, she prepared a completely new lecture entitled "Slavery in America," based, according to the advertisements, on "many years of personal observation and from an intimate acquaintance with life on the plantations." It was her most purely political lecture, and it was one she never repeated.

After opening the lecture with a humorous account of Americans' exaggerated boasts about their nation, Lola turned to the serious question of the possible dissolution of the Union. It will never happen, she said; it is far more likely that some kind of limited monarchy will evolve rather than that the Union should fail. "In the first place, a profound and almost sacred love of the Union is one of the most noticeable characteristics I have seen in all my travels in that country." Second, she argued, the only place where sentiment to dissolve the Union has any political strength, New England, was exactly the region that would be most seriously harmed by dissolution. The South, with its rich resources, could do quite well without the North, but New England would wither without the raw materials and markets of the South.

The abolitionists, Lola claimed, had discredited themselves by their radical attacks on Christianity and on the moral basis of society, and their following was now reduced to a handful. Not one inch of America had ever been freed from slavery by the abolitionists; every free state rejected slavery not out of principle but from economic pressure. "[Slavery] had to fade away before the competition of free labor and the necessities created by commerce and machinery, and by no other causes can it ever be routed from where it is now."

She had visited slave plantations, Lola said, and talked with the slaves, who they were fat, lazy, and contented, she declared. They pitied the free laborers of England, who they believed lived in abject poverty and heartless exploitation.

Finally, England should not believe that Americans were unaware of the moral issue in slavery or did not see the wrong being done:

> On this forbidden subject, the slavery is quite as much upon the thought and speech of the whites as it is upon the necks of the blacks. There are thousands of Christians and conscientious people in the Slave States whose secret hearts rebel against the enormity of the national sin, but there is the terror of the Lynch-Law, more dreadful than the code of Draco, which seals their lips in perpetual silence.
>
> But the justice of Heaven will not slumber forever The time will come when America will have redeemed herself from the sin that cries perpetu-

GOING HOME

ally to God against her; and when her national flag shall flutter in the breezes of heaven as free and proud an ensign of universal liberty as the banners that wave from the mastheads of the ships of free England!

Lola's lecture is likely to seem strange and equivocal today: slavery is an evil that cries to heaven, but it is best left alone to die an economic death. For the antebellum period, however, and particularly for the Democratic circles that Lola knew best, her viewpoint can be seen as the voice of reason and moderation. The abolitionists did represent a distinct minority even in the North, and nearly every stripe of politician not tied to the radical fringes was looking for a policy that would avert a national crisis over slavery.

Lola's lecture was enough to provoke a counter-lecture in London by a "lady of color" from the American Anti-Slavery Society. Lola took no notice of the protest and concluded her public appearances in Europe on the same evening as the counter-lecture, 15 June, repeating "Strong-Minded Women," this time with a short and satirical summary of her views on the "Women's Rights Movement in America." "At the conclusion of the lecture," the press reported, "the audience arose *en masse,* and continued cheering and waving their hats until long after she had retired."

Matters on Park Lane deteriorated. Lola found it impossible to generate and manage income sufficient to maintain the house and pay her debts. She was sued and then fell seriously ill. Judgments were executed, her furniture was seized and sold, and finally the lease itself was sold out from under her. Lola was saved by an elderly couple from Derby who had heard of her plight and offered her the use of their country home.

In the midst of forty acres of gardens, ponds, and orchards Lola recovered her health. She lived in a cottage covered with honeysuckle and ivy, amusing herself by fishing, gathering berries, and reading. Toward the end of the summer she began keeping a spiritual diary, making an entry every Saturday night. She was reading the religious essays of John Bunyan to guide her meditations, and her thoughts went back to the life she had lived even as she gave thanks for the faith she had found:

How many, many years of my life have been sacrificed to Satan, and my own love of sin! What have I not been guilty of, either in thought or in deed, during these years of misery and wretchedness! . . . What would I not give to have my terrible and fearful experience given as an awful warning to such natures as my own! . . . What is my worldly knowledge in Thy sight — an impediment to get to Thee. What has the world ever given to me? (And

I have known *all* that the world has to give—ALL!) Nothing but shadows, leaving a wound on the heart hard to heal—*a dark discontent.* . . .

I am afraid, sometimes, that I think too well of myself. But let me only look back to the past. Oh! how I am humbled! . . . Keep my tongue from evil speaking and lying. . . . Dear Lord, compel my hasty temper to be controlled, and give me an humble heart. . . . This week I have principally sinned through hastiness of temper and uncharitableness of feeling toward my neighbor.

Each Sunday she attended a Methodist chapel, where she was attracted by the simplicity of the service and of the parishioners. She longed to serve somehow, to visit the old, the sick, the poor. "But," she wrote in her diary, "that will be in the Lord's good time, when He thinks me *fit* for this happiness—that is, when *self* is *burned out of me completely.*"

The idyll in Derbyshire came to an abrupt halt at the end of September, when Lola quarreled with her host and returned to London. She later wrote to a friend that it "unfortunately happened that mankind, who are forever sinning, and who in the person of the gentleman took too much upon himself, you understand what I mean, and therefore I would not suffer this, packed up my trunk, and, as the Americans say, made 'tracks' for over the water." Yet this appears to be another example of Lola's improvement on facts to shift blame, for her diary seems to tell a different story: "It was cruel, indeed, of Mr. E to have said what he did; but I am afraid I was too hasty also. . . . Ought I to have resented what was said? No. I ought to have said not a word. The world would applaud me, but, oh! my heart tells me that for His sake I ought to bear the vilest reproaches, even unmerited. But I feel no anger in my heart. Why did I even for a moment?"

Lola departed Southampton on the steamship *Hammonia* on 4 October, arriving in New York on the 18th. The evening newspapers that day carried the frightening news of the seizure of a Federal arsenal in Virginia by a wild-eyed abolitionist named John Brown, who was attempting to incite a general slave rebellion. Lola must have begun to wonder about her confident assertions that the Union was secure.

Now she was using the name Mrs. Heald almost exclusively, both onboard the ship and after she arrived in New York. She took an apartment uptown, called on her old friends, and began attending a Methodist church, though she maintained her association with Thomas Harris's New Church.

If she wished to return to the repose she had enjoyed in Derbyshire, New York City was not the place to do it. Hardly a month had passed before Lola once more felt compelled to address the public in a letter to the editor of the *Herald*. She had been accused, she was told, of abusing America in her lectures in England, and she insisted on replying to this slander, particularly because she had become a naturalized American (through her marriage to Hull), choosing to be a citizen of that country above all others.

> I meant my lectures to be fair and truthful portraitures of this country, without the silly twaddle of adulation on the one hand or of misrepresentations on the other. And, surely, we may speak of faults in those we best love without incurring the charge of abusing them. I did not commit the useless folly of saying that America had no faults, but I did say, in these very words, that "take it all in all, there is no other spot on earth where man is making such giant strides towards civilization and perfection as in America." . . . When I say that my lectures were listened to with approval by Americans in England, I ought perhaps to except the one on "Slavery in the United States," which I understand gave offense to some very worthy gentlemen, who, I suppose, had certain partisan philanthropic views, which rendered it quite impossible that they should approve of the opinion of an impartial and unbiased observer who cares nothing for the partisanship or prejudices of either side. At any rate, the dark events which I predicted are already beginning to appear, and I am, even thus soon acquitted of the charge which was brought against my lecture, of abusing America, by saying that it was threatened with civil war and anarchy.

Whether from financial need or inability to retire from the limelight, the Countess of Landsfeld was soon back on the lecture platform. She prepared a new lecture, "John Bull at Home," and gave it for the first time before a standing-room audience of nearly three thousand at the Mozart Hall, 663 Broadway, on 15 December.

The lecture was largely a collection of anecdotal views of the English, but certain parts of it were revealing. Lola began by saying that she hoped that she would not be accused of abusing the English this time. She addressed the negative reaction in England to her lecture on slavery and accused the British of hypocrisy, claiming that the "coolyism" practiced in the British Empire was far more exploitive of native peoples than American slavery. At this point there is a canceled phrase in Lola's manuscript: "though mark that I declare that the *Soul* of the Negro I love, for Soul has no color."

Lola renewed her attack on the American women's movement, saying, "All that I have seen or heard in my time of this women's rights controversy does not intellectually amount to so much as Lady Mary Wortley Montagu said in England before these conventions were born. She was a genuine original *bas bleu* who took society by the nose and boxed its ears to some effect, not by boisterously trying to imitate the follies of men, in wrangling in public meetings about a great deal of abstract and nonsensical impossibilities, but by standing bravely up in her own sharp individuality and uttering her revolutionary and original ideas in words as hard as brickbats."

"John Bull at Home" was a success, and after New Year's Lola appeared again at Mozart Hall, this time to lecture on "Fashion," a modified version of "Comic Aspects of Fashion." Under the management of the Burrs again, she took her lectures on an extensive tour, opening on 25 January 1860 at the Musical Fund Hall in Philadelphia.

Once more Lola was able to draw overflowing houses almost everywhere, and critical reaction was generally flattering. In Philadelphia one critic wrote the "Fashion" lecture "is likely to place its talented author among the most competent and accomplished of living lecturers." From Maryland she sent a letter to a journalist friend back in Philadelphia, remarking that her health was bothering her again and that the chills, fever, and ague with which she made her entrance into Baltimore had made her feel "like the witches in Macbeth they were dancing in me."

In Washington she recognized another journalist friend, a man she had known in San Francisco, in her audience, which included Vice-President Breckinridge, senators, and ambassadors. She sent Chauncey Burr into the audience to ask the Californian to visit her at the conclusion of the lecture. After four years, Lola was happy to see her old friend and was eager for news of the Golden State, and she took him back to sit before a warm fire in the parlor of her suite in the National Hotel, where she rolled cigarettes and peppered him with questions about her West Coast friends. At 4:30 in the morning she finally let him go, but only after she had given him a letter of introduction to one of her contacts at the *New York Herald*, asking him to "show the Californian the elephant" and make a bohemian of him.

The tour schedule left Lola little time for rest, moving her through Pennsylvania and into Ohio, where Heman Burr arrived to take over management responsibilities from his son. In Cleveland, the *Daily Herald* printed an article claiming that Lola's real name was Betty Watson, that she had risen from dancing at penny sideshows in Ireland, and that her London debut as Lola Montez had been aborted by spectators rising and shouting, "Off, off! That won't do, Betty Watson!" The *Plain Dealer* called the *Herald*'s article "fabricated imbecility" and deemed it completely proper that "this magnificently gifted woman seeks to earn, in a praiseworthy manner, a living in this land of the free."

The Burrs were planning to take Lola through the Midwest and the South, and Lola hoped to be back in New York City by the end of March. The Midwestern winter was mild that year, but there was still plenty of unpleasant weather, which sometimes kept down the size of her crowds. On 6 March she wrote from Louisville to her friend Maria Buchanan:

> We have wended our way so far after a weary pilgrimage in the wilderness of Ohio and Indiana, and stopping at every class of town where people could squeeze out a 25 cent piece. We are *not* going down South but leave this for St. Louis tomorrow and prospect the whole of that section of the land to Chicago and environs, Detroit and environs till we retrace the homeward route, which will be at the end of next month.
>
> I have had to lecture with few exceptions *every night*—if I went South, there would not be the numerous towns there are west, and the distances are considerable between each place, so that all calculations made, it would not pay. . . .
>
> I have to lead a very monotonous life, shut up in my room in the daytime or traveling in cars and lecturing in the evenings to a lot of people that are not interesting to me—but I have a good piece of news to tell you. The Burrs are decided to get up a weekly paper in N.Y. They give me a quarter share in it and pay me $20 besides per week for services—this is a capital affair, as I do not invest a penny myself and I think it will be a better affair than the *Candy store*. I am going to write the whole history of my life in an extended form and old Burr is capable of making the best weekly in the country. I know that you will highly approve of the idea—the name is to be "The Thunderer." It shall be worthy of the name, as you will see.—The moment we arrive, as soon as possible, a first number will appear.
>
> I look forward with great pleasure to my return again to N.Y., for it is the only city in America where I prefer living. . . .
>
> I have been afflicted for 4 weeks with a most painful neuralgia affection on one side of my face, suffering great pain,—but now we have a perfect spring weather and I am much relieved. . . .
>
> The press everywhere is loud in my favor, which is very pleasant, though I don't care in reality much what they do say.

On her way from St. Louis to Chicago, Lola's tour brought her to Springfield, Illinois, on 14 March, the very day that the city's most famous lecturer, Abraham Lincoln, returned from his own successful speaking tour of the northeastern states, where his Cooper Union speech had made him a controversial national political figure. History does not record whether he joined more than four hundred of Springfield's "elite" in Cook's Hall on his first night home to hear Lola's less controversial remarks on "Comic Aspects of Fashion."

From Chicago, Lola's tour continued to Detroit, Toronto, Buffalo, Rochester, and innumerable towns in between, concluding with a single appearance on 11 April in Albany, and then she was home again in New York City. Lola was now trying to put money aside, to pay more attention to her finances, and even though her earnings from twelve weeks of lecturing did not compare with the great sums she had taken in when she was dancing, now she would husband it so that it would provide for her well in the modest life she intended to lead. Ultimately, she would simply put her affairs into Mrs. Buchanan's hands.

Lola rented a flat for herself at 15 Clinton Place (now Eighth Street) in Greenwich Village, just north of Washington Square, and lived quietly as Mrs. Heald. She had become a New Yorker; her visit to England had taught her that she felt more at home amid the financial aristocracy of the New World, with its greater tolerance for a self-made, independent woman, than she did in the rigid class structure in England. She had good friends and was happy in her church, and New York had a cosmopolitan atmosphere unknown in the rest of America's cities.

The Burrs' plan for the *Thunderer* did not materialize, but Lola kept busy. She was thinking about publishing her latest lectures, perhaps making another tour of England in 1861. The political situation, however, loomed over everything, and Lola had no illusions about what was coming: "Politically we are on the eve of a terrible disturbance between North and South," she wrote a friend in England. "One is as much at fault as the other."

To a great extent, Lola had now achieved the peace and stability that had come to mean more to her than the excitement and sensation she had enjoyed for so many years. Now she had the repose she had found in Grass Valley and in Derbyshire, but it was a repose that came from within. Her lectures had won Lola financial success, respect, and public attention, and there was every prospect that she could continue her career for years to come.

The New York summer had already turned hot at the end of June 1860; afternoon temperatures were climbing above 90 degrees, and it was approaching 80 degrees when Lola awoke on Saturday, 30 June. Shortly after rising she began to feel dizzy, and she lay back on her bed. In an instant she was paralyzed and speechless from a stroke. Her friends were called to her bedside, but they could only make her comfortable and wait to see how her condition changed. On Sunday and Monday, Lola sometimes gave signs that she recognized her friends, but on Tuesday she seemed to have slipped into a coma, and the doctors deemed it unlikely that she would survive the night.

Ships leaving that day for Europe carried the news that Lola Montez was dying, but by the Fourth of July her condition was improving. She was paralyzed on the left side and unable to speak, but by the end of the week, it was clear that the crisis had passed, and the Buchanans began to make plans to move her to their summer home and gardens in Astoria, opposite Eighty-Sixth Street in Manhattan, to convalesce.

The indomitable will that had made Lola famous was still strong, and she fought her illness as though she were going after an editor with a horsewhip. It was a daunting struggle, and by the end of August her condition was still pitiful: "Lola was costumed in a half night and half morning robe, and she sat in a pretty garden, her hollow cheeks, sunken eyes and cadaverous complexion forming a remarkable contrast to the gay flowers. She was unable to utter an intelligible word except spasmodically and after repeated effort. Her mouth was frothing like that of one in partial convulsions, and she was unconsciously wiping it as little boys do, by drawing it across the sleeve of her dress. In fact, she had the strange wild appearance and behavior of a quiet idiot, and is evidently lost to all further interest in the world around her or its affairs. And so ends her eventful history!"

But Lola's sharp mind was alive. In October, Mrs. Buchanan moved Lola back from Astoria into a room in a boarding house at 194 West Seventeenth Street, three blocks down from the Buchanan home. A widowed nurse named Margaret Hamilton was hired to be her attendant, and Lola's strength and control slowly grew. She once again was able to talk, and she could take steps with assistance. But now she was preparing for the fact that she might not recover; at the end of July, as soon as she could communicate her wishes, a will was drafted in which she left $250 to the Church of the Good Shepherd, for which she had lectured two years before, and everything else to Maria Buchanan and her son David.

In the fall of 1860, Lola had a visitor from England who was by all accounts unwelcome: her mother. Some witnesses said later that Eliza Craigie had come not out of compassion but in the hope that Lola might have a fortune to be claimed. One described her as a "cold passionless woman, who greeted and said adieu to her daughter, much as she might have made a fashionable call. She was greatly disappointed at finding Eliza without worldly wealth and visited her only twice, if I remember correctly, during her stay of two or three weeks."

The invalid probably made her mother feel anything but welcome. For years Lola had told anyone who would listen that Eliza Craigie's coldness and vanity had driven her only child to the path of sin, first by forcing her to flee into the arms of Lieutenant James and later by packing her off to England when she came to Calcutta seeking refuge from a failed marriage. After Mrs. Craigie returned to England, reportedly leaving behind a few dollars to help pay for Lola's medicine, Lola did not answer her letters. Perhaps to forestall an effort by her mother or anyone else to acquire property that could be hers, Lola executed a transfer to Isaac Buchanan of all legal interest she might still have to anything in Bavaria. With an enfeebled hand she signed herself one last time "Lola Montez, Countess of Landsfeld."

Lola's health improved rapidly throughout the fall. At last she felt ready to put herself into the service of her faith, perhaps, as she had written in her spiritual diary, "to have my terrible and fearful experience given as an awful warning to such natures as my own." She asked to be driven out to the New York Magdalen Society's refuge at Eighty-Eighth Street, where she did what she could to counsel and comfort the women who were trying to give up prostitution and regain a respected place in society. Lola believed that the society was doing good work, and she must have felt a kinship with women who suffered the same hypocritical scorn she had known and still had not entirely escaped. She told Mrs. Buchanan that rather than leave $250 to the Church of the Good Shepherd, she would like to give $300 to the Magdalen Society.

By the middle of December she was able to walk alone with little lameness, and there appeared to be hope for a full recovery. December was cold and windy, but Christmas Day was reasonably pleasant, and Lola made a holiday excursion in the open air. It proved to be a fatal mistake, for she quickly came down with pneumonia. Lola, whose lungs had always been weak, knew this was the end.

She asked Mrs. Buchanan to summon her minister, the Reverend Francis Lister Hawks of Calvary Episcopal Church, to help her prepare for death. Just two years earlier she had inveighed against the Episcopal bishop for his reported opposition to her benefit lecture for the Church of the Good Shepherd, but now all animosities were forgotten, and it was said that Bishop Potter himself called on Lola in her sickroom. Other friends who called on her during her final days found that the disease had made her large eyes stand out with even more magical beauty from her ravaged face. Around the room she had placed quotations of scripture in large characters so she would constantly have words of faith before her.

On his first visit to Lola's sickroom Hawks picked up her well-thumbed Bible, and it fell open to the story of Christ's forgiveness of the Magdalen in the house of Simon. Hawks spoke to her of "Christ's gentle pity and pardon" for that woman, and Lola exclaimed, "Ah, but she loved much. *Can I love enough?*" In the course of his visits to Lola, Hawks was moved by her fervor, her faith, and her desire to free her heart from sin: "She was a woman of genius, highly accomplished, and of great natural *eloquence*. I listened to her sometimes with admiration, as, with tears streaming from her eyes, her right hand uplifted, and her singularly expressive features (her keen black [*sic*] eye especially) speaking almost as plainly as her tongue, she would dwell upon Christ, and the almost incredible truth that He could show mercy to such a vile sinner as she felt herself to have been, until I would feel that *she* was the preacher, and not I.

"When she was near her end and could not speak, I asked her to let me know by a sign whether her soul was at peace, and she still felt that Christ would save her. She fixed her eyes on mine and nodded her head affirmatively."

As her lungs failed, she motioned for a friend to sit beside her and read from the Bible, and with her hand resting on the book, listening again to the words of hope, Lola Montez left on the last of her many journeys. It was Thursday, 17 January 1861.

29

EPILOGUE

One of Lola's friends went to Brooklyn the next day, in the midst of a winter storm, to pick out a plot in spacious Green-Wood Cemetery; the plot was on a hillside overlooking a small lake. Lola's coffin was brought down Seventeenth Street to the Buchanans' house, and there, among Lola's closest friends, the Reverend Hawks read the Episcopal funeral service early on Saturday morning. The news of Lola's death had been kept within a small circle of her friends so that the press and the curious would not disrupt her funeral, and it was only as the mournful procession made its way across Manhattan to the Brooklyn ferry that word began to spread that she was dead.

The party accompanied the coffin across the East River and followed it the two and a half miles to the fresh grave in the frozen earth. There the Reverend Hawks read the simple committal service, adding, "In the course of a long experience as a Christian minister I do not think I ever saw deeper penitence and humility, more real contrition of soul, and more bitter self-reproach, than in this poor woman." Even the hardened sexton was seen to wipe away a tear.

On Monday most newspapers published long obituaries, mixing fact and a great deal of fiction, much of it Lola's own creation, in recounting her adventures. "Her most eccentric actions were speedily reported," wrote the *New York Post*, "but her many acts of generosity, especially to poor people—and there are several of this class in New York who can bear testimony to this — were known only to the recipients of her careless bounty."

Those who knew her best spoke most affectionately of her. The author Charles Godfrey Leland, a friend of Lola's for years, wrote in his long obituary in *Frank Leslie's Illustrated Newspaper,* "She had many warm friends of many years' standing, with whom she never quarreled. She was generous to a fault, and as excitable to pity and kindly sympathies as to anger. Her nature was a stream which ran brilliantly until the depths were stirred. . . . Lola simply erred from a fiery and ungovernable temper. Few women living were so incapable of anything like a deliberately evil action or of calmly injuring another."

The *New York Times,* which had never been one of Lola's great admirers, called her "generous and high-tempered to a fault: irritable, too, as such natures are apt to be, but forgiving and affectionate. Her natural talents were of the highest order, her accomplishments manifold, and, in some respects, marvelous."

A few had nothing good to say about Lola. The *Albion* stiffly declared, "We do not think it desirable to narrate the adventures of unfortunates of her class, however prominent the position they may assume." And the *Irish American Weekly* was scornful of this daughter of Ireland: "Her life was neither creditable to her native land nor useful to society, so we choose not to inquire further into it."

In Europe, some newspapers that had run obituaries for her in the previous summer, when the premature news of her death had arrived, said nothing now. Others ran such headlines as "Lola Montez is Dead — Really Dead this Time" or "Lola Montez Dead Again!" Most papers contented themselves with republishing obituaries from the American press, but London's *Daily Telegraph* indulged in an enormous and scornful summary of "a strange and melancholy career," concluding, "Our involuntary reflection is, upon hearing of her abject death, that it was no unnatural termination to a life in which every brilliant hour of infamy had been purchased."

Most curious of all was a letter to the editor of London's *Morning Post* written by Dr. George Harrison, a fellow of the Royal College of Surgeons of England, on the very day news reached London of Lola's death stating, "Sir: Lola Montez having previously had a severe attack of paralysis, died of pneumonia, at New York, on the 17th ult. Her age, I believe, was 40; and she latterly subsisted entirely on charity, which I was selected to dispense."

In fact, Lola had two savings accounts totaling $1,247, a respectable sum in 1861. As she had requested on her deathbed, $300 was given to the New York Magdalen Society. The rest was used to pay her medical bills and funeral expenses and to purchase a white marble headstone in Green-Wood Cemetery reading, "Mrs. Eliza Gilbert, died January 17, 1861, Æ. 42." Perhaps it is only fitting for a woman who had so much difficulty telling the truth that her grave is marked with a name she never bore and that, after Lola spent most of her life lying to make herself younger, her tombstone declares her older than she was.

In Munich, seventy-four-year-old King Ludwig heard the news of the death of his Lolitta. In the thirteen years since he had last seen her there had been other loves for him, but nothing to compare with the hold she had had over his heart and mind. Queen Therese had died four years earlier of cholera, and her loss had been terrible for him. But he had never forgotten Lolitta. All of her letters to him and all of his letters to her were filed away with hundreds of other documents of her stay in Munich. Ambassador Wendland had continued to send him newspaper clippings of the adventures of Lola Montez, and now the ambassador sent him the obituaries of Lola Montez from the New York newspapers.

In April, one of the last documents for the Lolitta archive arrived in Munich. It was a small black-bordered letter from America.

Sire,
   In early childhood, having been school companion in Scotland with a young girl who I little thought would ever have requested me on her death bed to write to your Majesty.... She often spoke to me of your Majesty, and of your kindness and benevolence, which she deeply felt—And wished me to tell you she had changed her life and companions.
   And now I redeem the promise I made to the late Mme. Lola Montez, known to me as Eliza Gilbert, and to add that she wished me to let you know she retained a sincere regard for your great kindness to the end of her life.
   She died a true penitent, relying on her Savior for pardon and acceptance, triumphing only in His merit....
   I have the Honor to be your Majesty's Obedt. & Humble Sert.
   Maria E. Buchanan

The king took up his pen and, struggling with the English language, wrote his reply:

Mistress Maria Buchanan,
   With a great satisfaction I was hearing the repentance of L. M. of her

former behavior, and I'm very fond of it that she has given the commission to inform me. It is a great consolation to hear her dying as a Christian. L. M. was a much distinguished lady. My sincere thanks for your kind letter. . . .

Your much affect.,

Lewis

Perhaps Ludwig was even able to manage an ironic smile a few months later when a second letter arrived from Mrs. Buchanan, this one suggesting that the king who had lavished money on his beloved might wish to pay to erect a fence around her grave. Mrs. Buchanan received no reply.

Among the documents in Ludwig's archive were his letters to Papon, which the very strange marquis returned to him voluntarily in 1852 through Ambassador Wendland. Papon claimed to have entered a Dominican monastery and was calling himself Brother Antoine. Brother Antoine suggested that the king express in a monetary fashion his gratitude for this relinquishment of the blackmail material, but Ludwig preferred not to tempt the new brother from his vow of poverty. According to one source, Brother Antoine, whose health soon forced him to forswear the joys of monastic life, eventually went into business insuring Catholic churches in France against theft of their valuables. To justify an increase in premiums, Papon created losses by stealing the insured items himself, for which, it is said, the law took serious notice. But when the court decreed his punishment at ten years of hard labor, it was forced to sentence Papon in absentia.

King Ludwig's last years were not happy ones, but he persevered with his gritty determination. He lived to see King Max II, his son and successor, die, to be succeeded by King Ludwig II, his teenage grandson. Ludwig II promptly created a scandal by becoming obsessed beyond all reason with an arrogant and extravagant favorite—not a dancer but a composer, Lola's old acquaintance Richard Wagner, who also was forced to flee Munich, much to the distress of his royal patron.

The old king also lived to see Bavaria's military humiliation at the hands of Bismarck's Prussia in 1866. His isolation became ever greater as his hearing failed almost entirely and his friends, contemporaries, and more of his children preceded him in death. Yet his popularity grew with time; the Bavarians forgot his willfulness and his obsession with the Spanish woman, and they remembered the man who devoted his limitless energies to the good of his country, who had transformed Munich. King Ludwig had the rare honor of being present when a grand equestrian statue of him, erected by his faithful Munichers, was unveiled in the Ludwigstraße on his seventy-sixth birthday as thousands cheered. His bronze image still rides forth, lifting its hand in benediction over his city. He died in Nice on 29 February 1868.

Thousands of miles away, in Schenectady, New York, another of Lola's lovers is immortalized in bronze. Thanks to money from King Ludwig, Fritz Peißner had found refuge by emigrating to America, eventually joining the faculty of Union College as a professor of languages. He married an older professor's daughter, fathered three children, became a respected member of the faculty, and published a number of language textbooks that were quite successful. The death of an infant daughter in 1858 seems to have stirred Peißner to the same sort of personal religious quest that Lola was pursuing.

When the Civil War broke out, Professor Peißner became Colonel Peißner, leading a volunteer regiment that included many German immigrants fighting to preserve the Union. The colonel, eager to show the mettle of his men, requested that they be moved forward to the action. Their baptism by fire was a surprise attack on their position at the Battle of Chancellorsville, on 2 May 1863. Peißner was riding up and down the line, rallying his men to resist the Confederates, when he was shot from his horse; he died on the spot. He was thirty-seven years old. The members of the Union College Class of 1863 donated a bust of Lola's lover in his colonel's uniform to the school, inscribed "Accomplished Scholar, Beloved Friend, Heroic Soldier."

Lola's other notorious admirer in Munich, Lieutenant Friedrich Nußbammer, also came to an early and tragic end, but without heroics. Following his banishment from Munich he was placed on inactive duty with a meager pension and forbidden to engage in any trade or business. His repeated efforts to return to active duty or to take a job were invariably rebuffed. Living in internal exile with no hope of escaping his fate, Nußbammer finally went mad. He died at the age of thirty-nine in an asylum.

The other central figures in Lola's life slowly disappeared, too. Patrick Purdy Hull had suffered a paralytic stroke just a year after Lola left California, and he died six months later at the age of thirty-six. Her lover Lieutenant Lennox had returned to duty in India only to die a few months later of a fever at age twenty-three.

Only Thomas James, her first and only legal husband, survived her. Captain James was apparently no more popular with his fellow officers than he had been with his wife. Although most officers of the Indian Army received a new assignment every two or three years, James spent nearly fifteen years consigned to unofficial exile from his regiment at a remote outpost, ending his service with a reprimand because he had kept the books so badly that a substantial sum of money could not be accounted for.

Nevertheless, at retirement James was promoted to major and given an honorary appointment as a lieutenant-colonel so that he could enjoy a larger pension and be called "colonel" the rest of his life. The new major luckily retired to London just before the Sepoy Rebellion erupted to ravage the subcontinent and change the character of British India forever.

James seems to have occupied himself in retirement with his first loves, horses and shooting. He adopted a young girl whom he turned over to his spinster sister Wilhelmina to raise in Cheltenham. A few years after his return to England, when he was in his mid-fifties, James met a young woman with an illegitimate daughter, and he promptly began to father his own children by her, finally marrying her on New Year's Day 1870, when he was nearly sixty-three and she was pregnant with their third child. Just over a year later he died of a stroke in their home in the Bayswater district of London.

Lola's mother lived about a mile away, in Mrs. Smith's Boarding House at 36 Queen's Road (now Queensway). Mrs. Craigie was living a comfortable middle-class life as a retired military widow, keeping in touch with the Craigie family and with her own niece and nephew in Ireland, as well as enjoying a small circle of London friends. On the chill evening of 15 November 1875, passersby noticed dark smoke pouring from a first-floor window of the boarding house. A police constable rushed to the door of the room, but it was locked from the inside. After some hesitation, he and some other men broke it down.

Inside the rescuers found Eliza Craigie unconscious on the carpet, the clothes burned from her body; apparently her skirts had been ignited by her heating fire. The burned woman was carried out to a cab and rushed to St. Mary's Hospital, but she died without regaining consciousness six days later, aged seventy. The newspaper obituaries were unable even to get her name right, much less identify her as the mother of Lola Montez.

In death, Lola passed from being one of the most famous women in the world into the realm of legend. She had done so much to confuse the historical record that it is no surprise that the stories written after her death usually bore no greater relation to the facts of her life than her own accounts had. As the years passed, Lola became a popular subject for novelists and playwrights, even for composers of musicals, ballets, and operas. Lola Montez appeared as subject or character in a number of motion pictures, culminating in Max Ophüls's 1955 film *Lola Montes*, based on a French novel. The film has become a cinema classic, though the Lola it portrays displays a good deal more Gallic reserve and calculation than the original demonstrated.

The feminist movement has rarely regarded Lola as one of its heroines, and Lola never saw herself as a feminist. Lola always saw life's events in personal and specific terms rather than abstract and general ones; and though she was struggling to enjoy many of the same freedoms sought by feminists then and now, Lola fought primarily to free her own life from society's prejudices and restrictions, and only coincidentally was she blazing trails other women could follow.

Lola Montez did demonstrate that a woman of intelligence, daring, charm, and enormous will could succeed far beyond the constricted role conventionally allowed to women; and in this lies her contribution to feminism, that she defied scorn, ridicule, outrage, and all the obstacles society placed in her path, achieving fame and success on her own terms as a dancer, actress, lecturer, and author. The example of her life exhorts everyone to dare to live their dreams.

And yet in the end she came to realize that the egotism, vanity, and willfulness that had enabled her to trample bitter opposition to her as an ambitious, independent woman also caused her to ride roughshod over everyone around her. Her effort to learn humility, altruism, and piety was as immoderate and erratic as all her other enthusiasms; but if we can believe the memories of the friends who knew her best and the testimony of the minister who reported that on her deathbed she felt confident of God's acceptance of her efforts, Lola at last triumphed over even her own nature.

Her white tombstone still stands alone on the little knoll in Green-Wood Cemetery, the epitaph now illegible. If Lola at the last had chosen a final message to be engraved there for posterity, it might have been one of Christian faith and hope. But perhaps she best summed up the true motto of her life in her dedication to *The Arts of Beauty*:

TO
ALL MEN AND WOMEN
OF EVERY LAND
WHO ARE NOT AFRAID OF *THEMSELVES*,
WHO TRUST SO MUCH IN THEIR OWN SOULS THAT
THEY DARE TO STAND UP IN THE MIGHT OF THEIR
OWN INDIVIDUALITY
TO MEET THE TIDAL CURRENTS OF THE WORLD.

BIBLIOGRAPHY

Principal Manuscript Sources

GERMANY

Bayerisches Hauptstaatsarchiv, Munich
 Abteilung II: Nineteenth and twentieth centuries
 Abteilung III: Geheimes Hausarchiv
 Abteilung IV: Kriegsarchiv
Bayerisches Staatsarchiv (Oberbayern), Munich
Bayerische Staatsbibliothek, Munich
Stadtbibliothek, Monacensia Sammlung, Munich
Württemburgisches Hauptstaatsarchiv, Stuttgart

GREAT BRITAIN

British Library, India Office Library and Records, London
Greater London Record Office, London
Public Record Office, Kew

UNITED STATES

Harvard Theatre Collection, Cambridge

Selected Printed Sources

Adalbert, Prinz von Bayern. *Nymphenburg und seine Bewohner.* Munich: Prestel, 1949.

Albert Torrellas, A. *Como las hojas. Lola Montez, la amada del Rey Poeta.* Barcelona: Sociedad General de Liberia, 1944.

Albrecht, Dieter. "König Ludwig I. und Gottlieb Freiherr von Thon-Dittmer." In Andreas Kraus, ed., *Land und Reich, Stamm und Nation. Festgabe für Max Spindler zum 90. Geburtstag.* Munich: Beck, 1984.

Allgemeine deutsche Real-Encyklopädie für die gebildeten Stände, Conversations-Lexicon. Leipzig: Brockhaus, 1853.

Die allgemeine Studenten- und Volksbewegung in München am 8., 9., 10., 11., und 12. Februar 1848. Munich: Deschlen, [1848].

Anfang und Ende der Lola Montez in Bayern. Wahrheitsgetreue Schilderung der Zeit von Oktober 1846 bis Februar 1848. Munich: Kaiser, 1848.

"Aufzeichnungen eines Achtundvierzigers." *Österreichisches Rundschau* 16:57–63.

Augustin-Thierry, A. *Lola Montès. Favorite Royale.* Paris: Editions Bernard Grasset, 1936.

"Aus den Tagen der Lola Montez." *Neue Deutsche Rundschau* 1901:913–944.

"Der Beherrscher eines Kleinstaates." *Gartenlaube*, 1866: 591–595.

Bericht aus München über die Ereignisse des 9. 10. 11. Februar 1848. [Munich]: Henzel, [1848].

Beyer, L. [pseud.?]. *Glorreiches Leben und Taten der edelen Sennora Dolores.* Leipzig: Weller, 1847.

Blainey, Ann. *The Farthing Poet. A Biography of Richard Hengist Horne.* London: Longmans, 1968.

Blake, Charles. *An Historical Account of the Providence Stage.* Providence: Whitney, 1868.

Boisserée, Sulpiz. *Tagebücher.* Vol. 4. Darmstadt: Eduard Roether Verlag, 1985.

Bouchardon, Pierre. *Le duel du chemin de la Favorite.* Paris: Albin Michel, 1927.

Bray-Steinburg, Otto Graf von. *Denkwürdigkeiten aus meinem Leben.* Leipzig, 1901.

Bülow, Eduard von. *Novellen.* Stuttgart: Cotta, 1846.

Bülow, Hans von. *Briefe und Schriften.* Leipzig, 1904.

[Cannon, Michael]. *Lola Montes. The Tragic Story of a "Liberated Woman."* Melbourne: Heritage, 1973.

Chorley, Henry. *Modern German Music.* 1854; reprint, New York: Da Capo Press, 1973.

Chroust, Anton, ed. *Gesandtschaftsberichte aus München 1814–1848.*

   I. Abteilung: Die Berichte der französischen Gesandten. Munich: C. H. Beck, 1936.

   II. Abteilung: Die Berichte der österreichischen Gesandten. Munich: C. H. Beck, 1942.

   III. Abteilung: Die Berichte der preußischen Gesandten. Munich: Biederstein, 1951.

Cleland, Robert, ed. *Apron Full of Gold: The Letters of Mary Jane Megquier from San Francisco, 1849–1856.* San Marino, Calif.: Huntington Library, 1949.

"Colonel Elias Peissner." *Union College Magazine*, March 1867.

Corti, Egon Cäsar Conte. *Ludwig I. von Bayern.* Munich: Bruckmann, 1937.

Cotton, Julian James. *List of Inscriptions on Tombs or Monuments in Madras.* Madras: Superintendent of Government Press, 1905.

Coyne, J. Stirling. *Pas de Fascination: or, Catching a Governor! Originally Licensed by the Lord Chamberlain, and Performed at the Theatre Royal, Haymarket, under the Title Lola Montes: or, A Countess for an Hour.* London, [1848?].

Craemer, J. L. *Königs-Historien, Teil III, Residenz Geheimnisse.* Munich, 1896.

Criticisms on the performances of Harry Jackson, the Celebrated Comedian from the Sydney, Melbourne, Adelaide, Hobarttown, etc. Newspapers. Auckland, 1857.

Crowe, Catherine. *The Night Side of Nature.* London: Newby, 1848.

Cubitt, Geoffrey. *The Jesuit Myth. Conspiracy Theory and Politics in 19th Century France.* Oxford: Clarendon, 1993.

Danton, George H. "Elias Peissner." *Monatsheft für Deutschen Unterricht,* November 1940: 314–324.

Darling, Amanda [pseud.]. *Lola Montez.* New York: Stein and Day, 1972.

D'Auvergne, Edmund B. *Lola Montez: An Adventuress of the Forties.* London: T. Werner Laurie, 1909.

Dirr, Pius. "Sturmbewegte Zeiten." *Das Bayernland* 37 (1926): 653–664.

Disraeli, Benjamin. *Lord Beaconfield's Correspondence with His Sister 1832–1852.* London: John Murray, 1886.

Dobmayer, Ignaz [pseud.]. *See* Erdmann, Paul.

Dürck-Kaulbach, Josefa. *Erinnerungen an Wilhelm von Kaulbach und sein Haus.* Munich: Delphin, 1917.

[Dyer, Heman]. *The Story of a Penitent: Lola Montez.* New York: Protestant Episcopal Society for the Promotion of Evangelical Knowledge, 1867. (Often wrongly attributed to Francis L. Hawks.)

Ecquevilley, Victor d'. *Témoin dans un duel ou La verité sur le procès Victor d'Ecquevilley.* Frankfurt am Main, 1847.

Eden, Emily. *Up the Country.* London: Oxford University Press, 1930.

Erdmann, Paul [pseud.]. *Lola Montez und die Jesuiten. Eine Darstellung der jungsten Ereignisse in München.* Hamburg: Hoffmann und Campe, 1847. This book was originally published in Berlin by Herman Friedländer under the pseudonym Ignaz Dobmayer with the title *Zustände und Ereignisse in München im Jahre 1847.* The second version appears to be more widely distributed.

Farley, Porter. "The Day Peissner Fell." *Union College Alumni Monthly,* February 1914.

Fitzball, Edward. *Thirty-Five Years of a Dramatic Author's Life.* London: T. C. Newby, 1859.

Foley, Doris. *The Divine Eccentric. Lola Montez and the Newspapers.* Los Angeles: Westernlore Press, 1969.

Fournier, Alfred. "Lola Montez. Ein geheimer Bericht über Bayern im Jahre 1847." *Deutsche Revue,* August 1902: 214–230.

[Francis, George Henry]. "The King of Bavaria, Munich, and Lola Montez." *Fraser's Magazine,* January 1848: 89–104.

Fuchs, Eduard. *Ein vormärzliches Tanzidyll. Lola Montez in der Karikatur.* Berlin: Ernst Frensdorff, 1904.

Gash, Norman. *Sir Robert Peel.* London: Longman, 1970.

Genealogisches Taschenbuch der deutschen gräflichen Häuser auf des Jahr 1847. Gotha, 1847.

Giardina, Roberto. *Lola Montez. Ballerina e Avventuriera. La vita di Eliza Dolores Gilbert.* Milan: Rusconi, 1992.

Goldberg, Isaac. *Queen of Hearts. The Passionate Pilgrimage of Lola Montez.* New York: John Day, 1936.

Gollwitzer, Heinz. *Ein Staatsmann des Vormärz: Karl von Abel 1788–1859.* Göttingen: Vanderhoeck & Ruprecht, 1992.

———. *Ludwig I von Bayern. Königtum im Vormärz. Eine politische Biographie.* Munich: Süddeutscher Verlag, 1986.

Government of Bihar. *List of Pre-Mutiny Inscriptions in Christian Burial Grounds in the Patna District.* Patna, 1936.

Gower, F. Levenson. *Bygone Years.* London, 1905.

Guest, Ivor. *Romantic Ballet in Paris.* London: Pilman, 1966.

Hacker, Rupert. *Die Beziehungen zwischen Bayern und dem Hl. Stuhl in der Regierungszeit Ludwigs I.* Tübingen: Max Niemeyer, 1967.

Hase, Ulrika. *Joseph Stieler.* Munich: Prestel Verlag, 1971.

Hauser, Miska. *Aus dem Wanderbuch eines österreichischen Virtuosen. Briefe aus Californien, Südamerika, und Australien, gesammelt und herausgegeben von S. Hauser.* Leipzig: Herbig, 1859.

Hellerstein, Erna, Leslie Hume, and Karen Offen, eds. *Victorian Women.* Stanford: Stanford University Press, 1981.

Hingston, Edward P. *The Genial Showman.* London: John Camden, n.d.

Hodson, V. C. P. *List of the Officers of the Bengal Army 1758–1834.* London: Constable, 1927–1947.

Holdredge, Helen. *The Woman in Black. The Life of Lola Montez.* New York: Putnam, 1955.

Horn, O. *Chronik der Palatia. Zur fünfzigjährigen Jubelfeier des Corps Palatia.* Munich: J. Rösl, 1863.

Horstman, Allen. *Victorian Divorce.* New York: St. Martin's Press, 1985.

Hummel, Karl-Joseph. *München in der Revolution von 1848/49.* Göttingen: Vandenhoeck & Ruprecht, 1987.

Hutchings, Allis M. "The Most Famous Vamp Who Ever Lived." *Hobbies,* April 1945.

Ikonnikov, Nicolas, ed. *La Noblesse de la Russie.* Paris, 1959.

Jungmann-Stadler, Franziska. "Johann Nepomuk Wilhelm Freiherr von Pechmann." *Das Bayernland* 91, no. 3 (September 1989): 67–71.

K. G. M. [Kressner, General Major Erwin?]. "Das erste Auftreten von Lola Montez in Deutschland." *Velhagen und Klasing's Monatsheft* 1901 (February): 677–683.

Kinyon, Edmund. *The Northern Mines.* Grass Valley-Nevada City, [1949].

Kristl, Wilhelm Lukas. *Lola, Ludwig und der General*. Pfaffenhofen/Ilm: Ludwig, 1979.

Kurz, Ferdinand. *Der Anteil der Münchener Studentenschaft an den Unruhen der Jahre 1847 und 1848*. Munich: Academischer Verlag, [1893].

Leland, Charles Godfrey. *Memoirs*. New York: D. Appleton, 1893.

Leman, Walter. *Memories of an Old Actor*. San Francisco: A. Roman, 1886.

Lettre à Mr. A. P. à Nyon pour faire suite aux Offres et Ménaces. Geneva: Ramboz, 1849.

Lewald, Fanny. *Zwölf Bilder nach dem Leben*. Berlin: Janke, 1888.

Lola Montès. Aventures de la célèbre danseuse raconté par elle-même avec son portrait et facsimile de son écriture. Paris: Bauruche, 1847.

Lola Montez, Gräfin von Landsfeld. Munich: Deschlen, 1848.

Lola Montez or A Reply to the "Private History and Memoirs" of that celebrated Lady, recently published by the Marquis Papon. New York, 1851. (Sometimes attributed to a Johnson Richardson.)

Ludwig I, King of Bavaria. *Gedichte*. Pfaffenhofen: Ludwig, 1980.

Lumley, Benjamin. *Reminiscences of the Opera*. London: Hurst & Blackett, 1864.

Madras Almanac. Madras: Asylum Press, various years.

Maillier, Charles. *Trois Journalistes Drouais: Brisset, Dujarier, Bure*. Paris: Promotion et Edition, 1968.

Malmesbury, James Howard Harris, 3rd Earl of. *Memoirs of an Ex-Minister. An Autobiography of the Rt. Hon. Earl of Malmesbury*. London: Longmans, Green, 1884.

Mann, Golo. *Ludwig I, König von Bayern*. Schaftlach: Oreos, 1989.

Maretzek, Max. *Revelations of an Opera Manager in 19th Century America*. 1855; reprint, New York: Dover Publications, 1968.

Massett, Stephen. *"Drifting About" or What "Jeems Pipes of Pipesville" Saw and Did*. New York: G. W. Carlton, 1863.

Mirecourt, Eduard de [pseud. of Charles Jacquot]. *Les Contemporains. Parte 78, Lola Montès*. Paris: J. P. Roret, 1857.

Mola oder Tanz und Weltgeschichte. Leipzig: Ernst Keil, 1847.

Montez, Lola. *L'Arte de la Beauté*, etc. Paris, 1862.

———. *Anecdotes of Love. Being a true account of the most remarkable events connected with the history of love, all ages and among all nations*. New York: Dick & Fitzgerald, 1859.

———. *The Arts of Beauty or Secrets of a Lady's Toilet with Hints to Gentlemen on the Art of Fascinating*. New York: Dick & Fitzgerald, 1858.

———. *Lectures of Lola Montez including her Autobiography*. New York: Rudd & Carlton, 1858.

———. *Memoiren der Lola Montez*. Berlin: C. Schultzel, 1851; reprint, Frankfurt am Main: Zweitausendeins, 1986.

———. *Memoiren von Lola Montez, Gräfin von Landsfeld, aus dem Französischen übertragen von Ludwig Fort*. Grimma: Verlag des Verlags-Comptoirs, 1851 (vols. 43, 44, and 83, ser. 5, *Europaische Bibliothek der neuen belletristischen Literatur*).

Moore, Lilian. "George Washington Smith." *Dance Index* 4 (1945): 88–135.

Moreton de Chabrillan, Celeste Mogador de. *Un Deuil au Bout du Monde.* Paris: Librairie Nouvelle, 1877.

Moscheles, Ignatz. *Recent Music and Musicians.* New York: Henry Holt, 1875.

Moulin-Eckart, Richard. *Hans von Bülow.* Munich: Rosl, 1921.

Mourot, Suzanne. *This Was Sydney.* Sydney: Ure Smith, 1969.

Müller, Karl Alexander. *Am Rand der Geschichte.* Munich: Carl Hanser, 1957.

Das Nachtlager in Blutenburg, romantisches Schauspiel aus dem 19ten Jahrhundert in mehreren Aufzügen. [Munich, 1848].

[Oettinger, Eduard M.]. *Mollalontez.* Leipzig: Philipp Reclam Jr., 1847.

Ostini, Fritz. *Wilhelm von Kaulbach.* Bielefeld: Velhagen & Klasing, 1906.

Ottomeyer, Hans, ed. *Biedermeyers Glück und Ende. Die gestörte Idylle 1815–1848.* Munich: Hugendubel, 1987.

Papon, Auguste. *Lola Montès. Mémoires accompagné de lettres intimes de SM le roi de Bavière et de Lola Montès.* Nyon: J. Desoche, 1849.

Papon, Auguste, and others. *Lola Montez: Memoiren in Begleitung vertrauter Briefe des Königs von Bayern und Lola Montez.* Stuttgart: J. Schieble, 1849.

Phillips, Catherine Coffin. *Portsmouth Plaza. The Cradle of San Francisco.* San Francisco: John Henry Nash, 1932.

Plötz, Johann von. *Der verwunschene Prinz, Schwank in drei Aufzugen.* Munich, n.d.

Polksi Slownik Biograficzny. Krakow, 1935.

Praag, Marinus Maurits van. *Lola en Ludwig.* 's Gravenhage, 1962.

Pudelik, Janina. "The Warsaw Ballet Under the Directorships of Maurice Pion and Filippo Taglioni, 1832–1853." *Dance Chronicle* 11, no. 2 (1988): 219–273.

Q. *You Have Heard of Them.* New York: Redfield, 1854.

Rauh, Reinhold. *Lola Montez. Die königliche Mätresse.* Munich: Wilhelm Heyne Verlag, 1992.

Rogers, Andy. *A Hundred Years of Rip and Roarin' Rough and Ready.* Rough and Ready, Calif., 1952.

Ross, Ishbel. *The Uncrowned Queen. Life of Lola Montez.* New York: Harper & Row, 1972.

Sala, George A. *The Life and Adventures of George Sala.* New York: Scribner's Sons, 1895.

Schiller, Herbert, ed. *Briefe an Cotta, Von Vormärz bis Bismarck, 1833–1863.* Stuttgart: Cotta, 1934.

Schmeller, Johann Andreas. *Tagebücher 1801–1859.* Munich, 1954–1956.

Schmidt, Berthold, ed. *Die Reussen. Genealogie des Gesamthauses Reuß.* Schleiz: F. Webers Nachfolger, 1903.

Schorn, Karl. *Lebenserinnerungen.* Bonn: P. Hanstein, 1898.

Seitz, Max. "Die Februar- und Märzunruhen in München 1848." *Oberbayerisches Archiv für vaterländische Geschichte* 78 (1953): 1–104.

Seoighe, Mainchin. *The Story of Kilmallock.* Cill Mocheallog, 1987.

Sepp, Johann. *Ludwig Augustus, König von Bayern.* Schaffenhausen: Hurter, 1869.

Shoemaker, Samuel M. *Calvary Church, Yesterday and Today.* New York, 1936.

Sigma. "Lola Montez w Warszawie." *Tygodnik Illustrowany*, 1912, no. 21:409.

Simon, Ludwik. "L'extraordinaire aventure de Lola Montez." *Archives internationales de la danse*, October 1935, 133–135.

Spindler, Max. *Erbe und Verpflichtung. Aufsätze und Vorträge zur bayerischen Geschichte.* Munich, 1966.

———. "Die Politische Wendung von 1847/48 in Bayern." In Otto Schottenloher, ed., *Bayern, Staat und Kirche, Land und Reich.* Munich, [1961].

Stern, Madeleine B. *Purple Passage. The Life of Mrs. Frank B. Leslie.* Norman: University of Oklahoma Press, 1953.

Thiersch, Justus. *Carl Thiersch. Sein Leben.* Leipzig, 1922.

"Trial for Murder in France—Lola Montez." *American Law Journal*, July 1848.

Um Lola Montez. Blätter aus dem Kieler Theatermuseum. Kiel, 1930.

[Vandam, Albert D.]. *An Englishman in Paris.* New York: D. Appleton, 1892.

Varnhagen von Ense, K. H. *Tagebücher.* Bern: Lang, 1972.

[Vogt, Karl-Wilhelm]. *Lola Montez mit ihrem Anhange und Münchens Bürger und Studenten.* Munich, 1848.

[Vogt, Karl-Wilhelm?]. *Das Nachtlager in Blutenburg oder der Lola Montez letztes Verweilen in Münchens Nähe.* [Munich, 1848].

Wagner, Cosima. *Die Tagebücher.* Munich: R. Piper, 1976–1978.

Wagner, Richard. *Mein Leben.* Munich: Wilhelm Goldmann Verlag, 1983.

Walker, Alan. *Franz Liszt. The Virtuoso Years.* New York: Knopf, 1983.

Wernitz, Axel. "Lasaulx und die vorrevolutionäre Münchener Szene im Februar 1847." *Oberbayerisches Archiv für vaterländische Geschichte* 93 (1971): 185–189.

Whiting, Lillian. *Kate Field. A Record.* Boston: Little, Brown, 1900.

Wilmes, Jacqueline, and Jacques Prezelin. *Lola Montez. Pavane pour un roi poète.* Lausanne: Rencontre, 1967.

Withers, William Branwell. *History of Ballarat.* Ballarat: Niven, 1887.

Wolf, Jos. Heinrich. *Geschichtliche Walhalla der großen Fest- und Versöhnungs Woche zwischen König und Volk in München vom 6. bis 13. März 1848.* Munich, 1848.

Wyndham, Horace. *The Magnificent Montez. From Courtesan to Convert.* New York: Hillman-Curl, [1936?].

Xylander, R., and C. von Sutner. *Geschichte des 1. Feldartillerie Regiments, König Regent Luitpold.* Berlin: Mittler, 1911.

Zuber, Karl-Heinz. *Der "Fürst Proletarier." Ludwig von Oettingen-Wallerstein.* Munich: Beck, 1878.

ABBREVIATIONS

The following abbreviations are used in the notes:

AN   Archivist's Number
BAM   File RA 16177, Bayerisches Staatsarchiv (Oberbayern), Munich
BHS   Bayerisches Hauptstaatsarchiv, Munich, Abteilung II, Nineteenth and Twentieth Centuries
BSB   Bayerische Staatsbibliothek, Munich
CKL   Corti, Egon Cäsar Conte. *Ludwig I. von Bayern.*
FDE   Foley, Doris. *The Divine Eccentric.*
FGB   Chroust, Anton, ed. *Gesandtschaftsberichte aus München 1814–1848. I. Abteilung. Die Berichte der französischen Gesandten. Band V.*
GKL   Gollwitzer, Heinz. *Ludwig I. von Bayern.*
GHA   Bayerisches Hauptstaatsarchiv, Munich, Abteilung III, Geheimes Hausarchiv
IOBL   India Office Library and Records, British Library, London
JN   Journals of Sir Jasper Nicholls, India Office Library and Records, British Library, London, MSS Eur. F175
JSP   Jungmann-Stadler, Franziska. "Johann Nepomuk Wilhelm Freiherr von Pechmann."
JVJ   *James v. James*, File of the Consistory Court of London, Greater London Record Office, in Accession 73.77
KA   Bayerisches Hauptstaatsarchiv, Munich, Abteilung IV, Kriegsarchiv
KAM   Kurz, Ferdinand. *Der Anteil der Münchener Studentenschaft an den Unruhen.*

411

KL	King Ludwig I of Bavaria
KLA	King Ludwig I. Archiv in the Bayerische Staatsbibliothek, Munich
KLL	Kristl, Wilhelm Lukas. *Lola, Ludwig und der General.*
LM	Lola Montez
LML	Montez, Lola. *Lectures of Lola Montez Including Her Autobiography.*
MAR	Müller, Karl Alexander. *Am Rand der Geschichte.*
MD	Untitled anonymous diary transcript, 4°Mon 2660, Monacensia Sammlung, Stadtbibliothek, Munich
MEM	Montez, Lola. *Memoiren von Lola Montez, Gräfin von Landsfeld, aus dem französischen übertragen von Ludwig Fort* (Grimma).
MSB	Letter of KL to LM, 8 February 1849, Z-200/1936/37, Monacensia Sammlung, Stadtbibliothek, Munich
NL	Nachlaß Ludwig I. in GHA
ÖGB	Chroust, Anton, ed. *Gesandtschaftsberichte aus München 1814–1848. II. Abteilung: Die Berichte der österreichischen Gesandten.* Band III.
PGB	Chroust, Anton, ed. *Gesandtschaftsberichte aus München 1814–1848. III. Abteilung. Die Berichte der preußischen Gesandten.* Band IV.
PLM	Papon, Auguste. *Lola Montès. Memoires accompagné de lettres.*
PRO	Public Record Office, Kew
SFM	Seitz, Max. "Die Februar- und Märzunruhen in München 1848."
WGB	Württemburgisches Hauptstaatsarchiv, Stuttgart, *Gesandten Berichte aus München,* E73Vez.61–29

SOURCES

Text is identified by the page number and the first words of the passage. When a single paragraph of text contains more than one statement for which a source is cited, the sources are consolidated into a single entry.

1 The Reverend Francis: On the Reverend Hawks and his association with the dying LM, see [Dyer], *Penitent*, and Shoemaker, *Calvary Church*.

2 "I have known": [Dyer], *Penitent*, 21.

2 "our first feelings": MEM 1:93.

3 Gilbert was just: Government of Bihar, *List*, 48; PRO, WO25/65, *Commissioning Book*, 384; MEM 1:32.

3 He had arrived: PRO, WO12/4175, *Musterlist of the 25th Foot Regiment, 1818–1822;* MEM 1:32–33; on the age of Lola's mother, see her Entry of Death at the General Register Office, London, 1875, Middlesex County, Sub-District of St. Joan Paddington, No. 229; on the Olivers generally, see Seoighe, *Kilmallock*, 155; see Last Will and Testament of Charles Silver Oliver, dated and signed at Old Brompton, 3 May 1815, in the files of the Irish Land Commission, Dublin, Box 3643, schedule A, no. 2, record EC 4332; for the life of Charles Silver Oliver generally, see R. G. Thorne, *The House of Commons, 1790–1820* (London, 1986), 6:690.

3 Eliza, or Elizabeth: See Last Will and Testament of Charles Silver Oliver.

3 Ensign Gilbert was: See MEM 1:33 for a description of Lola's mother; LML 17.

4 If any record: See KLA 33 [AN 49], KL to LM, 13 February 1848.

4 At just about: See PRO, WO12/4175, *Musterlist of the 25th Foot Regiment,*

413

1818–1822; Parish Register, Holy Trinity Church (Christ Church), Cork, vol. 11: Marriages, 119; *Ennis Chronicle and Clare Advertiser,* 6 May 1820, 3c1.

4 For the first: See PRO, WO12/4175 and WO12/4176, *Musterlist of the 25th Foot Regiment,* 1818–1822, and *Government Gazette* [Calcutta], 22 May 1823, 7c1, General Order 2933.

4 So the Gilberts: PRO, WO25/3503, *Embarkation/Disembarkation Returns,* vol. 1819–1822:82.

5 After four months: PRO, WO12/5653, *Musterlist of the 44th Foot Regiment;* details of the voyage up the Ganges are from unpublished manuscripts in IOBL, particularly Eur.Ms.B242, *Journal of Travel on the Ganges,* and Eur.Ms.B208, *Journal of Capt. C. D. Aplin.*

5 Ensign Gilbert had: See PRO, WO25/1789, *Casualty List of the 44th Foot Regiment, Auction of the Effects of Ensign Edward Gilbert, Dinapore, 27 October 1823.*

5 But for Ensign: See PRO, WO25/1789, *Casualty List of the 44th Foot Regiment, Auction of the Effects of Ensign Edward Gilbert, Dinapore, 27 October 1823;* IOBL, N/1/vol. 12/617, *Dinapore Burial Records;* and Government of Bihar, *List,* 48, inscription 158.

6 According to Lola: MEM 1:44–45.

6 The other officers' wives: E.g., MEM 1:49–51, 61, 83.

6 A month after: See PRO, WO25/1789, *Casualty List of the 44th Foot Regiment, Auction of the Effects of Ensign Edward Gilbert,* 27 October 1823, and letter bound in at that point.

6 The mother and: See IOBL, L/mil/10/24/ff33, *Service Record of Patrick Craigie.*

6 Craigie was twenty-four: IOBL, L/mil/9/131/73–76, *Cadet Papers of Patrick Craigie;* Microfilm of Parish Records, Montrose Library; IOBL, L/mil/24/ff33, *Service Record of Patrick Craigie;* MEM 1:75.

7 A serious courtship: IOBL, L/mil/24/ff33, *Service Record of Patrick Craigie;* IOBL, N/1/13/189, *Parish Register of Dacca; Bengal Hukaru* [Calcutta], 24 August 1824, 2c3.

7 Craigie had become: MEM 1:99; JVJ, *Exhibits to the Summary of the Evidence of Robert McMullin* (two letters of Patrick Craigie to Robert McMullin, dated 28 September 1840 and 12 October 1840).

7 Lola recounts that: MEM 1:83.

8 Craigie arranged for: MEM 1:94.

8 Her mother set: MEM 1:93.

8 The family had: IOBL, L/Mar/B/70B, *Log of the "Malcolm";* MEM 1:95.

9 Eliza was traveling: This account of the voyage of the *Malcolm* taken from the surviving logbook (IOBL, L/Mar/B/70B) and Lola's brief account (MEM 1:95).

9 Lola received heartfelt: MEM 1:96.

10 To a child: See Microfilm of Parish Records, Montrose Library.

10 Lola recalled that: LML 21; *Edinburgh Evening Courant*, 20 August 1849, 3c5.

10 When she was: *Sunderland Herald*, 31 August 1849, 5c1–2.

11 Eliza's stay in: MEM 1:96–97; JN 40, 31 July 1837, and JN 38, 14 September 1832.

12 The Aldridge Academy: See the English Census of 1841 for 20 Camden Place, Bath, Somerset; MEM 1:Ch. 10.

13 How much contact: See MEM 1:Ch. 12.

13 The years at: MEM 1:104–105, 91; JN 40, 15 November 1837.

13 "At last we": JN 39, 14 February 1834.

14 So on 2 November: *Bengal Hukaru* [Calcutta], 2 November 1836, 2c4.

14 One of her: IOBL, L/mil/9/168/435–438, *Cadet Papers of Thomas James*, and IOBL, L/mil/10, *Service Record of Thomas James.*

14 It is impossible: MEM 1:138.

14 The relationship seems: MEM 1:138–140.

15 At some point: MEM 1:143; LML 22; on the Lumleys, see Hodson, *List*, 3:90 et seq.

15 Whatever the facts: MEM 1:Ch. 16.

16 The couple sailed: JVJ, *Summary of the Testimony of John James.*

16 "I am not": JN 40, 31 July 1837.

17 A few weeks: JN 40, 12 August and 15 November 1837.

17 If we are: MEM 1:161.

18 Lola was never: MEM 1:161, 163. On Ballycrystal, see MEM 1:Ch. 18.

18 Their return to: JVJ, *Summary of the Testimony of John James.*

18 But as the: JVJ, *Summary of the Testimony of Browne Roberts.*

18 "A long trip": MEM 1:164–165.

19 On the day: *Bengal Hakaru* [Calcutta], 26 February 1839, 3c1.

19 Lola compared the: For Lola's account of the voyage upriver, see MEM 2:Ch. 1–3.

20 In her later: KLA 34 [AN 172], LM to KL, 26 May 1850.

20 Social convention restricted: Eden, *Country*, 318.

20 "Sunday, Sept. 8": Eden, *Country*, 316–317.

21 "We were at": Eden, *Country*, 339.

22 "Little Miss J": Eden, *Country*, 341–342.

22 In February 1840: JVJ, *Allegation Five of the Complaint;* MEM 2:49.

22 "Days become centuries": MEM 2:49.

22 Lola later claimed: Compare LML 37–38 with MEM 2:49–50, and LML 38–39 with MEM 2:70–73.

23 On 5 August: IOBL, L/mil/10, *Service Record of Thomas James;* except where noted, from here to the end of this chapter all material is drawn from documents in JVJ.

23 Passage was secured: IOBL, Biographical card file, "Sturgis."

23 Major Craigie and: LML 39.

24 About ten days: IOBL, L/mil/9/185/247–255, *Cadet Papers of George Lennox*, and IOBL, L/mil/10, *Service Record of George Lennox.*

25 Major Craigie had: JVJ, *Exhibit to the Summary of the Testimony of Robert McMillan.*

27 Eliza left the: *Age* [London], 11 June 1843, 5c3.

27 The funds she: LML 40.

29 Lola never really: See *Times* [London], 9 April 1847, 5c5.

29 An acquaintance suggested: MEM 2:109.

30 Lola wrote that: LML 40–41.

30 And the trip: Although Lola usually spelled her new last name Montez, it was consistently spelled Montès in France, and she sometimes signed it Montes when she wrote in French.

30 Mrs. James sailed: New York Herald, 28 January 1850, 3c1; see the advertisement for her debut in London in the *Times*, 3 June 1843, 4c4.

31 Back in London: See *Morning Herald* [London], 7 December 1842, 7c3–4.

31 A little more: For the details of the divorce action, see JVJ; for a fascinating and thorough discussion of divorce in England, see Horstman, *Victorian Divorce.*

31 She took passage: Lola gave this date in her letter to the editor of the *Era* [London], 18 June 1843, 5c4–6c1; see *Allgemeine deutsche Real-Encyklopädie für die gebildeten Stände, Conversations-Lexikon* 10:628; Lord Malmesbury's account appears in his *Memoirs* 1:208, fn 1.

33 "Should I have": MEM 2:109–110.

33 The earl was: Lumley's account appears in his *Reminiscences*, 76–78.

33 He invited the: See the later account of the anonymous critic of the *Morning Post* (possibly Charles J. Rosenberg) in a book written under the pseudonym "Q" (*You Have Heard of Them*, 98–106).

33 Her figure was: Q, *You Have Heard of Them*, 101–102.

34 "Donna Lolah Montes": *Morning Post* [London], 3 June 1843, 5c5.

35 On the stage: *Morning Herald* [London], 5 June 1843, 3c5.

35 There was a: For the contemporary accounts from the London press, which form the basis for this description of Lola's debut, see *Morning Post*, 5 June 1843, 3c3; *Illustrated London News*, 10 June 1843, 405c1; *Examiner*, 10 June 1843, 357c3; *Evening Mail*, 2–5 June 1843, 8c5; *Planet*, 4 June 1843, 5c5; *Observer*, 4 June 1843, 2c6; *Bell's New Weekly Messenger*, 4 June 1843, 5c2; *Evening Chronicle*, 5 June 1843, 3c5; *English Chronicle*, 6 June 1843, 3c2; *Court Journal*, 10 June 1843, 377c1; *John Bull*, 10 June 1843, 363c2; *Weekly Chronicle*, 10 June 1843, 5c2; *British Queen & Statesman*, 10 June 1843, 10c3; *Spectator*, 10 June 1843, 537c2; *Weekly Dispatch*, 11 June 1843, 284c2; *Age*, 11 June 1843, 5c3–6c1; *Era*, 11 June 1843, 5c3; *Theatrical Journal*, 10 June 1843, 177–178; *Times*, 5 June 1843, 6c4. Some of the reviews cited are merely unacknowledged reprints of reviews in the other publications.

36 As Lumley watched: Lumley, *Reminiscences*, 78.

36 As her friends: Lumley, *Reminiscences*, 77–78.

37 "Her wonderfully supple": *Morning Post* [London], 5 June 1843, 3c3.

37 "The young lady": *Morning Herald* [London], 5 June 1843, 3c5.

37 "a Spanish dance": *Times* [London], 5 June 1843, 6c4.

38 "Donna Montez is": *Evening Chronicle* [London], 5 June 1843, 3c5.

38 "The only fault": *Era* [London], 11 June 1843, 5c3.

38 Unfortunately for Lola: Lumley, *Reminiscences*, 77–78; during Lola's lifetime the story appeared in print that her debut had been a fiasco because a group of young noblemen, led by Lord Ranelagh, hooted her off the stage as a fraud (see Q, *You Have Heard of Them*, 102–103). This myth has become the common version of Lola's debut, even though it is contradicted by every newspaper account and by Lumley's own memoirs.

39 Within a week: *Age* [London], 11 June 1843, 5c3–6c1.

39 "Sir: Since I": *Era* [London], 18 June 1843, 5c4–6c1.

40 "All this controversial": *Court Journal* [London], 17 June 1843, 394c1.

40 "Judging of Donna": *Spectator* [London], 17 June 1843, 564c1.

40 "The lady perched": *Age* [London], 18 June 1843, 5c2&3–6c1.

41 In late June: "Der Beherrscher eines Kleinstaates," 593c1.

41 At about the: See the notice of Lola's final London appearance, including mention of her departure for St. Petersburg, in Wyndham, *Magnificent Montez*, 60.

41 Before she could: For Fitzball's account of this incident, see Fitzball, *Thirty-Five Years*, 1:90–95.

43 In her memoirs: MEM 2:113–114.

47 Heinrich was one: The following account of Lola's visit to Ebersdorf is based primarily on K. G. M., "Das erste Auftretung von Lola Montez in Deutschland." Also valuable is "Der Beherrscher eines Kleinstaates," apparently by one of Heinrich's relatives. Lola's own account, in MEM 2:Ch. 21, appears unreliable.

47 "Donna Montez had": *Abend Zeitung* [Dresden], 17 August 1843, 56c2.

48 "At the moment": *Deutsche Allgemeine Zeitung* [Leipzig], 15 August 1843, 1327c1–2.

48 "In the matter": *Abend Zeitung* [Dresden], 24 August 1843, 59c2

48 On Friday the: *Abend Zeitung* [Dresden], 24 August 1843, 62c1–2.

48 Having danced her: *Gesellschafter* [Berlin], 13 September 1843, 728c1; *Journal des Débats* [Paris], 15 November 1843, 3c3–4.

49 Lola attracted many: Moulin-Eckart, *Hans von Bülow*, 29–30; E. von Bülow, *Novellen* 1:281–328. For the judgment of a contemporary observer on "Die neue Melusine" and the accuracy of its depiction of Lola, see ÖGB 409–410.

49 Lola was able: *Abend Zeitung* [Dresden], 21 November 1843, 407c1; *Berliner Illustrierte Zeitung*, 13 November 1927, 1853 et seq.; *Königliche Priviligierte Berlinerische Zeitung*, 22 August 1843.

50 Whatever the circumstances: *Münchener Conversationsblatt*, 5 October 1843, 319c1–2.

50 Her debut was: *Allgemeine Theater Chronique* [Leipzig], 6 September 1843, 426c1; *Königliche Priviligierte Berlinerische Zeitung*, 28 August 1843, suppl., 7c1.

50 "The guest appearance": *Münchener Conversationsblatt*, 5 October 1843, 319c1–2.

51 But whatever enthusiasm: *Abend Zeitung* [Dresden], 21 November 1843, 407c1.

51 To give the: *Königliche Priviligierte Berlinerische Zeitung*, 7 September 1843, suppl., (1c2).

51 But declining enthusiasm: *Königliche Priviligierte Berlinerische Zeitung*, 9 September 1843, 7c1.

51 The czar's visit: *Allgemeine Deutsche Zeitung* [Leipzig], 9 September 1843.

51 When the first: *Berlinische Nachrichten von Staats und gelehrter Sachen*, 9 September 1843, 2c3.

52 "During the entertainment": LML 42–43.

52 Bülow wrote, however: E. von Bülow, *Novellen*, 1:303.

52 As Lola stepped: *Königliche Priviligierte Berlinerische Zeitung*, 12 September 1843, suppl., 1c1; *Abend Zeitung* [Dresden], 21 November 1843, 407c1.

53 Whether she had: MEM 2:198.

53 The main attraction: *Galignani's Messenger* [Paris], 17 September 1843.

53 The police tried: *Allgemeine Deutsche Zeitung* [Leipzig], 15 September 1843, 1630c2.

53 Lola had spent: *Journal des Débats* [Paris], 7 October 1843, 3c5.

54 One report: *Journal des Débats* [Paris], 7 October 1843, 3c5.

54 The full significance: An excellent general survey of women's lives in England, France, and the United States during Lola's time is Hellerstein, Hume, and Offen, *Victorian Women*. Material on the lot of women in Biedermeyer Germany can be found in a number of the articles in Ottomeyer, *Biedermeyers Glück und Ende*.

55 Finally, it is: Hummel, *München*, 374–377.

55 The first repercussion: *Journal des Débats* [Paris], 15 November 1843, 3c3–4; *Allgemeine Theater Chronique* [Leipzig], 13 October 1843, 490c1–2; *Abend Zeitung* [Dresden], 24 October 1843, 328c1–2; *Dampfboot* [Danzig], 10 October 1843, 970c2; *Allgemeine Deutsche Zeitung* [Leipzig], 25 November 1843, 2318c2.

56 Strangely, Lola herself: MEM 2:201–206.

56 Craigie was only: IOBL, N/1/1844/1a, Will of Patrick Craigie, 29 September 1843.

57 On 8 October: Craigie's date of death is given as 3 October 1843 by Hodson (*List*, 1:406), but 8 October appeared on his tombstone (see Government of Bihar, *List*, 70, inscription 495) and was the date given in his obituary in *Asiatic Journal*, 3rd ser. vol. 2 (1844): 454–455. See the entry in Hodson for the description of Craigie toast.

57 Lola claimed that: LML 41.

58 On arriving in: The details of Lola's Warsaw sojourn are selected from the conflicting accounts given in Simon, "L'extraordinaire aventure"; Pudelek, "Warsaw Ballet"; Sigma, "Lola Montez w Warszawie"; *Sunday Times*, 21 Jan-

uary 1844, 3c5; *Era* [London], 21 January 1844, 5c4; *Allgemeine Theater Chronique* [Leipzig], 8 December 1843, 586c2; and *Dampfboot* [Danzig], 12 December 1843, 1186c1.

58 With the help: Pudelek, "Warsaw Ballet," 251–253; see also *Polski Slownik Biograficzny* 1:12–13.

59 The facts around: Pudelek, "Warsaw Ballet," 257; Simon, "L'extraordinaire aventure," 135; Sigma, "Lola Montez w Warszawie," 409; LML 45–47.

59 Perhaps it was: Simon, "L'extraordinaire aventure," 135.

59 "Before I left": *Journal des Débats* [Paris], 15 November 1843, 3c3–4.

60 Abramowicz received secret: Simon, "L'extraordinaire aventure," 135.

60 Lola danced on: *Sunday Times* [London], 21 January 1844, 3c5.

60 One version had: See *Abend Zeitung* [Dresden], 5 December 1843, 447–448.

61 When the prince: Simon, "L'extraordinaire aventure," 135.

62 "Lola Montez was": Simon, "L'extraordinaire aventure," 135.

62 Back in Warsaw: For a tribute by Lola to Poland and its people, see LML 158–159.

62 For the moment: *Stettiner Intelligenz-Blatt*, 25 November 1843, 2242, and 1 December 1843, 2277; *Allgemeine Theater Chronique* [Leipzig], 1 January 1844, 3c1.

62 After about two: *Allgemeine Politische Zeitung für die Provinz Preußen* [Danzig], 11 December 1843, 1160c2; *Schaluppe zum Dampfboot* [Danzig], 12 December 1843, 1188c2.

62 She performed three: *Schaluppe zum Dampfboot* [Danzig], 13 December 1843, 1204c1–2, and 16 December 1843, 1217c1.

63 Lola Montez began: *Königsbergische Preußische Staats-Kriegs-und-Friedens-Zeitung*, 4 January 1844, 28c2, and 6 January 1844, 40c2–41c1. See also *Allgemeine Theater Chronique* [Leipzig], 31 January 1844, 56c1.

63 "At the instant": *Königsbergische Preußische Staats-Kriegs-und-Friedens-Zeitung*, 6 January 1844, 40c2–41c1.

63 From Königsberg Lola: *Allgemeine Theater Chronique* [Leipzig], 31 January 1844, 56c2.

64 For the story: LML 49–52.

64 It appears that: Sigma, "Lola Montez w Warszawie"; MEM 2:159–166.

64 As she passed: *Königsbergische Preußische Staats-Kriegs-und-Friedens-Zeitung*, 21 February 1844, 393c1, quoting from *Echo am Memel* [Tilsit]. See also the Königsberg paper for 22 February 1844, 401c1.

64 "If the journey": MEM 2:167.

65 "A coincidence was": MEM 2:168.

65 In this case: MEM 2:169.

66 Lola wrote that: MEM 2:172–175; *Allgemeine Theater Chronique* [Leipzig], 6 March 1844, 116c1; *Dresdener Anzeiger*, 28 February 1844.

67 On Tuesday, 27 February: See Liszt's letter to the director of the Dresden Court Theater in the collection of the Library of Congress, ML 95.L68 (Mus) 86/20, 227, reel 1, letter 28; *Abend Zeitung* [Dresden], 19 March 1844, 228c2.

67 While in Dresden: R. Wagner, *Mein Leben*, 282.

67 "I had been": MEM 3:176.

67 Liszt's Tuesday evening: *Abend Zeitung* [Dresden], 14 March 1844, 42c2; R. Wagner, *Mein Leben*, 283; C. Wagner, *Die Tagebücher* 2:235–236.

68 In Tichatschek's dressing room: R. Wagner, *Mein Leben*, 283; C. Wagner, *Die Tagebücher* 1:32.

68 Lola had not: Moulin-Eckart, *Hans von Bülow*, 29–30; H. von Bülow, *Briefe und Schriften* 6 (vol. 5 of the letters), 503.

69 Liszt's last concert: MEM 3:43; *Abend Zeitung* [Dresden], 14 March 1844, 43c1.

69 According to Lola's account: For the following account, see MEM 3:42–56.

69 "At a dinner": *Königsbergische Preußische Staats-Kriegs-und-Friedens-Zeitung*, 26 March 1844, 641c2.

69 "A number of artists": *Abend Zeitung* [Dresden], 19 March 1844, 228c2.

70 A story that: For a discussion of this story, see Walker, *Franz Liszt* 1:393 and fn 28; MEM 2:180.

70 Their parting at the end: Lewald, *Zwölf Bilder*, 351.

70 The best evidence: *Journal du Dimanche* [Paris], 11 April 1847, 31c3; *Berliner Illustrierte Zeitung*, 13 November 1927, 1853 et seq.

71 In the city: *Abend Zeitung* [Dresden], 16 November 1844, 919c1–2.

71 Lola took to it: Ambassador Apponyi to Prince Metternich, 27 March 1847, quoted in *Berliner Illustrierte Zeitung*, 13 November 1927, 1853 et seq.

71 On 18 March: *Journal des Débats* [Paris], 18 March 1844, 2c5.

72 Lola had begun: Guest, *Romantic Ballet in Paris*, 230.

72 Lola's new friends: *Corsaire* [Paris], 24 March 1844, 1c2; *Journal des Théâtres*, 24 March 1844, 4c2.

72 The campaign worked: *Journal des Théâtres* [Paris], 28 March 1844, 3c1 and 4c1.

72 "There was no stall": *Courrier Français* [Paris], 1 April 1844, 1c3–2c1.

73 "After the first leap": *Siècle* [Paris], 4 April 1844, 2c2–3.

73 Whether the polka: *Courrier de Londres et de Paris* [London], 30 March 1844, 3c3.

73 That was the report: *Corsaire* [Paris], 29 March 1844, 3c1. *Presse* [Paris], 29 March 1844, 3c3.

74 The audience grew: *Allgemeine Theater Zeitung* [Vienna], 11 April 1844, 364c1.

74 "Mlle. Lola Montez is": *Estafette* [Paris], 2 April 1844, 1c3.

74 "It's perfectly excusable": *Journal des Théâtres* [Paris], 31 March 1844, 2c1.

74 "Mlle. Lola Montez has": *Presse* [Paris], 1 April 1844, 1c2–3.

75 The comtesse and Liszt: Walker, *Franz Liszt*, 395.

75 She went to the races: *Corsaire* [Paris], 7 August 1844, 3c1–2.

75 "Mlle. Lola Montez": *Era* [London], 28 July 1844, 5c2.

76 In late summer: *Coureur des Spectacles* [Paris], 20 August 1844, 2c2, and 3 September 1844, 3c1–2.

76 Lola ran with: The following discussion of Dujarier is based primarily on Maillier, *Trois Journalistes*. See also Bouchardon, *Le Duel*.

76 It was said: Bouchardon, *Le Duel*, 27.

77 "all of fashionable Paris": *Journal des Théâtres* [Paris], 5 March 1845, 2c2.

77 The Porte St. Martin: *Courrier Français* [Paris], 10 March 1845, 3c1; *Revue et Gazette des Théâtres* [Paris], 9 March 1845, 2c2; *Réform* [Paris], 10 Mar 1845, 2c2.

77 Lola displayed two: *Corsaire-Satan* [Paris], 8 March 1845, 3c3; *Constitutionnel* [Paris], 11 March 1845, 2c1.

77 "There is something": *Rabelais*, 9 March 1845, 2c1.

77 The critic of: *Siècle*, 10 March 1845, 3c3.

78 "She dances them": *Presse* [Paris], 10 March 1845, 2c2–3.

79 Lola had noticed: The following account is based primarily on the extensive transcripts and summaries of the testimony at Beauvallon's 1846 murder trial published in the Parisian press. This material can be found in *Presse*, 26, 27, 28, 29, 30, and 31 March 1846, in the *Journal des Débats* for 27, 28, 29, 30, and 31 March 1846, and in the *Gazette des Tribunaux* for 27, 28, 29, and 30 March 1846. For the most part, the accounts agree, though there are differences in the details. Another valuable source is Bouchardon, *Le Duel*, which appears to derive in part from unpublished material from the investigation of Dujarier's death.

81 "My dear Lola": From the original note, read into the record during Lola's testimony at the murder trial and reported in *Presse*, the *Journal des Débats*, and the *Gazette des Tribunaux*.

84 Whatever the reason: *Corsaire-Satan* [Paris], 23 March 1845, 3c3.

85 In the midst: *Corsaire-Satan* [Paris], 21 March 1845, 2c3. *Figaro* [Paris], 3 October 1858, 6c2; *Galignani's Messenger* [Paris], 14 April 1845, 4c1; *Journal des Théâtres* [Paris], 19 April 1845, 3c3; *Rabelais* [Paris], 20 April 1845, 2c3; *Revue des Théâtres* [Paris], 9 July 1845, 3c3; *Berliner Illustrierte Zeitung*, 13 November 1927, 1853 et seq.; LML 58.

85 Then as now: LM to "Mon cher Fiorentino," n.d., Harvard Theatre Collection.

86 Lola found much: See *Courrier de l'Europe* [London], 6 September 1845, 642c2 and 644c2.

86 Lola arrived at the Stern: Schorn, *Lebenserinnerungen* 1:200–201.

86 Lola finally found: *Bonner Wochenblatt*, 12 August 1845, [9c1]; Moscheles, *Recent Music*, 316.

87 On Wednesday, 13 August: The following account of the banquet relies on Schorn, *Lebenserinnerungen* 1:208–211; Chorley, *Modern German Music* 2:272–275; and Moscheles, *Recent Music*, 317–318.

87 Liszt spoke in German: On Liszt's German, see Lewald, *Zwölf Bilder*, 339.

88 With the festival: For an account of Lola's travels in the summer of 1845, see *Gazette des Tribunaux* [Paris], 26 July 1846, 1249c4–1250c1.

88 But whatever luck: See BAM, Police report of 17 February 1847, quoting the

report of the Baden-Baden incident in *Mannheimer Abendzeitung*, no. 28, February 1847; *Beobachter* [Stuttgart], 28 February 1847, 230c1–2.

89 It is difficult: See Cubitt, *Jesuit Myth*, 105–142.

89 According to a contemporary story: KLL 51–52.

89 In Paris, Lola was troubled: LM to a commissioner, 30 May 1846, Stadt- und Universitätsbibliothek, Frankfurt am Main; *Revue des Théâtres* [Paris], 14 February 1846, 2c2.

90 On her arrival: This account of the trial is based on the extensive reports in the Parisian press. See *Presse*, 26, 27, 28, 29, 30, and 31 March 1846; *Journal des Débats*, 27, 28, 29, 30, and 31 March 1846; and *Gazette des Tribunaux*, 27, 28, 29, and 30 March 1846.

91 Had she known: *Gazette des Tribunaux* [Paris], 28 March 1846.

92 "I don't know": *Gazette des Tribunaux* [Paris], 28 March 1846.

93 Lola must have: *Figaro* [Paris], 3 October 1858, 6c2. See also LM to Monsieur Vijand, n.d., carton 26, no. 6, Archives de la Ville de Reims, Collection Tarbe; and LM to a commissioner, 30 May 1846, Stadt- und Universitätsbibliothek, Frankfurt am Main. According to the army lists, Leigh had bought into the Tenth Hussars on 17 May 1844 and resold his commission early in 1845; see also LM to the proprietress of the Hotel de Suède, Brussels, of 18[?] August 1846, Harry Ransom Center for the Humanities, University of Texas, Austin. See Mirecourt, *Lola Montès*, facsimile letter of LM to Monsieur Bloque, 25 September 1847.

93 In June the: LM to the proprietress of the Hotel de Suède, Brussels, August 1846, Harry Ransom Center for the Humanities, University of Texas, Austin.

93 For a few: See article from the *Frankfurter Journal*, 27 February 1847, enclosed in a letter from Heinrich von der Tann to KL, 12 March 1847, to be found in NL85/3/7.

93 The intelligent young: Gash, *Sir Robert Peel*, 60, 176.

94 Lola found him: Beyer, *Glorreiches Leben*, 20; Wyndham, *Magnificent Montez*, 70.

94 Mid-August found Lola: *Allgemeine Zeitung* [Augsburg], 1 September 1846, 1949c2–1950c1; LM to proprietress of the Hotel de Suède, Brussels, 18[?] August 1846, Harry Ransom Center for the Humanities, University of Texas, Austin; *Allgemeine Zeitung* [Augsburg], 4 September 1846, 1976c1; LM to Monsieur Du Bois, n.d., Yale University Library, Theatrical Manuscripts Collection.

94 Lola spent September: *Beobachter* [Stuttgart], 28 February 1847, 230c1–2; Beyer, *Glorreiches Leben*, 20; MEM 3:67; *Atheneum* [London], 9 February 1861, 196–197 (notes Lola's departure from Stuttgart for Munich following the wedding festivities).

95 It was not: This sketch of King Ludwig's life, character, and accomplishments is based on the two best sources, GKL and CKL.

98 But Ludwig wanted: See KLA 33 [AN 128], KL to LM, 8 July 1848.

99 half a century: Mann, *Ludwig I*, 56.

99 And yet Bavaria: For a liberal Protestant's contemporary view of the situation, see Erdmann, *Lola*, 175–200.

100 Among them was: BHS Staatstheater file 13196, memorandum of Freiherr von Frays to KL, 6 October 1846, with notation by the king.

100 With typical energy: See KLA 33 [AN 199], KL to LM, 23 March 1849.

102 Lola had arrived: *Münchener Politische Zeitung*, 7 October 1846, 980.

102 Back at the: KLA 39, Freiherr von Maltzahn to KL, 31 December 1846.

103 One day after: *Bayerischer Volksfreund* [Munich], 7 October 1846, 648c1.

103 King Ludwig usually: With reference to the dress she wore when she first met King Ludwig, see KLA 33 [AN 162], KL to LM, 12 October 1848; KLA 33 [AN 164], KL to LM, 18 October 1848; and KLA 33 [AN 206], KL to LM, 30 April 1849. On Count Lerchenfeld, see Bray-Steinburg, *Denkwürdigkeiten*, 27.

103 A rumor about: See Fournier, "Lola Montez," 216, where an Austrian spy in Munich repeats the story in a report to Prince Metternich in March 1847. For another early rumor about the first meeting of LM and KL, see Boisserée, *Tagebücher* 4: 883–884.

104 "I told Lola": BHS Staatstheater file 13107, KL's notation of 8 October 1846.

104 Frays said that: BHS Staatstheater file 13196, Freiherr von Frays to KL, 8 October 1846, KL's notation of same date.

104 The messengers sped: BHS Staatstheater file 13196, second Memorandum of Freiherr von Frays to KL of 8 October 1846.

104 The notice to: BHS Staatstheater file 13196, copy of Letter from Court Theater Direction to LM, 8 October 1846.

105 In light of: Plötz, *Prinz*, 29–31.

105 The dance grew: *Münchener Morgenblatt*, 17 October 1846, 1; *Bayerischer Eilbote* [Munich], 16 October 1846, 1019c1.

105 One of the: *Bayerischer Eilbote* [Munich], 16 October 1846, 1019c1. Quoted in Hase, *Stieler*, 26. CKL 463; GKL 679; KLA 33 [AN 165], KL to LM, 22 October 1848.

106 But an unimpressed: MD 3.

106 Now there was: KLA 4.17, Pocketnotebook 1846–1847, 15 October 1846; KLA 33 [AN 121], KL to LM, 16 June 1848.

106 Ludwig could not: LM to Baron Frays, 22 October 1846, MS 1489, California Historical Society, San Francisco; Clipping from unidentified auction catalog of Walter R. Benjamin in May 1952 offering letter of LM to director of Augsburg Theater, 22 October 1846, Harvard Theatre Collection; KLA 33 [AN 165], KL to LM, 22 October 1848; KL to Tann, 5 June 1847, quoted in CKL 510.

107 Ludwig's heart leaped: PGB 201, 17 October 1846.

107 Munich was becoming: MD 2; CKL 464.

107 Word got around: ÖGB 425, 25 February 1847.

108 Within weeks, public: MD 2; *Bayerischer Eilbote* [Munich], 23 October 1846, 1042c2. BHS Staatstheater file 13196, Copy of message from theater director

to LM, 20 October 1846, and memorandum of 12 November 1846. ÖGB 396, 25 November 1846; Letter of Amalia Thiersch to her sister, 24 November 1846, reprinted in *Deutsche Allgemeine Zeitung* [Berlin], 25 July 1919, 2c1–3.

108 "More than twelve": KL to Tann, 17 November 1846, quoted in CKL 465.

109 Lola Montez began: MAR 101; Frau Ganser's first name, not mentioned elsewhere, can be found in the Munich city directories for the period. See KLA 39, Thierry file, Ulrich Thierry to KL, 20 October 1846, with notation by KL; and ÖGB 395–397, 25 November 1846.

109 One day early: PGB 209, 14 December 1846. Nußbammer (his real name, though he is usually referred to as Nußbaumer) was an orphan whose life was tragically altered by Lola. See his service file in KA file 80668. For a summary of his sad fate, see Xylander and Sutner, *Geschichte* 3:59, fn 2.

109 But Lola's most: A number of caricatures of Lola with Turk can be found in Fuchs, *Tanzidyll*.

110 Carl Wilhelm Baron: For a discussion of Heideck's previous life and his relations with the king, see KLL. Except where otherwise indicated, the account of Heideck's part in Lola's story is based on his thirteen-page unpublished memorandum on his relations with Lola, quoted at great length in KLL.

110 On 1 November: NL 88/4/2. See also the king's pocket account books in KLA 8, items 7 and 8; Hummel, *München*, 348; *Illustrated London News*, 30 October 1847, 283c3; KLA 39, Metzger file, KL's notation on Metzger's letter to him of 6 November 1846. KL later established the fund for the decoration of Lola's house at 20,000 florins; see KLL 100.

111 Although Heideck and: At least part of the police files on the incident are to be found in BAM.

112 But the story: See Nußbammer's personnel file in KA, file 80668.

112 The concert that: See Schmeller, *Tagebücher* 2:443 (entry for 16 November 1847); MD 4; Amalia Thiersch to her sister, 24 November 1846, reprinted in *Deutsche Allgemeine Zeitung* [Berlin], 25 July 1919, 2c1–3; "Aus den Tagen der Lola Montez," 923.

112 Nußbammer must have: KA file 80668; MD 3; Amalia Thiersch to her sister, 24 November 1846, reprinted in *Deutsche Allgemeine Zeitung* [Berlin], 25 July 1919, 2c1–3.

113 Ludwig chose to: See KLA 39, Curtius file, Dr. Curtius to KL, 23 December 1846, and Dr. Curtius to KL, n.d. but with notation by the king dated 20 January 1847.

113 Lola had another: The account of Lola's conflict with the police director is taken largely from MAR 96–125, which is based on Pechmann's unpublished diaries and memoranda. On this topic, see also JSP 67–71.

113 The king wrote: A facsimile of the note appears in JSP 70.

113 She had not: MAR 99.

114 The police director: For this meeting, see MAR 107.

115 "I would not": Quoted in CKL 467 from GHA.

115 "Lolitta (that's what)": Quoted in CKL 468–469, from KL to Tann, 27 November 1846.

115 The negotiation to: GHA Urkunde 54/4/32,4; see CKL 495, quoting from KL to Tann, 22 February 1847.

116 "I know everything": KLL 62.

116 Lola did intercede: MAR 112–113; PGB 203, 30 November 1846.

116 At Baron Pechmann's: MAR 109–110.

117 On 25 November: GKL 679, citing KL's diary.

117 "Let the poet": Erdmann, *Lola*, 54–55.

118 Minister Karl von Abel: KLL 61; see also PGB 209, 14 December 1846.

118 Abel's advice may: MAR 111.

118 At his weekly: The following dialogue is quoted from Pechmann's unpublished papers in MAR, 112–114.

120 That evening Pechmann: MAR 115.

120 "Well, dear Fiorentino": Reprinted in *Temps* [Paris], 26 February 1909, 2c3–6.

121 But Lola's resolve: MAR 115; CKL 472, quoting KL to Tann, 27 December 1846.

122 "Happiness is not": KLA 38, Heideck file, KL to Heideck, 5 December 1846.

122 The king told: The following account of events at the general's home is based on excerpts from Heideck's unpublished memorandum as cited in KLL and CKL's quotation (p. 472) of the 27 December 1846 letter from KL to Tann.

122 Ganser had also: See KLA 39, Seinsheim file, Seinsheim to KL, 5 December 1846 (first letter of this date). No copy of Ganser's reports seems to have survived, but the items mentioned, which appear to be typical of the whole, have been preserved in an undated note on Ganser's reports in BAM.

125 "If all the": CKL 473, quoting KL to Tann, 27 December 1846.

125 Back at the: Gollwitzer, *Abel*, 534. See KLA 39, Seinsheim File, two letters from Seinsheim to KL, both dated 5 December 1846; and NL XXI 586b, KL's notation on a memo from Abel, 20 December 1846, and, in the same place, KL's notation on Seinsheim's appeal, forwarded to KL through Abel on 21 December 1846.

125 When he called: KLL 70–71.

126 The next day: KLA 38, Maltzahn file, letter of KL to Maltzahn, 19 December 1846.

126 Although the bonds: GKL 679, citing KL's diary for 19 December 1846; PGB 203, 30 November 1846; GKL 891, fn 1520, citing KL's diary from 17 December 1846.

126 But only a few days: Erdmann, *Lola*, 20–21; KLA 34 [AN 1], LM to KL, 1 December 1846; KLA 33 [AN 3], KL to LM, 1 December 1846; KLA 39, Pechmann file, Pechmann to KL, 11 December 1846, enclosing copy of report 1998 of 10 December 1846; MAR 118.

127 Within the hour: This note, in German and not in Lola's handwriting, is reproduced in facsimile in JSP 71.

127 The next morning: For this and the following, see the affidavit of Ulrich Thierry in KLA 39, Pechmann file.

127 Now Lola played: MAR 119; a draft for this letter, together with a French translation, certainly for Lola to read, is found in KLA 38, Pechmann file.

128 Although he received: MAR 120; see also NL XXI, Pechmann to KL, 17 December 1846; Craemer, *Königs-Historien*, 28–29; Schmeller, *Tagebücher* 2:448, entry for 16 January 1847.

128 Ludwig was becoming: BAM, memorandum of 17 December with KL's notation of the same date; MD 4; KLA 34 [AN 19], LM to KL, n.d.; KLA 39, Thiersch file, Thiersch to KL, 23 December 1846; MD 4; Thiersch, *Carl Thiersch*, 46; KLA 39, Manostetter file, Manostetter to KL, 22 December 1846, Hörmann to Manostetter, 1 January 1847.

128 But far more: KLA 39, Empress Charlotte Auguste (Caroline) to KL, 15[?] December 1846; ÖGB 410, fn 1, 7 February 1847.

129 Ludwig wrote to his old friend: CKL 475–476, quoting KL to Tann, 12 December 1846.

129 Just before Christmas: KLA 39, Curtius file, Curtius to KL, 23 December 1846.

130 "In 48 years": CKL 477, quoting KL to Tann, 28 December 1846.

130 "My life is": KLA 39, Maltzahn file, Maltzahn to KL, 31 December 1846.

130 "May the New": KLA 34 [AN 3], LM to KL, 31 December 1846.

131 When Ludwig granted: KLA 39, Maltzahn file, Maltzahn to KL, 6 January 1847; see also PGB 213–214, 5 February 1847; ÖGB 405, 3 January 1847.

131 Later that day: WGB, 10 January 1847; see also Lola's letter to the editor of the *Times* [London], 18 March 1847, 6c2; WGB, 5 January 1847; PGB 240, 6 March 1847; see CKL 479, quoting KL to Tann, 6 January 1847 (though Corti fails to identify Maltzahn correctly). Also of interest is MS 1794, f. 287 and 288, KL to LM, 1 January 1848, *Bibliothèques Municipales de Besançon, Bibliothèque d'étude et de conservation*; in it he refers to her refusal of Maltzahn's bribe, saying, "What you did a year ago today is *imprinted* in *my heart.*"

132 Lola had become: "Aus der Tagen der Lola Montez," 924; BAM, Assignment of Bodyguards to Lola Montez, 3 January 1847.

132 Ludwig had ordered: ÖGB 404, 3 January 1847.

132 The portrait was: ÖGB 407, 6 January 1847; Dürck-Kaulbach, *Erinnerungen*, 53–54.

133 Ludwig was not: For the story of Kaulbach's portrait and its travels before coming home to Munich's Stadtmuseum, see *Süddeutsche Zeitung* [Munich], 5 August 1987, 13.

133 The police were: BHS Minn 45390, together with many other insulting and threatening letters and graffiti; also in PGB 214, fn 4, 5 February 1847; and WGB, 28 January, 10 January, and 24 January 1847.

133 The king was: KLA 39, Curtius file, Dr. Curtius to KL, n.d. but with notation by the king dated 20 January 1847; KA file 80668, two notes of KL dated 17 January 1847.

133 Two days later: KLA 3,9 Curtius file, Dr. Curtius to KL, n.d. but with notation by the king dated 20 January 1847.

133 Ludwig could not: CKL 484, quoting KL to Tann, 3 February 1847.

134 In spite of: KLA 33 [AN 7], KL to LM, 26 January 1847; Amalia Thiersch to her sister, 5 March 1847, reprinted in *Deutsche Allgemeine Zeitung* [Berlin], 26 July 1919, 2c1–3.

134 "Tell the king": KLA 39, Diepenbrock file, Cardinal Diepenbrock to KL, 29 January 1847.

135 "My lord prince-bishop": BSB, Autograph. Cim. Ludwig I, KL to Cardinal Diepenbrock, 9 February 1847.

135 The king gave: PGB 281, 13 July 1847.

135 On Wednesday, 3 February: BHS, Staatsrat file 4828.

135 Late that night: The following account is based on the police report of the incident in KLA 39, Manostetter file, 11 February 1847; BAM, Police Summary Report of 8 February 1847; MD 6; WGB, 4 February 1847; ÖGB 414, 11 February 1847; "Aus den Tagen der Lola Montez," 925.

136 Lola's first thought: The note is in KLA 34, anonymous to KL, dated "4 Feb 47 5 a.m." in KL's hand.

136 The king was: MD 6.

136 The immediate result: MD 6.

136 The Wednesday night: This account of the incident of 6 February is based on Police Director Mark's report to the king in KLA 39, Mark file, Mark to KL, 7 February 1847; BAM, Police report of 7 February 1847; MD 6; ÖGB 414–415, 11 February 1847; WGB, 8 February 1847; "Aus den Tagen der Lola Montez," 925; Schmeller, *Tagebücher* 2:449, entry for 10 February 1847.

137 After the incident: PGB 216, 5 February 1847.

137 Lola complained loudly: ÖGB 414–415, 11 February 1847; WGB, 8 February 1847; MD 7.

137 The meeting was: BHS Staatsrat 886, 8 February 1847; GKL 676.

138 That night a: WGB, 9 February 1847; ÖGB 416, 11 February 1847.

138 The Council of: BHS Staatsrat 887, 9 February 1847.

139 The following morning: KLA 39, Maurer file, Maurer to KL, 10 February 1847.

139 In the margin: BHS Staatsrat 887, KL's notation of 10 February 1847; Bray-Steinburg, *Denkwürdigkeiten*, 30–31.

139 The new problem: KLA 39, Maurer file, Maurer to KL, 10 February 1847 (second letter of this date).

139 Although Abel was: Austrian Ambassador Senfft, a close friend of Minister Abel's, wrote Metternich on 12 February concerning the plan for joint resignation, that "we are tensely awaiting further developments," which would seem to indicate that he, and perhaps Abel, thought the king might back down when confronted with the resignation of his entire council of ministers. ÖGB 416, fn 2.

139 In his memorandum: The original memorandum is in NL XXII and is reprinted in PGB 223–225.

140 "Abel remained adamant.": Quoted in CKL 490–491.

140 Lola had told Ludwig: See KLA 33 [AN 49], KL to LM, 13 February 1848.

141 As soon as: GKL 679–680, citing KL's diary for 13 February 1847; WGB, 17 and 23 February 1847.

141 Forming a new: See Spindler, "Die Politische Wendung," 333.

141 In the process: ÖGB 442, fn 3, 28 February 1847; WGB, 21 February 1847.

142 If the ultramontane: ÖGB 421–426, 25 February 1847; PGB 226–228, 24 February 1847; FGB 235–236, 21 February 1847; PRO, FO9/95 *Bavarian Correspondence*, 26 February 1847.

142 At the same: See Hacker, *Die Beziehungen*, 137; a copy of the false papal letter is in KLA 39; see also WGB, 26 February 1847. CKL assumed the letter was genuine.

142 At the university: See Lasaulx's own account of the meeting in his letter to Aloys Mayr of 18 February 1847, in Wernitz, "Lasaulx," 185–189.

143 The students at: Except as otherwise specified, this account of the events of 1 March 1847 is based on the following sources: MD 9; KA A XIII 3, *Justiz and Polizei, 1844–1869*, Memorandum on the disturbances of 1 March; WGB, 2 March 1847; FGB 238–239, 2 March 1847; PGB 233–234, 2 March 1847; ÖGB 427–432, 1, 2, and 3 March 1847; Amalia Thiersch to her sister, 5 March 1847, reprinted in *Deutsche Allgemeine Zeitung [Berlin]*, 26 July 1919, 2c1–3; NL XXI 586, Report of Minister Zu Rhein to KL on the excesses of 1 March, dated 9 March 1847; *Bayerischer Eilbote* [Munich], 5 March 1847, 230c2; Fournier, "Lola Montez," 214–230; Bray-Steinburg, *Denkwürdigkeiten*, 39–40; "Aus den Tagen von Lola Montez," 926–928.

143 Word of the: Reproduced in facsimile in *Um Lola Montez;* NL 21, Zu Rhein to KL, 1 March 1847.

143 At a little: FGB 239, 2 March 1847.

143 "She had a": "Aus den Tagen der Lola Montez," 927.

144 "ringing, mocking laughter": "Aus den Tagen der Lola Montez," 927.

145 Toward 6 o'clock: Amalia Thiersch to her sister, 5 March 1847, reprinted in *Deutsche Allgemeine Zeitung* [Berlin], 26 July 1919, 2c1–3; ÖGB 437, 5 March 1847.

145 "My nobles, the": Quoted in CKL 499.

146 "Ludwig, the otherwise": KLA 39, Österreich, Charlotte Auguste file, Charlotte to KL, 2 March 1847.

146 "The intoxication of": Quoted by Prince Metternich in a letter to Archbishop Diepenbrock, 29 March 1847, in ÖGB 435, fn 1.

147 The king had: KL to King Friedrich Wilhelm, 5 April 1847, quoted in CKL 502.

147 Ludwig was amazed: KLL 95; ÖGB 443, 29 March 1847; see LA 33 [AN 9], KL to LM, 7 April 1847; NL 85/3/7, Tann to KL, 14 March 1847.

147 Work progressed on: KLA 39, Heideck file, Heideck to KL, 24 December

1846. KLA 39, Heideck file, Bill from Ernestine Opitz, included in letter from Heideck to KL, 25 January 1847; KLL 97.

148 Heideck had to: KLL 100–102.

148 Lola actually was: ÖGB 443, 29 March 1847, and ÖGB 448, 6 April 1847; CKL 503; *Times* [London], 18 March 1847, 6c2; *National* [Paris], 21 March 1847, 2c1; KL to Tann, 28 December 1846, quoted in CKL 477; KLA 39, Diepenbrock file, Diepenbrock to KL, 27 March 1847.

149 on 20 March: *Pictorial Times* [London], 9:210 (20 March 1847), 185c1.

149 "Sir, In consequence": *Times* [London], 9 April 1847, 5c5; the letter also appeared in *Journal des Débats* [Paris], 6 April 1847, 2c5 and numerous other newspapers, but not all who received it deigned to publish it: see *National* [Paris], 7 April 1847, 2c1. See also LM to the editor of *Journal du Dimanche*, 31 March 1847, Bibliothéque Nationale, Paris, Nouvelles Acquisitions Françaises 1305, Lola Montés, no. 289; and LM to Girardin, 31 March 1847, Harry Ransom Center for the Humanities, University of Texas, Austin.

149 "You have driven": *Allgemeine Zeitung* [Augsburg], 17 June 1847, 1341.

150 Lola's house in: KLA 39, Metzger file, Metzger to KL, 20 July 1847. For a description of the house and its furnishings, see KLL 95–97; for the workmen's bills, see KLA 39, Metzger file; and for the inventory of Lola's house, see KLA 39, Rosmann file; GKL 685, fn 1532; KLA 33 [AN 194], KL to LM, 8 March 1849.

150 At last, on: ÖGB 452, 4 May 1847; CKL 506–507; *Allgemeine Zeitung* [Augsburg], 1 May 1847, 968.

150 In spite of: KLA 33 [AN 13], KL to LM, 22 May 1847; Adalbert, *Nymphenburg*, 114.

151 A riding accident: KA file 80668.

152 A more substantial: See an assessment of Berks in PGB 330, 30 November 1847.

152 King Ludwig was: PGB 279, 7 June 1847; ÖGB 457, 2 June 1847.

152 Two days later: KLA 33 [AN 121], KL to LM, 16 June 1848, undated small enclosure.

153 She even persuaded: PGB 282, 13 July 1847.

153 And on 18 June: See KLA 39, Peißner file, Peißner to KL, 29 December 1848; Horn, *Palatia*, 21–23; KAM.

154 According to one: See Amalia Thiersch to her sister, 30 June 1847, reprinted in *Deutsche Allgemeine Zeitung* [Berlin], 26 July 1919, 2c1–3.

154 Her itinerary called: Amalia Thiersch to her sister, 30 June 1847, reprinted in *Deutsche Allgemeine Zeitung* [Berlin], 26 July 1919, 2c1–3; KLA 39, Mussinan file, Mussinan to KL, 23 June 1847; *Kölnische Zeitung*, 3 July 1847, 7c1.

154 Ludwig was so: *Brüsseler Deutsche Zeitung*, 25 July 1847, 3c2; *Kölnische Zeitung*, 3 July 1847, 7c1; KLA 33 [AN 14], KL to LM, 4 July 1847.

155 When the king: CKL 512.

155 On the evening: CKL 512. The exact date can be established from KL's letter to LM of 18 July 1848 in KLA 33 [AN 132].

155 "My dear Tann": Quoted in CKL 513.

155 Lola made no: CKL 513–514.

156 Once Lola had: KLA 33 [AN 133], KL to LM, 21 July 1848.

156 There were many: On Ludwig's fascination with Lola's feet, in addition to regular remarks in his letters about kissing her feet, see the king's letters to Lola in KLA 33: [AN 134] 25 July 1848, [AN 142] 13 August 1848, [AN 150] 9 September 1848, [AN 165] 22 October 1848, [AN 167] 28 October 1848, [AN 173] 19 November 1848.

156 "You know I": BSB Kaulbach Archiv 1,8: Josephine von Kaulbach to Wilhelm von Kaulbach, 3 July 1847 and 22[?] July 1847.

157 "To L***": Ludwig I, *Gedichte* 246.

157 The illness was: See KLA 34 [AN 111], LM to KL, 23 July 1848.

157 The king and: Quoted in CKL 517. KLA 33 [AN 16], KL to LM, 4 August 1847.

157 Maurer replied to: NL XII 587e, Maurer to KL, 6 August 1847.

158 The king replied: NL XII 587e, Maurer to KL, 6 August 1847; notation of KL to Maurer, 9 August 1847.

158 Maurer saw that: NL XII 587e, Maurer to KL, 11 August 1847.

159 "I demand obedience": KL to Maurer, GHA, quoted in CKL 520.

159 In the meantime: On the Würzburg incident generally, see the following materials in KLA 39: Günther file, Günther to KL, undated; Berks file, Berks to KL, 8 August 1847; Mussinan file, Mussinan to KL, 8 August 1847; Hetzendorf file, Hetzendorf to KL, 10 August 1847.

160 Lola finally slipped: KLA 34 [AN 22], LM to KL, 6 August 1847.

160 Ludwig replied: KLA 33 [AN 19], KL to LM, 8 August 1847.

160 Although her fevers: KLA 39, Peißner file, Peißner to KL, 29 December 1848.

161 Ludwig was generous: BSB Kaulbach Archiv 1,8; Josephine von Kaulbach to Wilhelm von Kaulbach, 15 August 1847; PGB 203, 30 November 1846; compare with NL 88/4/2, and FGB 234, 16 February 1847.

161 King Ludwig's birthday: KLA 33 [AN 23], KL to LM, 21 August 1847; the original diploma is to be found in GHA Urkunde 54/4/32.

162 The king's birthday: KLA 34 [AN 29], LM to KL, 25 August 1847.

162 There were rumors: PGB 299, 4 September 1847; *Rheinischer Beobachter* [Cologne], 12 September 1847, 2c1.

162 Ludwig wrote to: KLA 33 [AN 25], 26 August 1847, and KLA 33 [AN 27], 1 September 1847.

162 "You should know": KLA 34 [AN 31], 2 September 1847.

163 As she did: WGB, 5 September 1847. KLA 34 [AN 37], 23 September 1847, and KLA 33 [AN 37], 27 September 1847.

164 There were even: PGB 332, 30 November 1847.

164 Lola apparently knew: KLA 34 [AN 38], 24 September 1847.

164 Ludwig himself tried: See KLA 33 [AN 27–37], 1 September to 27 September 1847.

165 In his last: KLA 33 [AN 38], 1 October 1847; the draft is AN 230.

165 On the first: KLA 33 [AN 118], KL to LM, "15 October 1848" (actually 15 November 1848).

165 On the evening: KLA 33 [AN 156], KL to LM, 1 October 1848.

166 "What a loving": KLA 39, Bayern, Königin Therese von file, 13 October 1847.

166 Ludwig's hopes for: "Aus den Tagen der Lola Montez," 931; WGB, 2 November 1847.

167 "Lola Montez is": *Berliner Illustrierte Zeitung*, 13 November 1927, 1853 et seq.

167 Lola's self-esteem was: *Bayerischer Volksfreund* [Munich], 11 October 1847, 672, Francis's arrival at the Goldener Hahn. [Francis], "King of Bavaria, Munich, and Lola Montez," 92.

168 "As is usual": [Francis], "King of Bavaria, Munich, and Lola Montez," 102–103.

168 On 15 October: GKL 684–685, citing KL's diary.

168 At the end: For de los Valles' visit to Lola, see KLA 41, de los Valles file, de los Valles to LM, 9 November 1847.

169 "recognize the abyss": KLA 41, de los Valles file, de los Valles to LM, 9 November 1847.

169 The Duke of Leuchtenberg: Amalia Thiersch to her sister, n.d. (probably from late November 1847), reprinted in *Deutsche Allgemeine Zeitung* [Berlin], 26 July 1919, 2c1–3; PGB 327, 23 November 1847.

170 The object of: KLA 39, Peißner file, Peißner to KL, 29 December 1848.

170 Fritz and Lola: KLA 39, Peißner file, Peißner to KL, 5 January 1849.

171 Wallerstein privately spread: PGB 332, 30 November 1847.

171 "It is impossible": PRO, FO9/100 Bavarian Correspondence, dispatch 79, 30 November 1847.

172 Even before the: FGB 313–316, 3 December 1847; PGB 333–334, 6 December 1847; KLA 39, Wallerstein file, Wallerstein to KL, 1 December 1847; WGB, 3 December 1847.

173 Perhaps it was: KLA 33 [AN 121], KL to LM, 16 June 1848, undated small enclosure; KLA 33 [AN 177], KL to LM, 1 December 1848.

173 Wallerstein would have: KLA 39, Wallerstein file, Wallerstein to KL, 2 December 1847.

174 Whether because she: PGB 333, 6 December 1847; FGB 316, 9 December 1847; KLA 39, Wallerstein file, Wallerstein to KL, 3 December 1847 and 4 December 1847; FGB 316, fn 1, 4 December 1847.

174 Mussinan was assigned: KLA 39 Mussinan file, Mussinan to KL, 4 December 1847 (two letters).

174 She dressed and: KLA 39, Berks file, Berks to KL, 4 December 1847.

174 The king had: KLA 39, Denker file, Denker to KL, 4 December 1847.

175 After the reports: PGB 335, 6 December 1847.

175 The next morning: KLA 39, Mussinan file, Mussinan to KL, 5 December 1847.

175 Munichers were forbidden: PGB 334, 6 December 1847.

176 As all this: KLA 39, Berks file, Berks to KL, 12 December 1847; KLA 39, Wallerstein file, Wallerstein to KL, 10 December 1847.

176 Wallerstein sent the: KLA 39, Mussinan file, Wallerstein to KL, 16 December 1847, to be found in letter of Mussinan to KL, 20 December 1847.

176 Wallerstein also composed: GHA ARO 35 I, Wallerstein to KL, 14 February 1848.

176 In fact, the: Schiller, *Briefe an Cotta* 3:163, Kolb to Cotta, 20 December 1847.

177 Despite the exception: GKL 705 fn 1605, citing KL's diary; KLA 34 [AN 59], LM to KL, 15 February 1848.

177 The concerted effort: MD 15; WGB, 4 January 1848.

177 Word reached the: KLA 39, Berks file, Berks to KL, n.d., referring to investigation of charges that students were not wearing their trousers.

178 But the issue: KLA 38, Berks file, KL to Berks, 3 January 1848; KLA 33 [AN 42], KL to LM, 3 January 1848; KLA 34 [AN 50], LM to KL, 3 January 1848.

178 The king's worst: See KLA 34 [AN 58], LM to KL, 14 February 1848.

178 Gossip in Munich: Amalia Thiersch to her sister, n.d. (probably about 1 February 1848), reprinted in *Deutsche Allgemeine Zeitung* [Berlin], 26 July 1919, 2c1–3.

178 "I come after": KLA 36, document in Spanish in KL's hand dated "Begun in the month of January and completed in February 1848."

179 Berks and Wallerstein: In reference to the Hohenhausen affair, see the following files in KLA 39: Berks file, Berks and Wallerstein to KL, 2 January 1848, and Berks to KL, 3 January 1848; Hohenhausen file, Hohenhausen to KL, 7 January 1848; Wallerstein file, Wallerstein to KL, 8 January 1848, 9 January 1848, and 19 January 1848. See also PGB 346–348, 11 January 1848; PGB 351–353, 18 January 1848; PGB 355, 25 January 1848; ÖGB 513–514, 7 January 1848.

179 The support of: PGB 349–350, 11 January 1848; FGB 326, 17 January 1848; WGB, 8 January 1848; MD 14.

179 In the street: WGB, 11 January 1848. PGB 331, 30 November 1847; PGB 363, 8 February 1848; ÖGB 514, fn 1, 24 January 1848.

180 Berks was having: WGB, 4 January 1848; *Allgemeine Studenten*, 5.

180 "If you wish": KLA 39, Berks file, Wallerstein memorandum to be found with letter from Berks to KL, 26 January 1848.

181 Wallerstein, left alone: KLA 39, Wallerstein file, Wallerstein to KL, 12 January 1848.

181 The hall was: MD 16; *Bayerische Landbötin* [Munich], 22 January 1848, 80c2.

182 Matters were made: SFM 18.

182 The funeral was: KLA 39, Hofbauer file, Hofbauer to KL, 10 February 1848; KAM 35; Amalia Thiersch to her sister, n.d. (probably about 1 February

1848), reprinted in *Deutsche Allgemeine Zeitung* [Berlin], 26 July 1919, 2c1–3.

183 Hohenhausen's replacement: PGB 360–361, 8 February 1848; ÖGB 519, 7 February 1848.

183 On the night: MD 18; WGB, 30 November 1847 and 8 February 1848; KLA 8:8, KL's expense book, December 1847. "Aus den Tagen der Lola Montez," 941.

183 As Rector Thiersch: From this point through the end of Chapter 19 the principal sources for the narrative, except as otherwise noted, are the following: KAM 52–64; SFM 23–39; "Aus den Tagen der Lola Montez," 913–944; "Lola Montez. Aus den Aufzeichnungen eines Achtundvierzigers," 57–63; KLA 39, Hagemann file, Hagemann to KL, n.d.; KLA 39, Weber file, Weber to KL, 12 February 1848; KLA 39, Mark file, Mark to KL, 19 February 1848; *Bayerische Landbötin* [Munich], 12 February 1848, 151c2–152c1–2; Memorandum of Burgermeister Steinsdorf, Munich Stadtarchiv, B.u.R. 1422, published in large part in Dirr, "Sturmbewegte Zeiten"; ÖGB 327–365; PGB 360–438; FGB 518–557; WGB, February and March 1848; PRO, FO149/38, dispatch 8, 11 February 1848; *Allgemeine Studenten*, 9–15; *Nachtlager in Blutenburg; Lola Montes, Gräfin von Landsfeld; Bericht aus München;* and Wolf, *Geschichtliche Walhalla*.

185 Berks sent the: NL 49/3/40, Verschiedene Gutakten, draft of decree closing the university, annotated and dated by KL on 8 February 1848; KAM 43–44.

186 When King Ludwig: MSB.

186 As King Ludwig: ÖGB 522, 9 February 1848.

188 To some onlookers: "Aus den Tagen der Lola Montez," 942.

188 He blamed the: See GHA ARO 35 I, Wallerstein to KL, 9 February 1848.

188 At about 11: "Aus der Tagen der Lola Montez," 939.

190 The countess was: MSB.

190 As 3:30 approached: The following account of the visit of the delegation relies particularly on Burgermeister Steinsdorf's memorandum, Munich Stadtarchiv, B.u.R. 1422.

192 The rioters, armed: "Aus den Tagen der Lola Montez," 937.

193 "I heard of": KLA 34 [AN 54], LM to KL, 10 February 1848.

194 "Just now a letter": KLA 33 [AN 45], KL to LM, 10 February 1848.

195 Ludwig began drafting: CKL 541–542.

196 Most dramatic of all: PGB 377, 15 February 1848.

196 A note arrived: KLA 39, Mussinan file, Mussinan to KL, [11 February 1848].

197 Kunft's announcement was: KLA 33 [AN 52], KL to LM, 15 February 1848, and [AN 62] 23 February 1848; see also Schiller, *Briefe*, 3:165.

197 Suddenly, to everyone's astonishment: In addition to the sources cited above, see KLA 39, Hagemann file, Hagemann to KL, n.d.

198 At that moment: KLA 33 [AN 46], KL to LM, 11 February 1848.

200 A delegation of: KLA 33 [AN 46], KL to LM, 11 February 1848.

201 She scribbled a note: KLA 34 [AN 56], LM to KL, [11 February 1848].

202 In Großhesselohe, Lola: In addition to sources cited in the previous chapter, see KLA 33 [AN 107], KL to L M, 11 May 1848.

202 Once back in: *Lola Montez, Gräfin*, 14; for what follows concerning Blutenburg, see particularly [Vogt?], *Nachtlager*, and an illustrated broadside entitled "Das Nachtlager."

203 In the meantime: KLA 33 [AN 46], KL to LM, 11 February 1848.

203 But news of: In addition to the previously cited sources see the following files in KLA 39: Mark file, Mark to KL, 12 February 1848; Berks file, Berks to KL, 12 February 1848; Weber file, Karl Weber to KL, n.d. Also see BSB Stieleriana 1,5, c. 1, protocol of Weber and Dichtl, 31 March 1848.

204 "My very ever": KLA 34 [AN 57], LM to KL, 12 February 1848.

205 The mood of: KLA 33 [AN 49], KL to LM, 13 February 1848; KLA 33 [AN 62], KL to LM, 23 February 1848; GHA ARO 35 I, Wallerstein to KL, 14 February 1848.

205 Wallerstein had sealed: KLA 33 [AN 50], KL to LM, 14 February 1848; KLA 33 [AN 46], KL to LM, 11 February 1848; although GKL reports a different story at page 688; *Bayerische Landesbötin* [Munich], 24 February 1848, 192c2.

206 "Don't they see": Varnhagen von Ense, *Tagebücher* 4:247, entry for 15 February 1848.

206 "I seem to": KLA 34 [AN 59], LM to KL, 14 February 1848.

207 When Mussinan took: KLA 39, Mussinan file, letters of Mussinan to KL dated 15 February 1848 and 18 February 1848, and KL's message to the three Alemannen in Lindau dated 19 February 1848.

207 "I was desperate": KLA 33 [AN 58 bis], draft letter of KL to LM, dated 18 February 1848.

208 "You are my": KLA 33 [AN 56], KL to LM, 18 February 1848.

208 Lola's reply treated: KLA 34 [AN 62], LM to KL, 19[?] February 1848.

209 "Very dear Lolitta": KLA 33 [AN 58], KL to LM, 19 February 1848 (apparently never sent).

209 Instead, when he: KLA 42, Mussinan to unknown addressee, probably Berks, 20 February 1848; KLA 34 [AN 63], LM to KL, 20 February 1848.

209 When Augusta Masson: KLA 34 [AN 60], LM to KL, 17 February 1848.

209 Lola then suggested: KLA 34 [AN 61], LM to KL, 18 February 1848.

210 "Read the free": KLA 34 [AN 59], LM to KL, 15 February 1848.

210 When Maria Denker: KLA 39, Mussinan file, Mussinan to KL, 22 February 1848 and 23 February 1848; KLA 39, Denker file, Denker to KL, n.d.; KLA 39, Peißner file, Peißner to KL, 5 January 1849; KLA 39, Denker file, Denker to KL, 25 February 1848.

210 At 9 A.M.: KLA 39, Poninski file, Poninski to KL, 25 February 1848; KLA 41, Robert Peel to LM, 21 February 1848.

211 "Things in France": KLA 34 [AN 70], LM to KL, 27 February 1848.

211 The next day: KLA 34 [AN 71], LM to KL, 28 February 1848.

212 Ludwig was told: CKL 553, quoting a letter from KL to his daughter Matilde, 6 March 1848, GHA.

212 He was afraid: KLA 33 [AN 73], KL to LM, 4 March 1848.

213 As the thousands: Spindler, "Die Politische Wendung," 337.

213 Lola had also: On the baron's identity, see his letter to KL in KLA 38 and the entry on the Meller-Zakomelsky family in Ikonnikov, *La Noblesse de la Russie* vol. J.1, j159–j171.

213 The news of: KLA 34 [AN 72 and 73], LM to KL, both dated 1 March 1848.

214 She wrote to: KLA 39, Peißner file, Peißner to KL, 5 January 1849; see also Lola's note reproduced in facsimile in Fuchs, *Tanzidyll*, 157.

214 With only bad: On Lola's return to Munich, see KLA 36, memoranda of KL dated 29 April 1854 and 27 January 1858; *Bayerische Landbötin* [Munich], 11 March 1848, 248c1–2; "Aus der Tagen der Lola Montez," 942–943; Wolf, *Geschichtliche Walhalla*, 11–13; and CKL 554–556, which appears to be based on an unidentified and unpublished source. Lola's own account is at LML 72–74.

216 Standing in her: LML 73.

216 With the newly: *Bayerische Landbötin* [Munich], 11 March 1848, 248c1–2; SFM 81.

216 In his mind: KLA 33 [AN 76], KL to LM, 10 March 1848, and [AN 77], 12 March 1848; Albrecht, "König Ludwig," 71.

217 The city celebrated: KLA 33 [AN 77], KL to LM, 12 March 1848.

217 Ludwig himself may: KLA 33 [AN 78], KL to LM, 15 March 1848; *Bayerische Landbötin* [Munich], 18 March 1848, 276c1–2.

219 "My very beloved": KLA 33 [AN 79], KL to LM, 17 March 1848.

219 As King Ludwig: KLA 39, Peißner file, Peißner to KL, 5 January 1849.

220 Apparently on the: KLA 34 [AN 75], LM to KL, 12 March 1848.

220 Lola also advised: KLA 34 [AN 77], LM to KL, 15 March 1848.

220 In Frankfurt, Peißner: KLA 39, Peißner file, Peißner to KL, 5 January 1849.

221 From her hotel: KLA 34 [AN 78], LM to KL, 16 March 1848.

221 On the 16th: KLA 33 [AN 79], KL to LM, 17 March 1848; GKL 716.

221 Rotenhan suggested to: Spindler, "Die Politische Wendung," 338.

222 "For 23 years": GKL 717.

222 "Very dear Lolitta": KLA 33 [AN 80 bis], KL to LM, 19 March 1848.

222 "God knows when": KLA 33 [AN 81], KL to LM, 19 March 1848, and [AN 83] KL to LM, 22 March 1848.

222 "Bavarians! A new": GKL 718–719.

224 When King Ludwig's farewell: PRO, FO 149/38 Bavarian Correspondence, dispatch 19, 23 March 1848.

224 In Frankfurt Lola: PGB 437, fn 1, 22 March 1848; *Examiner* [London], 8 April 1848, 236c2.

224 At the same: KLA 34 [AN 80], LM to KL, 18 March 1848; KLA 33 [AN 84], KL to LM, 23 March 1848.

225 Back in Bern: KLA 34 [AN 82], LM to KL, n.d.

225 "One last time": KLA 34 [AN 86], LM to King Maximilian, 24 March 1848; KLA 33 [AN 87], KL to LM, 29 March 1848.

225 Lola also told: KLA 34 [AN 83], LM to KL, 23 March 1848, with enclosures.

226 Then she wrote: KLA 34 [AN 87], LM to KL, 26 March 48; KLA 39, Peißner file, Peißner to KL, 29 December 1848; see also Letter of LM (not in her hand) to Carl Deil, 30 March 1848, Stadtarchiv, Hannover.

226 "I entreat you": KLA 33 [AN 88], KL to LM, 1 April 1848, and [AN 89] 3 April 1848.

226 He would see: KLA 33 [AN 92], KL to LM, 8 April 1848.

226 In the meantime: KLA 34 [AN 89], LM to KL, 2 April 1848, and [AN 90] 5 April 1848.

227 In the meantime: KLA 34 [AN 91], LM to KL, 7 April 1848; KLA 39, Peißner file, Peißner to KL, 29 December 1848.

227 In light of: KLA 39, Mussinan file, Mussinan to KL, 13 April 1848; and Vogt von Hunolstein file, Vogt von Hunolstein to KL, 9 April 1848 and 13 April 1848.

227 Finally, King Max: KLA 33 [AN 94], KL to LM, 11 April 1848, and [AN 95] 12 April 1848.

227 He wrote a sad letter: KLA 33 [AN 97], KL to LM, 17 April 1848.

228 Lola had had a bitter fight: KLA 39, Murray file, Murray to KL, 19 April 1848; KLA 33 [AN 99], KL to LM, 23 April 1848; KLA 34 [AN 96], LM to KL, 23 April 1848.

228 Lola's belongings were: KLA 34 [AN 95], LM to KL, 22 April 1848, enclosure by Frederic Bähler dated 20 April 1848.

228 The affair with: KLA 39, Peißner file, Peißner to KL, 29 December 1848.

229 "Dear Louis, one": KLA 34 [AN 98], LM to KL, 29 April 1848.

229 "When it comes": KLA 33 [AN 106], KL to LM, 9 May 1848.

229 "Its seems to": KLA 34 [AN 100], LM to KL, 9 May 1848.

230 Off in London: Coyne, *Pas de Fascination;* Playbill for the Theatre Royal, Haymarket, London, 29 April 1848, Harry Ransom Center for the Humanities, University of Texas, Austin; *Illustrated London News*, 29 April 1848, 281c1 ("'Lola Montès' will prove as attractive to the London public as she was to the Bavarian monarch"), and 6 May 1848, 296c3; *Satirist* [London], 29 April 1848, 152c1, 6 May 1848, 164c1, and 27 May 1848, 200c2.

230 "It's all the": KLA 34 [AN 105], LM to KL, 8 June 1848.

231 "How can you": KLA 34 [AN 106], LM to KL, 8 June 1848.

232 Her words were: KLA 33 [AN 121], KL to LM, 16 June 1848 (enclosure reading, "Once you have read this paper, burn it at once").

232 Lola kept encouraging: KLA 39, Rufenacht file, Rufenacht to KL, 8 August 1848 (draft); Peißner file, Peißner to KL, 29 December 1848.

232 Papon's grandfather had: On Papon, see KLA 39, Rufenacht file, Rufenacht to KL, 31 August 1848, 27 September 1848, and 10 January 1849. Rufenacht had the feeling that Lola and Papon might have known each other in Paris but had no evidence to support that idea. See also Archives d'Etat de Genève, Etrangers, 3 December 1848, 267, 461.

233 Among other things: KLA 34 [AN 109], LM to KL, 30 June 1848, enclosure
with note from KL on one side and reply from LM on the other.

233 During this time: KLA 39, Rufenacht file, Rufenacht to KL, 8 August 1848
and 8 August 1848 (draft).

234 In his letters: KLA 33 [AN 130], KL to LM, 13 July 1848; KLA 33 [AN 134]
25 July 1848; and KLA 33 [AN 142] 13 August 1848.

234 Instead, the letter: KLA 34 [AN 115], LM to KL, 17 August 1848.

234 He wrote her: KLA 33 [AN 144], KL to LM, 25 August 1848.

234 But it was: KLA 39, Rufenacht file, KL to Rufenacht, 27 August 1848 and 28
August 1848.

234 Lola borrowed the: KLA 39, Rufenacht file, Rufenacht to KL, 26 August
1848; KLA 33 [AN 145], KL to LM, 28 August 1848.

235 Enclosed with the: KLA 33 [AN 146], KL to LM, 29 August 1848.

235 "What great pain": KLA 34 [AN 116], LM to KL, 2 September 1848.

235 "You know, you": KLA 34 [AN 117], LM to KL, 7 September 1848.

236 What is your motive: KLA 33 [AN 151], KL to LM, 13 September 1848.

236 Rufenacht wrote the king: KLA 39, Rufenacht file, Rufenacht to KL, 14 September 1848 and 27 September 1848; KLA 34 [AN 118], LM to KL, 14 September 1848.

236 "It seems to me": KLA 33 [AN 154], KL to LM, 23 September 1848.

236 The only consolation: KLA 39, Rufenacht file, Rufenacht to KL, 27 September 1848, enclosing a copy of a letter to him from Peißner dated 23 September 1848; KLA 39, Peißner file, Peißner to KL, 29 December 1848.

237 "I know you"; KLA 34 [AN 119], LM to KL, 27 September 1848.

237 Ludwig received the: The following account of the meeting between Papon
and KL is based on the letters in the Papon files in KLA 38 and KLA 39; on
KLA 33 [AN 159], KL to LM, 7 October 1848; and on the account in PLM.

237 "Some day all": KLA 34 [AN 120], LM to KL, 2 October 1848.

238 Lola was right: KLA 34 [AN 158], LM to KL, 6 October 1848; and [AN 172]
KL to LM, "15 October 1848" (actually 15 November 1848, as the internal
dating of the letter clearly indicates).

238 "It is the duty": KLA 34 [AN 125], LM to KL, 20 October 1848.

238 "What a terrible": KLA 34 [AN 126], LM to KL, 1 November 1848.

239 Although months earlier: KLA 33 [AN 169], KL to LM, 5 November 1848.

239 At the theater: The story of Lola and Lord Julius is reconstructed from KLA
34 [AN 128], LM to KL, 20 November 1848, and [AN 129] 25 November 1848;
KLA 39, Papon file, Papon to KL, 24 November 1848, with enclosure of letter
from Charles Peschier to Papon of 23 November 1848, and Papon to KL, 1
December 1848; KLA 39, Rufenacht file, Rufenacht to KL, 10 January 1849.
See also *Genealogisches Taschenbuch der deutschen gräflichen Häuser auf
das Jahr 1847*, 582.

240 "I don't have": KLA 34 [AN 127], LM to KL, 8[?] November 1848.

240 What did the: KLA 38, Papon file, KL to Papon, 18 November 1848.

241 "He has sworn": KLA 34 [AN 128], LM to KL, 20 November 1848.

241 Just a week: KLA 33 [AN 173], KL to LM, 19 November 1848; KLA 33 [AN 174], KL to LM, 23 November 1848.

241 Lola returned triumphantly: See Peschier letter to Papon enclosed in KLA 39, Papon file, Papon to KL, 24 November 1848; KLA 33 [AN 119], KL to LM, 12 June 1848; KLA 34 [AN 108], LM to KL, 21 June 1848.

242 Lola and her: KLA 34 [AN 129], LM to KL, 25 November 1848 and [AN 130], 27 November 1848.

243 "I like it": KLA 34 [AN 132], LM to KL, 7 December 1848.

244 "Without lying": KLA 33 [AN 178], KL to LM, 13 December 1848.

244 As the first: KLA 33 [AN 177], KL to LM, 1 December 1848.

244 "The position in": KLA 39, Papon file, Papon to KL, 1 December 1848.

244 "Dear Louis, Geneva": KLA 34, LM to KL, 11 December 1848.

245 The first days: KLA 39, Peißner file, Peißner to KL, 5 January 1849.

245 "I very much": KLA 33 [AN 185 bis], KL to LM, 6 January 1849, draft.

245 "Had I but": Quoted in CKL 561, from the manuscript in GHA.

246 "It seems to": KLA 34 [AN 139], LM to KL, 19 January 1849.

246 "Louis of Bavaria": PLM, v.

247 Lola read a copy: KLA 39, Rufenacht file, copy of letter of LM to Rufenacht, 10 January 1849; KLA 34 [AN 138], LM to KL, 12 January 1849.

247 "It is most": KLA 33 [AN 188], KL to LM, 23 January 1849; KLA 38, Papon file, KL to Papon, 22 January 1849.

247 "After having so": PLM 53.

248 On the 11th: MSB; KLA 33 [AN 191], KL to LM, 15 February 1849.

248 "Please tell me": KLA 33 [AN 191], KL to LM, 15 February 1849.

248 "Because you have": KLA 33 [AN 191], KL to LM, 15 February 1849.

248 "I was never": KLA 34 [AN 141], LM to KL, 1 March 1849.

249 Ludwig was not: KLA 33 [AN 193], KL to LM, 1 March 1849.

249 "In London it": KLA 34 [AN 162], LM to KL, 20 February 1849; KLA 34 [AN 163], LM to KL, 24 February 1849; and KLA 34 [AN 142], LM to KL, n.d., enclosure by Dr. Thomas Watson, 1 March 1849.

249 To raise money: KLA 34 [AN 149], LM to KL, 22 March 1849; *Sunday Times* [London], 25 March 1849, 5c4; KLA 34 [AN 143], LM to KL, 5 March 1849; KLA 39, Rosmann file, Rosmann to KL, 27 March 1847.

250 She had repeatedly: KLA 34, LM to KL, 15 March 1849; KLA 34, [AN 148] 19 March 1849; KLA 34 [AN 150], 24 March 1849; KLA 33 [AN 198], KL to LM, 20 March 1849; KLA 33 [AN 199], 23 March 1849; KLA 33 [AN 200], 27 March 1849.

250 Most prominent among: KLA 34 [AN 162], LM to KL, 20 February 1849; Gower, *Bygone Years*, 116–117; Sala, *Life* 1:194–195.

250 The most extraordinary: KLA 34 [AN 153], LM to KL, 26 April 1849.

251 "If something were": KLA 34 [AN 151], LM to KL, 2 April 1849.

252 "Docile and confident": PLM 85–86.

252 "To work, Sire": PLM 96.

252 Even Ludwig felt: KLA 33 [AN 197], KL to LM, 16 March 1849; *Nouvelliste*

Vaudois, 31 March 1849, 1c1–2, quoted in *Journal de Genève*, 5 April 1849, 3c1.

252 The Swiss authorities: KLA 39, Rufenacht file, Rufenacht to KL, 12 May 1849.

252 Back in London: KLA 34 [AN 149], LM to KL, 22 March 1849; KLA 34 [AN 144], 6 May 1849; KLA 34 [AN 154], 12 May 1849; KLA 33 [AN 210], KL to LM, 24 May 1849.

253 "A voice inside": KLA 34 [AN 156], LM to KL, 15 June 1849.

253 "The opinion you": KLA 33 [AN 213], KL to LM, 16 June 1849.

253 Now Lola wrote: KLA 34 [AN 157], LM to KL, 28 June 1849.

254 She wrote him: KLA 34 [AN 157], LM to KL, 28 June 1849.

254 Lola had taken: MEM 3:188–191; *Assemblée Nationale* [Paris], 24 October 1849, 2c2–4; Disraeli, *Correspondence*, 228.

254 His name was: *Evening Mail* [London], 6–8 August 1849, 3c5; *Assemblée Nationale* [Paris], 24 October 1849, 2c3–4; General Registry Office, London, Entry of the Marriage of George Trafford Heald to Maria de los Dolores de Landsfeld, 19 July 1849.

255 Then, on 13 July: KLA 34 [AN 161], LM to KL, 16 July 1849.

255 Just four days: KLA 34 [AN 161], LM to KL, 16 July 1849.

256 "What happened in": KLA 33 [AN 218], KL to LM, 22 July 1849.

257 "You wrote me": KLA 33 [AN 219], KL to LM, 24 July 1849.

258 In fact, the: General Register Office, London, Registry of Marriages for Middlesex County, Parish of St. George Hanover Square, 1849; KLA 39, Cetto file, Cetto to KL, 4 August 1849; Catholic Archdiocese of Westminster, Register of Marriages in the French Chapel in King Street, 1849.

259 "Dear Louis, for": KLA 34 [AN 164], LM to KL, 1 August 1849.

259 On Monday, 6 August: The following account of Lola's arrest and booking are based on reports in *Era* [London], 19 August 1849, 2c2, and *Weekly Chronicle* [London], 12 August 1849, 5c3–4.

260 A hearing was: This account of Lola's hearing is based on reports in *Express* [London], 7 August 1849, 4c1–2; *Evening Mail* [London], 6–8 August 1849, 3c5; *Examiner* [London], 11 August 1849, 508c2–3 (this account was reprinted in *Sunday Times* [London], 12 August 1849, 2c3–4).

261 Representing the countess: Gower, *Bygone Years*, 116–117.

262 Lola and her: *Evening Mail* [London], 10–12 September 1849, 5c6; *Courrier de l'Europe* [London], 1 September 1849, 559c1; KLA 34 [AN 165], LM to KL, 15 September 1849.

262 From Rome they: *Evening Mail* [London], 10–12 September 1849, 5c6.

262 In England, the: *Express* [London], 8 August 1849, 3c1–2; *Weekly Chronicle* [London], 11 August 1849, 4c5–6. On the Divorce Act of 1857 and divorce in England in the nineteenth century, see Horstman, *Victorian Divorce*; *Punch* [London] 17 (1849):75c1; *News of the World* [London], 26 August 1849, 3c2.

263 The bigamy scandal: *Weekly Chronicle* [London], 16 September 1849, 6c1–2; *Lady's Newspaper* [London], 15 September 1849, 142c2–3, 154c2; *Court*

Journal [London], 1 September 1849, 742c2; *Sunderland Herald*, 31 August 1849, 5c1–2; *Express* [London], 11 August 1849, 3c3; *Evening Mail* [London], 13 August 1849, 2c4.

263 Lola and Heald: *Evening Mail* [London], 13 August 1849, 2c4; *Court Journal* [London], 15 September 1849, 785c2; *Courrier de l'Europe* [London], 15 September 1849, 582c1; *Evening Mail*, 12–14 September 1849, 3c5.

263 She had not: KLA 33 [AN 220], KL to LM, 30 July 1849 (draft); KLA 33 [AN 221], 10 August 1849 (draft).

264 Ignorant of all: KLA 34 [AN 165], LM to KL, 15 September 1849.

264 He replied that: KLA 33 [AN 223], KL to LM, 19 September 1849, enclosing [AN 222], 11 August 1849; KLA 8,8, KL's account book, 1847–1854, 1 October 1849.

264 Shortly after Heald: *Courrier de l'Europe* [London], 22 September 1849, 598c1–3.

265 Now she transformed: *Constitution* [Cork], 18 September 1849, 2c3; *Courrier de l'Europe* [London], 22 September 1849, 598c1–3.

265 The story went: *Assemblée Nationale* [Paris], 24 October 1849, 2c3–4; *New York Herald*, 19 November 1849, 1c3; KLA 34 [AN 166], LM to KL, 16 November 1849.

265 "I beg you": KLA 34 [AN 166], LM to KL, 16 November 1849.

266 Lola and Heald: *New York Herald*, 28 January 1850, 3c1; KLA 34 [AN 168], LM to KL, 31 December 1849; Letter of LM to Henry Vane, 31 December 1849, Harry Ransom Center for the Humanities, University of Texas, Austin.

266 "I told you": KLA 33 [AN 224], KL to LM, 23 December 1849.

266 Now she could: Letter of LM to Henry Vane, 31 December 1849, Harry Ransom Center for the Humanities, University of Texas, Austin.

266 Lola wrote to: KLA 34 [AN 169], LM to KL, 8 January 1850.

267 Late in January: KLA 33 [AN 227], KL to LM, 15 January 1850, returned as undeliverable; *Galignani's Messenger* [Paris], 11 February 1850, 3c1; KLA 34 [AN 170], LM to KL, 25 February 1850; KLA 33 [AN 226], KL to LM, 14 January 1850.

267 "The first thing": KLA 34 [AN 170], LM to KL, 25 February 1850.

267 "At this hour": KLA 33 [AN 228], KL to LM, 3 March 1850.

268 "Why do you": KLA 34 [AN 171], LM to KL, 8 March 1850.

268 "Enclosed are the": KLA 33 [AN 229], KL to LM, 13 March 1850.

268 The countess arrived: *National* [Paris], 17 August 1850, 3c3; *Galignani's Messenger* [Paris], 2 April 1850, 6c2; *New York Herald*, 22 April 1850, 1c4.

268 The notorious couple: *Gazette des Tribunaux* [Paris], 1 September 1850, 1039c1; KLA 39, Wendland file, Wendland to KL, 2 December 1850, enclosing anonymous police intelligence report.

268 The Healds did: KLA 39, Wendland file, Wendland to KL, 15 June 1850; *New York Herald*, 20 May 1850, 1c3, 7 June 1850, 2c2, and 2 July 1850, 2c3.

269 There were rumors: KLA 39, Wendland file, Wendland to KL, 15 June 1850; *Corsaire-Satan* [Paris], 16–17 August 1850, 1c1–2.

269 This life in: KLA 42, H. D. Davies to George Trafford Heald, 2 August 1850.

269 "My life is": KLA 34 [AN 172], LM to KL, 26 May 1850.

270 Ludwig decided that: GHA Wendland Nachlaß 50/I, KL to Wendland, 1 June 1850; KLA 39, Wendland file, Wendland to KL, 15 June 1850.

270 Ludwig wrote to: KLA 33 [AN 225], KL to LM, 9 June 1850 (draft; later version probably sent); KLA 34 [AN 173], LM to KL, 26 June 1850.

270 Instead, he peppered: GHA Nachlaß Wendland 50/I, KL to Wendland, 22 June 1850; KLA 39, Wendland file, Wendland to KL, 3 July 1850.

271 Lola had not: KLA 42, H. D. Davies to George Trafford Heald, 2 August 1850; KLA 39, Wendland file, Wendland to KL, 18 October 1850; *New York Herald*, 9 September 1850, 2c3, 7 October 1850, 4c2; GHA Urkunde 54/L4/32,6, LM to Henry Wellington Vallaince, 2 October 1850.

271 Lola was left: KLA 39, Wendland file, Wendland to KL, 18 October 1850; *New York Herald*, 9 September 1850, 2c3; *Sunday Times* [London], 25 August 1850, 4c3; GHA Urkunde 54/L4/32,6, LM to Henry Wellington Vallaince, 2 October 1850.

271 Heald finally agreed: *Galignani's Messenger* [Paris], 3 October 1850, 4c2–3; *New York Herald*, 21 October 1850, 1c3. *New York Herald*, 7 October 1850, 4c2; GHA Urkunde 54/L4/32,6, LM to Henry Wellington Vallaince, 2 October 1850; KLA39, Wendland file, Wendland to KL, 27 November 1850 and 8 December 1850, enclosing a police intelligence report; KLA 39, Wendland file, Wendland to KL, 8 December 1850, enclosing a police intelligence report.

272 There were even: *New York Herald*, 26 October 1850, 3c5; KLA39, Wendland file, Wendland to KL, 18 November 1850 and 8 December 1850; KLA 39, Wendland file, Wendland to KL, 18 November 1850.

272 Lola took to: KLA 39, Wendland file, Wendland to KL, 27 November 1850, 8 December 1850, 21 May 1851, 28 March [?] 1851; *New York Herald*, 23 December 1850, 1c2.

272 Now she wrote: KLA 34 [AN 174], LM to KL, 27 October 1850.

272 Corail seems to: KLA 39, Wendland file, Wendland to KL, 5 January 1851; *New York Herald*, 21 February 1851, 2c3.

273 Whether or not: KLA 39, Wendland file, Wendland to KL, 5 January 1851 and 8 February 1851.

273 In a final: KLA 39, Wendland file, de Lunel to KL with enclosed galley proofs and enclosure to Wendland's letter to KL of 8 January 1851.

273 The introduction set: MEM 1:1, 6, 8, 9.

274 She also managed: MEM 1:25–26.

274 Wendland was able: KLA 39, Wendland file, Wendland to KL, 8 February 1851.

274 She was said: KLA 39, Wendland file, Wendland to KL, 21 May 1851.

274 "Oh, Louis, if": KLA 34 [AN 175], LM to KL, undated but annotated by KL "Received 26 March 1851."

275 "Through you I": Ludwig I, *Gedichte*, 139, from the original manuscript in GHA.

276 What had brought: KLA 39, Pocci file, Pocci to KL, 2 May 1851; O'Brien file, O'Brien to KL, n.d. [5 May 1851?]; GHA Wendland Nachlaß 50/I, KL to Wendland, 7 May 1851.

276 He sent O'Brien: KLA 39, O'Brien file, O'Brien to KL, "Tuesday morning" [6 May 1851?] and [5 May 1851?].

276 "Tell the king": KLA 39, O'Brien file, O'Brien to KL, "Rome, Friday."

276 Wendland reported to: KLA 39, Wendland file, Wendland to KL, 20 June 1851; GHA Wendland Nachlaß 50/I, KL to Wendland, 30 July 1851; KLA 8,8, accounts book for 1847–54, July 1851; KLA 39, Pocci file, Pocci to KL, 1 August 1851.

277 She had moved: *New York Herald*, 30 July 1851, 3c6, 12 August 1851, 2c2, and 29 August 1851, 1c4.

277 Mabille choreographed several: *Sunday Times* [London], 21 September 1851, 3c4; *Courrier de l'Europe* [London], 20 September 1851, 710c2–3; KLA 39, Wendland file, Wendland to KL, 28 March 1851.

277 Her new apartment: *New York Herald*, 25 December 1851, 4c5.

278 Early in the spring: See Letter from George P. Morris to P. T. Barnum, 8 November 1851, Special Collections Department, Alderman Library, University of Virginia, Charlottesville.

278 "Thousands of Americans": *Boston Daily Evening Transcript*, 31 March 1852, 2c1.

278 "We shall be": *New York Times*, 26 September 1851, 2c3.

279 She signed a: *New York Herald*, 30 December 1851, 4c2–3.

279 About three hundred: *Courrier de l'Europe* [London], 20 September 1851, 710c2–3.

279 When at last: *Courrier des Etats Unis* [New York], 3 October 1851, 3c1; *Union* [Paris], 14 September 1851, 3c3; *Indépendence Belge* [Brussels], 20 September 1851, 1c1–4.

279 Four days later: *Revue et Gazette des Théâtres* [Paris], 21 September 1851, 3c3; *Deutsche Theater-Zeitung* [Berlin], 27 September 1851, 311c1; *New York Herald*, 28 October 1851, 2c1.

279 From Boulogne she: *Sunday Times* [London], 26 October 1851, 3c2; *Emancipation* [Brussels], 26 September 1851, 3c3, and 2 October 1851, 2c2; *Journal de la Belgique* [Brussels], 27 September 1851, 3c3; *Revue et Gazette des Théâtres* [Paris], 5 October 1851, 4c1.

280 She stayed at: *Galignani's Messenger* [Paris], 27 September 1851, 3c2; *Emancipation* [Brussels], 28 September 1851, 2c4, 3c1; *Augsburger Tagblatt*, 3 October 1851, 1542; *New York Herald*, 28 October 1851, 2c1.

280 After a one-night-stand: *Echo der Gegenwart* [Aachen], 1 October 1851, 3c2, 6 October 1851, 1c3, and 7 October 1851, 2c1; *New York Herald*, 28 October 1851, 2c1 and 4c4; *Augsburger Tagblatt*, 24 November 1851, 1880.

280 Lola's tour was: *Revue et Gazette des Théâtres* [Paris], 23 November 1851, 5c1.

281 From Bordeaux, the: *Union* [Paris], 17 October 1851, 3c4; *Galignani's Messenger* [Paris], 25 October 1851, 3c2.

281 The tour worked: *Deutsche Theater Zeitung* [Berlin], 1 November 1851, 355c2; *Galignani's Messenger* [Paris], 27 October 1851, 4c1.

282 Willis had booked: *New York Herald*, 13 January 1852, 4c6.

282 The voyage was: *New York Herald*, 5 December 1851, 2c5, 13 January 1852, 4c6.

282 She was going: *New York Post*, 5 December 1851, 2c1–3; *New York Herald*, 5 December 1851, 2c5; *Courrier des Etats Unis* [New York], 27 November 1851, 2c4.

283 In Manhattan, Lola: *New York Herald*, 6 November 1851, 4c3–4, 13 January 1852, 4c6, and 6 December 1851, 2c3; *New York Tribune*, 6 December 1851, 5c1.

284 To deal with: Moore, "George Washington Smith."

284 Smith also prepared: Moore, "George Washington Smith," 111.

285 Lola found time: Both a copy of the lithograph and a manuscript note of appreciation from Lola to Meade Brothers dated 22 December 1851 are in Harvard Theatre Collection.

285 In noting her: *Courrier des Etats Unis* [New York], 29 December 1851, 2c5; *New York Herald*, 29 December 1851, 1c6.

285 The Broadway Theater: This account of Lola's American debut is based on *New York Herald*, 30 December 1851, 4c2–3; *New York Post*, 30 December 1851, 2c4; *Courrier des Etats Unis* [New York], 30 December 1851, 3c1; and *Albion* [New York], 3 January 1852, 8c3.

286 "Ladies and gentlemen": *New York Herald*, 30 December 1851, 4c2–3.

286 The *Albion's* critic: *Albion* [New York], 3 January 1852, 8c3.

286 Her initial: *Sun* [Baltimore], 6 January 1852, 2c2; *New York Herald*, 13 January 1852, 4c6.

287 In the midst: *New York Herald*, 5 January 1852, 2c3, 6 January 1852, 4c4, 7 January 1852, 2c1, 10 January 1852, 5c2, and 13 January 1852, 4c6.

287 "Mr. Bennett": *New York Herald*, 15 January 1852, 4c5–6.

288 The wide republication: *Sun* [Baltimore], 28 January 1852, 2c3.

288 Her engagement at: *Public Ledger and Daily Transcript* [Philadelphia], 27 January 1852, 2c2.

289 From the beginning: Ware is a shadowy figure, and it has been suggested that the name was merely a pseudonym of a literary friend of William Bennett; but, on balance, the evidence seems to indicate he was a real, if obscure, playwright. See *New York Herald*, 6 April 1852, 3c5–6.

289 On the Monday: *Daily Pennsylvanian* [Philadelphia], 22 January 1852, 2c2, and 24 January 1852, 3c6; *Sunday Dispatch* [Philadelphia], 25 January 1852, 2c7; *Public Ledger and Daily Transcript* [Philadelphia], 3 February 1852, 2c3; *New York Herald*, 6 February 1852, 2c3–4, and 10 February 1852, 3c3.

289 She concluded her: *New York Herald*, 3 February 1852, 7c1, 6 February 1852, 2c3–4, and 15 February 1852, 1c2.

289 She went on: *New York Herald*, 25 February 1852, 2c1; *Richmond Dispatch*, 19 February 1852, 2c5; *Richmond Whig*, 20 February 1852, 2c1, and 25 February 1852, 2c1; *New York Herald*, 6 March 1852, 3c5.

289 After a one-night-stand: *Sun* [Baltimore], 27 February 1852, 2c1; *Boston Herald*, 12 March 1852, 2c5.

290 An incident during: *Boston Daily Evening Transcript*, 27 March 1852, 2c2, quoting *Boston Courier*.

290 The *Boston Daily*: *Boston Daily Evening Transcript*, 29 March 1852, 2c2; *Boston Herald*, 31 March 1852, 2c4; *Boston Daily Courier*, 1 April 1852, 1c8.

291 The *Transcript*, which: *Boston Daily Transcript*, 31 March 1852, 2c1–2, and 2 April 1852, 1c1–3; *New York Herald*, 31 March 1852, 1c6, and 1 April 1852, 6c3–4.

292 On the day: *Boston Daily Mail*, 3 April 1852, 2c1.

292 She and her: *Boston Herald*, 12 April 1852, 4c4; *Boston Transcript*, 12 April 1852, 2c5.

292 "Lola Montez is": *Boston Daily Mail*, 20 April 1852, 4c1, quoting *Hartford Times*.

292 Lola returned to: *New York Herald*, 30 April 1852, 7c2, 1 May 1852, 2c3, and 3 May 1852, 2c3; *New York Times*, 1 May 1852, 1c6.

293 Back in Europe: GHA Wendland Nachlaß 50/I, KL to Wendland, 14 June 1852.

293 Lola appeared before: *New York Herald*, 9 May 1852, 2c3; *Buffalo Daily Courier*, 11 May 1852, 2c5, and 12 May 1852, 2c5.

293 The role of: Thomas Barry to James Wright, 13 [18?] January 1852, Boston Public Library.

294 "Thus, in the": *New York Herald*, 27 May 1852, 7c4.

295 "Law may walk": *New York Herald*, 27 May 1852, 7c4.

295 The initial run: *New York Herald*, 27 May 1852, 4c4, 30 May 1852, 4c3; unidentified newspaper clipping quoting a review in *New York Mirror*, in Harvard Theatre Collection.

295 One critic remarked: *Public Ledger and Daily Transcript* [Philadelphia], 4 June 1852, 3c1.

296 "In this extraordinary": *Sunday Dispatch* [Philadelphia], 6 June 1852, 2c7.

296 Lola then took: *National Intelligencer* [Washington], 8 June 1852, 3c4, and 10 June 1852, 3c3; *Republic* [Washington], 9 June 1852, 3c2.

296 Then Lola was: *Daily Argus* [Baltimore], 19 June 1852, 3c1; *Sun* [Baltimore], 21 June 1852, 1c7; Moore, "George Washington Smith," 111.

297 Tom Hamblin, who: *New York Herald*, 12 June 1852, 4c4–5, 30 June 1852, 2c6, 2 July 1852, 4c4, and 5 July 1852, 2c5.

297 For the summer: *New York Herald*, 11 July 1852, 2c5, 25 August 1852, 2c3, and 27 August 1852, 1c6; *New York Times*, 6 September 1852, 3c6.

298 The *Daily Mail* thought: *Daily Mail* [Boston], 21 September 1852, 2c2 and 4c5, 23 September 1852, 2c4, and 25 September 1852, 2c3.

298 The world premiere: *Sunday Dispatch* [Philadelphia], 17 October 1852, 2c7; *Boston Herald*, 1 October 1852, 4c5.

298 The *Daily Mail* sent: *Daily Mail* (Boston), 29 September 1852, 2c2.

298 The *Daily Mail's* other: *Daily Mail* (Boston), 2 October 1852, 4c1.

298 *Maritana* was introduced: *Boston Daily Mail*, 2 October 1852, 4c1.

298 Lola opened in: *Sunday Dispatch* [Philadelphia], 24 October 1852, 2c5; *New York Herald*, 11 July 1852, 2c5.

299 The *Daily Pennsylvanian* declared: *Daily Pennsylvanian* [Philadelphia], 23 October 1852, 3c3; *Sunday Dispatch* [Philadelphia], 17 October 1852, 2c7.

299 *Charlotte Corday*, in: *Sunday Dispatch* [Philadelphia], 6 June 1852, 2c7, and 17 October 1852, 2c7.

299 He called *Maritana: Sunday Dispatch* [Philadelphia], 17 October 1852, 2c7, and 24 October 1852, 2c5.

300 "by its singing": Quoted by Charles Haywood in his introduction to Maretzek, *Revelations*, vii.

301 Her first engagement: Neither *Charleston Mercury* nor *Charleston Daily Courier* commented on Lola's performances except to note that attendance was good; *Charleston Daily Courier*, 7 December 1852, 2c2.

301 As she made: See Lola's comments on the South and its society in the manuscripts of her lecture on American slavery in Harvard Theatre Collection, vol. 3 of the manuscripts, 2nd lecture; *Mobile Daily Advertiser*, 23 December 1852, 3c1.

301 Her tour had: *Mobile Daily Advertiser*, 22 December 1852, 3c1, 23 December 1852, 3c1, 24 December 1852, 3c1, and 29 December 1852, 3c1; *Mobile Daily Register*, 23 December 1852, 3c1, 25 December 1852, 2c4, and 28 December 1852, 3c1; *New Orleans Daily Picayune*, 31 December 1852, 2c5; *Deutsche Zeitung* [New Orleans], 1 January 1853, 2c6.

302 On the second: James Sprigg to Elizabeth Linn, 5 January 1853, Lewis F. Linn Papers, Missouri Historical Society, St. Louis.

302 The reviews were: *New Orleans Daily Picayune*, 4 January 1853, 2c1; 5 January 1853, 2c1; *Courrier de la Louisiane* (New Orleans), 7 January 1853, 2c4–5.

302 It is possible: *New Orleans Daily Picayune*, 14 January 1853, 1c6, and 15 January 1853, 1c2; *New York Times* reported Heald's supposed death on its front page on 14 January but carried a correction on 22 January, also on the front page. No correction seems to have appeared in the New Orleans newspapers. An article in the *Boston Daily Mail*, 23 February 1853, copied from the *New Orleans Delta*, refers to Lola as being "rendered irritable by rumors of the loss of a husband," so she certainly heard the news.

303 Again the critics: *New Orleans Picayune*, 29 January 1853, 1c2, and 24 January 1853, 1c3.

303 The approaching departure: The following account is based on a story in the *Boston Daily Mail*, 23 February 1853, copied from the *New Orleans Delta*, and others in *Courrier de la Louisiane*, 10 February 1853, 2c2, and in *Deutsche Zeitung* [New Orleans], 10 February 1853, 3c1, and 11 February 1853, 3c1.

304 "We visited the": *Cincinnati Daily Commercial*, 5 March 1853, 2c3.

305 "The criticisms we": *Cincinnati Gazette*, 2 March 1853, 2c3.

305 "Up to now": *Deutscher Republicaner* [Cincinnati], 2 March 1853, 3c2.

306 On 21 March: *Missouri Republican* [St. Louis], 21 March 1853, 2c10.

306 "Well, Lola Montez": Quoted in Whiting, *Kate Field*, 33.

306 The St. Louis engagement: *St. Louis Democrat* quoted in *Liberty [Mo.] Weekly Tribune*, 15 April 1853, 1c5.

306 It seems to: *Louisville Daily Democrat*, 1 April 1853, 3c2; *Louisville Daily Journal*, 12 April 1853, 3c2.

307 They arrived back: The following account of the incident and the subsequent court hearing is based on an unidentified newspaper clipping in Harvard Theatre Collection, a clipping from the *Boston Daily Mail* of 26 April 1853 in the same collection, *Courrier de la Louisiane*, 10 April 1853, 2c3; *Deutsche Zeitung* [New Orleans], 15 April 1853, 3c2; and *New York Times*, 21 April 1853, 6c3, and 22 April 1853, 8c2–3; *Daily Panama Star*, 6 May 1853, 2c2–4; *Gazette des Tribunaux* [Paris], 13 May 1853, 458c4–459c1.

308 "At last she": *Boston Daily Mail*, 26 April 1853.

309 Lola took over: *New York Times*, 22 April 1853, 8c2–3.

309 Whether the matter: *New Orleans Daily Picayune*, 22 April 1853, 1c3 (evening edition).

310 After a week: *Panama Herald*, 3 May 1853, 2c4.

311 When a ship: *Panama Herald*, 6 May 1853, 3c2; *Deutsche Zeitung* [New Orleans], 24 May 1853, 2c6.

311 Lola took a: *Daily Panama Star*, 5 May 1853, 2c2.

311 Many of the: *Daily Panama Star*, 5 May 1853, 2c2.

312 In the course: See California Census of 1852, 4:222, also 4:252; unidentified newspaper clipping from a Philadelphia newspaper of 21 August 1853, quoting *New York Sunday Courier*, Harvard Theatre Collection; *San Francisco Bulletin*, 26 October 1895, 20c1–3.

312 Indeed, the gold: See *Pioneer* [San Jose, Calif.], 15 September 1900, 137.

312 Whether she arrived: *Golden Era* [San Francisco], 12 June 1853, 2c6.

313 Henning quit as: *Golden Era* [San Francisco], 22 May 1853, 4c1.

313 The first-night audience: *Alta California* [San Francisco], 27 May 1853, 2c4; *Placer Times & Transcript* [San Francisco], 27 May 1853, 3c1.

313 Her triumph in: Cleland, *Apron*, 80.

314 One editor who: *Shasta Courier* [Oroville], 16 July 1853, 2c2; *Sacramento Union*, 19 July 1853, 2c7;

314 On Monday, 30 May: *Daily Evening Herald* [San Francisco], 27 May 1853, 3c1; *Alta California* [San Francisco], 31 May 1853, 2c4.

314 And, as usual: Hauser, *Wanderbuch* 1:42.

314 One of the: *Alta California* [San Francisco], 13 June 1853, 3c7; *Sacramento Union*, 15 June 1853, 2c3; Hauser, *Wanderbuch* 1:42.

315 Lola asked Hauser: Hauser, *Wanderbuch* 1:41.

315 Lola had been: *Golden Era* [San Francisco], 7 November 1858, 4c5.

315 There had been: *Placer Times & Transcript* [San Francisco], 25 June 1853, 3c1; for accounts of the wedding see *Placer Times & Transcript* [San Fran-

cisco], 2 July 1853, 1c4, *Sacramento Union*, 4 July 1853, 2c3, and *Alta California* [San Francisco], 24 January 1874, 1c3.

315 Lola's conscience may: See a facsimile of the registry entry of the Mission Dolores in Phillips, *Portsmouth Plaza*, 292.

316 After spending their: *Sacramento Union*, 6 July 1853, 2c2–3.

316 "Boldly striding to": Hauser, *Wanderbuch* 1:47–50; in addition to Hauser's account of Lola's second performance in Sacramento, see *Daily Democratic State Journal* [Sacramento], 7 July 1853, 2c5, and 8 July 1853, 4c1–2; and *Sacramento Union*, 7 July 1853, 2c6.

318 The next day: Hauser, *Wanderbuch* 1:51.

318 "Ladies and gentlemen": *Sacramento Union*, 8 July 1853, 2c3.

319 The audience, a: *Sacramento Union*, 8 July 1853, 2c3.

319 The *Daily Californian: Alta California* [San Francisco], 9 July 1853, 2c2.

319 Lola's local debut: *Sacramento Union*, 18 July 1853, 2c2; *Democratic State Journal* [Sacramento], 18 July 1853, 2c4.

319 This time Lola: *Daily Evening Herald* [San Francisco], 19 July 1853, 2c1; *San Francisco Examiner*, 19 February 1899, 31.

320 Nevertheless, a second: *Sacramento Union*, 22 July 1853, 2:3.

320 Although it was: *Placer Times & Transcript* [San Francisco], 10 October 1853, 2c4.

320 According to a: M. Tellman Wright to M. E. Wright, 12 November 1853, Sophia Smith Collection, Smith College, Northampton.

320 Lola and Hull: *Nevada Journal*, 5 August 1853, 2c5; Jonas Wincester, Grass Valley correspondent of the *Nevada Journal*, implies in this story that Lola had danced naked at a private party in Grass Valley following the cancellation of a performance at the Alta, but nothing corroborates this story, and it would have been out of character for Lola. For evidence of Wincester's authorship of the anonymous article, see his letter to E. Wincester, 14 August 1853, Jonas Wincester papers, California State Library, Sacramento; *Sacramento Union*, 22 July 1853, 2c3.

321 After her second: FDE 71.

321 She purchased the: Jonas Winchester to E. Winchester, 14 August 1853, Wincester Papers, California State Library, Sacramento; M. Tellman Wright to M. E. Wright, 12 November 1853, Sophia Smith Collection, Smith College, Northampton.

321 Hull left Grass Valley: LM to "Paco," 14 September 1853, Catalogue 11 of L'Autographe, S. A., Geneva 1987, item 186; Lola would later testify that she had been married only twice, clearly referring to James and Heald (*New York Times*, 10 February 1858, 3c3). She probably realized that her marriage to Hull was void, even if she refused to admit the same was true of her marriage to Heald.

322 Lola left her: Gilmor Meredith to his sister Emma, 29 January 1854, quoted in FDE 107; *Democratic State Journal* [Sacramento], 22 October 1853, 2c4.

322 For the first: FDE 106–107.

322 The yard around: LM to "Paco," 14 September 1853, Catalogue 11 of L'Autographe, S. A., Geneva 1987, item 186; *New York Clipper*, 5 July 1879, 119c3–4; Kip, *Early Days*, 59–60.

322 Her cottage became: FDE 106–107.

322 Ole Bull, the: *Nevada Democrat*, 3 May 1854, 2c2.

322 "I found the": *New York Clipper*, 5 July 1879, 119c3–4.

323 Among her admirers: Gilmor Meredith to his sister Emma, 29 January 1854, quoted in FDE 107. Outside of a brief reference here to a "crazy German," there is no contemporary evidence to support the legend of Lola's affair or marriage with a German nobleman in Grass Valley, sometimes called Dr. Adler or Kirke Adler, who was supposedly killed in a hunting accident. The story seems to have appeared in print first in a premature obituary for Lola in *Europa, Chronik der gebildeten Welt* [Leipzig], 1860, second semester, c1122–1125, and was repeated in the first biography of King Ludwig by Johann Sepp (*Ludwig Augustus*, 497). Evidence that the legend originated in Germany and traveled back to the United States may be contained in the fact that even though the German accounts do not mention a name, they say the man was a physician of noble birth ("ein Arzt von Adel"), and this possibly became "Dr. Adler" when the story was picked up by English-speaking chroniclers; FDE 150; LM to Conrad Hotaling, 22 November 1854, Lola Montez Collection, Bancroft Library, University of California, Berkeley; Massett, "Drifting About," 247.

323 That winter in: *Nevada Journal*, 20 January 1854, 2c5.

323 At Christmas, Lola: FDE 121–122; *Daily National Gazette* [Nevada City], 1 July 1870, 2c1.

323 Two Grass Valley: FDE 123–126.

324 Lola's grizzly cub: *Sacramento Union*, 10 February 1854, 2c5; *Grass Valley Telegraph*, 9 March 1854, 2c3; *Shasta Courier* [Oroville], 18 February 1854, 2c2.

324 "Madame Lola Montez": *Grass Valley Telegraph*, 25 May 1854, 2c2.

324 Shortly after her: *Grass Valley Telegraph*, 13 July 1854, 2c1; *Golden Era* [San Francisco], 6 August 1854, 2c5

325 There had been: *Grass Valley Telegraph*, 18 May 1854, 2c3.

325 A letter was: *San Francisco Chronicle*, 27 December 1914, 29c3–5 and 31c6, and 28 December 1914, 8c1.

325 In November 1854: The following account of the Lola-Shipley encounter is based largely on an article in *San Francisco Examiner*, 23 September 1888, 10c6–8, quoting at length from the contemporary newspaper reports, most of which have not otherwise survived.

326 In the editor's: Quoted in *Democratic State Journal* [Sacramento], 22 November 1854, 3c1–2.

327 "I recollected the": Quoted in *San Francisco Examiner*, 23 September 1888, 10c6–8; also found in an abbreviated version in *Alta California* [San Fran-

cisco], 26 November 1854, 2c4, and in the same newspaper's Steamer Edition for 1 December 1854, 3c4.

327 "Madam Lola (as)": *National Gazette* [Nevada City], 11 November 1858, quoted in Kinyon, *Northern Mines*, 147–148.

328 There in Grass Valley: *New York Daily Tribune*, 30 January 1861, 7c1–2.

328 The tour was: *Alta California* [San Francisco], 21 May 1855, 2c3; see also the quoted letter of Noel Follin in Holdredge, *Woman in Black*, 254.

328 The company included: Noel Follin to Miriam Follin, 11 July 1854[?], quoted after Stern, *Purple Passage*, 18.

329 In his last: Noel Follin to Susan and Miriam Follin, 31 May 1855, quoted after Holdredge, *Woman in Black*, 254–255.

329 By June 1855: *Sacramento Union*, 7 June 1855, 2c6; *Golden Era* [San Francisco], 3 June 1855, 2c4.

329 "Lola was in": Leman, *Memories*, 257.

329 A large crowd: *Golden Era* [San Francisco], 10 June 1855, 2c4 and 5; *Placer Times & Transcript* [San Francisco], 7 June 1855, 2c1; *California Chronicle* [San Francisco], 7 June 1855, 2c3.

331 The *Fanny Major* stopped: *Sydney Morning Herald*, 17 August 1855, 4c1; *Argus* [Melbourne], 17 September 1855, 6c3.

331 The city itself: Mourot, *This Was Sydney*, 48.

332 *Bell's Life*: See *Bell's Life in Sydney and Sporting Reviewer*, 1 September 1855, 2c6, and 25 August 1855, 2c7. *Empire* [Sydney], 27 August 1855, 4c6.

332 "I am compelled": *Argus*, 31 August 1855, 9c3–4.

333 During that first: *Bell's Life in Sydney and Sporting Reviewer*, 1 September 1855, 2c6, and 8 September 1855, 2c5.

334 On Friday, 7 September: See Affidavit of James Simmonds, Exhibit to Action 2171 before the Supreme Court of New South Wales, 1855, Archives of New South Wales, Sydney.

334 One of the: Affidavit of James Simmonds, Exhibit to Action 2171 before the Supreme Court of New South Wales, 1855, Archives of New South Wales, Sydney.

335 Only the firm: See Writ of Capias ad Respondendum for £100 in the file of Action 2168 of 1855 in the Supreme Court of New South Wales, Archives of New South Wales, Sydney; the following account is based on Brown's statement to *Sydney Morning Herald*, 14 September 1855, 5c4; that of an officer of the steamship company who was on board the *Waratah*, in *Sydney Morning Herald*, 12 September 1855, 5c3; a letter from Lola's attorneys in the *Herald*, 12 September 1855, 5c3; and *Bell's Life in Sydney and Sporting Reviewer* 15 September 1855, 2c7–8. Folland gave a slightly different account in *Argus* [Melbourne], 17 September 1855, 6c3, and in *Age* [Melbourne], 17 September 1855, 6c1.

336 Crosby, described as: *Scotsman* [Edinburgh], 16 February 1861, 6c3.

336 The *Sydney Morning Herald*: *Sydney Morning Herald*, 11 September 1855, 5c2–3, and 14 September 1855, 5c4.

449

336 One of them: For the following account, see Hauser, *Wanderbuch* 2:102–105.

337 Lola opened in: *Geelong Advertiser & Intelligencer*, 15 September 1855, 2c6–7; *Age* [Melbourne], 14 September 1855, 4c3–4; *Herald* [Melbourne], 14 September 1855, 4c6.

337 "Why the stage": *Argus* [Melbourne], 20 September 1855, 5c3.

337 The critic of: *Geelong Advertiser*, 21 September 1855, 2c4.

338 The *Age*, however: *Age* [Melbourne], 20 September 1855, 4c6.

338 "I throw back": *Herald* [Melbourne], 21 September 1855, 6c3.

338 If any further: *Truth* [Melbourne], 12 August 1911, 7c1–2; *Herald* [Melbourne], 22 September 1855, 5c1; *Age* [Melbourne], 22 September 1855, 5c5; *Argus* [Melbourne], 24 September 1855, 6c1.

339 "simply ridiculous": *Age* [Melbourne], 22 September 1855, 4c6.

339 "A young Spanish Girl": *Geelong Advertiser & Intelligencer*, 28 September 1855, 2c7.

339 Lola Montez's best: *Herald* [Melbourne], 3 November 1855, 5c4.

340 Now she was: *Argus* [Melbourne], 1 October 1855, 5c5–6; Moreton de Chabrillan, *Un Deuil*, 136.

340 The critic for: *Adelaide Times*, 27 November 1855, 3c8; *Criticisms on the performances of Harry Jackson*, 27.

341 "I am very": *Adelaide Times*, 27 November 1855, 3c8; *Criticisms on the performances of Harry Jackson*, 29.

341 The company had: *South Australia Register*, 14 December 1855, 2c6.

341 The troupe was: *Age* [Melbourne], 24 December 1855, 6c4; *Herald* [Melbourne], 27 December 1855, 4c6.

342 Lola set herself: *Scotsman* [Melbourne], 16 February 1861, 6c3.

342 Amont the entertainments: *Scotsman* [Melbourne], 16 February 1861, 6c3; Blainey, *Farthing Poet*, 213.

342 On the first: *Sydney Morning Herald*, 14 January 1856, 4c6.

342 "Such deadly sin": *Bell's Life in Sydney and Sporting Reviewer*, 19 January 1856, 2c5.

342 "The press should": Quoted from the original criminal information against Seekamp, signed by LM, in the Archives Division of the State Library of Victoria, reproduced in [Cannon], *Lola Montes*.

343 Whether or not: *Bell's Life in Sydney and Sporting Reviewer*, 5 April 1856, 2c6; *Melbourne Punch*, 21 February 1856, 19c2.

343 On Tuesday afternoon: This account of the encounter between Lola and Seekamp is based on *Herald* [Melbourne], 22 February 1856, 5c3; *Age* [Melbourne], 23 February 1856, 3c1; and *Bell's Life in Sydney and Sporting Reviewer*, 1 March 1856, 2c5.

344 *Melbourne Punch* devoted: *Melbourne Punch*, 28 February 1856, 27; *Herald* [Melbourne], 23 February 1856, 6c4; Charles Eberle, Memoirs, MS 7569, Victoria State Library, 2:72–73.

344 Lola continued to: *Age* [Melbourne], 23 February 1856, 3c1; *Herald* [Melbourne], 28 March 1856, 5c3; Withers, *History*, 120–121.

S O U R C E S

344 Lola and her: *Herald* [Melbourne], 5 March 1856, 6c6, and 7 March 1856, 6c1;
Melbourne Punch, 6 March 1856, 35; *Age* [Melbourne], 7 March 1856, 4c6.

345 "In direct opposition": *Age* [Melbourne], 8 March 1856, 1c5.

345 "It would be": *Herald* [Melbourne], 10 March 1856, 5c2 and 5c3.

345 Lola had just: *Age* [Melbourne], 19 March 1856, 2c4.

346 In spite of: *Herald* [Melbourne], 28 March 1856, 5c3, and 31 March 1856, 7c2;
Age [Melbourne], 31 March 1856, 3c6, 3 April 1856, 5c2.

346 "From the front": Repeated in *Herald* [Melbourne], 4 April 1856, 7c1–2; see
also *Herald* [Melbourne], 7 April 1856, 6c5.

347 Lola pointedly remarked: *Age* [Melbourne], 11 April 1856, 3:2. Blainey, *Farthing Poet*, 210.

347 The performance went: *Mt. Alexander Mail*, 11 April 1856, 5c1–2.

347 "Lola indignantly condemned": *Mt. Alexander Mail*, 15 April 1856, 2c5.

347 The Castlemaine performance: *Mt. Alexander Mail*, 6 May 1856, 3c1;
Bendigo Courier, 10 May 1856, 3c2.

348 "Once I lived": LM to Miss Mitchell, 4 April 1859, New York Public Library,
Crane Family Papers.

349 On 7 July: *Pacific Commercial Advertiser* [Honolulu], 10 July 1856, 2c4 and
2c1; *Polynesian* [Honolulu], 12 July 1856, 39c5.

349 The ship was: *Golden Era* [San Francisco], 3 August 1856, 4c3; Typescript of
the diary of John H. McCabe 2:280, Sutro Library, San Francisco; *Alta California* [San Francisco], 4 April 1861, 1c2.

349 Whatever the circumstances: *Alta California* [San Francisco], 4 April 1861,
1c2; *Golden Era* [San Francisco], 3 August 1856, 4c3; [Dyer], *Penitent*, 26.

350 The newspapers reported: *Golden Era* [San Francisco], 2 August 1856, 4c3.

350 If she had: *Daily Evening Bulletin* [San Francisco], 23 August 1856, 3c3.

350 In the meantime: *Alta California* [San Francisco], 29 August 1856, 2c1, and
4 April 1861, 1c2.

351 The critics generally: *Alta California* [San Francisco], 14 August 1856, 2c4,
and 20 August 1856, 2c2.

351 "We have heard": Quoted in *Sacramento Union*, 14 August 1856, 3c3.

351 After a performance: *Daily Evening Bulletin* [San Francisco], 12 August
1856, 2c3; *Golden Era* [San Francisco], 24 August 1856, 5c1.

352 Her collection: *Alta California* [San Francisco], 6 September 1856, 2c1, and
9 September 1856, 2c3.

352 Lola opened at: *Democratic State Journal* [Sacramento], 13 September 1856,
2c4. An apocryphal letter signed "Lola Montes" appeared in a Parisian newspaper about this time and has led some biographers to conclude mistakenly
that Lola had somehow returned to Europe. See *Estafette* [Paris], 7 September 1856, 3c3, and 13 September 1856, 4c1.

352 The house and: *New York Times*, 26 April 1856, 2c4; *Golden Era* [San Fran-
cisco], 11 May 1856, 4c6.

352 More than a: *Alta California* [San Francisco], 11 July 1868, 1c6.

353 Lola was scheduled: *Age* [Sacramento], 17 September 1856, 2c2.

353 The second night: *Daily Evening Bulletin* [San Francisco], 16 October 1856, 3c2.

353 "It is very": *Daily Evening Bulletin* [San Francisco], 17 October 1856, 3c2.

353 Lola made out: *Alta California* [San Francisco], 4 April 1861, 1c2.

353 The California newspapers: *Wide West* [San Francisco], 21 September 1856, 3c1; Heald's entry of death, 20 June 1856, at the General Register Office, London.

354 She boarded the: *Alta California* [San Francisco], 20 November 1856, 2c2; *New York Times*, 23 January 1857, 6c3.

354 The son, Chauncey: See *Alta California*, 4 April 1861, 1c2; *New York Times*, 3 May 1883, 5c2; *New York Tribune*, 3 May 1883, 5c5.

355 She became quite: LM to Miss Mitchell, 4 April 1859, New York Public Library, Crane Family Papers.

355 This probably occurred: *Daily Territorial Enterprise* [Virginia City, Nev.], 14 July 1878, 1c1.

355 Miriam was twenty: See generally Stern, *Purple Passage*.

355 "Sweetest, . . .": LM to "Sweetest," n.d., Cornell University Library, Ithaca.

355 By the third: *New York Times*, 23 January 1857, 6c3; *Golden Era* [San Francisco], 5 April 1857, 4c5.

356 They caught the: *Frank Leslie's Illustrated Newspaper* [New York], 7 March 1857, 212–213.

356 On opening night: *Providence Journal*, 17 February 1857, 2c7, 16 February 1857, 2c5, 17 February 1857, 2c7.

356 "She remained one": Blake, *Historical Account*, 265–267.

357 Blake also writes: Blake, *Historical Account*, 268.

357 When Lola left: *Daily Territorial Enterprise* [Virginia City, Nev.], 14 July 1878, 1c1; Stern, *Purple Passage*, 23–26.

358 Lola's tour continued: *Pittsburgh Morning Post*, 28 February 1857, 3c1; *Freiheits Freund* [Pittsburgh], 2 March 1857, 3c1. *Golden Era* [San Francisco], 3 May 1857, 4c6; Missouri Historical Society, St. Louis, Playbill for the St. Louis Theatre, 12 March 1857, announcing the appearance of Lola Montez "recovered from her severe illness"; *Missouri Democrat* [St. Louis], 17 March 1857, 3c1.

358 After her engagement: *Anzeiger des Westens* [St. Louis], 24 March 1857, 3c3.

358 Five days after: *Louisville Daily Journal*, 6 April 1857, 3c1.

358 Outside of noting: *Daily Journal* [Chicago], 29 April 1857, 3c1; *Golden Era* [San Francisco], 28 June 1857, 4c6.

359 In May and: *Golden Era* [San Francisco], 28 June 1857, 4c6. In a letter in the Theatrical Manuscripts Collection of Yale University, Lola speaks of being "industriously and labouriously at work every day since I left Philadelphia in preparing a new lecture. . . . I am really better pleased with it than with any of my other writings." Undated letter to "My dear Dr." (actually written from Baltimore on 19 November 1858, to Robert Shelton MacKenzie, Irish-American author and journalist in Philadelphia).

359 The plan was: *Golden Era* [San Francisco], 28 June 1857, 4c6; *Buffalo Morning Express*, 18 July 1857, 3c2.

360 In the best: Clipping reprinting an old program of the Toronto performance from *New York Clipper*, n.d., in the collection of the Lincoln Center Branch of the New York Public Library; *Buffalo Morning Express*, 31 July 1857, 3c2.

360 "I know of": LML 122.

360 Lola drew a: *Buffalo Morning Express*, 31 July 1857, 3c2.

360 Two days later: *Buffalo Morning Express*, 1 August 1857, 3c2.

361 "I know not": LML 267, 276.

361 "It is that": LML 292.

361 "I cannot help": *Boston Post*, 2 September 1857, 2c2.

362 The first salvo: *Witness* [Montreal], 26 August 1857, 541c3.

362 "A feeling of": Reprinted in *New York Times*, 7 September 1857, 2c5.

362 "We write to": *Minèrve* [Montreal], 3 September 1857, 2c1–2.

362 The editor of: *Minèrve* [Montreal], 8 September 1857, 2c1–4.

363 The *Daily Argus* called: *Daily Argus* [Montreal], 29 August 1857, 2c1–2.

363 The *Boston Bee* declared: *Boston Bee*, 10 October 1857, 4c7; *Boston Herald*, 9 October 1857, 2c5; see the playbill for Lola's lecture in Newark, N.J., on 28 September 1857 in KLA 39, Wendland file.

363 In November Lola: *Philadelphia Press*, 9 November 1857, 2c3; KLA 34 [AN 75], LM to KL, 12 March 1848.

364 King Ludwig himself: LML 162, 165–166.

364 "That her lectures": *Philadelphia Press*, 16 November 1857, 2c3.

364 Lola certainly felt: "I am really better pleased with it than any of my other writings," Lola wrote in a letter in the Theatrical Manuscripts Collection, Yale University. The letter is undated and the salutation is only "Dear Dr.," but internal evidence indicates that it was written on 19 November 1857 from Baltimore to the Philadelphia author and journalist Dr. Robert Shelton MacKenzie.

365 Deeds, not words: LML 176–177; *New York Herald*, 16 February 1858, 6c1; *New York Times*, 16 February 1858, 5c3–4.

365 Lola had high: LML 185–186, 197–198.

365 Although she defended: Manuscript lectures of LM, Harvard Theatre Collection; *Philadelphia Press*, 5 December 1857, 2c4.

365 Lola had become: LML 43; Sulkowski's life, 1814–1879, can be followed in some detail in the annual editions of the Gothaischer genealogische Hof-Kalender published during his lifetime.

366 The evidence is: *New York Daily Tribune*, 19 January 1858, 7:1–2.

366 The next day: *New York Times*, 1 February 1858, 2c1–2; *Allgemeine Zeitung* [Augsburg], 31 December 1857, 5826c1–2.

366 When she returned: *Boston Daily Advertiser*, 18 January 1858, 1c5; *New York Herald*, 17 January 1858, 1c1; *New York Tribune*, 19 January 1858, 7c1–2.

366 It apparently was: *New York Times*, 10 February 1858, 3c3–4; *New York Herald*, 19 February 1858, 8c1; LML 43–44.

367 It was a: *New York Herald*, 21 January 1861, 8c1–2; *Sunday Dispatch* [Philadelphia], 21 February 1858, 2c4; LM to Maria Buchanan, "Friday morning" [9 April 1858], Harvard Theatre Collection; *New York Times*, 20 April 1858, 5c2.

367 But Lola had: *New York Herald*, 4 February 1858, 5c4–5; *New York Times*, 5 February 1858, 3c3–4.

368 Jobson was a: On Jobson see *Times* [London], 5 April 1842, 5c4, and 19 April 1842, 5c4; *New York Times*, 30 May 1876, 8c2; and the entries of his works in the British Library catalog.

368 "My name is": *New York Times*, 10 February 1858, 3c3–4.

369 "Madame, was your": *New York Herald*, 19 February 1858; *New York Times*, 19 February 1858, 8c1–3.

370 "The scene, had": *New York Times*, 19 February 1858.

371 Both Seely and: *New York Herald*, 27 February 1858, 1c1–2; 3 March 1858, 8c2; *New York Times*, 27 February 1858, 5c1–3; *Sunday Dispatch* [Philadelphia], 7 March 1858, 2c5; *New York Herald*, 17 March 1858, 7c5–6; *New York Times*, 19 March 1858, 1c6; *Courrier des Etats Unis* [New York], 20 March 1858, 1c5–2c1.

371 "Comic Aspects of": LML 219–220.

371 She subsequently delivered: *New York Herald*, 24 March 1858, 1c4.

372 "She must be": LML 15.

372 Lola declared herself: LML 14–15.

372 "Perhaps the noblest": LML 12–13.

372 "Run-away matches": LML 24.

372 As she came: LML 48–50.

372 Dujarier, she claimed: *Figaro* [Paris], 3 October 1858, 6c2; LML 69–73.

373 Toward the end: LML 81.

373 "A thousand thanks": LM to Maria Buchanan, "Friday morning" [9 April 1858], Harvard Theatre Collection.

373 "Some of them": *New York Herald*, 7 April 1858, 4c3.

374 She had now: *Evening Post* [New York], 9 November 1868, 1c1.

374 Her first book: *New York Herald*, 27 June 1858, 1c1; see the press notices of Lola's lectures on pp. iii–v of the Philadelphia edition, Harry Ransom Center for the Humanities, University of Texas, Austin; see also *New York Tribune*, 13 July 1858, 3c1, and *Frank Leslie's Illustrated Newspaper* [New York], 3 July 1858, 75c2; *Illustrated News of the World* [London], 14 August 1858, 107c2.

374 "I should not": *New York Herald*, 4 November 1858, 4c6.

374 "Lola Montez is": Quoted in *New York Daily News*, 17 September 1858, 5c4.

375 "the men have": Montez, *The Arts*, xvi.

375 The first New: See the editor's introduction to Montez, *L'Art;* there was a 1969 reprint by Chelsea Press, New York, and a 1978 reprint by Ecco Press, New York.

454

SOURCES

The success of: *Evening Post* [New York], 9 November 1868, 1c1; Wyndam, *Magnificent Montez*, 239, quoting a letter from LM to Charles G. Leland, 20 August 1858.

376 The diverse assemblage: *Golden Era* [San Francisco], 10 October 1858, 4c2; Leland, *Memoirs*, 225.

376 Lola was a: *Evening Post* [New York], 9 November 1868, 1c1; Leland, *Memoirs*, 225.

376 Lola was not: *New York Tribune*, 30 January 1861, 7c1–2.

376 Toward the end: This account of Lola's effort to help the Reverend Hoyt is based on unidentified newspaper clippings in the Manuscript Collection, New York Public Library.

377 "The idea of": See unidentified newspaper clippings in the Manuscript Collection, New York Public Library.

377 Although she had: Wyndam, *Magnificent Montez*, 239–240, quoting a letter of LM to Charles G. Leland from the first week of November 1858.

377 On Monday, 8 November: *Galway Vindicator*, 24 November 1858, 2c7.

377 "She spoke in": *Galway Vindicator*, 24 November 1858, 2c7.

378 Lola and the: *Dublin Evening Mail*, 26 November 1858, 3c1; *Munster News and Provincial Advertiser* [Limerick], 27 November 1858, 3c4.

378 It was to: *Freeman's Journal* [Dublin], 7 December 1858, 3c1.

378 Some of her: *Daily Express* [Dublin], 9 December 1858, 3c4–5.

379 The real subject: This account of her lecture is based on the newspaper reports in *Freeman's Journal* [Dublin], 9 December 1858, 3c2; *Daily Express* [Dublin], 9 December 1858; and the reading manuscript in Harvard Theatre Collection.

379 "The lecture was": *Freeman's Journal* [Dublin], 9 December 1858, 3c2; *Munster News and Provincial Advertiser* [Limerick], 15 December 1858, 3c3.

380 Two nights later: See the reading manuscript in Harvard Theatre Collection.

380 The third and: See the reading manuscript in Harvard Theatre Collection.

380 "But those stirring": See the reading manuscript in Harvard Theatre Collection.

381 From Dublin she: *Sunday Times* [London], 16 January 1859, 3c3.

381 In the Scottish: *Sunday Times* [London], 13 February 1859, 3c3.

381 In York's Concert: *Sunday Times* [London], 27 February 1859, 3c5.

382 "Oh blessed be": LM to Miss Mitchell, 4 April 1859, New York Public Library, Crane Family Papers.

382 "The Countess of": *British Spiritual Telegraph* [London], 1 May 1859, 252.

383 "She . . . was": *New York Tribune*, 30 January 1861, 7c1–2.

383 Although the press: *Morning Advertiser* [London], 8 April 1859, 3c2; *Morning Star* [London], 9 April 1859, 5c6.

383 "It is a": *Evening Journal* [London], 7–8 April 1859, 5c6.

383 Following her final: Much of this account of Lola's stay in England is based on *New York Tribune*, 30 January 1861, 7c1–2.

383 The plan soon: LM to "Camille" [probably Mrs. Sherard (Ellen) Osborn], 11

455

February 1860, Stadtbibliothek, Munich; LM to an unknown author, 13 [June 1859] [lithographic facsimile], Harry Ransom Center for the Humanities, University of Texas, Austin; *Era* [London], 5 June 1859, 1c1; see the account of this lecture in *Morning Post* [London], 13 June 1859, 3c2, and the reading manuscript in Harvard Theatre Collection.

384 "On this forbidden": Quoted from Lola's reading manuscript in Harvard Theatre Collection.

385 Lola's lecture was: *Morning Star* [London], 13 June 1859, 3c2; *Era* [London], 19 June 1859, 11c1.

385 Matters on Park Lane: *New York Tribune*, 30 January 1861, 7c1–2.

385 Toward the end: [Dyer], *Penitent*, 20–21, 23, 24, 26–27.

385 "How many, many": [Dyer], *Penitent*, 28.

386 She later wrote: LM to "Camille" [probably Mrs. Sherard (Ellen) Osborn], 11 February 1860, Stadtbibliothek, Monacensia Sammlung, Munich; [Dyer], *Penitent*, 29–30.

386 Now she was: *New York Herald*, 27 October 1859, 10c3; *New York Tribune*, 21 November 1859, 5c5; Lola gave Harris's New Church Publishing Company as her return address to a friend in February 1860. See LM to "Camille" [probably Mrs. (Ellen) Sherard Osborn] in the Stadtbibliothek, Monacensia Sammlung, Munich.

387 "I meant my": *New York Herald*, 30 November 1859, 4c5.

387 She prepared a: *New York Herald*, 18 December 1859, 2c3; Ames, *Outlines*, 124–126.

387 At this point: Reading manuscript in Harvard Theatre Collection.

387 "All that I": Reading manuscript in Harvard Theatre Collection.

388 In Philadelphia one: *Philadelphia Press*, 28 January 1860, 2c3.

388 In Washington she: *Alta California* [San Francisco], 4 April 1861, 1c2.

388 In Cleveland, the: *Cleveland Daily Herald*, 13 February 1860, 3c3; *Cleveland Plain Dealer*, 13 February 1860, 3c2.

389 The Burrs were: LM to "Camille" [probably Mrs. Sherard (Ellen) Osborn], 11 February 1860, Stadtbibliothek, Monacensia Sammlung, Munich.

389 "We have wended": LM to "My dear friend" [Maria Buchanan], 7 March 1860, Harvard Theatre Collection.

389 On her way: *Daily Illinois State Journal* [Springfield], 14 March 1860, 3c2, 15 March 1860, 2c1, 16 March 1860, 3c2–3, and 19 March 1860, 3c3.

390 Ultimately, she would: KLA 39, Buchanan file, Maria Buchanan to KL, 21 September 1861.

390 Lola rented a: See U.S. Census of 1860, New York City, 15th Ward, 3rd District, p. 339, Dwelling House 370, Family 462; *Montrose Standard & Angus & Mearns Register*, 27 July 1860, 3c1; LM to "Camille" [probably Mrs. Sherard (Ellen) Osborn], 11 February 1860, Stadtbibliothek, Monacensia Sammlung, Munich.

390 "Politically, we are": LM to "Camille" [probably Mrs. Sherard (Ellen)

Osborn], 11 February 1860, Stadtbibliothek, Monacensia Sammlung, Munich.

390 Shortly after rising: *New York Tribune*, 4 July 1860, 5c3.

391 Ships leaving that: *New York Tribune*, 7 July 1860, 5c3; *New York Herald*, 7 July 1860, 5c6; for examples of premature obituaries of Lola, see *Kölnische Zeitung*, 1 August 1860, 3c2; and *Europa, Chronik der gebildeten Welt* [Leipzig], 1860, c1122–1125; after Lola's death, a widely reprinted story alleged that the stroke had been brought on by the shock of being snubbed on the streets of New York by Follin's daughter, Caroline, whom, the story went, Lola had put through the Emma Willard Academy and who was now married to a former diplomat. Since Caroline Follin was too young to be married at this date (and there is no record of her enrollment at the Willard Academy) and Miriam Follin was now, as Mrs. E. G. Squier, married to a former diplomat, the story would appear to refer to the former "Minnie Montez." There is no independent evidence to support the story, and the fact that Lola and Miriam seem to have parted on unfriendly terms would appear to make it unlikely that Lola would have been seriously disturbed even if Miriam had snubbed her. See *Philadelphia Press*, 22 January 1861, 2c2, and *Alta California* [San Francisco], 29 March 1861, 1c6.

391 "Lola was costumed": *Sunday Dispatch* [Philadelphia], 9 September 1860, 2c6.

391 In October, Mrs. Buchanan: *New York Herald*, 21 January 1861, 8c1–2; New York City Department of Health, Register of Deaths, Borough of Manhattan, 1798–1865, microfilm reel 21, Death of Lola Montez on 17 January 1861. Her will is printed in Hutchings, "The Most Famous Vamp," 20.

391 In the fall: Unidentified newspaper clipping in Harvard Theatre Collection; see also Rodgers, *A Hundred Years*, 75–78.

392 After Mrs. Craigie: Eliza Craigie to Dr. John Cooper, 14 January 1861, printed in Rodgers, *A Hundred Years*, 78; BSB Auto. Cim Lola Montez.

392 She asked to: KLA 39, Buchanan file, Maria Buchanan to KL, 21 September 1861; *New York Clipper*, 16 September 1911, 17c4–5.

392 By the middle: Eliza Craigie to Dr. John Cooper, 14 January 1861, printed in Rodgers, *A Hundred Years*, 78; *New York Herald*, 21 January 1861, 8c1–2.

392 Other friends who: Hingston, *Genial Showman* 2:216.

393 On his first: [Dyer], *Penitent*, 35–40. A very different story of Lola's last months was told in Helen Holdredge, *Woman in Black*, in which Lola lived in a boarding house in Brooklyn and wandered half-crazed about the neighborhood. This account has been adopted by most subsequent biographers. It is based on an anonymous letter to the editor of the *Brooklyn Eagle*, 16 April 1894, 7c6. Every letter and contemporary newspaper account bearing on the last year of Lola's life, as well as the U.S. Census of 1860, which shows her living in Manhattan (15th Ward, 3rd District, page 339, Dwelling House 370,

Family 462, 22 June 1860), make it clear that this letter, written more than thirty years after Lola's death, is false.

394 One of Lola's: [Dyer], *Penitent*, 17; KLA 39, Buchanan file, Maria Buchanan to KL, 8 April 1861; *Sunday Dispatch* [Philadelphia], 27 January 1861, 1c8. Several months after Lola's death the New York correspondent of the *Sacramento Union* reported rumors that Mrs. Buchanan had cheated and abused Lola in her illness, that the nurse had brutalized her, and the reporter claimed to have seen himself that the room in which she died was filthy and squalid (*Sacramento Union*, 22. May 1861, 1c4). Although there is no question that Lola's room was modest, this story finds no support in any of the accounts of Lola's friends, all of whom speak of the good fortune Lola had to find such a good, Christian friend in her last days. See, e.g., the Reverend Hawks's testimony in [Dyer], *Penitent*, 35–36; Charles Leland's obituary in *Frank Leslie's Illustrated Newspaper*, 2 February 1861, 165c3; *Sun* [New York], 25 April 1897, sec. 3, 9c4; *New York Herald*, 20 January 1860, 4c6.

394 The party accompanied: [Dyer], *Penitent*, 36–37; *Evening Post* [New York], 19 January 1861, 3c6.

394 "Her most eccentric": *New York Evening Post*, 21 January 1861, 2c2–3.

395 "She had many": *Frank Leslie's Illustrated Newspaper* [New York], 2 February 1861, 164–165. The obituary is unsigned, but the details make clear the author is Leland.

395 "generous and high-tempered": *New York Times*, 21 January 1861, 8c1.

395 A few had: *Albion* [New York], 22 January 1861, 44c2; *Irish American Weekly* [New York], 26 January 1861, 2c2.

395 Others ran such: *Morning Star and Dial* [London], 7 February 1861, 5c2; *Sunderland Herald*, 8 February 1861, 6c7; *Daily Telegraph* [London], 9 February 1861, 4c5–6. and 5c1.

395 "Sir: Lola Montez": *Morning Post* [London], 7 February 1861, 4c6.

395 In fact, Lola: *Sun* [New York], 25 April 1897, sec. 3, 9c4.

396 Ambassador Wendland had: KLA 39. Wendland file, Wendland to KL, 15 February 1861.

396 "Sire, in early": KLA 39. Buchanan file, Maria Buchanan to KL, 16 March 1861.

396 "Mistress Maria Buchanan": KL to Maria Buchanan, 9 April 1861, Harvard Theatre Collection.

397 Among the documents: KLA 39. Papon file, Papon to KL, 6 August 1852, 6 September 1852, 3 February 1854; Mirecourt, *Lola Montès*, 64, fn 1.

398 Thousands of miles: On Peißner's life in America, see Danton, "Elias Peissner"; Farley, "The Day Peissner Fell"; "Colonel Elias Peissner"; and "History of the Class of 1863 of Union College," 76–79.

398 Lola's other notorious: KA File 80668; Xylander and Sutner, *Geschichte* 3:59, fn 2.

398 Patrick Purdy Hull: See FDE 92–93; Cotton, *List*, 343.

398 Although most officers: IOBL, E/4/840 ff171, 12 November 1856; Hodson, *List* 2:544.

399 James seems to: See his will, probated 8 June 1871, in the Principal Registry of the Family Division, Somerset House, London; and the records of his second marriage and death in the General Register Office, London.

399 Lola's mother lived: See *Paddington Times* [London], 20 November 1875, 3c2, and 27 November 1875, 3c1; and her will in the Principal Registry of the Family Division, Somerset House, London.

INDEX

461